THE LETTERS OF QUEEN VICTORIA

A SELECTION FROM HER MAJESTY'S CORRESPONDENCE BETWEEN THE YEARS 1837 and 1861

IN THREE VOLUMES

VOL. II.—1844-1853

by

Queen of Great Britain
Victoria

Printed on acid free ANSI archival quality paper.
ISBN: 978-1-78139-295-9/
© 2012 Benediction Classics, Oxford.

H.M. QUEEN VICTORIA, 1843

From the picture by F. Winterhalter at Windsor Castle

Frontispiece, Vol. II.

Contents

CHAPTER XIV

1845

The Spanish marriages—Position of the Prince—Title of
King Consort—Purchase of Osborne—Maynooth
grant—Religious bigotry—Public executions—Birthday
letter—Princess Charlotte—Vacant Deanery—Wine
from Australia—King of Holland—Projected visit to
Germany—Question of Lords Justices—Visit to the
Château d'Eu—Spanish marriages—The Prince criti-
cised—Governor-Generalship of Canada—Corn Laws—
Cabinet dissensions—Interview with Sir Robert Peel—
Lord John Russell suggested—Attitude of Lord Mel-
bourne—The Queen's embarrassment—Attitude of Sir
Robert Peel—Lord Stanley resigns—The Commander-
ship-in-Chief—Duke of Wellington—King Louis
Philippe—Anxiety for the future—Insuperable difficul-
ties—Lord Grey and Lord Palmerston—Lord John
Russell fails—Chivalry of Sir Robert Peel—He resumes
office—Cordial support—The Queen's estimate of Sir
Robert Peel—Lord Stanley—The Prince's Memoran-
dum—Comprehensive scheme—The unemployed—
Lord Palmerston's justification—France and the Syrian
War—Letter to King Louis Philippe—Ministry rein-
stated

CHAPTER XV

1846

CHAPTER XVI

1847

CHAPTER XVII

1848

CHAPTER XVIII

1849

CHAPTER XIX

1850

Grand Duchess Stéphanie—The Draft to Greece—Lord Palmerston's explanation—Lord John Russell's plan—Suggested rearrangement—*Status quo* maintained—Baron Stockmar's Memorandum—State of France—The Prince's speech—Lord Palmerston and Spain—Lord Howden—The Koh-i-noor diamond—A change imminent—Lord John Russell's report—Sunday delivery of letters—Prince George of Cambridge—The Earldom of Tipperary—Mr Roebuck's motion—Lord Stanley's motion—Holstein and Germany—Lord Palmerston's explanation—The Protocol—Christening of Prince Arthur—Don Pacifico Debate—Sir Robert Peel's accident—Letter from King of Denmark—Death of Sir Robert Peel—The Queen assaulted by Pate—Death of Duke of Cambridge—Prince of Prussia—The Foreign Office—Denmark and Schleswig—Sir Charles Napier's resignation—Lord Palmerston—Lord Clarendon's opinion—Duke of Bedford's opinion—Lord John Russell's report—Press attacks on Lord Palmerston—Duties of Foreign Secretary—Death of King Louis Philippe—Visit to Scotland—Illness of Queen Louise—Attack on General Haynau—Note to Baron Koller—The Draft gone—Lord Palmerston rebuked—Holstein—A great grief—Mr Tennyson made Poet Laureate—Ritualists and Roman Catholics—Unrest in Europe—England and Germany—Constitutionalism in Germany—Austria and Prussia—Religious strife—England and Rome—Lady Peel—The Papal aggression—Ecclesiastical Titles Bill

CHAPTER XX

1851

Life Peerages—Diplomatic arrangements—Peril of the Ministry—Negotiations with Sir J. Graham—Defeat of the Government—Ministerial crisis—The Premier's statement—Lord Lansdowne consulted—Lord Stanley sent for—Complications—Fiscal policy—Sir James Graham—Duke of Wellington—Difficulties—Lord Aberdeen consulted—Lord Stanley to be sent for—His letter—Lord Stanley's difficulties—Mr Disraeli—Question of dissolution—Explanations—Lord Stanley resigns—His reasons—The Papal Bill—Duke of Wellington—Appeal to Lord Lansdowne—Still without a Government—Lord Lansdowne's views—Further difficulties—Coalition impossible—Income Tax—Free Trade—Ecclesiastical Titles Bill—Confusion of Parties—New National Gallery—The great Exhibition—Imposing ceremony—The Prince's triumph—Enthusiasm in the City—Danish succession—The Orleans Princes—Regret at leaving Scotland—Extension of the Franchise—Louis Kossuth—Lord Palmerston's intentions—A dispute—Lord Palmerston defiant—He gives way—The Queen's anxiety—Lord Palmerston's conduct—The Queen's comment—Death of King of Hanover—The Suffrage—The *Coup d'État*—Louis Bonaparte—Excitement in France—Lord Palmerston and Lord Normanby—State of Paris—Lord Palmerston's approval—Birthday wishes—The crisis—Dismissal of Lord Palmerston—Inconsistency of Lord Palmerston—The Prince's Memorandum—Lord Clarendon—Discussion on new arrangements—Count Walewski informed—Lord Granville's appointment—The Queen's view of foreign affairs—Our policy reviewed—Difficulty of fixed principles—Prince Nicholas of Nassau—*Te Deum* at Paris 297-374

CHAPTER XXI

1852

CHAPTER XXII

1853

INTRODUCTORY NOTE
TO CHAPTER XIII

The new year (1844) opened with signs of improved trade, and a feeling of confidence, partly due to the friendly *entente* with France. In Ireland, soon after the collapse of the Clontarf meeting, O'Connell and some of his associates were indicted for seditious conspiracy, and convicted. The conviction was subsequently quashed on technical grounds, but O'Connell's political influence was at an end. In Parliament, owing chiefly to the exertions of Lord Ashley (afterwards Earl of Shaftesbury), an important Bill was passed restricting factory labour, and limiting its hours. The Bank Charter Act, separating the issue and banking departments, as well as regulating the note issue of the Bank of England in proportion to its stock of gold, also became law. Meanwhile the dissensions in the Conservative party were increasing, and the Ministry were defeated on a motion made by their own supporters to extend the preferential treatment of colonial produce. With great difficulty the vote was rescinded and a crisis averted; but the Young England section of the Tory party were becoming more and more an embarrassment to the Premier. Towards the end of the year the new Royal Exchange was opened amid much ceremony by the Queen.

The services rendered by Sir Charles Napier in India were the subject of votes of thanks in both Houses, but shortly afterwards Lord Ellenborough, the Governor-General, was recalled by the Directors of the East India Company: their action was no doubt due to his overbearing methods and love of display, but it was disapproved by the Ministry, and Lord Ellenborough was accorded an Earldom.

During the year there was a recrudescence of the friction between this country and France, due partly to questions as to the right of search of foreign ships, partly to a *brochure* issued by the Prince de Joinville, a son of Louis Philippe, partly to the assumption of French sovereignty over Tahiti and the seizure of the English consul there by the French authorities. Reparation however was made, and the ill-feeling subsided sufficiently to enable the King of the French to visit Queen Victoria,—the first friendly visit ever paid by a French king to the Sovereign of England. Louis Philippe was cordially received in this country.

Another historic royal visit also took place in 1844, that of the Emperor Nicholas, who no doubt was so much impressed with his friendly reception, both by the Court and by Aberdeen, the Foreign Secretary, that nine years later he thought he could calculate on the support of England under Aberdeen (then Premier) in a scheme for the partition of Turkey. Lord Malmesbury, who a few years later became Foreign Secretary, states in his memoirs that during this visit, the Czar, Sir Robert Peel, the Duke of Wellington, and Lord Aberdeen "drew up and signed a Memorandum, the spirit and scope of which was to support Russia in her legitimate protectorship of the Greek religion and the Holy Shrines, and to do so without consulting France," but the Memorandum was in reality only one made by Nicholas of his recollection of the interview, and communicated subsequently to Lord Aberdeen.

No events of special interest took place in other parts of Europe; the condition of affairs in the Peninsula improved, though the announcement of the unfortunate marriage of the Queen Mother with the Duke of Rianzares was not of hopeful augury for the young Queen Isabella's future; as a matter of fact, the marriage had taken place some time previously.

CHAPTER XIII

1844

Queen Victoria to the King of the Belgians.

Windsor Castle, *9th January 1844.*

My dearest Uncle,—I had the pleasure of receiving your kind letter of the 4th, which is written from Ardenne, where I grieve to see you are again gone without my beloved Louise.

Charlotte is the admiration of every one, and I wish much I could have seen the three dear children *en représentation.*

Our fat Vic or Pussette learns a verse of *Lamartine* by heart, which ends with "le tableau se déroule à mes pieds"; to show how well she had understood this difficult line which Mdlle. Charier had explained to her, I must tell you the following *bon mot.* When she was riding on her pony, and looking at the cows and sheep, she turned to Mdlle. Charier and said: "*Voilà* le tableau qui se déroule à mes pieds." Is not this extraordinary for a little child of three years old? It is more like what a person of twenty would say. You have no notion *what* a knowing, and I am sorry to say *sly*, little rogue she is, and so *obstinate.* She and *le petit Frère* accompany us to dear old Claremont to-day; Alice remains here under Lady Lyttelton's care. How sorry I am that you should have hurt your leg, and in such a provoking way; Albert says he remembers well your playing often with a pen-knife when you talked, and I remember it also, but it is really dangerous.

I am happy that the news from Paris are good; the really good understanding between our two Governments provokes the Carlists and Anarchists. Bordeaux[1] is not yet gone; I saw in a letter that it was *debated* in his presence whether he was on any favourable occasion *de se présenter en France!* Do you think that possible? Then again the papers say that there are fortifications being made on the coast of Normandy for fear of an invasion; is this so? These are many questions, but I hope you will kindly answer them, as they interest me. With Albert's love. Believe me, ever, your devoted Niece,

Victoria R.

Queen Victoria to the Earl of Aberdeen.

Claremont, *10th January 1844*.

The Queen understands that there is a negotiation with Sweden and Denmark pending about the cessation of their tribute to Morocco, likewise that Prince Metternich has sent a despatch condemning as unfair the understanding come to between us and France about the Spanish marriage;[2] that there is a notion of exchanging Hong Kong for a more healthy colony.

The Queen, taking a deep interest in all these matters, and feeling it her duty to do so, begs Lord Aberdeen to keep her always well informed of what is on the *tapis* in his Department.

Queen Victoria to the Earl of Aberdeen.

Claremont, *13th January 1844*.

The Queen has received Lord Aberdeen's letter of the 10th, and returns him the papers which he sent her, with her best thanks. She does not remember to have seen them before.

The Queen takes this opportunity to beg Lord Aberdeen to cause the despatches to be sent a little sooner from the Foreign Office, as drafts in particular have often come to the Queen a week or a fortnight after they had actually been sent across the sea.

With respect to the Hanoverian Orders, Lord Aberdeen has not quite understood what the Queen meant. It was Sir C. Thornton and others to whom the Queen had refused permission to accept the favour, on a former occasion, by which the King of Hanover was much affronted. The Queen would not like to have herself additionally fettered by any new regulation, but Lord Aberdeen will certainly concur with the Queen that it would not be expedient to give to the King of Hanover a power which the Queen herself does not possess, viz. that of granting orders as favours, or for personal services; as the number of the different classes of the Guelphic Order bestowed on Englishmen is innumerable, it would actually invest the King with such a power, which, considering how much such things are sought after, might be extremely inconvenient.

The Queen will not give a final decision upon this case until she returns to Windsor, where she has papers explanatory of the reasons which caused her to decline the King of Hanover's application in 1838.

Queen Victoria to the King of the Belgians.

Claremont, *16th January 1844.*

My dearest Uncle,—Many thanks for your kind letter of the 11th. Louise can give you the details of the little upset I and Lady Douro had, and which I did not think worth while to mention.[3] It was the strangest thing possible to happen, and the most *unlikely*, for we were going quite quietly, not at all in a narrow lane, with very quiet ponies and my usual postillion; the fact was that the boy looked the *wrong* way, and therefore did not perceive the ditch which he so cleverly got us into.

We leave dear Claremont, as usual, with the greatest regret; we are so peaceable here; Windsor is beautiful and comfortable, but it is a *palace*, and God knows *how willingly* I would *always* live with my beloved Albert and our children in the quiet and retirement of private life, and not be the constant object of observation, and of newspaper articles. The children (Pussette and Bertie) have been most remarkably well, and so have we, in spite of the very bad weather we had most days. I am truly and really grieved that good excellent Nemours is again *not* to get his *dotation*.[4] Really we constitutional countries are *too shabby*.

Now, dearest Uncle, I must bid you adieu, begging you to believe me, ever your devoted Niece,

Victoria R.

Queen Victoria to the King of the Belgians.

Windsor Castle, *30th January 1844.*

My dearest Uncle,—I must begin by thanking you for your kind letter of the 26th, and by wishing you joy that the fête went off *so* well. I am glad Leo will appear at the next ball; he is nearly nine years old, and it is good to accustom children of his rank early to these things.

Guizot's speech is exceedingly admired, with the exception of his having said more than he was justified to do about the right of search.[5] Our speech has been very difficult to frame; we should like to have mentioned our visits to France and Belgium, but it has been found impossible to do so; *France is* mentioned, and it is the first time since 1834!

To-morrow we go up to Town "pour ce bore," as the good King always said to me; whenever there were tiresome people to present he always said: "Je vous demande pardon de ce *bore*."

I have had a tiresome though not at all violent cold which *I was* alarmed might spoil the *sonorousness* of my voice for the speech on Thursday, but it promises well now.

I own I always look with horror to the beginning of a Parliamentary campaign.

With Albert's love. Ever your devoted Niece,

Victoria R.

Queen Victoria to the King of the Belgians.

Windsor Castle, *6th February 1844*.

My dearly beloved Uncle,—*You* must now be the father to us poor bereaved, heartbroken children.[6] To describe to you *all* that we *have* suffered, all that we *do* suffer, would be difficult; God has heavily afflicted us; we feel crushed, overwhelmed, bowed down by the loss of one who was so deservedly loved, I may say adored, by his children and family; I loved him and looked on him as my own father; his like we shall *not see again*; that youth, *that amiability*, and kindness in his own house which was the centre and rendezvous for the whole family, will never be seen again, and my poor Angel's fondest thought of beholding that *dearly beloved Vaterhaus*—where his thoughts continually were—*again* is for ever gone and his poor heart bleeds to feel *this* is for ever gone. Our promised visit, our dearest Papa's, and our fondest wish, all is put an end to. The violence of our grief may be over, but the desolate feeling which succeeds it is worse, and tears are a relief. I have never known real *grief* till now, and it has made a lasting impression on me. A father is *such* a *near* relation, you are a *piece* of him in fact,—and all (as my poor *deeply afflicted* Angel says) the earliest pleasures of your life were given you by a dear father; that can *never he replaced* though time may soften the pang. And indeed one loves to *cling* to one's grief; I can understand Louise's feeling in her overwhelming sorrows.

Let me now join my humble entreaties to Albert's, relative to the request about dearest Louise, which he has made. It is a sacrifice I ask, but if you *knew* the sacrifice I make in letting and urging Albert *to go*,

I am sure, if you *can* you *will* grant it. I have *never* been separated from him even for *one night*, and the *thought of such* a separation is quite dreadful; still, I feel I *could* bear it,—I have made up my mind to it, as the very *thought* of going has been a comfort to my poor Angel, and will be of such use at Coburg. Still, if I were to remain *quite* alone I do not think I *could* bear it quietly. Therefore *pray* do send me my dearly beloved Louise; she would be *such* a comfort to me; if you could come too—or afterwards (as you promised us a longer visit), that would be still more delightful. I may be indiscreet, but you must think of *what* the separation from my *all and all*, even only for a *fort-night*, will be to me!

We feel some *years* older since these days of mourning. Mamma is calm, but poor Aunt Julia[7] is indeed much to be pitied. Ever, dearest Uncle, your devoted and unhappy Niece and Child,

Victoria R.

Queen Victoria to the King of the Belgians.

Windsor Castle, *13th February 1844.*

My dearest Uncle,—I received your dear, kind but sad letter of the 8th on Sunday, and thank you much for it. God knows, poor dear Uncle, you have suffered *enough* in your life, but you should think, dearest Uncle, of *that blessed* assurance of *eternity* where we shall *all meet again never* to part; you should think (as we constantly do now) that those whom we have lost are far happier than we are, and *love us* still, and in a far more perfect way than *we can* do in this world! When the first moments and days of overwhelming grief are over these reflections are the greatest balm, the greatest consolation to the bleeding heart.

I hope you will kindly let me have a few lines of *hope* by the Tuesday's messenger. Ever your truly devoted Niece and Child,

Victoria R.

P.S.—O'Connell's being pronounced guilty is a great triumph.[8]

7

Viscount Melbourne to Queen Victoria.

South Street, *3rd April 1844.*

Lord Melbourne presents his humble duty to your Majesty, with many thanks for your Majesty's note of the 28th ult. Lord Melbourne believes that your Majesty is quite right in saying that Lord Melbourne has still some health left, if he will but take care of it. Lord Melbourne told Dr Holland, without mentioning your Majesty's name, that this had been said to him by a friend, and Dr Holland immediately said that it was very just and true, and very well expressed, and quite what he should have said himself. At the same time, the change from strength to weakness and the evident progress of decadence is a very hard and disagreeable trial. Lord Melbourne has been reading Cicero on old age, a very pretty treatise, but he does not find much consolation after it; the principal practical resources and alleviations which he recommends are agriculture and gardening, to both of which, but more particularly to the latter, Lord Melbourne has already had recourse. It is certainly, as your Majesty says, wrong to be impatient and to repine at everything, but still it is difficult not to be so. Lady Uxbridge's death[9] is a shocking event, a dreadful loss to him and to all. Lord Melbourne always liked her. Lord Melbourne is going down to Brocket Hall to-morrow, and will try to get Uxbridge and the girls to come over and dine.

Lord Melbourne has felt very much for the grief which your Majesty must feel at a separation, even short and temporary, from the Prince, and it is extremely amiable to feel comforted by the recollection of the extreme pleasure which his visit will give to his and your Majesty's relations. It is, of course, impossible that your Majesty should in travelling divest yourself of your character and dignity.

Lord Melbourne has just driven round the Regent's Park, where there are many almond trees in bloom, and looking beautiful.

Sir Robert Peel to Queen Victoria.

Whitehall, *23rd April 1844.*

Sir Robert Peel, with his humble duty to your Majesty, begs leave to acquaint your Majesty that he has every reason to believe that the Court of Directors will *to-morrow*, by an unanimous vote, resolve on the actual recall of Lord Ellenborough.[10]

Queen Victoria to Sir Robert Peel.

Buckingham Palace, *23rd April 1844.*

The Queen has heard with the greatest regret from Sir R. Peel that the Court of Directors, after all, mean to recall Lord Ellenborough. She cannot but consider this *very* unwise at this critical moment, and a very ungrateful return for the eminent services Lord Ellenborough has rendered to the Company in India. They ought not to forget so soon in what state Lord Ellenborough found affairs in 1842. The Queen would not be sorry if these gentlemen knew that this is her opinion.

The King of the Belgians to Queen Victoria.

Laeken, *3rd May 1844.*

My Dearest Victoria,—Whenever you wish to make me *truly happy*, you will have the power of doing so by repeating expressions as kind and affectionate as those contained in your dear little letter of the 30th. I have ever had the care and affection of a *real father* for you, and it has perhaps even been freer from many drawbacks which occasionally will exist betwixt parents and children, be they ever so well and affectionately together. With me, even from the moment in January 1820, when I was called by a messenger to Sidmouth, my care for you has been unremitting, and never has there been a cloud between us.... A thing which often strikes me, in a very satisfactory manner, is that we never had any bitter words, a thing which happens even with people who are very lovingly together; and the little row which we had in 1838 you remember well, and do not now think that *I* was wrong.[11] *De pareilles relations sont rares; may they ever continue!*

I cannot leave this more serious topic without adding that though you were always warm-hearted and right-minded, it must strike yourself how matured every kind and good feeling is in your generous heart. *The heart, and not the head, is the safest guide in positions like yours,* and this not only for this earthly and very short life, but for that which we must hope for hereafter. When a life draws nearer its close, how many earthly concerns are there that appear *still in the same light?* and how clearly the mind is struck that nothing has been and is still of *real* value, than the nobler and better feelings of the heart; the only good we can hope to keep as a precious store for the future. What

9

do we keep of youth, beauty, richness, power, and even the greatest extent of earthly possessions? Nothing!... Your truly devoted Uncle,

Leopold R.

Sir Robert Peel to Queen Victoria.

Whitehall, *5th May 1844.*

Sir Robert Peel, with his humble duty to your Majesty, and believing that he is acting in accordance with your Majesty's own opinion, begs leave to submit to your Majesty that it may be advisable that he should by the present mail inform Lord Ellenborough that it is your Majesty's intention to confer on him, at a very early period, as a mark of your Majesty's approval of Lord Ellenborough's conduct and services in India, the rank of an Earl and the Grand Cross of the Bath.

Lord Ellenborough may be at liberty (should your Majesty approve) to notify this publicly in India—and thus make it known that the general line of policy recently pursued has had the full sanction of your Majesty, and will not be departed from.

These were the honours conferred upon Lord Auckland.

If they were conferred *on the instant*, it might rather seem a rebuke to the East India Company than a deliberate approval of the conduct of Lord Ellenborough, but these honours might shortly follow the conclusion of the affair respecting the selection of Lord Ellenborough's successor, and any discussion that may arise in Parliament.

Queen Victoria to the King of the Belgians.

Claremont, *24th May 1844.*

Dearest Uncle,—Though *not* my day I must write you a line to say *how vexed* we are at this *most unfortunate* and *most imprudent brochure* of Joinville's;[12] it has made a *very bad* effect here, and will rouse all the envy and hatred between the *two Navies* again, which it was our great effort to subdue—and this *all* for *nothing!* I can't tell you how angry people are, and how poor Hadjy will get abused. And this *all* after our having been on such intimate terms with him and having *sailed* with him! If he comes here, *what* shall we do? Receive with open arms one who has talked of ravaging our coasts and burning our towns? Indeed it is most lamentable; you know how we like him, and that therefore it must be very annoying to us to see him get himself into such a scrape. *We* shall overlook it, but the people *here* won't! It *will* blow over, but it will do immense harm. We who wish to become more and more closely united with the French family are, of course, much put out by this return. We shall forgive and forget, and feel it was *not* intended to be published—but the public *here* will *not* so easily, and will put the worst construction on it all.

Pray, dearest Uncle, tell me what *could* possess Joinville to write it, and still more to have it printed? Won't it annoy the King and Nemours very much? *Enfin c'est malheureux, c'est indiscret au plus haut degré*—and it provokes and vexes us sadly. Tell me *all* you *know* and think about it; for you *can* do so with perfect safety by our courier.

I have written dearest Louise an account of my *old* birthday, which will please you, I think. The weather is very fine. Ever your *truly* devoted Niece and Child,

Victoria R.

Queen Victoria to the Earl of Aberdeen.

29th May 1844.

If Lord Aberdeen should not have read the Prince de Joinville's pamphlet, the Queen recommends him to do so, as one cannot judge fairly by the extracts in the newspapers. Though it does not lessen the extreme imprudence of the Prince's publishing what must do harm to the various French Governments, it certainly is *not* intentionally written to offend England, and on the contrary frankly proves *us* to be immensely superior to the French Navy in every way.

Queen Victoria to the King of the Belgians.

Windsor Castle, *4th June 1844.*

My beloved Uncle,—I gave Louise a long and detailed description of the Emperor,[13] etc. The papers are full of the details. A great event and a great compliment *his* visit certainly is, and the people *here* are extremely flattered at it. He is certainly a *very striking* man; still very handsome; his profile is *beautiful*, and his manners *most* dignified and graceful; extremely civil—quite alarmingly so, as he is so full of attentions and *politesses*. But the expression of the *eyes* is *formidable*, and unlike anything I ever saw before. He gives me and Albert the impression of a man who is *not* happy, and on whom the weight of his immense power and position weighs heavily and painfully; he seldom smiles, and when he does the expression is *not* a happy one. He is very easy to get on with. Really, it seems like a dream when I think that we breakfast and walk out with *this* greatest of all earthly Potentates as

11

quietly as if we walked, etc., with Charles or any one. We took him, with the dear good King of Saxony,[14] who is a great contrast to the *Czar* (and with whom I am *quite* at my ease), to Adelaide Cottage after breakfast. The grass here is just as if it had been burned with fire. *How* many different Princes have we not gone the same round with!! The children are much admired by the *Sovereigns*—(how *grand* this sounds!) —and Alice allowed the Emperor to take her in his arms, and kissed him *de son propre accord*. We are always so thankful that they are *not* shy. Both the Emperor and the King are *quite* enchanted with Windsor. The Emperor said very *poliment*: "C'est digne de vous, Madame." I must say the Waterloo Room lit up with that entire service of gold looks splendid; and the Reception Room, beautiful to sit in afterwards. The Emperor praised *my* Angel very much, saying: "C'est impossible de voir un plus joli garçon; il a l'air si noble et si bon"; which I must say *is very* true. The Emperor amused the King and me by saying he was so *embarrassé* when people were presented to him, and that he felt so "*gauche*" *en frac*, which certainly he is quite *unaccustomed* to wear. If we can do anything to get him to do what is right by you, we shall be most happy, and Peel and Aberdeen are very anxious for it. I believe he leaves on Sunday again. To-morrow there is to be a great review, and on Thursday *I* shall probably go with them to the races; *they* are gone there with Albert to-day, but I have remained at home.

I think it is time to conclude my long letter.

If the French are angry at this visit, let their dear King and their Princes come; *they* will be sure of a *truly affectionate* reception on our part. The one which Emperor Nicholas has received is cordial and civil, *mais ne vient pas du cœur*.

I humbly beg that any remarks which may *not* be favourable to our great visitor may *not* go *beyond* you and Louise, and *not* to *Paris*. Ever your devoted Niece,

Victoria R.

Queen Victoria to the King of the Belgians.

Buckingham Palace, *11th June 1844.*

My Dearest Uncle,—I received your very kind and long letter of the 7th on Sunday, and thank you very much for it. I am delighted that my accounts interested you, and I shall try and give you some more to-day, which you will see come from an unbiassed and impartial mind, and which I trust therefore *will* be relied upon. The excitement has ceased as suddenly as it had begun, and I am still confused about it. I will go back to where I last left you. The *Revue*[15] on the 5th was really very interesting, and our reception as well as that of the Emperor *most* enthusiastic. Louise tells me you had a review the same day, and that it also was so hot. Our children were there, and charmed. On the 6th we went with the Emperor and King to the races,[16] and I never saw such a crowd; again *here* the reception was *most brilliant*. Every evening a large dinner in the Waterloo Room, and the two last evenings in uniforms, as the Emperor disliked so being *en frac*, and was quite embarrassed in it. On the 7th we took him and the King back here, and in the evening had a party of 260 about. On Saturday (8th) my Angel took the Emperor and King to a very elegant breakfast[17] at Chiswick, which I for prudence' sake did *not* go to, but was very sorry for it. In the evening we went to the Opera (*not* in State), but they recognised us, and we were most brilliantly received. I had to force the Emperor forward, as he never would come forward when I was there, and I was obliged to take him by the hand and make him appear; it was impossible to be better bred or more respectful than he was towards me. Well, on Sunday afternoon at five, he left us (my Angel accompanied him to Woolwich), and he was much affected at going, and really unaffectedly touched at his reception and stay, the simplicity and quietness of which told upon his love of domestic life, which is very great. I will now (having told *all* that has passed) give you *my* opinion and feelings on the subject, which I may say are Albert's also. I was extremely against the visit, fearing the *gêne*, and bustle, and even at first, I did not feel at *all* to like it, but by living in the same house together quietly and unrestrainedly (and this Albert, and with great truth, says is the great advantage of these visits, that I not only *see* these great people but *know* them), I got to know the Emperor and he to know me. There is much about him which I cannot help liking, and I think his character is *one* which should be understood, and looked upon for *once* as it is. He is stern and severe—with fixed principles of *duty* which *nothing* on earth will make him change; very *clever* I do *not* think him, and his mind is an uncivilised one; his education has been neglected; politics and military concerns are the only things he takes great interest in; the arts and all softer occupations he is insensible to, but he is sincere, I am certain, *sincere* even in his most despotic acts, from a sense that that *is* the *only* way to govern; he is not, I am sure, aware of the dreadful cases of individual misery which he so often causes, for I can see by various instances that he is kept in utter ignorance of *many* things, which his people carry out in most corrupt ways, while he thinks that he is extremely just. He thinks of general measures, but does not look into detail. And I am sure *much* never reaches his ears, and (as you observed), how can it? He asked for *nothing* whatever, has merely expressed his great anxiety to be upon the best terms with us, but *not* to the *exclusion of others*, only let things remain as they are.... He is I should say, too frank, for he talks so openly before people, which he should not do, and with difficulty restrains himself. His anxiety *to be believed* is *very* great, and I must say his personal promises I *am inclined* to believe; then his feelings are very strong; he *feels* kindness deeply—and his love for his wife and children, and for all children, is *very* great. He has a strong feeling for domestic life, saying to me, when our children were in the room: "Voilà les doux moments de notre vie." He was not only civil, but extremely kind *to us both*, and spoke in the highest praise of dearest Albert to Sir Robert Peel, saying he wished any Prince in Germany had that ability and sense; he showed Albert great confidence, and I *think* it will do great good, as if *he* praises him abroad it will have great weight. He is *not* happy, and that melancholy which is visible in the countenance made me sad at times; the sternness of the eyes goes very much off when you know him, and changes according to his being put out (and he *can* be much embarrassed) or not, and also from his being heated, as he suffers with congestions to the head. My Angel thinks that he is a man inclined too much to give way to impulse and feeling, which makes him act wrongly often. His admiration for beauty is very great, and put me much in mind of you, when he drove out with us, looking out for pretty people. But he remains very faithful to those he admired *twenty-eight* years ago; for instance, Lady Peel, who has hardly any remains left. Respecting Belgium he did not speak to *me*, but to Albert and the Ministers. As for unkindly feeling towards *you*, he disclaims positively any, saying he knew you well, and that you had served in the Russian Army, etc., but he says those *unfortunate* Poles are the *only* obstacle, and that he positively cannot enter into direct communication *with Belgium* as long as they are *employed*. If you could only somehow or other get rid of them, I am sure the thing would be done at once. We all think he *need* not mind this, but I fear he has pledged himself. He admired Charlotte's picture. *Pour finir*, I must say one more word or two about his personal appearance. He puts us much in mind of his and our cousins the Würtembergs, and has altogether much of the Würtemberg family about him. He is bald now, but in his Chevalier Garde Uniform he is *magnificent* still, and very *striking*. I cannot deny that we were in great anxiety when we took him out lest some Pole might make an attempt, and I always felt thankful when we got him safe home again. His poor daughter is very ill, I fear. The good King of Saxony[18] remains another week with us, and we like him much. He is so unassuming. He is out sight-seeing *all* day, and enchanted with everything. I hope that you will persuade the King to come all the same in September. Our *motives* and politics are *not* to be exclusive, but to be on good terms with *all*, and why should we not? We make no secret of it.

Now I must end this very long letter. Ever your devoted Niece,

Victoria R.

You will kindly not *speak* of these details, but only in *allgemein* say the visit went off very satisfactorily on *both sides*, and that it was *highly pacific.*

Queen Victoria to the King of the Belgians.

Buckingham Palace, *18th June 1844.*

My Dearest Uncle,—I had the happiness of receiving your dear and kind letter of the 13th on Sunday; your *parties* at Ardenne must have been truly delightful; perhaps some day *we* may enjoy them too: that would be delightful! I can write to you with a light heart, thank goodness, to-day, for the Government obtained a majority, which *up* to the *last* moment last night we feared they would not have, and we have been in sad trouble for the last four or five days about it.[19] It is the more marvellous, as, if the Government asked for a *Vote* of Confidence, they would have a *Majority* of 100; but this very strength makes the supporters of the Government act in a *most* unjustifiable manner by continually acting and voting against them, *not* listening to the debates, but coming down and voting against the Government. So that we were really in the greatest *possible* danger of having a resignation of the Government *without knowing to whom to turn*, and this from the recklessness of a handful of foolish *half* "Puseyite" half "Young England"[20] people! I am sure you will agree with me that Peel's resignation would not only be for us (for *we cannot* have a better and a *safer* Minister), but for the whole country, and for the peace of Europe—a *great calamity.* Our present people are all *safe*, and not led away by impulses and reckless passions. We must, however, take care and not get into another crisis; for I assure you we have been quite miserable and *quite* alarmed ever since Saturday.

Since I last wrote to you, I spoke to Aberdeen (whom I should be equally sorry to lose, as he is so *very fair*, and has served *us personally*, so kindly and truly), and he told me that the Emperor has *positively pledged* himself to send a Minister to Brussels the moment those Poles are no longer employed;[21] that he is quite aware of the importance of the measure, and would be disposed to make the arrangement easy, and that he spoke very kindly of *you* personally. Aberdeen says it is not necessary to disgrace them in any way, but only for the present *de les éloigner*. The Emperor has evidently some time ago made some strong declaration on the subject which he feels he cannot get over, and, as I said before, he will not give up what he has once pledged his word to. *Then, no one* on earth *can* move him. *Au fond*, it is a fine *trait*, but he carries it too far. He wrote me a *very* kind and affectionate letter from the Hague. The Emperor has given Bertie the Grand Cross of St Andrew, which the boy was quite proud of.

Our kind and good King of Saxony leaves us to-morrow, after having seen more than anybody has done almost, and having enjoyed it of all things. He is quite at home with us and the children, whom he plays with much. Alice walks quite alone, and looks too funny, as she is so *very* fat. Now, ever your devoted Niece,

Victoria R.

Viscount Melbourne to Queen Victoria.

South Street, *19th June 1844.*

Lord Melbourne presents his humble duty to your Majesty, and thanks your Majesty much for the letter of the 14th inst. Lord Melbourne was very glad to have the opportunity of seeing the Emperor of Russia at Chiswick. Lord Melbourne humbly believes that the opinion, which your Majesty has formed and expresses of the Emperor's character is just, and he considers it extremely fortunate that a sovereign of such weight and influence in Europe, and with whom it is probable that Great Britain will have such near and intimate relations, should also be a man upon whose honour and veracity strong reliance may be safely and securely placed.

Lord Melbourne is very glad to believe that the late political movements, with which the public mind has been agitated, have subsided, and are entirely terminated by the last vote of the House of

Commons, and by the determination evinced to support the Administration.[22]

This finishes for the present a business which at one moment seemed likely to be troublesome, and out of which there did not appear to present itself any hope or practicable escape.

Lord Melbourne will not make any observation upon what is known and understood to have passed, further than to say that, as far as he is acquainted with the history of public affairs in this country, it is an entire novelty, quite new and unprecedented.[23] Many a Minister has said to the Crown, "My advice must be taken, and my measures must be adopted," but no Minister has ever yet held this language or advanced this pretension to either House of Parliament. However, it seems to be successful at present, and success will justify much. Whether it will tend to permanent strength or a steady conduct of public affairs, remains to be seen.

Lord Melbourne begs to be respectfully remembered to His Royal Highness.

The Earl of Ellenborough to Queen Victoria.

22nd June 1844.

Lord Ellenborough, with his most humble duty to your Majesty, humbly acquaints your Majesty that on the 15th of June he received the announcement of his having been removed from the office of Governor-General of India by the Court of Directors. By Lord Ellenborough's advice, letters were immediately despatched by express to every important native Court to assure the native Princes that this change in the person at the head of the Government would effect no change in its policy, and Lord Ellenborough himself wrote in similar terms to the British Representatives at the several Courts.... Lord Ellenborough has written a letter to the Earl of Ripon with reference to the reasons alleged by the Court of Directors for his removal from office, to which letter he most humbly solicits your Majesty's favourable and attentive consideration. It treats of matters deeply affecting the good government of India.

Amidst all the difficulties with which he has had to contend in India, aggravated as they have been by the constant hostility of the Court of Directors, Lord Ellenborough has ever been sustained by the knowledge that he was serving a most gracious Mistress, who would place the most favourable construction upon his conduct, and he now humbly tenders to your Majesty the expression of his gratitude, not only for those marks of Royal favour with which it has been intimated to him that it is your Majesty's intention to reward his services, but yet more for that constant support which has animated all his exertions, and has mainly enabled him to place India in the hands of his successor in a state of universal peace, the result of two years of victories, and in a condition of prosperity heretofore unknown.

The King of the Belgians to Queen Victoria.

Laeken, *28th June 1844.*

My beloved Victoria,—I have again to offer my warmest and best thanks for a very long and kind letter. I am truly and sincerely happy that a Ministerial crisis has been spared you; it is in all constitutional concerns an *awful* business; but in such a colossal machinery as the British Empire, it shakes the whole globe. For your sake, for the good of England, and for the quiet of the whole earth, we must most devoutly pray that *Sir Robert may remain for many, many years your trusty and faithful Minister.* Parliaments and Chambers are extremely fond of governing, particularly as long as it does not bore themselves. We have had an instance of it recently. I was anxious to keep the Chamber longer, as there are still many important things which it ought to have finished; but they were hot, they got tired, voted twelve *projets de loi* in one day, and disappeared afterwards, leaving one the trouble of managing the affairs of the State as best one may....

As a general political event, the Emperor's visit in England can only be useful; it is probable that he would *not* have made the visit if another had not been talked of. His policy is naturally to *separate* as much as possible the two great Western Powers; he is too weak to resist single-handed their dictates in the Oriental question; *but if they act not in concert*, it is evident that *he is the master*; in all this he acts wisely and in conformity with the great interests of his Empire. England has greater interests at stake at the mercy of Russia than at that of France. With France the questions are sometimes questions of jealousy, but, on the other hand, a tolerable understanding keeps France quiet and secures the peace of Europe, much more in the sense of the European policy of England than of that of France. The only consolation the French can find in it is that they are aware that *together* with England they have a great position, but they always lament that they can *get nothing by it.* A bad understanding with France opens not only the door to a European war, but also to revolution; and that is perhaps the most serious and most awfully dangerous part of the business.

England wants nothing from the Emperor than that he should leave the *status quo* of Europe and great part of Asia alone. At Paris they are not so much moved at the Emperor's visit as perhaps they ought to be, but they have put the flattering notion into their heads that he had made *fiasco*, which is *not true*; as, in fact, he has so far been rather *successful*, and has convinced people in England that he is a mild and good-natured man, himself and his Empire, without any ambition. Now it is high time I should finish my immense scrawl, for which I claim your forgiveness, remaining ever your devoted Uncle,

Leopold R.

Queen Victoria to the King of the Belgians.

Windsor Castle, *27th August 1844.*

My dearest Uncle,—Many thanks for your kind long letter, which I received yesterday, dated 23rd. I can report very well of ourselves. We are all well. The dear day of yesterday[24] we spent very quietly and happily and full of gratitude to Providence for so many blessings. I can only pray for the continuance of our present happiness.

The impending political cloud, I hope and trust, looks less black and lowering. But I think it very unwise in Guizot not to have at once disavowed D'Aubigny for what you yourself call an "outrage,"[25] instead of letting it drag on for *four weeks* and letting our people get excited. The Tangiers Affair[26] is unfortunate, and I hope that in future poor Joinville will not be exposed to such disagreeable affairs. What *can* be done will be, to get him justified in the eyes of the public here, but I fear that at first they will not be very charitable. Those letters in the *Times* are outrageous, and all that abuse very bad taste.[27] There is to be an investigation about the three officers, whose conduct is unworthy of Englishmen. Now, dearest Uncle, believe me always, your most affectionate Niece,

Victoria R.

Queen Victoria to the King of the Belgians.

Blair Athol, *15th September 1844.*

My Dearest Uncle,—I received your kind letter of the 6th the day we arrived here, and thank you very much for it. As I have written an account of our journey to Louise, I will *not* repeat it here.

The good ending of our difficulties with France is an immense blessing, but it is really and truly necessary that you and those at Paris should know that the danger was *imminent*, and that poor Aberdeen stood *almost alone* in trying to keep matters peaceable. We must try and prevent these difficulties for the future. I must, however, clear *Jarnac*[28] of all blame, for Aberdeen does nothing but praise him....

In Greece affairs look very black, and God knows how it all will end.

The Queen of the Belgians to Queen Victoria.

Laeken, *5th October 1844*.

My Dearly Beloved Victoria,—... I have not much to say about my father's *lodging habits* and *likings*.[29] My father is one of the beings *most easy* to *please*, *satisfy*, and to *accommodate*. His eventful life has used him to everything, and makes any kind of arrangements accept-able to him; there is only *one thing* which he *cannot easily do*, it is to be *ready very early*. He means notwithstanding to try to come to your breakfast, but you *must insist upon his not doing it*. It would disturb him in all his habits, and be bad for him, as he would certainly eat, a thing he is not used to do in the morning. He generally takes hardly what may be called a *breakfast*, and eats *only twice* in the day. It would be also *much better* for him if he only appeared to luncheon and dinner, and if you kindly dispensed him altogether of the breakfast. You must not tell him that I wrote you *this*, but you must manage it with Montpensier, and kindly order for him a bowl of *chicken broth*. It is the only thing he takes generally in the morning, and between his meals. I have also no observation to make, but I have told Montpensier to speak openly to Albert whenever he thought something ought to be done for my father, or might hurt and inconvenience him, and you may consult him when you are in doubt. He is entrusted with all the rec-ommendations of my mother, for my father is naturally *so imprudent* and *so little accustomed* to *caution and care*, that he must in some measure be *watched* to prevent his catching cold or doing what may be injurious to him. About his *rooms*, a hard bed and a large table for his papers are the only things he requires. He generally sleeps on a horse-hair mattress with a plank of wood under it: but *any kind* of bed will do, if it is not *too soft*. His liking will be to be entirely at *your com-mands* and to do *all you like*. You know he can take a great deal of exercise, and *everything* will *interest* and *delight* him, to see, as to do: this is not a compliment, but a *mere fact*. His only wish is, that you

should not go out of your way for him, and change your habits on his account. Lord Aberdeen will be, of course, at Windsor, and I suppose you will ask, as you told me, the Royal Family. My father hopes to see also Sir Robert Peel, Lord Stanley, and your other Ministers. You will probably ask most of them during his stay. He wishes very much to see again those he already knows, and to make the acquaintance of those he does not know yet. In writing all this I think I *dream, I cannot believe* yet that in a few days my dear father will have, God willing, the *unspeakable happiness* to see you again and at *Windsor*, a thing he had *so much wished* for and which for a *long time* seemed so *improbable*. You have *no notion* of the *satisfaction* it gives him, and *how delighted* he will be to see you again, and to be once more in England. God grant he may have a good passage, and arrive to you *safely* and *well. Unberufen*, as you will soon, I trust, be able to see, he is, notwithstanding the usual talk of the papers, *perfectly well....* Yours most devotedly,

Louise.

The Queen of the Belgians to Queen Victoria.

Laeken, *7th October 1844.*

My Dearly beloved Victoria,—... I wrote to my mother, to quiet her, all you kindly tell me about my dear father. We are *quite sure*, I assure you, that you and Albert will *take care of him*, and that he is with you *in safe hand*. And what makes my mother *uneasy* is the fear that, being at liberty without control, he will make *too much*, as she says, *le jeune homme*, ride, go about, and do everything as if he was still twenty years old. If I must tell you *all the truth*, she is afraid also he will *eat too much*. I am sure he will tell it to you himself, as he was so much amused with *this fear*; but to do her pleasure, being well assured by me that you would allow it, and that it was even *customary*, he has given up, of himself, all thought of attending your early breakfast: but I perceive I write as if *he was not already* under *your* roof. I will also only say, that though he has sent over his horses in case they should be wanted, my mother begs you to *prevent, if possible, his riding at all*. I wrote to her already that I supposed there would be *no occasion* for riding, and that your *promenades* would be either on foot or in carriage. I entrusted Montpensier with all my messages for you, my beloved Victoria and your dear children. He hopes you will permit him, during his stay at Windsor, to make *two* excursions—one to London, and one to Woolwich—he is very curious to see, as an artillery officer. I mention it as he would be, perhaps, *too shy* or *too discreet* to mention it himself. He might very well do those two trips by the railroad and be back for dinner-time, and I am sure you will have no objection to them.... Yours most devotedly,

Louise.

I am very glad that Lord Charles Wellesley is one of those who will attend my father. Montpensier and him will have surely capital fun together, and he was, you know, a great favourite with every one at Eu. If by chance Lord Hardwicke was in waiting during my father's stay, you must kindly put my father in mind to thank him for the *famous cheese*, which arrived safely, and was found very good....

Queen Victoria to the King of the Belgians.
Windsor Castle, *8th October 1844*.

Dearest Uncle,—You will, I am sure, forgive my writing but a few lines as I am all alone in the agitation of the dear King's arrival, and I will leave my letter open to announce it to you. My *dearest* master is gone to Portsmouth to receive him. The excitement and curiosity to see the dear King, and the desire to give him a most hearty reception, is *very great indeed*.

Many thanks for your kind letters of the 28th and 4th. I can't think who could have said that Peel, etc., would *not* have been here; for he, Aberdeen, and the old Duke are to be here the whole time, and all the other Ministers will come *during* his stay.

I am very glad Joinville is arrived, and avoided his *entrées triomphales*. I hope he will take great care of himself.

You will have heard from dear Louise of our voyage, etc. I cannot reconcile myself to be *here* again, and pine for my *dear* Highlands, the hills, the pure air, the quiet, the retirement, the liberty—*all*—more than is right. The children are well. I am sorry to hear that you are not quite so yet.

3.30.—The King and Montpensier arrived quite safely at two, and are both looking extremely well. We have just lunched with them. It seems like a dream to me, and a very pleasant one.

Albert sends his affectionate love. Ever your devoted Niece,

Victoria R.

Bertie has immediately taken a passion for Montpensier.

Viscount Melbourne to Queen Victoria.

Brocket Hall, *9th October 1844.*

Lord Melbourne presents his humble duty to your Majesty, and thanks your Majesty much for the letter of the 7th inst., which he has just received, and with very great satisfaction, as he had begun to think your Majesty's silence rather long. But he perfectly understands the reasons which prevented your Majesty from writing during your stay in the Highlands. Lord Melbourne is very glad to find that your Majesty enjoyed that country so much, and is so enthusiastically fond of it. Lord Melbourne believes that he was at the places which your Majesty mentions. In the year 1802 he stayed some months in Perthshire with the late Lord Kinnaird, and enjoyed it much. It annoys him sometimes to think how altered he is in strength since that time. Lord Melbourne has never yet thanked your Majesty for the pretty etchings of poor Islay and Eos, which your Majesty sent to Lord Melbourne when he was last at Windsor. Lord Melbourne has ordered them both to be framed, and will hang them up in his room here. They will afford Lord Melbourne most agreeable and pleasing souvenirs of the happiest period of his life, for he cannot say otherwise than that he continually misses and regrets the time when he had daily confidential communication with your Majesty. Lord Glenlyon[30] has one merit in Lord Melbourne's eyes, which is that he was a steady and firm supporter to the last of Lord Melbourne's Government. Lord Melbourne hopes and trusts that he feels no animosity against those who opposed him. But he does and always shall entertain a kindly and grateful recollection of those who supported him.

Lord Melbourne begs to be remembered to His Royal Highness.

The Queen of the Belgians to Queen Victoria.

Laeken, *12th October 1844.*

My dearly beloved Victoria,—... I thank you very much for attending to all my recommendations about *my* father: I only fear that they will lead you to believe that we consider him as a *great child* and treat him like one: but he is so *precious* and *dear* to *us all* that I am sure you will *understand* and *excuse* our being *over anxious*.... Yours most devotedly,

Louise.

Queen Victoria to the King of the Belgians.

Osborne House, *17th October 1844.*

My Dearest Uncle,—I had intended to have written to you on Monday, but you will since have heard of the great *confusion* of that day which prevented me from doing so. The dear King's visit went off to perfection, and I much and deeply regret its being passed. He was *delighted*, and was *most* enthusiastically and affectionately received wherever he showed himself. Our proceedings I wrote to good, dear Louise (whom you should not leave so long alone), who will no doubt have given you the details. What an extraordinary man the King is! What a wonderful memory, and how lively, *how sagacious!* He spoke very openly to us all, and is determined that our affairs should go on well. He wishes Tahiti *au fond de la mer.* He spoke also very openly about poor Hadjy's *brochure* which seems to have distressed him more than anything. The King praised my dearest Albert most highly, and fully appreciates his great qualities and talents—and what gratifies me *so much*, treats him completely as his equal, calling him "Mon Frère," and saying to me that *my husband* was the same as me, which it is— and "Le Prince Albert, c'est pour moi le Roi." The King is *very* sad to go, but he is determined, he says, *to see me every year.* Another *very* great thing is, that the officers of the two Navies staying at Portsmouth were on the best terms together and paying one another every sort of compliment. As Admiral La Susse (a very gentlemanlike man) and his squadron were sadly disappointed on Monday,[31] we thought it would please them if we went on board the *Gomer*, which we did, on Tuesday morning, and breakfasted there, and I drank the King's health. I am certain that the visit and everything connected with it can but do the *greatest good.*

We stay here till Monday. It is a very comfortable little house, and the grounds and place are delightful, so private—and the view so fine.

I must now conclude, begging you to believe me, ever your devoted Niece,

Victoria R.

I forgot to say how much we liked good Montpensier, who got on extremely well.

Queen Victoria to the King of the French.

Osborne House, *le 17 Octobre 1844.*

Sire, et mon très cher Frère,—Votre Majesté m'a écrit deux bien bonnes lettres de Douvres pour lesquelles je vous remercie de tout mon cœur. Les expressions de bonté et d'amitié que vous me vouez ainsi qu'à mon cher Albert nous touchent sensiblement; je n'ai pas besoin de vous dire encore, combien nous vous sommes attachés et combien nous désirons voir se raffermir de plus en plus cette *entente cordiale* entre nos deux pays qui existe si heureusement entre nous personnellement. C'était avec un vif regret que nous nous sommes séparés de votre Majesté, et de Montpensier, et ce sera une grande fête que de voir renouveler une visite dont le souvenir nous est si cher.

Albert se met à vos pieds, Sire, bien sensible ainsi que moi-même de l'amitié et la confiance que vous lui avez témoignées.

J'ose prier votre Majesté d'offrir mes plus tendres hommages à la Reine et à Madame votre Sœur et de me rappeler au souvenir de Montpensier. Je suis pour la vie, Sire et mon cher Frère, de votre Majesté la bien affectionnée Sœur et fidèle Amie,

Victoria R.

Queen Victoria to the King of the Belgians.

Windsor Castle, *29th October 1844.*

My dearest Uncle,—I had the happiness of receiving your kind letter of the 26th while I was dressing to go to the City for the opening of the Royal Exchange.[32] Nothing ever went off better, and the procession there, as well as all the proceedings *at* the Royal Exchange, were splendid and royal in the extreme. It was a fine and gratifying sight to see the myriads of people assembled—more than at the Coronation even, and all in such good humour, and so loyal; the articles in the papers, too, are most kind and gratifying; they say *no* Sovereign *was more* loved than I am (I am bold enough to say), and *that*, from our *happy domestic home*—which gives such a good example. The *Times* you have, and I venture to add a *Chronicle*, as I think it very pretty; you should read the accounts. *I* seldom remember being so gratified and pleased with any public show, and my beloved Albert was so enthusiastically received by the people. He is *so* beloved by all the really influential people, and by *all* right-thinking ones. We came back here yesterday evening. The accounts from Paris are excellent too. How long are the good Joinvilles to remain in the south, and where? By-the-by, dearest Uncle, have you read the continuation of Consuelo,[33] called the "Comtesse de Rudolstadt"? It is *dreadfully* interesting.

The Knights of the Garter did *not* wear the whole costume, but only the mantle. Being on this topic, shall tell you that I intend giving the Garter to Ernest, but pray do not mention it to E. or *any one*.

With Albert's affectionate love. Ever your devoted Niece and Child,

Victoria R.

The King of the French to Queen Victoria.

Saint Cloud, *le 15 Novembre 1844*.

Madame ma bien chère Sœur,—Mes souvenirs de Windsor sont de ceux dont aucun ne s'efface. Je n'oublie donc pas une petite question qui m'a été si joliment adressée, *Where is my gun?* et à présent j'en ai trouvé un qui serait indigne de la destinée que je prie votre Majesté de me permettre de lui donner, si le regret que la disparition du premier fusil avait causé, ne m'avait pas appris que le second devait être d'un genre à supporter tous les accidents que l'enfance aime à infliger à ses joujoux. C'est donc tout simplement un très modeste fusil de munition adapté a sa taille que j'adresse à votre Majesté pour son auguste et charmant enfant le Prince de Galles, comme ma réponse à sa question.

J'ai encore une autre dette dont je vous prie de me permettre de m'acquitter. Quelque vif que soit mon désir de revoir Windsor, ce serait un trop long retard que d'attendre cet heureux moment, pour offrir à la Princesse Royale cette petite boîte à ouvrage, de Paris, qu'elle m'a fait espérer lui serait agréable, et tout ce que je désire c'est que vos enfants se ressouviennent un jour d'avoir vu celui qui a été le fidèle ami de leur grand-père, comme il l'est et le sera toujours de leurs bien aimés parents.

Que votre Majesté me permette encore d'offrir ici au Prince Albert l'expression de la vive et sincère amitié que je lui porte et que je lui garderai toujours, et d'accepter celle de l'inaltérable attachement avec lequel je suis pour la vie, Madame ma bien chère Sœur, de votre Majesté, le bon Frère bien affectionné et fidèle Ami,

Louis Philippe R.

Sir Henry Hardinge to Queen Victoria.

23rd November 1844.

Sir Henry Hardinge[34] with his most humble duty to your Majesty, humbly submits for your Majesty's consideration the following observations on the state of affairs in this large portion of your Majesty's dominions.

The return of peace has also increased the desire of the native population to receive the advantages of English education. The literature of the West is the most favourite study amongst the Hindoos in their schools and colleges. They will discuss with accuracy the most important events in British History. Boys of fifteen years of age, black in colour, will recite the most favourite passages from Shakespeare, ably quoting the notes of the English and German commentators. They excel in mathematics, and in legal subtleties their acuteness is most extraordinary.

In order to reward native talent and render it practically useful to the State, Sir Henry Hardinge, after due deliberation, has issued a resolution, by which the most meritorious students will be appointed to fill the public offices which fall vacant throughout Bengal.

This encouragement has been received by the Hindoo population with the greatest gratitude. The studies in the Mohammedan schools and colleges have hitherto been confined to Arabic, the Koran, and abstruse studies relating to their religion, having always shown a marked aversion to English literature. Since the publication of the Resolution they have at once determined to change their system in order to participate in the benefits held out to native merit of every sect.

It is impossible throughout your Majesty's immense Empire to employ the number of highly paid European civil servants which the public service requires. This deficiency is the great evil of British Administration. By dispersing annually a proportion of well-educated natives throughout the provinces, under British superintendence, well-founded hopes are entertained that prejudices may gradually disappear, the public service be improved, and attachment to British institutions increased....

Sir Henry Hardinge, in closing these observations, most humbly ventures to assure your Majesty that he anticipates no occurrence as probable, by which the tranquillity of this portion of your Majesty's dominions is likely to be disturbed.

H. Hardinge.

ENDNOTES:

[1]:The Duc de Bordeaux, only son of the Duc de Berri, had by the death of Charles X. and the renunciation of all claims to the French Throne on the part of the Duc d'Angoulême, become the representative of the elder branch of the Bourbons. He had intended his visit to England to have a private character only.

[2]:*See ante*, vol. I.

[3]:On the 5th of January the Queen's phaeton was overturned at Horton, near Dachet, while driving to the meet of Prince Albert's Harriers.

[4]:On the occasion of the marriage of the Duc and Duchesse de Nemours (1840), the proposal made by the Soult Government for a Parliamentary grant of 500,000 francs had been rejected.

[5]:He insisted that French trade must be kept under the exclusive surveillance of the French flag.

[6]:The Duke of Saxe-Coburg Gotha died on 29th January.

[7]:The Grand Duchess Constantine of Russia, sister of the Duchess of Kent and of the deceased Duke of Saxe-Coburg.

[8]:He had been indicted with Charles Gavan Duffy and others for seditious conspiracy.

[9]:Henrietta Maria, daughter of Sir Charles Bagot, G.C.B.

[10]:This anomalous privilege was exercised by the Directors in consequence chiefly of what they considered Lord Ellenborough's overbearing demeanour in communication with them, his too aggressive policy, and his theatrical love of display.

[11]:*See* Letters of Queen Victoria and the King of the Belgians, *ante*, vol. I.

[12]:The *brochure* was entitled, *Notes sur les forces navales de la France*. The Prince de Joinville wrote as follows to the Queen: "Le malheureux éclat de ma brochure, le tracas que cela donne au Père et à la Reine, me font regretter vivement de l'avoir faite. Comme je l'écris à ton Roi, je ne renvoie que mépris à toutes les interprétations qu'on y donne; ce que peuvent dire ministre et journaux ne me touche en rien, mais il n'y a pas de sacrifices que je ne suis disposé à faire pour l'intérieur de la Famille."

[13]:The Emperor Nicholas of Russia had just arrived on a visit to England.

[14]:Frederick Augustus II.

[15]:In honour of the Emperor a Review was held in Windsor Great Park.

[16]:At Ascot.

[17]:Given by the Duke of Devonshire.

[18]:See *ante*, p. 11.

[19]:The Ministry had been defeated on Mr P. Miles's motion in favour of giving an increased preference to colonial sugar, but on the 17th this vote was rescinded by a majority of twenty-two, Mr Disraeli taunting the Premier with expecting that "upon every division and at every crisis, his gang should appear, and the whip should sound."

[20]:The name given to the group comprising Disraeli, George Smythe, Lord John Manners, etc. See *Coningsby*, which was published about this time.

[21]:See *ante*, p. 14.

[22]:See *ante*, p. 15.

[23]:Lord Melbourne refers to the House rescinding its own vote.

[24]:The Prince Albert's birthday. Prince Alfred was born on 6th August of this year.

[25]:The assumption of French sovereignty over Tahiti.

[26]:Hostilities had commenced between France and Morocco, and Tangiers was bombarded.

[27]:A series of letters had appeared in the *Times*, written by British naval officers who had witnessed the bombardment of Tangiers, and accused the French Admiral and Navy of being deficient in courage. The *Times* was much criticised for its publication of these letters.

[28]:*Chargé d'Affaires* in the absence of the French Ambassador.

[29]:The difficulty with France as to Tahiti having been satisfactorily disposed of, King Louis Philippe was enabled to visit England, the first French King to come on a visit to the Sovereign of England. The King was enthusiastically received in England, visited Claremont (which he was destined to occupy in exile), was installed as a Knight of the Garter at Windsor with great magnificence, and visited Eton College and Woolwich Arsenal.

[30]:*See* vol. I.

[31]:It had been intended that the King should return to France, as he had come, by way of Portsmouth, crossing in the frigate *Gomer*, but, in consequence of the wet and stormy weather, he returned by Dover and Calais.

[32]:On the preceding day.

[33]:The novel by George Sand (1804-1876), published in 1842.

[34]:Governor-General of India, in succession to Lord Ellenborough.

INTRODUCTORY NOTE
TO CHAPTER XIV

The new year (1845) opened auspiciously, trade improving owing to the great impetus given to it by the many lines of railway then in course of promotion. Over two hundred schemes were prepared at the commencement of the session to seek legislative sanction, and speculation outran all reasonable limits. The Income Tax (which in the ordinary course would have expired) was renewed, and the Anti-Corn Law Leaguers were more persistent than ever in their assaults on Protection, while the attacks on the Ministry from a section of their own party were redoubled. The most remarkable measure of the year was the Government Bill for increasing the grant to the Roman Catholic College of Maynooth, which was strongly opposed from the Conservative and the Protestant points of view; Mr Gladstone, though he approved of the measure, retired from the Ministry, as he had a few years before written in the opposite sense. Towards the close of the year the condition of Ireland, owing to the failure of the potato crop, became very alarming, and the Ministry greatly embarrassed. Lord John Russell wrote from Edinburgh to the electors of the City of London, announcing his conversion to the Repeal of the Corn Laws, and the *Times* announced that such a Bill would be brought in by the Ministry. Peel, reluctant to accept the task, resigned office in December, and a Whig Ministry was attempted. Owing to dissensions, the attempt had to be abandoned, and Peel returned to office, without Lord Stanley, but with Mr Gladstone, who however did not seek re-election for the seat vacated by his acceptance of office.

A dispute of great importance arose during the year with the United States, relating to the boundary line between English and American territory west of the Rocky Mountains. Twenty-five years earlier the same question had arisen, and had been settled on the footing of joint occupancy. The increased importance of the Pacific slope made the matter more vital, involving as it did the ownership of Vancouver Island and the mouth of the Columbia River; President Polk unequivocally claimed the whole, and said he would not shrink from upholding America's interests; the British Government was equally firm, and the matter was not adjusted till 1846.

In India, which during nearly the whole year enjoyed peace, the Sikhs in December assumed the aggressive, and crossed the Sutlej, invading British India. They were signally defeated by Sir Hugh Gough at Moodkee and Ferozeshah. In Scinde Sir Charles Napier prosecuted operations against the mountain desert tribes.

In New Zealand some disastrous collisions took place between the natives and the settlers; the former on two occasions either defeating or repulsing the British arms.

In France the most important events were the Bill for fortifying Paris, the campaign waged against Abd-el-Kader in Algeria, and a horrible act of cruelty perpetrated there. In Spain Don Carlos abdicated his claims to the throne in favour of his son; the Queen's engagement to Count Trapani was rumoured. In other parts of Europe little that was eventful occurred.

CHAPTER XIV

1845

Queen Victoria to the King of the Belgians.

Windsor Castle, *14th January 1845.*

My dearest Uncle,—What you say about Aquila[1] and Montpensier interests me. What madness is it then to force Trapani on Spain! Pray explain to me the cause of the King's obstinacy about that Spanish marriage, for *no* country has a right to dictate in that way to another. If Tatane[2] was *to think* of the Infanta, England would be extremely indignant, and would (and with right) consider it tantamount to a marriage with the Queen herself. Ever your devoted Niece,

Victoria R.

The King of the Belgians to Queen Victoria.

Laeken, *18th January 1845.*

My dearest Victoria,—... The Spanish marriage question is really very curious; in fact, all the other Bourbon branches are hostile to the Orleans family, but the idea that makes the King so constant in his views about it, is that he imagines it would create in France a bad impression if *now* any other than a Bourbon was to marry the Queen of Spain. That feeling they have *themselves created*, as in France they did not at all care about it; having, however, declared *quasi* officially in the French Chambers that they *will not have any but a Bourbon*, if circumstances should after all decide it otherwise it would now be a defeat, but certainly one of their own making.... Your devoted Uncle,

Leopold R.

Queen Victoria to the King of the Belgians.

Windsor Castle, *28th January 1845*.

...The feeling of loyalty in this country is happily *very* strong, and wherever we show ourselves we are most heartily and warmly received, and the civilities and respect shown to us by those we visit is *most* satisfactory. I mention merely a trifling instance to show *how* respectful they are—the Duke of Buckingham, who is immensely proud, bringing the cup of coffee after dinner on a waiter to Albert himself. And everywhere my dearest Angel receives the respect and honours I receive.

Many thanks for returning the list;[3] it was not Albert but *Tatane* who made the black crosses. Are not "Les 3 Mousquetaires," by Dumas, and "Arthur," by Eugène Sue, *readable* for *me*?

Now adieu, dearest, best Uncle. Ever your truly devoted Niece,

Victoria R.

Queen Victoria to Sir Robert Peel.

Pavilion, *10th February 1845*.

Though the Queen knows that Sir Robert Peel has already turned his attention to the urgent necessity of doing something to Buckingham Palace, the Queen thinks it right to recommend this subject herself to his serious consideration. Sir Robert is acquainted with the state of the Palace and the total want of accommodation for our little family, which is fast growing up. Any building must necessarily take some years before it can be safely inhabited. If it were to be begun this autumn, it could hardly be occupied before the spring of 1848, when the Prince of Wales would be nearly seven, and the Princess Royal nearly eight years old, and they cannot possibly be kept in the nursery any longer. A provision for this purpose ought, therefore, to be made this year. Independent of this, most parts of the Palace are in a sad state, and will ere long require a further outlay to render them *decent* for the occupation of the Royal Family or any visitors the Queen may have to receive. A room, capable of containing a larger number of those persons whom the Queen has to invite in the course of the season to balls, concerts, etc., than any of the present apartments can at once hold, is much wanted. Equally so, improved offices and servants' rooms, the want of which puts the departments of the household to great expense yearly. It will be for Sir Robert to consider whether it would not be best to remedy all these deficiencies at once, and to make use of this opportunity to render the exterior of the Palace such as no longer to be a *disgrace* to the country, which it certainly now is. The Queen thinks the country would be better pleased to have the question of the Sovereign's residence in London so finally disposed of, than to have it so repeatedly brought before it.[4]

Queen Victoria to Sir Robert Peel.

Pavilion, *18th February 1845*.

The Queen has received Sir Robert Peel's letter, and is glad that the progress in the House of Commons was so satisfactory.

The Queen was much hurt at Mr Borthwick's most impertinent manner of putting the question with respect to the title of King Consort, and much satisfied with Sir Robert's answer.[5] The title of King is open assuredly to many difficulties, and would perhaps be no *real* advantage to the Prince, but the Queen is positive that something must at once be done to place the Prince's position on a constitutionally recognised footing, and to give him a title adequate to that position.[6] *How* and *when*, are difficult questions....

Queen Victoria to Sir Robert Peel.

Windsor Castle, *24th March 1845*.

The Queen has received Sir Robert Peel's box containing his recommendation relative to the filling up of the vacant Bishopric of Ely. The Queen quite approves of the present Dean of Westminster[7] as the new Bishop. As Sir Robert has asked the Queen whether she would like to see Archdeacon Wilberforce succeed to the Deanery of Westminster in case the Dean should accept the Bishopric, she must say that such an arrangement would be *very satisfactory* to us, and the Queen believes would highly please the Archdeacon. This would again vacate, the Queen believes, a stall at Winchester, which she would like to see filled by a person decidedly adverse to Puseyism.

The Queen approves of the Bishop of Lichfield[8] being transferred to the See of Ely in case Doctor Turton should decline it.

It would give the Queen much pleasure to stand sponsor to Sir Robert Peel's little grandson, and perhaps Sir Robert would communicate this to Lady Villiers.

Queen Victoria to the King of the Belgians.

Windsor Castle, *25th March 1845*.

... I copied what you wrote me about Peel[9] in a letter I wrote him, which I am sure will please him much, and a Minister in these days *does* require a little encouragement, for the abuse and difficulties they have to contend with are dreadful. Peel works so hard and has so much to do, that sometimes he says he does not know *how* he is to get through it all!

You will, I am sure, be pleased to hear that we have succeeded in purchasing *Osborne* in the Isle of Wight,[10] and if we can manage it, we shall probably run down there before we return to Town, for three nights. It sounds so snug and nice to have a place of *one's own*, quiet and retired, and free from all Woods and Forests, and other charming Departments who really are the plague of one's life.

Now, dearest Uncle, adieu. Ever your truly devoted Niece,

Victoria R.

Queen Victoria to Viscount Melbourne.

Buckingham Palace, *3rd April 1845*.

The Queen had intended to have written to Lord Melbourne from Osborne to thank him for his last note of the 19th, but we were so occupied, and so delighted with *our new* and really delightful *home*, that she hardly had time for anything; besides which the weather was so beautiful, that we were out almost all day. The Queen refers Lord Melbourne to Mr Anson for particulars of the new property, which is very extensive, as she is not at all competent to explain about acres, etc. But she thinks it is impossible to imagine a prettier spot—valleys and woods which would be beautiful anywhere; but all this near the sea (the woods grow into the sea) is quite perfection; we have a charming beach quite to ourselves. The sea was so blue and calm that the Prince said it was like Naples. And then we can walk about anywhere by ourselves without being followed and mobbed, which Lord Melbourne will easily understand is delightful. And last, not least, we have Portsmouth and Spithead so close at hand, that we shall be able to watch what is going on, which will please the Navy, and be hereafter very useful for our boys.

The Children are all well. The Queen has just had a lithograph made after a little drawing which she did herself of the three eldest, and which she will send Lord Melbourne with some Eau de Cologne.

Fanny and Lord Jocelyn dined here last night; she is looking very well, and he seems much pleased at being in office, and being employed.

The Queen hopes Lord Melbourne is enjoying this fine weather, and here concludes with the Prince's kind remembrance.

Queen Victoria to the King of the Belgians.

Buckingham Palace, *15th April 1845*.

My beloved Uncle,—Here we are in a great state of agitation about one of the greatest measures ever proposed;[11] I am sure poor Peel ought to be *blessed by* all Catholics for the manly and noble way in which he stands forth to protect and do good to poor Ireland. But the bigotry, the wicked and blind passions it brings forth is quite dreadful, and I blush for Protestantism![12] A Presbyterian clergyman said very truly, "*Bigotry* is more *common than shame....*"

Queen Victoria to the King of the Belgians.

Buckingham Palace, *23rd April 1845*.

My dearest Uncle,—Our Maynooth Bill is through the second reading. I think, if you read Sir Robert's admirable speeches, you will see how good his plan is. The *Catholics* are quite delighted at it—full of gratitude, and behave extremely well; but the Protestants behave shockingly, and display a narrow-mindedness and want of sense on the subject of religion which is quite a disgrace to the nation. The case of Austria, France, etc., cannot be compared to this, as *this* is a *Protestant* country, while the others are Catholic; and I think it would never do to support a Roman Catholic Church with money belonging to the Protestant Church. The Protestant Establishment in Ireland must remain untouched, but let the Roman Catholic Clergy be well and handsomely educated.

The Duc de Broglie[13] dined with us last night; his *travaux* are going on satisfactorily; he asked when you were coming, and said you were "*beaucoup Anglais et un peu Français,*" which is true, I think.

With Albert's affectionate respects, believe me always, your devoted Niece,

Victoria R.

Mr Goulburn[14] to Queen Victoria.

Downing Street, *30th April 1845*.

Mr Goulburn submits with his humble duty to your Majesty that several representations have been made to the Treasury as to the convenience which the public would derive from the circulation of silver threepenny-pieces. Such pieces are lawfully current under your Majesty's Proclamation of the 5th July 1838. But as such pieces have been hitherto reserved as your Majesty's Maundy money, and as such especially belong to your Majesty's service, Mr Goulburn considers that a coinage of them for general use could not take place without a particular signification of your Majesty's pleasure.

Mr Goulburn therefore humbly submits for your Majesty's gracious consideration the signification of your Majesty's pleasure as to the issue of such a coinage.

Sir James Graham to Queen Victoria.

Whitehall, *13th May 1845*.

Sir James Graham, with humble duty, begs to lay before your Majesty the enclosed Memorial.

The proceedings in Newgate on the occasion of the last condemned sermon and on the morning of the execution have been fully investigated;[15] and the report established the necessity of legislative interference to prevent the recurrence of scenes so disgraceful and demoralising. The policy of depriving capital executions of their present publicity is well worthy of careful revision; and Sir James Graham, in obedience to your Majesty's desire, will bring the subject under the notice of his colleagues. He is disposed to think that the sentence might be carried into execution in the presence of a Jury to be summoned by the Sheriff with good effect; and that the great body of idle spectators might be excluded, without diminishing the salutary terror and awful warning which this extreme punishment is intended to produce on the public mind. In dealing, however, with a matter in which the community has so deep an interest, it is prudent not to violate public opinion, and caution is necessary before a change of the long-established usage is proposed.[16]

Sir James Graham deeply regrets the part taken by the newspapers in seeking to indulge the general curiosity with respect to all details of the conduct, habits, and demeanour of these wretched criminals in their last moments; but he fears that the license of the Press cannot be checked by any act of authority; if the public be excluded from witnessing the executions, they will probably become still more anxious to obtain a printed report of all that has taken place; and Sir James Graham is so thoroughly convinced that the punishment of death in certain cases must be maintained, that he would consider any course inexpedient which was likely to lead the public to desire the remission of capital executions in all cases without exception....

J. R. G. Graham.

The King of the Belgians to Queen Victoria.

Laeken, *21st May 1845*.

My dearest and most beloved Victoria,—Receive my sincerest and most heartfelt good wishes on the happy reappearance of your birthday. I need not dwell on my sentiments of devotion to you; they began with *your life, and will only end with mine*. The only claim I make is to be remembered with some little affection. Thank heaven, I have little to wish you, than that your present happiness may not be disturbed, and that those who are dear to you may be preserved for your happiness.

My gift is Charlotte's portrait. The face is extremely like, and the likest that exists; the hair is a little too fair, it had become also darker. I take this opportunity to repeat that Charlotte was a noble-minded and highly gifted creature. She was nervous, as all the family have been; she could be violent, but then she was full of repentance for it, and her disposition *highly generous* and *susceptible* of *great devotion*.

I am the more bound to say this, as I understood that you had some notion that she had been *very imperious*, and not mistress of her temper. Before her marriage some people by dint of flattery had tried to give her masculine tastes; and in short had pushed her to become one day a sort of Queen Elizabeth. These sentiments were already a little modified before her marriage. But she was particularly determined to be a *good* and *obedient* wife; some of her friends were anxious she should *not*; amongst these Madame de Flahaut must be mentioned *en première ligne*.

This became even a subject which severed the intimacy between them. Madame de Flahaut, much older than Charlotte, and of a sour and determined character, had gained an influence which partook on Charlotte's part a little of fear. She was afraid of her, but when once supported took courage.

People were much struck on the 2nd of May 1816 at Carlton House with the clearness and firmness with which she pronounced "*and obey*," etc., as there had been a *general belief* that it would be *for the husband* to give *these promises*. The Regent put me particularly on my guard, and said, "If you don't resist she will govern you with a high hand." Your own experience has convinced you that real affection changes many sentiments that may have been implanted into the mind of a young girl. With Charlotte it was the more meritorious, as from a very early period of her life she was considered as the heiress of the Crown; the Whigs flattered her extremely, and later, when she got by my intervention reconciled to the Tories, they also made great efforts to please her.

Her understanding was extremely good; she knew everybody, and I even afterwards found her judgment generally extremely correct. *She had read a great deal and knew well what she had read.* Generous she was almost *too much*, and her *devotion* was quite affecting, from a character so much pushed to be selfish and imperious.

I will here end my souvenir of poor dear Charlotte, but I thought that the subject could not but be interesting to you. Her constancy in wishing to marry me, which she maintained under difficulties of every description, has been the foundation of all that touched the family afterwards. You know, I believe, that your poor father was the chief promoter, though also the Yorks were; but our correspondence from 1814 till 1816 was entirely carried on through his kind intervention; it would otherwise have been impossible, as she was really treated as a sort of prisoner. Grant always to that good and generous Charlotte, who sleeps already with her beautiful little boy so long, where all will go to, an affectionate remembrance, and believe me she deserves it.

Forgive my long letter, and see in it, what it really is, a token of the great affection I have for you. Ever, my dearest Victoria, your devoted Uncle.

Leopold R.

Queen Victoria to Sir Robert Peel.

Windsor Castle, *12th June 1845*.

The Queen understands that the Deanery of Worcester has become vacant by some new arrangement. Believing that Sir Robert's brother, Mr John Peel, has a fair claim to such preferment, but being afraid that Sir Robert would perhaps hesitate to recommend him on account of his near relationship to him, the Queen wishes to offer herself this Deanery through Sir Robert to his brother.

Sir Robert Peel to Queen Victoria.

Windsor Castle, *12th June 1845*.

Sir Robert Peel, with his humble duty to your Majesty, hastens to acknowledge your Majesty's most kind and considerate communication, and to express his grateful acknowledgments for it.

He must, in justice to his brother, assure your Majesty that he never has expressed, and probably never would express, a wish to Sir Robert Peel on the subject of preferment in the Church.

Sir Robert Peel might have hesitated to bring the name of one so nearly connected with him under the notice of your Majesty, but as his brother was highly distinguished in his academical career at Oxford, and is greatly respected for the discharge of every professional duty, Sir Robert Peel could not feel himself justified in offering an impediment to the fulfilment of your Majesty's gracious intentions in his favour, if, when the vacancy shall have actually occurred in the Deanery of Worcester, no superior claim should be preferred.[17]

Lord Stanley to Queen Victoria.

Downing Street, *10th July 1845*.

Lord Stanley, with his humble duty, submits to your Majesty a despatch just received from the Governor of South Australia, enclosing the letter of a settler in the province, Mr Walter Duffield, who is anxious to be allowed the honour of offering for your Majesty's acceptance a case of the first wine which has been made in the colony.

Lord Stanley will not venture to answer for the quality of the vintage; but as the wine has been sent over with a loyal and dutiful feeling, and the importer, as well as the colonists in general, might feel hurt by a refusal of his humble offering, he ventures to hope that he may be permitted to signify, through the Governor, your Majesty's gracious acceptance of the first sample of a manufacture which, if successful, may add greatly to the resources of this young but now thriving colony.

The above is humbly submitted by your Majesty's most dutiful Servant and Subject,

Stanley.

Queen Victoria to the King of the Belgians.

Osborne, *29th July 1845*.

My dearest Uncle,—Accept my best thanks for your very kind little note of the 26th. As Albert writes to you about the King of Holland's visit[18] I will say but little, except that it really went off wonderfully well in our little house. We took him a sail in the *Victoria and Albert* on Saturday, which he admired amazingly, and after luncheon he went away, Albert taking him over to Gosport. He intends, I believe, to come here one morning for luncheon to take leave. He is grown old, and has lost all his front teeth, but he is as talkative and lively as he used to be, and seems very happy to be in England again. He was very anxious that we should pay him a visit this year, but was quite satisfied when we told him that this year it was impossible, but that we hoped some other time to do so. He was much struck at seeing me now independent and unembarrassed, and talking; as when he was here in 1836[19] I was extremely crushed and kept under and hardly dared say a word, so that he was quite astonished. He thought me grown. Believe me, always, dearest Uncle, your devoted Niece,

Victoria R.

Queen Victoria to Viscount Melbourne.

Osborne, *31st July 1845*.

The Queen thanks Lord Melbourne very much for his last kind letter of the 11th, by which she was truly rejoiced to see he was better. We are comfortably and peacefully established here since the 19th, and derive the greatest benefit, pleasure, and satisfaction from our little possession here. The dear Prince is constantly occupied in directing the many necessary improvements which are to be made, and in watching our new house, which is a constant interest and amusement. We are most anxiously waiting for the conclusion of the Session that we may set off on our much-wished-for journey to Germany. The Queen is extremely sorry to leave England without seeing Lord Melbourne, and without having seen him all this season; but something or other always prevented us from seeing Lord Melbourne each time we hoped to do so. We only return the night before the Prorogation and embark that same day. We have the children here. We went to the Undercliff—Ventnor, Bonchurch, etc.—on Monday, and were much delighted with all we saw. We had a visit from the King of Holland last week, who is grown old, but otherwise just the same as he used to be.

The Queen joins with Lord Melbourne in unfeigned satisfaction at the success of the Irish measures, after so much factious opposition. Lord Grey's death[20] will have shocked Lord Melbourne, as it has us. Poor Lord Dunmore's death is a very shocking event. The Prince wishes to be most kindly remembered to Lord Melbourne.

Sir Robert Peel to Queen Victoria.

Whitehall, *6th August 1845*.

Sir Robert Peel presents his humble duty to your Majesty, and begs leave to acquaint your Majesty that in the course of a long speech made by Lord John Russell last night, reviewing the policy of the Government and the proceedings of the Session, Lord John expressed himself strongly on the subject of your Majesty's absence from the country, without provision made for the exercise of the Royal authority by the appointment of Lords Justices.

Sir Robert Peel thinks it very probable that a motion will be made upon the subject in the course of the next Session—particularly in the event of any occurrence during your Majesty's absence, which might cause public inconvenience from the want of immediate access to the Royal authority, or compel any assumption of power on the part of your Majesty's servants of a questionable character.

The present Law Officers of the Crown were rather startled at the intention of departing from the precedent of George IV.'s reign, on seeing the legal opinions of their predecessors; they did not differ from the *legal* doctrines laid down by them, but were not very well satisfied on the point of discretion and policy.

Sir Robert Peel feels it to be his duty to state to your Majesty what has passed on this subject, and to apprize your Majesty of the possibility of a question being hereafter raised in Parliament upon it.

Sir Robert Peel thinks that in the case of a short absence, and a distance not precluding easy and rapid communication with your Majesty, the appointment of Lords Justices may be dispensed with; but he is humbly of opinion that were the distance greater or the period of absence longer than that contemplated by your Majesty, the reasons for the nomination of Lords Justices would preponderate.

Should the subject be again mentioned in Parliament and a direct question be put upon it, Sir Robert Peel will, of course, assume the entire responsibility for the non-appointment of Lords Justices; vindicating the departure from the precedent of George IV. on the ground of the shorter period of absence and the more easy means of communication.[21]...

The Earl of Aberdeen to Sir Robert Peel.

Château d'Eu, *8th September 1845.*

My dear Peel,—We left Antwerp very early yesterday morning, and anchored for a few hours off Flushing.[22] We passing down the Channel during the night, and as the weather was perfectly bright and fine, found ourselves off Tréport before nine o'clock this morning. The King came off to the yacht, and took the Queen in his barge to land. I need not say how joyfully she was received by all the Royal Family.

Although I shall have opportunities, both this evening and tomorrow morning, of speaking again with the King and Guizot, I have already discussed several subjects with each of them; and as the Queen particularly desires to send a messenger this evening, I will give you some notion of what has passed between us.

I think the marriage of the Queen of Spain is the subject on which the greatest interest is felt at this moment. It was the first introduced, both by the King and Guizot, and treated by both in the same manner. They said, that having promised to support the King of Naples, they were bound not to abandon the Count de Trapani, so long as there was a chance of his being successful in his suit. I said in answer to their desire, that we would assist this arrangement, that we had no objection to Count Trapani, and that we would take no part against him; but unless it should be the decided wish of the Spanish Government and people, we could give no support to the marriage, as we were honestly of opinion that it was not desired in Spain, and that we saw nothing in the proposal to call for our support under these circumstances. Both the King and Guizot said they had no objection to the Duke of Saville[23] (Don Enrique), and that if it should be found that Count Trapani was impossible, they would willingly support him.

With respect to the Infanta, they both declared in the most positive and explicit manner, that *until the Queen was married and had children*, they should consider the Infanta precisely as her sister, and that any marriage with a French Prince would be entirely out of the question. The King said he did not wish that his son should have the prospect of being on the throne of Spain; but that if the Queen had children, by whom the succession would be secured, he did not engage to preclude himself from the possibility of profiting by the great inheritance which the Infanta would bring his son. All this, however, was uncertain, and would require time at all events to accomplish; for I distinctly understood, that it was not only a marriage and a child, but *children, that were necessary to secure the succession.*

I thought this was as much as we could desire at present, and that the policy of a marriage with a French Prince might safely be left to be considered whenever the contingency contemplated should arrive. Many things may happen, both in France and Spain, in the course of a few years to affect this question in a manner not now apparent.

Aberdeen.

Sir Robert Peel to Queen Victoria.

Osborne, *15th September 1845.*

Sir Robert Peel, with his humble duty to your Majesty, begs leave to acquaint your Majesty that there remains the sum of £700 to be applied in the current year to the grant of Civil List Pensions.

Sir Robert Peel humbly recommends to your Majesty that another sum of £200 should be offered to Mr Tennyson, a poet of whose powers of imagination and expression many competent judges think most highly.

He was brought under the notice of Sir Robert Peel by Mr Hallam. His pecuniary circumstances are far from being prosperous.

There is a vacancy in the Deanery of Lincoln, but the preferment is less eligible from there being no residence, and the necessity for building one at the immediate expense of the new Dean.

Sir Robert Peel is inclined to recommend to your Majesty that an offer of this preferment should be made to Mr Ward, the Rector of St James's.

Should Mr Ward decline, there is a clergyman of the name of Maurice,[24] of whom the Archbishop says: "Of unbeneficed London clergy there is no one, I believe, who is so much distinguished by his learning and literary talent as the Rev. Frederick Maurice, Chaplain of St Guy's Hospital. His private character is equally estimable."

Should Mr Ward decline[25] the Deanery it might, should your Majesty approve of it, be offered to Mr Maurice. The Archbishop says that the appointment of Mr Maurice would be very gratifying to the *King of Prussia.*

The King of the Belgians to Queen Victoria.

St Cloud, *10th October 1845.*

My dearest Victoria,—... All you say about our dear Albert, whom I love like my own child, is perfectly true. The attacks, however unjust, have but one advantage, that of showing the points the enemy thinks *weakest* and best calculated to hurt. This, being the case, Anson, without boring A. with *daily* accounts which in the end become very irksome, should pay attention to these very points, and contribute to avoid what may be turned to account by the enemy. To hope to *escape* censure and calumny is next to impossible, but whatever is considered by the enemy as a fit subject for attack is better modified or avoided. The dealings with artists, for instance, require great prudence; they are acquainted with all classes of society, and for that very reason danger-ous; they are hardly *ever satisfied*, and when you have too much to do with them, you are sure to have *des ennuis*.... Your devoted Uncle,

Leopold R.

Queen Victoria to Lord Stanley.

Windsor Castle, *2nd November 1845.*

The Queen has read with great concern Lord Stanley's letter of the 1st November. From private information she had been led to ex-pect that Lord Metcalfe would not be able to continue at his irksome post.[26] He will be an immense loss, and the selection of a successor will be most difficult. The Queen hopes that there will not be too great a delay in making the new appointment, as experience has shown that nothing was more detrimental to the good government of Canada than the last interregnum after Sir Charles Bagot's death; it would certainly likewise be desirable that Lord Metcalfe should be able personally to make over his Government to his successor, whom he could verbally better put in possession of the peculiarities of his position than any instructions could do. It strikes the Queen to be of the *greatest impor-tance*, that the judicious system pursued by Lord Metcalfe (and which, after a long continuation of toil and adversities, only now just begins to show its effect) should be followed up by his successor.

The Queen knows nobody who would be as fit for the appoint-ment as Lord Elgin, who seems to have given great satisfaction in Jamaica, where he has already succeeded Lord Metcalfe, whose original appointment there had *likewise* taken place under circumstances of great difficulty, which his prudence and firmness finally overcame.[27]

Queen Victoria to Sir Robert Peel.

Osborne, *28th November 1845*.

The Queen is very sorry to hear that Sir Robert Peel apprehends further differences of opinion in the Cabinet, at a moment of impending calamity; it is more than ever necessary that the Government should be strong and united.

The Queen thinks the time is come when a removal of the restrictions upon the importation of food cannot be successfully resisted. Should this be Sir Robert's own opinion, the Queen very much hopes that none of his colleagues will prevent him from doing what it is *right* to do.

Sir Robert Peel to Queen Victoria.

Whitehall, *4th December 1845*.

Sir Robert Peel, with his humble duty to your Majesty, begs leave to acquaint your Majesty that a leading paragraph in the *Times* of to-day, asserting that your Majesty's servants had unanimously agreed to an immediate and total repeal of the Corn Laws, is quite without foundation.[28]

Sir Robert Peel to Queen Victoria.[29]

Whitehall, *5th December 1845*.

(*Friday evening.*)

Sir Robert Peel presents his humble duty to your Majesty, and will wait upon your Majesty to-morrow evening, leaving London by the half-past twelve train.

Sir Robert Peel will avail himself of your Majesty's kind proposal to remain at Osborne until Monday morning.

He will come to Osborne with a heart full of gratitude and devotion to your Majesty, but with a strong conviction (all the grounds for which he will, with your Majesty's permission, explain to your Majesty) that in the present state of affairs, he can render more service to your Majesty and to the country in a private than in a public station.

Memorandum by the Prince Albert.

Osborne, *7th December 1845.*

On receiving the preceding letter[30] ... we were, of course, in great consternation. Yesterday Sir Robert Peel arrived here and explained the condition of affairs.

On 1st November he had called his Cabinet, and placed before its members the reports of the Irish Commissioners, Dr Buckland, Dr Playfair and Dr Lindley, on the condition of the potato crop, which was to the effect that the half of the potatoes were ruined by the rot, and that no one could guarantee the remainder. Belgium, Holland, Sweden, and Denmark, in which states the potato disease had likewise deprived the poorer class of its usual food, have immediately taken energetic means, and have opened the harbours, bought corn, and provided for the case of a rise of prices. Sir Robert proposed the same thing for England, and, by opening the ports, a preparation for the abolition of the Corn Laws. His colleagues refused, and of the whole Cabinet only Lord Aberdeen, Sir James Graham, and Mr Sidney Herbert voted with him. Sir Robert hoped that in time the opinions of the others would change, and therefore postponed a final decision. In the meanwhile the agitation of the Anti-Corn Law League began; in every town addresses were voted, meetings were held, the *Times*—barometer of public feeling—became suddenly *violently* Anti-Corn Law, the meetings of the Cabinet roused attention, a general panic seized on the mass of the public. Sir Robert called anew his Cabinet. In the midst of their deliberation Lord John Russell issues from Edinburgh an address to the City of London.[31]

The whole country cries out: the Corn Laws are doomed.

Thereon Sir Robert declared to his Cabinet that nothing but unanimity could save the cause, and pressed for a decision.

The Duke of Buccleuch and Lord Stanley declared they could not take a part in a measure abolishing the Corn Laws, and would therefore have to resign. The other members, including the Duke of Wellington, showed themselves ready to support Sir Robert, yet, as the latter says, "apparently not willingly and against their feelings." Thereupon Sir Robert resolved to lay down his office as Minister.

When he arrived here he was visibly much moved, and said to me, that it was one of the most painful moments of his life to separate himself from us, "but it is necessary, and if I have erred it was from loyalty and too great an anxiety not to leave Her Majesty in a moment of such great difficulty. I ought to have gone when I was first left by my colleagues in a minority in my own Cabinet. I was anxious, however, to try my utmost, but it is impossible to retrieve lost time. As soon as I saw Lord John's letter I felt that the ground was slipping away from under me, and that whatever I might now propose would appear as dictated by the Opposition, as taking Lord John's measure. On the 1st of November the whole country was prepared for the thing; there had been no agitation, everybody looking to the Government, as soon as they saw this wavering and hesitating, the country decided for itself, and Lord John has the merit, owing to his most dexterous move and our want of unanimity."

On my observing that Sir Robert has a majority of one hundred in the House of Commons, and asking whether it was not possible for him to continue the Government, he said:—

"The Duke of Buccleuch will carry half Scotland with him, and Lord Stanley, leading the Protectionists in the House of Lords, would lead to great and immediate defections even in Her Majesty's household. The Duchess of Buccleuch, Lord Hardwicke, Lord Exeter, Lord Rivers, Lord Beverley, etc., would resign, and we should not be able to find successors; in the House of Commons I am sure I should be beat, the Tories, agriculturists, etc., in rage would turn round upon me and be joined by the Whigs and Radicals, who would say, 'This is *our* measure and we will not allow you to carry it.' It is better that I should go now, when *nobody has committed himself* in the heat of party contest, when no factions have been formed, no imprudent declarations been made; it is better for Her Majesty and for the country that it should be so."

After we had examined what possibilities were open for the Crown, the conclusion was come to that Lord John was the only man who could be charged with forming a Cabinet. Lord Stanley, with the aristocracy as his base, would bring about an insurrection [or riots], and the ground on which one would have to fight would be this: to want to force the mass of the people, amidst their great poverty, to pay for their bread a high price, in favour of the landlords.

It is a matter of the utmost importance not to place the House of Lords into direct antagonism with the Commons and with the masses of the people. Sir Robert says very correctly:—

"I am afraid of other interests getting damaged in the struggle about the Corn Laws; already the system of promotion in the Army, the Game Laws, the Church, are getting attacked with the aid of the league."

After Victoria had in consequence [of the foregoing] decided in favour of Lord John, and asked Sir Robert: "But how is it possible for him to govern with so exceedingly small a minority?" Sir Robert said: "He will have difficulties and perhaps did not consider what he was doing when he wrote that letter; but *I will support him*. I feel it my duty to your Majesty not to leave you without a Government. Even if Lord John goes to the full extent of his declaration in that letter (which I think goes too far), I will support him in Parliament and use all my influence with the House of Lords to prevent their impeding his progress. I will do more, if he likes it. I will say that the increase of the estimates which will become necessary are my work, and I alone am responsible for it."

Sir Robert intends to give me a memorandum in which he is to make this promise in writing.

He was greatly moved, and said it was not "the loss of power (for I hate power) nor of office," which was nothing but a plague for him, but "the breaking up of those relations in which he stood to the Queen and me, and the loss of our society,' which was for him a loss, for which there was no equivalent; we might, however, rely on his being always ready to serve us, in what manner and in what place it might be. Lord Aberdeen is said to feel the same, and very deeply so; and on our side the loss of two so estimable men, who possess our whole and perfect confidence in public as well as in private affairs, and have always proved themselves true friends, leaves *a great gap*.

Albert.

Victoria to Viscount Melbourne.

Osborne, *7th December 1845.*

Sir Robert Peel has informed the Queen that in consequence of differences prevailing in the Cabinet, he is very reluctantly compelled to solicit from the Queen the acceptance of his resignation, which she has as reluctantly accepted.

From the Queen's unabated confidence in Lord Melbourne, her first impulse was to request his immediate attendance here that she might have the benefit of his assistance and advice, but on reflection the Queen does not think herself justified, in the present state of Lord Melbourne's health, to ask him to make the sacrifice which the return to his former position of Prime Minister would, she fears, impose upon him.

It is this consideration, and this *alone*, that has induced the Queen to address to Lord John Russell the letter of which she sends a copy. The Queen hopes, however, that Lord Melbourne will not withhold from her new Government his advice, which would be so valuable to her.

It is of the *utmost importance* that the whole of this communication should be kept a *most profound secret* until the Queen has seen Lord John Russell.

Memorandum by the Prince Albert.

8th December 1845.

Sir Robert helped us in the composition of the letters to Lord John and to Lord Melbourne. We considered it necessary to write to the latter, in consideration of the confidential position which he formerly enjoyed.

Sir Robert Peel has not *resigned*, thinking it a matter of great strength for the Sovereign to keep his ministry until a new one can be got.

Albert.

Viscount Melbourne to Queen Victoria.

Brocket Hall, *9th December 1845.*

Lord Melbourne presents his humble duty to your Majesty; he has just received your Majesty's letter of the 7th inst., which, of course, has astonished him by the magnitude of the event which it announces, although something of this sort has been long pending and to be expected. Lord Melbourne returns your Majesty many thanks for this communication, and more for your Majesty's great kindness and consideration for him personally at the present moment. He is better, but so long a journey would still not have been convenient to him, and he has such a horror of the sea, that a voyage from Southampton to Cowes or from Portsmouth to Ryde seems to him in prospect as formidable as a voyage across the Atlantic.

Lord Melbourne will strictly observe your Majesty's injunction of secrecy.

With respect to the kind wishes about office which your Majesty is pleased to express, Lord Melbourne will of course give to your Majesty's new Government, if formed under Lord John Russell, all the support in his power, but as to taking office, he fears that he would find some difficulty. He would be very unwilling to come in pledged to a total and immediate reform of the Corn Law, and he also strongly feels the difficulty which has in fact compelled Sir Robert Peel to retire, viz. the difficulty of carrying on the Government upon the principle of upholding and maintaining the present law with respect to corn.

Lord Melbourne again thanks your Majesty for your great and considerate kindness.

Sir Robert Peel to Queen Victoria.

Whitehall, *10th December 1845.*

Sir Robert Peel presents his humble duty to your Majesty, and influenced by no other motive than the desire to contribute if possible to the relief of your Majesty from embarrassment, and the protection of the public interests from injury, is induced to make this confidential communication to your Majesty explanatory of his position and intentions with regard to the great question which is now agitating the public mind.

Your Majesty can, if you think fit, make this communication known to the Minister who, as successor to Sir Robert Peel, may be honoured by your Majesty's confidence.

On the first day of November last Sir Robert Peel advised his colleagues, on account of the alarming accounts from Ireland and many districts of Great Britain as to the failure of the potato crop from disease, and for the purpose of guarding against contingencies which in his opinion were not improbable, humbly to recommend to your Majesty that the duties on the import of foreign grain should be suspended for a limited period either by Order in Council, or by Legislative Enactment, Parliament in either case being summoned without delay.

Sir Robert Peel foresaw that this suspension, fully justified by the tenor of the reports to which he has referred, would compel, during the interval of suspension, the reconsideration of the Corn Laws.

If the opinions of his colleagues had been in concurrence with his own, he was fully prepared to take the responsibility of suspension, and of the necessary consequence of suspension, a comprehensive review of the laws imposing restrictions on the import of foreign grain and other articles of food, with a view to their gradual diminution and ultimate removal. He was disposed to recommend that any new laws to be enacted should contain within themselves the principle of gradual and ultimate removal.

Sir Robert Peel is prepared to support in a private capacity measures which may be in general conformity with those which he advised as a Minister.

It would be unbecoming in Sir Robert Peel to make any reference to the details of such measures.

Your Majesty has been good enough to inform him that it is your intention to propose to Lord John Russell to undertake the formation of a Government.

The principle on which Sir Robert Peel was prepared to recommend the reconsideration of the laws affecting the import of the main articles of food, was in general accordance with that referred to in the concluding paragraph of Lord John Russell's letter to the electors of the City of London.[32]

Sir Robert Peel wished to accompany the removal of restrictions on the admission of such articles, with relief to the land from such charges as are unduly onerous, and with such other provisions as in the terms of Lord John Russell's letter "caution and even scrupulous forbearance may suggest."

Sir Robert Peel will support measures founded on that general principle, and will exercise any influence he may possess to promote their success.

Sir Robert Peel feels it to be his duty to add, that should your Majesty's servants, after consideration of the heavy demands upon the Army of this country for colonial service, of our relations with the United States, and of the bearing which steam navigation may have upon maritime warfare, and the defence of the country, deem it advisable to propose an addition to the Army, and increased naval and military estimates, Sir Robert Peel will support the proposal, will do all that he can to prevent it from being considered as indicative of hostile or altered feeling towards France, and will assume for the increase in question any degree of responsibility present or retrospective which can fairly attach to him.

Robert Peel.

Lord Stanley to Queen Victoria.

St James's Square, *11th December 1845*.

... Lord Stanley humbly hopes that he may be permitted to avail himself of this opportunity to express to your Majesty the deep regret and pain with which he has felt himself compelled to dissent from the advice intended to have been tendered to your Majesty on the subject of the Corn Laws. He begs to assure your Majesty that he would have shrunk from making no personal sacrifice, short of that of principle, for the purpose of avoiding the inconvenience to your Majesty and to the country inseparable from any change of Administration; but being unconvinced of the necessity of a change of policy involving an abandonment of opinions formerly maintained, and expectations held out to political supporters, he felt that the real interests of your Majesty's service could not be promoted by the loss of personal character which the sacrifice of his own convictions would necessarily have involved; and that he might far more usefully serve your Majesty and the country out of office, than as the official advocate of a policy which he could not sincerely approve. Lord Stanley begs to assure your Majesty that it will be his earnest endeavour to allay, as far as may lie in his power, the excitement which he cannot but foresee as the consequence of the contemplated change of policy; and he ventures to indulge the hope that this long trespass upon your Majesty's much occupied time may find a sufficient apology in the deep anxiety which he feels that his regret at being compelled not only to retire from your Majesty's service, but also to take a step which he is aware may have had some influence on the course finally adopted by Sir Robert Peel, may not be still farther increased by the apprehension of having, in the performance of a most painful duty, incurred your Majesty's displeasure. All which is humbly submitted by your Majesty's most dutiful Servant and Subject,

Stanley.

Queen Victoria to Lord Stanley.

Osborne, *12th December 1845*.

The Queen, of course, *much regrets* that Lord Stanley could not agree in the opinions of Sir Robert Peel upon a subject of such importance to the country. However, Lord Stanley may rest assured that the

Queen gives full credit to the disinterested motives which guided Lord Stanley's conduct.

Queen Victoria to the Duke of Wellington.

Osborne, *12th December 1845.*

The Queen has to inform the Duke of Wellington that, in consequence of Sir Robert Peel's having declared to her his inability to carry on any longer the Government, she has sent for Lord John Russell, who is not able at present to state whether he can form an Administration, and is gone to Town in order to consult his friends. Whatever the result of his enquiries may be, the Queen has a *strong* desire to see the Duke of Wellington remain at the head of her Army. The Queen appeals to the Duke's so often proved loyalty and attachment to her person, in asking him to give her this assurance. The Duke will thereby render the greatest service to the country and to her own person.

The Duke of Wellington to Queen Victoria.

Strathfieldsaye, *12th December 1845.*

(*11 at night.*)

Field-Marshal the Duke of Wellington presents his humble duty to your Majesty; he has just now received your Majesty's commands from Osborne of this day's date.

He humbly submits to your Majesty that the duties of the Commander-in-Chief of your Majesty's Land Forces places him in constant confidential relations with all your Majesty's Ministers, and particularly with the one filling the office of First Lord of the Treasury.

Under these circumstances he submits to your Majesty the counsel, that your Majesty would be graciously pleased to consult the nobleman or gentleman who should be your Majesty's first Minister, before any other step should be taken upon the subject. He might think that he had reason to complain if he should find that it was arranged that the Duke of Wellington should continue to fill the office of Commander-in-Chief, and such impression might have an influence upon his future relations with that office.

Field-Marshal the Duke of Wellington believes that Lord John Russell and all your Majesty's former Ministers were aware, that during the whole period of the time during which Lord Hill was the

General Commanding-in-Chief your Majesty's Forces, the professional opinion and services of Field-Marshal the Duke of Wellington were at all times at the command and disposition of your Majesty's servants, and were given whenever required.

He happened to be at that time in political opposition to the Government in the House of Parliament, cf which he was a member; but that circumstance made no difference.

It is impossible for the Duke of Wellington to form a political connection with Lord John Russell, or to have any relation with the political course of the Government over which he should preside.

Such arrangement would not conciliate public confidence, be considered creditable to either party, or be useful to the service of your Majesty.

Nor, indeed, would the performance of the duties of the Commander-in-Chief of the Army require that such should exist; on the other hand, the performance of these duties would require that the person filling the office should avoid to belong to, or to act in concert with, a political party opposed to the Government.

Field-Marshal the Duke of Wellington has considered it his duty to submit these considerations, in order that your Majesty may be perfectly aware of the position in which he is about to place himself, in case Lord John Russell should counsel your Majesty to command Field-Marshal the Duke of Wellington to continue to hold the office of Commander-in-Chief of your Majesty s Land Forces.

He at once submits to your Majesty the assurance that he will cheerfully devote his service to your Majesty's command upon receiving the official intimation thereof, and that he will as usual make every effort in his power to promote your Majesty's service.

All of which is humbly submitted to your Majesty by your Majesty's most dutiful Subject and devoted Servant,

Wellington.

The King of the French to Queen Victoria.

St Cloud, *le 16 Décembre 1845*.

Madame ma très Chère Sœur,—J'ai à remercier votre Majesté de l'excellente lettre que ma bonne Clém m'a remise de sa part. Elle m'a été droit au cœur, et je ne saurais exprimer à quel point j'ai été touché de vos bons voeux pour ma famille, et de tout ce que vous me témoignez sur l'accroissement qu'il a plû à la Providence de lui donner dans mes *onze petits fils.*

Je me disposais à dire à votre Majesté que, quoiqu'avec un bien vif regret, je comprenais parfaitement les motifs qui vous portaient à remettre à une autre année, cette visite si vivement désirée, et que j'espérais toujours trouver une compensation à cette privation, en allant de nouveau Lui offrir en Angleterre, l'hommage de tous les sentiments que je Lui porte, et qui m'attachent si profondément à Elle, ainsi qu'au Prince son Epoux, lorsque j'ai reçu la nouvelle de la démission de Sir Robert Peel, de Lord Aberdeen et de tous leurs Collègues. Je me flattais que ces Ministres qui s'étaient toujours si bien entendus avec les miens pour établir entre nos deux Gouvernements, cette heureuse *entente cordiale* qui est la base du repos du monde et de la prospérité de nos pays, continueraient encore longtemps à l'entretenir, et à la consolider de plus en plus. Cet espoir est déçu!![33] Il faut s'y résigner; mais je suis empressé d'assurer votre Majesté, que quelque soit son nouveau Ministère, celui qui m'entoure aujourd'hui, et que je désire, et que j'espère conserver longtemps, n'omettra aucun effort pour cultiver et maintenir cet heureux accord qu'il est si évidemment dans notre intérêt commun de conserver intact.

Dans de telles circonstances, il me devient doublement précieux d'être uni à votre Majesté et au Prince Albert par tant de liens, et qu'il se soit formé entre nous cet attachement mutuel, cette affection et cette confiance, qui sont au dessus et indépendants de toute considération politique; mais qui pourront toujours plus ou moins exercer une influence salutaire sur l'action et la marche de nos deux Gouvernements. Aussi, je le dis à votre Majesté et à son Epoux avec un entier abandon, j'ai besoin de compter sur cette assistance occasionnelle, et j'y compte entièrement en vous demandant d'avoir la même confiance de mon côté, et en vous répétant que cette confiance ne sera pas plus déçue dans l'avenir, qu'elle ne l'a été dans le passé.

Votre Majesté me permettra d'offrir ici au Prince Albert l'expression de ma vive et sincère amitié. Je la prie aussi de recevoir celle de l'inviolable attachement avec lequel je suis, Madame ma très chère Sœur, de votre Majesté, le bon Frère et bien fidèle Ami,

Louis Philippe R.

Queen Victoria to Lord John Russell.

Windsor Castle, *16th December 1845.*

The Queen has just received Lord John Russell's letter of this day's date,[34] and considering that it is of great importance that no time should be lost, has immediately forwarded it to Sir Robert Peel.

The Queen fully understands the motives which guide Lord John in using every effort to ensure the success of the great measure which is impending before he undertakes to form a Government.

The Queen sees from Lord John's second letter that he has taken a copy of Sir R. Peel's letter of the 15th to her. As she does not feel to have been authorised to allow this, the Queen hopes that in case Sir Robert should have an objection to it Lord John will not retain the copy.

Queen Victoria to Sir Robert Peel.

Windsor Castle, *18th December 1845.*

Lord John Russell returned at five this evening, and informed the Queen that after considerable discussion, and after a full consideration of his position, *he will undertake to form a Government.*

As at present arranged, the Council is to be on Monday; the Queen much wishing to have a parting interview with Sir R. Peel, however painful it will be to her, wishes Sir Robert Peel to inform her when he thinks it best to come down here.[35]

Memorandum by the Prince Albert.

Windsor Castle, *20th December 1845.*

(*12 o'clock.*)

We just saw Lord John Russell, who came in order to explain why he had to give up the task of forming a Government. He had written to all his former colleagues to join him in his attempt, amongst others to Lord Grey, who answered, "that he could only belong to a Government which pledged itself to the principle of absolute free trade and abolition of all protection; that he had his own views upon the sugar question (as to which he advocated the admission of slave labour) and upon the Irish question (as to which his principle was to establish entire religious equality); that he hoped that in the formation of a new Government no personal considerations should stand in the way of a full attention to public Duty."

Lord John replied that he advocated free trade, but as the immediate question before them was the *Corn Laws*, he thought it wiser not to complicate this by other declarations which would produce a good deal of animosity; that the sugar question and Ireland might be discussed in Cabinet when circumstances required it; that he agreed entirely in the last sentence.

After this Lord Grey declared himself quite satisfied. Lord John considered now with his colleagues the peculiar measure to be proposed, and Mr Baring thought he could arrange a financial scheme which would satisfy Lord Lansdowne's demands for relief to the landed interest. They all felt it their duty to answer the Queen's call upon them, though they very much disliked taking office under such peculiar difficulties. Now Lord John undertook to apportion the different offices. He saw Lord Palmerston, and told him that the Queen had some apprehension that his return to the Foreign Office might cause great alarm in other countries, and particularly in France, and that this feeling was still more strongly manifested in the city; whether under these circumstances he would prefer some other office—for instance, the Colonies? Lord Palmerston declared that he was not at all anxious for office, and should much regret that his accession should in any way embarrass Lord John; that he was quite prepared to support him out of office, but that his taking another department than his former one would be a public recognition of the most unjust accusations that had been brought against him; that he had evinced throughout a long official life his disposition for peace, and only in one instance broke with France;[36] that that matter was gone by, and that nobody had stronger conviction of the necessity to keep in amity with that Power than himself. Upon this Lord John said that he could not form a Government without him, and showed himself quite satisfied with Lord Palmerston's declaration.

Suddenly Lord Grey, who had heard of this, cried out: "This was an infringement of their compact"; that no *personal* consideration should interfere with the discharge of public duty, and that he must decline entering the Government, as he considered Lord Palmerston's return to the Foreign Office as fraught with danger to the peace of Europe. Lord John could not, under these circumstances, form a Government. He read to us a long letter from Lord Grey, written with the intention that it should be seen by the Queen, in which Lord Grey enters more fully into his motives, and finishes by saying that therefore *he* was not answerable for the failure to form an Administration.[37]

Lord John gave the Queen a written statement[38] of the causes which induced him to relinquish the Government, and of the position he means to assume in Parliament. (He is most anxious that Sir R. Peel should re-enter and successfully carry his measures.)

The arrangements Lord John had contemplated have been—

Lord Palmerston,	*Foreign Secretary.*
Lord Grey,	*Colonial Secretary.*
Sir George Grey,	*Home Secretary.*

(Sir George was anxious later to retire from Parliament, and willing to go as Governor-General to Canada.)

Mr Baring,	*Chancellor of the Exchequer.*
Lord Clarendon,	*President of the Board of Trade.*

(The Vice-Presidency was to have been offered to his brother, Mr Villiers, but finally, by his advice, to Mr Cobden!! (Lord Grey wanted Mr Cobden to be in the Cabinet!!!) This Lord John thought quite out of the question.)

Lord Lansdowne,	*President of the Council.*

Memorandum by the Prince Albert.

Windsor Castle, *20th December 1845.*

(*4 o'clock* p.m.)

We saw Sir Robert Peel, who had been apprised by Sir James Graham (to whom Lord John Russell had written) of what had passed. He was much affected, and expressed his concern at the failure of Lord John to form a Government, seemed hurt at Lord John's not having shown more confidence in the integrity of his (Sir Robert Peel's) motives. He would have supported Lord John in *any* measure which he should have thought fit to introduce, and many would have followed his example. He blamed the want of deference shown to the Queen, by not answering her call with more readiness; he said it was quite new and unconstitutional for a man to take a week before he undertook to form a Government, and to pass that time in discussion with other people, to whom the Sovereign had not yet committed the task; and he had been certain it would end so, when so many people were consulted. He in 1834 had been called from Italy, had travelled with all haste and had gone straight to the King, had told him that he had seen nobody, consulted nobody, but immediately kissed the King's hand as his Minister.

He was now prepared to stand by the Queen, all other considerations he had thrown aside, he would undertake to deal with the difficulties, and should have to go down alone to the House of Commons. He had written to his colleagues that he would serve the Queen if she called upon him to do so, that he expected them to meet him at nine o'clock that evening, and that he would tell them what he meant to do. Those who would not go with him, he would dismiss at once. He did not wish to avail himself of any undue advantage, and therefore would not advise an Order in Council, but go at once to Parliament, laying his measure before it: "Reject it, if you please; there it is!"

He called the crisis an alarming one, which determination alone could overcome.

We showed him Lord John Russell's statement, with which he declared himself very much satisfied. He advised the Queen to write a letter to Lord John, announcing to him Sir Robert's consent to go on with the Government, and wrote a draft of it, which follows here.

He had heard strange instances of disagreement amongst the men whom Lord John had assembled in town.

Sir Robert seemed throughout much moved, and said with much warmth: "There is no sacrifice that I will not make for your Majesty, except that of my honour."

Queen Victoria to Lord John Russell.

Windsor Castle, *20th December 1845.*

Sir Robert Peel has just been here. He expressed great regret that Lord John Russell had felt it necessary to decline the formation of a Government.

He said he should have acted towards Lord John Russell with the most scrupulous good faith, and that he should have done everything in his power to give Lord John support.

He thinks many would have been induced to follow his example.

Sir Robert Peel did not hesitate a moment in withdrawing his offer of resignation. He said he felt it his duty at once to resume his office, though he is deeply sensible of the difficulties with which he has to contend.

Sir Robert Peel to Queen Victoria.

Whitehall, *21st December 1845.*

Sir Robert Peel presents his humble duty to your Majesty, and proceeds to give your Majesty an account of what has passed since he left your Majesty at four o'clock yesterday.

The Cabinet met at Sir Robert Peel's house in Downing Street at half-past nine.

Sir Robert Peel informed them that he had not summoned them for the purpose of deliberating on what was to be done, but for the purpose of announcing to them that he was your Majesty's Minister, and whether supported or not, was firmly resolved to meet Parliament as your Majesty's Minister, and to propose such measures as the public exigencies required.

Failure or success must depend upon their decision, but nothing could shake Sir Robert Peel's determination to meet Parliament and to advise the Speech from the Throne.

There was a dead silence, at length interrupted by Lord Stanley's declaring that he must persevere in resigning, that he thought the Corn Law ought to be adhered to, and might have been maintained.

The Duke of Wellington said he thought the Corn Law was a subordinate consideration. He was *delighted* when he received Sir Robert Peel's letter that day, announcing to the Duke that his mind was made up to place his services at your Majesty's disposal.

The Duke of Buccleuch behaved admirably—was much agitated—thought new circumstances had arisen—would not then decide on resigning.

Sir Robert Peel has received this morning the enclosed note from the Duke.[39]

He has written a reply very strongly to the Duke, stating that the present question is not one of Corn Law, but whether your Majesty's former servants or Lord Grey and Mr Cobden shall constitute your Majesty's Government. Sir Robert Peel defied the wit of man to suggest now another alternative to your Majesty.

Lord Aberdeen will see the Duke to-day.

All the other members of the Government cordially approved of Sir Robert Peel's determination not to abandon your Majesty's service.

There was no question about details, but if there is any, it shall not alter Sir Robert Peel's course.

The Duke of Buccleuch to Sir Robert Peel.

Montagu House, *20th December 1845.*

My dear Sir Robert,—That which has occurred this evening, and that which you have communicated to us, the very critical state in which the country now is, and above all the duty which I owe to her Majesty under the present circumstances, has made a most strong impression upon my mind. At the risk, therefore, of imputation of vacillation or of any other motive by others, may I ask of you to give me a few hours' time for further reflection, before finally deciding upon the course which I may feel it to be my duty to pursue? Believe me, my dear Sir Robert, yours most sincerely,

Buccleuch.

Sir Robert Peel to Queen Victoria.

Whitehall, *22nd December 1845.*

Sir Robert Peel presents his humble duty to your Majesty, and has the utmost satisfaction in informing your Majesty that Mr Gladstone is willing to accept the Seals of the Colonial Office should your Majesty be pleased to confide them to him.[40]

Sir Robert Peel thinks this of great importance, and that immediate decision in filling up so eminent a post will have a good effect.

Queen Victoria to the King of the Belgians.

Windsor Castle, *23rd December 1845.*

My dearest Uncle,—Many thanks for your two kind letters of the 17th and 19th, which gave me much pleasure. I have little to add to Albert's letter of yesterday, except my *extreme* admiration of our worthy Peel, who shows himself a man of unbounded *loyalty*, *courage*, patriotism, and *high-mindedness*, and his conduct towards me has been *chivalrous* almost, I might say. I never have seen him so excited or so determined, and *such* a good cause must succeed. We have indeed had an escape, for though Lord John's *own notions* were *very* good and moderate, he let himself be entirely twisted and twirled about by his *violent* friends, and *all* the moderate ones were crushed....

Victoria R.

Sir Robert Peel to the Prince Albert.

Whitehall, *23rd December 1845.*

Sir,—I think Her Majesty and your Royal Highness will have been pleased with the progress I have made in execution of the great trust again committed to me by Her Majesty.

It will be of great importance to conciliate Lord Stanley's support out of office, to induce him to *discourage* hostile combinations.

I would humbly recommend Her Majesty, when Her Majesty sees Lord Stanley to-day, to receive him with her usual kindness, to say that I had done full justice in my reports to Her Majesty to the motives by which he had been actuated, and to the openness and frankness of his conduct, to regret greatly the loss of his services, but to hope that he might be still enabled not to oppose and even to promote the accomplishment of what cannot now be safely resisted. I have the honour to be, etc., etc., etc.,

Robert Peel.

Memorandum by the Prince Albert.

Windsor Castle, *25th December 1845.*

We had a Council yesterday, at which Parliament was prorogued to the 22nd of January, then to meet for the despatch of business. Lord Stanley had an audience of the Queen before, and delivered up the Seals of his office. He was much agitated, and had told Sir Robert that he dreaded this interview very much. The Queen thanked him for his services, and begged he would do his best out of office to smooth down the difficulties her Government would have to contend with. At the Council Lord Dalhousie took his seat, and Mr Gladstone received the Colonial Seals. The Queen saw the Duke of Buccleuch and thanked him for the devotion he had shown her during these trying circumstances; the same to the Duke of Wellington, who is in excellent spirits. On my saying, "You have such an influence over the House of Lords, that you will be able to keep them straight," he answered: "I'll do anything; I am now beginning to write to them and to convince them singly of what their duty is."

We saw afterwards Sir Robert Peel, who stayed more than three hours. He is in the highest spirits at having got Mr Gladstone and kept the Duke of Buccleuch; he proposed that the Duke should be made President, and Lord Haddington Privy Seal in his stead. (Lord Haddington had behaved very well, had given up his place to Sir Robert, and told him he should do with him just as he liked—leave him out of the Cabinet, shift him to another place, or leave him at the Admiralty, as would suit him best.)

Sir Robert hinted to Lord Ripon that Lord Haddington had behaved so well, but got no more out of him, but "that he would *almost* have done the same." Sir Robert proposes to see Lord Ellenborough in order to offer him the Admiralty, received the Queen's sanction likewise to Lord St Germans (the Postmaster-General) being put into the Cabinet. I said: "With your Government that has no inconvenience, and even if you had a hundred members in the Cabinet, as you don't tell them but what is absolutely necessary, and follow your own course." He said in reply, that he should be very sorry if he had to have told his Cabinet that he meant to send for Lord Ellenborough. We could not help contrasting this conduct with the subjection Lord John has shown to his people. It is to his *own* talent and firmness that Sir Robert will owe his success, which cannot fail. He said he had been determined not to go to a general election with the fetters the last election had imposed upon him, and he had meant at the end of the next Session to call the whole Conservative Party together and to declare this to them, that he would not meet another Parliament pledged to the maintenance of the Corn Laws, which could be maintained no longer, and that he would make a public declaration to this effect before another general election came on. This had been defeated by events coming too suddenly upon him, and he had no alternative but to deal with the Corn Laws before a national calamity would *force* it on. The league had made immense progress, and had enormous means at their disposal. If he had resigned in November, Lord Stanley and the Protectionists would have been prepared to form a Government, and a Revolution might have been the consequence of it. Now they felt that it was too late.

Sir Robert has *an immense scheme in view*; he thinks he shall be able to remove the contest entirely from the dangerous ground upon which it has got—that of a war between the manufacturers, the hungry and the poor against the landed proprietors, the aristocracy, which can only end in the ruin of the latter; he will not bring forward a measure upon the Corn Laws, but a much more comprehensive one. He will deal with the whole commercial system of the country. He will adopt the principle of the League, *that of removing all protection and abolishing all monopoly*, but not in favour of one class and as a triumph over another, but to the benefit of the nation, farmers as well as manufacturers. He would begin with cotton, and take in all the necessaries of life and corn amongst them. The experiments he had made in 1842 and 1845 with boldness but with caution had borne out the correctness of the principle: the wool duty was taken off, and wool sold higher than ever before; foreign cattle were let in, and the cattle of England stood better in the market than ever. He would not ask for compensation to the land, but wherever he could give it, and at the same time promote the social development, there he would do it, but on that ground. For instance, one of the greatest benefits to the country would be the establishment of a rural police on the same principle as the metropolitan police. By taking this on the Consolidated Fund, the landowners would be immensely relieved in all those counties which kept a police. One of the heaviest charges on the land was the present administration of law and the carrying on of prosecutions. Sir Robert could fancy this to be very much improved by the appointment of a *public* prosecutor by the State, which would give the State a power to prevent vexatious, illegal, and immoral prosecutions, and reduce the expenses in an extraordinary degree. Part of the maintenance of the poor, according to the Poor Law, might be undertaken by the State. A great calamity must be foreseen, when the innumerable railroads now in progress shall have been terminated, which will be the case in a few years. This will throw an enormous labouring population suddenly out of employment. There might be a law passed which would provide employment for them, and improve the agriculture and production of the country, by enabling the State to advance money to the great proprietors for the improvements of their estates, which they could not obtain otherwise without charging their estates beyond what they already have to bear.

Sir Robert means to go with Mr Gladstone into all these details.

Albert.

Viscount Palmerston to Viscount Melbourne.[41]

Bowood, *26th December 1845.*

My dear Melbourne,—I return you with many thanks George Anson's letter, which was enclosed in yours of the 23rd, which I received just as we were setting off for this place. Pray, when next you write to George Anson, say how gratefully I appreciate the kind consideration on the part of H.R.H. Prince Albert, which suggested George Anson's communication. But I can assure you that although John Russell, in his Audience of the Queen, may inadvertently have overstated the terms in which he had mentioned to me what Her Majesty had said to him about my return to the Foreign Office, yet in his conversations with me upon that subject he never said anything more than is contained in George Anson's letter to you; and I am sure you will think that under all the circumstances of the case he could hardly have avoided telling me thus much, and making me aware of the impression which seemed to exist upon the Queen's mind as to the way in which other persons might view my return to the Foreign Office.

With regard to Her Majesty's own sentiments, I have always been convinced that Her Majesty knows me too well to believe for an instant that I do not attach the greatest importance to the maintenance, not merely of peace with all foreign countries, but of the most friendly relations with those leading Powers and States of the world with which serious differences would be attended with the most inconvenience. As to Peace, I succeeded, as the organ of Lord Grey's Government and of yours, in preserving it unbroken during ten years[42] of great and extraordinary difficulty; and, if now and then it unavoidably happened during that period of time, that in pursuing the course of policy which seemed the best for British interests, we thwarted the views of this or that Foreign Power, and rendered them for the moment less friendly, I think I could prove that in every case the object which we were pursuing was of sufficient importance to make it worth our while to submit to such temporary inconvenience. There never was indeed, during those ten years, any real danger of war except on three occasions; and on each of those occasions the course pursued by the British Government prevented war. The first occasion was just after the accession of the King of the French, when Austria, Russia, and Prussia were disposed and preparing to attack France, and when the attitude assumed by the British Government prevented a rupture. The second was when England and France united by a Convention to wrest the Citadel of Antwerp from the Dutch, and to deliver it over to the King of the Belgians.[43] If England had not then joined with France, Antwerp would have remained with the Dutch, or the attempt to take it would have led to a war in Europe. The third occasion was when Mehemet Ali's army occupied Syria, and when he was constantly threatening to declare himself independent and to march on Constantinople; while Russia, on the one hand, asserted that if he did so she would occupy Constantinople, and on the other hand, France announced that if Russia did so, she, France, would force the Dardanelles. The Treaty of July 1840, proposed and brought about by the British Government, and the operations in execution of that Treaty, put an end to that danger; and, notwithstanding what has often been said to the contrary, the real danger of war arising out of the affairs of Syria was put an end to, and not created by the Treaty of 1840.

I am well aware, however, that some persons both at home and abroad have imbibed the notion that I am more indifferent than I ought to be as to running the risk of war. That impression abroad is founded upon an entire mistake, but is by some sincerely felt, and being sincere, would soon yield to the evidence of contradictory facts. At home that impression has been industriously propagated to a limited extent, partly by the legitimate attacks of political opponents, and partly by a little cabal within our own ranks. These parties wanted to attack me, and were obliged to accuse me of something. They could not charge me with failure, because we had succeeded in all our undertakings, whether in Portugal, Spain, Belgium, Syria, China, or elsewhere; they could not charge me with having involved the country in war, because, in fact, we had maintained peace; and the only thing that was left for them to say was that my policy had a *tendency* to produce war, and I suppose they would argue that it was quite wrong and against all rule that it did not do so.

But notwithstanding what may have been said on this matter, the transaction which has by some been the most criticised in this respect, namely, the Treaty of 1840, and the operations connected with it, were entirely approved by the leaders of the then Opposition, who, so far from feeling any disposition to favour me, had always made a determined run at the Foreign Policy of the Whig Government. The Duke of Wellington, at the opening of the Session of 1841, said in the House of Lords that he entirely approved our policy in that transaction, and could not find that any fault had been committed by us in working it out; and I happen to know that Sir Robert Peel expressed to the representative of one of the German Powers, parties to the Alliance, his entire approval of our course, while Lord Aberdeen said to one of them, that the course I had taken in that affair made him forgive me many things of former years, which he had thought he never should have forgiven.

I am quite ashamed of the length to which this letter has grown, and shall only add, with reference to our relations with France, that I had some very friendly interviews with Thiers, who was my chief antagonist in 1840, and that although we did not enter into any conspiracy against Guizot and Peel, as the newspapers pretended, we parted on very good terms, and he promised to introduce me to all his friends whenever I should go to Paris, saying that of course Guizot would do me the same good office with his supporters. My dear Melbourne, yours affectionately,

Palmerston.

Queen Victoria to the King of the French.

Ch. de W., *le 30 Décembre 1845.*

Sire et mon très cher Frère,—Votre Majesté me pardonnera si je viens seulement maintenant vous remercier de tout mon cœur de votre lettre si bonne et si aimable du 16, mais vous savez combien j'étais occupée pendant ces dernières 3 semaines. La Crise est passée et j'ai tout lieu de croire que le Gouvernement de Sir R. Peel va s'affermir de plus en plus, ce que je ne puis que désirer pour le bien-être du pays. Je dois cependant dire à votre Majesté que si le Ministère eût changé, j'ai la certitude que le nouveau se serait empressé de maintenir, comme nous le désirons si vivement, cette entente cordiale si heureusement établie entre nos deux Gouvernements.

Permettez-moi, Sire, de vous offrir au nom d'Albert et au mien nos félicitations les plus sincères à l'occasion de la nouvelle Année, dans lequel vous nous donnez le doux espoir de vous revoir. Nous avons lu avec beaucoup d'intérêt le Speech de V.M., dans lequel vous parlez si aimablement du "friendly call" à Eu et des coopérations des 2 pays dans différentes parties du monde, et particulièrement pour l'Abolition de la Traite des noirs.

Ayez la grâce, Sire, de déposer nos hommages et nos félicitations aux pieds de la Reine et de votre Sœur. Agréez encore une fois, les expressions d'amitié et d'attachement sincère avec lesquelles je suis, Sire et mon bien cher Frère, de votre Majesté, la bien bonne Sœur et fidèle Amie,

Victoria R.

Queen Victoria to the King of the Belgians.

Windsor Castle, *30th December 1845.*

My dearest Uncle,—Many thanks for your kind letter of the 27th, by which I see how glad you are at our good Peel being again—and I sincerely and confidently hope for many years—my Minister. I have heard many instances of the confidence the country and *all* parties have in Peel; for instance, he was immensely cheered at Birmingham—a most Radical place; and *Joseph Hume* expressed great distress when Peel resigned, and the greatest contempt for Lord John Russell. The Members of the Government have behaved extremely well and with much disinterestedness. The Government has secured the services of Mr Gladstone and Lord Ellenborough,[44] who will be of great use. Lord E. is become very quiet, and is a very good speaker.

We had a very happy Christmas. This weather is extremely unwholesome. Now, ever your devoted Niece,

Victoria R.

ENDNOTES:

[1]:Louis Charles, Comte d'Aquila, a son of Francis I., King of the Two Sicilies, and brother of the Comte de Trapani and of Queen Christina; he and his brother were therefore uncles of Queen Isabella.

[2]:The Duc de Montpensier.

[3]:A list of French books which the Queen was proposing to read.

[4]:Peel replied that, as a renewal of the Income Tax was about to be proposed, it would be better to postpone the application to Parliament till the public feeling as to the tax had been ascertained.

[5]:A paragraph had appeared in the *Morning Chronicle*, giving credence to a rumour that this title was about to be conferred on the Prince, but, in answer to Mr Peter Borthwick, Sir Robert Peel positively contradicted it.

[6]:*Sir Robert Peel to the Prince Albert.*

Whitehall, *15th February 1845.*

Sir,--I received yesterday the accompanying note from Mr Borthwick, and in conformity with the notice therein given, he put the question to me in the House of Commons last evening respecting the paragraph which appeared in the *Morning Chronicle* respecting the intention of proposing to Parliament that your Royal Highness should assume the title of King Consort.

I very much regret that the *Morning Chronicle* inserted that paragraph.

The prominent place assigned to it in the newspaper, and a vague intimation that there was some authority for it, have caused a certain degree of credit to be attached to it. It has been copied into all the country newspapers and has given rise to a good deal of conjecture and speculation, which it is far from desirable to excite without necessity.

It appears to me that the editor of the *Morning Chronicle* acted most unwarrantably in inserting such a paragraph with a pretence of some sort of authority for it.

It has produced an impression which strongly confirms the observations which I took the liberty of making to your Royal Highness on Sunday evening.

I trust, however, that my decided contradiction of the paragraph will put a stop to further surmise and discussion on the subject.

To Mr Borthwick's note I add one of several letters addressed to me, which shows the proneness to speculate upon constitutional novelties.

I have the honour to be, Sir, with sincere respect, your Royal Highness's most faithful and obedient Servant,

Robert Peel.

[7]:Dr Thomas Turton (1780-1864), formerly Dean of Peterborough.

[8]:John Lonsdale (1788-1867) was Bishop of Lichfield from 1843 till his death.

[9]:See Peel's reply, *Life of the Prince Consort*, chap. XIII.

[10]:The purchase was suggested by Sir Robert Peel.

[11]:The Bill to increase the grant to the Roman Catholic College of Maynooth was carried by Peel in the teeth of opposition from half his party: another measure was passed to establish colleges for purely secular teaching ("godless colleges" they were nicknamed) in Cork, Belfast, and Galway, and affiliate them to a new Irish university.

[12]:As Macaulay had said during the previous night's debate: "The Orangeman raises his war whoop, Exeter Hall sets up its bray, Mr Macneile shudders to see more costly cheer than ever provided for the priests of Baal at the table of the Queen, and the Protestant operatives of Dublin call for impeachments in exceedingly bad English."

[13]:Achille Charles, Duc de Broglie, ex-Minister of Foreign Affairs.

[14]:Chancellor of the Exchequer.

[15]:The attraction these executions had for the general public was at this time a great scandal.

[16]:Public executions were abolished in 1868.

[17]:Dean Peel lived till 1875.

[18]:This visit lasted ten days, and included a visit to Goodwood races and a review of the Household troops in Hyde Park. His Majesty was also appointed a Field-Marshal.

[19]:*Ante*, vol. i. p. 47. He was then Prince of Orange, and succeeded his father, who abdicated in his favour in 1840.

[20]:Charles, second Earl Grey, had been Prime Minister, 1830-1834.

[21]:The Queen was accompanied by a Secretary of State (Lord Aberdeen), so that an act of State could be performed as well abroad as at home; see *Life of the Prince Consort*, vol. i. p. 272.

[22]:Parliament was prorogued on the 9th of August, and the Queen and Prince sailed in the evening for Antwerp in the Royal yacht. Sir Theodore Martin gives a very full description of the visit to Coburg. The Queen was especially delighted with the Rosenau and Reinhardtsbrunn. On the morning of the 8th of September the yacht, which had left the Scheldt on the previous evening, arrived at Tréport, and a second visit was paid to the King and Queen of the French at the Château d'Eu.

[23]:Younger son of Don Francisco de Paula, and first cousin to Queen Isabella, both through his father and his mother.

[24]:Frederick Denison Maurice (1805-1872), the friend of Kingsley, afterwards Chaplain of St. Peter's, Vere Street.

[25]:Mr Ward accepted the Deanery.

[26]:He retired from the Governor-Generalship of Canada through ill-health.

[27]:Lord Stanley, in reply, submitted a private letter from Lord Elgin, expressing a wish to return home; Earl Cathcart was provisionally appointed Governor-General.

[28]:See *Memoirs of the Life of Henry Reeve*, vol. i. p. 175, for Lord Dufferin's refutation of the story that Sidney Herbert confided the secret to Mrs Norton, and that she sold it to the *Times*. The story has obtained a wide currency through Mr Meredith's *Diana of the Crossways*. Lord Stanmore, in his *Life of Sidney Herbert*, substantially attributes the communication to Lord Aberdeen, but does not give the details.

[29]:Peel reported to the Queen the Cabinet discussions on the Corn Law question. The Queen wrote that the news caused her much uneasiness, and that she felt certain that her Minister would not leave her at a moment of such difficulty, and when a crisis was impending.

[30]:From Sir Robert Peel, 5th December, *ante.*

[31]:Declaring for the Repeal of the Corn Laws.

[32]:That paragraph urged that, with a revision of taxation to make the arrangement more equitable, and the safeguards suggested by caution and scrupulous forbearance, restrictions on the admission of the main articles of food and clothing used by the mass of the people should be removed.

[33]:The return of Palmerston to the Foreign Office was of course dreaded by the King and Guizot.

[34]:It is printed in the *Annual Register*, 1846, p. 17. Lord John considered the temporary suspension or repeal of duties, with the prospect of their re-imposition, open to grave objections.

[35]:Lord John Russell, however, found insuperable difficulties in forming the Cabinet; and, to quote Disraeli, "handed back with courtesy the poisoned chalice to Sir Robert."

[36]:In reference to affairs in Syria in 1840.

[37]:Lord Grey's attitude was condemned by Macaulay in a letter to a Mr Macfarlan, who unwisely communicated it to the Press.

[38]:Printed in *Annual Register*, 1846, p. 20.

[39]:*See* next letter.

[40]:Mr Gladstone, by accepting office, vacated the seat at Newark which he had held through the influence of the Protectionist Duke of Newcastle. He did not seek re-election, and though a Secretary of State, remained without a seat in Parliament.

[41]:Submitted to the Queen by Lord Melbourne.

[42]:1830-1834, and 1835-1841.

[43]:The English and French came in 1832 to the assistance of the Belgians, who some time before had entered Antwerp, but failed to take the Citadel.

[44]:Lord Ellenborough was one of the few Conservative statesmen of the day who, after remaining faithful to Sir Robert Peel till the middle of 1846, subsequently threw in his fortunes with Lord Derby and Mr Disraeli. He was President of the Board of Control with those Ministers in 1858 for the fourth time.

INTRODUCTORY NOTE
TO CHAPTER XV

The closing days of the year 1845 had been marked by startling political events, and Lord John Russell's failure to form a Government, and Sir Robert Peel's resumption of office, with Mr Gladstone substituted for Lord Stanley, were now followed by the Ministerial measure for the Repeal of the Corn Laws. Embarrassed as he now was by the attacks of his old supporters, led by Bentinck and Disraeli, Peel was supported whole-heartedly but in a strictly constitutional manner by the Queen and the Prince. Amid bitter taunts, the Premier piloted the measure through Parliament, but on the night that it finally passed the Lords he was defeated on an Irish Coercion Bill by a factious combination in the Commons between the Whigs and Protectionists, and resigned. Lord John Russell on this occasion was able to form an administration, though he failed in his attempt to include in it some important members of the outgoing Government.

Thus, owing to the Irish famine, the Tory party which had come into power in 1841 with a majority of ninety to support the Corn Laws, was shattered; after Peel's defeat it became clear that no common action could take place between his supporters in the struggle of 1846 and men like Bentinck and Disraeli, who now became leaders of the Protectionist party. For the remainder of the year Peel was on the whole friendly to the Russell Government, his chief care being to maintain them in office as against the Protectionists.

In India the British army was successful in its operations against the Sikhs, Sir Harry Smith defeating them at Aliwal, and Sir Hugh Gough at Sobraon. Our troops crossed the Sutlej, and terms of peace were agreed on between Sir Henry Hardinge (who became a Viscount) and the Sirdars from Lahore, peace being signed on 8th March.

On the continent of Europe the most important events took place in the Peninsula. The selection of husbands for the Queen of Spain and her sister, which had so long been considered an international question, came at last to a crisis; the policy of Great Britain had been to leave the matter to the Spanish people, except in so far as might be necessary to check the undue ambition of Louis Philippe; and neither the Queen, Prince Albert, Peel, nor Aberdeen had in any way supported the candidature of Prince Leopold of Saxe-Coburg.

It was common ground that no son of Louis Philippe should marry the Queen, but both that monarch and Guizot had further solemnly engaged at the Château d'Eu that no son should marry even the Infanta until the Queen was married and had children. The return of Palmerston to the Foreign Office, and his mention of Prince Leopold in a Foreign Office despatch as one of the candidates, gave the King and his Minister the pretext they required for repudiating their solemn undertaking. In defiance of good faith the engagements were simultaneously announced of the Queen to her cousin, Don Francisco de Asis, and of the Infanta to the Duc de Montpensier, Don Francisco being a man of unattractive, even disagreeable qualities, and feeble in *physique*. By this unscrupulous proceeding Queen Victoria and the English nation were profoundly shocked.

At the same time Queen Maria found some difficulty in maintaining her position in Portugal. She dismissed in a somewhat high-handed manner her Minister the Duc de Palmella, and had to bear the brunt of an insurrection for several months: at the close of the year her arms were victorious at the lines of Torres Vedras, but the Civil War was not entirely brought to an end.

In February a Polish insurrection broke out in Silesia, and the Austrian troops were driven from Cracow; the rising was suppressed by Austria, Russia, and Prussia, who had been constituted the "Protecting Powers" of Cracow by the Treaty of Vienna. This unsuccessful attempt was seized upon as a pretext for destroying the separate nationality of Cracow, which was forthwith annexed to Austria. This unjustifiable act only became possible in consequence of the *entente* between England and France (equally parties to the Treaty of Vienna) having been terminated by the affair of the Spanish marriages; their formal but separate protests were disregarded.

There remains to be mentioned the dispute between Great Britain and the United States as to the Oregon boundary, which had assumed so ominous a phase in 1845. Lord Aberdeen's last official act was to announce in the Lords that a Convention, proposed by himself for adjusting the question, had been accepted by the American President.

CHAPTER XV

1846

Queen Victoria to Sir Robert Peel.

Buckingham Palace, *23rd January 1846.*

The Queen must compliment Sir Robert Peel on his beautiful and indeed *unanswerable* speech of last night, which we have been reading with the greatest attention.[1] The concluding part we also greatly admire. Sir R. Peel has made a very strong case. Surely the impression which it has made must have been a good one. Lord John's explanation is a fair one;[2] the Queen has *not* a doubt that he will support Sir Robert Peel.

He has indeed pledged himself to it. He does not give a very satisfactory explanation of the causes of his failure, but perhaps he could not do so without exposing Lord Palmerston.

What does Sir Robert think of the temper of the House of Commons, and of the debate in the House of Lords? The debates not being adjourned is a good thing. The crowd was immense out-of-doors yesterday, and we were never better received.

Sir Henry Hardinge to Queen Victoria.[3]

Camp, Lullianee, 24 miles from Lahore,

18th February 1846.

The territory which it is proposed should be ceded in perpetuity to your Majesty is a fine district between the Rivers Sutlej and Beas, throwing our frontier forward, within 30 miles of Amritsar, so as to have 50 miles of British territory in front of Loodiana, which, relatively with Ferozepore, is so weak, that it appeared desirable to the Governor-General to improve our frontier on its weakest side, to curb the Sikhs by an easy approach towards Amritsar across the Beas River instead of the Sutlej—to round off our hill possessions near Simla—to weaken the Sikh State which has proved itself to be too strong—and to show to all Asia that although the British Government has not deemed it expedient to annex this immense country of the Punjab, making the Indus the British boundary, it has punished the treachery and violence of the Sikh nation, and exhibited its powers in a manner which cannot be misunderstood. For the same political and military reason, the Governor-General hopes to be able before the negotiations are closed to make arrangements by which Cashmere may be added to the possessions of Gholab Singh, declaring the Rajpoot Hill States with Cashmere independent of the Sikhs of the Plains. The Sikhs declare their inability to pay the indemnity of one million and a half, and will probably offer Cashmere as an equivalent. In this case, if Gholab Singh pays the money demanded for the expenses of the war, the district of Cashmere will be ceded by the British to him, and the Rajah become one of the Princes of Hindostan.

There are difficulties in the way of this arrangement, but considering the military power which the Sikh nation has exhibited of bringing into the field 80,000 men and 300 pieces of field artillery, it appears to the Governor-General most politic to diminish the means of this warlike people to repeat a similar aggression. The nation is in fact a dangerous military Republic on our weakest frontier. If the British Army had been defeated, the Sikhs, through the Protected States, which would have risen in their favour in case of a reverse, would have captured Delhi, and a people having 50,000 regular troops and 300 pieces of field artillery in a standing permanent camp within 50 miles of Ferozepore, is a state of things that cannot be tolerated for the future....

The energy and intrepidity displayed by your Majesty's Commander-in-Chief, Sir Hugh Gough, his readiness to carry on the service in cordial co-operation with the Governor-General, and the marked bravery and invincibility of your Majesty's English troops, have overcome many serious obstacles, and the precautions taken have been such that no disaster or failure, however trifling, has attended the arduous efforts of your Majesty's Arms.

Queen Victoria to the King of the Belgians.

Osborne, *3rd March 1846.*

My dearest Uncle,—I hasten to thank you for a most dear and kind letter of the 28th, which I received this morning. You know how I love and esteem my dearest Louise; she is the dearest friend, after my beloved Albert, I have.

I wish you could be here, and hope you will come here for a few days during your stay, to see the innumerable alterations and improvements which have taken place. My dearest Albert is so happy here, out all day planting, directing, etc., and it is so good for him. It is a relief to be away from all the bitterness which people create for themselves in London. Peel has a very anxious and a very peculiar position, and it is the force of circumstances and the great energy he *alone possesses* which will carry him through the Session. He certainly acts a most disinterested part, for did he not feel (as *every one* who is fully acquainted with the *real state* of the country must feel) that the line he pursues is the *only right* and sound one for the welfare of this country, he never would have exposed himself to all the annoyance and pain of being attacked by his friends. He was, however, determined to have done this before the next general election, but the alarming state of distress in Ireland forced him to do it now. I must, however, leave him to explain to you fully himself the peculiar circumstances of the present very irregular state of affairs. His majority was *not* a *certain* one *last year*, for on Maynooth, upwards of a *hundred* of his followers voted against him.

The state of affairs in India is very serious. I am glad you do justice to the bravery of our good people.

Queen Victoria to Sir Henry Hardinge.

Osborne, *4th March 1846.*

The Queen is anxious to seize the first opportunity of expressing to Sir Henry Hardinge, her admiration of his conduct on the last most trying occasion, and of the courage and gallantry of the officers and men who had so severe a contest to endure.[4] Their conduct has been in every way worthy of the British name, and both the Prince and Queen are deeply impressed with it. The severe loss we have sustained in so many brave officers and men is very painful, and must alloy the satisfaction every one feels at the brilliant successes of our Arms. Most deeply do we lament the death of Sir Robert Sale, Sir John M'Caskill,[5] and Major Broadfoot,[6] and most deeply do we sympathise with that high-minded woman, Lady Sale, who has had the misfortune to lose her husband less than three years after she was released from captivity and restored to him.

We are truly rejoiced to hear that Sir H. Hardinge's health has not suffered, and that he and his brave son have been so mercifully preserved. The Queen will look forward with great anxiety to the next news from India.

Memorandum by the Prince Albert.

Buckingham Palace, *1st April 1846.*

I saw this day Sir R. Peel, and showed him a memorandum, which I had drawn up respecting our conversation of the 30th.

It filled six sheets, and contained, as minutely as I could render it, the whole of the arguments we had gone through. Sir Robert read it through and over again, and, after a long pause, said: "I was not aware when I spoke to your Royal Highness that my words would be taken down, and don't acknowledge that this is a fair representation of my opinion." He was visibly uneasy, and added, if he knew that what he said should be committed to paper, he would speak differently, and give his opinion with all the circumspection and reserve which a Minister ought to employ when he gave responsible advice; but he had in this instance spoken quite unreservedly, like an advocate defending a point in debate, and then he had taken another and tried to carry this as far as it would go, in order to give me an opportunity of judging of the different bearings of the question. He did so often in the Cabinet, when they discussed important questions, and was often asked: "Well, then, you are quite against this measure?" "Not at all, but I want that the counter argument should be gone into to the fullest extent, in order that the Cabinet should not take a one-sided view."

He viewed the existence of such a paper with much uneasiness, as it might appear as if he had left this before going out of office in order to prepossess the Queen against the measures, which her future Minister might propose to her, and so lay secretly the foundation of his fall. The existence of such a paper might cause great embarrassment to the Queen; if she followed the advice of a Minister who proposed measures hostile to the Irish Church, it might be said, she knew what she undertook, for Sir R. Peel had warned her and left on record the serious objections that attached to the measure.

I said that I felt it to be of the greatest importance to possess his views on the question, but that I thought I would not have been justified in keeping a record of our conversation without showing it to him, and asking him whether I had rightly understood him; but if he felt a moment's uneasiness about this memorandum, I would at once destroy it, as I was anxious that nothing should prevent his speaking without the slightest reserve to me in future as he had done heretofore. I felt that these open discussions were of the greatest use to me in my endeavour to investigate the different political questions of the day and to form a conclusive opinion upon them. As Sir Robert did not say a word to dissuade me, I took it as an affirmative, and threw the memorandum into the fire, which, I could see, relieved Sir Robert.

Albert.

Mr Gladstone to Queen Victoria.

13 Carlton House Terrace, *1st April 1846.*

Mr William Gladstone presents his humble duty to your Majesty, and prays that he may be honoured with your Majesty's permission to direct that the Park and Tower Guns may be fired forthwith in celebration of the victory which was achieved by your Majesty's forces over the Sikh army in Sobraon on the 10th of February.[7]

Queen Victoria to Sir Henry Hardinge.

Buckingham Palace, *6th April 1846.*

The Queen must write a line to Sir Henry Hardinge in order to express her extreme satisfaction at the brilliant and happy termination of our severe contest with the Sikhs, which he communicated to her in his long and interesting letter of the 18th and 19th February. The Queen much admires the skill and valour with which their difficult operations have been conducted, and knows how much she owes to Sir Henry Hardinge's exertions. The Queen hopes that he will see an acknowledgment of this in the communication she has ordered to be made to him relative to his elevation to the Peerage.

The Prince, who fully knows all the Queen's feelings on this glorious occasion, wishes to be named to Sir Henry Hardinge.

The King of the French to Queen Victoria.

Paris, *5 Mai 1846.*

Madame ma très chère Sœur,—Quand le 1er de Mai, au moment où j'allais commencer les nombreuses et longues réceptions de mon jour de fête, on m'a remis la lettre si gracieuse que votre Majesté a eu l'aimable attention de m'écrire de manière à ce que je la reçoive ce jour là, j'en ai été pénétré, et j'ai pensé tout de suite aux paroles du Menuet d'Iphigénie comme exprimant le remercîment qu'à mon grand regret, je ne pouvais que sentir, et non exprimer par écrit dans un pareil moment. J'ai donc fait chercher tout de suite la partition de ce menuet, et celles du Chœur du même Opéra de Glück "*Chantons, célébrons notre Reine!*" mais on n'a pu, ou pas su se les procurer, et j'ai dû me contenter de les avoir arrangés pour le piano dans un livre (pas même relié) qui a au moins pour excuse de contenir toute la musique de cet Opéra. Je l'ai mis dans une grande enveloppe adressée à votre Majesté et j'ai fait prier Lord Cowley de l'expédier par le premier Courier qui pourrait s'en charger, comme Dépêche, afin d'éviter ces postages dont Lord Liverpool m'a révélé l'étonnant usage.

Que vous dirai-je, Madame, sur tous les sentiments dont m'a pénétré cette nouvelle marque d'amitié de votre part? Vous connaissez celle que je vous porte, et combien elle est vive et sincère. J'espère bien que l'année ne s'écoulera pas sans que j'aie été présenter mes hommages à votre Majesté....

Tout ce que j'entends, tout ce que je recueille, me donne de plus en plus l'espérance que la crise Parlementaire dans laquelle le Ministère de votre Majesté se trouve engagé, se terminera, comme Elle sait que je le désire vivement, c'est-à-dire que Sir Robert Peel, Lord Aberdeen, etc., will hold fast, et qu'ils seront encore ses Ministres quand j'aurai le bonheur de Lui faire ma Cour. Je vois avec plaisir que ce vœu est à peu près général en France, et qu'il se manifeste de plus en plus....

Que votre Majesté me permette d'offrir ici au Prince Albert l'expression de ma plus tendre amitié, et qu'elle veuille bien me croire pour la vie, Madame ma très chère Sœur, de votre Majesté, le bon Frère et bien fidèle Ami,

Louis Philippe, R.

J'ai volé ces feuilles de papier à ma bonne Reine pour échapper aux reproches trop bien fondés que Lord Aberdeen a faits à la dernière fourniture dont je me suis servi.

Sir Robert Peel to Queen Victoria.

House of Commons, *12th June 1846.*

(*Friday Night.*)

Sir Robert Peel, with his humble duty to your Majesty, begs leave to acquaint your Majesty that no progress has been made to-night with the Irish Bill.[8]

On reading the order of the day Sir Robert Peel took that opportunity of defending himself from the accusations[9] brought forward by Lord George Bentinck and Mr Disraeli against Sir Robert Peel for transactions that took place twenty years since. The debate on this preliminary question lasted until nearly half-past eleven.

Like every unjust and malignant attack, this, according to Sir Robert Peel's impressions, recoiled upon its authors.

He thinks the House was completely satisfied. Lord John Russell and Lord Morpeth behaved very well.

The vindictive motive of the attack was apparent to all but a few Protectionists.

Sir Robert Peel to Queen Victoria.

Whitehall, *22nd June 1846.*

Sir Robert Peel presents his humble duty to your Majesty, and assures your Majesty that he is penetrated with a deep sense of your Majesty's great kindness and your Majesty's generous sympathy with himself and Lady Peel.

Sir Robert Peel firmly believes that the recent attack made upon him was the result of a foul conspiracy concocted by Mr Disraeli and Lord George Bentinck, in the hope and belief that from the lapse of time or want of leisure in Sir Robert Peel to collect materials for his defence, or the destruction of documents and papers, the means of complete refutation might be wanting....

He hopes, however, he had sufficient proof to demonstrate the falseness of the accusation, and the malignant motives of the accusers.

He is deeply grateful to your Majesty and to the Prince for the kind interest you have manifested during the progress of this arduous struggle, which now he trusts is approaching to a successful termination.

Sir Robert Peel to Queen Victoria.

Downing Street, *26th June 1846.*

(*Two o'clock.*)

Sir Robert Peel, with his humble duty to your Majesty, begs leave to acquaint your Majesty that the members of the Government met in Cabinet to-day at one.

Sir Robert Peel is just returned from this meeting.

He stated to the Cabinet that after the event of yesterday (the rejection of the Irish Bill by so large a majority as 73) he felt it to be his duty as head of the Government humbly to tender his resignation of office to your Majesty. He added that, feeling no assurance that the result of a Dissolution would be to give a majority agreeing with the Government in general principles of policy, and sufficient in amount to enable the Government to conduct the business of the country with credit to themselves and satisfaction to your Majesty and the public at large, he could not advise your Majesty to dissolve the Parliament.

Sir Robert Peel said that, in his opinion, the Government generally ought to resign, but his mind was made up as to his own course.

There was not a dissenting voice that it was the duty of the Government to tender their resignation to your Majesty, and for the reasons stated by Sir Robert Peel, not to advise dissolution. If Sir Robert Peel does not receive your Majesty's commands to wait upon your Majesty in the course of to-day, Sir Robert Peel will be at Osborne about half-past three to-morrow.

Memorandum by the Prince Albert.

Osborne House, *28th June 1846.*

Sir Robert Peel arrived yesterday evening and tendered his resignation. He is evidently much relieved in quitting a post, the labours and anxieties of which seem almost too much for anybody to bear, and which in these last six months were particularly onerous. In fact, he said that he would not have been able to stand it much longer. Nothing, however, would have induced him to give way before he had passed the Corn Bill and the Tariff.[10] The majority upon the Irish Bill was much larger than any one had expected; Sir Robert was glad of this, however, as it convinced his colleagues of the necessity of resigning. He told them at the Cabinet that, as for himself personally, he had made up his mind to resign, and on being asked what he advised his Cabinet to do, he recommended them to do the same, which received general concurrence. The last weeks had not been without some intrigue. There was a party headed by Lord Ellenborough and Lord Brougham, who wished Sir Robert and Sir James Graham to retire, and for the rest of the Cabinet to reunite with the Protection section of the Conservatives, and to carry on the Government. Lord Ellenborough and Lord Brougham had in December last settled to head the Protectionists, but this combination had been broken up by Lord Ellenborough's acceptance of the post of First Lord of the Admiralty; Lord Brougham then declared for free trade, perhaps in order to follow Lord Ellenborough into office. The Duke of Wellington had been for dissolution till he saw the complete disorganisation of his party in the House of Lords. The Whigs, having been beat twice the evening before by large majorities on the Roman Catholic Bill, had made every exertion on the Coercion Bill, and the majority was still increased by Sir Robert's advising the Free Traders and Radicals, who had intended to stay away in order not to endanger Sir Robert's Government, not to do so as they would not be able to save him. Seventy Protectionists voted with the majority.

Before leaving Town Sir R. Peel addressed a letter to Lord John Russell, informing him that he was going to the Isle of Wight in order to tender his and his colleagues' resignation to the Queen, that he did not the least know what Her Majesty's intentions were, but that in case she should send for Lord John, he (Sir Robert) was ready to see Lord John (should he wish it), and give him any explanation as to the state of public affairs and Parliamentary business which he could desire. Sir Robert thought thereby, without in the least committing the Queen, to indicate to Lord John that he had nothing to fear on his part, and that, on the contrary, he could reckon upon his assistance in starting the Queen's new Government. He hoped likewise that this would tend to dispel a clamour for dissolution which the Whigs have raised, alarmed by their defeats upon the Catholic Bill.

Albert.

Sir Robert Peel to Queen Victoria.

House of Commons, *29th June 1846.*

Sir Robert Peel, with his humble duty to your Majesty, begs leave to acquaint your Majesty that he has just concluded his speech notifying to the House the resignation of the Government.

He thinks it was very well received.[11] Lord Palmerston spoke after Sir Robert Peel, but not very effectively, but no other person spoke. Sir Robert Peel is to see Lord John Russell at ten to-morrow morning.

Sir Robert Peel humbly congratulates your Majesty on the intelligence received *this day* from America. The defeat of the Government on the day on which they carried the Corn Bill, and the receipt of the intelligence from America[12] on the day on which they resign, are singular coincidences.

The Bishop of Oxford[13] to Mr Anson.

61 Eaton Place, *29th June 1846.*

(*Midnight.*)

My dear Anson,—Your kind letter reached me half an hour ago whilst Sir T. Acland was sitting with me; and I must say a few words in reply by the early post. I went down to hear Peel in the House of Commons, and very fine it was. The House crowded, Peers and Ambassadors filling every seat and overflowing into the House. Soon after six all private business was over; Peel not come in, all waiting, no one rose for anything; for ten minutes this lasted: then Peel came in, walked up the House: colder, dryer, more introverted than ever, yet to a close gaze showing the fullest working of a smothered volcano of emotions. He was out of breath with walking and sat down on the Treasury Bench (placing a small despatch box with the Oregon despatches on the table) as he would be fully himself before he rose. By-and-by he rose, amidst a breathless silence, and made the speech you will have read long ere this. It was very fine: very effective: really almost solemn: to fall at such a moment. He spoke as if it was his last political scene: as if he felt that between alienated friends and unwon foes he could have no party again; and could only as a shrewd bystander observe and advise others. There was but one point in the Speech which I thought doubtful: the apostrophe to "Richard Cobden."[14] I think it was wrong, though there is very much to be said for it. The opening of the American peace was noble; but for the future, what have we to look to? Already there are whispers of Palmerston and War; the Whig budget and deficiency. The first great question all men ask is: does Lord John come in, leaning on Radical or Conservative aid? Is Hawes to be in the Cabinet? the first Dissenter? the first tradesman? the Irish Church? I wish you were near enough to talk to, though even then you would know too much that must not be known for a comfortable talk. But I shall hope soon to see you; and am always, my dear Anson, very sincerely and affectionately yours,

S. Oxon.

Memorandum by the Prince Albert.

Osborne House, *30th June 1846.*

Lord John Russell arrived here this afternoon; he has seen Sir Robert Peel this morning, and is prepared to undertake the formation of a Government which he thinks will stand; at least, for the present session he anticipates no difficulty, as Sir R. Peel has professed himself ready not to obstruct its progress, and as the Protectionists have held a meeting on Saturday at which Lord Stanley has declared that he would let this Government go on smoothly unless the word "Irish Church" was pronounced. About men and offices, Lord John has consulted with Lord Lansdowne, Palmerston, Clarendon, and Cottenham, who were of opinion that the Liberal members of Sir Robert's Cabinet ought to be induced to retain office under Lord John, viz. Lord Dalhousie, Lord Lincoln, and Mr Sidney Herbert. Sir Robert Peel at the interview of this morning had stated to Lord John that he would not consider it as an attempt to draw his supporters away from him (it not being his intention to form a party), and that he would not dissuade them from accepting the offer, but that he feared that they would not accept. We concurred in this opinion, but Lord John was authorised by Victoria to make the offer. Mr F. Baring, the Chancellor of the Exchequer under the late Whig Government, has intimated to Lord John that he would prefer if no offer of office was made to him; Lord John would therefore recommend Mr Charles Wood for this office. Lord Grey was still a difficulty; in or out of office he seemed to be made a difficulty. It would be desirable to have him in the Cabinet if he could waive his opinions upon the Irish Church. His speech in the House of Lords[15] at the beginning of the session had done much harm, had been very extreme, and Lord John was decidedly against him in that. Lord Grey knew that everybody blamed it, but said everybody would be of those (his) opinions ten years hence, and therefore he might just as well hold them now. Mr Wood having great influence with him might keep him quiet, and so would the Colonial seals, as he would get work enough. About Lord Palmerston, he is satisfied, and would no more make any difficulty.

Lord John Russell told me in the evening that he had forgotten to mention one subject to the Queen: it was that Sir Robert Peel by his speech and his special mention of Mr Cobden as the person who had carried the great measure, had made it very difficult for Lord John not to offer office to Mr Cobden. The Whigs were already accused of being exclusive, and reaping the harvest of other people's work. The only thing he could offer would be a *Cabinet* office. Now this would affront a great many people whom he (Lord J.) had to conciliate, and create even possibly dissension in his Cabinet. As Mr Cobden was going on the Continent for a year, Lord John was advised by Lord Clarendon to write to Mr C., and tell him that he had heard he was going abroad, that he would not make any offer to him therefore, but that he considered him as entitled once to be recommended for office to the Queen. This he would do, with the Queen's permission....

Queen Victoria to Sir Robert Peel.

Osborne, *1st July 1846.*

The Queen returns these letters, with her best thanks. The settlement of the Oregon question has given us the greatest satisfaction. It does seem strange that at the moment of triumph the Government should have to resign. The Queen read Sir Robert Peel's speech with great admiration. The Queen seizes this opportunity (though she will see Sir Robert again) of expressing her *deep* concern at losing his services, which she regrets as much for the Country as for herself and the Prince. In whatever position Sir Robert Peel may be, we shall ever look on him as a kind and true friend, and ever have the greatest esteem and regard for him as a Minister and as a private individual.

The Queen will not say anything about what passed at Lord John Russell's interview, as the Prince has already written to Sir Robert. She does not think, however, that he mentioned the wish Lord John expressed that Lord Liverpool should retain his office, which however (much as we should personally like it) we think he would not do.

What does Sir Robert hear of the Protectionists, and what do his own followers say to the state of affairs?

Memorandum by the Prince Albert.

Buckingham Palace, *6th July 1846.*

Yesterday the new Ministry were installed at a Privy Council, and the Seals of Office transferred to them. We had a long conversation with Sir Robert Peel, who took leave. I mentioned to him that his word of "Richard Cobden" had created an immense sensation, but he was not inclined to enter upon the subject. When we begged him to do nothing which could widen the breach between him and his party, he said, "I don't think that we can ever get together again." He repeated that he was anxious not to undertake a Government again, that his health would not stand it, that it was better likewise for the Queen's service that other, younger men should be brought forward. Sir Robert, Lord Aberdeen, and Sir James Graham parted with great emotion, and had tears in their eyes when they thanked the Queen for her confidence and support. Lord Aberdeen means to have an interview with Lord Palmerston, and says that when he (Lord A.) came into office, Lord Palmerston and the *Chronicle* assailed him most bitterly as an imbecile Minister, a traitor to his country, etc., etc. He means now to show Lord P. the contrast by declaring his readiness to assist him in every way he can by his advice, that he would at all times speak to him as if he was his colleague if he wished it.

The new Court is nearly completed, and we have succeeded in obtaining a very respectable and proper one, notwithstanding the run which the Party made upon it which had been formerly used to settle these matters, to *their* liking only. The Government is not a united one, however, by any means. Mr Wood and Lord Clarendon take the greatest credit in having induced Lord Grey to join the Government,[16] and are responsible to Lord John to keep him quiet, which they think they will be able to do, as he had been convinced of the folly of his former line of conduct. Still, they say Lord Lansdowne will have the lead only nominally, that Lord Grey is to take it really in the House of Lords. There is the *Grey Party*, consisting of Lord Grey, Lord Clarendon, Sir George Grey, and Mr Wood; they are against Lord Lansdowne, Lord Minto, Lord Auckland, and Sir John Hobhouse, stigmatising them as old women. Lord John leans entirely to the last-named gentlemen. There is no cordiality between Lord John and Lord Palmerston, who, if he had to make a choice, would even forget what passed in December last, and join the Grey Party in preference to Lord John personally. The curious part of all this is that they cannot keep a secret, and speak of all their differences. They got the *Times* over by giving it exclusive information, and the leading articles are sent in and praise the new Cabinet, but the wicked paper added immediately a furious attack upon Sir John Hobhouse, which alarmed them so much that they sent to Sir John, sounding him, whether he would be hereafter prepared to relinquish the Board of Control. (This, however, is a mere personal matter of Mr Walter, who stood against Sir John at Nottingham in 1841 and was unseated.) Sir John Easthope, the proprietor of the *Morning Chronicle*, complains bitterly of the subserviency to the *Times* and treason to him. He says he knows that the information was sent from Lord John's house, and threatens revenge. "If you will be ruled by the *Times*," he said to one of the Cabinet, "the *Times* has shown you already by a specimen that you will be ruled by a rod of iron."

A Brevet for the Army and Navy is proposed, in order to satisfy Lord Anglesey with the dignity of Field-Marshal.

Albert.

The Protectionists, 150 strong, including Peers and M.P.'s, are to give a dinner to Lord Stanley at Greenwich, at which he is to announce his opinions upon the line they are to take. Lord George Bentinck is there to lay down the lead which the Party insisted upon. Who is to follow him as their leader in the Commons nobody knows.

Queen Victoria to the King of the Belgians.

Buckingham Palace, *7th July 1846.*

My dearest Uncle,—I have to thank you for your kind letter of the 3rd. It arrived yesterday, which was a very hard day for me. I had to part with Sir R. Peel and Lord Aberdeen, who are irreparable losses to us and the Country; they were both so much overcome that it quite overset me, and we have in them two devoted friends. We felt so safe with them. Never, during the five years that they were with me, did they *ever* recommend a *person* or a thing which was not for my or the Country's best, and never for the Party's advantage only; and the contrast *now* is very striking; there is much less respect and much less high and pure feeling. Then the discretion of Peel, I believe, is unexampled.

Stockmar has, I know, explained to you the state of affairs, which is unexampled, and I think the present Government *very* weak and extremely disunited. What may appear to you as a mistake in November was an inevitable evil. Aberdeen very truly explained it yesterday. "We had ill luck," he said; "if it had not been for this famine in Ireland, which rendered immediate measures necessary, Sir Robert would have prepared them gradually for the change." Then, besides, the Corn Law Agitation was such that if Peel had not wisely made this change (for which the *whole* Country blesses him), a convulsion would shortly have taken place, and we should have been *forced* to yield what has been granted as a boon. No doubt the breaking up of the Party (which *will* come together again, whether under Peel or some one else) is a very distressing thing. The only thing to be regretted, and I do not know exactly *why* he did it (though we *can* guess), was his praise of *Cobden*, which has shocked people a good deal.

But I can't tell you how sad I am to lose Aberdeen; you can't think what a delightful companion he was; the breaking up of all this intercourse during our journeys, etc., is deplorable.

We have contrived to get a *very* respectable Court.

Albert's use to me, and I may say to the *Country*, by his firmness and sagacity, is beyond all belief in these moments of trial.

We are all well, but I am, of course, a good deal overset by all these tribulations.

Ever your devoted Niece,

Victoria R.

I was much touched to see Graham so very much overcome at taking leave of us.

Queen Victoria to Viscount Hardinge.

Buckingham Palace, *8th July 1846.*

The Queen thanks Lord Hardinge for his interesting communications. Lord Hardinge will have learnt all that has taken place in the Country; one of the most brilliant Governments this Country ever had has fallen at the moment of victory! The Queen has now, besides mourning over this event, the anxiety of having to see the Government carried on as efficiently as possible, for the welfare of the Country. The Queen would find a guarantee for the accomplishment of this object in Lord Hardinge's consenting to continue at the head of the Government of India, where great experiments have been made which require unity of purpose and system to be carried out successfully.

Queen Victoria to Lord John Russell.

Osborne, *10th July 1846.*

... The Queen approves of the pensions proposed by Lord J. Russell, though she cannot conceal from him that she thinks the one to Father Mathew a doubtful proceeding. It is quite true that he has done much good by preaching temperance, but by the aid of superstition, which can hardly be patronised by the Crown.[17]

The Queen is sure that Lord John will like her at all times to speak out her mind, and has, therefore, done so without reserve.

Queen Victoria to the King of the Belgians.

Osborne, *14th July 1846.*

My dearest Uncle,—We are very happily established here since Thursday, and have beautiful weather for this truly enjoyable place; we drive, walk, and sit out—and the nights are so fine. I long for you to be here. It has quite restored my spirits, which were much shaken by the sad leave-takings in London—of Sir R. Peel, Lord Aberdeen, Lord Liverpool, etc. Lord L. could *not well* have stayed. Lord Aberdeen was very much overset.

The present Government is weak, and I think Lord J. does not possess the talent of keeping his people together. Most people think, however, that they will get through this Session; the only question of difficulty is the *sugar* question.

I think that the King of the French's visit is more than ever desirable—now; for if he were to be shy of coming, it would prove to the world that this *new* Government was hostile, and the *entente cordiale* no longer sure. Pray impress this on the King—and I *hope* and *beg* he will let the dear Nemours pay us a little visit in November. It would have the best effect, and be so pleasant, as we are so dull in the winter all by ourselves. I hope that in future, when the King and the Family are at *Eu*, some of them will frequently come over to see us *here*. It would be so nice and *so near.*

Now adieu, dearest Uncle. I hope I shall *not* have to *write* to you again, but have the happiness of *saying de vive voix*, that I am ever, your devoted Niece,

Victoria R.

Viscount Palmerston to Queen Victoria.

Foreign Office, *16th July 1846.*

... With regard to the marriage of the Queen of Spain, Viscount Palmerston has received a good deal of general information from persons who have conversed with him on the subject, but he has learnt nothing thereupon which was not already known to your Majesty. The state of that matter seems, in a few words, to be that the Count of Trapani is now quite out of the question, that the Count of Montemolin, though wished for by Austria, and in some degree supported by the Court of the Tuileries, would be an impossible choice, and that the alternative now lies between Don Enrique and the Prince Leopold of Coburg, the two Queens being equally set against the Duke of Cadiz, Don Enrique's elder brother. In favour of Prince Leopold seem to be the two Queens, and a party (of what extent and influence does not appear) in Spain. Against that Prince are arrayed, ostensibly at least, the Court of the Tuileries and the Liberal Party in Spain; and probably to a certain degree the Government of Austria.

In favour of Don Enrique are a very large portion of the Spanish nation, who would prefer a Spanish prince for their Sovereign's husband; and the preference, expressed only as an opinion and without any acts in furtherance of it, by your Majesty's late Administration. Against Don Enrique are the aversion of the Queen Mother, founded on her family differences with her late sister, and the apprehensions of the present Ministers in Spain, who would think their power endangered by the political connection between Don Enrique and the more Liberal Party. The sentiments of the King of the French in regard to Don Enrique seem not very decided; but it appears likely that the King of the French would prefer Count Montemolin or the Duke of Cadiz to Don Enrique; but that he would prefer Don Enrique to the Prince Leopold of Coburg, because the former would fall within the category of Bourbon princes, descended from Philip the Fifth of Spain, proposed by the King of the French as the limited circle within which the Queen of Spain should find a husband.

Queen Victoria to Viscount Palmerston.

16th July 1846.

The Queen has received Lord Palmerston's interesting letter, and is very much satisfied with his parting conversation with Ibrahim Pasha, which she conceives will not be lost upon him. The view Lord Palmerston takes about the present position of the Spanish marriage question appears to the Queen quite correct. She finds only one omission, which is Queen Isabella's personal objection to Don Enrique, and the danger which attaches to marriage with a Prince taken up by a Political Party in Spain, which makes him the political enemy of the opposite Party.[18]

The Queen thanks Lord Palmerston for his zeal about Portugal, which is really in an alarming state.[19] She sends herewith the last letter which she received from the King of Portugal. The Queen is sorry to have lost the opportunity of seeing Marshal Saldanha.

Queen Victoria to Lord John Russell.

Osborne House, *16th July 1846.*

The Queen has received Lord John Russell's communication of yesterday, and sincerely hopes that Lord John's sugar measure[20] may be such that the Committee of the Cabinet, as well as the whole Cabinet and *Parliament*, may concur in it, which would save the country another struggle this year. The Queen trusts, moreover, that late experience and good sense may induce the West Indians to be moderate and accommodating. As Lord John touches in his letter on the possibility of a Dissolution, the Queen thinks it right to put Lord John in possession of her views upon this subject *generally*. She considers the power of dissolving Parliament a most valuable and powerful instrument in the hands of the Crown, but which ought not to be used except in extreme cases and with a certainty of success. To use this instrument and be defeated is a thing most lowering to the Crown and hurtful to the country. The Queen strongly feels that she made a mistake in allowing the Dissolution in 1841; the result has been a majority returned against her of nearly one hundred votes; but suppose the result to have been nearly an equality of votes between the two contending parties, the Queen would have thrown away her last remedy, and it would have been impossible for her to get any Government which could have carried on public business with a chance of success.

The Queen was glad therefore to see that Sir Robert Peel did not ask for a Dissolution, and she *entirely concurs* in the opinion expressed by him in his last speech in the House of Commons, when he said:

"I feel strongly this, that no Administration is justified in advising the exercise of that prerogative, unless there be a fair, reasonable presumption, even a strong moral conviction, that after a Dissolution they will be enabled to administer the affairs of this country through the support of a party sufficiently powerful to carry their measures. I do not think a Dissolution justifiable to strengthen a party. I think the power of Dissolution is a great instrument in the hands of the Crown, and that there is a tendency to blunt that instrument if it be resorted to without necessity.

"The only ground for Dissolution would have been a strong presumption that after a Dissolution we should have had a party powerful enough in this House to give effect practically to the measures which we might propose. I do not mean a support founded on a concurrence on *one great question of domestic policy*, however important that may be, not of those who differ from us on almost all questions of public policy, agreeing with us in one; but that we should have the support of a powerful party united by a general concurrence of political opinions."

The Queen is confident that these views will be in accordance with Lord John Russell's own sentiments and opinions upon this subject.

Viscount Melbourne to Queen Victoria.

South Street, *21st July 1846.*

Lord Melbourne presents his humble duty to your Majesty. He has just received your Majesty's letter of yesterday, and is much delighted at again hearing from your Majesty.

What your Majesty says of the state of public affairs and of parties in Parliament is true. But in November last Sir Robert Peel had a party which might have enabled him to have long carried on the Government if he had not most unaccountably chosen himself to scatter it to the winds.

Lord Melbourne is much gratified by the intimation that your Majesty would not have been displeased or unwilling to see him again amongst your confidential servants, but your Majesty acted most kindly and most judiciously in not calling upon him in November last, and John Russell has done the same in forbearing to make to Lord Melbourne any offer at present. When Lord Melbourne was at Brocket Hall during the Whitsuntide holidays he clearly foresaw that Sir Robert Peel's Government must be very speedily dissolved; and upon considering the state of his own health and feelings, he came to the determination, which he communicated to Mr Ellice, who was with him, that he could take no active part in the then speedily approaching crisis. He felt himself quite unequal to the work, and also to that of either of the Secretaries of State, or even of the more subordinate and less heavy and responsible offices. He is very subject to have accesses of weakness, which render him incapable for exertion, and deprive his life of much of its enjoyment. They do not appear at present to hasten its termination, but how soon they may do so it is impossible to fore-tell or foresee.

Lord Melbourne hopes that he shall be able to wait upon your Majesty on Saturday next, but he fears the weight of the full dress uniform. He begs to be remembered to His Royal Highness.

Sir Robert Peel to the Prince Albert.

Drayton Manor, Fazeley, *August 1846.*

Sir,—I shall be very happy to avail myself of your Royal High-ness's kind permission occasionally to write to your Royal Highness. However much I am enjoying the contrast between repose and official life, I may say—I hope without presumption, I am sure with perfect sincerity—that the total interruption of every sort of communication with your Royal Highness would be a very severe penalty.

It was only yesterday that I was separating from the rest of my correspondence all the letters which I had received from the Queen and your Royal Highness during the long period of five years, in order that I might ensure their exemption from the fate to which in these days all letters seem to be destined, and I could not review them with-out a mixed feeling of gratitude for the considerate indulgence and kindness of which they contained such decisive proofs, and of regret that such a source of constantly recurring interest and pleasure was dried up.

I can act in conformity with your Royal Highness's gracious wishes, and occasionally write to you, without saying a word of which the most jealous or sensitive successor in the confidence of the Queen could complain.... Your faithful and humble Servant,

Robert Peel.

Queen Victoria to Lord John Russell.

Buckingham Palace, *3rd August 1846.*

The Queen has just seen Lord Bessborough, who presses very much for her going to Ireland; she thinks it right to put Lord John Rus-sell in possession of her views on this subject.

It is a journey which must one day or other be undertaken, and which the Queen would be glad to have accomplished, because it must be disagreeable to her that people should speculate whether she *dare* visit one part of her dominions. Much will depend on the proper moment, for, after those speculations, it ought to succeed if undertaken.

The Queen is anxious that when undertaken it should be a National thing, and the good which it is to do must be a permanent and not a transitory advantage to a particular Government, having the appearance of a party move.

As this is not a journey of pleasure like the Queen's former ones, but a State act, it will have to be done with a certain degree of State, and ought to be done handsomely. It cannot be expected that the main expense of it should fall upon the Civil List, nor would this be able to bear it.

The Prince Albert to Earl Grey.

Buckingham Palace, *3rd August 1846.*

My dear Lord Grey,—The Queen wishes me to return you the enclosed letter. The subject of the Government of Canada is one which the Queen has much at heart. Canada has been for a long time, and may probably *still* be for the future, a source of great weakness to this Empire, and a number of experiments have been tried. It was in a very bad state before the Union, continually embarrassing the Home Government, and the Union has by no means acted as a remedy, but it may be said almost to have increased the difficulties. The only thing that has hitherto proved beneficial was the prudent, consistent, and impartial administration of Lord Metcalfe. Upon the continuance and consistent application of the system which he has laid down and acted upon, will depend, in the Queen's estimation, the future welfare of that province, and the maintenance of proper relations with the mother country. The Queen therefore is most anxious that in the appointment of a new Governor-General (for which post she thinks Lord Elgin very well qualified), regard should be had to securing an uninterrupted development of Lord Metcalfe's views. The Queen thought it the more her duty to make you acquainted with her sentiments upon this subject, because she thinks that additional danger arises from the impressions which the different agents of the different political parties in Canada try to produce upon the Home Government and the imperial Parliament, and from their desire to mix up Canadian *party* politics with general English *party* politics.[21] Ever yours, etc.

Albert.

Lord John Russell to Queen Victoria.

Chesham Place, *4th August 1846.*

Lord John Russell presents his humble duty to your Majesty, and is greatly obliged to your Majesty for your Majesty's communication respecting a Royal visit to Ireland. He concurs in your Majesty's observations on that subject. He is of opinion that if the visit partook in any way of a party character, its effects would be mischievous, and not beneficial.

He is also doubtful of the propriety of either incurring very large expense on the part of the public, or of encouraging Irish proprietors to lay out money in show and ceremony at a time when the accounts of the potato crop exhibit the misery and distress of the people in an aggravated shape.

Queen Victoria to Lord John Russell.

7th August [.

With regard to the Statue[22] on the arch on Constitution Hill, the Queen is of opinion that if she is considered individually she is bound by her word, and must allow the Statue to go up, however bad the appearance of it will be. If the constitutional fiction is applied to the case, the Queen acts by the advice of her *responsible* advisers. One Government advised her to give her assent, another advises the withdrawal of that assent. This latter position has been taken in Lord Morpeth's former letter to the Committee, and in the debate in the House of Commons; it must therefore now be adhered to, and whatever is decided must be the act of the Government. It would accordingly be better to keep the word "Government" at the conclusion of Lord Morpeth's proposed letter, and that the Prince should not go to Town to give an opinion upon the appearance of the figure, when up.

The Prince Albert to Viscount Palmerston.

9th August 1846.

My dear Lord Palmerston,—The Queen is much obliged for Lord Howard de Walden's private letter to you, and begs you will never hesitate to send her such private communications, however unreserved they may be in their language, as our chief wish and aim is, by hearing all parties, to arrive at a just, dispassionate, and correct opinion upon the various political questions. This, however, entails a strict scrutiny of what is brought before us....

Queen Victoria to Lord John Russell.

Osborne, *17th August 1846.*

The Queen has received a draft to Mr Bulwer from Lord Palmerston. The perusal of it has raised some apprehensions in the Queen's mind, which she stated to Lord Palmerston she would communicate to Lord John Russell.

The draft lays down a general policy, which the Queen is afraid may ultimately turn out very dangerous. It is this:

England undertakes to interfere in the internal affairs of Spain, and to promote the development of the present constitutional Government of Spain in a more democratic direction, and this for the avowed purpose of counteracting the influence of France. England becomes therefore *responsible* for a particular direction given to the *internal* Government of Spain, which to control she has no sufficient means. All England can do, and will have to do, is: to keep up a particular party in Spain to support her views.

France, knowing that this is directed against her, must take up the opposite party and follow the opposite policy in Spanish affairs.

This must bring England and France to quarrels, of which we can hardly foresee the consequences, and it dooms Spain to eternal convulsions and reactions.

This has been the state of things before; theory and experience therefore warn against the renewal of a similar policy.

The natural consequence of this is that Don Enrique would appear as the desirable candidate for the Queen of Spain's hand, and Lord Palmerston accordingly for the first time deviates from the line hitherto followed by us, and *urges* Don Enrique, which in the eyes of the world must stamp him as "*an English Candidate.*" Lord Palmerston, from his wish to see him succeed, does, in the Queen's opinion, not sufficiently acknowledge the obstacles which stand in the way of this combination, and which all those who are on the spot and in the confidence of the Court represent as almost insurmountable.

The Queen desires Lord John Russell to weigh all this most maturely, and to let her know the result.

Lord John Russell to Queen Victoria.

Chesham Place, *19th August 1846.*

Lord John Russell presents his humble duty to your Majesty, and has the honour to state that he has maturely considered, together with Lord Palmerston, Lord Lansdowne, and Lord Clarendon, your Majesty's observations on the draft sent by Lord Palmerston for your Majesty's approbation.

Lord John Russell entirely concurs in your Majesty's wish that England and France should not appear at Madrid as countenancing conflicting parties. Lord John Russell did not attach this meaning to Lord Palmerston's proposed despatch, but he has now re-written the draft in such a manner as he trusts will obtain your Majesty's approval.

Lord John Russell will pay the utmost attention to this difficult and delicate subject.

Viscount Palmerston to Queen Victoria.

Foreign Office, *19th August 1846.*

Viscount Palmerston presents his humble duty to your Majesty, and has endeavoured to modify and rearrange his proposed instruction to Mr Bulwer in deference to your Majesty's wishes and feelings as expressed to Lord John Russell; and with this view also Viscount Palmerston has divided the instruction into two separate despatches— the one treating of the proposed marriage of the Queen, the other of the possible marriage of the Infanta. But with regard to these new drafts, as well as with regard to the former one, Viscount Palmerston would beg to submit that they are not notes to be presented to any Foreign Government, nor despatches to be in any way made public; but that they are confidential instructions given to one of your Majesty's Ministers abroad, upon matters upon which your Majesty's Government have been urgently pressed, to enable that Minister to give advice; and Viscount Palmerston would beg also to submit that in a case of this kind it would not be enough to communicate drily the opinion of the British Government, without stating and explaining some of the reasons upon which those opinions are founded.

It is quite evident from Mr Bulwer's communication, and especially from the postscript to his despatch of the 4th of this month, that Queen Christina, the Duke of Rianzares, and Señor Isturitz, are earnestly and intently bent upon marrying the Queen Isabella to Prince Leopold of Saxe-Coburg, and it is very difficult to find conclusive grounds for saying that such a match would not perhaps, on the whole, be the best for Queen Isabella and the Spanish nation. But still, all things considered, your Majesty's Government incline to the opinion that a Spanish Prince would be a preferable choice, and they are prepared to give that opinion to the Spanish Court.

There is however but one Spanish Prince whom it would be creditable to the British Government to recommend as husband to the Queen, and to that Prince Queen Christina is known to feel objections, principally founded upon apprehensions bearing upon her own personal interests. Viscount Palmerston has endeavoured to furnish Mr Bulwer with such arguments in favour of Don Enrique as appeared likely to meet Queen Christina's fears, and he has occasion to believe, from a conversation which he had a few days ago with Count Jarnac, that the French Government, impelled by the apprehension that your Majesty's Government intend to support Prince Leopold of Coburg, would be willing, in order to draw the British Government off from such a course, to give at least an ostensible though perhaps not a very earnest support to Don Henry. But your Majesty will no doubt at once perceive that although the British Government may come to an understanding with that of France as to which of the candidates shall be the one in whose favour an opinion is to be expressed, it would be impossible for the British Government to associate itself with that of France in any joint step to be taken upon this matter, and that each Government must act separately through its own agent at Madrid. For the two Governments have not only different objects in view in these matters, England wishing Spain to be independent, and France desiring to establish a predominant influence in Spain; but moreover, in regard to this marriage question, Great Britain has disclaimed any right to interfere except by opinion and advice, while France has assumed an authority of dictation, and it is essential that your Majesty's Government should so shape the mode of co-operating with France as not to appear to sanction pretensions which are founded in no right and are inconsistent with justice.

Viscount Palmerston is by no means confident that the joint advice of the British and French Governments in favour of Don Enrique will be successful, and especially because he fears that M. Bresson has taken so active a part in favour of other arrangements, that he will not be very eager in support of Don Enrique, and will perhaps think that if this arrangement can be rendered impossible the chances may become greater in favour of some other arrangement which he and his Government may prefer. But such future embarrassments must be dealt with when they arise, and Viscount Palmerston submits that for the moment, unless the British Government had been prepared to close with the offers of the Duke of Rianzares, and to follow at once the course recommended by Mr Bulwer, the steps suggested in the accompanying drafts are the safest and the best.

Viscount Palmerston has great pleasure in submitting the accompanying private letter from Mr Bulwer announcing the withdrawal of the Spanish troops from the frontier of Portugal.

Mr Bulwer to Viscount Palmerston.

Madrid, *29th August 1846.*

My Lord,—I have troubled your Lordship of late with many communications....

I have now to announce to your Lordship that the Queen declared last night at twelve o'clock that she had made up her mind in favour of His Royal Highness Don Francisco de Asis.... Your Lordship is aware under what circumstances Don Francisco was summoned here, the Court having been, when I wrote on the 4th, most anxious to conclude a marriage with Prince Leopold of Saxe-Coburg, and only induced to abandon this idea from the repeated intimations it received that it could not be carried out....

The same night a Council was held of the Queen Mother's friends, who determined to bring matters forthwith to a conclusion. Queen Christina, I understand, spoke to her daughter and told her she must choose one of two things, either marrying now, or deferring the marriage for three or four years. That the Prince of Saxe-Coburg was evidently impossible; that Count Trapani would be dangerous; that Don Henry had placed himself in a position which rendered the alliance with him out of the question, and that Her Majesty must either make up her mind to marry her cousin Don Francisco de Asis, or to abandon for some time the idea of marrying.

The Queen, I am told, took some little time to consider, and then decided in favour of her cousin. The Ministers were called in, and the drama was concluded....

H. L. Bulwer.

P.S.—I learn that directly the Queen had signified her intention of marrying her cousin, Count Bresson formally asked the hand of the Infanta for the Duke of Montpensier, stating that he had powers to enter upon and conclude that affair, and the terms of the marriage were then definitively settled between M. Isturitz and him.

H.L.B.

Queen Victoria to the King of the Belgians.

On Board the *Victoria and Albert*,
Falmouth Harbour, *7th September 1846.*

My dearest Uncle,—Though I have not heard from you for ages, you will perhaps be glad to hear from us, and to hear that our trip has been most successful. We left Osborne on the 2nd, at eight in the morning, and reached Jersey at seven that evening. We landed at St Heliers the next morning, and met with a most brilliant and enthusiastic reception from the good people. The island is beautiful, and like an orchard.

The settlement of the Queen of Spain's marriage, *coupled with Montpensier's,* is *infamous,* and we *must* remonstrate. Guizot has had the barefacedness to say to Lord Normanby that though *originally* they said that Montpensier should *only* marry the Infanta *when* the Queen *was married* and *had children,* that Leopold's being named one of the candidates had changed all, and that they must settle it now! This is *too* bad, for *we* were so honest as *almost to prevent* Leo's marriage (which *might* have been, and which Lord Palmerston, as matters now stand, regrets much did not take place), and the return is this unfair *coupling* of the *two* marriages which have nothing, and ought to have nothing, to do with one another. The King should know that *we* are extremely indignant, and that this conduct is *not* the way to keep up the *entente* which *he* wishes. It is done, moreover, in such a *dishonest* way. I must do Palmerston the credit to say that he takes it very quietly, and will act very temperately about it.

I must now conclude. Ever your devoted Niece,

Victoria R.

Vicky and Bertie enjoy their tour very much, and the people here are delighted to see "the Duke of Cornwall."

The Queen of the French to Queen Victoria.

Neuilly, *8 Septembre 1846.*

Madame,—Confiante dans cette précieuse amitié dont votre Majesté nous a donné tant de preuves et dans l'aimable intérêt que vous avez toujours témoigné à tous nos Enfants, je m'empresse de vous annoncer la conclusion du mariage de notre fils Montpensier avec l'Infante Louise Fernanda. Cet événement de famille nous comble de joie, parce que nous espérons qu'il assurera le bonheur de notre fils chéri, et que nous retrouverons dans l'Infante une fille de plus, aussi bonne et aussi aimable que ses Aînées, et qui ajoutera à notre bonheur intérieur, le seul vrai dans ce monde, et que vous, Madame, savez si bien apprécier. Je vous demande d'avance votre amitié pour notre nouvel Enfant, sûre qu'elle partagera tous les sentiments de dévouement et d'affection de nous tous pour vous, pour le Prince Albert, et pour toute votre chère Famille. Madame, de votre Majesté, la toute dévouée Sœur et Amie,

Marie Amélie.

Queen Victoria to the Queen of the French.

Osborne, *10 Septembre 1846.*

Madame,—Je viens de recevoir la lettre de votre Majesté du 8 de ce mois, et je m'empresse de vous en remercier. Vous vous souviendrez peut-être de ce qui s'est passé à Eu entre le Roi et moi, vous connaissez, Madame, l'importance que j'ai toujours attachée au maintien de Notre Entente Cordiale et le zèle avec lequel j'y ai travaillé, vous avez appris sans doute que nous nous sommes refusés d'arranger le mariage entre la Reine d'Espagne et notre Cousin Léopold (que les deux Reines avaient vivement désiré) dans le seul but de ne pas nous éloigner d'une marche qui serait plus agréable à votre Roi, quoique nous ne pouvions considérer cette marche comme la meilleure. Vous pourrez donc aisément comprendre que l'annonce soudaine de ce *double mariage* ne pouvait nous causer que de la surprise et un bien vif regret.

Je vous demande bien pardon de vous parler de politique dans ce moment, mais j'aime pouvoir me dire que j'ai toujours été *sincère* envers vous.

En vous priant de présenter mes hommages au Roi, je suis, Madame, de votre Majesté, la toute dévouée Sœur et Amie,

Victoria R.

Viscount Palmerston to Queen Victoria.

Carlton Terrace, *12th September 1846.*

Viscount Palmerston presents his humble duty to your Majesty, and returns with many acknowledgments the accompanying letters which your Majesty has been pleased to send him, and which he has thought your Majesty would wish him also to communicate to Lord John Russell.

The letter of the Queen of the French seems to Viscount Palmerston to look like a contrivance to draw your Majesty on to express, in regard to the Montpensier marriage in its character as a domestic arrangement, some sentiments or wishes which might be at variance with the opinions which your Majesty might entertain regarding that marriage in its political character and bearing. But your Majesty's most judicious answer has defeated that intention, if any such existed, and has stated in a firm, but at the same time in the friendliest manner, the grounds of complaint against the conduct of the French Government in this affair.

Viscount Palmerston had yesterday afternoon a very long conversation with the Count de Jarnac upon these matters.

Viscount Palmerston said that with regard to the marriage of the Queen of Spain, that was a matter as to which the British Government have no political objection to make. They deeply regret that a young Queen should have been compelled by moral force, and to serve the personal and political interests of other persons, to accept for husband a person whom she can neither like nor respect, and with whom her future life will certainly be unhappy at home, even if it should not be characterised by circumstances which would tend to lower her in the estimation of her people. But these are matters which concern the Queen and people of Spain more than the Government and people of England. But that the projected marriage of the Duke of Montpensier is a very different matter, and must have a political bearing that must exercise a most unfortunate effect upon the relations between England and France.

Queen Victoria to the King of the Belgians.

Osborne, *14th September 1846.*

My dearest Uncle,—I have to thank you for a most kind letter of the 31st from Basle, by which I was sorry to see that your journey had been delayed, and that you were still not well.

We are, alas! sadly engrossed with this Spanish marriage, which, though it does not threaten *war* (for the English care very little about the Spanish marriages) threatens complications. Albert has told you all that passed between the dear Queen and me, and the very absurd ground on which the French make their stand. The details of the story are very bad—and I grieve to say that the good King, etc., have behaved *very dishonestly.*

We have protested, and mean to protest very strongly, against Montpensier's marriage with the Infanta, *as long as she is presumptive heiress to the Throne of Spain.* The King departs from his principle, for *he insisted* on a *Bourbon, because* he declared he would *not* marry one of his sons to the Queen; and now he effects the Queen's marriage with the worst Bourbon she could have, and marries his son to the Infanta, who in all probability will become Queen! It is very bad. Certainly at Madrid [Palmerston] mismanaged it—as Stockmar says— by forcing Don Enrique, in spite of all Bulwer could say. If our dear Aberdeen was still at his post, the whole thing would not have happened; for he would *not* have forced Enriquito (which enraged Christine), and secondly, Guizot would not have *escamoté* Aberdeen with the wish of triumphing over him as he has done over Palmerston, who has behaved most openly and fairly towards France, I must say, in this affair. But say what one will, it is *he again* who *indirectly* gets us into a squabble with France! And it is such a personal sort of a quarrel, which pains and grieves me so; and I pity the poor good Piat,[23] whom we are very fond of. One thing, however, I feel, that in opposing this marriage, we are not really affecting his happiness, for he has never seen the Infanta—and she is a child of fourteen, and not pretty. The little Queen I pity so much, for the poor child dislikes her cousin, and she is said to have consented *against her will.* We shall see if she really does marry him. Altogether, it is most annoying, and must ruffle our happy intercourse with the French family for a time at least.

I was obliged to write very strongly and openly to poor dear Louise too. You may rely upon nothing being done rashly or intemperately on our part. Lord Palmerston is quite ready to be guided by us. In haste, ever your devoted Niece,

Victoria R.

We go into our new house to-day.

H.M. MARIE AMÉLIE, QUEEN OF THE FRENCH, 1828.

From the miniature by Millet at Windsor Castle

Baron Stockmar to Queen Victoria.

18th September 1846.

Baron Stockmar has been honoured with your Majesty's kind note of the 17th instant. The very day the Baron heard of the Spanish news, he wrote to a man at Paris, whom the King sees as often as he presents himself at the palace. In this letter the Baron stated *fairly and moderately but without palliation* in what light M. Bresson's conduct must necessarily appear *in London*, and what very naturally and most probably *must be the political consequences of such conduct.*

The Baron's statement was read to the King, word for word, the very evening it reached Paris.

His Majesty listened to it most attentively, and said after some pause: "Notwithstanding all this, the marriage will take place. I don't consider Montpensier's marriage an affair between nations, and the English people, in particular, care very little about it; it is much more a private affair between myself and the English Secretary, Lord Palmerston, *and as such* it will not bring on important political consequences."

Queen Victoria to the Queen of the Belgians.

Osborne, *18 Septembre 1846.*

Ma bien chère Louise,—Je te remercie pour ton retour de franchise; je ne désire pas que cette controverse entre de plus dans notre correspondance privée, comme elle est le sujet et le sera je crains encore davantage de discussion politique. Je veux seulement dire qu'il est *impossible* de donner à cette affaire le cachet d'une simple affaire de famille; l'attitude prise à Paris sur cette affaire de mariage dès le commencement était une fort étrange; il fallait toute la discrétion de Lord Aberdeen pour qu'elle n'amenât un éclat plutôt; mais ce dénouement, si contraire à la parole du Roi, qu'il m'a donnée lors de cette dernière visite à Eu *spontanément*, en ajoutant à la complication, pour la *première fois*, celle du projet de mariage de Montpensier, aura mauvaise mine devant toute l'Europe.

Rien de plus pénible n'aurait pu arriver que toute cette dispute qui prend un caractère si personnel....

Victoria R.

Queen Victoria to the King of the Belgians.

Osborne, *21st September 1846.*

My Dearest Uncle,—I have to thank you very much for your very kind letter of the 5th from Zurich. It is very unfortunate that you should be so far off at this moment. Since I wrote to you we have decided to remonstrate both at Madrid (this went a week ago), and at Paris, but this last not in a formal note but in a despatch to Lord Normanby, against this very unjustifiable breach of faith on the part of France. We have seen these despatches, which are very firm, but written in a very proper and kind tone, exposing at the same time the fallacy of what has been done; for the King himself declared that he would *never* let *one of his sons marry* the Queen, he *insisted* on her marrying a descendant of Philip V. This has been done, and at the same moment he says his *son* is to marry the *Infanta*, who may *become Queen to-morrow!* And to all this he says, "C'est seulement une affaire de famille"! The King is very fond of England, and still more of peace, and he never *can* sacrifice this (for though it would not be immediate war it would cause coolness with us and with other Powers, and would probably lead to war in a short time), for a breach of faith and *for one of his sons'* marriages. No quarrel or misunderstanding in the world *could be more disagreeable* and to me *more cruelly painful*, for it is *so personal*, and has come into the midst of all our communications and correspondence, and is too annoying. It is so sad, too, for dear Louise, to whom one cannot say that her father has behaved dishonestly. I hope, however, another ten days will show us some *daylight*. I will not mention anything about Leopold's[24] answer, as Albert will, I doubt not, write to you all about it. It is very satisfactory, however.

We are since this day week in our charming new house, which is delightful, and to-morrow we go, alas! to Windsor, where we expect the Queen-Dowager and the Princess of Prussia, who will remain a week with us. Ever your devoted Niece,

Victoria R.

I received this afternoon your kind letter from Gais of the 12th. One word more I must just add. No doubt if Lord Aberdeen had been at his post what has happened would *not* have taken place, and suspicion of Lord Palmerston *has* been the cause of the *unjustifiable* conduct of the French Government. But just as they *did* suspect him, they should have been more cautious to do anything which could bring on a quarrel, which is surely not what the King can wish.

Queen Victoria to the King of the Belgians.

Windsor Castle, *29th September 1846.*

My dearest Uncle,—I received last week your very kind and *satisfactory* letter of the 16th. Your opinion on this truly unfortunate and, on the part of the French, disgraceful affair is a great support to us. Stockmar has, I know, communicated to you what has passed, and he will send you copies of the King's letter and my answer. Our conduct has been throughout *honest*, and the King's and Guizot's the contrary. *How* the King *can* wantonly throw away the friendship of one who has stood by him with such sincere affection, for a *doubtful* object of personal and family aggrandizement, is to me and to the whole country inexplicable. Have *confidence* in *him* I fear I never can again, and Peel, who is here on a visit, says a *war may* arise any moment, *once* that the good understanding is disturbed; think, then, that the King has done this in his 74th year, and leaves this inheritance to his successor; and to whom—to a *Grandchild*, and a *Minor!* And for Nemours and Paris, *our* friendship is of the greatest importance, and yet he prefers the troubles of governing Spain, which will be a source of constant worry and anxiety, to the happy understanding so happily existing between our two countries! I cannot comprehend him. Guizot behaves shamefully, and so totally without good faith. Our protests have been presented. I feel more than ever the loss of our valuable Peel.

I wish, dearest Uncle, you would not go to Paris at all at present.

The Queen-Dowager and the Princess of Prussia[25] have left us this morning after a week's stay, and I have been delighted with the Princess. I find her so clever, so amiable, so well informed, and so good; she seems to have some enemies, for there are whispers of her being *false*; but from all that I have seen of her—from her discretion, her friendship through thick and thin, and to her own detriment, for Hélène, and for the Queen-Dowager who has known her from her birth, I *cannot* and will not believe it. Her position is a very difficult one; she is too enlightened and liberal for the Prussian Court not to have enemies; but *I believe* that she is a friend to us and our family, and I do believe that *I* have a friend in her, who may be most useful to us. I must conclude, envying your being in Tyrol. Ever your devoted Niece,

Victoria R.

Queen Victoria to Viscount Palmerston.

Windsor Castle, *1st October 1846.*

The Queen wishes to express her approval of the step taken by Lord Palmerston in urging the Three Northern Powers to join in the protest against the Montpensier marriage on the ground of the Treaty of Utrecht and the Declaration of Philip V. She thinks, however, that it is necessary to do more, and wishes Lord Palmerston should send a note to the Cabinets of the three Powers, explanatory of the whole of the proceedings relative to the Spanish marriages, showing the attitude taken by us from the first, and disclosing the facts which led to this unfortunate termination. The three Powers ought to be enabled to see the whole of the transaction if we wish them to sympathise with us.

Lord John Russell to Queen Victoria.

1st October 1846.

Lord John Russell saw Count Jarnac to-day, and told him that your Majesty's displeasure had not been removed. He had in his hands a memorandum, which is apparently word for word the letter of the King of the French to the Queen of the Belgians.[26]

Lord John Russell observed that it was admitted that the Duke of Montpensier was not to marry the Infanta till the Queen of Spain had children, and that voluntary engagement had been departed from. We might expect the same departure from the professions now made not to interfere in the affairs of Spain.

Count Jarnac protested against this inference, and repeated that the promise with regard to the Infanta was only conditional.

Lord John Russell expects that in consequence of the remonstrances of England, and the attention of Europe to the question, France will be cautious in her interference with the internal government of Spain, and may probably not be able to direct her external policy.

M. Bresson has written a long letter to Lord Minto, defending his own conduct.

Queen Victoria to the King of the Belgians.

Windsor Castle, *6th October 1846.*

My dearest Uncle,—I thank you very much for your last kind letter from Gais of the 23rd. This unfortunate Spanish affair has gone on, heedlessly—and our *entente wantonly* thrown away! I mourn over it, and feel deeply the ingratitude shown; for—without boasting—I must say they never had a *truer* friend than we; and one who *always* stood by them. When Hadjy wrote that foolish *brochure*, who stood by him through thick and thin, but we? and our friendship for the children will ever continue, but how can we *ever* feel at our ease with L. P. again? Guizot's conduct is beyond *all* belief shameful, and so *shabbily* dishonest. Molé and Thiers both say he cannot stand. It is the King's birthday to-day, but I thought it better *not* to write to him, for to say *fine words* at *this* moment would be mockery. For my beloved Louise my heart bleeds; it is *so* sad....

I must now conclude. Begging you to believe me, ever your devoted Niece,

Victoria R.

Queen Victoria to the King of the Belgians.

Windsor Castle, *17th November 1846.*

My Dearest Uncle,—I yesterday received your long and interesting letter of the 14th. I would much rather not say anything more about this truly unfortunate and painful Spanish business; but in justice to myself I must make a few observations. You say that the King thinks me *resentful*; this is extraordinary, for I have no such feeling; my feelings were and are *deeply* wounded at the unhandsome and secret manner (so totally, in *letter* and in *meaning*, contrary to an *entente cordiale*) in which this affair was settled, and in which the two marriages were incorporated.

What can I do?

The King and French Government never *expressed regret* at the sudden and *unhandsome* manner, to say the *least*, in which they behaved to their *best ally* and *friend*, and *we* really *cannot admit* that *they have to forgive us for duping us!* Why have they not tried to make *some* sort of apology? What do I do, but remain silent *for the present*?

It is a sad affair, but *resentment* I have none whatever, and this accusation is a new version of the affair.

With respect to Portugal, I refute most positively the unfounded accusations against us; we *cannot* interfere in internal dissensions beyond ensuring the personal safety of the King, Queen, and Royal Family. The Constitution may be, and I believe is, an unfortunate thing in those Southern countries; but once it is established, the Queen must abide by it; but, unfortunately, the *coup de main* in sending away Palmella's Government (which would inevitably have crumbled to pieces of itself), was both unconstitutional and unsafe, and I fear they are in a much worse position *vis-à-vis* of the country than they ever were.[27]

We are all going to-morrow to Osborne for four weeks. Ever your truly devoted Niece,

Victoria R.

Lord John Russell to Queen Victoria.

Downing Street, *19th November 1846.*

... Lord John Russell breakfasted with Dr Hawtrey yesterday, and had much conversation with him. He finds Dr Hawtrey strongly impressed with the evils of Montem, and he declared himself as decidedly against its continuance. He thinks your Majesty would please the Etonians equally by going to the boats once a year, which he said the late King was in the habit of doing. The Chancellor of the Exchequer,[28] who was at Eton, wishes to see Montem abolished. Lord Morpeth would prefer seeing it regulated. Upon the whole, Lord John Russell thinks it would not be advisable for your Majesty to interpose your authority against the decided opinion of Dr Hawtrey, the Provost, and the assistants.[29]

Queen Victoria to the Duke of Wellington.

Osborne, *25th November 1846.*

The Queen has learned from various quarters that there still exists a great anxiety amongst the officers and men who served under the Duke of Wellington's orders in the Peninsula to receive and wear a medal as a testimony that they assisted the Duke in his great undertaking. The Queen not only thinks this wish very reasonable, considering that for recent exploits of infinitely inferior importance such distinctions have been granted by her, but she would feel personally a great satisfaction in being enabled publicly to mark in this way her sense of the great services the Duke of Wellington has rendered to his country and to empower many a brave soldier to wear this token in remembrance of the Duke.

The Duke of Wellington to Queen Victoria.

Strathfieldsaye, *27th November 1846.*

Field-Marshal the Duke of Wellington presents his humble duty to your Majesty.

He has just now received your Majesty's most gracious commands from Osborne, dated the 26th instant.

He does not doubt that many of the brave officers and soldiers who served in the armies in the Peninsula under the command of the Duke are anxious to receive and wear a medal, struck by command of the Sovereign, to commemorate the services performed in that seat of the late war.

Many of them have, upon more than one occasion, expressed such desire, in their letters addressed to the Duke, in their petitions to Parliament, and, as the Duke has reason to believe, in petitions presented to your Majesty.

Although the Duke has never omitted to avail himself of every occasion which offered to express his deep sense of the meritorious services of the officers and soldiers of the Army which served in the Peninsula, he did not consider it his duty to suggest to the Sovereign, under whose auspices, or the Minister under whose direction the services in question were performed, any particular mode in which those services of the Army should be recognised by the State.

Neither has he considered it his duty to submit such suggestion since the period at which the services were performed, bearing in mind the various important considerations which must have an influence upon the decision on such a question, which it was and is the duty of your Majesty's confidential servants alone to take into consideration, and to decide.

Neither can the Duke of Wellington now venture to submit to your Majesty his sense of a comparison of the services of the Army which served in the Peninsula, with those of other armies in other parts of the world, whose recent services your Majesty has been most graciously pleased to recognise by ordering that medals should be struck, to commemorate each of such services, one of which to be delivered to each officer and soldier present, which your Majesty was graciously pleased to permit him to wear.

Field-Marshal the Duke of Wellington humbly solicits your Majesty, in grateful submission to your Majesty upon the subject of the last paragraph of your Majesty's most gracious letter, that, considering the favour with which his services were received and rewarded by the gracious Sovereign, under whose auspices they were performed; the professional rank and the dignity in the State to which he was raised, and the favour with which his services were then and have been ever since received, that your Majesty would be graciously pleased to consider upon this occasion only the well-founded claims upon your Majesty's attention of the officers and soldiers who served in the Army in the Peninsula; and to consider him, as he considers himself, amply rewarded for any service which he might have been instrumental in rendering; and desirous only of opportunities of manifesting his gratitude for the favour and honour with which he has been treated by his Sovereign.

All of which is humbly submitted to your Majesty by your Majesty's most dutiful and devoted Servant and Subject,

Wellington.

Queen Victoria to Viscount Palmerston.

Osborne, *28th November 1846.*

The Queen has just received Lord Palmerston's draft to Mr Southern,[30] and must observe that she does not quite approve the tone of it, as it will be likely only to irritate without producing any effect. If our advice is to be taken, it must be given in a spirit of impartiality and fairness. Lord Palmerston's despatch must give the impression that we entirely espouse the cause of the rebels, whose conduct is, to say the least, illegal and very reprehensible. Lord Palmerston likewise takes the nation and the Opposition to be one and the same thing. What we must insist upon is a return to Constitutional Government. And what we may advise is a compromise with the Opposition. What Ministry is to be formed ought to be left to the Portuguese themselves. It being the 28th to-day, the Queen is afraid the despatch went already yesterday. The Queen hopes in future that Lord Palmerston will not put it out of her power to state her opinion in good time.

Queen Victoria to the Duke of Wellington.

Arundel Castle, *1st December 1846.*

The Queen has not yet acknowledged the Duke of Wellington's last letter.

She fully appreciates the delicacy of the Duke in not wishing to propose himself a step having reference to his own achievements, but the Queen will not on that account forgo the satisfaction of granting this medal as an acknowledgment on her part of those brilliant achievements.

The Queen has been assured by Lord John Russell that her confidential servants will be ready to assume the responsibility of advising such a measure.

The Duke of Wellington to Queen Victoria.

Arundel castle, *2nd December 1846.* (*Morning.*)

Field-Marshal the Duke of Wellington presents his humble duty to your Majesty. He did not receive your Majesty's commands, dated

113

the 1st instant, in this Castle, till seven o'clock in the afternoon; and being under the necessity of attending at [? Dover] in the evening, he has not had it in his power till this time to express his acknowledgment of the receipt of them.

He submits to your Majesty that he has always been aware that it would be impolitic to confer upon the officers and soldiers who served in the Peninsula the wished-for distinction without the concurrence of your Majesty's confidential servants.

They alone can give the orders to carry into execution the measure, and can adopt means to remedy any inconvenience which may result from it; and it is satisfactory to him to learn, from the perusal of your Majesty's note, that Lord John Russell is disposed to adopt it, notwithstanding that the Duke has no personal wish or feeling in the adoption of the measure, excepting to see gratified the wishes of so many gallant officers and brave soldiers, who have so well served.

The few words which he addressed to your Majesty in his last letter of the 27th of November in relation to himself, referred to the expressions in that of your Majesty of the 26th November, to the Duke; from which it appeared to be your Majesty's intention "to empower many a brave soldier to wear this token, in remembrance of the Duke."

Having stated to your Majesty that he would serve your Majesty, and would promote the objects of your Majesty's Government, to the utmost of his power, he has faithfully performed his engagement, as he believes, to the satisfaction of your Majesty's servants.

His whole life being devoted to your Majesty's service, he is most anxious to deserve and receive your Majesty's approbation.

But he wishes that it should be conveyed only when it may be convenient to your Majesty's Government. Your Majesty and your Majesty's servants must be the best judges upon this point, as well as whether the medal in question shall be struck and granted at all or not.

If granted, or whatever may be the mode in which granted, or whether the Duke's name is recalled to recollection or not, the Duke will be equally satisfied, and grateful for your Majesty's gracious favour, and desirous to merit a continuance of it, by his devotion to your Majesty's service.

All of which is humbly submitted by your Majesty's most dutiful Subject and most devoted Servant,

Wellington.

Queen Victoria to Lord John Russell.

Osborne, *14th December 1846.*

The Queen has still to acknowledge Lord John Russell's letter of the 11th. She has carefully read the Duke of Wellington's letter to Lord John, which evinces all the Duke's honourable feelings. He should certainly be relieved from the appearance of having refused honours to others, but agreed to the granting of them the moment it was intended to couple the measure with an honour conferred upon himself. On the other hand, the Queen still wishes the step to be taken as a means of doing honour to the Duke. His name should, therefore, certainly be connected with it. The introduction of the names of other commanders, even of that of Sir John Moore, the Queen does not think advisable. She does not quite understand from Lord John's letter whether he proposes to adopt the Duke's recommendation to *re*-issue all the medals formerly granted, or to adhere to the original idea of striking a new one. In the latter case, which appears the most natural, the word "Peninsula" would cover all the campaigns, and in these the Duke of Wellington had by far so much the greatest share that his name being introduced on *all* the medals cannot be considered as anomalous.

Queen Victoria to Viscount Palmerston.

Osborne, *14th December 1846.*

The Queen returns the enclosed private letters.[31] The view Lord Palmerston takes of the affair of Cracow appears to the Queen a very sound one, and she would much wish to see the plan of a conference realised against which Lord Ponsonby does not bring any very relevant reasons. Prince Metternich's plan of a declaration "that the case is to be considered an exceptional one and not to afford a precedent to other powers" is too absurd. The Prince very justly compared it to the case of a person giving another a box on the ear and declaring at the same time that he is to consider it as exceptional, and that it is in no way to afford him a precedent for returning it. The Queen hopes the Cabinet will well consider the question, and contrive to find means to prevent the evil consequences of the unjustifiable step against Cracow by speaking out in time, before Russia or France may have decided on acts of further infraction of the Treaty of Vienna. It seems quite clear that Russia was at the bottom of the measure relative to Cracow, and it is therefore but reasonable to expect that she has an ulterior object in view.

ENDNOTES:

[1]:The Queen had opened Parliament in person; the Prime Minister took the unusual course of speaking immediately after the seconder of the Address, and in his peroration, after laying stress on the responsibilities he was incurring, proceeded: "I do not desire to be Minister of England; but while I am Minister of England I will hold office by no servile tenure; I will hold office unshackled by any other obligation than that of consulting the public interests and providing for the public safety."

[2]:He explained that the attitude of Lord Grey made the difficulties attending the formation of a Whig Ministry insuperable.

[3]:The Sikhs were defeated at Sobraon on 10th February by the British troops under Sir Hugh Gough, reinforced by Sir Harry Smith, fresh from his victory at Aliwal. *See* p. 73.

[4]:At Moodkee on 18th December, and Ferozeshah on 21st and 22nd December.

[5]:Who had commanded a brigade under Pollock in the second Afghan campaign.

[6]:Major George Broadfoot, C.B., Political Agent on the north-western frontier.

[7]:In September 1882 Mr Gladstone quoted this as a precedent for firing the Park Guns after the victory of Tel-el-Kebir. See *Life of Right Hon. Hugh C. E. Childers*, by Colonel Childers, C.B., R.E., vol. ii p. 127.

[8]:In consequence of a serious increase of crime in Ireland, a Coercion Bill had been introduced.

[9]:This refers to the Catholic Emancipation discussions of 1827, when Bentinck and Disraeli accused Peel of having hounded Canning to death.

[10]:By a remarkable coincidence the Corn Bill passed through the Lords on the same night that the Ministry were defeated in the Commons.

[11]:He expressed his hope to be remembered with goodwill "in the abodes of those whose lot it is to labour, and to earn their daily bread by the sweat of their brows, when they shall recruit their exhausted strength with abundant and untaxed food, the sweeter because no longer leavened with a sense of injustice."

[12]:The Convention for adjusting the dispute as to the Oregon boundary had been accepted by the United States Government.

[13]:Dr S. Wilberforce.

[14]:"Sir, the name which ought to be, and which will be, associated with the success of these measures, is the name of a man who, acting, I believe, from pure and disinterested motives, has advocated their cause with untiring energy, and by appeals to reason, enforced by an eloquence the more to be admired because it was unaffected and unadorned—the name which ought to be and which will be associated with the success of these measures is the name of Richard Cobden."

[15]:On the 23rd of March, in the course of a long speech on the state of Ireland, Earl Grey had contrasted the poverty of the Roman Catholic Church in that country with the affluence of the Establishment, diverted, as he said, by the superior power of England from its original objects; adding that the Protestant Church was regarded by the great mass of the Irish people as an active cause of oppression and misery.

[16]:In spite of the opposition of the latter to Palmerston's re-appointment to the Foreign Office. See *ante*, p. 58.

[17]:The pension was, however, granted.

[18]:On the 18th of July Lord Palmerston wrote his celebrated despatch to Mr Bulwer, and unfortunately showed a copy of it to Jarnac, the French Ambassador in London. The mention of Prince Leopold in it, as a possible candidate for the Queen of Spain's hand, gave the French King and Minister the opportunity they wanted, and brought matters to a crisis. See *Life of the Prince Consort*, vol. i. chap. xvii.; Dalling's *Life of Lord Palmerston*, vol. iii. chaps. vii. and viii.

[19]:Owing to the insurrection, a run took place on the Bank of Lisbon. The Ministry (in which Saldanha was War Minister) had some difficulty in raising a loan.

[20]:In pursuance of the policy of free trade, the Ministry introduced and passed a Bill reducing the duties on foreign slave-grown sugar, with the ultimate intention of equalising them with those on Colonial produce.

[21]:In the event, Lord Elgin was appointed.

[22]:The equestrian statue of the Duke of Wellington at Hyde Park Corner was much criticised at the time of its erection: it is now at Aldershot.

[23]:A name by which the Duc de Montpensier was sometimes called in the family circle.

[24]:Prince Leopold of Saxe-Coburg.

[25]:Marie Louise Augusta, daughter of the Grand Duke Charles of Saxe-Weimar, subsequently Empress of Germany, mother of Prince Frederick William, afterwards the Emperor Frederick, who in 1858 married the Princess Royal.

[26]:See Louis Philippe's long letter of the 14th of September, printed in the *Life of the Prince Consort*, vol. i. Appendix B. Queen Victoria's complete and unanswerable reply will be found there also.

[27]:The Duke de Palmella's Ministry was abruptly dismissed by the Queen of Portugal on the 10th of October, in consequence of their inability to raise money on loan. Civil war broke out, Das Antas, Loulé, Fornos, and Sà da Bandeira being the chief rebel leaders. The British Fleet was ordered to the Tagus to support the Queen against her subjects, with the ulterior object of restoring Constitutional Government.

[28]:Mr (who a few weeks later became Sir) Charles Wood.

[29]:Montem, the triennial Eton ceremony, the chief part of which took place at Salt Hill (*ad montem*), near Slough, was abolished in 1847.

[30]:Secretary of Legation at Lisbon, and Chargé d'Affaires in the absence of Lord Howard de Walden.

[31]:The first ill fruits of the disruption of the *entente* between England and France were seen in the active co-operation of Russia, Prussia, and Austria to destroy Polish independence. See *ante*, p. 74.

INTRODUCTORY NOTE
TO CHAPTER XVI

During the year 1847 the Parliament which had been elected in 1841 with a great Tory majority was dissolved, and, as a result, the position of the Whig Ministry was slightly improved; but they were still dependent on the support of Sir Robert Peel. A Factory Act limiting the labour of women and children to ten hours a day was passed. An autumn session was rendered necessary by an acute financial crisis, the Ministry having authorised the Bank of England to infringe the provisions of the recent Bank Charter Act, and as a consequence being compelled to ask Parliament for an indemnity. The knowledge of the Bank's authority to issue notes beyond the prescribed limits was of itself sufficient to allay the panic. The Church of England was convulsed by the promotion of Dr Hampden, whom Lord Melbourne had made Regius Professor of Divinity at Oxford, to the See of Hereford; his orthodoxy was impugned in a memorial presented by thirteen bishops to the Prime Minister, and an unsuccessful application was made to the Queen's Bench (the Court being divided in opinion) to compel the Primate to hear objections to Dr Hampden's consecration. The new House of Lords was used for the first time this year.

Perhaps the most important event in France was the cold-blooded murder of the Duchesse de Praslin (daughter of Count Sebastiani, formerly French Ambassador in England) by her husband, an incident which, like the Spanish intrigue of 1846, contributed subsequently to the downfall of the Orleanist dynasty.

Switzerland was torn by internecine strife, partly owing to the existence, side by side, of Catholic and Protestant cantons; the proposed expulsion of Jesuits and the formation of the "Sonderbund" were the questions of the day. The latter was an offensive and defensive confederation of seven cantons, and civil war raged round the question of its legality.

In Italy the death of Pope Gregory XVI. and the election of a more liberal successor induced Lord John Russell to send his father-in-law, Lord Minto, the Lord Privy Seal, on a special mission to the new Pope Pius IX., to encourage him in the path of Reform. But more violent measures were in progress, and it was soon clear that Lombardy and Venetia were rising against Austria, and the way being paved for the Unity of Italy.

Spain was in a ferment, frequent changes of Ministry taking place, and the miserable marriage of the Queen having all the evil results anticipated in England. Portugal continued in a state of civil war, the British attempting to mediate, but the revolutionary Junta refused to abide by their terms, and ultimately armed intervention became necessary.

CHAPTER XVI

1847

Queen Victoria to Lord John Russell.

Windsor Castle, *7th January 1847.*

The turn which the Portuguese affairs are now likely to take is really very satisfactory. The Queen is sure that the Court will not allow violent measures of revenge to be taken against the vanquished party nor the overthrow of a Constitutional Government; but the Queen of Portugal will have to punish those who have broken their oath of allegiance, and will have to remove from the country those who would infallibly ere long plunge the country afresh into those *horrors* from which it is just emerging. The further infusion of democracy into the Charter would at this moment be quite misplaced, but this opportunity should be taken by the Queen of Portugal to *establish* a *state* of *legality* and *security*, by compelling any new Ministry to lay the accounts every year before the Cortes (which has not been done for the last ten years, either by Progressistas, Septembristas, or others), by establishing irremovable judges, and appointing thereto incorruptible persons, by *honestly and fairly* distributing the patronage in the Army—apart from the party—which will now be possible as the King has the command himself, and by adopting such measures of *internal* improvement as will promote the *material* welfare of the people.

These are the principles which the Queen would wish to see *her* representative urge upon the Portuguese Court and Government, and she has no doubt that they are in perfect conformity with Lord John Russell's own views. The Queen cannot help repeating that the tone and bearing of Mr Southern are more those of a Portuguese Demagogue than of an English Representative.

The King of the Belgians to Queen Victoria.

Tuileries, *15th January 1847.*

My Dearest Victoria,—I am truly happy to learn what you say about your feelings on those troublesome politics; I can assure you that many people who are, in fact, quite indifferent to politics, *renchérissent* in expressions of dislike and contempt *seulement*, because they believe that you have those opinions. Many wise people repeat sayings which they assume to come from your own mouth, such, for instance, "that Louis Philippe could never be trusted, being, after all, an old fox," etc.

The King's Speech was as unobjectionable as possible. I trust that there will be no *bitterness* in yours. It is as much, if not more, in the interest of Great Britain to keep France quiet and continuing a peaceable policy than in that of France. France, as the old Duke once said with great truth, has been already *under water several times, what could be spoiled has been spoiled*, what remains *is pretty solid*. To attack France in France would lead to the most dangerous consequences. In general, if we get once a great war again you will be sure to have everywhere revolutions, and to imagine that you will escape in England all reactions would be a grievous mistake. When one looks to the changes, brought about in England in consequence of the Revolution of July, one is quite astounded. Here they changed nothing but the dynasty, in England *the very spirit of the old Monarchy has been abolished*, and what will be, in the course of time, the consequences, it is not easy to tell. A bad Constitution acts strongly on the people. Look to America, even to Belgium. Ever, my dearest Victoria, your devoted Uncle,

Leopold R.

Queen Victoria to Lord John Russell.

Buckingham Palace, *14th February 1847.*

Lord John Russell's memorandum contains two different questions. The one is this: how far the interests of England require an interference in the affairs of Portugal for the restoration of peace in that country and the preservation of its Throne, and how far England is bound by existing treaties to interfere.

As to this question, it appears from Lord John's memorandum that the ancient treaties having reference to *foreign* invasion only are inapplicable to the present case, that the Quadruple Treaty would revive on the appearance of Dom Miguel in Portugal, that an understanding with Spain ought to be come to for its execution, but Lord John does not make any specific proposal.

The other question is, what wrongs the Queen, the Ministers, and the rebels may have done to bring about the present state of affairs. This the Queen conceives can only be decided by a *most minute, impartial, and anxious scrutiny.* She indignantly rejects the notion to leave this decision to Mr Southern.... Lord John's statement contains, however, nothing but the echo of his reports.

Lord John will upon reflection admit that to say "that recent events exhibit a spirit of tyranny and cruelty in the Portuguese Government *without a parallel* in any part of Europe," there, where not *one* execution has taken place, is rather a strong expression.

That the cruelties and miseries inseparable from a Civil War are to be deplored, there can be no doubt of, and it is in order to stop a further continuance and perhaps aggravation of these horrors, that the Queen is so anxious to see the struggle brought to an early termination.

The Queen hopes to see Lord John to-morrow at three o'clock, when she hopes that he will be able to submit a definitive step.

Queen Victoria to Lord John Russell.

14th March 1847.

The Queen wishes again to call Lord John Russell's serious attention to the state of Spain and Portugal, and to the policy which has been pursued with regard to them, and the result of this policy. In Spain we have taken up the cause of the Progressistas, and what has been the consequence? They desert us.

We have no longer the slightest influence in that country; France has it all her own way, and we shall see the Cortes confirm the succession of the Infanta and her children without being able to prevent it. Of the Progressistas, on whom Lord Palmerston, Lord Clarendon, and others always placed their hopes, Mr Bulwer says *now*: "The fact is, that though they are the party least servile to France, they are the most impracticable party, and belonging to a lower class of society, who have not the same feelings of honourable and gentlemanlike conduct which sometimes guide a portion, though a very small one, of their opponents."

In Spain therefore it is, the Queen fears, *too late*; but let us not throw away this lesson, and, if it is still possible, not also lose Portugal. Our influence there is fast going, and Sir H. Seymour[1] confirms what *every one* but Mr Southern has stated for the last two months, viz. that we are believed to be favourable to the rebels; consequently, that no advice of ours will be listened to. Sir H. Seymour further says: "I should have been glad to have gained a little time, and not at the outset of my mission to be obliged to call the Government to account upon various scores. Your orders, however, leave me no option, and I shall be obliged to administer a series of reproofs which will, I fear, confirm the notion as to our unfriendly feelings." This is the course the Queen thinks so very unfortunate; trifles about two horses, the beating of a gardener of Lord Howard's by some soldiers on a march in times of Civil War, etc., are made topics of serious complaint. Most peremptory notes are written, threatening the Government with our men-of-war, whilst it is held to be unwise to threaten the insurgents.

Then, the Court is told to believe *our feelings of attachment* for them!

Sir H. Seymour says that his position is rendered very difficult in consequence. We have now the results before us. Let us, therefore, before Portugal, our ancient ally, turns also away from us, and leans to France or Spain in preference, as she *must*, if we give her such doubtful support, try to pursue a more conciliatory course; these peremptory and dictatory notes, these constant complaints, produce the worst and most unfortunate effect.

These very Septembristas have been always the greatest enemies of England, and would be the first to turn against us should they succeed.

There should more latitude be given to the resident Minister not to press things at moments when they produce embarrassment to a Government already *tottering*, but to give him the option of waiting for a fit opportunity, and for the manner in which it is to be done, which a person on the spot can be a better judge of than we can in England.

Once more the Queen earnestly warns Lord John of the imminent danger of England losing *all* legitimate influence in Portugal, which ought now, more than ever, to be of the greatest *importance* to us.

The Queen has in all this *spoken* solely of English influence, but this influence becomes of still greater importance to her when the Sovereigns of that country are her near and dear relations.[2]

Lord John Russell to Queen Victoria.

Chesham Place, *19th March 1847.*

Lord John Russell presents his humble duty to your Majesty. Lord John Russell thinks it right to state to your Majesty that the prevailing opinion in the Cabinet is that when the necessary business in the House of Commons has been finished, a Dissolution of Parliament should take place.

This course would be conformable to the usage from the passing of the Septennial Act till 1830. From 1830 to the present year no House of Commons has been allowed to continue six years. The Dissolutions of Lord Grey in 1831 and 1832, of Sir Robert Peel in 1834, the death of William the Fourth in 1837, Lord Melbourne's Dissolution in 1841, have all interrupted the natural life of Parliaments. But all Governments since the accession of the House of Hanover have been of opinion (with one or two exceptions) that it is hazardous to allow a Parliament to continue seven years, as circumstances may arise making a Dissolution very detrimental to the public welfare.

These being general considerations, Lord John Russell would reserve any decision on the subject till the moment shall arrive when a Dissolution may appear to your Majesty's advisers to be the course most likely to secure moderate and fair elections.

Queen Victoria to Lord John Russell.

25th March 1847.

The Queen with pleasure approves the appointment of Lord Clarendon's brother to the vacant stall at St Paul's. The Queen would, however, draw Lord John's attention generally to the mode of filling up those Church sinecures. She is quite aware how necessary it is for a Minister to be able to recommend to such places persons of political connections, but she thinks that where it can be done, it would be of great use both to the Church and the country to give these places of emolument to Churchmen distinguished for their *scientific attainments*, who have neither the means nor the time to prosecute their researches, whilst their labours might be of the greatest importance to the country. Such person of this kind, for instance, the Prince thinks, is a Mr Cureton, who has just published the *real* epistles of St Ignatius, which he translated from the Syriac, and is about to produce a Gospel of St Matthew which is considered the undoubted original in the Coptic dialect, and other most important documents lately acquired for the British Museum.

Queen Victoria to Viscount Palmerston.

Buckingham Palace, *17th April 1847.*

The Queen has several times asked Lord Palmerston, through Lord John Russell and personally, to see that the drafts to our Foreign Ministers are not despatched *previous* to their being submitted to the Queen. Notwithstanding, this is still done, as for instance to-day with regard to the drafts for Lisbon. The Queen, therefore, once more repeats her desire that Lord Palmerston should prevent the recurrence of this practice.

Lord John Russell to Queen Victoria.

Chesham Place, *18th May 1847.*

Lord John Russell has the painful duty of announcing to your Majesty the death of the Earl of Bessborough.[3] The firmness and kindness of his temper, together with his intimate knowledge of Ireland and his sound judgment, make this event a public misfortune.

It appears to Lord John Russell very desirable that his successor should be named without loss of time, and as the Cabinet agreed yesterday that the Earl of Clarendon was the fittest person for the office, Lord John Russell would suggest that a Council should be held on Thursday next, at the hour your Majesty may appoint, for a Council for the purpose of the declaration of your Majesty's pleasure.

It was the opinion of the Cabinet that although it is advisable finally to abolish the office of Lord-Lieutenant, it is not advisable to propose any measure, or make any announcement for the present.

Queen Victoria to the King of the Belgians.

Buckingham Palace, *12th June 1847.*

My dearest Uncle,—We are here in terrible hot water, though *I* think we shall get out of it.[4] But only think that the Radicals *and* Protectionists join to attack Government for our interference in Portugal! A change of Government on such a subject would be *full* of mischief for the future, independent of the great momentary inconvenience; but it would cripple all future Governments in their future conduct respecting Foreign Affairs, would create distrust abroad in our promises, and is totally contrary to England's ancient policy of upholding Portugal.

In short, it would be *very* bad. The old Duke will do *every* thing to set matters right.

To-night we are going to the Opera in state, and will hear and see Jenny Lind[5] (who is perfection) in *Norma*, which is considered one of her best parts. Poor Grisi is quite going off, and after the pure angelic voice and extremely quiet, perfect acting of J. Lind, she seems quite *passée*. Poor thing! she is *quite* furious about it, and was excessively impertinent to J. Lind.

To-morrow we go to a ball at Stafford House, and on Thursday to one at Gloucester House. Ever your truly devoted Niece,

Victoria R.

The Duke of Wellington to Queen Victoria.

London, *12th July 1847.*
(*Five in the afternoon.*)

Field-Marshal the Duke of Wellington presents his humble duty to your Majesty. He submits to your Majesty the expression of his sorrow and shame that your Majesty should be troubled for a moment by anything so insignificant as a statue of himself.

When he first heard of the intention to remove the statue from the pedestal on which it had been placed, he was apprehensive that the measure might be misconstrued and misrepresented in this country as well as abroad.

That feeling was increased when the probable existence of such misconstruction was adverted to in one of the printed papers circulated by the Committee for the erection of the statue; and still farther when the removal became the subject of repeated discussions in Parliament. His daily experience of your Majesty's gracious reception of his endeavours to serve your Majesty; and the events of every day, and the repeated marks which he received of your Majesty's consideration and favour proved clearly, as the Duke stated in his letter to Lord John Russell, that there was no foundation for the misconstruction of the intended act—which undoubtedly existed. The apprehension of such misconstruction had from the first moment created an anxious wish in the mind of the Duke that the removal should be so regulated and should be attended by such circumstances as would tend to relieve the transaction from the erroneous but inconvenient impression which had been created.

The Duke apprehended that he might find it impossible to perform the duties with which he had been entrusted, and therefore, when Lord John Russell wrote to him, he deprecated the measure in contemplation; and he rejoices sincerely that your Majesty has been most graciously pleased to countermand the order for the removal of the statue.

All of which is most humbly submitted to your Majesty by your Majesty's most dutiful Subject and most devoted Servant,

Wellington.[6]

Queen Victoria to Lord Palmerston.

Buckingham Palace, *12th July 1847.*

The Queen has been informed by Lord John Russell that the Duke of Wellington is apprehensive that the removal of his statue from the Arch to another pedestal might be construed as a mark of displeasure on her part. Although the Queen had hoped that her esteem and friendship for the Duke was so well known to the public in general as not to render such a construction possible, and although she had thought that another pedestal would have been more suitable for *this* statue, and that the Arch might have been more becomingly ornamented in honour of the Duke than by the statue *now* upon it, she has given immediate direction that the Statue should remain in its present situation, and only regrets that this monument should be so unworthy of the great personage to whose honour it has been erected.

Viscount Hardinge to Queen Victoria.

27th July 1847.

Lord Hardinge, with his most humble duty to your Majesty, humbly acknowledges the letter in which your Majesty has been graciously pleased to approve of his conduct in the Government of your Majesty's Eastern Empire, and to sanction his return to Europe the end of this year.

It will always be a source of happiness to Lord Hardinge to have contributed his efforts towards maintaining the stability of your Majesty's Indian possessions committed to his charge, and he feels, in the performance of these duties, that the approbation of his Sovereign is the most grateful distinction to which honourable ambition can aspire.

The Governor-General entertains the most sanguine expectations that peace has been securely established beyond the north-west frontiers, as well as throughout India, and in this confidence he has ordered nearly 50,000 men of the native force to be reduced, which reductions have caused no discontent, being for the most part voluntary on the part of the men and accompanied by gratuities in proportion to the service performed.

As regards internal dangers, there is no native power remaining able to face a British army in the field. The people are very generally engaged in trade and agriculture, and to a great extent in the British Provinces no longer carry arms. Confidence in the protection of the Government has superseded the necessity. Formerly trade and wealth were concentrated in a few large cities—and Indian manufactures have been ruined by cheaper goods sent from England; but wealth and comfort have, under British rule, been more extensively diffused through the agricultural districts, and all classes, including the warlike tribes, are becoming more devoted to the happier and safer pursuits of peace.

In this state of things Lord Hardinge entertains a very confident expectation that the Government of India, by judicious attention to the native army in time of peace—which may have its peculiar dangers—will maintain due subordination in its ranks; and by abstaining from all interference in the religious prejudices of the people, will secure their loyal attachment to your Majesty, and their willing obedience to the Governor acting in your Majesty's behalf.

Lord Hardinge has the honour to subscribe himself your Majesty's most humble and dutiful Subject and Servant,

Hardinge.

Lord John Russell to Queen Victoria.
Pembroke Lodge, *5th August 1847.*

Lord John Russell presents his humble duty to your Majesty, and has the honour to state that he considers the elections which have taken place since he last addressed your Majesty as satisfactory.

The Liberal gains, upon the whole, have been upwards of thirty, and when the elections are concluded will probably be upwards of forty.

The rejection of so distinguished a man as Mr Macaulay[7] is the most disgraceful act in the whole election. It has only a parallel in the rejection of Mr Burke by the city of Bristol.

The result of the whole elections will be, even if Sir George Grey is defeated in Northumberland, that neither Lord John Russell or any other Minister will have the command of a regular party majority.

But it is probable that Government will be sufficiently strong to resist both a reaction against free trade, and any democratic movement against the Church or the aristocracy.

Lord John Russell to Queen Victoria.

Pembroke Lodge, *21st August 1847.*

Lord John Russell presents his humble duty to your Majesty, and has the honour to state that Lord Fitzwilliam writes that he shall feel hurt if the Earldom of Strafford should be given to Lord Strafford.

To save his feelings on this subject (Lord Fitzwilliam having the first Wentworth Earl of Strafford's property), Lord John Russell would humbly propose that Lord Strafford should be created Earl of Middlesex.

But as the relations of the late Duke of Dorset might also object, Lord John Russell will adhere to his original proposal if your Majesty should deem it best.

In fact, many titles have been given in succession to different families. Leinster, Orford, Westmorland, are familiar instances.

Lord John Russell has drawn up a paper respecting the Irish elections, on which the Prince wished to have his remarks. The subject is a dark and a dreary one....

Changes of Ministry may occur, but it is to be hoped that your Majesty may be enabled to keep the present Parliament for five or six years. For nothing tends so much to favour such reformations, to impede sober improvements, and to make members stand in servile awe of their constituents, as frequent General Elections.

Lord John Russell is happy to see in the newspapers the successful progress of your Majesty's journey. It has occurred to Lord John Russell that as the harvest is very promising, and the election heats will have subsided, it may be desirable that your Majesty should go for three days to Ireland on your Majesty's return. The want of notice might in some respects be favourable, and would be an excuse to many Irish peers, who might otherwise complete their ruin in preparations.

Queen Victoria to Earl Fitzwilliam.

3rd September 1847.

The Queen has received Lord Fitzwilliam's letter of the 31st.[8] As she sees Lord Strafford's elevation to an Earldom already announced in the *Gazette* of the same day, it will be impossible for the Queen to have the question of Lord Fitzwilliam's adverse claim reconsidered.

She thinks it right, however, to say, that, knowing that the Wentworth property came to Lord Fitzwilliam, it was only after the Heralds College had proved that Lord Strafford was the representative of the Earl of Strafford of the Second Creation, whilst Lord Fitzwilliam was not properly considered the representative of the first, that the Queen approved the selection of the title of Earl of Strafford for the present Lord. The Queen is very sorry to find that this step should have been annoying to Lord Fitzwilliam, for whom she has ever entertained a sincere regard. She has sent his letter on to Lord John Russell.

"The name and history of the first Earl of Strafford is, of course, familiar to your Majesty, and I venture to conclude that your Majesty is not unaware of my being his descendant, his heir, and his successor. I own his lands, I dwell in his house, I possess his papers, and, if neither my father nor myself have ever applied to the Crown for a renewal of his titles, it has not been because either of us was indifferent to those honours or to the favour of the Sovereign, but because we were well aware of the embarrassment which such applications frequently occasion to the Crown and its advisers."

Queen Victoria to Lord John Russell.

Ardverikie, *3rd September 1847.*

The Queen has received Lord John Russell's two letters of the 31st and 1st inst., and is glad to find that the views expressed in the Prince's Memorandum coincide with those entertained by Lord John and Lord Palmerston, and also by Lord Minto, as she infers. As it seems difficult to find a person of inferior rank and position than Lord Minto, and of equal weight, the Queen sanctions his undertaking the mission on the understanding that the object of it will be communicated beforehand to the Courts of Vienna and Paris, and that both these Governments will be made fully acquainted with the position England thinks herself bound to take with regard to the Italian controversy.[9] After this shall have been done, the sending of Sir William Parker with his fleet to the West Coast of Italy strikes the Queen as a very proper measure to give countenance to the Sovereigns engaged in Liberal Reform, and exposed alike to the inroads of their absolutist neighbour, and to the outbreaks of popular movements directed by a republican party, and perhaps fostered by the Austrian Government.

Queen Victoria to the King of the Belgians.

Ardverikie, *7th September 1847.*

My dearest Uncle,—I thank you much for your kind letter of the 28th. Mamma writes me *such* a good report of you both, which gives us the greatest pleasure. I hope you like young Ernest? This horrid Praslin tragedy [10] is a subject one cannot get out of one's head. The Government can in no way be accused of these murders, but there is *no* doubt that the *standard of morality* is *very low* indeed, in France, and that the higher classes are extremely unprincipled. This must shake the security and prosperity of a nation. In my opinion, nothing has gone on so well since the *unfortunate* false move of the Spanish marriages, and I think you will admit *que cela n'a pas porté bonheur au Roi.* I am very anxious to explain that I was out of spirits, and, I fear, humour, when I wrote to you last, for I *love* this place dearly, and the quiet, simple and wild life we lead here, particularly, in spite of the *abominable* weather we have had; and I *am not* the enemy of *La Chasse,* as I expressed myself—on the contrary, I am very keen about it, and am only annoyed at being unable to see it all. Really, when one thinks of the *very dull life,* and particularly the life of constant *self-denial,* which my poor, dear Albert leads, he deserves *every* amusement in the world, and even about his amusements he is so accommodating that I am deeply touched by it. He is very fond of shooting, but it is all with the greatest moderation. Do you know that you never wished Albert joy of his birthday?

The state of politics in Europe is very critical, and one feels *very* anxious for the future.

With my dearest Albert's love, and mine, to my beloved Louise. Believe me, ever your devoted Niece,

Victoria R.

Queen Victoria to Viscount Palmerston.

Windsor Castle, *9th October 1847.*

The Queen has just received these drafts, which she has read attentively, and thinks very proper; she only perceives *one* omission which should be rectified, viz. the one in which Lord Palmerston directs Sir H. Seymour and the Admiral to remain perfectly neutral in case of a conflict, and that is that our Fleet should naturally give protection to the persons of the King and Queen and Royal Family in case of danger, for we cannot allow them to be *murdered*, even if we should not be able to prevent their losing their Crown (which God forbid).

The Queen must *again* observe that the drafts have since some weeks past been sent to her *after* they were gone, so that she can make no remark upon them. The Queen wishes to have copies of these drafts.

Lord John Russell to Queen Victoria.

Chesham Place, *14th October 1847.*

Lord John Russell presents his humble duty to your Majesty. He has seen the Governor (Mr Morris) and Deputy-Governor (Mr Prescott) of the Bank, Mr Jones Loyd[11] and Mr Newman. Sir Charles Wood has seen many others connected with the City, and they have both made statements to the Cabinet.

The general result is: That an unsound state of trade has prevailed for some time.

More failures may be expected.[12]

The funds may fall still lower.

Any interference by Government in the way of issuing more notes might postpone but would aggravate the distress.

The railway calls add much to the present difficulty.

No forcible interference with railways would be justifiable, but a voluntary postponement of the execution of their Acts might be proposed to Parliament.

It will be seen by this short summary that the persons who by official position, practical experience, and much reflection are most capable of giving an opinion think that little or nothing can be done by Parliament or by Government.

It is one of those revulsions in trade which take place periodically, increased in extent by the expansion of commerce, but controlled in its operation by the sound principles of currency which have lately prevailed.

The Act of 1844 is generally blamed, but without the least reason. The accommodation afforded by the Bank has been large, liberal, and continuous. The circulation of notes approaches nineteen millions.

Upon fully considering the difficulty of finding a person of ability and experience to place at the head of the Poor Law Commission, Lord John Russell has come to the conclusion that the best course he can take is to propose to Mr Cobden to accept the Presidency with a seat in the Cabinet, and to propose to the Duke of Bedford at the same time a seat in the Cabinet without office.

Various reasons for making this offer to Mr Cobden will occur to your Majesty. His ability, his popularity with the working classes, and his knowledge of sound principles of political economy are undoubted. Sir Robert Peel's tribute to him has raised him both on the Continent and in this country, so that his presence in the Cabinet would give satisfaction to many.

On the other hand, the landed nobility and gentry would be glad to see the Duke of Bedford take part in the deliberations of the Government.

With your Majesty's permission Lord John Russell will propose these arrangements to the Cabinet to-morrow.

He has sent for Mr Lee[13] to offer him the Bishopric of Manchester. It is with great regret he states that Mr Stephen[14] is obliged from ill health to retire from the Colonial Office. He has asked Lord Grey to be made a Privy Councillor, having received an assurance from Lord Stanley that Sir Robert Peel would propose it to your Majesty on his retirement. Lord John Russell submits the proposal to your Majesty as an honour due to Mr Stephen's long, able, and calumniated[15] public services.

Lord John Russell has the honour to submit a letter of Lord Clarendon's in reference to a Memorandum of His Royal Highness Prince Albert.

Lord John Russell thinks that in the present state of affairs, the abolition of the Lord-Lieutenancy must not be thought of, and that with the exception noticed by Lord Clarendon, the suggestions made by the Prince would be the best measures for adoption, when that event takes place.

It is possible the Prince may not have a copy of the Memorandum.

Queen Victoria to Lord John Russell.

Windsor Castle, *14th October 1847.*

The Queen has received Lord John Russell's letter, bringing several very important subjects before her. She regrets that the state of the Money Market should still be so uncomfortable, but is sure that the Government cannot by any interference do much to mend matters, though it might easily render them still more complicated, and make itself responsible for a crisis, which it has in no way either brought on or been able to avert.[16]

As to Mr Cobden's appointment to the Poor Law Board, the Queen thinks that he will be well qualified for the place in many respects, and that it will be advantageous to the Government and the Country that his talents should be secured to the service of the State, but the elevation to the Cabinet directly from Covent Garden[17] strikes her as a very sudden step, calculated to cause much dissatisfaction in many quarters, and setting a dangerous example to agitators in general (for his main reputation Mr Cobden gained as a successful agitator). The Queen therefore thinks it best that Mr Cobden should first enter the service of the Crown, serve as a public functionary in Parliament, and be promoted subsequently to the Cabinet, which step will then become a very natural one.

The Duke of Bedford's entrance into the Cabinet the Queen would see with great pleasure.

The Queen returns the Prince's Memorandum to Lord John, whilst she has retained Lord Clarendon's letter upon it, which the Prince is anxious to keep if Lord John will allow him. The Queen must agree with Lord John and Lord Clarendon that the present moment is not a favourable one for the experiment of abolishing the Lord-Lieutenancy.

Mr Stephen's elevation to the Privy Council will be a very proper reward for his long and faithful services. Would he not be a proper person for one of the new Civil degrees of the Bath?[18]

Queen Victoria to Lord John Russell.

Windsor Castle, *18th October 1847.*

The Queen cannot resist drawing Lord John Russell's attention to the enclosed paragraph taken from the *Revue des Deux Mondes*, which gives an account of the late events in Spain. How little honourable our line of policy appears according to this version, which the Queen is afraid is so very plausible that it will be received as the truth by the whole French public and a great part of the European public at large! It is, no doubt, perverted, but still the Queen must admit that our policy, and especially Mr Bulwer's conduct at Madrid, lays itself open to similar construction. After the gross duplicity and immorality which characterised the conduct of France with respect to the Spanish marriages, though she had all the profit and we all the loss, still we had a very strong position on the side of integrity, morality, and honour. The

Queen is afraid that the diplomatic intrigues and counter intrigues at Madrid have made us lose daily more of that advantageous position without *any* compensation on the other side. The Queen entreats Lord John Russell not to underrate the importance of keeping our foreign policy beyond reproach. Public opinion is recognised as a ruling power in our domestic affairs; it is not of less importance in the society of Europe with reference to the conduct of an individual state. To possess the *confidence* of Europe is of the utmost importance to this country. That is the reason why the Queen is uneasy about our dealings in Greece, and anxious that we should not be misunderstood with respect to Italy. The Queen is sorry to perceive that the French complain of unfair dealing on our part with reference to the negotiations in the River Plate.[19] Have they any right to do so? Have Lord Howden's private instructions been at variance in any way with the public instructions which had been agreed upon with the French Government? The Queen would consider any advantage gained at the expense of an ally as a loss.

Queen Victoria to Viscount Palmerston.

Windsor Castle, *24th October 1847.*

The Queen has perused with eagerness Mr Bulwer's accounts of the late extraordinary events in Spain, but must confess that she has in vain looked for an explanation of the real motives and causes of the crisis. Has Lord Palmerston received any private letters throwing more light upon the matter? There seems to prevail the greatest mystery about the affair. Is the Queen reconciled with her husband? Has she sent for him? Have all the accounts of her hatred for Don Francisco and the Queen-Mother been false? All these questions are unanswered.

Viscount Palmerston to Queen Victoria.

Foreign Office, *30th October 1847.*

Viscount Palmerston presents his humble duty to your Majesty, and has many apologies to make for not having attended your Majesty's Council to-day, and the more so as his absence arose from an inadvertence which he is almost ashamed to mention. But having got on horseback to ride to the station, with his thoughts occupied with some matters which he was thinking of, he rode mechanically and in a fit of absence to the Nine Elms Station,[20] and did not recollect his mistake till he had got there; and although he made the best of his way afterwards to the Paddington Station, he could not get there in time for any train that would have taken him early enough to Windsor.

Viscount Palmerston received this morning your Majesty's remarks upon his proposed drafts to Sir Hamilton Seymour, and has modified some of the expressions in those drafts; but those drafts are only private and confidential answers in his own name to private and confidential communications from Sir Hamilton Seymour, and they express only his own personal opinions, and not those of the Government.

Viscount Palmerston is sorry to say that the circumstances lately mentioned by Sir Hamilton Seymour, coupled with the course pursued at Lisbon almost ever since the successful interference of the Allied Powers, have brought Viscount Palmerston to the painful convictions expressed in the above-mentioned drafts, and he feels desirous, for his own sake, to place those convictions at least upon record in this Office. He will be most happy to find that he is mistaken, and will most truly and heartily rejoice if events should prove that the confidence which your Majesty reposes in the sincerity and good faith of the Queen of Portugal is well founded; but in a matter of this importance Viscount Palmerston feels that it is his bounden duty to your Majesty not to conceal his opinions, even though they should, as in the present case, unfortunately differ from those which your Majesty entertains.

Queen Victoria to Viscount Palmerston.

Windsor Castle, *21st October 1847.*

The Queen acknowledges Lord Palmerston's letter of yesterday. She can have no objections to Lord Palmerston's putting on record his opinion that the Queen of Portugal is leaning to the Chartist Party, and exposing herself, her Throne and country, to great danger by so doing; but she would *much* deprecate the putting on record the grave accusation "that the Queen of Portugal is in a secret and perfect understanding with the Cabrals,"[21] which is really not warranted by the facts of the case, and is likely to mislead both our Government and the Minister at Lisbon. Since the Queen wrote yesterday the Prince received a letter from the King of Portugal (which he sent to Lord Palmerston), and which quite explains the position and views of the Court: we must not forget either that Sir Hamilton Seymour acknowledges that a change of Ministry at this moment would provoke a fresh Revolution at Lisbon. Although this would come from the Cabralists, the Queen of Portugal very naturally may not feel inclined to run that risk to avoid a danger the existence of which she does not see or comprehend.

Lord John Russell to Queen Victoria.

Chesham Place, *10th November 1847.*

Lord John Russell presents his humble duty to your Majesty, and after reflecting on the various reasons in favour of, and objections against, different Bishops for promotion to the Archbishopric of York, he humbly submits to your Majesty the name of Dr Musgrave, Bishop of Hereford, to be appointed Archbishop of York. The Bishop of Hereford is a man of sound information, good judgment, and business habits. It is of such consequence to have an Archbishop of York, who will, like the late Archbishop, avoid quarrels and crotchets, and live peaceably with all men.

Should your Majesty approve, he would then submit the name of Dr Hampden to be the new Bishop, and that of the Bishop of Oxford[22] as Queen's Almoner.

The Bishop of Oxford to Mr Anson.

16th November 1847.

My dear Anson,—I enclose you a letter from Lord John Russell, offering me the Lord Almonership. I have ventured to write direct to Her Majesty, to express to her my grateful feelings at this notice of me. But I have been so afraid of offending by anything like freedom of expression that I much fear I have instead said coldly and formally what, if I had said it naturally, would have expressed the deepest and most exuberant feelings of what I trust I may venture to say is not an ungrateful heart. Ungrateful it would be most certainly if it did not feel to its deepest core the uniform and great kindness I have received now for so many years from Her Majesty and from the Prince. I wish I could better show them my feelings....

You have read no doubt the *Times* article on Dr Hampden. I am afraid it is too true. I cannot conceive *what* was Dr Hampden's recommendation. He was not a persecuted man, for he had got a station far higher than he ever dreamed of already; he is not an able, or an active man, or one popular with any party, and unless Lord John Russell wished for an opportunity of shocking the young confidence of the Church in him, I cannot conceive why he should have made it. I deeply lament it. Pray let me hear of your health, if it be only a single line (to Cuddesdon), and believe me to be, ever your truly affectionate,

S. Oxon.

Queen Victoria to Viscount Palmerston.

17th November 1847.

The Queen has been struck by the concluding passage of the accompanying draft to Mr Bulwer. It gives an official declaration of the views of England with respect to a point of the greatest gravity and importance, and upon which the Queen apprehends that the mind of the Cabinet is not yet made up. The Queen herself has come to no determination upon it, and it may involve the question of peace or war. Surely our line of policy under future and uncertain contingencies ought not to be pledged beforehand and in such an indirect way. The Queen wishes Lord Palmerston to speak to Lord John Russell upon the subject, and to show him the draft and these remarks of the Queen upon it.

Viscount Palmerston to Queen Victoria.

Foreign Office, *17th November 1847.*

Viscount Palmerston presents his humble duty to your Majesty, and in compliance with your Majesty's wishes he has omitted the whole of the latter part of the proposed despatch to Mr Bulwer.

Queen Victoria to Lord John Russell.

(*Undated.*)

The Queen has seen with surprise in the *Gazette* the appointment of Mr Corigan,[23] about which she must complain to Lord John Russell. Not only had her pleasure not been taken upon it, but she had actually mentioned to Lord Spencer that she had her doubts about the true propriety of the appointment. Lord John will always have found the Queen desirous to meet his views with regard to all appointments and ready to listen to any reasons which he might adduce in favour of his recommendations, but she must insist upon appointments in her Household not being made *without* her previous sanction, and least of all such as that of a *Physician to her person.*

The King of Prussia to Queen Victoria.

[Translation.]

25th November 1847.

... I hear with delight and thankfulness that it has pleased your Majesty to agree to a Conference for regulating the dreadful Swiss quarrels.[24] I took the liberty to propose my beloved and truly amiable town of Neuchâtel as the place for the Conference, not only because its position in neutral territory and in Switzerland herself qualifies it above every other place for that purpose, but *particularly* because this meeting of the representatives of the great Powers there would protect it and the courageous and faithful country of Neuchâtel from indignities, spoliation, and all the *horrors* which oppress at this moment the unfortunate and far from courageous Fribourg. I am afraid that your Majesty has not a full appreciation of the people and the partisans who fill Switzerland with murders and the miseries of the most abominable Civil War. Your Majesty's happy realms have centuries ago passed through the "phase" of such horrors, and with you the state of parties has been (as one says here) grown in bottles,[25] under the glorious Constitution given by God and History, but *not* "made"; but there, in Switzerland, a party is becoming victorious!!! which, notwithstanding the exercise of Christian charity, can only be called "*Gottlos und Rechtlos*" (without God and without right). For Germany, the saving of Switzerland from the hands of the Radicals is *simply* a *vital question.* If they are victorious there, in Germany likewise torrents of blood will flow; I will answer for that. The murder of Kings, Priests, and Aristocrats is no empty sound with them, and Civil War in song, writing, word, and deed, is their watchword. "Toute charité bien entendue commence par soi-même." So they begin with their own country, true to this "Christian" (!) motto. If they are allowed to proceed, surely they *won't stop there.* Thousands of emigrated malefactors wait only for a sign (which their comrades and allies in Germany will not be backward in giving) to pour forth beyond the German frontier. In Germany the PEOPLE are just as little fond of them as they were in Switzerland, but the experience of Switzerland teaches us that that alone cannot stem their victorious march, if circumstances are favourable to them. The German people rely upon their Governments, and do nothing, but Governments are weakened by the modern Liberalism (the precursor of Radicalism, as the dying of chickens precedes the Cholera) and will have to take the consequences of their own negligence. Notwithstanding people and princes, that godless band will march through Germany, because, though small, it is strong through being united and determined. All this I have pondered in my head and heart (led, so to say, by the hand of History), and that has prompted me now to propose that the German Confederation (which *en parenthèse* includes a population of more than forty millions) should appear as one of the great Powers of Europe at the settlement of the Swiss dispute, and should be admitted as such by the other great Powers. *Would your Majesty do justice, and give* PROTECTION *to this idea?...*

F. W.

Queen Victoria to the King of Prussia.

Osborne, *5th December 1847.*

Since your letter was written events have followed each other so rapidly that at this moment the war in Switzerland may be considered as terminated; by the capitulations of the Cantons formerly constituting the Sonderbund, *two* parties, between which a mediation of the great Powers could have taken place, have ceased to exist, and consequently mediation and the Conference resulting from it are in fact no longer necessary or possible. I had proposed London as the place of conference, but should with pleasure have waived this proposition to adopt the place which you have expressed a wish of seeing fixed for that purpose, viz. Neuchâtel, and I should have felt truly happy if by so doing I could have met your wishes, and given further protection to the principality against possible aggressions on the part of the Federal Government of Switzerland. As matters now stand, the only complication which might arise is that between Neuchâtel and the Diet. I have, in anticipation of any such event, instructed Sir Stratford Canning to exert himself to his utmost to dissuade the Diet from any plan of aggression on your territory, and he has been furnished with an able and elaborate state paper for his guidance, which Chevalier Bunsen had drawn up, discussing the legal merits of the case. Should events prove that Sir S. Canning did not arrive in time, or had not the power of averting a hostile step against Neuchâtel, you may rely upon my readiness at all times to put my good offices at your disposal. Should a conference upon Swiss affairs still become necessary, I conceive that the only plea upon which the great Powers could meet in conference would be their having guaranteed the independence and neutrality of Switzerland, and by implication the Federal Compact amongst the

Cantons. This has not been the case with regard to the German Confederation, and I do not readily see in consequence how the Confederation could be admitted into this Conference, however much I confess I would like to see Germany take her place amongst the Powers of Europe, to which her strength and population fairly entitle her. I may say that my Government are equally impressed with me with the importance of German unity and strength and of this strength weighing in the balance of power of Europe; I am sure that the English public generally share this feeling, but I must not conceal from your Majesty that much would depend upon the manner in which this power was represented. Much as the English would like to see this power represented by the enlightened councils of your Majesty, they would be animated with very different feelings in seeing it in the hands of Prince Metternich....

Victoria R.

Queen Victoria to Lord John Russell.

Osborne, *19th December 1847.*

The Queen has to acknowledge the receipt of several letters from Lord John Russell. She was pleased to see that the Debates have been brought to such a satisfactory conclusion, all the propositions of the Government having passed with such good majorities. The Queen must mention to Lord John that she was a little shocked at Sir Charles Wood in his speech upon the Commission of Inquiry, designating the *future Government*, and selecting Lord George Bentinck, Mr Disraeli(!), and Mr Herries as the persons destined to hold *high offices* in the next Government.

The Bishops behave extremely ill about Dr Hampden, and the Bishop of Exeter[26] is gone so far, in the Queen's opinion, that he might be prosecuted for it, in calling the Act settling the supremacy on the Crown a *foul act* and *the Magna Charta of Tyranny.*

The Queen is glad to hear that Lord John is quite recovered. We are going to Windsor the day after to-morrow.

Viscount Melbourne to Queen Victoria.

Brocket Hall, *30th December 1847.*

Lord Melbourne presents his humble duty to your Majesty. He has received with great pleasure your Majesty's letter of this morning, and reciprocates with the most cordial heartiness your Majesty's good wishes of the season, both for your Majesty and His Royal Highness. Lord Melbourne is pretty well in health, perhaps rather better than he has been, but low and depressed in spirits for a cause which has long pressed upon his mind, but which he has never before communicated to your Majesty. Lord Melbourne has for a long time found himself much straitened in his pecuniary circumstances, and these embarrassments are growing now every day more and more urgent, so that he dreads before long that he shall be obliged to add another to the list of failures and bankruptcies of which there have lately been so many. This is the true reason why Lord Melbourne has always avoided the honour of the Garter, when pressed upon him by his late Majesty and also by your Majesty. Lord Melbourne knows that the expense of accepting the blue ribbon amounts to £1000, and there has been of late years no period at which it would not have been seriously inconvenient to Lord Melbourne to lay down such a sum.[27]

ENDNOTES:

[1]:Envoy Extraordinary at Lisbon.

[2]:This letter at once bore fruit, a conference being held in London between the representatives of Great Britain, Spain, France, and Portugal, and armed co-operation to enforce the acceptance of certain terms by the Revolutionary Junta being decided upon.

[3]:John William, formerly Lord Duncannon, 4th Earl, born 1781; Lord-Lieutenant of Ireland.

[4]:The Government were severely attacked by a coalition of Radicals and Protectionists for their intervention in Portugal. A hostile motion of Lord Stanley's in the House of Lords was opposed by the Duke of Wellington and defeated, while one of Mr Hume's in the House of Commons was talked out, Sir Robert Peel supporting the Ministry.

[5]:She made her *début* in London on the 4th of May in *Roberto il Diavolo*. The Queen had heard her sing previously at Stolzenfels. In May 1849, after singing for two years to enthusiastic audiences, she retired from the stage, and made extended concert tours in Europe and America.

[6]:The Duke of Wellington wrote to Croker, 19th of December 1846:—"I should desire never to move from my principles of indifference and non-interference on the subject of a statue of myself to commemorate my own actions."

And again, on the 14th of June 1847, the Duke wrote to Croker:—"It has always been my practice, and is my invariable habit, to say nothing about myself and my own actions.

"More than forty years ago Mr Pitt observed that I talked as little of myself or my own acts as if I had been an assistant-surgeon of the army....

"I follow the habit of avoiding to talk of myself and of what I have done; with the exception only of occasions when I am urging upon modern contemporaries measures which they don't like, and when I tell them I have some experience, and have had some success in these affairs, and feel they would experience the benefit of attending to my advice, I never talk of myself.

"These are the reasons for which they think that I don't care what they do with the statue.

"But they must be idiots to suppose it possible that a man who is working day and night, without any object in view excepting the public benefit, will not be sensible of a disgrace inflicted upon him by the Sovereign and Government whom he is serving. The ridicule will be felt, if nothing else is!"...

[7]:In consequence of his vote on Maynooth. The poem he wrote on the present occasion will be remembered.

[8]:On John, Baron Strafford, who as Sir John Byng had been distinguished in the Peninsula and at Waterloo, receiving the Earldom of Strafford, Lord Fitzwilliam had written: "Your Majesty has, undoubtedly, the power of conferring this, or any other titular dignity, according to your good pleasure, but I venture to hope that, if it be your Majesty's pleasure to revive the Earldom of Strafford, it will not be bestowed upon any other person than the individual who has now the honour of addressing your Majesty.

[9]:Lord John Russell proposed that Lord Minto should be sent on a special mission to the Vatican. *See* Introductory Note for the Year, *ante*, p. 115.

[10]:The sensational murder in Paris of the Duchesse de Praslin, daughter of the diplomatist, Sebastiani, by her husband, who committed suicide. This event, as well as the affair of the Spanish marriages, largely contributed to the Orleanist catastrophe of 1848, for it was suspected that the Court and the police had not merely connived at, but had actually furnished the means for, the Duke's suicide, in order to prevent certain exposures which would have resulted from his trial.

[11]:Afterwards Lord Overstone.

[12]:There had been many failures in London, Liverpool, and elsewhere.

[13]:James Prince Lee, then Headmaster of King Edward's School, Birmingham, Bishop of Manchester, 1847-1869.

[14]:James Stephen, Under-Secretary for the Colonies, 1836-1847, afterwards Professor of Modern History at Cambridge.

[15]:He had made enemies by supporting the abolition of slavery.

[16]:Matters, however, became worse, and Lord John Russell and Sir Charles Wood wrote recommending that the Bank should enlarge their discounts and advances, for which they would propose a bill of indemnity. By degrees the panic subsided.

[17]:Free Trade meetings had taken place in Covent Garden Theatre.

[18]:He was made a K.C.B.

[19]:Sir John Hobart Caradoc, second Lord Howden, British Minister at Rio Janeiro, was, together with Count Walewski, the French Minister there, engaged in a special mission to the River Plate and Uruguay; Buenos Ayres was blockaded by the British Fleet.

[20]:The former terminus of the London and South-Western Railway.

[21]:The Ministry in which Castro Cabral had been Premier, and his brother, José, Minister of Justice, had resigned in May 1846.

[22]:Samuel Wilberforce.

[23]:Dominic John Corigan, M.D., Physician-in-Ordinary to Her Majesty in Ireland.

[24]:*See* Introductory Note for the year, *ante,* p. 119.

[25]:As old wine improves by being kept in bottles.

[26]:Henry Phillpotts, Bishop of Exeter, 1830-1869.

[27]:The Queen, through the agency of Mr Anson, advanced Lord Melbourne a considerable sum of money, which seems to have been repaid at his death. Apparently Lord Melbourne's declining health caused him to magnify his difficulties. The report which Mr Anson made shows that he was in no sense seriously embarrassed.

INTRODUCTORY NOTE
TO CHAPTER XVII

At the outset of the year 1848 great alarm was felt throughout England at the supposed inadequacy of her defences, a panic being caused by the indiscreet publication of a confidential letter from the Duke of Wellington to Sir John Burgoyne, to the effect that in his judgment the whole South Coast was open to invasion, and that there were no means of opposing a hostile force. The Government turned its attention to reconstructing the Militia, and raising the Income Tax for the purpose. But the outlook was completely changed by the French Revolution; Louis Philippe, who had just lost his sister and counsellor, Madame Adélaïde, impulsively abdicated, on a rising taking place, and escaped with his family to this country. England and Belgium were unaffected by the outburst of revolution which convulsed Europe: the Emperor of Austria was forced to abdicate, and Metternich, like Guizot, became a fugitive; Prussia was shaken to her foundation, and throughout Germany the movement in favour of representative institutions made rapid headway; a National Assembly for Germany was constituted, and Schleswig was claimed as an integral part of the German dominions. In Italy also the Revolution, though premature, was serious. The Pope, not yet reactionary, declared war against Austria; the Milanese rose against Radetzky, the Austrian Governor, and King Charles Albert of Sardinia marched to their assistance. A republic was proclaimed in Venice, but these successes were afterwards nullified, and a Sicilian rising against Ferdinand II. of Naples was suppressed. In France the revolutionary movement held steadily on its course, a National Assembly was elected, and national workshops established; Louis Bonaparte, who had been a fugitive in England, was allowed to return, and was elected President of the Republic by an immense majority of the popular vote.

The friends of Revolution had no success in England; a very serious riot at Glasgow was dispersed, and the meeting convened by Feargus O'Connor for the 10th of April on Kennington Common, which was to carry a huge petition in favour of the People's Charter to the House of Commons, proved a ridiculous *fiasco*. Ireland was much disturbed during the year by what was known as the Young Ireland agitation, a movement organised by youthful, and for the most part cultivated, leaders, and utterly different from the sturdy Repeal movement of O'Connell. Smith O'Brien, brother of Lord Inchiquin, was the ringleader, and was backed by Mitchel, Duffy, Meagher, and others, as well as by the *Nation* and *United Irishman* newspapers. Like Chartism, the movement ignominiously collapsed and its leaders were convicted of treason. An Act was at the same time passed reducing some offences (till then legally defined as treason) to felonies, and improving the law as to offences against the person of the Sovereign.

The treacherous murder of two Englishmen in the Punjab led to operations against the Sikhs, Lord Dalhousie—who had recently become Viceroy—after some hesitation, reinforcing Lord Gough, the Commander-in-Chief, and proceeding in person to the frontier; a British force sustained a reverse at Ramnuggur on 22nd November, and a decisive result was not arrived at till 1849.

In South Africa, a proclamation by Sir Harry Smith, the Governor of the Cape of Good Hope, extending British sovereignty over the country between the Orange and Vaal rivers, led to a collision with the Boers, and ultimately to the founding of the Transvaal State. Sir Harry Smith defeated the Boers on the 29th of August at Boom Platz.

CHAPTER XVII

1848

The King of the Belgians to Queen Victoria.

Laeken, *1st January 1848.*

My dearest Victoria,—This is a most melancholy beginning of the year. Our poor Aunt Adélaïde,[1] so kind to us, has departed this life yesterday morning. Poor Louise feels it dreadfully, as nothing could be more affectionate and more motherly than she was for Louise. She was always very kind and friendly to me, and I must confess I feel the blow much. I am very much alarmed about the poor King; he must feel the loss of a sister and friend so entirely devoted to him deeply; it is the thing most likely to hurt and shake his health. You will forgive if I cut short here, as I am much disturbed by this melancholy event. I think you would act kindly in writing to the King. We are too nearly connected not to do it, and it will soothe him, who has been enough persecuted since last year. I trust you begin better than we do this most melancholy January. My best love to Albert, and believe me ever, my dearest Victoria, your truly and devoted Uncle,

Leopold R.

Queen Victoria to Lord John Russell.[2]

Windsor Castle, *3rd January 1848.*

The Queen sends Lord John Russell a letter from her Uncle, the King of the Belgians, which will show how dreadful a blow Mme. Adélaïde's death will be to the King of the French and Royal Family. The Queen's first thought was to write to the King, which she would not have done without first mentioning it to Lord John; but upon reflection she thought it quickest and best to write *at once* to her cousin Clémentine (Princess Augustus of Saxe-Coburg), to convey in her name to the King her sincere sympathy at this melancholy event. The King of the Belgians' letter has, however, brought back to the Queen her first thought of writing to the King, and she wishes to know what Lord John thinks of it. The Queen thinks it as undignified as unfeeling to carry on political coolness at moments like these, when her own feelings of sympathy are so strong and so sincere. The Queen would certainly under other circumstances have instantly written to the King. On the other hand, her first letter to her cousin (the King's daughter) may be sufficient, as it conveys a direct message; and there may be people who will construe this into a political act, but the Queen thinks that this risk should rather be run than that she should appear unfeeling and forgetful of former kindness and intimacy.

The Queen would be glad to have Lord John's opinion on this subject as soon as possible.

The Queen of the Belgians to Queen Victoria.

Laeken, *3rd January 1848.*

My dearly beloved Victoria,—I thank you *most sincerely* for your kind last letter, and all your good wishes for the New Year. Alas! the year *ended* and *began* in a *most painful* and *heartrending way for us.* The loss of my good, excellent, beloved Aunt is an *immense misfortune* for *us all*, and the most *dreadful blow* for my poor Father. We are all broken-hearted by this, at last *unexpected* event. Some years we were uneasy about my poor Aunt's health, and of late I had been particularly alarmed by what I heard of her increasing weakness; but I was very far from believing that her end was *so near.* I was only anxious for the winter. At least her end was peaceful. She went to sleep and did not wake more. She died without a struggle; the horror of death, and the still greater pang of the last farewell, of the last leave-taking of her beloved brother, was spared her. I thank God for *this* proof of His mercy, and hope He will keep up my Father under *such a heavy affliction.* To him the loss is *irretrievable.* My Aunt lived *but* for him; one may almost say that her affection alone had kept her alive these last years, and a devotion like hers—that devotion of all instants—so complete, so full of self-denial—cannot, will never, be replaced. A heart *like hers*, so true, so noble, so warm, so loving, so devoted, is *rarely* seen. To us also, independently of my Father, the loss is a *dreadful* one. My Aunt was a second mother for us; we loved her and looked up to her in this way, and certainly few mothers do for their children what she did for us, or loved them better. We are overwhelmed with grief by the sudden disappearance of a being *so dear* and *so necessary* to us all, and we go to-morrow to Paris, to mourn with the remainder of the family, and offer my poor Father the only consolation he can feel at this cruel moment, that of being surrounded by all those he loves. I have still so much to do previous to our melancholy journey that I cannot say more to-day. I am sure you will excuse me. I shall, God willing, write in a more proper way the next time. In the meanwhile I thank God that you are *unberufen* all well, and, in sorrow or in joy, I am equally, my beloved Victoria, from the bottom of my heart, yours most devotedly,

Louise.

Lord John Russell to Queen Victoria.

Woburn Abbey, *4th January 1848.*

Lord John Russell presents his humble duty to your Majesty, and has no hesitation in saying that he thinks your Majesty will do well to follow your own kind impulse to write a letter to the King of the French. There will be some persons, and M. Guizot perhaps among the number, who will construe this into a political act; but it is better to be subject to such misconstructions than to leave undone any act of sympathy to the King of the French in his sore affliction.

Should the King attempt to found upon your Majesty's letter any political intercourse, Lord John Russell has no doubt that your Majesty will explain to him that your present proceeding is entirely founded upon private regard, and past recollections of intimacy, and is not intended as an opening for political correspondence.

Queen Victoria to the King of the French.

Ch. de Windsor, *5 Janvier 1848.*

Sire et mon bon Frère,—Je ne voulais pas suivre l'impulse de mon cœur, dans les premiers instants de la vive douleur de votre Majesté, en vous écrivant—mais maintenant où la violence de cette rude secousse peut-être sera un peu adoucie, je viens moi-même exprimer à votre Majesté la part sincère que nous prenons, le Prince et moi, à la cruelle perte que vous venez d'éprouver, et qui doit vous laisser un vide irréparable. Ayez la bonté, Sire, d'offrir nos expressions de condoléance à la Reine, et faisant des vœux pour le bonheur de V.M., je me dis, Sire et mon bon Frère, de V.M., la bonne Sœur,

V. R.

A S.M. le Roi des Français.

The King of the French to Queen Victoria.

Paris, *8 Janvier 1848.*

Madame ma bonne Sœur,—Dans la profonde douleur où m'a plongé le coup cruel qui vient de me frapper, une des plus douces consolations que je pusse recevoir, est la lettre que votre Majesté a eu la bonté de m'adresser, tant en son nom qu'en celui du Prince son Epoux. L'expression de la part que vous prenez tous deux à mon malheur, et de l'intérêt que vous continuez à me porter, m'a vivement ému, et quelque douloureuse qu'en soit l'occasion, qu'il me soit permis, Madame, de vous en remercier, et de dire à votre Majesté que mon cœur et mes sentimens pour elle, sont et seront toujours les mêmes que ceux que j'étais si heureux de Lui manifester à Windsor et au Château d'Eu.

Je prie votre Majesté de vouloir bien être, auprès du Prince son Epoux, l'interprète de toute ma sensibilité. La Reine est bien touchée de ce que votre Majesté m'a chargé de Lui témoigner, et je la prie de croire que je suis toujours, Madame, ma bonne Sœur, de votre Majesté, le bon Frère,

Louis Philippe R.

Queen Victoria to Viscount Palmerston.

Claremont, *11th January 1848.*

The Queen has this morning seen a draft addressed to Lord Cowley, in which he is desired to advise the Sultan to give Abd-el-Kader a command in his Army—a step which the Queen cannot approve, not because it is not good advice to the Porte, but because it is uncalled for on our part, and might be considered by France as a hostile step towards her. What would we say if the French were to advise M. Ali to give Akbar Khan the command of his army? [3]

Queen Victoria to the King of the Belgians.

Claremont, *11th January 1848.*

My dearest Uncle,—I always write with pleasure to you from this *so* very dear old place, where we are safely and happily housed with our *whole* little family since yesterday. The weather is very cold, and it is the third night of a black frost which is likely to continue for some days. Many thanks for your kind letter of the 7th, which, according to the new arrangement, I received already on the 8th. Your visit will, I fear, have been a very melancholy one. Poor Mme. Adélaïde's death was so extremely sudden, it must be a dreadful blow to the poor King. I *have* written to him. Louise will have told you that poor Aunt Sophia[4] is decidedly sinking.

I wish, dearest Uncle, if even Louise feels unequal to coming to us now (which would be a *sad disappointment*), *you* would come to see us. Why not come while she is at Paris? It would be such a pleasure to us. You will of course have no balls, and you might come even sooner than you originally intended. Pray do see if you could manage this. I am sure you could. If Louise could come, of course that would be still better.

Albert desires me to ask you the following favour, viz. if you would give us the picture that is here of Grand Uncle Frederic (the Field-Marshal), that we might hang it up in London, where we have made a fine collection of his contemporaries, and we would replace it by a faithful copy, which could be hung up in the frame here. Will you grant this?

We are very desirous of getting the Woods and Forests to build a small *glass dome* to the greenhouse here where the palm-trees are, and (if you approved) there could be no difficulty in getting this done; the palm-trees are beautiful, and will be quite stunted and spoilt if not allowed to grow. We shall stay here till Monday next. With Albert's love, ever your truly devoted Niece,

Victoria R.

The King of the Belgians to Queen Victoria.

Laeken, *12th January 1848.*

My dearest Victoria,—A messenger of my own going to England, I take advantage of it to write you a few words. Your kind letter to the poor King was an act for which I thank you from the bottom of my soul, because it made him so happy. I was still in his rooms—where the family has been breakfasting and dining till now—when your letter arrived; he was so delighted with it that he *kissed it most tenderly*. I left him tolerably well on Monday, but with rather a severe cold. He had certainly at the end of December the Grippe, which perhaps was the immediate cause of poor Aunt's death, as from over-anxiety for her beloved brother, she got up in the night to find out how he was. His cold had been better when he went to Dreux, then he met the procession, and walked with it bareheaded to the church; this seems to have given him a new cold. His nerves are also a good deal shaken, and this renders him very irritable. He is much occupied about some of the arrangements connected with poor Aunt's fortune; she left her landed property to Nemours, Joinville, and Montpensier, charged with the various sums she left to nearly all the branches of her family. The King is to have, however, the enjoyment of the whole of this fortune for his life. His great wish would be to employ the revenues, from the whole of the succession legacies as well as landed property, to free the landed property of the mortgage of the various legacies. This will require a good many years, and I told him that it would force him to live till it would be arranged, which will easily require ten years. In France a good feeling has been shown on this occasion. I heard from trustworthy quarters that even people who were known to be personally not very kind to the King, expressed themselves most anxious for his preservation. Whenever that sad event will take place, the reaction in Europe will be great, as all the bad passions which are kept down by him will then of course try to get the over hand. The Queen is much affected by all this, and thinks much of her own end. The children, including good Hélène, have all behaved with the utmost affection to their parents, and nothing can equal particularly good Nemours' devotion and attention. My beloved Child, your truly devoted Uncle,

Leopold R.

The King of the Belgians to Queen Victoria.

Laeken, *12th February 1848.*

My dearest Victoria,—... From Paris the news are alarming;[5] the struggle of the Liberal Party leaning towards radicalism, or in fact merely their own promotion; principles are *out* of the question. This state of affairs reacts in a very lamentable way upon the well-being of the great European community. Great complaints are made that the working classes are deprived of work and at the same time political agitation is kept up, which must have the effect of stopping transactions of every description. The human race is a *sad* creation, and I trust the other planets are better organised and that we may get there hereafter.... Your devoted Uncle,

Leopold R.

Lord John Russell to Queen Victoria.

Downing Street, *23rd February 1848.*

Lord John Russell presents his humble duty to your Majesty, and will have the honour of waiting upon your Majesty at three o'clock to-morrow.

Lord Normanby's letters from Paris give a little information.[6]

There has been some fighting in the streets, and some apprehension for the night. But it does not appear probable that any serious danger will be incurred, with the troops in such force in Paris.

Hereafter there may be a serious struggle between the Government of the King, and the Republicans. But in that case such men as M. Odilon Barrot will shrink from the contest.

The King of the Belgians to Queen Victoria.

Laeken, *26th February 1848.*

My dearest Victoria,—I am very unwell in consequence of the *awful* events at Paris. How will this end? Poor Louise is in a state of despair which is pitiful to behold. What will soon become of us God alone knows; great efforts will be made to revolutionise this country; as there are poor and wicked people in all countries it may succeed.

Against France we, of course, have a right to claim protection from England and the other Powers. I can write no more. God bless you. Ever your devoted Uncle,

Leopold R.

The Queen of the Belgians to Queen Victoria.

Brussels, *27th February 1848.*

My dearly beloved Victoria,—I understand by an account arrived this morning, and which seems to be correct, that my unfortunate parents arrived in England before yesterday evening: but I don't know *where* they are. (I don't know anything of them since the 23rd, evening!!!) But you will surely know, and kindly forward the letter to my poor mother. I have just received your kind letter of the 25th, but I am unable to say more to-day. You will easily conceive my agony and anguish. What an *unbelievable* clap of thunder! I know still nothing of what Nemours and Montpensier are become. I rely on your interest and sympathy, and remain as ever, yours most devotedly,

Louise.

I hear this moment with an *extreme relief* that my parents were to arrive yesterday at London, and thank God from the bottom of my heart for their safety! In my agony I did not wish for anything else.

The King of Prussia to Queen Victoria.

[Translation.]

27th February 1848.

Most gracious Queen and Sister,—Even at this midnight hour of the day, on the evening of which the awful news from Paris has arrived, I venture to address these lines to your Majesty. God has permitted events which decisively threaten the peace of Europe.

It is an attempt to "spread the principles of the Revolution by *every* means throughout the whole of Europe." This programme binds together both these individuals and their parties. The consequences for the peace of the world are *clear* and *certain*. If the revolutionary party carries out its programme, "The sovereignty of the people," my minor crown will be broken, no less certainly than the mighty crowns of your Majesty, and a fearful scourge will be laid upon the nations; a century [will follow] of rebellion, of lawlessness, and of godlessness. The late King did not dare to write "by the Grace of God." *We*, however, call ourselves King "by the Grace of God," because it is true. Well, then, most gracious Queen, let us now show to men, to the peoples threatened with disruption and nameless misery, both *that* we understand our sacred office and *how* we understand it. God has placed in your Majesty's hands, in the hands of the two Emperors, in those of the German Federation, and in mine, a power, which, if it now acts in union and harmony, with reliance on Heaven, is able humanly speaking, to enforce, with certainty, the maintenance of the peace of the world. This power is *not that of arms*, for these, more than ever, must only afford the *ultima ratio*.

The power I mean is "the power of united speech." In the year 1830 the use of this immeasurable power was criminally neglected. But now I think the danger is much more pressing than it was then. This power is divided among *us* in equal portions. I possess the smallest portion of it, and your Majesty has by far the greatest share. That share is so great that your Majesty, by your powerful word, might alone carry out the task. But the certainty of victory lies, subject to the Divine blessing, solely in our utterance being united. This must be our message to France; "that all of us are cordial well-wishers to France; we do not grudge her all possible welfare and glory; we mean never to encroach on it, and we will stand by the new Government as by the old, *foi de gentils-hommes*. But the first breach of the peace, be it with reference to Italy, Belgium, or Germany would be, undoubtedly and at the same time, a breach with 'all of us,' and we should, with all the power that God has given us, let France feel by *sea* and by *land*, as in the years '13, '14, and '15, what our union may mean."

Now I bless Providence for having placed Lord Palmerston at the head of your Foreign Office, and keeping him there at this very moment. During the last quarter of the past year I could not always cordially agree with him. His genuine British disposition will honour this open confession. All the more frankly may I now express the hopes which rise in me, from the very fact of *his* holding that office at the present moment; for a more active, more vivid, more energetic Minister of foreign affairs, a man that would more indefatigably pursue great aims, your Majesty could probably never have. If at this grave hour he sets himself to proclaim that our forces are united; if he himself utters his message as befits St George, he will earn the blessing of millions, and the blessing of God and of the world will rest on your Majesty's sacred head. That I am your Majesty's and *Old England's* most faithful and most devoted brother and companion, you are aware, and I mean to prove it. On both, knees I adjure you, use, for the welfare of Europe, "*Engellands England*."

With these words I fall at your Majesty's feet, most gracious Queen, and remain your Majesty's most faithfully devoted, most attached Servant and good Brother,

Frederic William.

P. S.—The Prince I embrace. He surely feels with me, and justly appraises my endeavours.

Post scriptum, 28th, in the evening.

I venture to open my letter again, for this day has brought us news from France, which one can only call *horrible*. According to what we hear, there is no longer left a King in France. A regency, a government, and the most complete anarchy has ensued, under the name of the Republic—a condition of things in which, at first, there will be no possibility of communicating with the people, infuriated with crime. In case a Government should evolve itself out of this chaos, I conscientiously hold that the "united word" of the great Powers, such as I have indicated in the preceding pages, should be made known, *without any modification, to the new holders of power.* Your Majesty's gracious friendship will certainly not take amiss this addition to my letter, though it be not conformable to strict etiquette.

The fate of the poor old King, of the Duchess of Orleans, of the whole honourable and amiable family, cuts me to the heart, for up to this time we do not know what has become of any of them. We owe Louis Philippe eighteen happy years of peace. No noble heart must forget that. And yet—who would not recognise the avenging hand of the King of kings in all this?

I kiss your Majesty's hands.

The Queen of the Belgians to Queen Victoria.

Brussels, *28th February 1848.*

My dearly beloved Victoria,—*What a misfortune! What* an *awful, overwhelming, unexpected* and *inexplicable catastrophe. Is it possible* that we should witness *such events,* and that *this* should be the end of nearly eighteen years of courageous and successful efforts to maintain order, peace, and make France happy, what *she was*? I have heard, I read hourly, *what has happened: I cannot believe it yet*; but if *my beloved parents* and the remainder of the family are at least *safe* I won't mind the rest. In the hours of agony we have gone through I asked God *only* to spare *the lives,* and I ask still *nothing else*: but we don't know

157

them yet *all* saved, and till I have heard of my unfortunate parents, of my unhappy brothers far away, of all those for whom I would lay my life at any moment and whose danger I could not even share or alleviate, I cannot exist.

I was *sure*, my beloved Victoria, of all *you* would *feel for us* when you would hear of these awful events. I received yesterday your two kind, warm, sympathising letters of the 25th and 26th, and thank you with *all my heart* for them, and for yours and Albert's share and sympathy.

Our anguish has been *undescribable*. We have been *thirty-six hours without any news*, not knowing even if my parents and the family were still alive or not, and what had been their fate. Death is not worse than what we endured during these horrible hours. We don't know yet what to think, what to believe, I would almost say, what to wish; we are *stunned* and *crushed* by the awful blow. What has happened is *unaccountable, incomprehensible*; it appears to us like a *fearful* dream. Alas! I fear my dear beloved father was led away by his *extreme courage*; by that same courage which had made his success and a part of his strength; for it is strange to say that even those that deplored most his resolution never to yield on certain things gave him credit for it. The exaggeration of the system of peace and resistance, or rather *immobility*, lost him, as that of war lost Napoleon. Had he shunned less war *on all occasions*, and granted in time some trifling reforms, he would have satisfied public opinion, and would probably be still where he was *only eight days ago*, strong, beloved, and respected! Guizot's accession has been *as fatal* as his fall, and is perhaps the *first cause* of our ruin, though my father cannot be blamed for having kept him in office, as he had the majority in the Chamber, and an overwhelming one. *Constitutionally*, he could not have been turned out, and it was *impossible to foresee* that when all was quiet, the country prosperous and happy, the laws and liberty respected, the Government strong, a *Revolution*—and *such a Revolution*—would be brought on by a few imprudent words, and the resistance (lamentable as it was) to a manifestation which, in fact, the Government had a right to prevent. *It was the Almighty's will: we must submit.* He had decreed our loss the day He removed my beloved brother[7] from this world. Had he lived still, all this would have turned otherwise. It has been also an immense misfortune that Joinville and Aumale were both away. They were both popular (which poor dear *never-to-be-sufficiently-respected* Nemours was *not*), energetic, courageous, and capable of turning chance in our favour. Oh! *how I long* to know what is become of them! I cannot live till then, and the thought of my unfortunate parents *annihilates* me! Poor dear Joinville had foreseen and foretold almost all that has happened, and it was the idea of the crisis he apprehended which made him so unhappy to go. He repeated it to me several times six weeks ago. Alas! *nobody* would believe him, and who *could believe* that in *a day*, almost without struggle, *all would be over*, and the past, the present, the future carried away on an unaccountable storm! *God's will be done!* He was at least *merciful* to my dear Aunt, and I hope He will preserve all those dear to me!

Here everything is quiet: the horror general, and the best feeling and spirit prevailing. There is still now nothing to fear: but if *a republic really established* itself in France, it is impossible to tell what may happen. For this reason your Uncle thinks it right that we should remove to some place of safety what we have of precious. If you permit I will avail myself of the various messengers that are going now to send *under your care* several boxes, which you will kindly send to Claremont to Moor, to keep with those your Uncle already sent. They contain your Uncle's letters and those of my parents—the treasure I most value in the world.

29th.—My dearly beloved Victoria,—This was written yesterday, in a moment of comparative quiet, when I thought my parents at least safe and in security in England. Albert's letter to your Uncle of the 27th, which arrived yesterday evening, says they were *not arrived yet*, and I am again in the most horrible agony. I had also yesterday evening details of their flight (*my father flying!!!*) by Madame de Murat, Victoire's lady, who has gone to England, which quite distracted me. Thank God that Nemours and Clém at least *are safe!* I am quite unable to say more, and I hope the Duchess and Alexandrine will excuse me if I don't write to them. Truly, I *can't.* I thank you only once more, my beloved Victoria, *for all your kindness* and *interest* for my unfortunate family, and trust all the anxiety you feel for us won't hurt you. God bless you ever, with all those dear to you. Believe me always, my beloved Victoria, yours most devotedly,

Louise.

I send you no letter for my mother in the present uncertainty.

Lord John Russell to Queen Victoria.

Chesham Place, *29th February 1848.*

Lord John Russell presents his humble duty to your Majesty, and has the honour to transmit a short note from Lord Normanby, which is very satisfactory.

Lord John Russell declared last night that your Majesty would not interfere in the internal affairs of France. But in repeating this declaration, in answer to Mr Cobden, he added that the sacred duties of hospitality would be, as in all times, performed towards persons of all opinions. Both declarations were generally cheered. In extending this hospitality to members of the Royal Family of France, it is only to be observed that no encouragement should be given by your Majesty to any notion that your Majesty would assist them to recover the Crown. In this light it is desirable that no *Prince* of the House of Orleans should inhabit one of your Majesty's palaces in or near London.

Queen Victoria to Viscount Palmerston.

(*Undated.*)[8]

The Queen has perused the enclosed despatches and the proposed Minutes of a draft to Lord Normanby with Lord John Russell's remarks. She approves generally of the Minutes, but would like that amongst the laudable intentions of the new French Government, *that* of keeping *inviolate* the European Treaties should be brought in in some way. In the paper No. 2, the expression "*most cordial friendship*" strikes the Queen as rather too strong. We have just had sad experience of *cordial* understandings. "Friendly relations" might do better or the whole sentence might run thus: "that not peace only but cordial friendship with France *had been at all times* [instead of "is one of the," etc.] one of the first wishes of the British Government, and that this *will* remain," etc., etc., etc.

Queen Victoria to the King of the Belgians.

Buckingham Palace, *1st March 1848.*

My dearest Uncle,—Every hour seems to bring fresh news and events. Victoire and her children and Montpensier are at Jersey, and are expected to arrive to-morrow. About the King and Queen, we still know nothing, but we have some clue, and think *he may be* somewhere on the coast, or even *in* England. We do everything we can for the poor dear Family, who are indeed most dreadfully to be pitied; but you will naturally understand that we cannot *make cause commune* with them and cannot take a hostile position opposite to the new state of things in France; we leave them alone, but if a Government which has the approbation of the country be formed, we shall feel it necessary to recognise it, in order to pin them down to maintain peace and the existing Treaties, which is of great importance. It will not be pleasant for us to do this, but the public good and the peace of Europe go before one's feelings. God knows what *one feels* towards the French. I trust, dear Uncle, that you will maintain the fine and independent position you are now in, which is so gratifying to us, and I am sure you will feel that much as we all must sympathise with our poor French relations, you should not for that quarrel with the existing state of things, which however is very uncertain. There were fresh reports of great confusion at Paris, which is sure to happen. All our poor relations have gone through is worthy only of a *dreadful* romance, and poor Clém behaves beautifully, courageously, and calmly, and is full of resignation; but she can get no sleep, poor thing—and hears the horrid cries and sees those *fiend-like faces* before her! The children are very happy with ours, but very unmanageable. I saw the Duchesse de Montpensier to-day.

Now, with every wish for *all* going on well, believe me ever, your devoted Niece,

Victoria R.

Mr Featherstonhaugh[9] to Viscount Palmerston.

Havre, *3rd March 1848.*

My dear Lord Palmerston,—It was a hair-trigger affair altogether, but thanks be to God everything has gone off admirably. I was obliged to abandon the plan of trusting the King in a fishing-boat from Trouville. The weather was very stormy; had he attempted to find the steamer, he might have failed, for the sea was in a furious state and the wind ahead. There was also the danger of the fishing-boat being lost, a contingency the very idea of which made me miserable.

I therefore abandoned the plan altogether, and after much and careful reflection determined to execute one more within my control, and the boldness of which, though trying to the nerves, was its very essence for success. It was to bring the King and Queen into Havre itself before anybody could suspect such a dangerous intention, and have everything ready for their embarkation to a minute. To carry out the plan, I wanted vigilant, intelligent, and firm agents, and I found them as it turned out. It was known to me that the lower classes suspected it was M. Guizot concealed at Trouville, and as some sinister occurrence might reasonably be expected there, I sent a faithful person into Calvados. It was high time. The mob had assembled at the place where the King was, who had to slip out at the back door and walk two leagues on foot. At length he reached a small cottage belonging to a gardener at Honfleur, where the Queen was. This was half-past six o'clock A.M. yesterday. My agent saw the King and Queen, who, after some conversation, sent him back with this message, that they "would wait where they were until they again heard from me, and would carry out my final arrangements with exactitude, as far as it depended upon them." I now instructed Captain Paul to be ready at half-past seven P.M., when it would be dark, to have his water hot, ready to get up steam; to have only a rope moored to the quay with an anchor astern; to expect me with a party a little before eight P.M., and as soon as I had got on board with my party and told him to push off, he was to let me go on shore, cut his rope and cable, get into the middle of the Basin, up with his steam and jib and push for England. Not a word was to be spoken on board.

To get the King here from Honfleur the following method was adopted: M. Bresson, a loyal and intelligent officer in the French Navy and well known to the King, and Mr Jones, my Vice-Consul and principal Clerk, went in the steam ferry-boat a quarter before five P.M. to Honfleur. From the landing-place it is three-quarters of a mile to the place where the King and Queen were concealed. The ferry-boat was to leave Honfleur for Havre a quarter before seven o'clock. I had given M. Bresson a passport for Mr and Mrs Smith, and with this passport the King was to walk to the landing-place, where he was to be met by my Vice-Consul and be governed by him.

If the *gens d'armes* disputed his passport Mr Jones was to vouch for its regularity, and say that he was sent by me to conduct Mr Smith to Havre, who was my Uncle. M. Bresson was to follow with the Queen, and the rest of the suite were to come to the ferry-boat one after another, but none of the party were to know each other. The ferry-boat was to arrive in Havre about half-past seven, and I was to do the rest. A white pocket-handkerchief was to be twice exhibited as a signal that all was right so far. The difficulty of the *gens d'armes* being infinitely more to be provided against and apprehended here, I first confidentially communicated to the greatest gossips in the town that I had seen a written statement from an official person that the King had reached England in a fishing-boat from the neighbourhood of Tréport, and then got some persons whom I could rely upon, sons of my tradesmen here who are in the National Guard, to be near the steamer that was to receive the King, to give me their assistance if it should be necessary, on account of the turbulence of the crowd, to embark some friends of mine who were going to England. And if an extraordinary number of *gens d'armes* were stationed at the steamer, and they hesitated about letting my Uncle go on board, then about one hundred yards off I had two persons who were to pretend a quarrel and a fight, to which I knew the *gens d'armes* would all go as well as the crowd. In the meantime I hoped that as Captain Paul made no noise with his steam that the crowd would not assemble, and that we might find no *gens d'armes*. The anxiously expected moment at length arrived. The ferry-boat steamer came to the quay; it was almost dark, but I saw the white pocket-handkerchief. There was a great number of passengers, which favoured the debarkation. When half of them were out, the trembling Queen came up the ladder. I took her hand, told her it was me, and M. Bresson walked with her towards our steamer. At last came the King, disguised, his whiskers shaved off, a sort of casquette on his head, and a coarse overcoat, and immense goggles over his eyes. Not being able to see well, he stumbled, when I advanced, took his hand and said, "Ah, dear Uncle, I am delighted to see you." Upon which he answered, "My dear George, I am glad you are here." The English about me now opened the crowd for their Consul, and I moved off to a quiet and shaded part of the quay. But my dear Uncle talked so loud and so much that I had the greatest difficulty to make him keep silence. At length we reached the steamer; it was like a clock-work movement. The crowd was again opened for me. I conducted the King to a state-room below, gave him some information, and having personally ascertained that the Queen was in her cabin, and being very much touched with her tears and her grateful acknowledgments, I respectfully took my leave, gave the Captain the word to cut loose, and scrambled ashore. In twenty minutes the steamer was outside, steaming away for England. I drove down to the jetty, and had that last satisfaction of seeing her beyond all possibility of recall, and then drove home. Much has been said this morning about the mysterious departure of Captain Paul, and I have been obliged to confess that the gentleman I was seen conducting on board was a brother of the King of Naples, who was immensely frightened without cause, and that I had engaged the steamer for him and his family. Many think, however, that it was the King, but then again that could not be if he crossed over from Tréport in a fishing-boat. We have got everybody completely mystified, and there are only four persons in the secret, who will all remain in the same story.

I have scribbled, amidst the most hurried engagements, this little narrative, believing that it would interest your Lordship. It has the interest of romance and the support of truth. I have the honour to be, etc.

G. W. Featherstonhaugh.

Information has just reached me that one hour after the King and Queen left their hiding-place last night, and just when I was embarking them, an officer and three *gens d'armes* came to the place to arrest him. They were sent by the new Republican *Préfet*. It appears that the man who gave him refuge had confessed who he was as soon as the King had left Trouville, and had betrayed the King's hiding-place at Honfleur. What an escape! Your Lordship will see a paragraph in the enclosed newspaper not altogether false. We in the secret know nothing about Louis Philippe; we know something about the Count of Syracuse and something about Mr William Smith. If it leaks out, it must come from England. Here no one has any proof. In the meantime almost everybody here is delighted to think that he may have escaped.

Viscount Palmerston to Queen Victoria.

Carlton Gardens, *3rd March 1848.*

(*3 P.M.*)

Viscount Palmerston presents his humble duty to your Majesty, and begs to state that General Dumas has just been with him to announce that the King and Queen of the French landed this morning at Newhaven, having been brought over in the Steam Packet Express, in which they embarked at Havre yesterday evening about eight o'clock.

General Dumas says that till the morning of their arrival at Dreux the King and the Queen imagined that the Comte de Paris had succeeded to the Throne, and that the Duchess of Orleans had been declared Regent; that when they heard that a Republic and a Provisional Government had been declared they thought it unsafe to remain at Dreux; and that they then separated in order to go by different roads to Honfleur, where they were to meet at a small house belonging to a friend of General Dumas. At that house they remained for some days, until Mr Featherstonhaugh opened a communication with them. The King then removed to Trouville in order to embark from thence in a manner which Mr Featherstonhaugh had arranged, and he remained there two or three days for that purpose; but the weather was too stormy, and prevented his departure. In the meanwhile the people of Trouville found out who he was, and their demonstrations of attachment became inconvenient. He therefore returned to Honfleur, and the arrangements were altered. Yesterday evening at seven o'clock the King, the Queen, and General Dumas came to the ferry-boat which plies between Honfleur and Havre, and were met by the Vice-Consul, who treated the King as uncle of the Consul. On landing at Havre the King walked straight down to the Express Packet, which was lying ready; the Queen went separately, and after making a slight round through the streets of Havre embarked also; the Packet then immediately started, and went into Newhaven in preference to any other port, because no Packets start from thence for the French coast. General Dumas says that the whole party were unprovided with anything but the clothes they wore, and he was going to the King's banker to provide funds to enable him to come to town, and said that the King begged him to apologise for his not having at once written to your Majesty to thank your Majesty for the great interest which your Majesty has taken in his safety, and for the assistance, which he has received for his escape, but that he would do so this evening.

General Dumas said that the King's present intention is to remain in England in the strictest *incognito*, and that he and the Queen will assume the title of Count and Countess of Neuilly.

Viscount Palmerston explained to General Dumas that your Majesty has made arrangements for the King's reception at Claremont, and that your Majesty intended to send down an officer of your Majesty's Household to communicate with the King.

General Dumas said that the King would most gratefully avail himself of the arrangement as to Claremont, but that under all circumstances, and as the King wished to remain in entire privacy, he thought it would be better that no person from your Majesty's Household should go down to the King at Newhaven, and that he was sure the King would rather find his own way from the railway station at London Bridge to Claremont than attract attention by being met at the station by any of your Majesty's carriages.

165

The King would remain to-night at Newhaven, and would come up to-morrow morning. General Dumas said that the King and the Queen had gone through much personal fatigue and mental anxiety, but are both well in health. The General was going to Count Jarnac before he returned to Newhaven.

The King of the French to Queen Victoria.

Newhaven, Sussex, *3ème Mars 1848.*

Madame,—Après avoir rendu grâces à Dieu, mon premier devoir est d'offrir à votre Majesté l'hommage de ma reconnaissance pour la généreuse assistance qu'elle nous a donnée, à moi et à tous les miens et que la Providence vient de couvrir d'un succès complet, puisque j'apprends qu'ils sont tous à présent sur la terre hospitalière de l'Angleterre.

Ce n'est plus, Madame, que *le Comte de Neuilly* qui, se rappelant vos anciennes bontés, vient chercher sous ses auspices, un asyle et une retraite paisible et aussi éloignée de tout rapport politique que celle dont il y a joui dans d'autres temps, et dont il a toujours précieusement conservé le souvenir.

On me presse tellement pour ne pas manquer le train qui emportera ma lettre que j'ai à peine le temps de prier votre Majesté d'être mon interprète auprès du Prince votre auguste Époux.

Ma femme, accablée de fatigue par la vie que nous venons de mener depuis dix jours! écrira un peu plus tard à votre Majesté. Tout ce qu'elle a pu faire, est de tracer quelques mots pour notre bien aimée Louise que je recommande à votre bonté. On me presse encore, Madame, je ne puis que me souscrire avec mon vieil attachement pour vous, de votre Majesté, très affectionné,

Louis Philippe.

The Queen of the French to Queen Victoria.

Newhaven, *3ème Mars 1848.*

Madame,—A peine arrivée dans cette contrée hospitalière après 9 jours d'une cruelle agonie, mon premier sentiment, après avoir béni la Divine Providence, c'est de remercier, du fond de mon cœur, votre Majesté, pour les facilités qu'elle a bien voulu nous donner pour venir dans ce pays terminer nos vieux jours dans la tranquillité et l'oubli. Une vive inquiétude me tourmente, c'est d'apprendre le sort de mes enfants chéris desquels nous avons dû nous séparer; j'ai la confiance qu'ils auront trouvé aussi un appui dans le cœur généreux de votre Majesté, et qu'ils auront été également sauvés comme leur admirable Père, mon premier trésor. Que Dieu vous bénisse, Madame, ainsi que le Prince Albert et vos enfants, et vous préserve de malheurs pareils aux nôtres, c'est le vœu le plus sincère de celle qui se dit, Madame, de votre Majesté, la toute dévouée,

Marie Amélie.

Lord John Russell to Queen Victoria.

House of Commons, *3rd March 1848*.

Lord John Russell presents his humble duty to your Majesty: he has read with deep interest the affecting letter of the fallen King.

After the vicissitudes of a long life, it may be no irremediable calamity if a Prince of great powers of mind and warm domestic affections is permitted by Providence to end his days in peace and tranquillity.

Of course all enmity to his projects as a King ceases with his deposition.

M. Guizot came to London from Dover at half-past six.

Queen Victoria to the King of the French.

Palais de Buckingham, *3ème Mars 1848*.

Sire et mon cher Frère,—C'était une consolation bien vive pour moi de recevoir la bonne lettre de votre Majesté qui m'a bien touchée. Nous avons tous été dans de vives inquiétudes pour vous, pour la Reine et toute la famille, et nous remercions la Providence pour que vous soyez arrivés en sûreté sur le sol d'Angleterre, et nous sommes bien heureux de savoir que vous êtes ici loin de tous ces dangers qui vous ont récemment menacés. Votre Majesté croira combien ces derniers affreux événements si inattendus nous ont péniblement agités. Il nous tarde de savoir que vos santés n'ont pas été altérées par ces derniers jours d'inquiétude et de fatigue. Albert me charge d'offrir les hommages à votre Majesté, et je vous prie de déposer les nôtres aux pieds de la Reine, à qui je compte répondre demain. Je me dis, Sire et mon bon Frère, de votre Majesté, la bien affectionnée Sœur,

Victoria R.

Queen Victoria to the Queen of the French.

Palais de Buckingham, *4ème Mars 1848*.

Madame,—Votre Majesté aura excusé que je ne vous ai pas de suite remercié de votre bonne et aimable lettre de hier. C'est des fonds de mon cœur que je me réjouis de vous savoir en sûreté à Claremont avec le Roi. Mes pensées étaient auprès de votre Majesté pendant tous ces affreux jours, et je frémis en pensant à tout ce que vous avez souffert de corps et d'âme.

Albert sera le Porteur de ces lignes; j'aurais été si heureuse de l'accompagner pour vous voir, mais je n'ose plus quitter Londres.

Avec l'expression de l'affection et de l'estime, je me dis toujours, Madame, de votre Majesté, la bien affectionnée Sœur,

Victoria R.

Viscount Palmerston to Queen Victoria.

Carlton Gardens, *5th March 1848*.

Viscount Palmerston presents his humble duty to your Majesty, and cannot see that there could be any objection to the King and Queen of the French coming to town to visit your Majesty, and indeed, on the contrary, it would seem under all the circumstances of the case natural that they should be anxious to see your Majesty, and that your Majesty should be desirous of receiving them.

Viscount Palmerston was sure that your Majesty would read with interest Mr Featherstonhaugh's account of the manner in which he managed the escape of the King and Queen of the French. It is like one of Walter Scott's best tales, and the arrangements and the execution of them do great credit to Mr Featherstonhaugh, who will be highly gratified to learn, as Viscount Palmerston proposes to inform him, that your Majesty has approved his conduct. Mr Featherstonhaugh has also probably rendered a good service to the Provisional Government, who would have been much embarrassed if their Commissioner had arrested the King and Queen.

Queen Victoria to the King of the Belgians.

Buckingham Palace, *7th March 1848*.

My dearest Uncle,—Albert has written to you so constantly that I have little to add; he just tells me this is not quite true. However, there is nothing very new except that we have seen the King and Queen;

Albert went down to Claremont to see them on Saturday, and yesterday they came here with Montpensier. They both look very *abattus*,
and the poor Queen cried much in thinking of what she had gone
through—and what dangers the King had incurred; in short, humbled
poor people they looked. Dearest Vic I saw on Sunday; *she* has also
gone through much, and is so dear and good and gentle. She looked
wonderfully well *considering*. They are still *very* much in want of
means, and live on a very reduced scale.

Queen Victoria to the King of the Belgians.

Buckingham Palace, *11th March 1848.*

My dearest Uncle,—I profit by the departure of Andrews to write
to you a few lines, and to wish you joy of the continued satisfactory
behaviour of my friends, the good Belgians; fervently do I hope and
really trust all will go on well; but what an extraordinary state of
things everywhere! *"Je ne sais plus où je suis,"* and I fancy really that
we have gone back into the *old* century. But I also feel one must not be
nervous or alarmed at these moments, but be of good cheer, and mus-
ter up courage to meet all the difficulties.

Our little riots are mere nothing, and the feeling here is good....
What is *your* opinion as to the late events at Paris? Do you not think
the King ought to have retired to Vincenness or somewhere else a day
or two before, and put himself at the head of the army? Ought not
Montpensier at least to have gone to Vincennes? I know Clém even
thinks this—as also that *one* ought to have foreseen, and ought to have
managed things better. Certainly at the *very last*, if they had not gone,
they would all have been massacred; and *I* think they were quite right,
and in short could not avoid going as quickly as they could; but there
is an impression they *fled* too quickly. Still the recollection of Louis
XVI.... is enough to justify all, and everybody will admit that; but the
Princes, they think, ought to have remained. *What* do *you* think of all
this? I think the blunders were *all* on the last three or four days—and
on the last day, but were no longer to be avoided at last; there seemed
a *fatality*, and *all* was lost. Poor Nemours did his best till he could *no
longer* get to the troops. People here also abuse him for letting Victoire
go alone—but he *remained* to do his *duty*; a little more *empressement*
on her arrival here I would have wished. Albert told you all about the
Montpensiers' journey. It would do the King irreparable mischief if
they went now to Spain; the feeling of anger would all return. Poor
people! they are all in a sad state of *want* at present.

I must conclude. Hoping to hear from you, and to have your opinion.

Ever your devoted Niece,

Victoria R.

Queen Victoria to Viscount Melbourne.

Buckingham Palace, *15th March 1848.*

The Queen cannot let this day pass without offering Lord Melbourne hers and the Prince's best wishes for many happy returns of it in health and strength.

Lord Melbourne will agree with the Queen that the last three weeks have brought back the times of the last century, and we are in the midst of troubles abroad. The Revolution in France is a sad and alarming thing.... The poor King and his Government made many mistakes within the last two years, and were obstinate and totally blind at the last till flight was inevitable. But for *sixteen* years he did a great deal to maintain peace, and made France prosperous, which should *not* be forgotten.... Lord Melbourne's kind heart will grieve to think of the *real want* the poor King and Queen are in, their dinner-table containing barely enough to eat. And the poor Nemours hardly know which way to turn. If the private property be not restored God only knows what is to become of these distinguished young Princes and their little children. What will be their *avenir*? It breaks one's heart to think of it, and the Queen, being so nearly related to them and knowing them all, feels it very much. Surely the poor old King is sufficiently punished for his faults. Lord Beauvale will surely be shocked at the complete ruin of the family. Has he seen or heard from his old friend Madame de Montjoye, who is here with the Queen of the French? The poor dear Queen of the Belgians is quite broken-hearted, but, thank God, Belgium goes on admirably. In Germany also there are everywhere disturbances, but the good Germans are at bottom very loyal....

The state of Paris is very gloomy; the rabble armed—keeping the Government in awe—failures in all directions, and nothing but ruin and misery. This is too gloomy a letter for a birthday, and the Queen must apologise for it. The Prince wishes to be kindly remembered to Lord Melbourne.

The Emperor of Russia to Queen Victoria.

St. Petersburg, le 22 Mars – 3 Avril, 1848

Madame ma Sœur,—Veuillez me permettre, Madame, d'offrir à votre Majesté mes sincères félicitations de son heureuse délivrance.[10] Puisse le bon Dieu conserver votre Majesté et toute son auguste famille, c'est mon vœu de tous les jours. Plus que jamais, Madame, au milieu des désastres qui renversent l'ordre social, l'on éprouve le besoin de relier les liens d'amitié que l'on a été heureux de former dans de meilleurs temps; ceux-là au moins nous restent, car ils sont hors de la portée des hommes, et je suis fier et heureux de ce que votre noble cœur me comprendra. En jettant les yeux sur ce qui se passe, peut-être votre Majesté accordera-t-elle un souvenir à ce que j'eus l'honneur de lui prédire, assis à table près d'elle: depuis, 4 années à peine se sont écoulées, et que reste-t-il encore debout en Europe? La Grande-Bretagne et la Russie!

Ne serait-il pas naturel d'en conclure que notre union intime est appelée peut-être à sauver le monde? Excusez, Madame, cet épanchement d'un cœur qui vous est dévoué et qui a pris l'habitude de souvenir à vous.

J'ose avec une entière confiance compter sur l'amitié de votre Majesté, et la prie de recevoir l'assurance de l'inviolable attachement avec lequel je suis, Madame, de votre Majesté, le tout dévoué et fidèle bon Frère et Ami,

Nicolas.

Veuillez, Madame, me rappeler au souvenir de son Altesse Royale Monsieur le Prince Albert.

The King of the Belgians to Queen Victoria.

Brussels, *25th March 1848.*

My dearest Victoria,—... England seems quiet, and even the attempt in Ireland seems to have passed over. But Germany is in an awful state, beyond what I ever should have thought possible in that country, and with such a good nation. For years, however, all sorts of people had been stirring them up, and half measures, seeming dishonest, of the Sovereigns have done harm. Curious enough that I, who in fact was desirous of retiring from politics, should be on the Continent the only Sovereign who stood the storm, though I am at ten hours' distance from Paris. I trust we shall be able to go on with our money matters to enable us to keep up; our working classes are at this moment what occupies us most, and much has been done, and our Banks, which were much threatened, are now safe.

We work hard, and with these few days I suffered a little, but I am better to-day. Louise is tolerably well; the poor children are attentive and amiable. Poor things! *their existence* is a good deal on the cards, and fortunes, private and public, are in equal danger.

Now I will leave you that you should not be tired. Ever, my beloved child, your devoted Uncle,

Leopold R.

Queen Victoria to the King of the Belgians.

Buckingham Palace, *4th April 1848.*

My dearest Uncle,—I have to thank you for three most kind letters, of the 18th and 25th March, and of the 1st. Thank God, I am *particularly strong* and *well* in *every possible respect*, which is a blessing in these *awful, sad, heart-breaking* times. From the first I heard all that passed, and my only thoughts and talk were—Politics; but I never was calmer and quieter or less nervous. *Great* events make me quiet and calm, and little trifles fidget me and irritate my nerves. But *I feel* grown old and serious, and the future is very dark. God, however, will come to help and protect us, and we must keep up our spirits. *Germany* makes me so sad; on the other hand, Belgium is a real pride and happiness.

We saw your poor father and mother-in-law with the Nemours, Joinville, and Aumale yesterday. Still a dream to see them *thus, here!* They are well in health, and the young people's conduct most praiseworthy; really the three Princesses are astonishing, and a beautiful lesson to every one. They are so much admired and respected for it. My beloved Vic, with her lovely face, is perfection, and so cheerful. She often comes to see me, and this is a great pleasure to me, if only it was not caused by such misfortunes!

Now good-bye. With fervent prayers for the continuation of your present most flourishing position, ever your devoted Niece,

Victoria R.

Lord John Russell to the Prince Albert.

Chesham Place, *9th April 1848.*

Sir,—The Cabinet have had the assistance of the Duke of Wellington in framing their plans for to-morrow.

Colonel Rowan[11] advised that the procession should be formed, and allowed to come as far as the bridge they may choose to pass, and should there be stopped. He thinks this is the only way to avoid a fight. If, however, the Chartists fire and draw their swords and use their daggers, the Military are to be called out.

I have no doubt of their easy triumph over a London mob.

But any loss of life will cause a deep and rankling resentment. I trust, for this and every reason, that all may pass off quietly. I have the honour to be, your Royal Highness's most obedient Servant,

J. Russell.

"THE COUSINS."

H.M. QUEEN VICTORIA AND THE DUCHESS OF NEMOURS

From the picture by F. Winterhalter at Buckingham Palace

The Prince Albert to Lord John Russell.

Osborne, *10th April 1848.*

My dear Lord John,—To-day the strength of the Chartists and all evil-disposed people in the country will be brought to the test against the force of the law, the Government, and the good sense of the country. I don't feel doubtful for a moment who will be found the stronger, but should be exceedingly mortified if anything like a commotion was to take place, as it would shake *that* confidence which the whole of Europe reposes in our stability at this moment, and upon which will depend the prosperity of the country. I have enquired a good deal into the state of employment about London, and I find, to my great regret, that the number of workmen of all trades out of employment is *very* large, and that it has been increased by the reduction of all the works under Government, owing to the clamour for economy in the House of Commons. Several hundred workmen have been discharged at Westminster Palace; at Buckingham Palace much fewer hands are employed than are really wanted; the formation of Battersea Park has been suspended, etc., etc. Surely this is not the moment for the taxpayers to economise upon the working classes! And though I don't wish our Government to follow Louis Blanc in his system of *organisation du travail*,[12] I think the Government is bound to do what it can to help the working classes over the present moment of distress. It may do this consistently with real economy in its own works, whilst the reductions on the part of the Government are followed by all private individuals as a sign of the times. I have before this spoken to Lord Morpeth[13] upon this subject, but I wish to bring it specially under your consideration at the present moment. Ever yours truly,

Albert.

Lord John Russell to Queen Victoria.

Downing Street, *10th April 1848.*

(*2 p.m.*)

Lord John Russell presents his humble duty to your Majesty, and has the honour to state that the Kennington Common Meeting has proved a complete failure.

About 12,000 or 15,000 persons met in good order. Feargus O'Connor, upon arriving upon the ground in a car, was ordered by Mr Mayne[14] to come and speak to him. He immediately left the car and came, looking pale and frightened, to Mr Mayne. Upon being told that the meeting would not be prevented, but that no procession would be allowed to pass the bridges, he expressed the utmost thanks, and begged to shake Mr Mayne by the hand. He then addressed the crowd, advising them to disperse, and after rebuking them for their folly he went off in a cab to the Home Office, where he repeated to Sir George Grey his thanks, his fears, and his assurances that the crowd should disperse quietly. Sir George Grey said he had done very rightly, but that the force at the bridges should not be diminished.

Mr F. O'Connor—"Not a man should be taken away. The Government have been quite right. I told the Convention that if they had been the Government they never would have allowed such a meeting."

The last account gave the numbers as about 5,000 rapidly dispersing.

The mob was in good humour, and any mischief that now takes place will be the act of individuals; but it is to be hoped the preparations made will daunt those wicked but not brave men.

The accounts from the country are good. Scotland is quiet. At Manchester, however, the Chartists are armed, and have bad designs.

A quiet termination of the present ferment will greatly raise us in foreign countries.

Lord John Russell trusts your Majesty has profited by the sea air.

Lord John Russell to Queen Victoria.

Chesham Place, *15th April 1848.*

Lord John Russell has a letter from Lord Clarendon to-day in better spirits, but somewhat fearing an outbreak in Dublin to-night. He speaks confidently of the disposition of the troops.

Lord John Russell cannot wonder that your Majesty has felt deeply the events of the last six weeks. The King of the French has brought upon his own family, upon France, and upon Europe a great calamity. A moderate and constitutional Government at home, coupled with an abstinence from ambitious projects for his family abroad, might have laid the foundation of permanent peace, order, and freedom in Europe. Selfishness and cunning have destroyed that which honesty and wisdom might have maintained. It is impossible not to pity the innocent victims of the misconduct of Louis Philippe. Still less can one refrain from regarding with dread the fearful state of Germany, of her princes, her nobles, and her tempest-tossed people.

The example of Great Britain, may, however, secure an interval of reflection for Europe. The next six months will be very trying, but they may end with better prospects than we can now behold. It was impossible that the exclusion of free speaking and writing which formed the essence of Prince Metternich's system could continue. It might have been reformed quietly; it has fallen with a crash which spreads ruin and death around.

Lady John is deeply grateful for the congratulations of your Majesty and the Prince.[15] She is going on well to-day.

Queen Victoria to Lord John Russell.

Osborne, *16th April 1848.*

The Queen has received Lord John Russell's letter. The state of Ireland is most alarming and most anxious; altogether, there is so much inflammable matter all around us that it makes one tremble. Still, the events of Monday must have a calming and salutary effect. Lord John Russell's remarks about Europe, and the unfortunate and calamitous policy of the Government of the poor King of the French are most true. But is he not even most to be pitied for being the cause of such misery? (Though perhaps he does not attribute it to himself), for, to see all his hopes thus destroyed, his pride humbled, his children—whom he loves dearly—ruined—is not this enough to make a man wretched? and indeed much to be pitied; for *he* cannot feel *he* could *not* have prevented all this. Still Guizot is more to blame; *he* was the responsible adviser of all this policy: he is *no* Bourbon, and he ought to have behaved differently. Had the poor King died in 1844 after he came here, and before that most unfortunate Spanish marriages question was started, he would have deservedly gone down to posterity as a great monarch. *Now*, what will be his name in history? His fate is a great *moral!*

With regard to Germany, Prince Metternich is the cause of half the misfortune. His advice was taken by almost all the sovereigns of that country, and it has kept them from doing in time what has now been torn from them with the loss of many rights which they need not have sacrificed. We heard yesterday that the Archduke John[16] had arrived at Frankfort. This is a wise measure, and may do much good and prevent much evil, as he is a popular and most distinguished prince....

Queen Victoria to Viscount Palmerston.

Osborne, *17th April 1848.*

The Queen not having heard anything from Lord Palmerston respecting foreign affairs for so long a time, and as he must be in constant communication with the Foreign Ministers in these most eventful and anxious times, writes to urge Lord Palmerston to keep her informed of what he hears, and of the views of the Government on the important questions before us.

She now only gets the Drafts when they are gone.

The acceptance of the mediation between Denmark and Holstein is too important an event not to have been first submitted to the Queen.

Viscount Palmerston to Queen Victoria.

Carlton Gardens, *18th April 1848.*

Viscount Palmerston presents his humble duty to your Majesty, and regrets much that he has not lately had an opportunity of giving your Majesty verbally such explanations as your Majesty might wish to receive with respect to the progress of foreign affairs, but Viscount Palmerston hopes to be able to get down to Broadlands for a few days on Saturday next, and he could easily from thence wait upon your Majesty on any morning and at any hour your Majesty might be pleased to appoint.

Although events of the greatest importance have been passing in rapid succession in almost every part of Europe, the position of your Majesty's Government has been one rather of observation than of action, it being desirable that England should keep herself as free as possible from unnecessary engagements and entanglements, in order that your Majesty may be at liberty to take such decisions as the state of things may from time to time appear to render most advisable.

Queen Victoria to the King of the Belgians.

Barton, *18th April 1848.*

Dearest Uncle,—Detained here by a heavy shower of rain, I begin my letter to you and thank you warmly for your dear and kind letter of the 15th, which I received yesterday.

Truly proud and delighted are we at the conduct of the Belgians,[17] and at their loyalty and affection for you and yours, which I am sure must be a reward for all that you have done these seventeen years. I must beg to say that you are wrong in supposing that no mention is made of what took place on the 9th in our papers; on the contrary, it has been *most gratifyingly* mentioned in the *Times*, *Chronicle*, *John Bull, etc. You* are held up as a pattern to the German Sovereigns, and the Belgians as a pattern to the German people.

In France, really things go on *dreadfully....* One does not like to attack those who are fallen, but the poor King, Louis Philippe, *has* brought much of this on by that ill-fated return to a *Bourbon Policy*. I always think he *ought not* to have abdicated; every one seems to think he *might* have stemmed the torrent *then* still. On the other hand, Joinville says it was sure to happen, for that the French want constant change, and were quite tired of the present Government. *Qu'en dites-vous?* How is poor, dear Louise? I hope her spirits are better.

Our weather is terribly rainy, though very fine between. We have got nightingales in the pleasure ground, and in the wood down near the sea. We are all extremely well, and expect the Prince of Prussia here to-day for two nights. Ever your devoted and attached Niece,

Victoria R.

Queen Victoria to Viscount Palmerston.

Osborne, *1st May 1848.*

The Queen has this morning received Lord Palmerston's letter.[18] She cannot see any reason for deviating from the established rules, and inviting to Court Frenchmen who are not recognised in their official capacity, and have no natural representatives to present them as private individuals. As an invitation cannot be claimed by them, the omission of it ought not to lead to any misrepresentation; whilst the contrary, under the fiction of their being private individuals, might lead to misconstruction and to most inconvenient precedents.

Queen Victoria to the King of the Belgians.

Buckingham Palace, *9th May 1848.*

My dearest Uncle,—Many thanks for your very kind letter of the 6th. How delightful it is to hear such good accounts of Belgium! If only dear Germany gets right and if all our interests (those of the smaller Sovereigns) are not sacrificed! I cannot say *how* it distresses and vexes me, and *comme je l'ai à cœur*. My good and dear Albert is much worried and works *very* hard....

I had a curious account of the opening of the *Assemblée* from Lady Normanby.[19] No *real* enthusiasm, dreadful confusion, and the Blouses taking part in everything, and stopping the Speakers if they did not please them. The opinion is that it cannot last.

I enclose another letter from Lady Normanby, with an account of the poor Tuileries, which is very curious and sad; but the respect shown for poor Chartres is very touching, and might interest poor dear Louise, if you think fit to show it her. But why show such hatred to poor Nemours and to the Queen? Montpensier's marriage may cause *his* unpopularity, possibly. I shall beg to have the letter back.

I must conclude, as we are going to pay a visit at Claremont this afternoon. Ever your truly devoted Child and Niece,

Victoria R.

Queen Victoria to the King of the Belgians.

Buckingham Palace, *16th May 1848.*

My dearest Uncle,—I have just heard the news of the extraordinary confusion at Paris, which must end in a *Blutbad.* Lamartine has quite lost all influence by yielding to and supporting Ledru Rollin![20] It seems inexplicable! In Germany, too, everything looks most anxious, and I *tremble* for the result of the Parliament at Frankfort.[21] I am *so* anxious for the fate of the poor smaller Sovereigns, which it would be infamous to sacrifice. I feel it *much* more than Albert, as it would break my heart to see Coburg *reduced.*

Many thanks for your kind and dear letter of the 13th. Thank God! that with you everything goes on so well. I will take care and let Lord Normanby know your kind expressions. The visit to old Claremont was a touching one, and it seemed an incomprehensible dream to see them all there. They bear up wonderfully. Nothing can be kinder than the Queen-Dowager's behaviour towards them all. The poor Duchess of Gloster is again in one of her nervous states, and gave us a dreadful fright at the Christening by quite forgetting where she was, and coming and kneeling at my feet in the midst of the service. Imagine our horror!

I must now conclude. The weather is beautiful, but too hot for me. Ever your devoted Niece,

Victoria R.

Queen Victoria to Viscount Palmerston.

(*No date.*)

The Queen has carefully perused the enclosed papers, and wishes to have a copy of Baron Hummelauer's[22] note sent to her to keep.

The basis laid down in it is quite inadmissible, and the Queen was struck by the light way in which the claims of the Dukes of Parma and Modena are spoken of (as disposed of by the events), whilst their position and that of Austria are in every respect identical.[23] The Queen thinks Lord Palmerston's proposition the one which is the most equitable, still likely to be attained, but it does not go far enough; the position which Austria means to take *in Italy* with her Italian province ought to be explained, and a declaration be made that Austria will, with this province, join any Italian league which the other states of Italy may wish to establish. This will be useful to Italy, and much facilitate the acceptance of the Austrian proposal, as the Queen feels convinced that as soon as the war shall be terminated, the question of the political constitution of Italy (as a whole) will have to be decided. Why Charles Albert ought to get any additional territory the Queen cannot in the least see. She thinks it will be better to proceed at once upon the revised Austrian proposal, than to wait for Italian propositions, which are sure to be ridiculously extravagant.

Queen Victoria to Viscount Palmerston.

Osborne, *23rd May 1848.*

The Queen has received Lord Palmerston's letter respecting Spain and Italy this morning. The sending away of Sir H. Bulwer[24] is a serious affair, which will add to our many embarrassments; the Queen is, however, not surprised at it, from the tenor of the last accounts from Madrid, and from the fact that Sir H. Bulwer has for the last three years almost been sporting with political intrigues. He invariably boasted of at least being in the confidence of every conspiracy, "though he was taking care not to be personally mixed up in them," and, after their various failures, generally harboured the chief actors in his house under the plea of humanity. At every crisis he gave us to understand that he had to choose between a "revolution and a palace intrigue," and not long ago only he wrote to Lord Palmerston, that if the Monarchy with the Montpensier succession was inconvenient to us, he could get up a Republic. Such principles are sure to be known in Spain, the more so when one considers the extreme vanity of Sir H. Bulwer, and his probable imprudence in the not very creditable company which he is said to keep. Lord Palmerston will remember that the Queen has often addressed herself to him and Lord John, in fear of Sir H. getting us into some scrape; and if our diplomatists are not kept in better order, the Queen may at any moment be exposed to similar insults as she has received now in the person of Sir H. Bulwer; for in whatever way one may wish to look at it, Sir Henry still is *her* Minister.

The Queen wishes Lord Palmerston to show this letter to Lord John Russell, and to let her know what the Government mean to propose with respect to this unfortunate affair.

The Prince of Prussia to Queen Victoria.

[Translation.]

Brussels *30th May 1848.*

Most gracious Cousin,—I obey the impulse of my heart in seizing my pen, without any delay, in order to express to you my warmest and most heartfelt thanks for the infinitely gracious and affectionate way with which you and the Prince have treated me during my stay in London.[25] It was a melancholy time, that of my arrival. By the sympathetic view which you took of my situation, most gracious Cousin, it became not only bearable, but even transformed into one that became proportionately honourable and dignified. This graciousness of yours has undoubtedly contributed towards the change of opinion which has resulted in my favour, and so I owe to you, to the Prince, and to your Government, a fortunate issue out of my calamities. So it is with a heavy heart that I have now left England, not knowing what future lies before me to meet—and only knowing that I shall need the strengthening rest and tranquillity which my stay in England and an insight into her institutions have afforded me in full measure.

Offering my most cordial remembrances to the Prince, to whom I shall write as soon as possible, I remain, most gracious Cousin, your faithful and most gratefully devoted Cousin,

Prince of Prussia.

Queen Victoria to Lord John Russell.

Buckingham Palace, *1st June 1848.*

The Queen had not time the other day to talk to Lord John Russell on the subject of the French Royal Family, and therefore writes to him now. As it seems now most probable that they, or at least some of them, will take up their residence for a lengthened period in this country, and as their position is now a defined one, viz. that of *exiles*, their treatment should be defined and established.

At first everything seemed temporary, and the public were much occupied with them, inclined to criticise all that was done or was omitted by the Court; all their movements were recorded in the papers, etc. The lapse of three months has a good deal altered this. They have lived in complete retirement, and are comparatively forgotten; and their poverty and their resignation to their misfortunes have met with much sympathy! The Queen is consequently anxious to take the right line; particularly desirous to do nothing which could hurt the interests of the country, and equally so to do everything kind towards a distinguished Royal Family in severe affliction, with whom she has long been on terms of intimacy, and to whom she is very nearly related. She accordingly wishes to know if Lord John sees any objection to the following: She has asked her Cousin, the Duchess of Nemours, to come for two or three nights to see her at Osborne when she goes there, *quite* privately; the Duchess of Kent would bring her with her. The Duke will not come with the Duchess, as he says he feels (very properly) it would be unbecoming in him till their fate (as to *fortune*, for *banished* they already are) is decided, to be even for a day at Osborne. The Duchess herself wishes not to appear in the evening, but to remain alone with the Queen and the Prince.

The Queen considers that when she is *staying* in the country during the summer and autumn, and any of the branches of the French Royal Family should wish to visit her and the Prince, as they occasionally do here, she might lodge them for one or two nights, as the distance might be too great for their returning the same day. They are exiles, and *not Pretenders*, as the Duc de Bordeaux and Count de Montemolin are (and who are *for that reason only not received at Court*). In all countries where illustrious exiles related to the Sovereign have been they have always been received at Court, as the Duc de Bordeaux, the Duchesse d'Angoulême, etc., etc., invariably have been at Vienna (even on public occasions), there being a French Ambassador there, and the best understanding existing between France and

Austria. The Duke of Orleans (King Louis Philippe) in former times was constantly received by the Royal Family, and was the intimate friend of the Duke of Kent. Probably, if their fortunes are restored to them, the French Royal Family will go out into society in the course of time, and if the state of France becomes consolidated there may no longer exist that wish and that necessity for *extreme* privacy, which is so obvious now. What the Queen has just mentioned, Lord John must well understand, is not what is *likely* to take place (except in the case of her cousin, the Duchess of Nemours) immediately, but only what might occasionally occur when we are permanently settled in the country. Of course events *might* arise which would change this, and which would render it inadvisable, and then the Queen would communicate with Lord John, and ask his advice again upon the subject. All she has suggested refers to the present state of affairs, and, of course, merely to *strictly* private visits, and on *no state occasion*. This is a long letter about such a subject, but the Queen wishes to be quite safe in what she does, and therefore could not have stated the case and her opinion in a smaller space.

Queen Victoria to Viscount Palmerston.

Buckingham Palace, *4th June 1848.*

The Queen returns the enclosed draft. She has written upon it, in pencil, a passage which she thinks ought to be added, if the draft— though civil—is not to be a mere refusal to do anything for Austria, and a recommendation that whatever the Italians ask for ought to be given, for which a mediation is hardly necessary.[26] The Queen thinks it most important that we should try to mediate and put a stop to the war, and equally important that the boundary which is to be settled should be such a one as to make a recurrence of hostilities unlikely. The Queen has only further to remark that Lord Palmerston speaks in the beginning of the letter only of the Cabinet, and adverts nowhere to the proposition having been submitted to her.

Lord John Russell to Queen Victoria.

Chesham Place, 14th June 1848.

Lord John Russell presents his humble duty, and thanks your Majesty for the perusal of this interesting letter.

An Emperor with a rational Constitution might be a fair termination of the French follies; but Louis Napoleon, with the Communists, will probably destroy the last chance of order and tranquillity. A despotism must be the end.

May Heaven preserve us in peace!

Queen Victoria to Viscount Palmerston.

Buckingham Palace, *15th June 1848.*

The Queen has received Lord Palmerston's letter explaining his views as to the reparation we may be entitled to receive from the Spanish Government. She considers them as quite fair, but does not wish to have Sir H. Bulwer again as her Minister at Madrid, even if it should be necessary that he should repair there in order to be received by the Queen of Spain. It would not be consulting the permanent interests of this country to entrust that mission again to Sir H. Bulwer, after all that has passed. When the Queen considers the position we had in Spain, and what it ought to have been after the constitution of the French Republic when we had no rival to fight and ought to have enjoyed the entire confidence and friendship of Spain, and compares this to the state into which our relations with that country have been brought, she cannot help being struck how much matters must have been mismanaged.

Queen Victoria to Lord John Russell.

Buckingham Palace, *16th June 1848.*

The Queen sends the enclosed draft,[27] and asks whether this note is what Lord John directed Lord Palmerston to send to Lisbon as a caution to Sir H. Seymour not to mix himself up with party intrigues to upset a particular Ministry?[28] ...

Viscount Palmerston to Lord John Russell.

Carlton Gardens, *17th June 1848.*

My dear John Russell,—The draft to Seymour was written in consequence of what you said to me, and what the Queen wrote to you; but my own opinion certainly is that it would be best to leave the things with him as they are. It must, however, be remembered that the Portuguese Government have not in reality fulfilled the engagements taken by the Queen in the Protocol of last year....

Palmerston.

Queen Victoria to Lord John Russell.

Buckingham Palace, *17th June 1848.*

The Queen returns Lord Palmerston's letter. The country is at this moment suffering, particularly with regard to Spain, under the evil consequence of that system of diplomacy, which makes the taking up of party politics in foreign countries its principal object. This system is condemned alike by the Queen, Lord John, the Cabinet, and, the Queen fully believes, public opinion in and out of Parliament. Lord Palmerston's objection to caution our Minister in Portugal against falling into this fault brings it to an issue, whether that *erroneous* policy is to be maintained to the detriment of the real interests of the country, or a wiser course to be followed in future. Does Lord John consider this so light a matter as to be surrendered merely because Lord Palmerston is not to add to such a caution a gratuitous attack upon the Queen and Government of Portugal? The Queen thinks it of the utmost importance that in these perilous times this question with regard to the basis of our foreign policy should be *settled*, and has no objection to Lord John showing this letter to Lord Palmerston.

Lord John Russell to Queen Victoria.

Pembroke Lodge, *18th June 1848.*

Lord John Russell presents his humble duty to your Majesty; he begs to assure your Majesty that if he was disposed to rest on the known discretion and temper of Sir Hamilton Seymour without specific instruction, it was not from regarding the matter lightly, but from a sense of the inconvenience which might arise to your Majesty's service from raising a question with Lord Palmerston in the present critical state of Europe which might induce a belief that he had not conducted foreign affairs to the satisfaction of his colleagues or of his Sovereign.

Lord John Russell feeling, however, that on the particular point at issue your Majesty has just reason to expect that precautions should be taken against the chance of intrigue with foreign parties against a foreign government, with which this country is on terms of friendship, is ready to insist on an instruction to Sir Hamilton Seymour similar to that which was given to Sir Henry Bulwer to take no part in the struggle of parties, and to refrain from any interference with respect to which he has not specific directions from your Majesty's Government.

But in this case he must take upon himself the whole responsibility of requiring such a note from Lord Palmerston. It would not be conducive to your Majesty's service, nor agreeable to the wholesome maxims of the Constitution to mix your Majesty's name with a proceeding which may lead to the most serious consequences.

It is just to Lord Palmerston to say that his general course of policy has met with the warm approval of the Cabinet, and that the cases of difference of judgment have been rare exceptions.

Lord John Russell submits to your Majesty the letter he proposes to write before sending it to Lord Palmerston. He would wish to have it returned as soon as your Majesty can do so.

Queen Victoria to Lord John Russell.

Buckingham Palace, *18th June 1848.*

The Queen returns to Lord John Russell his letter to Lord Palmerston,[29] which is excellent, and shows that the Queen's and Lord John's views upon the important question of our foreign policy *entirely coincide*. The Queen is sorry that the trouble of such an altercation should be added to the many anxieties which already press upon Lord John, but she feels sure that his insisting upon a *sound* line of policy will save him and the country from *far greater* troubles....

Viscount Palmerston to Queen Victoria.

Carlton Gardens, *26th June 1848.*

Viscount Palmerston presents his humble duty to your Majesty, and is sorry he is not able to submit to your Majesty the proposed draft to Sir Hamilton Seymour to go by to-night's mail, as he has not succeeded in settling the wording of it with Lord John Russell, and is therefore obliged to defer it till the next mail.

Queen Victoria to Lord John Russell.

Buckingham Palace, *26th June 1848.*

The Queen sends this letter, which she has just received from Lord Palmerston. No remonstrance has any effect with Lord Palmerston. Lord John Russell should ask the Duke of Bedford to tell him of the conversation the Queen had with the Duke the other night about Lord Palmerston.

Queen Victoria to Viscount Palmerston.

Buckingham Palace, *1st July 1848*.

The Queen has not yet answered Lord Palmerston's letter of the 29th. She cannot conceal from him that she is ashamed of the policy which we are pursuing in this Italian controversy in abetting wrong, and this for the object of gaining *influence* in Italy.[30] The Queen does not consider influence so gained as an advantage, and though this influence is to be acquired in order to do good, she is afraid that the fear of losing it again will always stand in the way of this. At least in the countries where the greatest stress has been laid on that influence, and the greatest exertions made for it, the *least good* has been done—the Queen means in Spain, Portugal, and Greece. Neither is there any kind of consistency in the line we take about Italy and that we follow with regard to Schleswig; both cases are perfectly alike (with the difference perhaps that there is a question of right mixed up in that of Schleswig); whilst we upbraid Prussia, caution her, etc., etc., we say nothing to Charles Albert except that if he did not wish to take *all* the Emperor of Austria's Italian Dominions, we would not lay any *obstacles* in the way of his moderation. The Queen finds in Lord Palmerston's last despatch to Chevalier Bunsen the following passage: "And it is manifest and indisputable that no territory or state, which is not now according to the Treaty of 1815 included in the German Confederation, can be added to that territory without the consent of the Sovereign of that territory or state." How does this agree with our position relative to the incorporation of Lombardy into the states of the King of Sardinia?

Queen Victoria to Viscount Palmerston.

Buckingham Palace, *6th July 1848*.

The Queen has to acknowledge Lord Palmerston's long Memorandum respecting our relations with Italy, the length of which, however, was fully justified by the importance of the subject.

The mission of Lord Minto has had the Queen's approval at the time, and the policy pursued by him has never been called in question; but it certainly was prejudicial to the Austrians, and imposes upon us additional care not to appear now as the abettors of the anti-Austrian movement, and nothing in Lord Minto's mission can prevent our endeavouring to facilitate and forward a speedy settlement of the present Italian difference.[31] If, therefore, the Italians should be inclined to be moderate, there can be no dereliction of principle in encouraging them to be so. The danger of French interference increases with the delay and is equally great, whether the Austrians maintain themselves in the Venetian Territory or whether Charles Albert unite it to his proposed kingdom of Northern Italy; indeed, the French seem to be anxious for a cause of interference from the line they pursue even with regard to Naples.

Lord Palmerston seeks to establish a difference between the case of Schleswig and of Lombardy, on the fact that Schleswig is to be incorporated into a confederation of States; but this makes the case of Lombardy only the stronger, as this is to be incorporated into the dominions of another Sovereign. With regard to the "Revue Retrospective," the perusal of it has left a different impression upon the Queen from that which it seems to have made upon Lord Palmerston. It proved to her, that while the retiring attitude which the late Government took with regard to the Spanish marriages, left the French Government to try their different schemes and intrigues and to fail with every one of them, the attempt of Lord Palmerston to re-organise the Progressista Party and regain the so-called *English influence*, brought Queen Christina and King Louis Philippe (who had before seriously quarrelled) immediately together, and induced them to rush into this unfortunate combination, which cannot but be considered as the origin of all the present convulsions in Europe.

Queen Victoria to the King of the Belgians.

Buckingham Palace, *11th July 1848.*

My dearest Uncle,—For another kind and dear letter of the 8th, I have much to thank you. The prosperity of dear little Belgium is a bright star in the stormy night all around. May God bless and prosper you all, for ever and ever!

Since the 24th February I feel an uncertainty in everything existing, which (uncertain as all human affairs must be) one never felt before. When one thinks of one's children, their education, their future—and prays for them—I always think and say to myself, "Let them grow up fit for *whatever station* they may be placed in—*high or low*." This one never thought of before, but I *do* always now. Altogether one's whole disposition is so changed—*bores* and trifles which one would have complained of bitterly a few months ago, one looks upon as good things and quite a blessing—provided one can *keep one's position in quiet!*

I own I have not much confidence in Cavaignac,[32] as they fear his mother's and brother's influence, the former being a widow of a regicide, and as *stern* and severe as can be imagined.

I saw the King and Queen on Saturday; he is wonderfully merry still and quite himself, but *she* feels it deeply—and for *her* there is here the greatest sympathy and admiration.

Albert is going to York to-morrow till Friday; *how* I wish you and Louise could be with me, as in '44 and '46! I have, however, got dear Victoire to come and spend a night with me; it does her always good, and we are just like sisters, and feel as we did in 1839, when you know how very fond we were of each other. She is a dear, noble, and still *beautiful* child.

I venture to send you a snuff-box with poor Aunt Charlotte's picture as a child, which also belonged to poor Aunt Sophia. Ever your devoted Niece,

Victoria R.

Queen Victoria to Lord John Russell.

Buckingham Palace, *13th July 1848.*

The Queen was glad to hear of the majorities the other night. She concludes Lord John Russell cannot at all say *when* the Session is likely to end? Is it not much to be regretted that the measure relative to the Navigation Laws is given up, and was it unavoidable? The Queen sends Lord John Col. Phipps's report of the Prince's reception at York, which she thinks will interest him. Does Lord J. Russell think, if we should not go to Ireland, that we could go to Balmoral for ten days or a fortnight, without shocking the Irish very much? It strikes the Queen that to go to see *our own place* makes a difference, and is in fact a natural thing; it is, however, impossible to say if we *can* get away even for so short a time.

The Queen concludes that there can be no possible objection to the Duc de Nemours bringing or fetching the Duchess to and from Osborne? He is the Queen's Cousin, and consequently in a different position to any of the others; moreover, he does *not* wish *at present* to spend one *night* there even, but merely to pay a morning visit.

Lastly, the Queen wishes to know if the King and Queen and the other Princes and Princesses *should themselves* ask to come and pay the Queen a morning visit at Osborne, and return again the same day (as they do here), there would be any objection to it? The Queen

189

merely wishes to know, in *case they* should ask leave to do so, what she can answer.

Queen Victoria to Sir George Grey.

Buckingham Palace, *14th July 1848.*

The Queen has received Sir George Grey's letter of yesterday, and has considered the proposed alteration in the mode of preparing Commissions for Officers in the Army. The Queen does not at all object to the amount of trouble which the signature of so many Commissions has hitherto entailed upon her, as she feels amply compensated by the advantage of keeping up a personal connection between the Sovereign and the Army, and she very much doubts whether the Officers generally would not feel it as a slight if, instead of their Commissions bearing the Queen's sign-manual, they were in future only to receive a certificate from the Secretary at War that they have been commissioned.

She therefore prefers matters to remain on their old footing.

The Secretary at War speaks in his Memorandum of his responsibility to Parliament with respect to allowing Appointments to go on; the Queen apprehends that his responsibility does not extend beyond the appropriation of the money voted by Parliament for the use of her Army.

The Princess Charlotte of Belgium to Queen Victoria.

Laeken, *18th July 1848.*

My dearest Cousin,—I have received the beautiful dolls' house you have been so kind as to send me, and I thank you very much for it. I am delighted with it; every morning I dress my doll and give her a good breakfast; and the day after her arrival she gave a great rout at which all my dolls were invited. Sometimes she plays at drafts on her pretty little draft-board, and every evening I undress her and put her to bed.

Be so good, my dearest Cousin, as to give my love to my dear little Cousins, and believe me always, your most affectionate Cousin,

Charlotte.

Queen Victoria to Viscount Palmerston.

Osborne, *24th July 1848.*

The Queen has received Lord Palmerston's letter[33] reporting his conversation with M. de Tallenay. She can only repeat her opinion that a negotiation with France in order to agree with her upon a common line of policy to be followed with regard to the Italian question can lead to no good; it will make us the ally of a Government which is not even legally constituted, and which can accordingly not guarantee the fulfilment of any engagement it may enter into, and it will call upon the very power to judge the Italian dispute which it is the interest of Europe to keep out of it. M. de Tallenay seems to have admitted that the French Republic, if called upon to act, will neither allow Austria to keep the Venetian territory nor Sardinia to acquire it, but that she will strive to set up a Venetian Republic. It can really not be an object for us to assist in such a scheme, or even to treat upon it.

Lord Cowley the Queen means to invite to dinner to-day, and she wishes Lord Palmerston to let her know the day on which he is to leave for Frankfort in order that she may prepare her letter for the Archduke accordingly.

Queen Victoria to Lord John Russell.

Osborne, *25th July 1848.*

The Queen sends Lord John Russell the enclosed Despatch from Lord Normanby, with a draft in answer to it which was sent for her approval, but which she really cannot approve. The Queen must tell Lord John what she has repeatedly told Lord Palmerston, but without apparent effect, that the establishment of an *entente cordiale with the French Republic,* for the purpose of driving the Austrians out of *their dominions* in Italy, would be a *disgrace* to this country. That the French would attach the greatest importance to it and gain the greatest advantage by it there can be no doubt of; but how will England appear before the world *at the moment* when she is struggling to maintain her supremacy in Ireland, and boasts to stand by treaties with regard to her European relations, having declined all this time to interfere in Italy or to address one word of caution to the Sardinian Government on account of its attack on Austria, and having refused to mediate when called upon to do so by Austria, because the terms were not good enough for Sardinia, if she should now ally herself with the arch-enemy of Austria to interfere *against her* at the moment when she has recovered in some degree her position in the Venetian territory?

The notion of establishing a Venetian State under French guarantee is too absurd. Lord Palmerston in his draft says that we believe that the French plan would be agreed to by Austria. Now this is completely at variance with every account, report, or despatch we have received from Verona, Innspruck, or Vienna; however, Lord Palmerston hints that the King of Sardinia might expect still better terms. The French Republic seems *not* to be anxious for war, not able to conduct it, and the country appears to be decidedly against it; all M. Bastide says is: "There were two extremes which it would be very difficult for them to admit without opposition, viz. the restoration of Lombardy to the Dominion of Austria on the one side, and the union under one powerful state under Charles Albert of all the principalities into which the north of Italy has hitherto been divided." With this explicit declaration, it would surely be best for the interests of Europe that we should name *this* to Charles Albert, and call upon him to rest satisfied with his conquest, and to conclude a peace with Austria, leaving her what he cannot take from her, and thus avoid calling in France as an arbiter. Why this has not been done long ago, or should not be done now, the Queen cannot comprehend.

Queen Victoria to Lord John Russell.

Osborne, *27th July 1848.*

The Queen has to acknowledge Lord John Russell's two letters with respect to Italy. The alterations in the draft meet many of the Queen's objections, giving to the whole step another appearance. The Queen ... must acknowledge the advantage of our trying to bind [the French] to good conduct; only this must be done in a way not to appear as a league with them against a friendly Power, struggling to preserve to herself a territory granted to her by a Treaty to which we were a party.

As the amended draft secures us against these appearances, and leaves us free for the future, the Queen approves it.

Queen Victoria to the King of the Belgians.

Osborne, *1st August 1848.*

My dearest Uncle,—I had yesterday the happiness of receiving your kind letter of the 29th, for which I return my best thanks.

There are ample means of crushing the Rebellion in Ireland,[34] and I think it now is very likely to go off without any contest. ...Lord

Hardinge is going over there to serve on the Staff, which is very praiseworthy of him.

I do not think the fate of the Minor Princes in Germany is so completely decided as Charles[35] ... is *so* anxious to make one believe. There is only a question of taking certain powers and rights away, and not at all of getting rid of them; and I think you will see that the *Ausführung* of the Unity will be an impossibility, at least in the sense they propose at Frankfort. The Archduke John has spoken very reassuringly both to Ernest and the Duke of Meiningen, and the attachment in many of those smaller principalities is still extremely great, and I am sure they will never consent to being *ausgewischt*. Coburg, for instance, on the occasion of the suppression of a very small riot, showed the greatest attachment and devotion to Ernest; at Gotha the feeling of independence is *very* great, and at Strelitz, on the occasion of Augusta's confinement with a *son*, the enthusiasm and rejoicing was universal. All this cannot be entirely despised.

We are as happy as possible here, and would be perfectly so, if it was not for the sorrow and misfortunes of so many dear to us, and for the state of the world in general.

I have always forgotten to tell you that we bought a fine marble bust of you quite by accident in London the other day. It is in armour and with moustaches, but quite different to the one the Gardners have at Melbourne; Albert saw it at the window of a shop, and heard it had been bought in a sale of a General Somebody. Now, with Albert's best love, ever your devoted Niece,

Victoria R.

We have just heard that there has been an *action* in Ireland in which some of the insurgents have been killed; *fifty* Police dispersed *four thousand* people. Smith O'Brien is, however, not yet taken.

Queen Victoria to Viscount Palmerston.

Osborne, *8th August 1848.*

... The Queen has attentively perused the statement of Lord Palmerston in favour of accrediting an Ambassador at Paris. As the proposed arrangement for the present is to be only a *provisional* one, the Queen thinks that the appointment of a *Minister* now will leave it quite open to have an Ambassador hereafter, if it should be found necessary or advantageous, whilst it would set that matter at rest for the moment. Withdrawing an Ambassador and substituting a Minister hereafter, would be much more difficult. The French Republic would no doubt like to have an Ambassador here, and perhaps take immediate steps to secure that object if Lord Normanby were accredited Ambassador at Paris, against which we would be secured in having only a Minister there.... Lord Normanby's acquaintance with the public men at Paris is as much an inconvenience as it may be a convenience in some respects; his having been the great admirer and friend of M. Lamartine, for instance, etc., etc. The possibility of mixing freely with persons of various kinds, which Lord Palmerston adduces as an important consideration will, in the Queen's opinion, be more easy for a Minister than for a person of the high rank of Ambassador. All things considered therefore, the Queen will prefer to have temporarily a Minister accredited at Paris.

M. de Tallenay the Queen would receive in London on Tuesday next at six o'clock, when the Queen will be in Town.

Queen Victoria to Viscount Palmerston.

Osborne, *11th August 1848.*

The Queen has to acknowledge Lord Palmerston's letter of yesterday. The Queen was quite surprised to hear from Lord Palmerston in his last communication that he had written to Lord Normanby to offer him to stay as Minister at Paris, after his having before stated to the Queen that this would never do and could not be expected from Lord Normanby; Lord Normanby's answer declining this offer therefore does in no way alter the matter, and must have been foreseen by Lord Palmerston. By the delay and Lord Normanby's various conversations with M. Bastide[36] and General Cavaignac it has now become difficult to depart from the precedent of the Belgian and Sardinian Missions without giving offence at Paris. The Queen must, however, insist upon this precedent being fully adhered to. She accordingly sanctions Lord Normanby's appointment as Ambassador Extraordinary, on the *distinct understanding* that there is to be no Ambassador sent in return to London now, and that a Minister is to be appointed to Paris when the diplomatic intercourse is permanently to be settled. The Queen wishes Lord Palmerston to bear this in mind, and to submit to her the arrangement which he thinks will be best calculated to carry this into effect.

Queen Victoria to Lord John Russell.

Osborne, *11th August 1848.*

The Queen has to acknowledge Lord John Russell's letter of to-day. The Queen is highly indignant at Lord Palmerston's behaviour now again with respect to Lord Normanby's appointment; he knew perfectly well that Lord Normanby could not accept the post of Minister, and had written to the Queen before that such an offer could not be made, and has now made it after all, knowing that, by wasting time and getting the matter entangled at Paris, he would carry his point. If the French are so anxious to keep Lord Normanby as to make any sacrifice for that object, it ought to make us cautious, as it can only be on account of the ease with which they can make him serve their purposes. They, of course, like an *entente cordiale* with us at the expense of Austria;... but this can be no consideration for us....

Threatening the Austrians with war, or making war upon them in case they should not be inclined to surrender their provinces at his bidding [Lord Palmerston] knows to be impossible; therefore the *entente* with the Republic is of the greatest value to him, enabling him to threaten the Austrians at any time with the French intervention which he can have at command if he agrees to it.[37] The Queen has read the leading articles of the *Times* of yesterday and to-day on this subject with the greatest satisfaction as they express almost entirely the same views and feelings which she entertains. The Queen hopes that Lord John Russell will read them; indeed, the whole of the Press seem to be unanimous on this subject, and she can hardly understand how there can be two opinions upon it....

Queen Victoria to Viscount Palmerston.

Osborne, *20th August 1848.*

The Queen has received an *autograph* letter from the Archduke John (in answer to the private letter she had written to him through Lord Cowley), which has been cut open at the Foreign Office. The Queen wishes Lord Palmerston to take care that this does not happen again. The opening of official letters even, addressed to the Queen, which she has *of late* observed, is really not becoming, and ought to be discontinued, as it used never to be the case formerly.

Queen Victoria to Lord John Russell.

Osborne, *21st August 1848.*

The Queen has received Lord John Russell's letter of yesterday, but cannot say that she has been satisfied by the reasons given by Lord Palmerston. The union of Lombardy and Piedmont cannot be considered as a concession to France for the maintenance of peace, because we know that it is the very thing the French object to. The Queen quite agrees that the principal consideration always to be kept in sight is the preservation of the peace of Europe; but it is precisely on that account that she regrets that the terms proposed by Lord Palmerston (whilst they are not in accordance with the views of France) are almost the only ones which must be most offensive to Austria. Lord Palmerston *will* have his kingdom of Upper Italy under Charles Albert, to which every other consideration is to be sacrificed, and Lord Normanby's alteration of the terms certainly serve *that* purpose well; but it is quite independent of the question of mediation, and the only thing in the whole proceeding which is indefensible in principle.

It will be a calamity for ages to come if this principle is to become part of the international law, viz. "that a people can at any time transfer their allegiance from the Sovereign of one State to that of another by universal suffrage (under momentary excitement)," and this is what Lord Normanby—no doubt according to Lord Palmerston's wishes—has taken as the basis of the mediation. For even the *faits accomplis*, which are a convenient basis to justify any act of injustice, are here against Charles Albert.

Lord Palmerston's argument respecting Schleswig,[38] which the Queen quoted in her last letter, had no reference to the Treaty of 1720.

Queen Victoria to the King of the Belgians.

Osborne, *29th August 1848.*

My dearest Uncle,—Most warmly do I thank you for your very kind and dear letter of the 26th, with so many good wishes for that *dearest* of days. It is indeed to me one of eternal thankfulness, for a purer, more perfect being than my beloved Albert the Creator could *not* have sent into this troubled world. I feel that I could *not* exist without him, and that I should sink under the troubles and annoyances and *dégoûts* of my *very* difficult position, were it not for *his* assistance, protection, guidance, and comfort. Truly do I thank you for your *great* share in bringing about our marriage.

Stockmar I do not quite understand, and I cannot believe that he *really wishes to ruin* all the smaller States, though his principal object is that unity which I fear he will *not* obtain.

I do not either at all agree in his wish that Prussia should take the lead; his love for Prussia is to me incomprehensible, for it is the country of all others which the *rest* of Germany dislikes. Stockmar cannot be my good old friend if he has such notions of injustice as I hear attributed to him. But whatever they may be, I do *not* believe the *Ausführung* to be possible.

I have great hopes of soon hearing of something decided about the fortunes of the poor French family. You will have seen how nobly and courageously good Joinville and Aumale behaved on the occasion of the burning of that emigrant ship off Liverpool.[39] It will do them great good. I must now conclude. Ever your devoted Niece,

Victoria R.

Queen Victoria to Viscount Palmerston.

Osborne, *2nd September 1848.*

The Queen has read in the papers the news that Austria and Sardinia have nearly settled their differences, and also "that it was confidently stated that a French and *British* squadron, with troops on board, *are to make a demonstration in the Adriatic.*"

Though the Queen cannot believe this, she thinks it right to inform Lord Palmerston without delay that, should such a thing be thought of, it is a step which the Queen could *not* give her consent to.

Queen Victoria to Viscount Palmerston.

Buckingham Palace, *4th September 1848.*

The Queen since her arrival in Town has heard that the answer from Austria declining our mediation has some days ago been communicated to Lord Palmerston. The Queen is surprised that Lord Palmerston should have left her uninformed of so important an event. The Queen has received Lord Palmerston's letter respecting the proposal to mediate on the part of the central power of Germany,[40] and does not see why that power, which has a responsible Government, is to be precluded from taking part in a negotiation because the Archduke John might be friendly towards Austria—whereas the French republic, which had in public documents espoused the Italian Cause, is to be a party to it.

Neither France nor England are neighbours to or directly interested in Lombardy, whereas Germany is both.[41]

Queen Victoria to Lord John Russell.

On board the *Victoria and Albert,*

Aberdeen, *7th September 1848.*

The Queen must send the enclosed draft to Lord John Russell, with a copy of her letter to Lord Palmerston upon it. Lord Palmerston has as usual pretended not to have had time to submit the draft to the Queen before he had sent it off. What the Queen has long suspected and often warned against is on the point of happening, viz. Lord Palmerston's using the new *entente cordiale* for the purpose of wresting from Austria her Italian provinces by French arms. This would be a most iniquitous proceeding. It is another question whether it is good policy for Austria to try to retain Lombardy, but that is for her and not for us to decide. Many people might think that we would be happier without Ireland or Canada. Lord John will not fail to observe how very intemperate the whole tone of Lord Palmerston's language is.

Queen Victoria to the King of the Belgians.

Balmoral Castle, *13th September 1848.*

My dearest Uncle,—I yesterday received your dear and kind letter of the 9th (it having arrived in London only the day before), which is very quick, and I thank you much for it. The Schleswig affair at Frankfort is *very* unfortunate, and there seems a lamentable want of *all* practical sense, foresight, or even *common* prudence.[42]

The poor Austrians seem now to accept the (to me *very* doubtful) mediation. It reminds me of the wolf in the lamb's skin. *Nous verrons,* how matters will be arranged....

My letter to Louise will have informed you of our voyage and our arrival here. This house is small but pretty, and though the hills seen from the windows are not *so* fine, the scenery all around is the finest almost I have seen anywhere. It is very wild and solitary, and yet cheerful and *beautifully wooded,* with the river Dee running between the two sides of the hills. Loch Nagar is the highest hill in the immediate vicinity, and belongs to us.

Then the soil is the driest and best known almost anywhere, and all the hills are as sound and hard as the road. The climate is also dry, and in general not very cold, though we had one or two very cold days. There is a deer forest—many roe deer, and on the opposite hill (which does not belong to us) grouse. There is also black cock and ptarmigan. Albert has, however, no luck this year, and has in vain been after the deer, though they are continually seen, and often quite close by the house. The children are very well, and enjoying themselves much. The boys always wear their Highland dress.

I must now wish you good-bye, and repeat how much delighted we are that everything goes on so well in Belgium. Ever your devoted Niece,

Victoria R.

Memorandum by Queen Victoria.

Balmoral, *19th September 1848.*

I said to Lord John Russell, that I must mention to him a subject, which was a serious one, one which I had delayed mentioning for some time, but which I felt I must speak quite openly to him upon now, namely about Lord Palmerston; that I felt really I could hardly go on with him, that I had no confidence in him, and that it made me seriously anxious and uneasy for the welfare of the country and for the peace of Europe in general, and that I felt very uneasy from one day to another as to what might happen. Lord John replied that he was aware of it; that he had considered the matter already, having heard from his brother (the Duke of Bedford) how strongly I felt about it; that he felt the truth of all that I had said, but that, on the other hand, Lord Palmerston was a very able man, entirely master of his office and affairs, and a very good colleague, never making any difficulties about other questions, but (certainly *unreasonably*) complaining of other people mixing with and interfering in the affairs of his office. I said that ... I fully believed that that Spanish marriage question, which had been the original cause of so many present misfortunes, would never have become so *embrouillé* had it not been for Lord Palmerston. This led Lord John to say, that though he disapproved the length of Lord Palmerston's correspondence, still that we could not have done otherwise than object to the marriage. This is true enough. I repeated that all that had been done in Italy last winter had also done harm, as it was done by *Lord Palmerston*, who was distrusted everywhere abroad, which Lord John regretted. I said that I thought that he often endangered the honour of England by taking a very prejudiced and one-sided view of a question;... that his writings were always as bitter as gall and did great harm, which Lord John entirely assented to, and that I often felt quite ill from anxiety; that I wished Lord Clarendon (who, I had heard, was tired of Ireland) could come over and be Secretary of State for Foreign Affairs, and Lord Palmerston go to Ireland as Lord-Lieutenant. Lord John said nothing would be better, for that he was sure that Lord Palmerston would make an admirable Lord-Lieutenant, but that another thing to be considered was the danger of making Lord Palmerston an enemy by displacing him, that Lord Minto (who was formerly a great friend and admirer of Lord Palmerston's) had told Lady John when she spoke to him on the subject of placing Lord Palmerston in another office, that *he* (Lord Palmerston) would certainly turn against the Government if displaced. I said that might be, but that sometimes there were great interests at stake which exceeded the danger of offending one man, and that this was here the case; Lord John said it was very true, but that at moments like these one of course was anxious not to do anything which could cause internal trouble. I admitted this, but repeated my anxiety, which Lord John quite understood, though he thought I a little overrated it, and said I was afraid that some day I should have to tell Lord John that I could not put up with Lord Palmerston any longer, which might be very disagreeable and awkward.

It ended by Lord John's promising to bear the subject in mind, and I must say that he took it all just as I could wish.

Victoria R.

Minute by the Governor-General of India.

30th September 1848.

... The course of events, as they have developed themselves, and long and anxious considerations of this important subject, have finally and immovably confirmed in my mind the conviction which the earlier events of the insurrection at Mooltan long since had founded, that there will be no peace for India, nor any stability of Government in the Punjab, nor any release from anxiety and costly defensive preparations on our frontier, unless the British Government, justly indignant at the unprovoked and treacherous aggression once again committed against them by the Sikhs, shall now effectually provide against future dangers by subverting for ever the Dynasty of the Sings, by converting the Punjab into a British province, and by adopting the only measure which will secure the observance of peace by the Sikhs, namely, depriving them utterly of all the means of making war. I continue as fully convinced as ever that the establishment of a strong, friendly, Hindoo Government in the Punjab would be the best settlement that could be made for the interests of British India, if it could be formed. But I am convinced that such a Government cannot be formed.[43]

The Chiefs of the Punjab are utterly powerless and worthless. The great body of the nation is adverse to all control, and in no degree submissive to the authority of those who are professedly their rulers.

Even admitting, which I am by no means prepared to do, that the Sirdars are not treacherously or hostilely disposed to the British Government, of what advantage, what defence to us is the fidelity of the Chiefs, if they are confessedly unable to control the army which is as avowedly hostile to us? That which we desire to secure is a peaceful and well-governed neighbour, and a frontier free from alarms, nor demanding a permanent garrison of 50,000 men. If their army are able to disturb and eager to disturb on every occasion the peace we seek to render permanent, of what profit to us is the assumed fidelity of the Chiefs, who cannot repress their soldiers' turbulence, or command their obedience?

I discredit altogether the assurances of the fidelity of the Chiefs on the evidence of the facts before us....

To all these recommendations my colleagues in the Council have yielded their ready assent.

I have to the last sought to avert, or to avoid, the necessity, if it could prudently or fitly be avoided.

The Sikh nation have forced the necessity upon us. Having resolved at once, and fully, to meet it, I shall proceed with all speed to the frontier, and shall endeavour by every exertion, and by all the means in my power, to carry into effect vigorously the measures on which the Government of India has resolved, and which, in my conscience I believe, are imperatively called for by regard to the peace of India, to the security of our Empire there, and to the happiness of the people over whom we rule.

Dalhousie.

Queen Victoria to Lord John Russell.

Osborne, *7th October 1848.*

The Queen sends Lord Palmerston's answer to her last letter, of which the Queen has sent a copy to Lord John Russell, and encloses likewise a copy of her present answer. The partiality of Lord Palmerston in this Italian question really *surpasses all conception*, and makes the Queen *very uneasy* on account of the character and honour of England, and on account of the danger to which the peace of Europe will be exposed. It is now clearly proved by Baron Wessenberg that upon the conclusion of the Armistice with Sardinia, negotiations for peace would have speedily been entered into, had our *mediation* not been offered to the King, to whom the offer of Lombardy was too tempting not to accept, and now that promise is by fair or unfair means to be made good. The Queen cannot see any principle in this, as the principle upon which Lord Palmerston goes is *Italian Nationality and Independence from a foreign Yoke and Tyranny*. How can the Venetian territory then be secured to Austria? and if this is done, on what ground can Lombardy be wrung from her? It is really not safe to settle such important matters without principle and by personal *passion* alone. When the *French* Government say they cannot control public feeling, Lord Palmerston takes this as an unalterable fact, and as a sufficient reason to make the Austrians give up Lombardy; when, however, the *Austrian* Government say they cannot give up Lombardy on account of the feeling of the Army which had just reconquered it with their blood and under severe privations and sufferings, Lord Palmerston flippantly tells the Austrian Government, "if that were so, the Emperor had better abdicate and make General Radetzky Emperor." When Charles Albert burned the whole of the suburbs of Milan to keep up the delusion that he meant to defend the town, Lord Palmerston said nothing; and now that the Austrian Governor has prohibited revolutionary placards on the walls, and prolonged the period at which arms are to be surrendered, at the end of which persons concealing arms are to be tried by court-martial, he writes to Vienna: "that this savage proclamation, which savours more of the barbarous usages of centuries long gone by than of the spirit of the present times, must strike everybody as a proof of the fear by which the Austrian Commander is inspired," etc., etc., etc.

Venice was to have been made over to Austria by the Armistice, and now that this has not been done, Austria is not even to retake it, in order (as Lord Normanby says) to keep something in hand against which Austria is to make further concessions. Is all this fair? In the meantime, from the account of our Consul at Venice, the French agents are actively employed in intrigues against Austria in that town, and have asked him to assist, which he refused. Lord Palmerston merely approved his conduct, and did not write a line to Paris about it.

Now the question at issue is not even to be submitted to a Conference of European powers, but to be settled by the French Republic and Lord Palmerston alone, Lord Normanby being the instrument who has pledged himself over and over again for Italian *independence* (so called). If Austria makes peace with Sardinia, and gives her Italian provinces separate National Institutions with a liberal constitutional Government, *who can force* upon her another arrangement?

Queen Victoria to Viscount Palmerston.

Osborne, *8th October 1848.*

The Queen cannot refrain from telling Lord Palmerston what a painful impression the perusal of a draft of his to Lord Normanby referring to the affairs of Greece has made upon her, being so little in accordance with the calm dignity which she likes to see in all the proceedings of the British Government; she was particularly struck by the language in which Lord Palmerston speaks of King Otho, a Sovereign with whom she stands in friendly relations, and the asperity against the Government of the King of the French, who is really sufficiently lowered and suffering for the mistakes he may have committed, and that of all this a copy is to be placed in the hands of the Foreign Minister of the French *Republic*, the Queen can only see with much regret.[44]

Queen Victoria to the King of the Belgians.

Windsor Castle, *10th October 1848.*

My dearest Uncle,—Our voyage yesterday was much saddened by a terrible accident at Spithead, which delayed us half an hour, and which still fills us with horror. The sea was running very high, and we were just outside what is called The Spit, when we saw a man in the water, sitting on the keel of a boat, and we stopped, and at that moment Albert discerned *many heads* above the sea, including a poor woman. The tide was running so strong that we could only stop an instant and let a boat down, but you may imagine our horror. We waited at Gosport to hear if the people had been saved, and we learnt that three had, two of whom by our *Fairy's* boat, and that four were drowned. Very horrid indeed.

The state of Germany is dreadful, and one does feel quite ashamed about that once really so peaceful and happy people. That there are still good people there I am sure, but they allow themselves to be worked upon in a frightful and shameful way.... In France a crisis seems at hand. *What* a very bad figure we cut in this mediation! Really it is quite immoral, with Ireland quivering in our grasp, and ready to throw off her allegiance at any moment, for us to force Austria to give up her lawful possessions. What shall we say if Canada, Malta, etc., begin to trouble us? It hurts me terribly. This ought to be the principle in *all actions*, private as well as public: "Was du nicht willst, dass dir geschieht, das thu' auch einem andern nicht." ...

I must now conclude. With every good wish, ever your devoted Niece,

Victoria R.

Earl Grey to Queen Victoria.

Colonial Office, *25th October 1848.*

Earl Grey presents his humble duty to your Majesty, and begs to inform your Majesty that no official accounts have been received of the engagement on the Cape Frontier between your Majesty's forces under Sir H. Smith and the insurgent Dutch farmers, of which an account is published in the newspapers.[45] Lord Grey has, however, seen a private letter, which mentions, in addition to what is stated in the Government notice in the Cape newspapers, that Sir Harry Smith exposed himself very much, and was slightly wounded; most fortunately, he was merely grazed in the leg; his horse was also struck by a bullet in the nose. A very large proportion of those who were hit by the fire of the rebels were officers, who appear to have been particularly aimed at.

Queen Victoria to Earl Grey.

Windsor Castle, *26th October 1848.*

The Queen has received Lord Grey's letter, and is glad to hear that Sir H. Smith's wound was not of a serious nature. The loss of so many officers, the Queen is certain, proceeds from their wearing a blue coat whilst the men are in scarlet; the Austrians lost a great proportion of officers in Italy from a similar difference of dress.

As to the Medal for Major Edwardes, the Queen did not approve but disapprove the step, and wished the Bath to be given instead, which has been done. The medals for troops in general (given by the East India Company) are a new and doubtful thing, and now it is proposed to reward even a special case of personal distinction by the *Company's* conferring a mark of honour. Lord Grey will agree with the

Queen that it will be better not to establish two fountains of honour in the Realm. If the East India Company wish to mark their approbation, perhaps they might send Major Edwardes a fine sword or something of that kind.

Earl Grey to Queen Victoria.

Colonial Office, *26th October 1848.*

Earl Grey presents his humble duty to your Majesty, and has just had the honour of receiving your Majesty's letter. Lord Fitzroy Somerset happened to be here when it arrived, and Lord Grey read to him that part of it which relates to the danger occasioned to officers in action from wearing a dress of a different colour from that of the men. Lord Fitzroy observed that although there can be no doubt of the objection to the blue coats worn by officers, in this instance their having suffered so much cannot be attributed to that cause, as it appears that all the officers who were wounded but one, belonged to regiments (the Rifle Battalion or the Cape Mounted Rifles) in which the officers are dressed in the same colour as the men....

Lord Grey begs to submit to your Majesty that the usual time for relieving the present Governor of Gibraltar is now come, and that he thinks it very desirable to appoint a successor to Sir Robert Wilson, who now fills that situation. It appears to Lord Grey that, considering the nature of the appointment and also the great advantage which would result from affording greater encouragement to the officers serving under the Ordnance, it would be very proper to confer this government upon a General Officer belonging to the Royal Artillery or Engineers. There is some difficulty in making a selection from the officers of these Corps, because, from their retiring only by seniority, they seldom attain the rank of General Officer while they are still in possession of sufficient strength and activity for employment. Lord Grey, however, believes from the information he has been able to obtain, that Sir Robert Gardiner might, with advantage, be appointed to this command, which he therefore begs leave to recommend to your Majesty to confer upon him. Lord Grey has had no communication with Sir R. Gardiner, and is entirely ignorant whether he would accept this employment.[46]

Queen Victoria to Lord John Russell.

Windsor Castle, *27th October 1848.*

The Queen has not yet acknowledged the receipt of Lord John Russell's communication of the views of the Cabinet on the Italian affairs.[47] She is very glad that the Cabinet should have considered this important question, and that she should have received an assurance "that she will not be advised to have recourse to forcible intervention." The Queen understands this principle to apply to Lombardy as well as to Sicily, and that, of course, "forcible intervention" will not only be avoided as to British means, but likewise as to French means, with British consent and concurrence. Though Lord John Russell does not enter so much into particulars with regard to the opinions of the Members of the Cabinet as the Queen might have wished, she infers from the proposition that Lombardy should be constituted separately under an Archduke, that the idea of making it over to the King of Sardinia is finally abandoned.

Lord John Russell to Queen Victoria.

Pembroke Lodge, *19th November 1848.*

Lord John Russell presents his humble duty to your Majesty.

It will probably be necessary to send troops to India, who will then be no longer chargeable to this country. But Lord John Russell thinks it his duty to state that however unwilling he may be to diminish the Military and Naval force, it is still more essential to keep our income within our expenditure.

The whole matter will be under the consideration of the Cabinet next week.

The approaching election of a President in France must decide the question of the future Government of France. Louis Bonaparte may probably play the part of Richard Cromwell.

Queen Victoria to the King of the Belgians.

Windsor Castle, *21st November 1848.*

My dearest Uncle,—I write to thank you for your kind letter of the 18th on your god-daughter's *eighth* birthday! It does seem like an incredible dream that Vicky should already be so old! She is very happy with all her gifts.

In Vienna things are much better. Louis Napoleon's election seems certain, and I own I wish for it as I think it will lead to something else.

You will grieve to hear that our good, dear, old friend Melbourne is dying; there is *no* hope, and I enclose a pretty letter of Lady Beauvale's,[48] which I think will interest you, and which I beg you to return. One cannot forget how good and kind and amiable he was, and it brings back so many recollections to my mind, though, God knows! I never wish that time back again.

We go to-morrow for four weeks to our dear, peaceful Osborne.

I will now take my leave. Begging you to believe me ever your devoted Niece,

Victoria R.

Viscount Palmerston to Queen Victoria.

Brocket Hall, *23rd November 1848.*

Viscount Palmerston is here engaged in the melancholy occupation of watching the gradual extinction of the lamp of life of one who was not more distinguished by his brilliant talents, his warm affections, and his first-rate understanding, than by those sentiments of attachment to your Majesty which rendered him the most devoted subject who ever had the honour to serve a Sovereign.

Viscount Palmerston to Queen Victoria.

Brocket Hall, *25th November 1848.*

Viscount Palmerston presents his humble duty to your Majesty, and has to state that Viscount Melbourne was released from further suffering at about six o'clock yesterday afternoon. His bodily strength had been rapidly declining during the last few days, and it was only at intervals that he retained any degree of apparent consciousness. The last transition took place quietly and with almost imperceptible gradation.

Lord John Russell to Queen Victoria.

Pembroke Lodge, *26th November 1848.*

Lord John Russell presents his humble duty to your Majesty: he sees no political objection to a visit to Osborne on the part of the Duke and Duchess of Nemours. The election of a President in France is so completely absorbing attention that any mark of regard to the Duke of Nemours may well pass unnoticed.

Lord John Russell had the honour of seeing Louis Philippe in this house on Friday. He was in much better spirits, owing to the convalescence of the Queen; but the illness has been a very serious one.

Lord John Russell had understood that the affairs of property belonging to the Orleans family were arranged, and that Louis Philippe would ultimately be possessed of more than a million sterling.

Louis Philippe expressed his opinion in favour of Louis Bonaparte as a candidate for the Presidency. He feels confident that France cannot go to war on account of the state of her finances.

Queen Victoria to the King of the Belgians.

Osborne, *21th November 1848.*

My dearest Uncle,—Thank God! that the news from Berlin are better. It is to be hoped that this may have a good effect elsewhere.

In France there ought really to be a Monarchy before long, *qui que ce soit.*

Our poor old friend Melbourne died on the 24th. I sincerely regret him, for he was truly attached to me, and though not a firm Minister he was a noble, kind-hearted, generous being. Poor Lord Beauvale and Lady Palmerston feel it very much. I wish it might soften the *caro sposo* of the latter-named person.

Victoria R.

Pope Pius IX. to Queen Victoria.[49]

To the Most Serene and Potent Sovereign Victoria, the Illustrious Queen of England, Pius Papa Nonus.

Most Serene and Most Potent Queen, Greeting! Your Royal Majesty has already learned what a subversion of public affairs has taken place at Rome, and what utterly unheard-of violence was, on the 16th of the late month of November, offered to us in our very Palace of the Quirinal, in consequence of a nefarious conspiracy of abandoned and most turbulent men. Hence, in order to avoid more violent commotions and more serious dangers, as likewise for the purpose of freely performing the functions of our apostolic Ministry, we, not without the deepest and most heartfelt sorrow, have been constrained to depart for a time from our Holy City, and from the whole state of our pontifical dominions; and in the meanwhile we come as far as Gaëta, where, as soon as we had arrived, our first care was to declare to our subjects the sentiments of our mind and will, by a public edict, a copy of which we transmit to your Royal Majesty, together with these our letters. Without doubt, through your own wisdom, you will perfectly understand, Most Serene and Potent Sovereign, that amongst the other most cruel difficulties by which we are pressed, we must be chiefly solicitous concerning those subject to our temporal rule and the rights and possessions of the Roman Church, which, moreover, your august Uncle and the other Princes of Europe protected with so much zeal. But we do not in the least doubt that, in conformity with your exalted magnanimity, your justice, and your known desire to maintain order in public affairs, you will by no means suffer this same to be wanting to us at this most lamentable time. Trusting indeed in this hope, we do not cease, in the humility and affliction of our heart, from earnestly beseeching God, the All Good and All Great, that He may heap upon your Royal Majesty and your whole House all true and solid prosperity, and that He may unite you with us in perfect charity.

Given at Gaëta, the 4th day of December 1848, in the third year of our Pontificate.

Pius PP. IX.[50]

Queen Victoria to the King of the Belgians.

Osborne, *13th December 1848.*

My beloved Uncle,—Pray accept my warmest and *best* wishes for *many, many happy* returns of your birthday—a day so *dear* to so many, and which will be hailed with such joy in Belgium. You have indeed reason to look with satisfaction on all around you, though it is a painful thing to think how many have been ruined and made miserable since this day twelvemonths. Let us hope that another year may bring many things round again.

The weather is beautiful, and I wish much we could fly over to pay our respects to you on your dear birthday.

The papers are just come, and I see there is no doubt of Louis Napoleon's election, which I am very glad of, as it is a sign of better times. But that one *should have to wish for him* is really wonderful.

Now good-bye, dearest Uncle. Ever your devoted Niece,

Victoria R.

Queen Victoria to the King of the Belgians.

Osborne, *19th December 1848.*

My dearest, kindest Uncle,—Your dear letter, full of interesting topics, which I received yesterday, gave me great pleasure, and I thank you much for it. The success of Louis Napoleon[51] is an extraordinary event, but valuable as a universal condemnation of the Republic since February.

It will, however, perhaps be more difficult to get rid of him again than one at *first* may imagine. Nemours thinks it better that none of themselves should be *called* into action for some time to come. I fear that *he feels* now that they *ought* to have *foreseen* the dangers in February, and *ought not* to have yielded; when I said to him that the Pope had declared that he would *never* quit Rome, and *did so do* the *very next day*, he said: "Ah! mon Dieu, on se laisse entraîner dans ces moments." Louise said to me that *her Father* had so *often declared he would never quit Paris alive*, so that when she heard of his flight she always believed it was untrue and he must be dead....

Queen Victoria to Lord John Russell.

Windsor Castle, *22nd December 1848.*

The Queen has been waiting to receive an answer from Lord John Russell upon her last letter, and has therefore delayed sending the enclosed letter from Lord Palmerston.[52] But lest any further delay might cause future inconvenience, she sends it now without having received Lord John's answer. The Queen is sure Lord John will feel that neither Lord Palmerston nor Lord Normanby have shown a proper regard for the Queen's wishes and opinion in this matter. Lord Normanby's Despatch shows that the step to be taken with reference to an Ambassador to be sent here is avowedly for the purpose of controlling the future action of the Queen's Government, and to *oblige her* to keep a *permanent* Ambassador at Paris in the person of Lord Normanby. It is not very delicate in Lord Normanby to convey such a message, nor in Lord Palmerston to urge it so eagerly. M. de Beaumont's departure from this country without taking leave of the Queen was neither very becoming.

The Queen has already, on Lord Palmerston's account, received two public affronts: the one by her Minister in Spain having been sent out of that country,[53] the other now, by the new Emperor of Austria not announcing to her by special mission his accession to the Throne, which he did to all other Sovereigns, avowedly, as it appears, to mark the indignation of Austria at the inimical proceedings of the British Foreign Secretary. The Queen does not think that, in the face of such slurs, the dignity of England will be vindicated by a race between her representative and that of Spain, who is to present his credentials first to the new President of the French Republic, which Lord Palmerston considers of such importance as to render an *immediate* decision indispensable.

Should Lord John think that we cannot do less now for Louis Napoleon than has been done in the case of General Cavaignac, the Queen will not object to renewing Lord Normanby's credentials as Ambassador-Extraordinary on a special mission.

ENDNOTES:

[1]:Sister of King Louis Philippe.

[2]:This letter is headed "Reproduction—Substance of a letter to Lord John Russell, written from recollection."

[3]:See *ante*, vol. i. p. 254.

[4]:Fifth daughter of George III., born 1777. She died in May 1848.

[5]:The Republican movement had been making rapid headway in Paris, and the leader of the Opposition, M. Odilon Barrot, proposed Guizot's impeachment on the 22nd of February. Louis Philippe, when it was unfortunately too late, consented to a change of Ministry, but the formation of a new Government proved impossible. The Revolution could have been quelled, had it not been for the King's reluctance to shed blood in defence of the Throne to which he had been elected; even to the agitators themselves the completeness of the Revolution was a surprise.

[6]:A letter from Lord Normanby on the 13th of March to Lord Palmerston (published in Ashley's *Life of Palmerston*, vol. i. chap. iii.) gives an account of the situation on the eve of the 22nd of February. On the 25th of February he wrote:—

"The National Guards, mixed with the people, were in full march upon the Tuileries, and the latter threatening the life of the King, when Emile Girardin, the editor of the *Presse* newspaper, who was in advance as an officer of the National Guard, hastily drew up an Act of Abdication, and placed it before the King as the only means of safety. The King at first refused, saying that he would rather die; but the Duc de Montpensier urged him, not only for his own sake, but to save his country from confusion. The King at last signed it, and threw it impatiently at the Duc de Montpensier, who, I believe, has been in favour of conciliatory counsel throughout. The Royal Family then retired through the garden, the King saying to every one as he passed, 'J'abdique, j'abdique.'"

[7]:The Duc d'Orléans, who was killed on 13th July 1842.

[8]:Apparently written at the end of February.

[9]:British Consul at Havre. This letter was submitted to the Queen by Lord Palmerston.

[10]:The Princess Louise was born on 18th March.

[11]:Chief Commissioner of Police, afterwards Sir C. Rowan, K.C.B. The Chartist meeting had been fixed for the 10th.

[12]:Alluding to the *Ateliers Nationaux*, to be established under the guidance of a Council of Administration.

[13]:Chief Commissioner of Woods and Forests.

[14]:Mr Richard Mayne, Commissioner of Police, created a K.C.B. in 1851.

[15]:On the birth of a second son.

[16]:Uncle of the Emperor (Ferdinand I.) of Austria, born 1782.

[17]:A party of French Republicans entered Belgium with the intention of exciting an insurrection; the attempt signally failed.

[18]:M. de Tallenay had arrived in London with a letter from M. Lamartine, accrediting him as provisional *chargé d'affaires* of the French Government, and Lord Palmerston had suggested to the Queen that etiquette would not be violated by inviting him to a Court Ball.

[19]:The National Assembly commenced its sittings on 4th May, when the Oath of Allegiance was abolished, and the Republic proclaimed in the presence of 200,000 citizens.

[20]:Lamartine and Ledru Rollin were members of the Provisional Government, and subsequently of the Executive Committee. The mob, holding that the promises of general employment had been broken, invaded the Assembly *en masse*, and attempted a counter-revolution.

[21]:Out of the revolutionary movement in Germany had grown their National Assembly, which after a preliminary session as a *Vor-Parlament*, was to reassemble on 18th May.

[22]:The Austrian Government, in its efforts to maintain its ascendency in Lombardy, had sent Baron Hummelauer to negotiate with Lord Palmerston.

[23]:The Dukes had both been driven from their dominions, while the King (Charles Albert) of Sardinia threw in his lot with the cause of United Italy as against Austria, which then ruled Lombardy.

[24]:Lord Palmerston had written a letter to Bulwer (which the latter showed to the Spanish Premier), lecturing the Spanish Queen on her choice of Minister. This "assumption of superiority," as Sir R. Peel called it, led to a peremptory order to Bulwer to leave Spain in twenty-four hours. His own account of the affair appears in his *Life of Palmerston*, vol. iii. chap. vii.

[25]:The Prince of Prussia, afterwards the Emperor William I., having become intensely unpopular at Berlin, had been obliged in March to fly for his life, in disguise, *viâ* Hamburg, to England.

[26]:War was now raging in Lombardy between the Austrians under Marshal Radetzky and the Piedmontese under the King of Sardinia.

[27]:The draft ran:—"As it is evident that the Queen and the Government of Portugal will listen to no advice except such that agrees with their own wishes, I have to instruct you to abstain in future from giving any longer

any advice to them on political matters, taking care to explain both to the Queen and the Government your reasons for doing so. You will, however, at the same time positively declare to the Portuguese Government that if by the course of policy they are pursuing they should run into any difficulty, they must clearly understand that they will not have to expect any assistance from England."

[28]:Lord John Russell replied that he would write immediately to Lord Palmerston respecting Portuguese affairs. He added that he did not approve of the proposed draft.

[29]:The letter was to the effect that Sir H. Seymour was to take no part in the struggle of parties in Portugal, and to refrain from confidential communications with members of the Opposition.

[30]:Lord Palmerston's sympathy had been with the anti-Austrian movement in Northern Italy. For some time after Radetzky's evacuation of Milan, the operations of the King of Sardinia in support of the Lombards were successful, and he had assistance from Tuscany, Naples, and Rome. The Austrians suffered reverses at Peschiera and Goito, and the independence of Northern Italy seemed to be accomplished. But the tide had begun to turn.

[31]:Lord Minto, the Lord Privy Seal, and father-in-law of the Prime Minister, had been sent to encourage in the path of reform Pope Pius IX., who was halting between progress and reaction: on the sanguinary risings taking place in Lombardy and Venetia, his mission naturally appeared hostile to Austria.

[32]:General Cavaignac, Minister for War, had been given *quasi*-dictatorial powers during the insurrection. These powers, on the suppression of the revolt, he resigned, and was thereupon almost unanimously made President of the Council.

[33]:Lord Palmerston had reported an interview with de Tallenay, who sought the co-operation of England with France in Northern Italy; the Austrian force in Italy to be withdrawn or reduced, the union of Lombardy and Piedmont to be accepted as a *fait accompli*, and Venetian territory erected into a separate republic.

[34]:*See* Introductory Note for the year, *ante*, p. 146.

[35]:The Frankfort Assembly, in pursuance of the policy of German consolidation, had placed the central executive power in the hands of a Reichsverweser, or Vicar of the Empire. The Archduke John, uncle of the Emperor of Austria, was elected to this position, and the Queen's halfbrother Charles, Prince of Leiningen, was entrusted with the Department of Foreign Affairs.

[36]:Minister of Foreign Affairs.

[37]:The success of the Piedmontese in Northern Italy had not continued through the summer, and the States whose assistance they had hitherto received began to fall away from them. The King of Naples, successful within his own dominions, had withdrawn his troops; the Pope hesitated to

attack Austria; even undivided support from Venetia could no longer be counted upon. After several reverses, Charles Albert, now left virtually alone in the contest, was decisively defeated by Radetzky, at Custozza, and retreated across the Mincio. With what was left of his troops he entered Milan, which he was eventually forced to surrender, being unable to maintain himself there. Italy now turned to France for assistance, but Cavaignac, virtually Dictator in Paris, would not go further than combining with England to effect a peaceful mediation. Austria was not in a frame of mind to relinquish any part of the provinces she had had so severe a struggle to retain.

[38]:The first act of the *Vor-Parlament*, a body which had existed temporarily at Frankfort, to pave the way for the National Assembly of a Consolidated Germany, had been to treat Schleswig, theretofore part of the Danish dominions, as absorbed in the German Confederation, and Lord Palmerston's objections to this proceeding had been treated by the Queen in a letter of 19th August as inconsistent with his attitude towards Austria.

[39]:One hundred and seventy-eight persons perished in the burning of the *Ocean Monarch*; the French Princes were on board a Brazilian steam frigate, which saved one hundred and fifty-six lives.

[40]:See *ante*, p. 193, note 35.

[41]:Lord Palmerston's object, in which he ultimately succeeded, was, by obtaining the French Government's co-operation in mediating between Austria and Piedmont, to prevent the aggressive party in France from maturing any designs on Italy.

[42]:The incorporation of Schleswig had been forcibly resisted, and Sweden determined on armed intervention; but a temporary armistice was arranged in August. This the National Assembly attempted to disavow, but a few days after this letter was written it was ratified.

[43]:*See* Introductory Note for 1849, *post*, p. 208.

[44]:Lord Palmerston replied that his observations on the two Kings lay at the very root of his argument, and were necessary to conciliate the present Government of France.

[45]:In July, Pretorius, the Boer leader, had in consequence of the British annexation of territory, expelled the British Resident from Bloemfontein. *See* Introductory Note, *ante*, p. 142. Sir Harry Smith decisively defeated the Boers on the 29th of August.

[46]:Sir Robert Gardiner, K.C.B.. was appointed Governor and Commander-in-Chief of Gibraltar on the 21st of November, and held that post till 1855.

[47]:Lord John had written to the effect that, while no definite decision had been arrived at with regard to Italy, it was thought by the Cabinet that every means should be used to induce Austria to give up Lombardy to an Austrian Prince, as most conformable to the interests of Austria herself. The question of Sicily (he added) was more difficult, but if no agreement could be arrived at by amicable negotiation, the Cabinet would not be disposed to advise the Queen to have recourse to forcible intervention.

[48]:See Greville's appreciative description of Lady Beauvale in his Journal for the 30th of January 1853.

[49]:Official translation.

[50]:This letter was suitably acknowledged in general terms. *See* p. 210.

[51]:He was elected President on the 10th of December, by an immense majority.

[52]:Lord Palmerston had written to say that Lord Normanby's credentials were provisional, and regular credentials would become necessary. The new French Government were sending Ambassadors to Vienna, Rome, and other capitals, which in return would send Ambassadors to Paris, so that it would be injurious for this country's representative to be of inferior diplomatic rank. "It would," he wrote subsequently, "be derogatory to the dignity of your Majesty, and to the character of your Majesty's Government if, in the present state of things between the British and Spanish Governments the Spanish Ambassador should, by a dilatoriness on the part of your Majesty's Government, be allowed to raise a question about precedence with your Majesty's representative at Paris; it would be very inconvenient if that question were decided unfavourably to your Majesty's representative, and very undesirable that he should appear to be under obligation to the French Government for a decision in his favour."

[53]:See *ante*, p. 175.

INTRODUCTORY NOTE
TO CHAPTER XVIII

The opening of Parliament (1849) was noteworthy for the appearance of Mr Disraeli as leader of the Opposition in the House of Commons, in place of Lord George Bentinck, who had died suddenly in the recess; the Peelites, though influential, were numerically few, and they continued by their support to maintain the Whigs in office, the principal measure of the session being the Act for the repeal of the Navigation Laws, a natural corollary to Peel's free trade policy. A Royal visit was paid to Ireland in August, and at Cork, Waterford, Dublin, and Belfast, the Queen and Prince were received with great enthusiasm.

Abroad, the cause of United Italy suffered a severe check. The Sicilian revolt came to an end, and Austrian ascendency was re-established in Northern Italy. King Charles Albert was defeated at Novara, and abdicated in favour of his son, Victor Emmanuel. The Pope, who had fled from Rome in disguise, in November 1848, and was living at Gaëta, was now under the protection of Austria and France, and General Oudinot occupied the Papal city on his behalf in June. Austrian influence restored Tuscany, Parma, and Modena to their rulers, and in Central Europe operated to prevent the acceptance by the King of Prussia of the Imperial Crown of Germany. Hungary, in consequence of the help rendered to the Viennese insurrectionists in 1848, was reduced to submission, but only with Russian co-operation. Heavy retribution was inflicted on the Hungarians; Kossuth and other revolutionaries fled to Turkey, the Russian and Austrian Governments unsuccessfully demanding their extradition.

The British operations against the Sikhs were brought to a successful termination; the Commander-in-Chief, Lord Gough, with inferior numbers, had engaged the enemy at Chillianwalla, with indecisive and virtually unfavourable results, and Sir Charles Napier was sent out to supersede him. Mooltan, where the outrage of the previous year had taken place, had been besieged, and fell on the 22nd of January. Dalhousie had established himself at Ferozepore. A week or two later the Sikhs and Afghans were overwhelmingly defeated at Gujerat, and on the 29th of March the Punjab was incorporated in the British Empire; the "Koh-i-noor" was, in token of submission, presented by the Maharajah to the Queen. Lord Dalhousie received a Marquisate, and the thanks of both Houses of Parliament were voted to all concerned.

CHAPTER XVIII

1849

Memorandum on Matters connected with the Form of addressing the Pope in Answer to his Letter to Her Majesty of 4th December 1848.

Foreign Office, *5th January 1849.*

The accompanying draft of answer to the letter which the Pope addressed to Her Majesty from Gaëta on the 4th of December is in the same form as letters which were written to Pope Pius VII. by George the Fourth while Prince Regent, and after he came to the Throne. They address the Pope as "Most Eminent Sir," style him "Your Holiness," and finish with the mere signature after the date of the conclusion of the letter. Copies of those letters are annexed.

Other forms of writing Royal letters are:—

1st. Commencing "Sir my Brother" (or "Sir my Cousin," etc., as the case may be), and ending thus:

"Sir my *Brother*,

Your *Majesty's*

Good *Sister*."

This is the form used between Sovereign and Sovereign.

2nd. Commencing with the Queen's titles. In these letters the plural "we" and "our" are employed instead of "I" and "my," and the letters terminate thus:—

"Your Good Friend,

. . . ."

This form is now used almost exclusively for Royal letters to Republics.

In the State Paper Office there is, with only one exception, no record of any letter from a Sovereign of England to the Pope from the time of Henry VIII., when the State Paper Office records commence. The single exception is an original letter from Queen Mary in 1555 to Pope Paul IV. It seems that when the time of her expected confinement drew nigh, she caused letters to be prepared announcing the birth of a son, and signed them in anticipation of the event. When no birth took place, the letters were of course not sent off; but they have been preserved to the present day, and among them is the letter to the Pope. The accompanying paper contains a copy of the beginning and conclusion of it.

There is no trace in the State Paper Office of any letter of credence having been given by James II. to Lord Castlemaine in 1685. The correspondence of the reign of James II. is, however, very defective, and much of it must either have been suppressed or have got into private hands.

[Draft] Queen Victoria to Pope Pius IX.[1]

Most Eminent Sir,—I have received the letter which your Holiness addressed to me from Gaëta on the 4th of December last, and in which you acquaint me that in consequence of the violent proceedings of certain of your subjects, you had felt yourself obliged to depart from Rome, and for a time to quit your dominions. I assure your Holiness that I have been deeply pained at the intelligence of the events to which your letter refers, and that I do the fullest justice to the motives which induced your Holiness to withdraw for a time from your capital. Your Holiness has given so many proofs of being animated by a sincere desire to improve the condition of the people whom, under Divine Providence, you have been chosen to govern, and the clemency of your heart and the rectitude of your intentions are so well known and so truly appreciated, that I cannot but hope that the trials which you have experienced in consequence of popular commotion will speedily come to an end, and will be succeeded by a cordial, good understanding between your Holiness and the Roman people. I request your Holiness to believe that it would afford me real pleasure to be able in any degree to contribute to a result so much to be desired; and I am happy in having this opportunity of assuring you of my sincere friendship, and of the unfeigned respect and esteem which I entertain for your person and character.

Given at Windsor Castle the [   ] day of January 1849.

The President of the French Republic to Queen Victoria.

Elysée National, *le 22 Janvier 1849.*

Très chère et grande Amie,—Une de mes premières pensées lorsque le vœu de la nation Française m'appela au pouvoir fut de faire part à votre Majesté de mon avènement et des sentiments que j'apportais dans ma nouvelle position.

Des circonstances particulières ont retardé le départ de l'ambassadeur qui devait porter ma lettre; mais aujourd'hui que l'Amiral Cécile se rend à Londres je désire exprimer à votre Majesté la respectueuse sympathie que j'ai toujours éprouvée pour sa personne; je désire surtout lui dire combien je suis reconnaissant de la généreuse hospitalité qu'elle m'a donnée dans ses états lorsque j'étais fugitif ou proscrit et combien je serais heureux si ce souvenir pouvait servir à resserrer les liens qui unissent les gouvernements et les peuples de nos deux pays.

Je prie votre Majesté de croire à mes sentiments. Votre ami,

Louis Napoléon Bonaparte.

Lord John Russell to Queen Victoria.

Chesham Place, *22nd January 1849.*

Lord John Russell presents his humble duty to your Majesty, and would now wish to consult Lord Lansdowne on the propriety of offering to Lord Palmerston to exchange the Foreign Office for the Lord-Lieutenancy of Ireland.[2]

As Lord John Russell has always approved in the main of the foreign policy of Lord Palmerston, he could only make this offering in a mode honourable to Lord Palmerston—that is to say, for instance, by offering him at the same time an English Earldom, or an English Barony with the Garter. Nor could he proceed in the matter without Lord Lansdowne's concurrence.

Queen Victoria to Lord John Russell.

Windsor Castle, *22nd January 1849.*

The Queen has just received Lord John Russell's letter and enclosures, the contents of which have deeply grieved her, as the honour of her Government has always been nearest to her heart. She feels deeply the humiliation to have to make an apology to the Government of Naples, which stands so very low in public estimation, and she naturally dreads the effect this disclosure about the guns will have in the world, when she considers how many accusations have been brought against the good faith of this country latterly by many different Governments. Of course they will all consider their suspicions and accusations, however absurd they may have been, as justified and proved.

The Queen supposes that the proposition Lord John makes to her about moving Lord Palmerston to Ireland is the result of his conviction that after this disclosure it will be no longer to the advantage of the public service to leave the direction of the Foreign Affairs in these critical times in Lord Palmerston's hands. The Queen will be anxious to see Lord John upon this subject. All she wishes for is, that matters may be so managed as to reflect the least possible discredit upon the Government and Lord Palmerston himself.

Queen Victoria to the King of the Belgians.

Windsor Castle, *6th February 1849.*

My dearest Uncle,—We are well. All went off extremely well on Thursday, but the Government must expect difficulties upon their (very doubtful) Foreign Policy. I own I do *not* feel reassured about peace. *Italy* and the Pope, etc., are very ticklish subjects.

Everybody says Louis Napoleon has behaved extremely well in the last crisis—full of courage and energy, and they say that he is decidedly straightforward, which is not to be despised. I will not admit that the *Gemüthlichkeit ist für immer begraben* in Germany; it will surely return when this madness is over, but how soon no one can tell. Ever your devoted Niece,

Victoria R.

Queen Victoria to the Earl of Dalhousie.

Windsor Castle, *6th February 1849.*

The Queen has not yet thanked Lord Dalhousie for his long and interesting letter which she received in the summer. Since that period many important events have taken place in India, and the last news have naturally made the Queen feel very anxious. She deeply laments the loss of General Cureton and Colonel Havelock, officers who will not be easily replaced. The Queen thinks that Lord Dalhousie has throughout acted most judiciously and has thwarted more mischief being done. She will abstain from remarking upon the conduct of the Commander-in-Chief, as she knows that the Duke of Wellington has written fully to Lord Dalhousie on this painful subject.[3] The Queen concludes with expressing her hopes that Lord and Lady Dalhousie are in good health, and with the Prince's kindest remembrances to Lord Dalhousie.

The King of the Belgians to Queen Victoria.

Laeken, *10th February 1849.*

My dearest Victoria,—I have to offer my most affectionate thanks for your dear letter of the 6th. The state of the Queen seems better, though I fear not so solidly as to be beyond mischief; but the improvement is real, and will act as a moral support. They have been severely tried, those poor exiles, and Heaven knows what is still in store for them. I don't think that in Italy there will be war. The French cannot think of it for some months, probably not before June or July, and the Italians cannot make it alone without being licked; the better informed know that. The Pope ought to be replaced on his seat for the sake of every one; and his ultra-Liberal policy entitles him to be supported by all Governments and by all right-minded people.

Louis Bonaparte has not ill-behaved, it seems; negatively he might have done much harm. The position continues to be abominable. There is for every one an *absence d'avenir* which ruins everything and everybody—that is the real difficulty.

Die Gemüthlichkeit in Germany was the consequence of its political existence these last thousand years; that is now all going to ruin, and the *Gemüthlichkeit* will be as little found again *que l'urbanité Française* so much talked of formerly and now unknown.

This part of February puts me always in mind of my dear little *séjour* with you in 1841. How far that period is now, though but eight years from us; the very features of everything changed, I fear for ever, and *not* for the better.... Now I must conclude, and remain ever, my dearest Victoria, your truly devoted Uncle,

Leopold R.

Memorandum by Queen Victoria.

Buckingham Palace, *19th February 1849.*

Admiral Cécile, who dined here for the first time after the presentation of his credentials as Ambassador from the French Republic, with whom I spoke for some time after dinner, said: "Nous en avons fait de tristes expériences en France," but that he hoped "que les choses s'amélioraient"; that the Government was very firm and decided, and determined not to allow order to be disturbed; "Paris a maintenant fait quatre Révolutions que la France a subies; votre Majesté sait qui a proclamé la République au mois de Février? Une centaine de coquins! Personne s'en doutait, et cependant la France s'y est soumise!" That the Government was however determined, and so were all the Departments, that this should never happen again; no doubt the danger from the Socialists was great, all over the world; that *that* was the *real danger*, and that they would readily make another attempt like the fearful one in June (the result of which for three days was uncertain), but that they had not the power; that he was continually impressing upon all his friends in France the necessity of supporting *whatever* form of Government there was *whose object* was the *maintenance of order*, and to unite "contre cet ennemi commun." The President, he continued, had risen amazingly in the opinion of every one by his firmness, courage, and determination—which he had shown in those critical days a fortnight or three weeks ago—and that in these two months he had acquired "une grande aptitude pour les affaires; tout le monde est étonné, parce que personne ne s'y attendait." He spoke with great delight of Belgium—and how it had stood the shock of the events in France—and also of England. Italy, he considered, was by far the greatest object of danger.

Victoria R.

Queen Victoria to the Marquis of Lansdowne.

Osborne, *3rd March 1849.*

The Queen sends Lord Lansdowne the book[4] she mentioned to him. It is an extraordinary production for people of the working classes, and there are a great many sound and good observations in it on education; the observations on the deficiency in the religious instruction and in the *preaching* the Queen thinks are particularly true. It likewise shows a lofty and enlarged *view* of education which is often overlooked.

The Queen takes this occasion of repeating her hope that *Gaelic* will be taught in future in the Highland schools, as well as English, as it is really a great mistake that the people should be constantly *talking* a language which they often cannot read and generally not write. Being very partial to her loyal and good Highlanders, the Queen takes much interest in what she thinks will tend more than anything to keep up their simplicity of character, which she considers a great merit in these days.

The Queen thinks equally that Welsh should be taught in Wales as well as English.[5]

Queen Victoria to the King of the Belgians.

Osborne, *6th March 1849.*

My dearest Uncle,—Your dear letter reached me yesterday, and I thank you warmly for it. I wish you could be here, for I never remember finer weather than we have had since we came here; perfect summer, and so sweet, so enjoyable, and then with all the pleasures and beauties of Spring you have that beautiful sea—so blue and smooth as it has been these three days. If we have no mountains to boast of, we have the *sea*, which is ever enjoyable. We have camelias which have stood out two winters covered with *red* flowers, and scarlet rhododendrons in brilliant bloom. Does this not sound tempting? It seems almost wrong to be at home, and Albert really hardly is.

I wish you joy of your *twenty-four* foxes. If there was a black one amongst them I should beg for one, as the skin you sent me last year was *not* a black one.

The news from India are very distressing, and make one very anxious, but Sir Charles Napier is instantly to be sent out to supersede Lord Gough, and he is so well versed in Indian tactics that we may look with safety to the future *after* his arrival.

The Italian Question remains very complicated, and the German one a very perplexing, sad one. Prussia must protect the poor Princes and put herself at the head, else there is no hope. Austria should behave better, and not oppose the consolidation of a central Power, else I know not what is to become of poor Germany.

Pray use your influence to prevent more fatal mischief.

Now adieu, dearest Uncle. Ever your devoted Niece,

Victoria R.

Lord John Russell to Queen Victoria.

Chesham Place, *16th March 1849.*

Lord John Russell presents his humble duty to your Majesty, and has the honour to state that the debate last night was brought to a close.[6]

Mr Cobden and Mr Disraeli made very able speeches at the end of the debate.

The debate has been a remarkable one, and the division shows tolerably well the strength of parties. The Protectionists, animated by the cry of agricultural distress, are disposed to use their power to the utmost. Mr Disraeli shows himself a much abler and less passionate leader than Lord George Bentinck.

On the other hand, the friends of Sir Robert Peel and the party of Mr Cobden unite with the Government in resisting the Protectionist party. The House of Commons thus gives a majority, which, though not compact, is decided at once against the extreme Tory and the extreme Radical party. With such a House of Commons the great interests of the Throne and the Constitution are safe. An abrupt dissolution would put everything to hazard.

The Earl of Dalhousie to Queen Victoria.

Camp, Ferozepore, *24th March 1849.*

The Governor-General presents his most humble duty to your Majesty, and has the honour of acknowledging the receipt of the letter which your Majesty most graciously addressed to him on the 5th of February.

He is deeply sensible of your Majesty's goodness, and most grateful for the expression of approbation which it has conveyed.

The Governor-General is not without fear that he may have intruded too often of late upon your Majesty's time. But he is so satisfied of the extreme pleasure which your Majesty would experience on learning that the prisoners who were in the hands of the Sikhs, and especially the ladies and children, were once again safe in the British camp, that he would have ventured to convey to your Majesty that intelligence, even though he had not been able to add to it—as happily he can—the announcement of the surrender of the whole Khalsa army, and the end of the war with the Sikhs.

Major-General Gilbert pushed on rapidly in pursuit of the Sikhs, who were a few marches in front of him, carrying off our prisoners with them.

At Rawul Pindee, half-way between the Jhelum and Attock, the Sikh troops, as we have since heard, would go no further. They received no pay, they were starving, they had been beaten and were disheartened; and so they surrendered.

All the prisoners were brought safe into our camp. Forty-one pieces of artillery were given up. Chuttur Singh and Shere Singh, with all the Sirdars, delivered their swords to General Gilbert in the presence of his officers; and the remains of the Sikh army, 16,000 strong, were marched into camp, by 1000 at a time, and laid down their arms as they passed between the lines of the British troops.

Your Majesty may well imagine the pride with which British Officers looked on such a scene, and witnessed this absolute subjection and humiliation of so powerful an enemy.

How deeply the humiliation was felt by the Sikhs themselves may be judged by the report which the officers who were present have made, that many of them, and especially the grim old Khalsas of Runjeet's time, exclaimed as they threw their arms down upon the heap: "This day Runjeet Singh has died!"

Upwards of 20,000 stands of arms were taken in the hills. Vast quantities were gathered after the flight of the Sikhs from Gujerat. As a further precaution, the Governor-General has ordered a disarming of the Sikhs throughout the Eastern Doabs, while they are yet cast down and afraid of punishment. He trusts that these measures may all tend to ensure the continuance of peace.

The Sirdars will arrive at Lahore to-day, where they will await the determination of their future places of residence. The officers who were prisoners have also reached Lahore, together with Mrs George Lawrence and her children.

It is impossible to speak too highly of the admirable spirit which this lady has displayed during many months of very arduous trial.

By the kindness of others, the Governor-General has had the opportunity of seeing constantly the little notes which were secretly despatched by her from her prison. The gallant heart she kept up under it all, the cheerful face she put upon it, and the unrepining patience with which she bore the privations of captivity and the dangers which it threatened to her children, her husband, and herself, must command the highest respect and make one proud of one's countrywomen.

General Gilbert, by the latest intelligence, had seized the fort of Attock, had crossed the Indus, and was advancing on Peshawur, whither the Afghans had retired.

By next mail the Governor-General trusts that he will be able to announce that every enemy has been swept away by your Majesty's Armies, and that the Afghans have either been crushed like the Sikhs or have fled to Cabul again.

He has the honour to subscribe himself, your Majesty's most obedient, most humble and very faithful Subject and Servant,

Dalhousie.

The King of Sardinia (Victor Emanuel) to Queen Victoria.

Turin, *le 30 Mars 1849.*

Ma très chère Sœur,—La participation officielle que je m'empresse de vous donner de mon avènement au trône m'offre une occasion que je suis heureux de saisir pour vous exprimer dans une lettre de ma main les sentiments de ma vive gratitude pour l'affection dont ma maison a reçu des preuves marquantes et réitérées de votre part, comme pour le bienveillant intérêt que votre Gouvernement a témoigné à ce pays particulièrement dans les graves événements qui ont eu lieu pendant cette dernière année.

Je vous prie d'être persuadée que rien n'est plus sincère que la reconnaissance que j'en conserve, et de me laisser nourrir la confiance que je puis compter sur la continuation de ces dispositions si aimables.

En vous renouvelant les sentiments d'amitié la plus parfaite, je suis, votre très cher Frère,

Victor Emanuel.

Queen Victoria to the King of the Belgians.

Windsor Castle, *10th April 1849.*

My dearest Uncle,—You will, I am sure, share our joy at Ernest's *wonderful* success at Eckerforde.[7] It is a marvellous piece of good fortune *pour son baptême de feu*, but it alarmed and agitated us all to think that he might have been wounded, *to say the least*, for he had his horse killed under him. At all events, he has done honour to the poor race to which he belongs, and it makes us both very happy. I think it will tend decidedly to shorten the war. Poor dear Alexandrine! in what anxiety she will have been.

The victory of Novara[8] seems to have been one of the hardest fought and most brilliant battles known for years and years, and old Radetzky says that he must name every individual if he was to do justice to officers and men. But the loss was very severe. The regiment of Kinsky lost *twenty-four* officers! The Archduke Albert distinguished himself exceedingly, which is worthy of his noble father. I could work myself up to a great excitement about these exploits, for there is nothing I admire more than great military exploits and daring.

Queen Victoria to the Duke of Wellington.

1st May 1849.

The Queen cannot let this day pass without offering to the Duke of Wellington her warmest and sincerest wishes for many happy returns of this day. She hopes the Duke will place the accompanying trifle on his table, and that it will recall to his mind *one* who ever reflects with gratitude on the services he has rendered and always does render to his Sovereign and his country.

Queen Victoria to the King of the Belgians.

Buckingham Palace, *8th May 1849.*

My dearest Uncle,—Alas! poor Germany, I am wretched about her; those news from Dresden are very distressing.[9] Really with such an excellent man as the poor King, it is too wicked to do what they have done. If only *some sort* of arrangement could be made; then afterwards there might be modifications, both in the Constitution, etc., for that Constitution never will work well.

Our Navigation Laws debate in the House of Lords began last night, and is to be concluded to-night. There seems to be almost a certainty that there will be a majority, though a very small one, and the danger of course exists that any accident may turn it the other way.

Knowing your esteem for our worthy friend, Sir Robert Peel, you will, I am sure, be glad to hear that his second son, Frederick,[10] made such a beautiful speech—his maiden speech—in the House of Commons last night; he was complimented by every one, and Sir Robert was delighted. I am so glad for him, and also rejoice to see that there is a young man who promises to be of use hereafter to his country.

Albert is again gone to lay a first stone. It is a delight to hear people speak of the good he does by always saying and doing the right thing....

Queen Victoria to the King of the Belgians.

Buckingham Palace, *22nd May 1849*.

My dearest Uncle,—I could not write to you yesterday, my time having been so entirely taken up by kind visitors, etc., and I trust you will forgive these hurried lines written just before our departure for Osborne.[11] I hope that you will not have been alarmed by the account of the occurrence which took place on Saturday, and which I can assure you did *not* alarm *me* at all. *This* time it is quite clear that it was a wanton and wicked wish merely to *frighten*, which is very wrong, and will be tried and punished as a *misdemeanour*. The account in the *Times* is quite correct. The indignation, loyalty, and affection this act has called forth is very gratifying and touching.

Alice gives a very good account of it, and Lenchen[12] even says, "Man shot, tried to shoot dear Mamma, must be punished." They, Affie, and Miss Macdonald were with me. Albert was riding, and had just returned before me. Augustus and Clém had left us just two hours before....

Many thanks for your kind letter of the 19th. *What* a state Germany is in!—I mean *Baden*, but I hope that this violent crisis may lead to good.

I must conclude. Ever your truly devoted Niece,

Victoria R.

Queen Victoria to Lord John Russell.

Osborne, *26th May 1849*.

The Queen has to say, in answer to Lord John Russell's communication respecting India, that she quite approves the annexation of the Punjab, and is pleased to find that the Government concur in this view. The elevation of Lord Dalhousie to a Marquisate is well deserved, and almost the only thing that can be offered him as a reward for his services; but considering his want of fortune, the Queen thinks that it should be ascertained in the first instance whether the increase of rank will be convenient to him. Lord Gough's elevation to the dignity of Viscount has the Queen's sanction.

Lord John Russell to the Prince Albert.

Chesham Place, *19th June 1849.*

Sir,—I have spoken to Lord Palmerston respecting the draft to Mr Buchanan.[13]

It appears that he converted it into a private letter, as I suggested, but he thought fit to place it on record, as it contained information derived from authentic sources, and of importance.

It appears the drafts are still sent to the Queen at the same time as to me, so that my remarks or corrections, or even the cancelling of a despatch, as not infrequently happens, may take effect after the Queen's pleasure has been taken.

This appears to me an inconvenient course.

Lord Palmerston alleges that as 28,000 despatches were received and sent last year, much expedition is required; but he professes himself ready to send the despatches to me in the first instance, if the Queen should desire it.

It appears to me that all our despatches ought to be thoroughly considered, but that Her Majesty should give every facility to the transaction of business by attending to the drafts as soon as possible after their arrival.

I would suggest therefore that the drafts should have my concurrence before they are submitted to the Queen, and in case of any material change, that I should write to apprise Her Majesty of my views, and, if necessary, submit my reasons, I have the honour to be, your Royal Highness's most obedient Servant,

J. Russell.

The Prince Albert to Lord John Russell.

20th June 1849.

My dear Lord John,—Your proposal with respect to the mode of taking the Queen's pleasure about the drafts is perfectly agreeable to the Queen. She would only require that she would not be pressed for an answer within a few minutes, as is now done sometimes.

Lord Palmerston could always manage so that there are twelve or twenty-four hours left for reference to you, and consideration, and there are few instances in which business would suffer from so short a delay. As Lord Palmerston knows when the Mails go, he has only to write in time for them, and he must recollect that the 28,000 despatches in the year come to you and to the Queen as well as to himself.

Should the Queen in future have to make any remark, she will make it to you, if that will suit you. Ever yours truly,

Albert.

Lord John Russell to Viscount Palmerston.

21st June 1849.

My dear Palmerston,—I wrote the substance of what you wrote to me to the Prince, and proposed that the drafts should, in the first instance, be sent to me. You will see by the enclosed letter from the Prince that the Queen approves of this proposal.

It may somewhat abridge the circuit if, when I have no remark to make, I forward the drafts with the Foreign Office direction to the Queen at once.

I cannot pretend to say that I paid the same attention to the 28,000 despatches of 1848 that you are obliged to do. Still I agree in the Prince's remark that directions to Foreign Ministers ought to be very maturely weighed, for the Queen and the Government speak to foreign nations in this and no other manner. Yours truly,

J. Russell.

Queen Victoria to Viscount Palmerston.

Buckingham Palace, *21st June 1849.*

The Queen returns the enclosed drafts, which she will not further object to, but she feels it necessary to say a few words in answer to Lord Palmerston's letter. The union of Schleswig and Holstein[14] is not an ideal one, but *complete* as to Constitution, Finance, Customs, Jurisdiction, Church, Universities, Poor Law, Settlement, Debts, etc., etc., etc. It is *not established* by the Kings-Dukes, but has existed for centuries. To defend Holstein against the attack made by Denmark upon this union, Germany joined the war. It is true that it is now proposed in the new Constitution for Germany to consent to the separation of Schleswig and Holstein, although last year the Frankfort Parliament had desired the incorporation of Schleswig into Germany with Holstein; but the question for Germany is now not to begin a war, but to close one by a lasting peace. In this she has, in the Queen's opinion, a right and a duty to see that the independence of Schleswig is secured before she abandons that country. The comparison with Saxony does not hold good for a moment, for the Schleswig Revolution was not directed against the Duke, but against the King of Denmark, who invaded the rights of the Duke of Schleswig-Holstein; the assistance of Prussia could therefore not be given to Denmark, but to Schleswig-Holstein. The case of Hungary has neither any similitude. Hungary is not to be torn from its connection with the German States by the Austrian Government, but just the reverse.

Lord Palmerston cannot be more anxious for a speedy termination of the Danish war than the Queen is, but she thinks that the mediation will not effect this as long as the mediating power merely watches which of the two parties is in the greatest difficulties for the moment, and urges it to give way; but by a careful and anxious discovery of the rights of the question and a steady adherence to the recommendation that what is right and fair ought to be done. The cause of the war having been the unlawful attempt to incorporate Schleswig into Denmark, the peace cannot be lasting unless it contains sufficient guarantees against the resumption of that scheme.[15]

Lord John Russell to the Earl of Clarendon.
23rd June 1849.

I have the satisfaction to inform your Excellency that I have received the Queen's commands to acquaint you that Her Majesty hopes to be able in the course of the present summer to fulfil the intention, which you are aware she has long entertained, of a visit to Ireland. The general distress unfortunately still prevalent in Ireland precludes the Queen from visiting Dublin in state, and thereby causing ill-timed expenditure and inconvenience to her subjects; yet Her Majesty does not wish to let another year pass without visiting a part of her dominions which she has for so long a time been anxious personally to become acquainted with. She accordingly will, at some sacrifice of personal convenience, take a longer sea voyage, for the purpose of visiting in the first instance the Cove of Cork, and from thence proceed along the Irish coast to Dublin. After remaining there a few days, during which time Her Majesty will be the guest of your Excellency, she would continue her cruise along the Irish coast northward and visit Belfast, and from thence cross to Scotland. Although the precise time of Her Majesty's visit cannot yet be fixed, it will probably take place as early in August as the termination of the session of Parliament will permit, and

I feel assured that this early announcement of her intentions will be received with great satisfaction by Her Majesty's loyal and faithful subjects in Ireland.

Queen Victoria to Lord John Russell.

Osborne, *19th July 1849.*

The Queen has received Lord John Russell's letters. She returns Lord Clarendon's, and the very kind one of the Primate.[16]

With respect to Lord Clarendon's suggestion that the Prince of Wales should be created Duke, or rather, as Lord John *says*, *Earl* of Dublin—the Queen thinks it is a matter for consideration whether such an act should *follow* the Queen's visit as a compliment to Ireland, but she is decidedly of opinion that it should *not precede* it.

We are sorry that Lord John does not intend going to Ireland, but fully comprehend his wishes to remain quiet for three weeks. We shall be very glad to see him at Balmoral on the 20th or 22nd of August.

We hope Lady John and the baby continue to go on well.

Queen Victoria to the King of the Belgians.

Lodge, Phœnix Park, *6th August 1849.*

My dearest Uncle,—Though this letter will only go to-morrow, I will begin it to-day and tell you that everything has gone off beautifully since we arrived in Ireland, and that our entrance into Dublin was really a magnificent thing. By my letter to Louise you will have heard of our arrival in the Cove of Cork. Our visit to Cork was very successful; the Mayor was knighted *on deck* (on board the *Fairy*), like in times of old. Cork is about seventeen miles up the River Lee, which is beautifully wooded and reminds us of Devonshire scenery. We had previously stepped on shore at *Cove*, a small place, to enable them to call it *Queen's Town*; the enthusiasm is immense, and at Cork there was more firing than I remember since the Rhine.

We left Cork with fair weather, but a head sea and contrary wind which made it rough and me very sick.

7th.—I was unable to continue till now, and have since received your kind letter, for which I return my warmest thanks. We went into Waterford Harbour on Saturday afternoon, which is likewise a fine, large, safe harbour. Albert went up to Waterford in the *Fairy*, but I did not. The next morning we received much the same report of the weather which we had done at Cork, viz. that the weather was fair but the wind contrary. However we went out, as it could not be helped,

233

and we might have remained there some days for no use. The first three hours were very nasty, but afterwards it cleared and the evening was beautiful. The entrance at seven o'clock into Kingston Harbour was splendid; we came in with ten steamers, and the whole harbour, wharf, and every surrounding place was *covered* with *thousands* and thousands of people, who received us with the greatest enthusiasm. We disembarked yesterday morning at ten o'clock, and took two hours to come here. The most perfect order was maintained in spite of the immense mass of people assembled, and a more good-humoured crowd I never saw, but noisy and excitable beyond belief, talking, jumping, and shrieking instead of cheering. There were numbers of troops out, and it really was a wonderful scene. This is a very pretty place, and the house reminds me of dear Claremont. The view of the Wicklow Mountains from the windows is very beautiful, and the whole park is very extensive and full of very fine trees.

We drove out yesterday afternoon and were followed by jaunting-cars and riders and people running and screaming, which would have amused you. In the evening we had a dinner party, and so we have to-night. This morning we visited the Bank, the Model School (where the Protestant and Catholic Archbishops received us), and the College, and this afternoon we went to the Military Hospital. To-morrow we have a Levée, where 1,700 are to be presented, and the next day a Review, and in the evening the Drawing-Room, when 900 ladies are to be presented.

George[17] is here, and has a command here. He rode on one side of our carriage yesterday. You see more ragged and wretched people here than I ever saw anywhere else. *En revanche*, the women are really very handsome—quite in the lowest class—as well at Cork as here; such beautiful black eyes and hair and such fine colours and teeth.

I must now take my leave. Ever your most affectionate Niece,

Victoria R.

The Earl of Clarendon to Sir George Grey.

Vice-Regal Lodge, *14th August 1849.*

My dear Grey,—If I had known where to direct I should have thanked you sooner for your two welcome letters from Belfast, where everything seems to have gone off to our hearts' desire, and the Queen's presence, as the Stipendiary Magistrate writes word, has united all classes and parties in a manner incredible to those who know the distance at which they have hitherto been kept asunder.

The enthusiasm here has not abated, and there is not an individual in Dublin that does not take as a personal compliment to himself the Queen's having gone upon the paddle-box and having ordered the Royal Standard to be lowered three times.

Even the ex-Clubbists,[18] who threatened broken heads and windows before the Queen came, are now among the most loyal of her subjects, and are ready, according to the police reports, to fight any one who dare say a disrespectful word of Her Majesty.

In short, the people are not only enchanted with the Queen and the gracious kindness of her manner and the confidence she has shown in them, but they are pleased with themselves for their own good feelings and behaviour, which they consider have removed the barrier that hitherto existed between the Sovereign and themselves, and that they now occupy a higher position in the eyes of the world. Friend Bright was with me to-day, and said he would not for the world have missed seeing the embarkation at Kingston, for he had felt just the same enthusiasm as the rest of the crowd. "Indeed," he added, "I'll defy any man to have felt otherwise when he saw the Queen come upon the platform and bow to the people in a manner that showed her heart was with them." He didn't disguise either that the Monarchical principle had made great way with him since Friday. Ever yours truly,

Clarendon.

Queen Victoria to Lord John Russell.

Osborne, *3rd October 1849.*

The Queen has received Lord John Russell's explanation respecting the brevet promotions on the occasion of her visit to Ireland, but cannot say that his objections have convinced her of the impropriety of such a promotion (to a limited extent). To Lord John's fears of the dangerous consequences of the precedent, the Queen has only to answer, that there can be only *one first visit* to Ireland, and that the *first* visit to Scotland in 1842 was followed by a few promotions, without this entailing promotions on her subsequent visits to that part of the country; that even the first visit to the Channel Islands was followed by a few promotions, and this under Lord John's Government. All the precedents being in accordance with the proposition made by the Duke, an opposition on the part of the Government would imply a declaration against all brevets except in the field, which would deprive the Crown of a most valuable prerogative. If such a brevet as the one proposed were to lead to great additional expense, the Queen could understand the objection on the ground of economy; but the giving brevet rank to a few subaltern officers is too trifling a matter to alarm the Government. Perhaps the number might be reduced even, but to deviate from the established precedents for the first time altogether in this case, and that after the excellent behaviour of the Army in Ireland under very trying circumstances, would be felt as a great injustice.

The Queen therefore wishes Lord John to ask the Duke to send him the former precedents and to consider with his colleagues whether a modified recommendation cannot be laid before her.[19]

Lord John Russell to Queen Victoria.

Woburn Abbey, *4th October 1849.*

Lord John Russell presents his humble duty to your Majesty, and will consider, in communication with the Duke of Wellington, whether any modified list can be proposed by him to your Majesty.

The economy, as your Majesty truly observes, is not a matter of much consideration. But to reward Officers on the Staff, who are already favoured by being placed on the Staff in Ireland, is a practice which tends but too much to encourage the opinion that promotions in the Army and Navy are given not to merit, but to aristocratical connection and official favour.

In the midst of the degradation of Thrones which the last two years have seen in Europe, it will be well if the English Crown preserves all its just prerogatives, and has only to relinquish some customary abuses, which are not useful to the Sovereign, and are only an equivocal advantage to the Ministers of the day.

Queen Victoria to Lord John Russell.

Windsor Castle, *31st October 1849.*

The Queen has just received Lord John Russell's letter, and was much rejoiced at everything having gone off so well yesterday;[20] she was very much annoyed at being unable to go herself, and that the untoward chicken-pox should have come at this moment; she is, however, quite recovered, though still much marked.

With respect to the proposition about the Thanksgiving, the Queen quite approves of it, and (*if it is generally preferred*) that it should be on a week-day. As to the Bishop of London's proposal,[21] the

Queen thinks that Lord John may have misunderstood him; she supposes that he meant that she should attend *some* place of *public worship*, and not in her domestic chapel, in order to join in the public demonstration. The Queen is quite ready to go with her Court to St George's Chapel here; but she would like it to take place on an earlier day than the 27th of November, when she would probably be already in the Isle of Wight, where we think of going as usual on the 22nd or 23rd.

Lord John Russell to Queen Victoria.

Eaton Square, *29th November 1849.*

Lord John Russell presents his humble duty to your Majesty. In answer to your Majesty's enquiry, he has to state that a very short conversation took place in the Cabinet on the affairs of Germany upon an enquiry of Lord John Russell whether the Diet of Erfurt[22] might not be considered a violation of the Treaties of 1815. Lord Palmerston thought not, but had not examined the question.

The affairs of Germany are in a critical position; Austria will oppose anything which tends to aggrandise Prussia; Prussia will oppose anything which tends to free Government; and France will oppose anything which tends to strengthen Germany. Still, all these powers might be disregarded were Germany united, but it is obvious that Bavaria and Würtemberg look to Austria and France for support, while Hanover and Saxony will give a very faint assistance to a Prussian League.

The matter is very critical, but probably will not lead to war.

Viscount Palmerston to Queen Victoria.

Foreign Office, *30th November 1849.*

Viscount Palmerston presents his humble duty to your Majesty, and in reply to your Majesty's enquiry as to what the measures would be which Sir William Parker[23] would have to take in order to support Mr Wyse's[24] demands for redress for certain wrongs sustained by British and Ionian subjects, begs to say that the ordinary and accustomed method of enforcing such demands is by reprisals—that is to say, by seizing some vessels and property of the party which refuses redress,[25] and retaining possession thereof until redress is granted.

Another method is the blockading of the ports of the party by whom redress is refused, and by interrupting commercial intercourse to cause inconvenience and loss. Viscount Palmerston, however, does not apprehend that any active measures of this kind will be required, but rather expects that when the Greek Government finds that the demand is made in earnest, and that means are at hand to enforce it, satisfaction will at last be given. The refusal of the Greek Government to satisfy these claims, and the offensive neglect with which they have treated the applications of your Majesty's representative at Athens have, as Viscount Palmerston is convinced, been the result of a belief that the British Government never would take any real steps in order to press these matters to a settlement.

Queen Victoria to the King of the Belgians.

Osborne, *11th December 1849.*

My dearest Uncle,—Thank you much for your kind letter of the 6th; you will have received mine of the 4th shortly after you wrote. I know *how* you would mourn with us over the death of our beloved Queen Adelaide. *We* have lost the kindest and dearest of friends, and the *universal* feeling of sorrow, of regret, and of *real* appreciation of her character is very touching and gratifying. *All* parties, *all* classes, join in doing her justice. Much was done to set Mamma against her, but the dear Queen ever forgave this, ever showed love and affection, and for the last eight years their friendship was as great as ever. Ever yours affectionately,

Victoria R.

ENDNOTES:

[1]:*See* p. 208.
[2]:Hostilities were in progress between the Sicilian insurgents and their Sovereign. An agent for the former came to England to purchase arms, but was informed by the contractor to whom he applied that the whole of his stock had been pledged to the Ordnance Office. Lord Palmerston, without consulting the Cabinet, allowed this stock to be transferred to the insurgents. The matter became public property, and the Premier brought it before the Cabinet on the 23rd of January, when, somewhat unexpectedly, the Foreign Secretary consented to make an apology to the Neapolitan Government; so that the crisis terminated for the time.
[3]:*See* Introductory Note for the year, *ante*, p. 216.
[4]:This book was probably *Popular Education, as regards Juvenile Delinquency*, by Thos. Bullock, 1849.

[5]:Lord Lansdowne, in his reply, undertook "to combine instruction in the Gaelic with the English language in the Highland as well as the Welsh schools, and to have a view to it in the choice of Inspectors."

[6]:On Mr Disraeli's motion for payment of the half of local rates by the Treasury, which was defeated by 280 to 189.

[7]:In this engagement with the Danes, arising out of the Schleswig-Holstein dispute, Prince Ernest greatly distinguished himself.

[8]:In which Marshal Radetzky defeated the Piedmontese.

[9]:The King of Prussia, finding Saxony, Bavaria, Würtemberg, and Hanover opposed to the ascendency of Prussia in the Confederation, declined the Imperial Crown of Germany; fresh disturbances thereupon ensued, and at Dresden, the King of Saxony had to take refuge in a fortress.

[10]:Afterwards the Right Hon. Sir Frederick Peel, who died in 1906.

[11]:The Queen, while driving down Constitution Hill, was fired at by one William Hamilton, the pistol being charged only with powder. He was tried under the Act of 1842, and sentenced to seven years' transportation.

[12]:Princess Helena (now Princess Christian), born 25th May 1846.

[13]:Mr (afterwards Sir) Andrew Buchanan (1807-1882), Secretary of Legation at St. Petersburg.

[14]:Schleswig had been claimed by Germany as an integral part of her territory, and a war between Germany and Denmark was in progress.

[15]:In reply, Lord Palmerston expressed entire concurrence in the justice of the principles which the Queen indicated as being those which ought to guide a mediating Power.

[16]:Lord John George de la Poer Beresford (1773-1862) was Archbishop of Armagh from 1822 until his death.

[17]:The late Duke of Cambridge.

[18]:Seditious clubs had been an important factor in the Irish disturbances of 1848.

[19]:The Duke of Wellington had submitted a list of Officers for brevet promotion, which received the Queen's sanction; but the list was afterwards reduced.

[20]:The ceremony of opening the new Coal Exchange, at which, besides Prince Albert, the Prince of Wales and Princess Royal were present.

[21]:There had been a severe epidemic of cholera in the country. In twelve months 14,000 deaths, in London alone, were due to this malady. The 15th of November was appointed for a general Day of Thanksgiving for its cessation, and the Bishop of London had suggested that the Queen should attend a public service at St Paul's. Lord John Russell was in favour of Westminster Abbey.

[22]:In order to effect the consolidation of Germany, the King of Prussia had summoned a Federal Parliament to meet at Erfurt.

[23]:Commanding the Mediterranean Fleet.

[24]:British Envoy at Athens.

[25]:*See* Introductory Note for 1850, *post*, p. 240.

INTRODUCTORY NOTE
TO CHAPTER XIX

The Ministry were still (1850) able, relying on the support of Sir Robert Peel, to resist the attacks of the Protectionists in the House of Commons, though their majority on a critical occasion fell to twenty-one; but they were rehabilitated by the discussions on foreign policy. One Don Pacifico, a Portuguese Jew, a native of Gibraltar and a British subject, had had his house in Athens pillaged by a mob; he, with Mr Finlay, the historian, who had a money claim against the Greek Government, instead of establishing their claims in the local courts, sought the intervention of the home Government; Lord Palmerston, whose relations with the Court were even more strained than usual, resolved to make a hostile demonstration against Greece, and a fleet was sent to the Piræus with a peremptory demand for settlement. The House of Lords condemned this high-handed action, but a friendly motion of confidence was made in the Commons, and Lord Palmerston had an extraordinary triumph, by a majority of forty-six, notwithstanding that the ablest men outside the Ministry spoke against him, and that his unsatisfactory relations with the Queen were about to culminate in a severe reprimand.

Sir Robert Peel's speech in this debate proved to be his last public utterance, his premature death, resulting from a fall from his horse, taking place a few days later; Louis Philippe, who had been living in retirement at Claremont, passed away about the same time. Another attack on the Queen, this time a blow with a cane, was made by one Robert Pate, an ex-officer and well-connected; the plea of insanity was not established, and Pate was transported.

Public attention was being drawn to the projected Exhibition in Hyde Park, Prince Albert making a memorable speech at the Mansion House in support of the scheme; the popular voice had not been unanimous in approval, and subscriptions had hung fire, but henceforward matters improved, and Mr Paxton's design for a glass and iron structure was accepted and proceeded with.

The friction with Lord Palmerston was again increased by his action in respect to General Haynau, an Austrian whose cruelty had been notorious, and who was assaulted by some of the *employés* at a London brewery. The Foreign Office note to the Austrian Government nearly brought about Palmerston's resignation, which was much desired by the Queen.

At the close of the year the whole country was in a ferment at the issue of a Papal Brief, re-establishing the hierarchy of Bishops in England with local titles derived from their sees; and Cardinal Wiseman, thenceforward Archbishop of Westminster, by issuing a pastoral letter on the subject, made matters worse. The Protestant spirit was aroused, the two Universities presented petitions, and the Prime Minister, in a letter to the Bishop of Durham, helped to fan the "No Popery" flame. Just at a time when a coalition of Whigs and Peelites was beginning to be possible, an Ecclesiastical Titles Bill, almost fatal to mutual confidence, became necessary.

CHAPTER XIX

1850

Queen Victoria to the King of the Belgians.

Windsor Castle, *5th February 1850.*

My dear Uncle,—We had the house full for three days last week on account of our theatrical performances on Friday, which went off extremely well. The Grand Duchess Stephanie was here, *très aimable*, and not altered. She spoke much of Germany and of politics, and of *you* in the highest terms—"Comme le Roi Léopold s'est bien tenu"— and that she had mentioned this at Claremont, and then felt shocked at it, but that the poor King had answered: "Il avait mon exemple devant lui, et il en a profité!" She thought the whole family *très digne* in their *malheur*, but was struck with the melancholy effect of the whole thing.

Our affairs have gone off extremely well in Parliament, and the Protectionists have received an effective check; the question of the Corn Laws seems *indeed settled*. This is of great importance, as it puts a stop to the excitement and expectations of the farmers, which have been falsely kept up by the aristocracy....

I must now conclude. Ever your devoted Niece,

Victoria R.

Viscount Palmerston to Lord John Russell.

Carlton Gardens, *15th February 1850.*

My dear John Russell,—I have altered this draft so as I think to meet the views of the Queen and of yourself in regard to the continuance of the suspension.[1] I should not like to put into a despatch an instruction to accept less than we have demanded, because that would imply what I don't think to be the fact, viz. that we have demanded more than is due. If the demands were for the British Government, we might forego what portions we might like to give up, but we have no right to be easy and generous with the rights and claims of other people. Besides, if we get anything, we shall get all. The whole amount is quite within the power of the Greek Government to pay. Yours sincerely,

Palmerston.

Queen Victoria to Viscount Palmerston.

Buckingham Palace, *17th February 1850.*

The Queen sent the day before yesterday the proposed draft to Mr Wyse back to Lord Palmerston, enclosing a Memorandum from Lord John Russell, and telling Lord Palmerston "that she entirely concurred with Lord John, and wished the draft to be altered accordingly." She has not yet received an answer from Lord Palmerston, but just hears from Lord John, in answer to her enquiry about it, that Lord Palmerston has *sent* the draft off *unaltered.*[2] The Queen must remark upon this sort of proceeding, of which this is not the first instance, and plainly tell Lord Palmerston that this must not happen again. Lord Palmerston has a perfect right to state to the Queen his reasons for disagreeing with her views, and will always have found her ready to listen to his reasons; but she cannot allow a servant of the Crown and her Minister to act contrary to her orders, and this without her knowledge.

Viscount Palmerston to Queen Victoria.

Carlton Gardens. *17th February 1850.*

Viscount Palmerston presents his humble duty to your Majesty, and in reply to your Majesty's communication of this day, he begs to state that upon receiving, the day before yesterday, your Majesty's Memorandum on the proposed draft to Mr Wyse, together with the accompanying Memorandum[3] from Lord John Russell, he altered the draft, and sent it to Lord John Russell, and received it back from Lord John Russell with the accompanying note in answer to that which he wrote to Lord John Russell. It was important that the messenger should go off that evening, and the time occupied in these communications rendered it just, but barely, possible to despatch the messenger by the mail train of that evening. The despatch thus altered coincided with the views of your Majesty and Lord John Russell as to the question in

regard to the length of time during which reprisals should be suspended to give scope for the French negotiation. The other question as
to giving Mr Wyse a latitude of discretion to entertain any proposition
which might be made to him by the Greek Government was considered by the Cabinet at its meeting yesterday afternoon, and Viscount
Palmerston gave Mr Wyse a latitude of that kind in regard to the claim
of Mr Pacifico, the only one to which that question could apply, in a
despatch which he sent by the overland Mediterranean mail which
went off yesterday afternoon. That despatch also contained some instructions as to the manner in which Mr Wyse is to communicate with
Baron Gros,[4] and those instructions were the result of a conversation
which Viscount Palmerston had with the French Ambassador after the
meeting of the Cabinet. Viscount Palmerston was only waiting for a
copy of the despatch of yesterday evening, which, owing to this day
being Sunday, he has not yet received, in order to send to your Majesty
the altered draft of yesterday evening, with an explanation of the circumstances which rendered it impossible to submit them to your
Majesty before they were sent off.[5]

Memorandum by the Prince Albert.

Windsor Castle, *3rd March 1850.*

Before leaving Town yesterday we saw Lord John Russell, who
came to state what had passed with reference to Lord Palmerston. He
premised that Lord Palmerston had at all times been a most agreeable
and accommodating colleague; that he had acted with Lord John ever
since 1831, and had not only never made any difficulty, but acted most
boldly and in the most spirited manner on all political questions; besides, he was very popular with the Radical part of the House of
Commons as well as with the Protectionist, so that both would be
ready to receive him as their Leader; he (Lord John) was therefore
most anxious to do nothing which could hurt Lord Palmerston's feelings, nor to bring about a disruption of the Whig Party, which at this
moment of Party confusion was the only one which still held together.
On the other hand, the fact that the Queen distrusted Lord Palmerston
was a serious impediment to the carrying on of the Government. Lord
John was therefore anxious to adopt a plan by which Lord Palmerston's services could be retained with his own goodwill, and the
Foreign Affairs entrusted to other hands. The only plan he could think
of was to give Lord Palmerston the lead in the House of Commons—
the highest position a statesman could aspire to—and to go himself to

the House of Lords. He had communicated his views to Lord Lansdowne, who agreed in them, and thought he could do nothing better than speak to Lord Palmerston at once. Lord Palmerston said that he could not have helped to have become aware that he had forfeited the Queen's confidence, but he thought this had not been on *personal* grounds, but merely on account of his line of policy, with which the Queen disagreed. (The Queen interrupted Lord John by remarking that she distrusted him on *personal* grounds also, but I remarked that Lord Palmerston had so far at least seen rightly; that he had become disagreeable to the Queen, not on account of his person, but of his political doings, to which the Queen assented.) Lord Palmerston appeared to Lord John willing to enter into this agreement.

On the question how the Foreign Office should be filled, Lord John said that he thought his father-in-law, Lord Minto, ought to take the Foreign Office.... As the Queen was somewhat startled by this announcement, I said I thought that would not go down with the public. After Lord Palmerston's removal (who was considered one of the ablest men in the country) he ought not to be replaced but by an equally able statesman; the Office was of *enormous* importance, and ought not to be entrusted to any one but Lord John himself or Lord Clarendon. On the Queen's enquiry why Lord Clarendon had not been proposed for it, Lord John said he was most anxious that the change of the Minister should not produce a change in the general line of policy which he considered to have been quite right, and that Lord Clarendon did not approve of it; somehow or other he never could agree with Lord Clarendon on Foreign Affairs; he thought Lord Clarendon very anti-French and for an alliance with Austria and Russia. The Queen replied she knew Lord Clarendon's bad opinion of the mode in which the Foreign Affairs had been conducted, and thought that a merit in him, but did not think him Austrian or Russian, but merely disapproving of Lord Palmerston's behaviour. I urged Lord John to take the Foreign Affairs himself, which he said would have to be done if the Queen did not wish Lord Minto to take them; he himself would be able to do the business when in the House of Lords, although he would undertake it unwillingly; with the business in the House of Commons it would have been impossible for him.

The Queen insisted on his trying it with a seat in the House of Lords, adding that, if he found it too much for him, he could at a later period perhaps make the Department over to Lord Clarendon.

I could not help remarking that it was a serious risk to entrust Lord Palmerston with the lead in the House of Commons, that it might be that the Government were defeated and, if once in opposition, Lord Palmerston might take a different line as leader of the Opposition from that which Lord John would like, and might so easily force himself back into office as Prime Minister. Lord John, however, although admitting that danger, thought Lord Palmerston too old to do much in the future (having passed his sixty-fifth year); he admitted that Sir George Grey was the natural leader of the Commons, but expected that a little later the lead would still fall into his hands.

The arrangements of the Offices as proposed would be that Lord Palmerston would take the Home Office, and Sir George Grey the Colonial Office, and Lord Grey vacate this office for the Privy Seal. If Lord Minto, however, was not to have the Foreign Office, the arrangement must be recast. Lord Clarendon would become Secretary of State for Ireland, after the abolition of the Lord-Lieutenancy. Possibly also Sir George Grey might take the office, and Lord Clarendon take the Colonies, which Lord Grey would be glad to be rid of. On my observing that I had thought the Colonies would have done best for Lord Palmerston, leaving Sir George Grey at the Home Office, Lord John acknowledged that he would likewise prefer this arrangement, but considered it rendered impossible from its having been the very thing Lord Grey had proposed in 1845, and upon which the attempt to form a Whig Government at that time had broken down, Lord Palmerston having refused to enter the Cabinet on those terms. Lord John ended by saying that Lord Palmerston having agreed to the change, it was intended that nothing should be done about it till after the close of the Session, in order to avoid debates and questions on the subject; moreover, Lord Lansdowne had agreed to continue still this Session his labours as Leader in the House of Lords, and begged for the *utmost secrecy* at present.

Albert.

Lord John Russell already last year had spoken to me of his wish to go to the House of Lords, finding the work in the House of Commons, together with his other business, too much for him, and Lord Lansdowne being desirous to be relieved from the lead in the Upper House.

Albert.

Memorandum by Baron Stockmar.[6]

12th March 1850.

The least the Queen has a right to require of her Minister is:—

1. That he will distinctly state what he proposes in a given case, in order that the Queen may know as distinctly to what she has to give her royal sanction.

2. Having given once her sanction to a measure, the Minister who, in the execution of such measure alters or modifies it arbitrarily, commits an act of dishonesty towards the Crown, which the Queen has an undoubted constitutional right to visit with the dismissal of that Minister.

Stockmar.

Queen Victoria to the Marquis of Lansdowne.

Buckingham Palace, *16th March 1850.*

The Queen wishes to remark to Lord Lansdowne, that his answer to Lord Stanley in the House of Lords last night might possibly lead to the misapprehension that Lord Palmerston's delay in sending the despatch to Mr Wyse had been caused by the time it took to get the Queen's approval of it. She must protest against such an inference being drawn, as being contrary to the fact, Lord Palmerston indeed having sent out in the first instance a different despatch from that which she had approved.

The King of the Belgians to Queen Victoria.

Laeken, *25th March 1850.*

My dearest Victoria,— ... King Louis Philippe seems better, but still he is evidently breaking; there is no wonder when one considers all he has gone through, and is still to suffer! No one can tell a day [ahead] what may happen in France, and if all the family have, which is but[7] in France, may not be confiscated. The thirst for spoliation is great; the people who lead have no other view, they are not fanatics, their aim is to rise and to enrich themselves; the remainder is mere humbug, exactly as you have it very near home. Never was there a nation in a worse and a more helpless state, and the numerous parties who will *not* unite render all solutions impossible, and the republic will be maintained for that very reason. It is but a name and no substance, but that *name of republic* encourages every extravagant or

247

desperate proceeding, and turns people's heads in the old monarchies; every doctor or magistrate sees himself president of some republic, and the ambitions of so many people who see all the impediments which existed formerly removed, and who, according to their *own opinion*, are wonderful people, will be insatiable and much more dangerous than you imagine in England. On the Continent every man thinks himself fit to be at the head of the Government; there is no political measure or scale, and the success of some bookseller or doctor or advocate, etc., turns the heads of all those in similar positions—*on ne doute de rien*. When you consider that a *banqueroutier* like Ledru Rollin[8] ruled over France *for six months* almost with *absolute power,* merely because he took it, you may imagine how many thousands, even of workmen, cooks, stage people, etc., look to be taken to rule over their fellow-citizens; *toujours convaincu de leur propre mérite*. I am happy to see that you escaped a ministerial crisis; the peril was great, and it would have been dreadful for you at such a moment.

Albert made a fine long speech, I see.[9] Did he read it? *ex tempore*, it would have been very trying. I trust we may come to that unity of mankind of which he speaks, and of universal peace which our friend Richard Cobden considers as very near at hand; if, however, the red benefactors of mankind at Paris get the upper hand, *universal war* will be the order of the day. We are so strongly convinced of this that we are very seriously occupied with the means of defence which this country can afford, and we imagine that if we are not abandoned by our friends, it will be impossible to force our positions on the Schelde.

I must now quickly conclude. Remaining ever, my beloved Victoria, your devoted Uncle,

Leopold R.

BARON STOCKMAR.

From the portrait by John Partridge at Buckingham Palace

Queen Victoria to Viscount Palmerston.

Buckingham Palace, *25th March 1850.*

The Queen approves these drafts, but thinks that in the part alluding to M. Pacifico, should be added a direction to Mr Wyse to satisfy himself of the *truth* of M. Pacifico's statements of losses before he grounds his demands upon them.[10] The draft merely allows a subdivision of the claims, but takes their validity for granted.

Queen Victoria to the King of the Belgians.

Windsor Castle, *26th March 1850.*

My dearest Uncle,—Albert made a really beautiful speech the other day, and it has given the greatest satisfaction and done great good. He is indeed *looked up to and beloved*, as *I* could *wish* he should be; and the *more* his *rare qualities* of mind and heart are *known*, the *more* he will be understood and appreciated. People are much struck at his great powers and energy; his great self-denial, and constant wish to work for others, is so striking in his character; but it is the *happiest* life; pining for what one cannot have, and trying to run after what is pleasantest, *invariably* ends in disappointment.

I must now conclude. Ever your devoted Niece,

Victoria R.

Queen Victoria to the King of the Belgians.

Windsor Castle, *29th March 1850.*

My dearest Uncle,—I write only a few lines to-day, begging you to give the accompanying drawing of her little *namesake* to dearest Louise *on* her birthday.

I shall duly answer your dear letter of the 25th on Tuesday, but am anxious to correct the impression that Albert read his fine speech. He *never* has done so with any of his fine speeches, but speaks them, having first prepared them and written them down,—and does so *so well*, that no one believes that he is ever nervous, which *he is*. This last he is said to have spoken in so particularly English a way.

We have still sadly cold winds. Ever your devoted Niece,

Victoria R.

Queen Victoria to Lord John Russell.

Buckingham Palace, *14th April 1850.*

The Queen has received Lord John Russell's letter with the drafts, which he mentioned last night to her, and she has sent his letter with them to Lord Palmerston.

Lord Palmerston's conduct in this Spanish question[11] in not communicating her letter to Lord John, as she had directed, is really too bad, and most disrespectful to the Queen; she can really hardly communicate with him any more; indeed it would be better she should not.

Queen Victoria to Lord John Russell.

Buckingham Palace, *27th April 1850.*

In order to save the Government embarrassments, the Queen has sanctioned the appointment of Lord Howden[12] to Madrid, although she does not consider him to be quite the stamp of person in whom she could feel entire confidence that he will be proof against all spirit of intrigue, which at all times and now particularly is so much required in Spain. But she must once more ask Lord John to watch that the Queen may be quite openly and considerately dealt by. She knows that Lord Howden has long been made acquainted with his appointment, and has been corresponding upon it with General Narvaez; the correspondent of the *Times* has announced his appointment from Madrid already three weeks ago, and all that time Lord Palmerston remained silent upon the matter to the Queen, not even answering her upon her letter expressing her wish to see Lord Westmorland[13] appointed. Lord John must see the impropriety of this course, and if it were not for the Queen's anxiety to smooth all difficulties, the Government might be exposed to most awkward embarrassments. She expects, however, and has the right to claim, equal consideration on the part of her Ministers. She addresses herself in this matter to Lord John as the head of the Government.

Lord John Russell to Queen Victoria.

Pembroke Lodge, *28th April 1850.*

... Lord John Russell cannot but assent to your Majesty's right to claim every consideration on the part of your Majesty's Ministers. He will take care to attend to this subject, and is much concerned to find that your Majesty has so frequently occasion to complain of Lord Palmerston's want of attention.

The Marquis of Dalhousie to Queen Victoria.

Simla, *15th May 1850.*

... When the Governor-General had the honour of addressing your Majesty from Bombay, the arrangements for the transmission of the Koh-i-noor were incomplete. He therefore did not then report to your Majesty, as he now humbly begs leave to do, that he conveyed the jewel himself from Lahore in his own charge, and deposited it in the Treasury at Bombay. One of your Majesty's ships had been ordered to Bombay to receive it, but had not then arrived, and did not arrive till two months afterwards, thus causing delay. The *Medea*, however, sailed on 6th April, and will, it is hoped, have a safe and speedy passage to England.

By this mail the Governor-General transmits officially a record of all that he has been able to trace of the vicissitudes through which the Koh-i-noor has passed. The papers are accurate and curious.

In one of them it is narrated, on the authority of Fugueer-ood-deen, who is now at Lahore, and who was himself the messenger, that Runjeet Singh sent a message to Wufa Begum, the wife of Shah Sooja, from whom he had taken the gem, to ask her its value. She replied, "If a strong man were to throw four stones, one north, one south, one east, one west, and a fifth stone up into the air, and if the space between them were to be filled with gold, all would not equal the value of the Koh-i-noor." The Fugueer, thinking probably that this appraisement was somewhat imaginative, subsequently asked Shah Sooja the same question. The Shah replied that its value was "good fortune; for whoever possessed it had conquered their enemies."

The Governor-General very respectfully and earnestly trusts that your Majesty, in your possession of the Koh-i-noor, may ever continue to realise its value as estimated by Shah Sooja.

He has the honour to subscribe himself, with deep respect, your Majesty's most obedient, most humble, and most faithful Subject and Servant,

Dalhousie.

The Prince Albert to Lord John Russell.

Buckingham Palace, *18th May 1850.*

My dear Lord John,—I return you the enclosed letters which forbode a new storm, this time coming from Russia.[14] I confess I do not understand that part of the quarrel, but one conviction grows stronger and stronger with the Queen and myself (if it is possible), viz. that Lord Palmerston is bringing the whole of the hatred which is borne to him—I don't mean here to investigate whether justly or unjustly—by all the Governments of Europe upon England, and that the country runs serious danger of having to pay for the consequences. We cannot reproach ourselves with having neglected warning and entreaties, but the Queen may feel that her duty demands her not to be content with mere warning without any effect, and that for the sake of one man the welfare of the country must not be exposed....

Albert.

Lord John Russell to the Prince Albert.

Pembroke Lodge, *18th May 1850.*

Sir,—I feel very strongly that the Queen ought not to be exposed to the enmity of Austria, France, and Russia on account of her Minister. I was therefore prepared to state on Monday that it is for Her Majesty to consider what course it will be best for her and for the country to pursue.

1. I am quite ready to resign my office, but I could not make Lord Palmerston the scapegoat for the sins which will be imputed to the Government in the late negotiations.

2. I am ready, if it is thought best, to remain in office till questions pending in the two Houses are decided. If unfavourably, a solution is obtained; if favourably, Lord John Russell will no longer remain in office with Lord Palmerston as Foreign Secretary.

These are hasty and crude thoughts, but may be matured by Monday.

Memorandum by the Prince Albert.

Buckingham Palace, *20th May 1850.*

Lord John Russell came to-day to make his report to the Queen on his final determination with respect to the Greek question and Lord Palmerston. He said it was quite impossible to abandon Lord Palmerston upon this question, that the Cabinet was as much to blame (if there were cause for it) as Lord Palmerston, and particularly he himself, who had given his consent to the measures taken, and was justly held responsible by the country for the Foreign Policy of the Government. Admitting, however, that Lord Palmerston's personal quarrels with all Governments of foreign countries and the hostility with which they were looking upon him was doing serious injury to the country, and exposing the Crown to blows aimed at the Minister, he had consulted Lord Lansdowne.... Lord Lansdowne fully felt the strength of what I said respecting the power of the Leader of the House of Commons, and the right on the part of the Queen to object to its being conferred upon a person who had not her entire confidence. I said I hoped Lord Lansdowne would consider the communication of the letter as quite confidential, as, although I had no objection to telling Lord Palmerston anything that was said in it myself, I should not like that it should come to his ears by third persons or be otherwise talked of. Lord John assured me that Lord Lansdowne could be entirely relied upon, and that he himself had locked up the letter under key the moment he had received it, and would carefully guard it.

The result of our conference was, that we agreed that Lord Clarendon was the only member of the Government to whom the Foreign Affairs could be entrusted unless Lord John were to take them himself, which was much the best. Lord John objected to Lord Clarendon's intimate connection with the *Times*, and the violent Austrian line of that paper; moreover, Lord Clarendon would be wanted to organise the new department of Secretary of State for Ireland. The Colonial Office was much the best for Lord Palmerston, and should Lord John go to the House of Lords, Sir George Grey was to lead in the Commons. Lord John would take an opportunity of communicating with Lord Palmerston, but wished nothing should be said or done about the changes till after the close of the Session.[15]

Albert.

Queen Victoria to Lord John Russell.

Osborne, *9th June 1850.*

The Queen has received Lord John Russell's two letters. If the Cabinet *think* it impossible to do otherwise, of course the Queen consents—though *most reluctantly*—to a compliance with the vote respecting the Post Office.[16] The Queen thinks it a very *false* notion of obeying God's will, to do what will be the cause of much annoyance and possibly of great distress to private families. At any rate, she thinks decidedly that great caution should be used with respect to any alteration in the transmission of the mails, so that at least *some means* of communication may still be possible.

Queen Victoria to the Duke of Cambridge.

Osborne, *10th June 1850.*

My dear Uncle,—I have enquired into the precedents, and find that though there are none exactly similar to the case of George, there will be no difficulty to call him up to the House of Lords; and I should propose that he should be called up by the name of Earl of Tipperary, which is one of your titles. Culloden, which is your other title, would be from recollections of former times obviously objectionable. There are several precedents of Princes being made Peers without having an establishment, consequently there can be no difficulty on this point.

I feel confident that George will be very moderate in his politics, and support the Government whenever he can. Princes of the Royal Family should keep as much as possible aloof from *Party Politics*, as I think they else invariably become mixed up with Party violence, and frequently are made the tools of people who are utterly regardless of the mischief they cause to the Throne and Royal Family. Believe me, always, your affectionate Niece,

Victoria R.

The Duke of Cambridge to Queen Victoria.

Cambridge House, *10th June 1850.*

My dearest Victoria,—I seize the earliest opportunity of thanking you for your very kind letter, which I have this moment received, and to assure you at the same time that I do most fully agree with you in your observations concerning the line in politics which the members of the Royal Family ought to take. This has always been my principle since I entered the House of Lords, and I am fully convinced that George will follow my example.

I must also add that I have felt the great advantage of supporting the Government, and I have by that always been well with all Parties, and have avoided many difficulties which other members of my family have had to encounter.

I shall not fail to communicate your letter to George, who will, I trust, never prove himself unworthy of the kindness you have shown him.

With the request that you will remember me most kindly to Albert, I remain, my dearest Victoria, your most affectionate Uncle,

Adolphus.

Prince George of Cambridge to Queen Victoria.

St James's Palace, *15th June 1850.*

My dear Cousin,—I have not as yet ventured to address you on a subject of much interest personally to myself, and upon which I am aware that you have been in correspondence with my father; but as I believe that the question which was brought to your notice has been settled, I cannot any longer deprive myself of the pleasure of expressing to you my most sincere and grateful thanks for the kind manner in which you have at once acceded to the anxious request of my father and myself, by arranging with the Government that I should be called up to the House of Lords. This has been a point upon which I have long been most anxious, and I am truly and sincerely grateful that you have so considerately entered into my feelings and wishes. I understand that it is your intention that I should be called up by my father's second title as Earl of Tipperary; at the same time I hope that though I take a seat in the House as Earl of Tipperary, I may be permitted to retain and be called by my present name on all occasions not connected with the House of Lords. As regards the wish expressed by yourself, that I should not allow myself to be made a political partisan, I need not, I trust, assure you that it will be ever my endeavour to obey your desires upon this as on all other occasions; but I trust I may be permitted to add, that even before this desire expressed by you, it had been my intention to follow this line of conduct. I conceive that whenever they conscientiously can do so, the members of the Royal Family should support the Queen's Government; and if at times it should happen that they have a difficulty in so doing, it is at all events not desirable that they should place themselves prominently in opposition to it. This I believe to be your feelings on the subject, and if you will permit me to say so, they are also my own.

Hoping to have the pleasure soon of expressing to you my gratitude in person, I remain, my dear Cousin, your most dutiful Cousin,

George.

Queen Victoria to Prince George of Cambridge.

Osborne, *17th June 1850.*

My dear George,—Many thanks for your kind letter received yesterday. I am glad to hear that you are so entirely of my opinion with respect to the political conduct of the Princes of the Royal Family who are peers, and I feel sure that your conduct will be quite in accordance with this view. With respect to your wish to be called as you have hitherto been, I do not think that this will be possible. It has never been done, besides which I think the Irish (who will be much flattered at your being called up by the title of Tipperary) would feel it as a slight if you did not wish to be called by the title you bear. All the Royal Peers have always been called by their titles in this and in other countries, and I do not think it would be possible to avoid it. Ever, etc.,

Victoria R.[17]

Buckingham Palace. *8th July 1850.*

I kept this warrant back from the Queen's signature on account of the Duke of Cambridge's illness. The Duke died yesterday evening, without a struggle, after an attack of fever which had lasted four weeks. So the summons of Prince George has never been carried out.

Albert.

Lord John Russell to Queen Victoria.

Chesham Place, *21st June 1850.*

Lord John Russell presents his humble duty to your Majesty, and has the honour to report that Mr Roebuck asked him yesterday what course the Government intends to pursue after the late vote of the House of Lords.[18]

The newspapers contain the report of Lord John Russell's answer.

Mr Roebuck has proposed to move on Monday a general approbation of the Foreign Policy of the Government.

What may be the result of such a Motion it is not easy to say, but as Lord Stanley has prevailed on a majority in the House of Lords to censure the Foreign Policy of the Government, it is impossible to avoid a decision by the House of Commons on this subject.

The misfortune is that on the one side every detail of negotiation is confounded with the general principles of our Foreign Policy, and on the other a censure upon a Foreign Policy, the tendency of which has been to leave despotism and democracy to fight out their own battles, will imply in the eyes of Europe a preference for the cause of despotism, and a willingness to interfere with Russia and Austria on behalf of absolute government. The jealousy of the House of Commons would not long bear such a policy.

Be that as it may, Lord Stanley has opened a beginning of strife, which may last for many years to come.

Queen Victoria to Lord John Russell.

Buckingham Palace, *21st June 1850.*

The Queen has received Lord John Russell's letter and read his speech in the House of Commons. She regrets exceedingly the position in which the Government has been placed by the Motion of Lord Stanley in the House of Lords. Whichever way the Debate in the House of Commons may terminate, the Queen foresees great troubles. A defeat of the Government would be *most inconvenient*. The Queen has always approved the *general* tendency of the policy of the Government to let despotism and democracy fight out their battles abroad, but must remind Lord John that in the execution of this policy Lord Palmerston has *gone a long way* in taking up the side of democracy in the fight, and this is the "detail of negotiations" which Lord John is afraid may be confounded with the general principle of our Foreign Policy. Indeed it is already confounded by the whole of the foreign and the great majority of the British public, and it is to be feared that the discussion will place despotic and democratic principles in array against each other in this country, whilst the original question turns only upon the justice of Don Pacifico's claims.

Lord John Russell to Queen Victoria.

Chesham Place, *22nd June 1850.*

Lord John Russell deeply regrets that your Majesty should be exposed to inconvenience in consequence of Lord Stanley's Motion. He has copied Mr Roebuck's Motion as it now stands on the votes. The word "principles" includes the general policy, and excludes the particular measures which from time to time have been adopted as the objects of approbation.

It is impossible to say at this moment what will be the result. Lord Stanley, Lord Aberdeen, Mr Gladstone, and Mr Disraeli appear to be in close concert.

Lord Stanley can hardly now abandon Protection. Mr Gladstone, one should imagine, can hardly abandon Free Trade. The anger of the honest Protectionists and the honest Free-Traders will be very great at so unprincipled a coalition.

Mr Roebuck's Motion: That the principles on which the Foreign Policy of Her Majesty's Government has been regulated have been such as were calculated to maintain the honour and dignity of this country, and in times of unexampled difficulty to preserve peace between England and the various nations of the world.

Queen Victoria to Viscount Palmerston.

Buckingham Palace, *22nd June 1850.*

The Queen has received Lord Palmerston's letter of yesterday, but cannot say that his arguments in support of his former opinion, that the Germanic Confederation should be omitted from amongst the Powers who are to be invited to sign a protocol, the object of which is to decide upon the fate of Holstein, have proved successful in convincing her of the propriety of this course. As Holstein belongs to the Germanic Confederation and is only accidentally connected with Denmark through its Sovereign, a Protocol to ensure the integrity of the Danish Monarchy is a direct attack upon Germany, if carried out without her knowledge and consent; and it is an act repugnant to all feelings of justice and morality for third parties to dispose of other people's property, which no diplomatic etiquette about the difficulty of finding a proper representative for Germany could justify. The mode of representation might safely be left to the Confederation itself. It is not surprising to the Queen that Austria and Prussia should complain of Lord Palmerston's agreeing with Sweden, Russia, Denmark, and France upon the Protocol before giving Prussia and Austria any notice of it.

Viscount Palmerston to Lord John Russell.

Carlton Gardens, *23rd June 1850.*

My dear John Russell,—The Queen has entirely misconceived the object and effect of the proposed Protocol. It does not "decide upon the fate of Holstein," nor is it "an attack upon Germany." In fact, the Protocol is to *decide* nothing; it is to be merely a record of the wishes and opinions of the Power whose representatives are to sign it....[19]

How does any part of this decide the fate of Holstein or attack Germany?

Is not the Queen requiring that I should be Minister, not indeed for Austria, Russia, or France, but for the Germanic Confederation? Why should we take up the cudgels for Germany, when we are inviting Austria and Prussia, the two leading powers of Germany, and who would of course put in a claim for the Confederation if they thought it necessary, which, however, for the reasons above stated, they surely would not?...

As to my having *agreed* with Sweden, Russia, Denmark, and France before communicating with Prussia and Austria, that is not the course which things have taken. Brunnow proposed the Protocol to me, and I have been in discussion with him about it. It is *he* who has communicated it to the French Ambassador, to Reventlow, and to Rehausen; I sent it privately several weeks ago to Westmorland, that he might show it confidentially to Schleinitz, but telling Westmorland that it was not a thing settled, but only a proposal by Russia, and that, at all events, some part of the wording would be altered. I have no doubt that Brunnow has also shown it to Koller; but I could not send it officially to Berlin or Vienna till Brunnow had agreed to such a wording as I could recommend the Government to adopt, nor until I received the Queen's sanction to do so.

The only thing that occurs to me as practicable would be to say to Austria and Prussia that if, in signing the Protocol, they could add that they signed also in the name of the Confederation, we should be glad to have the additional weight of that authority, but that could not be made a *sine quâ non*, any more than the signature of Austria and Prussia themselves, for I think that the Protocol ought to be signed by as many of the proposed Powers as may choose to agree to it, bearing always in mind that it is only a record of opinions and wishes, and does not decide or pretend to decide anything practically. Yours sincerely,

Palmerston.

Queen Victoria to Lord John Russell.

Buckingham Palace, *25th June 1850.*

The Queen has received Lord John Russell's letter enclosing those of Lord Palmerston and Lord Lansdowne. The *misconception* on the Queen's part, which Lord Palmerston alleges to exist, consists in her taking the essence of the arrangement for the mere words. Lord Palmerston pretends that the Protocol "does not decide upon the fate of Holstein nor attack Germany." However, the only object of the Protocol is the fate of Holstein, which is decided upon—

(1.) By a declaration of the importance to the interests of Europe to uphold the integrity of the Danish Monarchy (which has no meaning, if it does not mean that Holstein is to remain with it).

(2.) By an approval of the efforts of the King of Denmark to keep it with Denmark, by adapting the law of succession to that of Holstein.

(3.) By an engagement on the part of the Powers to use their "*so-ins*" to get the constitutional position of Holstein settled in a peace according to the Malmoe preliminaries, of which it was one of the conditions that the question of the succession was to be left untouched.

(4.) To seal the whole arrangement by an act of European acknowledgment.

If the declarations of importance, the approval, the "*soins*" and the acknowledgments of *all* the great Powers of Europe are to decide nothing, then Lord Palmerston is quite right; if they decide anything, it is the fate of Holstein.

Whether this will be an attack upon Germany or not will be easily deduced from the fact that the attempt on the part of Denmark to incorporate into her polity the Duchy of Schleswig was declared by the Diet in 1846 to be a declaration of war against Germany merely on account of its intimate connection with the Duchy of Holstein.

The Queen does not wish her Minister to be Minister for Germany, but merely to treat that country with the same consideration which is due to every country on whose interests we mean to decide.

The Queen would wish her correspondence upon this subject to be brought before the Cabinet, and will abide by their deliberate opinion.

Queen Victoria to the King of the Belgians.

Buckingham Palace, *25th June 1850.*

My dearest Uncle,—Charles will have told you how kindly and amiably the Prince of Prussia has come here, travelling night and day from St Petersburg, in order to be in time for the christening of our little *Arthur*.[20] I wish you could (and you will, for he intends stopping at Brussels) hear him speak, for he is so straightforward, conciliatory, and yet firm of purpose; I have a great esteem and respect for him. The poor King of Prussia is recovered,[21] and has been received with great enthusiasm on the first occasion of his first reappearance in public.

We are in a *crisis*, no one knowing how this debate upon this most unfortunate Greek business will end. It is most unfortunate, for whatever way it ends, it must do great harm.

I must now conclude, for I am quite overpowered by the heat. Ever your truly devoted Niece,

Victoria R.

Lord John Russell to Queen Victoria.

Chesham Place, *26th June 1850*.

Lord John Russell presents his humble duty to your Majesty, and has the honour to report that in the debate of last night Viscount Palmerston defended the whole Foreign Policy of the Government in a speech of four hours and three quarters.[22] This speech was one of the most masterly ever delivered, going through the details of transactions in the various parts of the world, and appealing from time to time to great principles of justice and of freedom.

The cheering was frequent and enthusiastic. The debate was adjourned till Thursday, when it will probably close.

The expectation is that Ministers will have a majority, but on the amount of that majority must depend their future course.

Lord John Russell to Queen Victoria.

Chesham Place, 27th June 1850.

Lord John Russell presents his humble duty to your Majesty, and has the honour to state that the prospects of the division are rather more favourable for Ministers than they were.

Ministers ought to have a majority of forty to justify their remaining in office.[23]

Mr Gladstone makes no secret of his wish to join Lord Stanley in forming an Administration.

Lord John Russell would desire to have the honour of an audience of your Majesty on Saturday at twelve or one o'clock.

The division will not take place till to-morrow night.

Queen Victoria to the King of the Belgians.

Buckingham Palace, *2nd July 1850*.

My dearest Uncle,—For two most kind and affectionate letters I offer my warmest and best thanks. The good report of my beloved Louise's improvement is a great happiness. By my letter to Louise you will have learnt all the details of this certainly very disgraceful and very inconceivable attack.[24] I have not suffered except from my head, which is still very tender, the blow having been extremely violent, and the brass *end* of the stick fell on my head so as to make a considerable noise. I own it makes me nervous out driving, and I start at any person coming near the carriage, which I am afraid is natural. We have, alas! now another cause of much greater anxiety in the person of our excellent Sir Robert Peel,[25] who, as you will see, has had a most serious fall, and though going on well at first, was very ill last night; thank God! he is better again this morning, but I fear still in great danger. I cannot bear even to think of losing him; it would be the greatest loss for the whole country, and irreparable for us, for he is so trustworthy, and so entirely to be depended on. *All* parties are in great anxiety about him. I will leave my letter open to give you the latest news.

Our good and amiable guest[26] likes being with us, and will remain with us till Saturday. We had a concert last night, and go to the opera very regularly. The *Prophète* is quite beautiful, and I am sure would delight you. The music in the *Scène du Couronnement* is, I think, finer than anything in either *Robert* or the *Huguenots*; it is highly dramatic, and really very touching. Mario sings and acts in it quite in perfection. His *Raoul* in the Huguenots is also most beautiful. He improves every year, and I really think his voice is the finest tenor I ever heard, and he sings and acts with such *intense* feeling.

What do you say to the conclusion of our debate? It leaves things just as they were. The House of Commons is becoming very unmanageable and troublesome....

I must now conclude. With Albert's love, ever your most affectionate Niece,

Victoria R.

I am happy to say that Sir Robert, though still very ill, is freer from pain, his pulse is less high, and he feels himself better; the Doctors think there is *no* vital injury, and nothing from which he cannot recover, but that he must be for some days in a precarious state.

The King of Denmark to Queen Victoria.

Copenhague, *4 Juillet 1850.*

Madame ma Sœur,—Je remplis un devoir des plus agréables, en m'empressant d'annoncer à votre Majesté que la paix vient d'être signée le 2 de ce mois à Berlin entre moi et Sa Majesté le Roi de Prusse, en Son nom et en celui de la Confédération Germanique.[27]

Je sais et je reconnais de grand cœur combien je suis redevable à votre Majesté et à Son Gouvernement de ce résultat important, qui justifie mon espérance de pouvoir bientôt rendre à tous mes sujets les bienfaits d'une sincère réconciliation et d'une véritable concorde.

Votre Majesté a par la sollicitude avec laquelle Elle a constamment accompli le mandat de la médiation dans l'intérêt du Danemark et de l'Europe, ajouté aux témoignages inappréciables de sincère amitié qu'elle n'a cessé de m'accorder durant la longue et pénible épreuve que le Danemark vient de nouveau de traverser, mais qui paraît, à l'aide du Tout-Puissant, devoir maintenant faire place à un meilleur avenir, offrant, sous les auspices de votre Majesté, de nouvelles garanties pour l'indépendance de mon antique Couronne et pour le maintien de l'intégrité de ma Monarchie, à la défense desquelles je me suis voué entièrement.

Je suis persuadé que votre Majesté me fera la justice de croire que je suis on ne peut plus reconnaissant, et que mon peuple fidèle et loyal s'associe à moi et aux miens, pénétré de ces mêmes sentiments de gratitude envers votre Majesté.

Je m'estimerais infiniment heureux si Elle daignait ajouter à toutes Ses bontés, celle que de me fournir l'occasion de Lui donner des preuves de mon dévouement inaltérable et de la haute considération avec lesquels je prie Dieu qu'il vous ait, Madame ma Sœur, vous, votre auguste Époux et tous les vôtres, dans sa sainte et digne garde, et avec lesquels je suis, Madame ma Sœur, de votre Majesté, le bon Frère,

Frederick.

The King of the Belgians to Queen Victoria.

Laeken, *5th July 1850.*

My dearest Victoria,—It gave me the greatest pain to learn of the death of our true and kind friend, Sir Robert Peel. That he should have met with his end—he so valuable to the whole earth—from an accident so easily to be avoided with some care, is the more to be lamented. You and Albert lose in him a friend whose moderation, correct judgment, great knowledge of everything connected with the country, can never be found again. Europe had in him a benevolent and a truly wise statesman....

Give my best thanks to Albert for his kind letter. I mean to send a messenger probably on Sunday or Monday to write to him. I pity him about the great Exhibition. I fear he will be much plagued, and I was glad to see that the matter is to be treated in Parliament. Alas! in all human affairs one is sure to meet with violent passions, and Peel knew that so well; great care even for the most useful objects is necessary.

I will write to you a word to-morrow. God grant that it may be satisfactory.[28] Ever, my beloved, dear Victoria, your devoted Uncle,

Leopold R.

Queen Victoria to the King of Prussia.

Buckingham Palace, *6th July 1850.*

Sire, my most honoured Brother,—I have to express to you my thanks for the pleasure which the visit of your dear brother has given us, who, as I hope, will remit these lines to you in perfect health. That things go so well with you, and that the healing of your wound has made undisturbed progress, has been to us a true removal of anxiety. You will no doubt have learnt that I too have been again the object of an attempt, if possible still more cowardly. The criminal is, *as usual*, this time too, insane, or will pretend to be so; still the deed remains.

All our feelings are, in the meanwhile, preoccupied by the sorrow, in which your Majesty and all Europe will share, at the death of Sir Robert Peel. That is one of the hardest blows of Fate which could have fallen on us and on the country. You knew the great man, and understood how to appreciate his merit. His value is now becoming clear even to his opponents; all Parties are united in mourning.

The only satisfactory event of recent times is the news of your conclusion of peace with Denmark. Accept my most cordial congratulations on that account.

Requesting you to remember me cordially to the dear Queen, and referring you for detailed news to the dear Prince, also recommending to your gracious remembrance Albert, who does not wish to trouble you, on his part, with a letter, I remain, in unchangeable friendship, dear Brother, your Majesty's faithful Sister,

Victoria R.

Queen Victoria to the King of the Belgians.

Buckingham Palace, *9th July 1850.*

My Dearest Uncle,—We live in the midst of sorrow and death! My poor good Uncle Cambridge breathed his last, without a struggle, at a few minutes before ten last night. I still saw him yesterday morning at one, but he *did not see me*, and to-day I saw him lifeless and cold. The poor Duchess and the poor children are very touching in their grief, and poor Augusta,[29] who arrived just *five hours too late*, is quite heartbroken. The end was most peaceful; there was no disease; only a gastric fever, which came on four weeks ago, from over-exertion, and cold, and which he neglected for the first week, carried him off.

The good Prince of Prussia you will have been pleased to talk to and see. Having lived with him for a fortnight on a very intimate foot-ing, we have been able to appreciate his *real* worth fully; he is so honest and frank, and so steady of purpose and courageous.

Poor dear Peel is to be buried to-day. The sorrow and grief at his death are most touching, and the country mourns over him as over a father. Every one seems to have lost a personal friend.

As I have much to write, you will forgive me ending here. You will be glad to hear that poor Aunt Gloucester is wonderfully calm and resigned. My poor dear Albert, who had been so fresh and well when we came back, looks so pale and fagged again. He has felt, and feels, Sir Robert's loss *dreadfully*. He feels he has lost a second father.

May God bless and protect you all, you dear ones! Ever your de-voted Niece,

Victoria R.

Queen Victoria to Viscount Palmerston.

Osborne, *19th July 1850.*

Before this draft to Lord Bloomfield about Greece is sent, it would be well to consider whether Lord Palmerston is justified in call-ing the Minister of the Interior of Greece "a notorious defaulter to the amount of 200,000 drachms,"[30] and should he be so, whether it is a proper thing for the Queen's Foreign Secretary to say in a public des-patch!

Queen Victoria to Lord John Russell.

Osborne, *28th July 1850.*

The Queen will have much pleasure in seeing the Duke and Duchess of Bedford here next Saturday, and we have invited them. She will be quite ready to hear the Duke's opinions on the Foreign Of-fice. Lord John may be sure that she fully admits the great difficulties in the way of the projected alteration, but she, on the other hand, feels the duty she owes to the country and to herself, not to allow a man in whom she can have no confidence, who has conducted himself in *anything but* a straightforward and proper manner to herself, to remain in the Foreign Office, and thereby to expose herself to insults from other nations, and the country to the constant risk of serious and alarming complications. The Queen considers these reasons as much graver than the other difficulties. Each time that we were in a difficulty, the Government seemed to be determined to move Lord Palmerston, and as soon as these difficulties were got over, those which present themselves in the carrying out of this removal appeared of so great a magnitude as to cause its relinquishment. There is no chance of Lord Palmerston reforming himself in his sixty-seventh year, and after having considered his last escape as a triumph.... The Queen is personally convinced that Lord Palmerston at this moment is secretly planning an armed Russian intervention in Schleswig, which may produce a renewal of revolutions in Germany, and possibly a general war.

The Queen only adduces this as an instance that there is no question of delicacy and danger in which Lord Palmerston will not arbitrarily and without reference to his colleagues or Sovereign engage this country.

Queen Victoria to the King of Denmark.

Osborne, *29 Juillet 1850.*

Sire et mon bon Frère,—La lettre dont votre Majesté a bien voulu m'honorer m'a causé un bien vif plaisir comme témoignage que votre Majesté a su apprécier les sentiments d'amitié pour vous et le désir d'agir avec impartialité qui m'ont animée ainsi que mon Gouvernement pendant tout le cours des longues négociations qui out précédé la signature de la Paix avec l'Allemagne. Votre Majesté peut aisément comprendre aussi combien je dois regretter le renouvellement de la guerre avec le Schleswig qui ne pourra avoir d'autre résultat que l'accroissement de l'animosité et l'affaiblissement des deux nobles peuples sur lesquels vous régnez. Dieu veuille que cette dernière lutte se termine pourtant dans une réconciliation solide, basée sur la reconnaissance des droits et des obligations des deux côtés. Je me trouve poussée à vous soumettre ici, Sire, une prière pour un Prince qui s'est malheureusement trouvé en conflit avec votre Majesté, mais pour lequel les liens de parenté me portent à plaider, le Duc de Holstein-Augustenburg. Je suis persuadée que la magnanimité de votre Majesté lui rendra ses biens particuliers, qu'elle a jugé nécessaire de lui ôter pendant la guerre de 1848, ce que je reconnaîtrais bien comme une preuve d'amitié de la part de votre Majesté envers moi.

En faisant des vœux, pour son bonbeur et en exprimant le désir du Prince, mon Epoux, d'être mis aux pieds de votre Majesté, je suis, Sire et mon bon Frère, de votre Majesté la bonne Sœur,

Victoria R.

Queen Victoria to Lord John Russell.

Osborne, *31st July 1850.*

The Queen must draw Lord John Russell's attention to the accompanying draft[31] with regard to Schleswig, which is evidently intended to lay the ground for future foreign armed intervention. This is to be justified by considering the assistance which the Stadthalterschaft of Holstein may be tempted to give to their Schleswig brethren "as an invasion of Schleswig by a German force."

Lord John seems himself to have placed a "?" against that passage. This is, after two years' negotiation and mediation, *begging the question* at issue. The whole war—Revolution, mediation, etc., etc.— rested upon the question whether Schleswig was part of Holstein (though not of the German Confederation), or part of Denmark and not of Holstein.

Queen Victoria to Lord John Russell.

Osborne, *31st July 1850.*

The Queen has considered Lord Seymour's memorandum upon the Rangership of the Parks in London, but cannot say that it has convinced her of the expediency of its abolition. There is nothing in the management of these parks by the Woods and Forests which does not equally apply to all the others, as Greenwich, Hampton Court, Richmond, etc. There is certainly a degree of inconvenience in the divided authority, but this is amply compensated by the advantage to the Crown, in appearance at least, to keep up an authority emanating personally from the Sovereign, and unconnected with a Government Department which is directly answerable to the House of Commons. The last debate upon Hyde Park has, moreover, shown that it will not be safe not to remind the public of the fact that the parks are Royal property. As the Ranger has no power over money, the management will always remain with the Office of Woods.

The Duke of Wellington to Queen Victoria.

London, *3rd August 1850.*

Field-Marshal the Duke of Wellington presents his humble duty to your Majesty. He regrets to be under the necessity of submitting to your Majesty the enclosed letter from General Sir Charles Napier, G.C.B., in which he tenders his resignation of the office of Commander-in-Chief of your Majesty's Forces in the East Indies.[32]

Upon the receipt of this paper Field-Marshal the Duke of Wellington considered it to be his duty to peruse all the papers submitted by Sir Charles Napier; to survey the transaction which had occasioned the censure of the Governor-General in Council complained of by Sir Charles Napier; to require from the India House all the information which could throw light upon the conduct complained of, as well as upon the motives alleged for it; the reasons given on account of which it was stated to be necessary.

He has stated in a minute, a memorandum of which he submits the copy to your Majesty, his views and opinions upon the whole subject, and the result which he submits to your Majesty is that he considers it his duty humbly to submit to your Majesty that your Majesty should be graciously pleased to accept the resignation of General Sir Charles Napier thus tendered.

Before he should submit this recommendation to your Majesty in relation to an office of such high reputation in so high and important a station, Field-Marshal the Duke of Wellington considered it his duty to submit his views to your Majesty's servants, who have expressed their concurrence in his opinion.

It is probable that the President of the Board of Control will lay before your Majesty the papers transmitted to the Secret Committee of the Court of Directors, by the Governor-General in Council, which are adverted to in the paper drawn up by the Duke, and of which the substance alone is stated.

All of which is humbly submitted to your Majesty by your Majesty's most dutiful Subject and most devoted Servant,

Wellington.

Memorandum by the Prince Albert.

Osborne, *5th August 1850.*

Lord John Russell having lately stated that Lord Clarendon, who had always been most eager to see Lord Palmerston moved, had lately expressed to him his opinion that it would be most dangerous and impolitic to do so under present circumstances, we thought it right to see Lord Clarendon here.... In conversation with me, Lord Clarendon spoke in his old strain of Lord Palmerston, but very strongly also of the danger of turning him out and making him the leader of the Radicals, who were anxiously waiting for that, were much dissatisfied with Lord John Russell, and free from control by the death of Sir Robert Peel. I said that if everything was done with Lord Palmerston's consent there would be no danger, to which Lord Clarendon assented, but doubted that he would consent to giving up what was his hobby. He added, nobody but Lord John could carry on the Foreign Affairs, but he ought not to leave the House of Commons under present circumstances, where he was now the only authority left.

We saw the Duke of Bedford yesterday, whom Lord John had wished us to invite. He is very unhappy about the present state of affairs, frightened about things going on as at present, when Lord John can exercise no control over Lord Palmerston, and the Queen is exposed year after year to the same annoyances and dangers arising from Lord Palmerston's mode of conducting the affairs; but on the other hand, equally frightened at turning him loose. The Duke was aware of all that had passed between us and Lord John, and ready to do anything *he* could to bring matters to a satisfactory solution, but thought his brother would not like to leave the House of Commons now. He had very much changed his opinion on that head latterly, and the more so as he thought something ought to be done next year with the franchise, which he alone could carry through. On my questioning whether it was impossible to persuade him to take the Foreign Office and stay in the Lower House, with a first-rate under-secretary, at least for a time, the Duke thought he might perhaps temporarily, as he felt he owed to the Queen the solution of the difficulty, but expressed again his fears of Lord Palmerston's opposition. I replied that if Lord John would make up his mind to take the Foreign Office, and to stay in the House of Commons, I saw no danger, as Lord John would be able to maintain himself successfully, and Lord Palmerston would not like to be in opposition to him, whilst he would become most formidable to anybody who was to *gain* only the leadership in the House; moreover,

Lord John, having done so much for Lord Palmerston, could expect and demand a return of sacrifice, and a variety of posts might be offered to him—the Presidency of the Council, the office of Home Secretary, or Secretary for the Colonies, Chancellor of the Exchequer, etc., etc., which places I was sure any member of the Cabinet would vacate for him. The Duke of Bedford added the Lieutenancy of Ireland, as Lord Clarendon had told him he was ready to give it up for the purpose, but only under *one* condition, viz. that of not having to succeed to Lord Palmerston at the Foreign Office. Observing our surprise at this declaration, the Duke added that Lord Clarendon acted most considerately, that he was ready to have no office at all, and would support the Government independently in the House of Lords if this were to facilitate arrangements. The Queen rejoined that a peerage was of course also at Lord John's disposal for Lord Palmerston. We then agreed that Lord Granville would be the best person to become Lord John's Under-Secretary of State, a man highly popular, pleasing, conciliatory, well versed in Foreign Affairs, and most industrious; trained under Lord John, he could at any time leave him the office altogether, if Lord John should find it too much for himself. Lord Granville had a higher office now, that of Vice-President of the Board of Trade and Paymaster-General, but would be sure to feel the importance of taking a lower office under such circumstances and with such contingencies likely to depend upon it. I have seen a great deal of him latterly, as he is the only working man on the Commission for the Exhibition of 1851, and have found him most able, good-natured, and laborious. The Duke liked the proposal very much, and is going to communicate all that passed between us to Lord John on Tuesday.

Albert.

Memorandum by the Prince Albert.

Osborne, *8th August 1850.*

Lord John Russell came down here yesterday in order to report to the Queen what had passed between him and Lord Palmerston the day before, on whom he had called in order to have an explanation on the Foreign Affairs.

Lord John reminded him of former communications, but admitted that circumstances were much changed by the recent debates in both Houses of Parliament; still, it was necessary to come to an understanding of the position. The *policy* pursued with regard to the Foreign

Affairs had been right and such as had the approval of Lord John himself, the Cabinet generally, and he believed the greater part of the country. But the manner in which it had been executed had been unfortunate, led to irritation and hostility; although peace had actually been preserved, and England stood in a position requiring no territorial aggrandisement or advantage of any kind, yet all Governments and Powers, not only Russia and Austria, but also France and the liberal states, had become decidedly hostile to us, and our intercourse was not such as was desirable. Lord John could instance many cases in which they had been unnecessarily slighted and provoked by Lord Palmerston, like M. Drouyn de Lhuys in the Greek affair. Lord Palmerston's conduct towards the Queen had been disrespectful and wanting in due attention and deference to her, and had been much complained of.

In consequence of all this Lord John had before proposed to Her Majesty that the Foreign Affairs should be entrusted to Lord Minto, he himself should go to the House of Lords, and Lord Palmerston should have the lead in the House of Commons. The Queen had, however, objected to this arrangement, [thinking] the lead in the Lower House to be more properly given to Sir George Grey, who had as Home Secretary conducted all internal business in the House. Now had come Sir R. Peel's death, which made it impossible for Lord John to leave the House of Commons without endangering the position of Government and of the parties in the House.

Lord Palmerston was much pleased to hear of Lord John's intention to stay in the House of Commons, said all was changed now; there had been a great conspiracy against him, he had been accused in Parliament, put on his trial and acquitted. The acquittal had produced the greatest enthusiasm for him in the country, and he was now supported by a strong party; he owned, however, that his success had been chiefly owing to the handsome manner in which Lord John and his colleagues had supported him in the debate. That he should incur the momentary enmity of those states whose interests and plans he might have to cross was quite natural; he had never intended any disrespect to the Queen, and if he had been guilty of any he was quite unconscious of it and sorry for it.

Lord John reminded him that although the Government had got a majority in the House of Commons in the Foreign debate, it was not to be forgotten that the fate of the Government had been staked upon it, and that many people voted on that account who would not have supported the Foreign policy; that it was remarkable that all those who had the strongest reason to be anxious for the continuance of the Government, but who could not avoid *speaking*, were obliged to speak and vote against the Government. Sir R. Peel's speech was a most remarkable instance of this.

Lord Palmerston saw in Sir Robert's speech nothing but a reluctant effort to defend Lord Aberdeen, whom he was bound to defend. If he (Lord Palmerston) were to leave the Foreign Office, there must be a ground for it, such as his having to take the lead in the House of Commons, which was evidently impossible with the conduct of Foreign Department at the same time. (It had killed Mr Canning, and after that failure nobody ought to attempt it.) But without such a ground it would be loss of character to him, which he could not be expected to submit to. There was not even the excuse of wishing to avoid a difficulty with a foreign country, as all was smooth now. Those who had wished to injure him had been beat, and now it would be giving them a triumph after all. If the Queen or the Cabinet were dissatisfied with his management of the Foreign Affairs, they had a right to demand his resignation, and he would give it, but they could not ask him to lower himself in public estimation. Lord John answered that his resignation would lead to a further split of parties: there were parties already enough in the House, and it was essential that at least the Whig party should be kept together, to which Lord Palmerston assented. He (Lord Palmerston) then repeated his complaints against that plot which had been got up in this country against him, and urged on by foreigners, complained particularly of Lord Clarendon, Mr Greville of the Privy Council, Mr Reeve, ditto, and their attacks upon him in the *Times*, and of Mr Delane, the Editor of the *Times*, of Guizot, Princess Lieven, etc., etc., etc. However, they had been convinced that they could not upset him, and Mr Reeve had declared to him that he had been making open and honourable (?!!) war upon him; now he would make a lasting peace. With Russia and France he (Lord Palmerston) had just been signing the Danish Protocol, showing that they were on the best terms together.

Lord John felt he could not press the matter further under these circumstances, but he seemed much provoked at the result of his conversation. We expressed our surprise that he had not made Lord Palmerston any offer of any kind. Lord John replied he had not been sure what he could have offered him....

Albert.

Queen Victoria to Lord John Russell.[33]

Osborne, *12th August 1850.*

With reference to the conversation about Lord Palmerston which the Queen had with Lord John Russell the other day, and Lord Palmerston's disavowal that he ever intended any disrespect to her by the various neglects of which she has had so long and so often to complain, she thinks it right, in order *to prevent any mistake* for the *future*, shortly to explain *what it is she expects from her Foreign Secretary.* She requires: (1) That he will distinctly state what he proposes in a given case, in order that the Queen may know as distinctly to *what* she has given her Royal sanction; (2) Having *once given* her sanction to a measure, that it be not arbitrarily altered or modified by the Minister; such an act she must consider as failing in sincerity towards the Crown, and justly to be visited by the exercise of her Constitutional right of dismissing that Minister. She expects to be kept informed of what passes between him and the Foreign Ministers before important decisions are taken, based upon that intercourse; to receive the Foreign Despatches in good time, and to have the drafts for her approval sent to her in sufficient time to make herself acquainted with their contents before they must be sent off. The Queen thinks it best that Lord John Russell should show this letter to Lord Palmerston.

Viscount Palmerston to Lord John Russell.

Foreign Office, *13th August 1850.*

My dear John Russell,—I have taken a copy of this memorandum of the Queen and will not fail to attend to the directions which it contains. With regard to the sending of despatches to the Queen, they have sometimes been delayed longer than should have been the case, in consequence of my having been prevented by great pressure of business, and by the many interruptions of interviews, etc., to which I am liable, from reading and sending them back into the Office so soon as I could have wished. But I will give orders that the old practice shall be reverted to, of making copies of all important despatches as soon as they reach the Office, so that there may be no delay in sending the despatches to the Queen; this practice was gradually left off as the business of the Office increased, and if it shall require an additional clerk or two you must be liberal and allow me that assistance.—Yours sincerely,

Palmerston.

The Duc de Nemours to Queen Victoria.

Claremont, *26 Août 1850.*

Madame ma chère Cousine,—La main de Dieu vient de s'appesantir sur nous. Le Roi notre Père n'est plus.[34] Après avoir reçu hier avec calme et résignation les secours de la religion, il s'est éteint ce matin à huit heures au milieu de nous tous. Vous le connaissiez ma chère Cousine, vous savez tout ce que nous perdons, vous comprendrez donc l'inexprimable douleur dans laquelle nous sommes plongés; vous la partagerez même je le sais!

La Reine brisée, malgré son courage, ne trouve de soulagement que dans une retraite absolue où ne voyant personne elle puisse laisser cours à sa douleur.

Veuillez faire part à Albert de notre malheur et recevoir ici, ma chère Cousine, l'hommage des sentiments de respect et d'attachement, de votre bien affectionné Cousin,

Louis d'Orléans.

Queen Victoria to Viscount Palmerston.

Osborne, *26th August 1850.*

The Queen wishes Lord Palmerston to give directions for a Court mourning according to those which are usual for an abdicated King. She likewise wishes that every assistance should be given, and every attention shown to the afflicted Royal Family, who have been so severely tried during the last two years, on the melancholy occasion of the poor King of the French's death.

The Queen starts for Scotland to-morrow.

The King of the Belgians to Queen Victoria.

Laeken, *30 August 1850.*

... I have offered to the poor Queen of the French to remain at Claremont and *d'en disposer* as long as Heaven does not dispose of myself. She, of course, dislikes the place, but will keep the family with her at least for some time.

Lord John Russell to Queen Victoria.

Taymouth Castle, *5th September 1850.*

Lord John Russell presents his humble duty to your Majesty, and was happy to receive your Majesty's gracious letter, which reached him the night before last.

The proofs of attachment to your Majesty, which are everywhere exhibited, are the more gratifying as they are entirely spontaneous.

It is fit and becoming that your Majesty should inhabit the royal Palace of Holyrood, and this circumstance gives great satisfaction throughout Scotland.

Lord John Russell is glad to learn that the family of the late King of the French will continue to reside in England.

The reflection naturally occurs, if Napoleon and Louis Philippe were unable to consolidate a dynasty in France, who will ever be able to do it? The prospect is a succession of fruitless attempts at civil Government till a General assumes the command, and governs by military force.

Lord John Russell to Queen Victoria.

Dunkeld, *7th September 1850.*

... Lord John Russell has had the honour of receiving at Taymouth a letter from the Prince. He agrees that the office of Poet Laureate ought to be filled up. There are three or four authors of nearly equal merit, such as Henry Taylor, Sheridan Knowles, Professor Wilson, and Mr Tennyson, who are qualified for the office.

The King of the Belgians to Queen Victoria.

Ostend, *7th October 1850.*

My dearest Victoria,—I write a few words only to tell you how our dear patient is.[35] Yesterday was a most perilous, truly dreadful day; our dear angelic Louise was so fainting that Madame d'Hulst, who was with her, felt the greatest alarm. She afterwards was better, and her mother, Clém, Joinville, and Aumale having arrived, she saw them with more composure than could have been expected. Still, she would in fact wish to be left quiet and alone with me, and we try to manage things as much as possible so that their visit does not tire her too much.

Her courage and strength of mind are most heart-breaking when one thinks of the danger in which she is, and her dear and angelic soul seems even to shine more brightly at this moment of such great and imminent danger. I am in a dreadful state when I am with her. She is so contented, so cheerful, that the possibilities of danger appear to me impossible; but the physicians are very much alarmed, without thinking the state absolutely hopeless. That one should write such things about a life so precious, and one in fact still so young, and whose angelic soul is so strong! You will feel with me as you love her so dearly. God bless you and preserve you from heart-breaking sufferings like mine. Ever, my dearest Victoria, your devoted Uncle,

Leopold R.

Viscount Palmerston to Queen Victoria.

Broadlands, *8th October 1850.*

Viscount Palmerston presents his humble duty to your Majesty, and has had the honour to receive your Majesty's communication of the 4th instant, expressing your Majesty's wish that an alteration should be made in his answer to Baron Koller's[36] note of the 5th of September, on the subject of the attack made upon General Haynau;[37] but Viscount Palmerston begs to state that when Baron Koller was at this place about ten days ago, he expressed so much annoyance at the delay which had already taken place in regard to the answer to his note of the 5th September, and he requested so earnestly that he might immediately have the reply, that Viscount Palmerston could do no otherwise than send him the answer at once, and Baron Koller despatched it the next day to Vienna.

Viscount Palmerston had put the last paragraph into the answer, because he could scarcely have reconciled it to his own feelings and to his sense of public responsibility to have put his name to a note which might be liable to be called for by Parliament, without expressing in it, at least as his own personal opinion, a sense of the want of propriety evinced by General Haynau in coming to England at the present moment.[38]

The state of public feeling in this country about General Haynau and his proceedings in Italy and Hungary was perfectly well known; and his coming here so soon after those events, without necessity or obligation to do so, was liable to be looked upon as a bravado, and as a challenge to an expression of public opinion.

Baron Koller indeed told Viscount Palmerston that Prince Metternich and Baron Neumann had at Brussels strongly dissuaded General Haynau from coming on to England; and that he (Baron Koller) had after his arrival earnestly entreated him to cut off those long moustachios which rendered him so liable to be identified.

With regard to the transaction itself, there is no justifying a breach of the law, nor an attack by a large number of people upon one or two individuals who cannot resist such superior force; and though in the present case, according to Baron Koller's account, the chief injury sustained by General Haynau consisted in the tearing of his coat, the loss of a cane, and some severe bruises on his left arm, and though four or five policemen proved to be sufficient protection, yet a mob who begin by insult lead each other on to outrage; and there is no saying to what extremes they might have proceeded if they had not been checked.

Such occurrences, however, have taken place before; and to go no further back than the last summer, the attacks on Lord Talbot at the Stafford meeting, and on Mr Bankes, Mr Sturt, and others at the Dorchester meeting, when a man was killed, were still more violent outrages, and originated simply in differences of political opinion; whereas in this case the brewers' men were expressing their feeling at what they considered inhuman conduct on the part of General Haynau.

The people of this country are remarkable for their hospitable reception of foreigners, and for their forgetfulness of past animosities. Napoleon Bonaparte, the greatest enemy that England ever had, was treated while at Plymouth with respect, and with commiseration while at St Helena. Marshal Soult, who had fought in many battles against the English, was received with generous acclamation when he came here as Special Ambassador. The King of the French, Mons. Guizot, and Prince Metternich, though all of them great antagonists of English policy and English interests, were treated in this country with courtesy and kindness. But General Haynau was looked upon as a great moral criminal; and the feeling in regard to him was of the same nature as that which was manifested towards Tawell[39] and the Mannings,[40] with this only difference, that General Haynau's bad deeds were committed upon a far larger scale, and upon a far larger number of victims. But Viscount Palmerston can assure your Majesty that those feelings of just and honourable indignation have not been confined to England, for he had good reason to know that General Haynau's ferocious and unmanly treatment of the unfortunate inhabitants of Brescia and of other towns and places in Italy, his savage proclamations to the people of Pesth, and his barbarous acts in Hungary excited almost as much disgust in Austria as in England, and that the nickname of "General Hyæna" was given to him at Vienna long before it was applied to him in London.

Queen Victoria to Lord John Russell.

Buckingham Palace, *11th October 1850.*

The Queen having written to Lord Palmerston in conformity with Lord John Russell's suggestion respecting the draft to Baron Koller, now encloses Lord Palmerston's answer, which she received at Edinburgh yesterday evening. Lord John will see that Lord Palmerston has not only *sent* the draft, but passes over in silence her injunction to have a corrected copy given to Baron Koller, and adds a vituperation against General Haynau, which clearly shows that he is not sorry for what has happened, and makes a merit of sympathising with the draymen at the brewery and the Chartist Demonstrations....

The Queen encloses likewise a copy of her letter to Lord Palmerston, and hopes Lord John will write to him.[41]

Lord John Russell wrote to the Prince Albert that he would be "somewhat amused, if not surprised, at the sudden and amicable termination of the dispute regarding the letter to Baron Koller. The same course may be adopted with advantage if a despatch is ever again sent which has been objected to, and to which the Queen's sanction has not been given." See the Queen's letter of the 19th of October.

Queen Victoria to Viscount Palmerston.

Buckingham Palace, *12th October 1850.*

The Queen has received Lord Palmerston's letter respecting the draft to Baron Koller. She cannot suppose that Baron Koller addressed his note to Lord Palmerston in order to receive in answer an expression of his *own personal opinion*; and if Lord Palmerston could not reconcile it to his own feelings to express the regret of the Queen's Government at the brutal attack and wanton outrage committed by a ferocious mob on a distinguished foreigner of past seventy years of age, who was quietly visiting a private establishment in this metropolis, without adding *his censure of the want of propriety* evinced by General Haynau in coming to England—he might have done so in a private letter, where his personal feelings could not be mistaken for the opinion of the Queen and her Government. She must repeat her request that Lord Palmerston will rectify this.

The Queen can as little approve of the introduction of Lynch Law in this country as of the *violent* vituperations with which Lord Palmerston accuses and condemns public men in other countries, acting in most difficult circumstances and under heavy responsibility, without having the means of obtaining correct information or of sifting evidence.

Queen Victoria to Viscount Palmerston.

Osborne, *16th October 1850.*

The Queen is glad to hear from Lord Palmerston that he has given no countenance to the French and Russian proposal at the suggestion of Denmark, that England, France, and Russia should, after having signed the Protocol in favour of Denmark, now go further and send their armies to aid her in her contest with Holstein.[42] The Queen does not expect any good result from Lord Palmerston's counter proposal to urge Prussia and Austria to compel the Holsteiners to lay down their arms. The mediating power ought rather to make Denmark feel that it requires more than a cessation of hostilities, a plan of reconciliation, and a solution of the questions in dispute, before she can hope permanently to establish peace. The mediating power itself, however, should strive to arrive at some opinion on the matter in dispute, based, not on *its own* supposed interests, as the Protocol is, but on an anxious, careful, and impartial investigation of the rights and pretensions of the disputing parties; and if it finds it impossible to arrive at such an opinion, to fix upon some impartial tribunal capable of doing so, to which the dispute could be submitted for decision. Common principles of morality would point out such a course, and what is morally right only can be politically wise.

Queen Victoria to the King of the Belgians.

Osborne, *18th October 1850.*

My dearest Uncle,—*This* was the day I *always* and for so *many years* wrote to *her*, to *our adored Louise*, and I *now* write to *you*, to thank you for that *heart-breaking*, touching letter of the 16th, which you so *very kindly* wrote to me. It is *so* kind of you to write to us. *What* a day Tuesday must have been! *Welch einen Gang!* and *yesterday!* My *grief* was *so great* again yesterday. To *talk* of her is my *greatest consolation!* Let us *all try* to imitate *her!* My poor dear Uncle, we wish so to be with you, to be of *any use* to you. You will allow us, in three or four weeks, to go to you for two or three days, *quite quietly* and alone, to Laeken without *any* one, without *any* reception anywhere, to cry with you and to talk with you of *Her*. It will be a great comfort to us— a *silent tribute* of *respect and love to her*—to be able to mingle our tears with yours over *her* tomb! And the affection of your two devoted children will perhaps be *some slight balm*. My *first* impulse was to *fly at once* to you, but perhaps a few weeks' delay will be better. It will be a *great* and melancholy satisfaction to us. *Daily* will you feel more, my poor dear Uncle, the *poignancy* of *your dreadful* loss; my *heart breaks* in thinking of *you* and the poor dear children. *How* beautiful it must be to see that *your whole country* weeps and mourns *with* you! For this country and for your children you must *try* to bear up, and feel that in *so doing* you are doing *all* she wished. If only *we* could be of use to you! if *I* could do *anything* for dear little Charlotte, whom our blessed Louise talked of *so* often to me.

May I *write* to *you* on *Fridays* when I used to write to her, as well as on Tuesdays? You need *not* answer me, and whenever it bores you to write to me, or you have no time, let one of the dear children write to me.

May God bless and protect you ever, my beloved Uncle, is our anxious prayer. Embrace the dear children in the name of one who has almost the feelings of a mother for them. Ever your devoted Niece and loving Child,

Victoria R.

Queen Victoria to Lord John Russell.

Osborne, *19th October 1850.*

The Queen is very glad of the result of the conflict with Lord Palmerston, of which Lord John Russell apprised her by his letter of yesterday's date. The correspondence, which the Queen now returns, shows clearly that Lord Palmerston in this transaction, as in every other, remained true to his principles of action.... But it shows also that Lord John has the power of exercising that control over Lord Palmerston, the careful exercise of which he owes to the Queen, his colleagues, and the country, if he will take the necessary pains to remain firm. The Queen does not believe in *resignation* under almost any circumstances.

The Queen is very anxious about the Holstein question, and sends a copy of her last letter to Lord Palmerston on the subject.

Lord John Russell to the Prince Albert.

Pembroke Lodge, *21st October 1850.*

Sir,—I have just received this note from Lord Palmerston.[43]

The French Ambassador, who has been here, confirms the news. We must consider the whole affair on Wednesday, and I shall be glad to learn what the Queen thinks can be done.

Mr Tennyson is a fit person to be Poet Laureate.

I have the honour to be, your Royal Highness's most obedient Servant,

J. Russell.

Lord John Russell to Queen Victoria.

Bishopthorpe, *25th October 1850.*

Lord John Russell presents his humble duty to your Majesty; he has read with attention the letter of the Duchess of Norfolk.[44] He has also read the Pope's Bull. It strikes him that the division into twelve territorial dioceses of eight ecclesiastical vicariats is not a matter to be alarmed at. The persons to be affected by this change must be already Roman Catholics before it can touch them.

The matter to create rational alarm is, as your Majesty says, the growth of Roman Catholic doctrines and practices within the bosom of the Church. Dr Arnold said very truly, "I look upon a Roman Catholic as an enemy in his uniform; I look upon a Tractarian as an enemy disguised as a spy."

It would be very wrong to do as the Bishop of Oxford proposed, and confer the patronage of the Crown on any of these Tractarians. But, on the other hand, to treat them with severity would give the whole party vigour and union.

The Dean of Bristol is of opinion that the Tractarians are falling to pieces by dissension. It appears clear that Mr Denison and Mr Palmer have broken off from Dr Pusey.

Sir George Grey will ask the Law Officers whether there is anything illegal in Dr Wiseman's assuming the title of Archbishop of Westminster. An English Cardinal is not a novelty.[45]

In September, Pius IX. (now re-established in the Vatican) promulgated a papal brief, restoring the Roman Catholic hierarchy in England, and dividing it territorially into twelve sees, and in October Cardinal Wiseman, as Archbishop of Westminster, issued his Pastoral, claiming that Catholic England had been restored to its orbit in the ecclesiastical firmament. The Duchess of Norfolk, writing from Arundel, had criticised the proselytising action of certain Roman Catholic clergy. *See* the Queen's reply, *post*, p. 277.

Lord John was pictorially satirised in *Punch* as the boy who chalked up "No popery" on the door and ran away.

The King of the Belgians to Queen Victoria.

Ardenne, *10th November 1850.*

My dearest Victoria,—I write already to-day that it may not miss to-morrow's messenger. I came here yesterday by a mild sunshine, and the valley of the Meuse was very pretty. I love my solitude here, and though the house is small and not what it ought to have been, still I always liked it. There seems in most countries danger of agitation and convulsions arising. I don't know how it will end in Germany. In France it is difficult that things should not break up some way or other. I trust you may be spared religious agitation. These sorts of things begin with one pretext, and sometimes continue with others. I don't think Europe was ever in more danger, *il y a tant d'anarchie dans les esprits.* I don't think that can be cured *à l'eau de rose*; the human race is not naturally good, very much the contrary; it requires a strong hand, and is, in fact, even pleased to be led in that way; the memory of all the sort of Césars and Napoléons, from whom they chiefly got blows, is much dearer to them than the benefactors of mankind, whom they crucify when they can have their own way. Give my best love to Albert; and I also am very anxious to be recalled to the recollection of the children, who were so very friendly at Ostende. How far we were then to guess what has since happened.... My dearest Victoria, your devoted Uncle,

Leopold R.

Queen Victoria to the Countess of Gainsborough.[46]

Thursday morning [*November* ...] *1850.*

Dearest Fanny,—This is a case of positive necessity, and as *none* of the ladies are forthcoming I fear I must call upon you to attend me *to-night.* You did so once *in state* before, and as it is not a *matter of pleasure*, but of duty, I am sure you will at once feel that you can have no scruple.

Whenever the Mistress of the Robes does not attend, I *always* have three ladies, as they must take turns in standing behind me. Ever yours affectionately,

Victoria R.

Queen Victoria to Viscount Palmerston.

Windsor Castle, *18th November 1850.*

The Queen is exceedingly sorry to hear that Lord Westmorland[47] is gone, as she was particularly anxious to have seen him before his return to Berlin, and to have talked to him on the present critical events in Germany; but she quite forgot the day of his departure. What is the object of his seeing the President at Paris? and what are his instructions with regard to Germany?[48]

Having *invariably encouraged Constitutional* development in other countries,... and having at the beginning of the great movement in 1847, which led to all the catastrophes of the following years, *sent* a Cabinet Minister to Italy to *declare* to all Italian states that *England* would *protect* them from Austria if she should attempt by threats and violence to debar them from the *attainment* of their *Constitutional* development, *consistency* would require that we should *now*, when that great struggle is at its end and *despotism* is to be *re-imposed* by Austrian arms upon Germany, throw *our weight* into the scale of *Constitutional* Prussia and Germany.... The Queen is afraid, however, that all our Ministers abroad,—at Berlin, Dresden, Munich, Stuttgart, Hanover, etc. (with the exception of Lord Cowley at Frankfort)—are warm partisans of the *despotic* league against Prussia and a German Constitution and *for* the maintenance of the old Diet under Austrian and Russian influence. Ought not Lord Palmerston to make his agents understand that their sentiments are at variance with those of the English Government? and that they are doing *serious mischief* if they express them at Courts which have *already* every inclination to follow their desperate course?

Lord Palmerston is of course aware that the old Diet once reconstituted and recognised, one of the main laws of it is that "*no organic change can be made* without *unanimity* of voices," which was the cause of the nullity of that body from 1820 to 1848, and will now enable Austria, should Prussia and her confederates recognise the Diet, to condemn Germany to a further life of stagnation or new revolution.

Viscount Palmerston to Queen Victoria.

Foreign Office, *18th November 1850.*

Viscount Palmerston presents his humble duty to your Majesty. With respect to the maintenance of Constitutional Government in Germany, Viscount Palmerston entirely subscribes to your Majesty's opinion, that a regard for consistency, as well as a sense of right and justice, ought to lead your Majesty's Government to give to the Constitutional principle in Germany the same moral support which they endeavoured to afford it in Italy, Spain, Portugal, and elsewhere; but though he is conscious that he may be deceived and may think better of the Austrian Government in this respect than it deserves, yet he cannot persuade himself that rational and sound Constitutional Government is at present in danger in Germany, or that the Austrian Government, whatever may be their inclination and wishes, can think it possible in the present day to re-establish despotic government in a nation so enlightened, and so attached to free institutions as the German people now is. The danger for Germany seems to lie rather in the opposite direction, arising from the rash and weak precipitation with which in 1848 and 1849 those Governments which before had refused everything resolved in a moment of alarm to grant everything, and, passing from one extreme to the other, threw universal suffrage among people who had been, some wholly and others very much, unaccustomed to the working of representative Government. The French have found universal suffrage incompatible with good order even in a Republic; what must it be for a Monarchy?

Viscount Palmerston would, moreover, beg to submit that the conflict between Austria and Prussia can scarcely be said to have turned upon principles of Government so much as upon a struggle for political ascendency in Germany. At Berlin, at Dresden, and in Baden the Prussian Government has very properly no doubt employed military force to reestablish order; and in regard to the affairs of Hesse, the ground taken by Prussia was not so much a constitutional as a military one, and the objection which she made to the entrance of the troops of the Diet was that those troops might become hostile, and that they ought not, therefore, to occupy a central position in the line of military defence of Prussia.

The remark which your Majesty makes as to unanimity being required for certain purposes by the Diet regulations is no doubt very just, and that circumstance certainly shows that the free Conference which is about to be held is a better constructed body for planning a new arrangement of a central organ.[49]

Queen Victoria to the King of the Belgians.

Windsor Castle, *22nd November 1850.*

My dearest Uncle,—Accept my best thanks for your kind letter of the 17th, and the dear little English one from dear little Charlotte, which is so nicely written, and shows such an amiable disposition. I send her to-day a little heart for the hair of our blessed Angel, which I hope she will often wear. Our girls have all got one. I have written to the dear child. You should have the dear children as much with you as possible; I am *sure* it would be so *good and useful* for *you* and *them*. Children ought to have great confidence in their parents, in order for them to have any influence over them.

Yesterday Vicky was ten years old. It seems a dream. If she lives, in eight years more she may be married! She is a very clever child, and I must say very much improved.

The state of the Continent is deplorable; the folly of Austria and the giving way of Prussia are lamentable. *Our* influence on the Continent is *null....* Add to this, we are between two fires in *this* country: a furious Protestant feeling and an enraged Catholic feeling in Ireland. I believe that Austria fans the flame at Rome, and that the *whole movement* on the Continent is *anti-Constitutional, anti-Protestant, and anti-English*; and this is so complicated, and we have (thanks to Lord Palmerston) contrived to quarrel *so happily*, separately with each, that I do not know *how* we are to stand against it all!

I must now conclude. Trusting soon to hear from you again. Ever your devoted Niece,

Victoria R.

My longing for dearest Louise seems only to increase as time goes on.

Queen Victoria to the Duchess of Norfolk.

Windsor Castle, *22nd November 1850.*

My dear Duchess,—It is very remiss in me not to have sooner answered your letter with the enclosure, but I received it at a moment of great grief, and since then I have been much occupied.

I fully understand your anxiety relative to the proceedings of the Roman Catholic Clergy, but I trust that there is no *real* danger to be apprehended from that quarter, the more so as I believe they see that they have been misled and misinformed as to the feeling of this country by some of the new converts to their religion. The real danger to be apprehended, and what I am certain has led to these proceedings on the part of the Pope, lies in *our own* divisions, and in the extraordinary conduct of the Puseyites. I trust that the eyes of many may now be opened. One would, however, much regret to see any acts of intolerance towards the many innocent people who I believe entirely disapprove the injudicious conduct of their Clergy.

Hoping that you are all well, believe me, always, yours, affectionately,

Victoria R.

Queen Victoria to the King of the Belgians.

Windsor Castle, *29th November 1850.*

My dearest Uncle,—I have no dear letter to answer, but write to keep to the dear day, rendered so peculiarly dear to me by the recollection of our dearly beloved Louise.

We are well, but much troubled with numberless things. Our religious troubles are great, and I must just say that Cardinal Wiseman *himself* admits that Austria not only approves the conduct of the Pope but is urging *on* the *Propaganda*. I *know this* to be so. Our great difficulty must be, and will be, to steer clear of both parties—the violent Protestants and the Roman Catholics. We wish in no way to infringe the rights of the Roman Catholics, while we must protect and uphold our own religion.

We have seen General Radowitz,[50] with whom we have been much interested; his accounts are very clear and very able, and I must say, very fair and strictly constitutional. You know him, I suppose? Might I again ask, dearest Uncle, if you would like to have a copy of Ross's picture of our angel Louise or of Winterhalter's?

Lady Lyttelton, who is returned, is very anxious in her enquiries after you.

I must now conclude, my dearest Uncle. Ever your devoted Niece,

Victoria R.

Queen Victoria to the King of the Belgians.

Windsor Castle, *3rd December 1850.*

My beloved Uncle,—Two of your dear letters are before me, of the 29th November and of yesterday. In the former you *give me a promise*, which I consider *most* valuable, and which I shall *remind* you of if you get desponding, viz. "I will to please you *labour on, and do all the good I can.*" It is so pleasing to feel that one *does* good and does one's duty. It sweetens so many bitter trials.

The state of Germany is indeed a very anxious one. It is a mistake to think the *supremacy of Prussia* is *what is wished for*. General Radowitz himself says that what is necessary for Germany [is] that she should take the lead, and should redeem the pledges given in '48. Unless this be *done* in a moderate and determined way, a *fearful reaction* will take place, which will *overturn Thrones*; to use Radowitz's own words: "*und nicht vor dem Thron stehen bleiben.*" Prussia is the *only large* and powerful *really German* Power there is, and therefore she must take the lead; but her constant vacillation—one day doing one thing and another day another—has caused her to be entirely distrusted. You are quite right in saying things should be done *d'un commun accord*, and I think that the other great Powers ought to be consulted. Unfortunately, *Lord Palmerston* has contrived to make us *so hated* by all parties abroad, that we have lost our position and our influence, which, considering the flourishing and satisfactory state of this country during all the European convulsions, *ought* to have been *immense*. This it is which pains and grieves me so deeply, and which I have so plainly been speaking to Lord John Russell about. What a noble position we *might* have had, and how wantonly has it been thrown away!

Good Stockmar is well, and always of the *greatest* comfort and use to us. His judgment is so sound, so unbiassed, and so dispassionate. Ever your devoted Niece,

Victoria R.

Queen Victoria to Lord John Russell.

Windsor Castle, *8th December 1850.*

The Queen received Lord John Russell's letter and the draft yesterday. He must be a better judge of what the effect of Mr Sheil's[51] presence in Rome may be than she can; but for her own part, she thinks it entirely against her notions of what is *becoming* to *ask* the *Pope* for a *favour* (for it is tantamount to that) at a moment when his name is being vilified and abused in every possible manner in this country. It strikes the Queen as an *undignified* course for this Government to pursue.

The Queen is glad to hear of what passed between the Archbishop and Lord John.[52] She trusts that something may be done, as the desire for it seems to be so great. On the other hand, the Queen deeply regrets the great abuse of the Roman Catholic religion which takes place at all these meetings, etc. She thinks it unchristian and unwise, and trusts that it will soon cease....

Queen Victoria to the King of the Belgians.

Windsor Castle, *10th December 1850.*

My beloved Uncle,—My letter must, I fear, be a somewhat hurried and short one, for my morning has been taken up in receiving in state Addresses from the City and Universities about this *unfortunate* "Papal Aggression" business, which is still keeping people in a feverish state of wild excitement.[53] *One* good effect it has had, viz. that of directing people's serious attention to the very alarming tendency of the *Tractarians*, which was doing *immense* harm....

Many, many thanks for your two dear and kind letters of the 6th and of yesterday. All you *say* about *Louise*, and about the disappearance *for ever* of *all* that *she loved* and was *proud of*, is so true, so *dreadful*. One fancies (foolishly and wrongly, but still one *does*) that the lost one has been hardly used in no longer enjoying these earthly blessings, and one's grief seems to break out afresh in bitter agony upon *small and comparatively trifling* occasions. Poor Lady Peel (whom I saw for the first time yesterday at Buckingham Palace, whither I had gone for an hour) expressed *this* strongly. *Hers* is indeed a *broken heart*; she is so *truly* crushed by the *agony* of *her* grief; it was *very* touching to see and to hear her. Poor thing! she *never* can be happy again!

What you say about *me* is far too kind. I am very *often* sadly dissatisfied with myself and with the little self-control I have.

Your long letter interested us much. I fear the German affairs are very bad.... That everlasting "backwards and forwards," as you say, of my poor friend the King of Prussia is *calamitous*; it causes *all* parties to distrust him, and gives *real* strength only to the Republicans. Since

'48 that has been his conduct, and the *misfortune* for Germany. A *steady* course, *whatever* it may be, is *always* the best.

What you say about poor Hélène[54] and France is true and sad. I really wish you would caution Hélène as to her language; she is much attached to you. I *pity* her very much; her position is very trying, and her religion renders it more difficult even.

I must now end my letter. I grieve to hear of your going *alone* to Ardenne; it is BAD for you to be alone, and your poor children also ought not to be alone. Ever your devoted Niece,

Victoria R.

Lord John Russell to Queen Victoria.

Downing Street, *11th December 1850.*

Lord John Russell presents his humble duty to your Majesty, and has the honour to state that the Cabinet to-day considered at great length the question of the steps to be taken in respect to the Papal Aggression.

The inclination of the majority was not to prosecute, but to bring a Bill into Parliament to make the assumption of any titles of archbishop, etc., of any place in the United Kingdom illegal, and to make any gift of property conveyed under such title null and void.

Queen Victoria to the Duchess of Gloucester.

Windsor Castle, *12th December 1850.*

My dear Aunt,—Many thanks for your kind letter; you are quite right not to distress the Duchess of Cambridge by mentioning to her what I wrote to you about the Bishop of London.[55] I am glad that you are pleased with my answers to the Addresses; I thought them very proper.[56]

I would never have consented to say anything which breathed a spirit of intolerance. Sincerely Protestant as I always have been and always shall be, and indignant as I am at those who *call themselves Protestants*, while they in fact *are* quite the *contrary*, I much regret the unchristian and intolerant spirit exhibited by many people at the public meetings. I cannot bear to hear the violent abuse of the Catholic religion, which is so painful and cruel towards the many good and innocent Roman Catholics. However, we must hope and trust this excitement will soon cease, and that the wholesome effect of it on our own *Church* will be the lasting result of it. Ever yours ...

Victoria R.

Queen Victoria to Lord John Russell.

Windsor Castle, *14th December 1850.*

The Queen has received Lord John Russell's letter of yesterday. She sanctions the introduction into Parliament of a Bill framed on the principles agreed upon at yesterday's Cabinet, presuming that it will extend to the whole United Kingdom. What is to be done, however, with respect to the Colonies where the Roman Catholic bishoprics are recognised by the Government under territorial titles? and what is to be done with Dr Cullen, who has assumed the title of Archbishop of Armagh, Primate of all Ireland, which is punishable under the Emancipation Act? If this is left unnoticed, the Government will be left with the "*lame*" argument in Parliament of which we conversed here. Could the Government not be helped out of this difficulty by the Primate himself prosecuting the obtruder? The Queen hopes that the meeting of the archdeacons with Dr Lushington may do some good; she cannot say that she is pleased with the Archbishop's answer to the laity published in to-day's *Times*, which leaves them without a remedy if the clergymen persist in Puseyite Rituals! The Queen will return Lord Minto's letter with the next messenger.

Queen Victoria to Lord John Russell.

Windsor Castle, *22nd December 1850.*

The Queen now returns Lord Seymour's letter respecting the New Forest, and sanctions the proposed arrangement. Considering, however, that she gives up the deer, and all patronage and authority over the Forest, she wishes the shooting, as the only remaining Royalty, not to be withdrawn from her authority also. It will be quite right to give Deputations[57] to shoot over the various divisions and walks of the Forest to gentlemen of the neighbourhood or others; but in order that this may establish no right on their part, and may leave the Sovereign a voice in the matter, she wishes that a list be prepared every year of the persons recommended by the Office of Woods to receive Deputations and submitted for her approval.

ENDNOTES:

[1]:*I.e.* of hostilities against the Greek Government, designed to extract compensation for the injuries inflicted on British subjects. See *ante*, p. 240.

[2]:*See* Ashley's *Palmerston*, vol. i. chap. v.

[3]:Lord John Russell's opinion was that three weeks should be allowed to Mr Wyse and Sir W. Parker to accept terms as satisfactory as they could obtain, and that Sir W. Parker should not be obliged to resume coercive measures, if the concessions of the Greek Government should appear to afford a prospect of a speedy settlement of the affair.

[4]:Baron Gros was the Commissioner despatched by the French Government to Athens to assist in arranging the dispute.

[5]:See subsequent correspondence between Lord John and Lord Palmerston, Walpole's *Russell*, vol. ii. chap. xix.

[6]:Compare this with the Memorandum ultimately drawn up on the 12th of August.

[7]:*I.e.* "only."

[8]:He was President in 1848.

[9]:At the Mansion House banquet to the Commissioners for the Exhibition of 1851. See quotation from it in Sir T. Martin's *Life*, vol. ii, p. 247.

[10]:Don Pacifico claimed £31,500—£4,900 being for effects destroyed, and £26,600 in respect of certain claims against the Portuguese Government, the vouchers for which he stated had been destroyed by the mob which pillaged his house. His valuation of the various items was of the most extravagant description.

[11]:The question was the selection of a Minister for Madrid.

[12]:Lord Howden had been recently Minister at Rio Janeiro.

[13]:Minister at Berlin, 1841-51.

[14]:Russia as well as France had been appealed to by Greece against the pressure brought to bear upon her. On the 18th of April a Convention was signed in London disposing of the whole dispute, and referring Don Pacifico's claims against Portugal to arbitration. Lord Palmerston was remiss in communicating the progress of those negotiations to Mr Wyse, who persisted in his coercive measures, disregarding the intelligence on the subject he received from Baron Gros, and Greece accordingly submitted to his terms. France and Russia were incensed, the French Ambassador was recalled, and on the 18th of May Baron Brunnow intimated the imminence of similar action by the Czar.

[15]:The question of the relations of Lord Palmerston with the Crown had to be postponed owing to the debates in both Houses on Foreign Policy. In the Lords, Lord Stanley moved a vote of censure on the Government for enforcing by coercive measures various doubtful or exaggerated claims against the Greek Government.

[16]:Lord Ashley carried a resolution forbidding the Sunday delivery of letters; a Committee of Inquiry was appointed, and reported against the proposed change, which was abandoned.

[17]:The patent was made out, but not signed, a memorandum of Prince Albert recording:—

[18]:Lord Stanley's Motion of Censure was carried by a majority of 37 in a House of 301.

[19]:The Protocol was to record the desirability of the following points:—(1) that the several states which constituted the Danish Monarchy should remain united, and that the Danish Crown should be settled in such manner that it should go with the Duchy of Holstein; (2) that the signatory Powers, when the peace should have been concluded, should concert measures for the purpose of giving to the results an additional pledge of stability, by a general European acknowledgment.

[20]:The present Duke of Connaught, born on the 1st of May, the birthday of the Duke of Wellington, who was one of the sponsors, and after whom he was named.

[21]:From an attempt to assassinate him.

[22]:It lasted from dusk till dawn, and the Minister asked for a verdict on the question whether, "as the Roman in days of old held himself free from indignity when he could say, *Civis Romanus sum*, so also a British subject, in whatever land he may be, shall feel confident that the watchful eye and the strong arm of England will protect him against injustice and wrong." Peel, who made his last appearance in the House, voted against Palmerston.

[23]:In the result, Ministers succeeded by 310 to 264, although opposed to them in the debate were Mr Gladstone, Mr Cobden, Sir Robert Peel, Mr Disraeli, Sir James Graham, and Sir William Molesworth. Next to the speeches of Lord Palmerston and Lord John Russell, the most effective speech on the Government side was that of Mr Alexander Cockburn, afterwards Lord Chief Justice of England.

[24]:The Queen, as she was leaving Cambridge House, where she had called to inquire after the Duke of Cambridge's health, was struck with a cane by one Robert Pate, an ex-officer, and a severe bruise was inflicted on her forehead. The outrage was apparently committed without motive, but an attempt to prove Pate insane failed, and he was sentenced to seven years' transportation.

[25]:On the day following the Don Pacifico debate, Sir Robert Peel, after attending a meeting of the Exhibition Commissioners, had gone out riding. On his return, while passing up Constitution Hill, he was thrown from his horse, and, after lingering three days in intense pain, died on the 5th of July.

[26]:The Prince of Prussia.

[27]:Denmark and the Schleswig-Holstein Duchies were still at war. Germany was bent on absorbing the Duchies, but Prussia now concluded a peace

with Denmark: the enlistment of individual Germans in the insurgent army continued.

[28]:The Princess Charlotte of Belgium was seriously ill.

[29]:See *ante*, vol. i. p. 437.

[30]:The Convention of the 18th of April (see *ante*, p. 242, note 1) had decided that £8500 should be distributed among the claimants, and that Don Pacifico's special claim against Portugal should be referred to arbitration. Ultimately he was awarded only an insignificant sum.

[31]:In this draft, Lord Palmerston was remonstrating with the Prussian Government against the orders given by the Holstein Statthalters to their army to invade Schleswig, after the signature of the peace between Prussia and Denmark.

[32]:This was in consequence of Sir Charles Napier's action in exercising powers belonging to the Supreme Council, on the occasion of a mutiny of a regiment of the Native Army.

[33]:Compare the memorandum suggested by Baron Stockmar, *ante*, p. 238. This letter was, after much forbearance, written in the hope of bringing Lord Palmerston to a proper understanding of his relation to the Sovereign. Even when the catastrophe came, and its tenor had to be communicated by the Premier to Parliament, the Preamble was generously omitted; but in consequence of its description by Lord Palmerston, in a letter published by Mr Ashley, as an *angry* memorandum, it was printed in full in *The Life of the Prince Consort*.

[34]:King Louis Philippe was in his seventy-seventh year when he died: his widow, Queen Marie Amélie, lived till 1866, when she died at the age of eighty-four.

[35]:The Queen of the Belgians died on the 11th of October, at the age of thirty-eight.

[36]:The Austrian Ambassador.

[37]:General Haynau had earned in the Hungarian War an odious reputation as a flogger of women. When visiting the brewery of Barclay & Perkins, the draymen mobbed and assaulted him; he had to fly from them, and take refuge in a neighbouring house. Lord Palmerston had to send an official letter of apology to the Austrian Government, which, as originally despatched, without waiting for the Queen's approval, contained a paragraph offensive to Austria.

[38]:See Lord Palmerston's letter to Sir G. Grey, Ashley's *Life of Lord Palmerston*, vol. i. chap. vi.

[39]:Executed for the Salt Hill murder.

[40]:Marie Manning (an ex-lady's maid, whose career is said to have suggested Hortense in *Bleak House* to Dickens) was executed with her husband, in 1849, for the murder of a guest. She wore black satin on the scaffold, a material which consequently became unpopular for some time.

[41]:Lord John insisted on the note being withdrawn, and another substituted with the offensive passage omitted. After threatening resignation, Lord Palmerston somewhat tamely consented.

[42]:A strenuous attempt was being made by the Danish Government to bring pressure to bear on Austria and Prussia, to put down the nationalist movement in the Duchies, either by active intervention, or by reassembling the Conference which had negotiated the Treaty of Berlin. Lord Palmerston discountenanced both alternatives, but wrote to the Queen that he and the representatives of France, Russia, and Denmark thought that Austria and Prussia should be urged to take all feasible steps to put an end to the hostilities.

[43]:The note was in reference to the affairs of Hesse-Cassel, and to the rumours of a Conference to be held in Austria for the settlement of German affairs.

[44]:Two important events in the history of the English Church had just occurred. The Bishop of Exeter had refused to institute Mr Gorham to a Crown living in his diocese, on the ground that his teaching on baptism was at variance with the formularies of the Church. This decision, though upheld in the Court of Arches, was reversed (though not unanimously) by the Privy Council. High Church feeling was much aroused by the judgment.

[45]:Lord John wrote on the 4th of November to Dr Maltby, Bishop of Durham, denouncing the assumption of spiritual superiority over England, in the documents issued from Rome. But what alarmed him more (he said) was the action of clergymen within the Church leading their flocks dangerously near the brink, and recommending for adoption the honour paid to saints, the claim of infallibility for the Church, the superstitious use of the sign of the cross, the muttering of the liturgy so as to disguise the language in which it was said, with the recommendation of auricular confession and the administration of Penance and absolution.

[46]:Frances, Countess of Gainsborough, daughter of the third Earl of Roden, a Lady of the Bedchamber, and known till 1841 as Lady Barham.

[47]:Minister at Berlin.

[48]:Lord Palmerston may have had this letter of the Queen's in mind when he wrote on the 22nd of November to Lord Cowley: "Her (*i.e.* Prussia's) partisans try to make out that the contest between her and Austria is a struggle between constitutional and arbitrary Government, but it is no such thing." Ashley's *Life of Lord Palmerston*, vol. 1. chap. vi.

[49]:War was staved off by the Conference; but the relative predominance of Prussia and Austria in Germany was left undecided for some years to come.

[50]:General Radowitz, who had been Minister for Foreign Affairs in Prussia, had just arrived in England on a special mission from the King of Prussia.

[51]:Minister at the Court of Tuscany.

[52]:The Government were preparing for the introduction of their Ecclesiastical Titles Bill.

[53]:These Addresses were presented at Windsor, Prince Albert and the Duke of Wellington representing the Universities of Cambridge and Oxford.

[54]:The Duchess of Orleans.

[55]:The Bishop of London had taken the same view as Lord John Russell of the Papal action, though they had disagreed over the Gorham controversy.

[56]:See *ante*, p. 288.

[57]:A deputation, *i.e.*, a deputed right to take game.

INTRODUCTORY NOTE
TO CHAPTER XX

The Ministry were in difficulties at the very beginning of the session (1851), being nearly defeated on a motion made in the interest of the agricultural party; and though the Ecclesiastical Titles Bill was allowed to be brought in, they were beaten in a thin House chiefly by their own friends, on the question of the County Franchise. A crisis ensued, and a coalition of Whigs and Peelites was attempted, but proved impracticable. Lord Stanley having then failed to form a Protectionist Ministry, the Whigs, much weakened, had to resume office.

The Exhibition, which was opened in Hyde Park on the 1st of May, was a complete success, a brilliant triumph indeed, for the Prince, over six million people visiting it; it remained open till the Autumn, and the building, some time after its removal, was re-erected at Sydenham, at the Crystal Palace.

The Ecclesiastical Titles Bill, much modified, was proceeded with, and, though opposed by the ablest Peelites and Radicals, became law, though its effect, while in operation, was virtually *nil*. It was in after-years repealed.

Kossuth, the champion of Hungarian independence, visited England in October, and Lord Palmerston had to be peremptorily restrained from receiving him publicly at the Foreign Office. A little later, Kossuth's ultra-liberal sympathisers in London addressed the Foreign Secretary in language violently denunciatory of the Emperors of Austria and Russia, for which Lord Palmerston failed to rebuke them. The cup was filled to the brim by his recognition of the President's *coup d'état* in France. Louis Napoleon, after arresting M. Thiers and many others, proclaimed the dissolution of the Council of State and the National Assembly, decreed a state of siege, and re-established universal suffrage, with a Chief Magistrate elected for ten years, and a Ministry depending on the executive alone. Palmerston thereupon, though professing an intention of non-interference, conveyed to the French Ambassador in London his full approbation of the proceeding, and his conviction that the President could not have acted otherwise. Even after this indiscreet action, the Premier found some difficulty in bringing him to book; but before the end of the year he was dismissed from office, with the offer, which he declined, of the Irish Lord-Lieutenancy and a British Peerage. Greatly to the Queen's satisfaction, Lord Granville became Foreign Secretary.

At the Cape, Sir Harry Smith was engaged in operations against the Kaffirs, which were not brought to a successful termination till the following year, when General Cathcart had superseded him.

CHAPTER XX

1851

Queen Victoria to Lord John Russell.

Windsor Castle, *25th January 1851.*

The Queen approves of the elevation of Mr. Pemberton Leigh[1] to the Peerage, which she considers a very useful measure, and not likely to lead to any permanent increase of the Peerage, as he is not likely to marry at his present age, and considering that he has only a life interest in his large property.

With regard to the creation of Dr Lushington[2] as a Peer, without remainder, the Queen has again thoroughly considered the question, and is of opinion that the establishment of the principle of creation for life—in cases where public advantage may be derived from the grant of a Peerage, but where there may be no fortune to support the dignity in the family—is most desirable. The mode in which the public will take the introduction of it will however chiefly depend upon the merits of the first case brought forward. Dr Lushington appears to the Queen so unobjectionable in this respect that she cannot but approve of the experiment being tried with him.

It would be well, however, that it should be done quietly; that it should not be talked about beforehand or get into the papers, which so frequently happens on occasions of this kind, and generally does harm.

Queen Victoria to Viscount Palmerston.

Windsor Castle, *31st January 1851.*

The Queen has received Lord Palmerston's letter of the 29th, in which he proposes a change in those diplomatic arrangements which she had already sanctioned on his recommendation, and must remark that the reasons which Lord Palmerston adduces in support of his present proposition are in direct contradiction to those by which he supported his former recommendation.[3]

The principle which the Queen would wish to see acted upon in her diplomatic appointments in general, is, that the *good of the service* should precede every other consideration, and that the selection of an agent should depend more on his personal qualifications for the particular post for which he is to be selected than on the mere pleasure and convenience of the person to be employed, or of the Minister recommending him.

According to Lord Palmerston's first proposal, Sir H. Seymour was to have gone to St Petersburg, Lord Bloomfield to Berlin, and Sir Richard Pakenham to Lisbon; now Lord Palmerston wishes to send Lord Cowley to St Petersburg.

The Queen has the highest opinion of Lord Cowley's abilities, and agrees with Lord Palmerston in thinking that Russia will, for some time at least, exercise a predominating influence over all European affairs. She would accordingly not object to see that Agent accredited there in whom she herself places the greatest confidence. But according to the same principle, she must insist that the posts of Berlin and Frankfort, which in her opinion are of nearly equal importance, should be filled by men capable of dealing with the complicated and dangerous political questions now in agitation there, and the just appreciation and judicious treatment of which are of the highest importance to the peace of Europe, and therefore to the welfare of England.

Before the Queen therefore decides upon Lord Palmerston's new proposals, she wishes to know *whom* he could recommend for the post of Frankfort in the event of Lord Cowley leaving it, and thinks it but right to premise that in giving her sanction to the proposals Lord Palmerston may have to submit, she will be guided entirely by the principle set forth above.

Lord John Russell to Queen Victoria.

Chesham Place, *12th January 1851.*

Lord John Russell presents his humble duty to your Majesty, and has the honour to state that Mr Disraeli brought forward his Motion yesterday.[4] His speech was long and elaborate, but not that of a man who was persuaded he was undertaking a good cause.

He proposed nothing specific, but said nothing offensive.

The doubts about the division increase. Mr Hayter reckoned yesterday on a majority of three! Sir James Graham is of opinion Lord

Stanley will not undertake anything desperate. He will speak in favour of Government to-morrow, when the division will probably take place.

Queen Victoria to Viscount Palmerston.

Buckingham Palace, *15th February 1851.*

The Queen has received Lord Palmerston's letter of yesterday, and has to state in answer her decision in favour of the original plan of appointments, viz. of Sir H. Seymour to Petersburg, Lord Bloomfield to Berlin, and Sir R. Pakenham to Lisbon. The Queen quite agrees with Lord Palmerston in the opinion that the post at Petersburg is more important than that of Frankfort, and had Lord Palmerston been able to propose a good successor to Lord Cowley she would have approved his going to Petersburg; Sir R. Pakenham, however, would not take Frankfort if offered to him, as it appears, and the two other persons proposed would not do for it, in the Queen's opinion. It must not be forgotten that at a place for action like Petersburg, the Minister will chiefly have to look to his instructions from home, while at a place of observation, as Lord Palmerston justly calls Frankfort, everything depends upon the acuteness and impartiality of the observer, and upon the confidence with which he may be able to inspire those from whom alone accurate information can be obtained. Lord Cowley possesses eminently these qualities, and Sir H. Seymour has at all times shown himself equal to acting under most difficult circumstances. The desire of the Emperor to see Lord Cowley at Petersburg may possibly resolve itself in the desire of Baron Brunnow to see him removed from Germany.... The Queen had always understood that Sir H. Seymour would be very acceptable to the Emperor, and that Count Nesselrode called him a diplomatist "de la bonne vieille roche."

Memorandum by Queen Victoria.

Buckingham Palace. *17th February 1851.*

Lord John Russell came at half-past three. He had had a long conversation with Sir James Graham, had stated to him that from the tone of his speech (which Lord John explained to us yesterday was of so very friendly a character and pointed directly to supporting the Government)—its friendliness, and the manner in which he advocated the union of those who opposed a return to Protection, that he proposed to him to join the Government; that Sir G. Grey had offered to resign his office in order that Sir J. Graham might have it. Before I go farther I ought to say that Lord John yesterday explained the importance of obtaining support like Sir J. Graham's in the Cabinet, and that he thought of proposing the Board of Control to him, which Sir J. Hobhouse was ready to give up—receiving a Peerage, and retaining a seat in the Cabinet or the Admiralty, which Sir F. Baring was equally ready to give up.

Well, Sir J. Graham said that before he answered he wished to show Lord John a correspondence which had passed between him and Lord Londonderry. In the course of conversation in the country, Sir James had said to Lord Londonderry that parties never could go on as they were, and that they must ultimately lapse into *two*; this, Lord Londonderry reported to Mr Disraeli, who told it to Lord Stanley; and Mr Disraeli wrote to Lord Londonderry, stating that if certain advantages and reliefs were given to the landed interests, he should not cling to Protection; in short, much what he said in his speech—and that he was quite prepared to give up the lead in the House of Commons to Sir J. Graham. Sir James answered that he never meant anything by what he had said, and that he had no wish whatever to join Lord Stanley; that if he had, he was so intimate with Lord Stanley that he would have communicated direct with him.

Sir James said that as soon as he heard from Lord John, he thought *what* he wished to see him for, and that he had been thinking over it, and had been talking to Lord Hardinge and Mr Cardwell. That he did wish to support the Government, but that he thought he could be of more use if he did not join the Government, and was able to give them an independent support; that he had not attempted to lead Sir Robert Peel's followers; that many who had followed Sir Robert would *not* follow *him*; that he thought the Government in great danger; that the Protectionists, Radicals, and Irish Members would try to take an opportunity to overset them (the Government); that should the Government be turned out, he would find no difficulty in joining them; or should they go on, that by-and-by it might be easier to do so; but that at this moment he should be injuring himself without doing the Government any real service; besides which, there were so many measures decided on which he was ignorant of, and should have to support. Lord John told him that were he in the Cabinet, he would have the means of stating and enforcing his opinions, and that at whatever time he joined them, there would always be the same difficulty about measures which had already been decided on. He (Sir James) is not quite satisfied with the Papal Aggression Bill, which he thinks will exasperate the Irish; he also adverted to the report of our having protested against Austria bringing her Italian Provinces, etc., into the German Confederation.

Lord John told him that this had not been done, but that we meant to ask for explanations.

In short, Lord John said it was evident that Sir James thought the Government in great danger, and "did not wish to embark in a boat which was going to sink." Still, he was friendly, and repeated that it would be very easy when in opposition to unite, and then to come in together.

Victoria R.

Lord John Russell to Queen Victoria.

Chesham Place, *21st February 1851.*

Lord John Russell presents his humble duty to your Majesty, and has the honour to report that on a motion of Mr Locke King's[5] yesterday the Government was defeated by a hundred to fifty-two.

This is another circumstance which makes it probable the Ministry cannot endure long. The Tories purposely stayed away.

Queen Victoria to the King of the Belgians.

Buckingham Palace, *21st February 1851.*

My dearest Uncle,—I have only time just to write a few hasty lines to you from Stockmar's room, where I came up to speak to Albert and him, to tell you that we have got a Ministerial crisis; the Ministers were in a great minority last night, and though it was not a question *vital* to the Government, Lord John feels the support he has received so meagre, and the opposition of so many parties so great, that he must *resign!* This is very bad, because there is no chance of any other good Government, poor Peel being no longer alive, and not one man of talent except Lord Stanley in the Party;... but Lord John is *right* not to go on when he is so ill supported, and it will raise him as a political man, and will strengthen his position for the future.

Whether Lord Stanley (to whom I must send to-morrow *after* the Government have resigned) will be able to form a Government or not, I cannot tell. Altogether, it is very vexatious, and will give us trouble. It is the more provoking, as this country is so very prosperous.

On Tuesday I hope to be able to say more....

With Albert's love, ever your truly devoted Niece,

Victoria R.

303

Memorandum by the Prince Albert.

Buckingham Palace, *22nd February 1851.*

Lord John Russell having been for a few minutes with the Queen, in order to prepare her for the possibility of the Government's resignation (yesterday, at two o'clock), went to Downing Street to meet the Cabinet, and promised to return at four in order to communicate the decision the Cabinet might have arrived at. On his return he explained that after the vote at the beginning of the Session on the Orders of the Day, which went directly against the Government, after the small majority (only fourteen) which they had on the motion of Mr Disraeli on the landed interest, and now the defeat on the Franchise, it was clear that the Government did not possess the confidence of the House of Commons. He complained of the Protectionists staying away in a body on Mr King's motion, and he (Lord John) himself being left without a supporter even amongst his colleagues in the debate, but most of all of the conduct of the Radicals; for when Mr King, hearing Lord John's promise to bring in a measure next Session, wanted to withdraw his Motion, as he ought to have done on such a declaration by the head of the Government, Mr Hume insisted upon his going on, "else Lord John would withdraw his promise again in a fortnight"; and when the result of the vote was made known the shouting and triumph of the hundred was immense.

Lord John had declared to the Cabinet that he could not go on, that the Income Tax would have to be voted the next day, and a defeat was probable; it were much better therefore not to hesitate, and to resign at once. The Cabinet agreed, although some Members thought with Lord Palmerston that the occasion was hardly sufficient. Lord John begged to be allowed till to-day, in order to see Lord Lansdowne, whom he had sent for from the country, and to be able to tender then his resignation; he would go down to the House to adjourn it, promising explanations on Monday.

We agreed with Lord John that he owed to his station personally, and as the Queen's Minister, not to put up with ignominious treatment, praised his speech on the Suffrage, which is admirable, and regretted that his colleagues had prevented him from bringing in a measure this year. We talked of the difficulty of forming any Government, but agreed that Lord Stanley and the Protection Party ought to be appealed to; they longed for office, and would not rest quiet till they had had it if for ever so short a time only.

We further went over the ground of a possible demand for a Dissolution, which might bring on a general commotion in the country. Lord John agreed in this, but thought the responsibility to be very great for the Crown to refuse an appeal to the country to the new Government; he thought a decision on that point ought to depend on the peculiar circumstances of the case.

Lord Lansdowne, who had come from Bowood by the express train, arrived at twelve o'clock, and came at once to meet Lord John Russell here at the Palace.

In the audience which the Queen gave him he expressed his entire concurrence with the decision the Cabinet had come to, as the resignation could at any rate only have been delayed. It was clear that the Cabinet had lost the confidence of the House of Commons; what had happened the other night was only the last drop which made the cup flow over, and that it was much more dignified not to let the Government die a lingering and ignominious death; he [thought] that Lord Stanley would have great difficulties, but would be able to form a Government; at least the Protectionist Party gave out that they had a Cabinet prepared.

We then saw Lord John Russell, who formally tendered his resignation, and was very much moved on taking leave; he said that, considering Lord Stanley's principles, it would not be possible for him to hold out any hope of support to that Government, except on the estimates for which he felt responsible, but he would at all times be ready vigorously to defend the Crown, which was in need of every support in these days.

At three o'clock came Lord Stanley, whom the Queen had summoned.

The Queen informed him of the resignation of the Government, in consequence of the late vote, which had been the result of the Protectionists staying away, of the small majority which the Government had had upon Mr Disraeli's Motion, and of the many symptoms of want of confidence exhibited towards the Government in the House of Commons. The Queen had accepted their resignation, and had sent for him as the head of that Party, which was now the most numerous in Opposition, in order to ask him whether he could undertake to form a Government.

Lord Stanley expressed great surprise. The impression had been that the Government had not been in earnest in their opposition to Mr L. King's Motion; in the minority had voted only twenty-seven members of the Government side, the rest had been of his Party. He asked if the whole Cabinet had resigned, or whether there had been dissension in the Cabinet upon it? The Queen replied that the resignation had been unanimously agreed upon in the Cabinet, and that Lord Lansdowne, who had only come up from Bowood this morning, had given his entire approval to it. Lord Stanley then asked whether anybody else had been consulted or applied to, to which the Queen replied that she had written to him a few minutes after Lord John's resignation, and had communicated with no one else. Lord Stanley then said that he hoped the Queen's acceptance had only been a conditional one; that he felt very much honoured by the Queen's confidence; that he hoped he might be able to tender advice which might contribute to the Queen's comfort, and might relieve the present embarrassment.

In order to be able to do so he must enter most freely and openly into his own position and that of his Party. It was quite true that they formed the most numerous in Parliament after the supporters of what he hoped he might still call the *present* Government, but that there were no men contained in it who combined great ability with experience in public business. There was one certainly of great ability and talent—Mr Disraeli—but who had never held office before, and perhaps Mr Herries, who possessed great experience, but who did not command great authority in the House of Commons; that he should have great difficulties in presenting to the Queen a Government fit to be accepted, unless he could join with some of the late Sir R. Peel's followers; that he considered, for instance, the appointment of a good person for Foreign Affairs indispensable, and there was scarcely any one fit for it except Lord Palmerston and Lord Aberdeen. Lord Aberdeen had told him that he had no peculiar views upon Free Trade, and that he did not pretend to understand the question, but that he had felt it his duty to stand by Sir R. Peel; this might now be different, but it ought first to be ascertained whether a combination of those who agreed in principle, and had only been kept asunder hitherto by *personal* considerations, could not be formed; that Sir James Graham had in his last speech declared it as his opinion that the ranks of those who agreed ought to be closed; when such a combination had taken place, those of Sir R. Peel's followers who could not agree to it might not be unwilling to join him (Lord Stanley). As to his principles, he would frankly state that he thought that the landed interest was much depressed by the low state of prices; that an import duty on corn would be absolutely necessary, which, however, would be low, and only a revenue duty; such a duty, he thought, the country would be prepared for; and if they were allowed to state their honest opinion, he felt sure the greatest part of the present Government would be heartily glad of. He would require Duties upon sugar for revenue, but he could not conceal that if the revenue after a diminution in the direct taxation, which he would propose, should considerably fall off, he might be driven to raise the Import duties on other articles. He thought the present House of Commons could hardly be expected to reverse its decision upon the financial and commercial policy of the country, and that accordingly a Dissolution of Parliament would become necessary. Such a Dissolution, however, could not be undertaken at this moment for the sake of public business. The Mutiny Bill had not been voted nor the Supplies, and it would require more than eight weeks before the new Parliament could be assembled, and consequently the Crown would be left without Army or money. A Dissolution could accordingly not take place before Easter. He felt, however, that if he were to take office now, he would between this and Easter be exposed to such harassing attacks that he should not be able to withstand them; moreover, it would subject the members of his Government to two elections in two months. He hoped therefore that the Queen would try to obtain a Government by a coalition of the Whigs and Peelites, but that this failing, if the Queen should send again for him, and it was clear no other Government could be formed, he would feel it his duty as a loyal subject to risk everything, except his principles and his honour, to carry on the Government; and he hoped that in such a case the Queen would look leniently on the composition of the Cabinet which he could offer, and that the country would, from the consideration of the circumstances, give it a fair trial. He begged, however, that he might not be called upon to take office except as a *dernier ressort*, a *necessity*.

I interrupted him when he spoke of his financial measures, and begged him further to explain, when it appeared that a duty of about six shillings on corn was the least he could impose to bring up the price to forty-five shillings, which Sir R. Peel had stated to the House of Commons was in his opinion the lowest price wheat would fall to after the abolition of the Corn Laws.

We expressed our doubts as to the country agreeing to such a measure, and our apprehension of the violent spirit which would be roused in the working classes by a Dissolution for that purpose, which Lord Stanley, however, did not seem to apprehend; on the contrary, he thought the distress of the farmers would lead to the destruction of the landed interest, which was the only support to the Throne.

I told him that the Queen and certainly myself had been under a delusion, and that I was sure the country was equally so, as to his intention to return to Protection. Sometimes it was stated that Protection would be adhered to, sometimes that it was given up, and that it was *compensation* to the landed interest which the Protectionists looked to. His last speeches and the Motion of Mr Disraeli led to that belief, but that it was of the highest importance that the country should know exactly what was intended; the Queen would then have an opportunity of judging how the nation looked upon the proposal. I hoped therefore that the declaration of his opinions which Lord Stanley had now laid before the Queen would be clearly enunciated by him in Parliament when the Ministerial explanations should take place, which would naturally follow this crisis.

Lord Stanley merely answered that he hoped that no explanations would take place before a Government was formed. He said he should wish the word "Protection" to be merged, to which I rejoined that though he might wish this, I doubted whether the country would let him.

Before taking leave, he repeated over and over again his advice that the Coalition Ministry should be tried.

Albert.

Queen Victoria to Lord Stanley.

22nd February 1851.

In order to be able to be perfectly accurate in stating Lord Stanley's opinions, which the Queen feels some delicacy in doing, she would be very thankful if he would write down for her what he just stated to her—as his advice in the present difficulty. Of course she would not let such a paper go out of her hands.

Memorandum by the Prince Albert.

Buckingham Palace, *23rd February 1851.*

Sir James Graham, who had been out of Town, came at six o'clock, having received my letter on his return. Lord John Russell had been here before that time.

After having stated to him (Lord John) what had passed with Lord Stanley, we told him that Sir James Graham was here; Lord John seemed much surprised at Lord Stanley's refusal to form an Administration, declared himself ready to do what he could towards the formation of a new Government on an extended basis, but thought that Sir James Graham and Lord Aberdeen should have the first offer.

I went accordingly over to my room, where Sir James was waiting. He was entirely taken by surprise by the announcement of the resignation of the Government, and begged to be able to state to me how he was situated before he saw the Queen and Lord John.

I then communicated to him what had passed with Lord Stanley, upon which we had a conversation of more than an hour, of which the chief features were:

1. Apprehension on the part of Sir James Graham lest the attempt on the part of Lord Stanley to re-impose Protective duties should produce universal commotion in the country, which would be increased by the Dissolution, without which Lord Stanley would not be able to proceed.

2. His disbelief that Lord Aberdeen would be able to join in any Government abandoning Sir R. Peel's principles, as he had been consulted before and after Sir James's late speech in which he expressed his entire concurrence.

3. His own utter weakness, calling himself the weakest man in England, who had lost his only friend in Sir R. Peel, and had for the last fifteen years not exercised an independent judgment, but rested entirely on his friend.

4. His disagreement with some of his late colleagues—the Duke of Newcastle, Mr Gladstone, and Mr Sidney Herbert—in religious opinions.

5. His disagreement with Lord John's Government upon some most important points.

He could not take office with Lord Palmerston as Foreign Secretary, whose policy and mode of conducting business he disapproved, who was now protesting against the admission of Austria into the German Confederation; he disapproved the Papal Aggression Bill, finding it militating against the line which he had taken as Secretary of State with regard to the Roman Catholic Bishops in Ireland, and particularly the Bequest Act, and considering that after Lord John's letter the Bill would fall short of the high expectations formed in the minds of the English public.

He disapproved of the abolition of the Irish Lord-Lieutenancy, and the making a fourth Secretary of State had been considered by Sir Robert Peel and himself as introducing into England all the Irish malpractices, while Ireland was still kept wholly separate from England.

Lord John had raised a new difficulty by his declaration upon Reform. He had been thunderstruck when he read the announcement on the part of the chief author of the Reform Bill, who had stood with him (Sir J. Graham) hitherto upon *finality*, condemning his own work, and promising at a year's distance important alterations, in which interval great agitation would be got up, great expectations raised, and the measure when brought forward would cause disappointment. Sir Robert Peel had always been of opinion that it was most dangerous to touch these questions, but if opened with the consent of the Crown, a measure should at once be brought forward and passed.

After my having replied to these different objections, that the Queen felt herself the importance of Lord Palmerston's removal, and would make it herself a condition with Lord John that he should not be again Foreign Secretary; that the protest to Austria had not gone, and that upon studying the question Sir James would find that the entrance of the whole Austrian Monarchy, while giving France a pretext for war and infringing the Treaties of 1815, would not tend to the strength and unity of Germany, which held to be the true English interest, but quite the reverse; that I did not think the Papal Aggression Bill touched the Bequest Act or militated against toleration; that the Lieutenancy would perhaps be given up, and a measure on the Franchise be considered by the *new* Government and brought forward at once. I thought it would be better to discuss the matters with Lord John Russell in the Queen's presence, who accordingly joined us.

The discussion which now arose went pretty much over the same ground, Lord John agreeing that Lord Palmerston ought to form no difficulty, that the Papal Aggression Bill would be further modified, that the Lieutenancy Bill might be given up, that he agreed to Sir James's objection to the declaration about reform, but that he had intended to bring forward a measure, if he had been able to get his colleagues to agree to it, that he would be ready to propose a measure at once. This Sir J. Graham thought important as a means of gaining at a General Election, which he foresaw could not be long delayed, whoever formed a Government.

In order to obtain some result from this long debate I summed up what might be considered as agreed upon, viz. That there was *tabula rasa*, and for the new Coalition a free choice of men and measures, to which they assented, Lord John merely stating that he could not take office without part of his friends, and could not sacrifice his *personal* declarations. Dinnertime having approached, and Lord Aberdeen having written that he would be with us after nine o'clock, we adjourned the further discussion till then, when they would return.

Whilst the Queen dressed I had an interview with the Duke of Wellington, who had come to dine here, in which I informed him of the nature of our crisis. He expressed his regret and his dread of a Protectionist Government with a Dissolution, which might lead to civil commotion. He could not forgive, he said, the high Tory Party for their having stayed away the other night on Mr Locke King's Motion, and thus abandoned their own principles; he had no feeling for Lord John Russell's Cabinet, measures, or principles, but he felt that the Crown and the country were only safe in these days by having the Liberals in office, else they would be driven to join the Radical agitation against the institutions of the country.

After dinner we resumed our adjourned debate in my room, at a quarter to ten, with Lord Aberdeen, and were soon joined by Lord John and Sir James Graham. We went over the same ground with him. Lord Stanley's letter was read and discussed. Lord Aberdeen declared his inability to join in a Protectionist Ministry; he did not pretend to understand the question of Free Trade, but it was a point of honour with him not to abandon it, and now, since Sir R. Peel's death, a matter of piety. He thought the danger of a Dissolution on a question of food by the Crown, for the purpose of imposing a tax upon bread, of the utmost danger for the safety of the country. He disapproved the Papal Bill, the abolition of the Lieutenancy, he had no difficulty upon the Franchise, for though he was called a *despot*, he felt a good deal of the Radical in him sometimes.

Lord John put it to Lord Aberdeen, whether *he* would not undertake to form a Government, to which Lord Aberdeen gave no distinct reply.

As Sir James Graham raised nothing but difficulties, though professing the greatest readiness to be of use, and as it was getting on towards midnight, we broke up, with the Queen's injunction that *one* of the three gentlemen *must* form a Government, to which Lord Aberdeen laughingly replied: "I see your Majesty has come into[6] the Président de la République." Lord John was to see Lord Lansdowne *to-day* at three o'clock, and would report progress to the Queen at five o'clock. On one point we were agreed, viz. that the Government to be formed must not be for the moment, but with a view to strength and stability.

Albert.

311

Queen Victoria to Lord John Russell.

23d February 1851.

The Queen has seen Lord Aberdeen and Sir J. Graham, but is sorry to say that her doing so was premature, as they had no opportunity of seeing each other after they left Lord John Russell, and therefore had not considered the Memorandum[7] which Lord John had handed to them. Lord Aberdeen has in the interval seen Lord Stanley, and declared to him that he must undeceive him as to the possibility of his ever joining a Protection Government. What further resulted from the conversation the Queen would prefer to state to Lord John verbally to-morrow. Perhaps Lord John would come in the forenoon to-morrow, or before he goes to the House; he will be so good as to let her know.

Memorandum by the Prince Albert.

Buckingham Palace, *23rd February 1851.*

(*Sunday.*)

Lord John Russell came at half-past five, much fatigued and depressed. On the Queen's asking whether he could report any progress, he said he thought he could; he had met Lord Aberdeen and Sir James Graham, together with Sir George Grey (Lord Lansdowne being ill). That he had informed them that he had received the Queen's commands to form a Government (?) and handed to them a Memorandum which follows here and which they had promised to take into consideration.

We asked him whether he had chalked out a Government. He said he had not thought of it yet; he added, however, that *he* could not undertake the Foreign Affairs with the lead in the House of Commons and Government (which the Queen had pressed upon him); Lord Palmerston might be leader in the House of Lords; he would not like Lord Aberdeen at the Foreign Office; Lord Clarendon and Lord Granville were equally acceptable to him.

I suggested that it might be well if the Queen were to see Sir James and Lord Aberdeen again, which he approved, but thought it better he should not be present himself, and that the Queen might tell Sir James that he might have any Office he liked; perhaps *he* would take the Foreign Affairs.

Lord John's relations and private friends evidently are distressed at his resuming office; the Radicals were very much pleased with the idea of Sir James Graham being in office.

Albert.

Memorandum by the Prince Albert.

24th February 1851.
(Monday evening.)

Lord John came at three o'clock before making his statement to the House of Commons. We communicated to him what had passed with Sir James Graham and Lord Aberdeen yesterday evening. He thought his Memorandum had been misunderstood: the nature of the Reform Bill was left open to discussion, and what he had said about filling the Offices only meant that the Offices should not be divided according to number, and each party left to fill up its share, as had been done in former Coalition Ministries. He had seen Lord Palmerston, who was not willing to give up the Foreign Office—spoke of retiring from business at his age, of his success in conducting Foreign Affairs, and of its being a self-condemnation if he accepted another Office. Lord John told him that he did not agree in this view, that the Lord-Lieutenancy of Ireland was to be maintained, and thought it best to leave it there. He thought Lord Palmerston had given up the idea of leading the House of Commons. We ascertained from him in conversation that he could not agree to Lord Aberdeen taking the Foreign Office nor that he could serve under Lord Aberdeen or Sir James Graham in case any one of these were to form a Government.

At half-past six Lord John returned from the House of Commons, and reported that two very important events had taken place: the one that upon his making his statement to the House that the Government had resigned, that Lord Stanley had been sent for, had declared *his inability then to form a Government* (words agreed upon between Lord Lansdowne, Lord John, and Sir George Grey), and that he was now charged with the formation of a Government, Mr. Disraeli got up, and denied that Lord Stanley had declined forming a Government, which was received with cheers from the Protectionists. Lord John had merely answered that when Lord Stanley would make his explanations, what he had stated would be found to be correct, relying entirely, not upon what the Queen had communicated, but on Lord Stanley's own letter. The second event was a letter from Lord Aberdeen and Sir James Graham,[8] which put *an end* to all *thoughts* of a Coalition. It stated that they could agree to no legislation whatever on the Papal Aggressions, and ended with a hint that Sir James Graham was prepared to go farther in reductions than Lord John was likely to consent to.

Lord John had at once answered that although he did not understand the latter objection, the difference on the Papal Bill must put an end to their negotiation. We much lamented the result, and after some discussion agreed that the only thing to be done now was to send for Lord Aberdeen. Lord Stanley could not pretend to be consulted before every other means of forming a Government had been exhausted.

Queen Victoria to Lord John Russell.

Buckingham Palace, *24th February 1851.*

(*Half-past ten* p.m.)

The Queen returns these papers, as Lord John Russell wished. She has just seen Lord Aberdeen and Sir James Graham, who, though ready to do anything which could be of any use to the Queen and the country, have stated it as their decided opinion that Lord Stanley should be asked to form a Government. Under these circumstances the Queen intends to send to Lord Stanley to-morrow. The Queen did ask Lord Aberdeen if he could undertake to form a Government, but he said that he thought it would not be successful, and that the Papal Aggression would be an insurmountable difficulty for him and Sir James Graham.

The Queen rejoices to hear from them, and from Lord John and Lord Lansdowne, the expression of cordiality of feeling, which it is so essential for the Crown and the country that there should be.

Queen Victoria to the King of the Belgians.

Buckingham Palace, *25 February 1851.*

My dearest Uncle,—Through Van der Weyer, you will have heard what was the state of the *long* and anxious crisis yesterday evening.

Alas! the hope of forming a strong Coalition Government has failed—*for the present.* I say for the present, as they are all so entirely agreed on the Commercial Policy that another time they hope there will be no difficulty, when they have *fought together.* The *Papal Ag-*

gression has in fact been the only insurmountable difficulty. We sent to Lord Aberdeen last night (both he and Sir James Graham have been most kind to us), and asked if *he* could not try to form a Government; but with the greatest readiness to serve me, he said he could not, on account of this self-same Papal Aggression. He equally declares that he cannot join Lord Stanley. Accordingly this morning I have seen Lord Stanley, and he means to try if he can form any fit sort of Government, but he has *no* men of talent, and his difficulties are gigantic. I shall only know to-morrow *definitely* if he *can* form an Administration. I am calm and courageous, having such support and advice as my dearest Albert's; but it is an anxious time, and the uncertainty and suspense very trying. More details you will have later on. Ever your devoted Niece,

Victoria R.

Memorandum by the Prince Albert.

Buckingham Palace, *26th February 1851.*

Lord Aberdeen and Sir James Graham came yesterday evening at nine o'clock; the Queen put it to them whether *they* could form a Government, to which they replied that they had turned it in their heads a hundred times, that there was nothing they would not do to show their readiness to serve the Queen, but that they did not see a possibility of forming an Administration which could stand a day. They were most likely at that moment the two most unpopular men in England, having declared that nothing should be done in Parliament against the Papal Aggression, which the whole country clamoured for; the Whigs would be very angry with them for their having broken up the new combination; they might find favour with the Radicals, but that was a support upon which no reliance could be placed. There was a growing opinion that Lord Stanley ought to have a chance of bringing forward his measures; that it was perilous, but that it was an evil which must be gone through; that this opinion had been strongly expressed by Lord Lansdowne, whose moderation nobody could doubt; that it was shared by the Duke of Newcastle, Mr Sidney Herbert, and others of Sir James's friends whom he had had time to consult.

Upon the Queen's expression of her great apprehension as to the consequence of such a step on the country, they said there would no doubt spring up a most violent opposition, that there would be attempts to stop the supplies and dissolve the Army, but that Lord John

Russell and Sir James Graham together would do their utmost to preach moderation, and would refer the House of Commons to the Queen's example, who had taken strictly the Constitutional course throughout the crisis, whose opinions on Free Trade were well known (as far as subjects could allow themselves to pretend to know their Sovereign's *private* opinions) from the hearty support she had given to Sir Robert Peel's and Lord John's Governments. That upon the first proposition of a Stanley Government the junction of Parties would be completed, and there would be only *one* strong opposition. After having fought together, there would be no longer any difficulty about forming a strong Government out of their joint ranks, whilst now it was impossible not to see that every Minister displaced would feel personally aggrieved, that then they stood on a footing of perfect equality. Sir James had seen Lord John since he had tendered his second resignation, and found him quite altered; whilst he was embarrassed and *boutonné* before, he was open and unreserved now, and they could speak on terms of private friendship. Lord Aberdeen would save his influence in the House of Lords, which he would probably have lost if he had joined the Whigs in office; in future all this would be different.

Lord John Russell's letter with the Memoranda came and interrupted us. From these papers, and what Sir James and Lord Aberdeen said, it is clear that all parties are relieved by the failure of their attempt to form a Coalition Government, but determined to form a positive junction, which will be most salutary to the country. The Queen will therefore send for Lord Stanley.

We discussed further the means Lord Stanley would have to form an Administration, for which the material was certainly sad. Disraeli's last scene in the House of Commons would render the publication of Lord Stanley's letter necessary. Mr Gladstone might possibly join him; at least no pains would be spared to bring him in. Lord Palmerston had often so much secret understanding with Disraeli that he might be tempted with the bait of keeping the Foreign Office, particularly if personally offended.

Whether the Queen should allow or refuse a Dissolution was debated; the latter declared a most heavy responsibility for the Sovereign to undertake, but a subject upon which the decision should only be taken at the time, and on a due consideration of the circumstances.

Albert.

Lord John Russell to Queen Victoria.

Chesham Place, *25th February 1851.*

Lord John Russell presents his humble duty to your Majesty, and has the honour to state that having seen the letter which Lord Stanley addressed to your Majesty, and feeling himself precluded from entering into any details, he announced to the House of Commons that Lord Stanley had in reply to your Majesty's offer declared "he was not *then* prepared to form a Government."

Mr Disraeli disputed the accuracy of this statement.

Your Majesty's word cannot be called in question, but Lord John Russell now feels it due to his own honour humbly to ask your Majesty for a copy of Lord Stanley's letter. He does not propose to read the letter to the House of Commons, but to refer to it in the statement he is compelled to make.

Lord John Russell humbly requests that this representation may be shown to Lord Stanley. He will feel what is due to the honour of a public man.

Memorandum by the Prince Albert.

25th February 1851.
(*Tuesday.*)

Lord Stanley obeyed the Queen's summons at eleven o'clock, and seemed very much concerned when she informed him that Lord John Russell had given up his task, as differences of opinion, particularly on the Papal Bill, had prevented a junction between him, Lord Aberdeen, and Sir James Graham; that an appeal to Lord Aberdeen had been equally unsuccessful from the same cause, viz. their difficulty in dealing with the Papal Question; that consequently the contingency had arisen under which Lord Stanley had promised to undertake the formation of a Government.

Lord Stanley said his difficulties were immense, and he could not venture to approach them unless he was sure of every support on the part of the Crown; that he would have arrayed against him a formidable opposition of all the talent in the country.

The Queen assured him that he should have every Constitutional support on her part, of which Lord Stanley repeated he had felt sure, although the total change must be very trying to the Queen.

On his question, whether there was any hope of Lord Aberdeen joining him and taking the Foreign Office, we had to tell him that he must quite discard that idea. He replied, with a sigh, that he would still

317

try and see him; he had thought of the Duke of Wellington taking the Foreign Office *ad interim*, but felt that he could hardly propose that, considering the Duke's age and infirmity; he would make an attempt to see Lord Canning with the Queen's permission, and that failing, could only think of Sir Stratford Canning, now at Constantinople, which the Queen approved.

He still hoped he might get Mr Gladstone to take the lead in the House of Commons, without which assistance he must not conceal that it was almost impossible for him to go on. Mr Gladstone was on his way home from Paris, and he had written to him to see him as soon as he arrived; till then he could not promise that he would succeed to form an Administration, and he only undertook it for the good of his country, but was afraid of ruining his reputation.

To this I rejoined that who tried to do the best by his country need never be afraid for his reputation.

The Queen showed Lord Stanley Lord John Russell's letter respecting Mr Disraeli's denial of the truth of Lord John's statement in the House of Commons yesterday.

Lord Stanley said it had been a very unfortunate misunderstanding, that he had been sorry Lord John and Lord Lansdowne should have felt it necessary to say that "he had not *then* been prepared to form a Government," as the knowledge of this fact, as long as there was a chance of his being called back, could not but act injuriously to him and dispirit those with whom he acted. He would explain all this on Friday in the House of Lords, and had no objection to sending Lord John a copy of his letter.

We now came to *Measures*. Lord Stanley hopes to obviate the Papal Question by a Parliamentary declaration and the appointment in both Houses of a Committee to enquire into the position of the Roman Catholic Church in this country; he would diminish the Income Tax by a million, and exempt temporary incomes; he would allow compounding for the Window Tax and levy a moderate duty on corn, which he called a Countervailing Duty, and tried to defend as good political economy, on the authority of Mr M'Culloch's last edition of "Ricardo." (I had some discussion with him, however, on that point.)

Returning to the offices to be filled, Lord Stanley said he should have to propose Mr Disraeli as one of the Secretaries of State. The Queen interrupted him by saying that she had not a very good opinion of Mr Disraeli on account of his conduct to poor Sir R. Peel, and what had just happened did not tend to diminish that feeling; but that she felt so much Lord Stanley's difficulties, that she would not aggravate them by passing a sentence of exclusion on him. She must, however, make Lord Stanley responsible for his conduct, and should she have cause to be displeased with him when in office, she would remind Lord Stanley of what now passed. Lord Stanley promised to be responsible, and excused his friend for his former bitterness by his desire to establish his reputation for cleverness and sharpness; nobody had gained so much by Parliamentary schooling, and he had of late quite changed his tone.

Mr Herries would make a good Chancellor of the Exchequer.

As to Ireland, he had thought of having a more ostensible Lord-Lieutenant, whilst the business should be done by the Secretary for Ireland. He asked the Queen whether the Duke of Cambridge might be offered that post, which she took *ad referendum*. The Duke of Northumberland, though not of his Party, he should like to offer the Admiralty to.

At the conclusion of the interview he broached the important question of Dissolution, and said that a Dissolution would anyhow become necessary; that, if it was thought that the Queen would withhold from him the privilege of dissolving, he would not have the slightest chance in the House of Commons; he would be opposed and beat, and then his adversaries would come in and dissolve. He avowed that it could not be said that the Queen had refused him the power of dissolving, but he required some assurance.

On the Queen's objecting to giving him a contingent positive promise, but declaring her readiness fairly to discuss the question when the emergency arose, he contented himself with the permission to deny, if necessary, that she would *not* consent to it, putting entire confidence in the Queen's intention to deal fairly by him.

I tried to convince Lord Stanley, and I hope not without effect, of the advantage, both to the Queen and Lord Stanley himself, that they should not be hampered by a positive engagement on that point, which might become very inconvenient if circumstances arose which made a Dissolution dangerous to the country.

Albert.

Queen Victoria to Lord John Russell.

Buckingham Palace, *25th February 1851.*

The Queen has seen Lord Stanley, who will let Lord John Russell have a copy of the letter. He wishes it not to be known or considered that he has formally undertaken to form a Government till to-morrow, on account of the House of Lords meeting to-day. He feels the difficulty of his position, and is not sure yet that he will be able to complete a Ministry. To-morrow he will give the Queen a positive answer.

Queen Victoria to Lord Stanley.

Buckingham Palace, *25th February 1851.*

The Queen has just received Lord Stanley's letter. She had forgotten the Levée, and was just going to write to him to inform him that she wished to see him at eleven o'clock to-morrow.

The Queen cannot but regret that Lord Stanley should think Lord John Russell's explanation led to a wrong inference; for Lord Stanley will himself recollect that he stated his objections to her much more strongly in his first interview than he did in writing, and as Lord Stanley so strongly advised the Queen to try if no other arrangement could first be come to, she hardly knows how this could otherwise have been expressed than by the words used by Lord Lansdowne and Lord John Russell.

Memorandum by Queen Victoria.

26th February 1851.
(*Wednesday.*)

Lord Stanley came again at eleven. The first part of the audience, which was not long, was occupied by Lord Stanley's trying to explain away Mr Disraeli's contradiction of Lord John Russell, though he termed it "very unfortunate," by saying that he wished Lord John had *not mentioned* that *he* (Lord Stanley) "was not *then* prepared" to form a Government, for that, though true in fact, he had *not* absolutely *refused*, but had only advised me to *try* and make other arrangements first. I said I thought the distinction "a very nice one," which he admitted. What passed between us on the subject the correspondence between Albert and Lord John will best explain.

Lord Stanley then told us that he had seen the Duke of Northumberland, who wished for time to consider; that he was to see Lord Canning again to-day, but had no hopes of his accepting; and that he found so many people out of Town that he must ask for *forty-eight* hours more before he could give me a positive answer, viz. till Friday. He added he "must not conceal" from me that he was "not very sanguine" of success; almost all depended on Mr Gladstone, who was expected to arrive to-day; but that it might *now* be said (in answer to a question of Albert's "whether in these days of nice distinctions one *might* say that he had *undertaken* to form a Government"), that he had *attempted* to *undertake* to *form a Government*.

Victoria R.

Lord Stanley to Queen Victoria.

St James's Square, *27th February 1851.*

(*Four o'clock* p.m.)

Lord Stanley, with his humble duty, awaits your Majesty's commands at what hour he may be honoured with an audience, to explain the grounds on which, with the deepest regret, he feels himself under the necessity of resigning the important trust with which your Majesty has honoured him.

Queen Victoria to Sir James Graham.

Buckingham Palace, *27th February 1851.*

The Queen sanctions Sir James Graham's making any statement to the House of Commons which he thinks necessary, to explain the part which he and Lord Aberdeen took in the late Ministerial negotiations, and indeed hopes that these explanations will be as full as possible on all parts, in order that the country may fully appreciate the difficulties of the crisis.

Memorandum by the Prince Albert.

Buckingham Palace, *27th February 1851.*

Lord Stanley arrived at half-past five o'clock. We were struck by the change of his countenance, which had lost all the expression of care and anxiety which had marked it at the previous interviews.

He assured the Queen that he had been labouring incessantly since he had seen her last, but that he was sorry to say without any success.

He had seen Mr Gladstone, who declined joining his Government on account of his previous pledges in Parliament respecting the Commercial Policy of Sir R. Peel, but evidently also on account of his peculiar views with respect to the Papal Aggression, which he did not seem disposed to look upon as in any way objectionable.

Lord Canning had given him some hope at one time, but finally declined in order not to risk his credit for political consistency.

Mr H. Corry, whose opinions on Free Trade were by no means decided, and who had only filled a very subordinate situation in Sir R. Peel's Government, he had offered high office, but was refused, Mr Corry expressing his fears that the Government had no chance of standing against the opposition it would have to meet in the House of Commons.

The Duke of Northumberland was the only person not properly belonging to the Protection Party who had accepted office (First Lord of the Admiralty). At one time Lord Ellenborough had accepted, but having been sent on a mission to Mr Goulburn in order to see whether he could convert him, he came home himself converted, and withdrew his acceptance again.

In this situation Lord Stanley called his friends together, and after some discussion concurred in their opinion that it was not possible for them to form such an Administration as ought to be offered to the Queen. Lord Stanley then qualified this expression again, and said that though he could have offered a very respectable Government if he had had a majority in the House of Commons, or the means of strengthening himself by an immediate Dissolution, he could not form such a one which could have withstood an adverse majority and such a formidable array of talent in the Opposition. He therefore returned the trust which had been committed to him into the Queen's hands, expressing at the same time his deep sense of gratitude for the kindness with which she had treated him, the support and confidence she had given him, sorry only that it should have led to no result. He thought, however, that the prolongation of the crisis had not inconvenienced the public service, as Her Majesty's *present* Government were constitutionally enabled to carry on all necessary business.

The Queen rejoined that she was very sorry that this attempt had also failed, that she had tried every possible combination, and still was without a Government. Lord Stanley answered as if he considered it natural that Lord John Russell's Government should now quietly proceed; but on the Queen's observation, that it was now necessary that all Parties should join in the support of some measures at least, and particularly the Papal Bill, he stated what he was prepared to support, and would have been prepared to propose had he taken office, viz. a fuller recital in the preamble of the Bill and no penal clause in the body of it.

(The present Bill looked pettish and undignified, as if framed in anger as a return for the insult, and not a correction of the state of the law.) He thought the Law very complex and obscure, and never found it acted upon. He would have proposed therefore that Committees of both Houses should enquire into the whole subject; the state of the Convents; whether subjects were detained against their will; whether people were forced to bequeath their property to the Church on the deathbed, etc., etc.; he knew that the Roman Catholic laity felt severely the oppression which the Priests exercised over them, and would be willing to give evidence.

Lord Stanley asked whether it could be of use if he were to state all this in his explanation to-day, which the Queen strongly affirmed. I added that I hoped he would explain what he was prepared to do on all the subjects in dispute—the Commercial and Financial Policy as well. He promised to do so, and entered into his views on the Income Tax, which he called a War Tax, which had been imposed for temporary purposes only in 1842, and ought to be taken off again when practicable in order to keep faith with the public; but if, as often as there was a surplus, this was immediately absorbed by remission of other burdens, this object could never be fulfilled. He would propose that by degrees, as surpluses arose, the Income Tax should be decreased, and so on to its final repeal.

I disputed with him for some time on the advantages of an Income Tax, but without coming to any result.

On his enquiry whether there was anything else the Queen might wish him to state—perhaps the rumour that he had been refused the power of dissolving—we agreed that he should say the question had never been seriously entertained, but that the Queen had been ready to give him the same support and advantages which any other Government might have enjoyed.[9]

Albert.

The Prince Albert to the Duke of Wellington.

Buckingham Palace, *28th February 1851.*

My dear Duke,—Lord Stanley has likewise resigned his task, not being able to gain over any of Sir R. Peel's friends, and being incapable of forming a Government out of his Party alone.

So Lord John Russell has declared his inability to carry on the Government. Lord Stanley has then declared his inability to form one until every other combination should have failed. We have tried all possible combinations between Whigs and Peelites, and have not succeeded, and now Lord Stanley throws up the game a second time! The Queen would be happy to consult you and hear your advice in this dilemma. Possibly to-night's Debate may define the position of Parties more clearly, and give a clue to what may be best to be done under the circumstances. Ever yours, etc.

Albert.

Lord John Russell to the Prince Albert.

Chesham Place, *28th February 1851.*

Sir,—The former Cabinet meet at eleven, at Lansdowne House.

It appears to me that the Queen might with advantage see Lord Lansdowne. He was in office with Mr Fox and Lord Grenville in 1806; he has been distinguished and respected in political life ever since; he is now desirous of retiring, and has therefore no personal object to gain. If the Queen approves, Lord Lansdowne might wait on Her Majesty soon after twelve o'clock. I have the honour to be, Sir, your Royal Highness's very dutiful Servant,

J. Russell.

Queen Victoria to Lord Lansdowne.

Buckingham Palace, *28th February 1851.*

It would be a great satisfaction to the Queen to hear Lord Lansdowne's advice in the present critical state of affairs, and she would be glad if he could come to her at twelve this morning. The Queen has sent to the Duke of Wellington in order to hear his opinion also; but he cannot be here before to-night, being at Strathfieldsaye.

Memorandum by the Prince Albert.

Friday, *28th February 1851.*

Lord Lansdowne, who arrived at twelve o'clock, was asked by the Queen what advice he could offer her in the present complication. His answer was: "I wish indeed I had any good advice to offer to your Majesty." He expressed his delight at the Queen having sent for the Duke of Wellington. We talked generally of the state of affairs; he agreed in a remark of mine, that I thought the Queen should be entirely guided in her choice of the person to construct a Government, by the consideration which Party would now appear to be the strongest in the House of Commons. On my asking, however, whether he knew if, on the failure of Lord Stanley to form a Government, part of his followers would now give up Protection as past hope, and be prepared in future to support the Peelite section of the Conservative Party, Lord Lansdowne said he had heard nothing on the subject, nor could he give us more information on the chance of the Radicals and Irish members now being more willing to support Lord John Russell in future. He liked Lord Stanley's plan of dealing with the Papal Question, of which the Queen communicated to him the outlines, was afraid of Sir J. Graham's excessive leaning towards economy, shook his head at Lord John Russell's letter to the Bishop of Durham[10] which had been instrumental in bringing on the present crisis, and confessed that he had been amongst those in the Cabinet who had prevented the bringing forward of a measure of reform in the present Session. He offered to do whatever might be most conducive to the Queen's comfort—stay out of office, or come into office—as might be thought the most useful.

Albert.

Queen Victoria to the King of the Belgians.

Buckingham Palace, *1st March 1851.*

My dearest Uncle,—I did not write to you yesterday, thinking I could perhaps give you some more positive news to-day, but I *cannot.* I am still without a Government, and I am still trying to hear and pause before I actually call to Lord John to undertake to form, or rather more to continue, the Government. We have passed an anxious, exciting week, and the difficulties are very peculiar; there are so many conflicting circumstances which render coalition between those who agree in almost everything, and in particular on *Free Trade*, impossible, but the "Papal Question" is the real and almost insuperable difficulty.

Lord Lansdowne is waiting to see me, and I must go, and with many thanks for your two kind letters, ever your devoted Niece,

Victoria R.

Memorandum by the Prince Albert.

Buckingham Palace, *2nd March 1851.*

(*Sunday.*)

Lord Lansdowne, who arrived after church, had seen Lord John Russell and discussed with him the Memorandum which we left with him yesterday. He had since drawn up a Memorandum himself which embodied his views, and which he had not yet communicated to any one. He was very apprehensive lest to begin a new Government with an open question would produce the greatest prejudice against it in the public; he was still inclined therefore to recommend the continuance of the present Government avowedly for the purpose of passing the Papal Bill, after which the Coalition might take place, which, however, should be agreed upon and settled at this time. As the Duke of Wellington has not yet sent his promised Memorandum, and Lord Lansdowne was anxious to hear his opinion, the Queen commissioned him to appoint Lord John Russell to come at three o'clock, and to go himself to the Duke of Wellington.

Lord John Russell, who arrived at the appointed time, and had not seen Lord Lansdowne's Memorandum yet, read it over, and expressed great misgivings about the execution of the proposal. He said he saw in fact, like Sir J. Graham, nothing but difficulties. He had ascertained that his Party by no means liked the idea of a fusion, and had been much relieved when the attempt to form a Coalition Ministry had failed. He was afraid that in the interval between their resuming office and giving it up again every possible surmise would be current who were the Ministers to be displaced, and every possible intrigue would spring up for and against particular members of the Cabinet. He would prefer not to make any arrangements for the Coalition now, but merely to engage to resign again after having carried the Papal Bill, when the Queen could try the Coalition, and that failing, could entrust Lord Aberdeen and Sir J. Graham with the carrying on of the Government, whose chief difficulty would then be removed. I objected to this—that his Party might feel justly aggrieved if after their having carried him through the difficulty of the Papal Measure, he were to throw them over and resign, and asked him whether his Cabinet would not repent in the meantime and wish to stay in.

He answered that it would be entirely in his and Lord Lansdowne's hands to carry out the proposed arrangements.

We asked him whether it would strengthen his hands if, instead of his only *accepting* the task of continuing the Government till the Papal Measure had been passed, the Queen were to make it a *condition* in *giving* him the Commission, that it should terminate then. He replied, "Certainly." He begged, however, to be understood not to have given a decided opinion that the plan of "the open Question" proposed in our Memorandum was not preferable, although he saw great objections to that also, particularly as Sir J. Graham had reserved the statement of his principal objections to the Papal Bill for the second reading. He promised to draw up a Memorandum, which he would bring to-morrow at twelve o'clock, after having consulted some of his colleagues, and begged that it might not be considered that he had accepted the Government till then.

One of the difficulties which we likewise discussed was the position of the financial measures which required almost immediate attention, and still ought to be left open for the consideration of the future Government.

We agreed that the pressing on the Papal Measure was the chief point, and that it ought to be altered to meet the objections (as far as they are reasonable) of its opponents, strengthening the declaratory part, however, to please Lord Stanley; and the Queen promised to call upon Lord Stanley to give this so modified Bill the support of himself and his Party, which we thought she could in fairness claim after all that had happened.

The Queen reiterated her objections to Lord Palmerston, and received the renewed promise that her wishes should be attended to.

Albert.

Memorandum by the Prince Albert.

Buckingham Palace, *3rd March 1851.*

Lord John Russell arrived at the hour appointed (twelve o'clock), and was sorry to inform the Queen that all hope of a Coalition must be given up. He had found that his Party was very much averse to it. On proposing to his former colleagues the plan of keeping Office now, and vacating it after the Aggression Bill had passed, many of them, amongst which were Lord Grey, Sir Charles Wood, Sir Francis Baring, declared they would not be *warming-pans* (an expression used at the time of the Grey-Grenville Coalition), and would resign at once. The Duke of Wellington, whose opinion the Queen had asked, had recommended the return of the old Cabinet to power. He (Lord John) could therefore only advise that course, although he was conscious that it would be a very weak Government, and one not likely to last any length of time.

He then read the Memorandum which he had drawn up and which follows here.[11]

The Queen now asked whether Lord John proposed a modification of his own Cabinet, to which Lord John replied, None, except perhaps an exchange of Office between Sir C. Wood and Sir F. Baring, if Sir Charles were to refuse bringing in a different budget from the one he had already propounded; he was for maintaining the Income Tax, whilst Sir Francis was for repealing it by degrees. The Queen then reminded Lord John of her objections to Lord Palmerston, and his promise that Lord Palmerston should not again be thrust upon her as Foreign Secretary. Lord John admitted to the promise, but said he could not think for a moment of resuming office and either expel Lord Palmerston or quarrel with him. He (Lord John) was in fact the weakness and Lord Palmerston the strength of the Government from his popularity with the Radicals.... He said he was very anxious that he and Lord Lansdowne should bear the responsibility of removing Lord Palmerston from the Foreign Office and not the Queen; her refusal now could only go to the country as a personal objection on her part, and the country would be left without a Government in consequence. On the Queen's reiterating that she wanted to keep Lord John and get rid of Lord Palmerston, and that it was too painful to her to be put into the situation of having actually to *wish* the fall of her own Government, Lord John promised to move Lord Palmerston in the Easter recess, or to resign then himself if he should meet with difficulties; in the meantime he must apprise Lord Palmerston of this intention, which he could explain to him as a wish to make a general modification of his Government. He would offer him the Lieutenancy of Ireland or the Presidency or lead in the House of Lords, which Lord Lansdowne would be ready to resign. He might at that period perhaps get some of the Radicals into office or some Peelites. The Queen finally entrusted Lord John with the Government on these conditions.

Albert.

Memorandum by Lord John Russell.

3rd March 1851.

Her Majesty having tried in vain the formation of a Government—first, by Lord Stanley; second, by Lord John Russell, Lord Aberdeen, and Sir James Graham; third, by Lord Aberdeen; fourth, by Lord Stanley a second time—had recourse to the advice and opinion of the Duke of Wellington. The Duke, admitting the great qualifications for office of the adherents of the late Sir Robert Peel, yet advises the Queen to restore her former Ministers to office.

But supposing Her Majesty to follow that advice, a further question naturally arises: the late Government having fallen from want of Parliamentary support, can they upon their return be in any way strengthened, and be enabled to carry on the public business with more power and efficiency?

This might be done in three ways: first, by a Coalition sooner or later with the Peel Party; secondly, by admitting to office some of their own Radical supporters; thirdly, by seeking aid from the Party which has followed Lord Stanley.

The first of these courses appears the most natural. The present Ministers are agreed with the adherents of Sir Robert Peel on Free Trade, and on the policy which has regulated our finances of late years. The difference between them is of a temporary nature. But it may be doubted whether any strength would be gained by an immediate junction with that Party.

If such junction took place now, the Ministers coming in must oppose their colleagues on the Ecclesiastical Titles Bill—an unseemly spectacle, a source of weakness, and probably the beginning of strife, which would not end with the Bill in question.

If, on the other hand, the junction were delayed till the Ecclesiastical Titles Bill is disposed of, the existing Ministry would be divided into two portions, one of which would have only a temporary tenure of office. Rumours, cabals, and intrigues would have ample room to spread their mischief in such a state of things.

But finally the Whig Party in the House of Commons would not be cordial supporters of the junction; jealousy and discontent would soon break up the Ministry.

Secondly, by admitting to office some of their Radical supporters. This course must lead to concessions on measures as well as men, and those concessions would provoke hostility in other quarters. The great question of the defence of the country is besides one of too great importance to be made a matter of compromise.

Third, by seeking aid from the Party which has followed Lord Stanley. This cannot be done by means of official connection; but something might be effected by adopting measures calculated to convince the Landed Interest that their sufferings were not disregarded.

Upon the whole, if the late Ministers are invited by your Majesty to resume office, the easiest course would be to proceed at once with the Ecclesiastical Titles Bill. That question disposed of, it would be seen whether the Ministry had sufficient strength to go on; if they had, they might, as occasion arose, seek assistance from other quarters, looking to those with whom there is the greatest agreement of opinion.

Should the Ministry, on the other hand, not receive Parliamentary support sufficient to enable them to carry on the Government, the Queen would be in a position to form a new Government free from the obstacles which have lately been fatal.

Queen Victoria to Lord John Russell.

Buckingham Palace, *4th March 1851.*

... The Queen was in hopes to have heard from Lord John Russell this morning relative to what passed in the House of Commons last night. She wishes likewise to hear what takes place at the meeting of Lord John's supporters to-day. The Queen must ask Lord John to keep her constantly informed of what is going on, and of the temper of parties in and out of Parliament; for no one *can* deny that the present state of affairs is most critical; and after all that has happened it is absolutely necessary that the Queen should not be in a state of uncertainty, not to say of ignorance, as to what is passing. She can else not form a just opinion of the position of affairs.

Queen Victoria to the King of the Belgians.

Buckingham Palace, *4th March 1851.*

My dearest Uncle,—Pray receive my warmest thanks for two kind letters of the 28th, and my excuses for the terribly incoherent scrawl of last Saturday. The *dénouement* of ten days of the greatest anxiety and excitement I cannot call satisfactory, for it holds out only the prospect of another crisis in a very short time, and the so much wished-for union of Parties has been again frustrated. I have been speaking *very strongly* about Lord Palmerston to Lord John, and he has *promised* that if the Government should still be in at Easter, then to make a change.... Lord Stanley can never succeed *until* he gives up Protection, which he would do, if the country decides against him;[12] he has failed solely from the *impossibility* of finding *one* single man capable to take the important Offices. He said last night to Lord John Russell, "I am *l'homme impossible*; they cannot come to me again." Still it would be very desirable that there should be a strong Conservative Party; nothing but the abandonment of Protection can bring this to pass, and Lord Stanley cannot abandon it with honour till *after* the *next Election*. This is the state of Parties, which is greatly *erschwert* by the Papal Question, which divides the Liberals and Conservatives. In short, there *never* was *such* a *complicated* and difficult state of affairs. Ever your devoted Niece,

Victoria R.

Stockmar has been an immense comfort to us in our trials, and I hope you will tell him so.

Memorandum by the Queen.

Buckingham Palace, *5th March 1851.*

The Queen would give every facility to the selection of a good site for a new National Gallery, and would therefore not object to its being built on to Kensington Palace or anywhere in Kensington Gardens; but does not see why it should exactly be placed upon the site of the present Palace, if not for the purpose of taking from the Crown the last available set of apartments. She is not disposed to trust in the disposition of Parliament or the public to give her an equivalent for these apartments from time to time when emergencies arise. The surrender of Kensington Palace will most likely not be thanked for at the moment, and any new demand in consequence of such surrender would be met with lavish abuse. As to economy in the construction, it will most likely be best consulted by building on a spot perfectly free and unencumbered.

Lord John Russell to the Prince Albert.

Chesham Place, *14th March 1851.*

Sir,—I cannot undertake to make any change in the Foreign Office. Our Party is hardly reunited, and any break into sections, following one man or the other, would be fatal to us. I need not say that the Queen would suffer if it were attributed to her desire, and that as I have no difference of opinion on Foreign Policy, that could not fail to be the case.

Upon the whole, the situation of affairs is most perplexing. A Dissolution I fear would not improve it.

I can only say that my Office is at all times at the Queen's disposal.

I have the honour to be, Sir, your Royal Highness's most dutiful Servant,

J. Russell.

Queen Victoria to Sir George Grey.

Buckingham Palace, *30th March 1851.*

The Queen approves of the draft of a letter to the Archbishop of Canterbury. With respect to the Archbishop's letter and the address, the Queen will receive it in the Closet. It seems strange to propose as a remedy for the present evils in the Church, and for its evident great disunion, *600* more churches to be built! There ought clearly to be some security given to those who are to encourage such a scheme against the extension of those evils.

Lord John Russell to the Prince Albert.

Pembroke Lodge, *19th April 1851.*

Sir,—Lord Granville came here yesterday to speak to me upon the order for opening the Exhibition at one o'clock on the 1st of May. He is anxious to have the order changed, and the season-ticket bearers admitted at eleven o'clock.

I did not give him any positive opinion on the subject. But the account he gave me of the route which the Queen will follow in going to the Exhibition takes away the main objection which I felt to the admission of visitors before one o'clock. It appears there cannot well be any interruption to Her Majesty's progress to and from the Crystal Palace on the 1st of May.

I conclude that Her Majesty will not go in the State Coach, but in the same manner that Her Majesty goes in state to the theatres....

I feel assured there will be no undue and inconvenient pressure of the crowd in the part of the building in which Her Majesty may be. Colonel Wemyss and Colonel Bouverie might easily be in attendance to request the visitors not to crowd where the Queen is. At the same time, I am ready to abide by the existing order, if Her Majesty wishes it to be enforced.

I have the honour to submit two private letters sent by Lord Palmerston. I have the honour to be, Sir, your Royal Highness's most dutiful Servant,

J. Russell.

The Duchess of Gloucester to Queen Victoria.

Gloucester House, *2nd May 1851.*

My dearest Victoria,—It is impossible to tell you how warmly I do participate in all you must have felt yesterday, as well as dear Albert, at everything having gone off so beautifully. After so much anxiety and the trouble he has had, the joy *must* be the greater.[13]

The sight from my window was the gayest and the most gratifying to witness, and to me who loves you so dearly as *I do*, made it the more delightful. The good humour of all around, the fineness of the day, the manner you were received in both going and coming from the Exhibition, was quite perfect. Therefore what must it have been in the inside of the building!

Mary and George came away in perfect *enchantment*, and every soul I have seen describes it as the fairest sight that ever was seen and the best-conducted *fête!* Why, G. Bathurst told me it far surpassed the *Coronation* as to magnificence, and we all agreed in rejoicing that the *Foreigners should* have witnessed the affection of the *People* to *you* and *your Family*, and how the *English people* do *love* and respect the *Crown*. As to Mary, she was in *perfect enchantment*, and full of how pretty your dear little Victoria looked, and how nicely she was dressed, and so grateful to your Mother for all her kindness to her. I should have written to you last night, but I thought I would not plague you with a letter until to-day, as I think you must have been tired last night with the *excitement* of the day. I shall ever lament the having missed such a sight, but I comfort myself in feeling sure I could not have followed you (as I ought) when you walked round. Therefore I was *better* out of the way. We drank your health at dinner and *congratulation* on the *complete success* of *Albert's plans* and *arrangements*, and also dear little Arthur's health. Many thanks for kind note received last night. Love to Albert. Yours,

Mary.

Queen Victoria to the King of the Belgians.

Buckingham Palace, *3rd May 1851.*

My dearest Uncle,—... I wish you *could* have witnessed the *1st May 1851*, the *greatest* day in our history, the *most beautiful* and *imposing* and *touching* spectacle ever seen, and the triumph of my beloved Albert. Truly it was astonishing, a fairy scene. Many cried, and all felt touched and impressed with devotional feelings. It was the *happiest, proudest* day in my life, and I can think of nothing else. Albert's dearest name is immortalised with this *great* conception, *his* own, and my *own* dear country *showed* she was *worthy* of it. The triumph is *immense*, for up to the *last hour* the difficulties, the opposition, and the ill-natured attempts to annoy and frighten, of a certain set of fashionables and Protectionists, were immense; but Albert's temper, patience, firmness, and energy surmounted all, and the feeling is universal. *You* will be astounded at this great work when you see it!—the beauty of the building and the vastness of it all. I can never thank God enough. I feel *so* happy, so proud. Our dear guests were much pleased and impressed. You are right to like the dear Princess, for she is a noble-minded, warm-hearted, distinguished person, much attached to you, and who revered dearest Louise. Oh! *how* I thought of *her* on that great day, how kindly she would have rejoiced in our success! Now good-bye, dearest Uncle. Ever your devoted Niece,

Victoria R.

Queen Victoria to the Emperor of Austria.[14]

Palais de Buckingham, *5 Mai 1851.*

Sire et mon bon Frère,—C'est avec un vif empressement que je viens remercier votre Majesté Impériale des superbes objets de l'industrie et des arts de votre Empire, que vous avez eu l'extrême bonté de m'envoyer et qui me seront bien précieux à plus d'un titre d'abord comme venant de votre Majesté, et puis à cause de leur grande beauté et comme un souvenir à une époque où il a plu au Tout-Puissant de permettre une réunion pacifique de tous les peuples du monde et de leurs produits.

La cérémonie de l'inauguration de l'Exposition a fait une profonde impression sur mon cœur et je regrette d'avoir été le seul Souverain qui ait pu jouir de cette scène à la fois imposante et parlant au cœur. Nous avons déjà fait plusieurs visites au département Autrichien et le Prince et moi avons eu occasion d'admirer beaucoup les produits qui nous sont venus de vos États. Puisse leur exposition contribuer à la prospérité du commerce de l'Empire Autrichien.

Agréez l'expression de ma sincère amitié, qui j'espère pourra un jour être cimentée par la connaissance personnelle de votre Majesté, et croyez-moi toujours, Sire, de votre Majesté Impériale, la bonne Sœur,

Victoria R.

Queen Victoria to Lord John Russell.

Buckingham Palace, *2nd June 1851.*

The Queen will see the Judge Advocate on Saturday at three.

The place of the late Mr Mill is already filled up.

Mr Sheil's death is very sudden, and must be a great shock to his family....

We go to Windsor this afternoon to stay till Friday. We hope that Lord John Russell's little girl is going on quite well.

The Queen has had good accounts from the dear Princess of Prussia from Coblentz. Her letter is full of England, her great happiness here, and her great sorrow at having left it. The Princes have expressed the same, so this dangerous journey has gone off without *one* single unpleasant circumstance, which is very gratifying.

The Prince and Prince Frederic are gone to Berlin, where the statue of Frederic the Great was to be inaugurated yesterday.

Queen Victoria to Lord John Russell.

Buckingham Palace, *18th June 1851.*

The Queen returns the papers signed. We are both much pleased at what Lord John Russell says about the Prince's speech yesterday.[15] It was on so ticklish a subject that one could not feel sure beforehand how it might be taken; at the same time the Queen felt sure that the Prince would say the right thing, from her entire confidence in his great tact and judgment.

The Queen, at the risk of not appearing sufficiently modest (and yet, why should a wife ever be modest about her husband's merits?), must say that she thinks Lord John Russell will admit now that the Prince is possessed of very extraordinary powers of mind and heart. She feels so proud at being his wife that she cannot refrain from herself paying a tribute to his noble character.

Queen Victoria to Lord John Russell.

Buckingham Palace, *10th July 1851.*

The Queen hastens to tell Lord John Russell how amiably every-thing went off last [night], and how enthusiastically we were received by an almost *fearful* mass of people in the streets;[16] the greatest order prevailed, and the greatest and most gratifying enthusiasm.

Not being aware whether Sir George Grey is equal to any busi-ness, the Queen writes to Lord John to direct that a proper letter be written without delay to the Lord Mayor, expressing not only the Queen's and Prince's thanks for the splendid entertainment at the Guildhall, but also our high gratification at the hearty, kind, and enthu-siastic reception we met with during our progress through the City, both going and returning. Our only anxiety is lest any accident should have occurred from the great pressure of the dense crowds.

The Queen would likewise wish to know what distinction should be conferred in honour of the occasion on the Lord Mayor.

Queen Victoria to Lord John Russell.

Buckingham Palace, *15th July 1851.*

The Queen has received Lord John Russell's letter. She has no ob-jection on this particular occasion to knight the two Sheriffs, this year being so memorable a one.

But the Queen would wish it clearly to be *understood* that they have no right or claim to be knighted whenever the Queen goes into the City.

On the occasion of the opening of the Royal Exchange the Sher-iffs were not knighted....

We regret to hear of Lord John's continued indisposition.

Queen Victoria to Lord John Russell.

Osborne, *25th August 1851.*

The Queen wishes to draw Lord John Russell's attention to the enclosed draft, which she does not think can go in its present shape. We argued in innumerable despatches that the *choice of the successor* to the Danish Crown was entirely an internal question for Denmark, in which foreign Powers could not interfere. Here, however, it is laid down that the German Diet has no right to treat the succession in Hol-stein (a German State) as an *internal* question, as it ought to be decided on—not according to the *German law of succession*, but according to the interests of Europe. Nor is it true, as stated in the despatch, that the Duke of Augustenburg has *no* claim to the Danish Crown. His mother was the daughter of Christian VII. and of Queen Matilda.

Queen Victoria to the King of the Belgians.

Balmoral Castle, *16th September 1851.*

My dearest Uncle,—Accept my best thanks for your kind and dear letter of the 8th. It is a good thing for Leo to begin to follow in your footsteps, but (if I may speak out plainly), I think that anything like *fonctions* and *représentation* is agreeable and *not* difficult to Leo. It is the common contact with his fellow-creatures, the being put on a par with him, the being brought to feel that he is as much *one* of them as any other, in spite of his birth, which I think of such great importance for him, and I therefore hope you will send him to *Bonn*.

My letter is terribly *décousu*, for it has been twice interrupted. I was out the whole day with Albert, in the forest in a perfectly tropical heat. Since we went to Allt-na-Giuthasach, our little bothy near Loch Muich on the 12th, the heat of the sun has been daily increasing, and has reached a pitch which makes it almost sickening to be out in it, though it is beautiful to behold. The sky these last two evenings has been like an Italian one, and for the last few days—at least the last four—without the slightest particle of cloud, and the sun blazing. With this, not a breath of air. The mountains look quite crimson and lilac, and everything glows with the setting sun. The evenings are quite a *relief.* Really one cannot undertake expeditions, the heat is so great. We thought of you, and wished you could be here; you would fancy yourself in Italy.

Albert got a splendid stag to-day. I must hastily conclude, hoping to hear from you that you *will come.* Our moonlights have been magnificent also. Ever your devoted Niece,

Victoria R.

Queen Victoria to the King of the Belgians.

Balmoral Castle, *22nd September 1851.*

My dearest Uncle,—I write to you on purpose on this large paper in order that you may see and admire it. Landseer did it also on pur-

pose, and I think it is even finer than the other. It is so truly the character of the noble animal.

That abuse of the poor Orleans family in our papers is abominable, and Lord John is equally shocked at it, but won't interfere. Don't
you think Joinville should not have left it open for him to accept it, for
it is *impossible* for *him* to be *President* of the French Republic? Still, I
feel convinced that he and they *all* do what they think best for *France*.

I must conclude. Ever your devoted Niece,

Victoria R.

Queen Victoria to the King of the Belgians.

Shiel of Allt-na-Giuthasach, *30th September 1851.*

My dearest Uncle,—I write to you from our little bothy in the
hills, which is quite a wilderness—where we arrived yesterday evening after a long hill expedition to the Lake of Loch Nagar, which is
one of the wildest spots imaginable. It was very cold. To-day it pours
so that I hardly know if we shall be able to get out, or home even. We
are not *snowed*, but *rained up*. Our little Shiel is very snug and comfortable, and we have got a little piano in it. Lady Douro is with us.

Many thanks for your kind letter of the 22nd. Our warm, fine
weather left us on the 25th, and we have had storm and snow in the
mountains ever since then.

The position of Princes is no doubt difficult in these times, but it
would be much less so if they would behave honourably and straightforwardly, giving the people gradually those privileges which would
satisfy all the reasonable and well-intentioned, and would weaken the
power of the Red Republicans; instead of that, *reaction* and a return to
all the tyranny and oppression is the cry and the principle—and all
papers and books are being seized and prohibited, as in the days of
Metternich!...

Vicky was kicked off her pony—a quiet beast—but not the least
hurt; this is more than three weeks ago. Alfred (whom you will recollect I told you was so terribly heedless and entirely indifferent to all
punishment, etc.) tumbled downstairs last week. He was not seriously
hurt at all, and quite well the next morning, only with a terribly black,
green, and yellow face and very much swelled. He might have been
killed; he is always bent upon self-destruction, and one hardly knows
what to do, for he don't mind being hurt or scolded or punished; and

the very next morning he tried to go down the stairs leaning over the banisters just as he had done when he fell.

Alas! this will be my last letter but one from the dear Highlands. We start on the 7th, visiting Liverpool and Manchester on our way back, and expect to be at Windsor on the 11th.

I must now conclude. Ever your devoted Niece,

Victoria R.

Queen Victoria to the King of the Belgians.

Balmoral Castle, *6th October 1851.*

My dearest Uncle,—Only two words can I write to you, as we are to start to-morrow morning. My heart is *bien gros* at going from here.

I love my peaceful, wild Highlands, the glorious scenery, the dear good people who are much attached to us, and who feel their *Einsamkeit* sadly, very much. One of our Gillies, a young Highlander who generally went out with me, said, in answer to my observation that they must be very dull here when we left: "It's just like death come all at once." In addition to my sorrow at leaving this dear place, I am in great sorrow at the loss of a dear and faithful, excellent friend, whom you will sincerely lament—our good Lord Liverpool. He was well and in the highest spirits with us only six weeks ago, and in three days he was carried away. I cannot tell you *how* it has upset me; I have known him so long, and he was such an intimate friend of ours. We received the news yesterday.

Many thanks for your kind letter of the 29th. I am glad all went off so well, but it must have been dreadful to miss dearest Louise. This time reminds me so much of all our sorrow last year on her dear account.

Victoria R.

Queen Victoria to Lord Palmerston.

Windsor Castle, *13th October 1851.*

The Queen returns Lord Howden's letter, and thinks that the best answer to the Queen of Spain's request will be that the Statutes do not allow the Garter to be bestowed upon a lady; that the Queen herself possesses no order of knighthood from any country.[17]

With reference to the claim for the King arising out of the Prince having received the Fleece, it may be well to say that the offer of the Fleece had in the first instance been declined for fear of establishing a ground for the necessity of giving the Garter in return, and was at its second offer accepted by the Prince, together with the first orders of almost every country, on the understanding that no return would be expected. It would have been impossible to give the Garter to every Sovereign, and very difficult to make a selection. The Queen of Spain ought to be made aware of the fact that among the reigning Sovereigns, the Emperors of Austria and Brazil, and the Kings of Sweden, Denmark, Bavaria, Holland, Sardinia, Naples, Greece, etc., etc., have not got the Garter, although many of them have expressed a wish for it, and that amongst the Kings Consort, the King of Portugal, the Queen's first cousin, has not received it yet, although the Queen has long been anxious to give it to him.

Anything short of these explanations might offend, or leave the claim open to be repeated from time to time.

Lord John Russell to Queen Victoria.

Downing Street, *14th October 1851.*

Lord Carlisle, Lord Minto, and Sir Charles Wood are appointed a Committee to consider of the extension of the Suffrage. They meet to-morrow. Lord John Russell expects to see Mr Peel to-morrow. It is proposed that Parliament should meet on the 3rd or 5th of February....

Queen Victoria to Lord John Russell.

Windsor Castle, *14th October 1851.*

The Queen does not consider the Committee appointed to con-sider the extension of the Franchise a very strong one. Will Lord Carlisle be up to the peculiar business?

Queen Victoria to Lord John Russell.[18]

Windsor Castle, *29th October 1851.*

The Queen concludes Lord John Russell has read the accounts of Kossuth's arrival in to-day's papers.

She wishes Lord John could still try to prevent Lord Palmerston from receiving him. The effect it will have abroad will do us immense harm. At all events, Lord John should take care to have it understood that the Government have not sanctioned it, and that it is a private act of Lord Palmerston's.

The Queen will else have again to submit to insults and affronts, which are the result of Lord Palmerston's conduct.

Lord John Russell to Queen Victoria.

Windsor Castle, *24th October 1851.*

Lord John Russell presents his humble duty to your Majesty, and is sorry to say he can interfere no further with respect to Lord Palmerston's reception of Kossuth.

With respect to the manner of the reception, however, he will write to Lord Palmerston to desire him to take care that nothing is said which goes beyond the strict expression of thanks for the efforts made by the British Government to procure first the safety, and next the liberty, of Kossuth.

As for the reception, it is to be considered that Kossuth is considered the representative of English institutions against despotism.

If this were so the public feeling would be laudable.

Lord John Russell to Queen Victoria.

Pembroke Lodge, *31st October 1851.*

Lord John Russell presents his humble duty to your Majesty; he has the honour to submit to your Majesty a correspondence[19] which has taken place between Lord Palmerston and himself.

After Lord Palmerston's answer, Lord John Russell can have but little hope that Lord Palmerston will not see M. Kossuth. Lord John Russell cannot separate the private from the public man in this instance; the reception of Kossuth, if it takes place, will be a reception by your Majesty's Secretary of State for Foreign Affairs. Whether that reception is to take place in Downing Street or Carlton Terrace does not appear to him material.

Lord John Russell would, as a last resource, humbly advise your Majesty to command Lord Palmerston not to receive M. Kossuth.

It appears to him that your Majesty owes this mark of respect to your Majesty's ally, and generally to all States at peace with this country.

Lord John Russell has no other copy of this letter to Lord Palmerston.

Queen Victoria to Lord John Russell.

Windsor Castle, *31st October 1851.*

The Queen has received Lord John Russell's letter, and returns the enclosures. She likewise sends him her letter to Lord Palmerston, which she begs him to send on, merely changing the label. She must tell Lord John, however, that although *he* may go on with a *colleague*, even after having received an answer like the one Lord Palmerston has returned to the many entreaties not to compromise the Government by his personal act, the Queen cannot expose herself to having her positive commands disobeyed by one of her public servants, and that should Lord Palmerston persist in his intention he cannot continue as her Minister. She refrains from any expression upon Lord Palmerston's conduct in this matter, as Lord John is well aware of her feelings.

Queen Victoria to Viscount Palmerston.[20]

Windsor Castle, *31st October 1851.*

The Queen mentioned to Lord Palmerston when he was last here at Windsor Castle that she thought it would not be advisable that he should receive M. Kossuth upon his arrival in England, as being wholly unnecessary, and likely to be misconstrued abroad. Since M. Kossuth's arrival in this country, and his violent denunciations of two Sovereigns with whom we are at peace, the Queen thinks that she owes it as a mark of respect to her Allies, and generally to all States at peace with this country, not to allow that a person endeavouring to excite a political agitation in this country against her Allies should be received by her Secretary of State for Foreign Affairs. Whether such a reception should take place at his official or private residence can make no difference as to the public nature of the act. The Queen must therefore demand that the reception of M. Kossuth by Lord Palmerston should not take place.

Lord John Russell to Queen Victoria.

Pembroke Lodge, *31st October 1851.*

Lord John Russell presents his humble duty to your Majesty. Since writing to your Majesty this morning it has occurred to him that it will be best that your Majesty should not give any commands to Lord Palmerston on his sole advice.

With this view he has summoned the Cabinet for Monday, and he humbly proposes that your Majesty should await their advice.

Queen Victoria to Lord John Russell.

Windsor Castle, *31st October 1851.*

The Queen has just received Lord John Russell's letter. She thinks it natural that Lord John should wish to bring a matter which may cause a rupture in the Government before the Cabinet, but thinks his having summoned the Cabinet only for Monday will leave Lord Palmerston at liberty in the intermediate time to have his reception of Kossuth, and then rest on his *fait accompli.* Unless, therefore, Lord John Russell can bind him over to good conduct, all the mischief which is apprehended from this step of his will result; and he will have, moreover, the triumph of having carried his point, and having set the Prime Minister at defiance....

Lord John Russell to Queen Victoria.

Pembroke Lodge, *1st November 1851.*

Lord John Russell presents his humble duty to your Majesty; he is deeply sensible of your Majesty's kindness and indulgence. He feels that he is at times overwhelmed by the importance and variety of the questions of which the principal weight lies upon him.

He now lays before your Majesty a copy of the letter he has written to Lord Palmerston.[21] With a grateful sense of your Majesty's confidence, he is now of opinion that the Cabinet should decide, and that no part of the burden should be placed upon your Majesty.

He therefore returns the letter to Lord Palmerston.

He summoned the Cabinet for Monday, as so many members of it are at a distance. He does not think Lord Palmerston will come to town before Monday.

Queen Victoria to Lord John Russell.

Windsor Castle, *1st November 1851.*

The Queen has to acknowledge Lord John Russell's letter of this day, and returns the copy of his to Lord Palmerston. She feels that she has the right and the duty to demand that one of her Ministers should not by his private acts, compromise her and the country, and therefore omitted in her letter to Lord Palmerston all reference to Lord John Russell's opinion; but she of course much prefers that she should be protected from the wilful indiscretions of Lord Palmerston by the attention of the Cabinet being drawn to his proceedings without her personal intervention.[22]

Queen Victoria to Lord John Russell.

Windsor Castle, *3rd November 1851*.

The Queen has just received Lord John Russell's letter. She is very glad to hear that this matter has been amicably arranged, and she trusts that Lord Palmerston will act according to his promises.

Queen Victoria to Lord John Russell.

Windsor Castle, *11th November 1851*.

The Queen sends this draft to Lord John Russell, as she thinks the tone in which it is written so very ironical, and not altogether becoming for a public despatch from the English Secretary for Foreign Affairs, to be given to the Minister of another State. The substance is quite right, and a dignified explanation of the absurdity of the conduct of the Parma officials would very likely produce its effect, but some expressions in this draft could only tend to irritate, and therefore prevent that readiness to comply with our demand, which is to be produced.[23]

Queen Victoria to Lord John Russell.

Windsor Castle, *20th November 1851*.

The Queen must write to-day to Lord John Russell on a subject which causes her much anxiety. Her feelings have again been deeply wounded by the official conduct of her Secretary of State for Foreign Affairs since the arrival of M. Kossuth in this country. The Queen feels the best interests of her people, the honour and dignity of her Crown, her public and personal obligations towards those Sovereigns with whom she *professes* to be on terms of peace and amity, most unjustifiably exposed. The Queen has unfortunately very often had to call upon Lord John to check his colleague in the dangerous and unbecoming course which at various times he has so wilfully persevered in pursuing. But Lord John Russell, although agreeing on most of these occasions with the view taken by the Queen, has invariably met her remonstrances with the plea that to push his interference with Lord Palmerston beyond what he had done would lead to a rupture with him, and thus necessarily to a breaking up of the Cabinet. The Queen, considering a change of her Government under present political cir-cumstances dangerous to the true interests of the nation, had only to choose between two evils, without possessing sufficient confidence in her own judgment to decide which in its political consequences would turn out the least. But if in such a contingency the Queen chooses rather not to insist upon what is due to her, she thinks it indispensable at the same time to express to her Cabinet that she does so on their account, leaving it to them to reconcile the injuries done to her with that sound policy and conduct which the maintenance of peace and the welfare of the country require. These remarks seem to be especially called for after the report of the official interview between Lord Palm-erston and the deputation from Finsbury,[24] and the Queen requests Lord John Russell to bring them under the notice of the Cabinet.

Lord John Russell to Queen Victoria.

Pembroke Lodge, *21st November 1851.*

Lord John Russell presents his humble duty to your Majesty. He had the honour of receiving last night your Majesty's communication respecting Lord Palmerston.

Lord John Russell presumes that it is the substance of this com-munication which your Majesty wishes to be laid before the Cabinet.

But before doing so he cannot refrain from mentioning some cir-cumstances which appear to him to weigh materially in the consideration of Lord Palmerston's conduct.

In many instances Lord Palmerston has yielded to the remon-strances of Lord John Russell, supported as they have been by your Majesty.

He did so on the question of furnishing guns to the Sicilians.

He did so in respect to the letter to Baron Koller on the affair of Count Haynau.

He gave way likewise in this last instance, when, after assuring Lord Dudley Stuart that he would see Kossuth whenever he chose to call upon him, he consented to intimate privately to Lord Dudley that he requested him not to call.

This last concession must have been mortifying to Lord Palm-erston, and he has consoled himself in a manner not very dignified by giving importance to the inflated addresses from some meetings in the suburbs of London.

But it appears to Lord John Russell that every Minister must have a certain latitude allowed him which he may use, perhaps with indiscretion, perhaps with bad taste, but with no consequence of sufficient importance to deserve notice.

Lord John Russell must, however, call your Majesty's attention to an article in the *Morning Post*, which denies the accuracy of the report of Lord Palmerston's answer to what is there called "the froth and folly of an address to Downing Street."

Lord John Russell, in admitting that he has more than once represented to your Majesty that the expulsion of Lord Palmerston would break up the Government, begs to explain that he has always done so upon one of two grounds:

First, if Lord Palmerston should be called upon by your Majesty to resign on account of a line of Foreign Policy of which his colleagues had approved, and for which they were, with him, responsible.

Second, in case no difference of opinion had arisen, and the transaction should bear the character of an intrigue, to get rid of an inconvenient colleague.

It must be remembered that Lord Palmerston was recommended to the late King by Lord Grey as Foreign Secretary, and remained in that Office from 1830 to 1834; that he was afterwards replaced in the same Office by Lord Melbourne, and remained from 1835 to 1841.

He has thus represented the Foreign Policy of the Whig Party fifteen years, and has been approved not only by them but by a large portion of the country. In the advice which Lord John Russell has humbly tendered to your Majesty, he has always had in view the importance of maintaining the popular confidence which your Majesty's name everywhere inspires. Somewhat of the good opinion of the Emperor of Russia and other foreign Sovereigns may be lost, but the good will and affection of the people of England are retained, a great security in these times.

Lord John Russell has made out a note of his address to the Cabinet for your Majesty's information. He prays to have it returned.

Queen Victoria to Lord John Russell.

Windsor Castle, *21st November 1851.*

The Queen has received Lord John Russell's letter and returns the note on his former communication to the Cabinet. If Lord John felt on the 3rd of November that "above all, it behoves us to be particularly cautious and not to afford just ground of complaint to any Party, and that we cannot be too vigilant or weigh our proceedings too scrupulously"—the Queen cannot suppose that Lord John considers the official reception by the Secretary of State for Foreign Affairs of addresses, in which allied Sovereigns are called Despots and Assassins, as within that "latitude" which he claims for every minister, "which he may use perhaps with indiscretion, perhaps with bad taste, but with no consequence of sufficient importance to deserve notice."

The Queen leaves it to Lord John Russell whether he will lay her letter, or only the substance of it, before the Cabinet;[25] but she hopes that they will make that careful enquiry into the justice of her complaint which she was sorry to miss altogether in Lord John Russell's answer. It is no question with the Queen whether she pleases the Emperor of Austria or not, but whether she gives him a just ground of complaint or not. And if she does so, she can never believe that this will add to her popularity with her own people. Lord John's letter must accordingly have disappointed her as containing a mere attempt at a defence of Lord Palmerston. Lord John sees one cause of excuse in Lord Palmerston's natural desire to console himself for the mortification of having had to decline seeing M. Kossuth; the Queen has *every reason to believe* that he has seen him after all.

Queen Victoria to Viscount Palmerston.

Windsor Castle, *21st November 1851.*

The Queen has just received Lord Palmerston's letter with the Memorandum relative to the mourning of her Uncle, the late King of Hanover,[26] and she has to say in reply that she thinks the mourning ought not to be for a Foreign Sovereign but for a Prince of the Blood Royal, which was the nearest relation in which he stood to the Throne.

Queen Victoria to the King of Hanover.

Windsor Castle, *21st November 1851.*

My dear George,—Your kind letter of the 18th, announcing to me the melancholy news of the death of your Father, was given to me yesterday by Mr Somerset, and I hasten to express to you in both our names our sincere and heartfelt condolence, and beg you to do so in our names to our dear Cousin Mary.[27]

It must be a consolation to you that the end of the King was peaceful and so free from pain and suffering. Most truly do I enter into your feelings as to the responsible position into which you are now placed, and my best wishes for your welfare and happiness as well as that of Hanover will ever accompany you. I am happy to hear from Mr

Somerset that you were well, as well as your dear Mary and dear children.

Albert desires me to say everything kind from him to you as well as to our cousins, and with every possible good wish for your health and prosperity, believe me always, my dear George, your very affectionate Cousin,

Victoria R.

Viscount Palmerston to Queen Victoria.

Carlton Gardens, *22nd November 1851.*

Viscount Palmerston presents his humble duty to your Majesty and has taken the proper steps according to your Majesty's commands, about the mourning for the late King of Hanover; and he would wish to know whether it is your Majesty's desire that he should have letters prepared for your Majesty's signature, announcing to Foreign Sovereigns the decease of the late King.

Queen Victoria to Viscount Palmerston.

Osborne, *22nd November 1851.*

The Queen has just received Lord Palmerston's letter.

The Queen does not think it necessary for her to announce the King of Hanover's death to other Sovereigns, as there is a head of that branch of her Family who would have to do so. She declared the present King's marriage in Council, but she does not think that she announced it. This Lord Palmerston would perhaps be able to ascertain at the Office.

Queen Victoria to Lord John Russell.

Osborne, *3rd December 1851.*

The Queen has received Lord John Russell's letter of the 30th ult., and has carefully considered his Memorandum on the report of the Committee of the Cabinet; she now returns Sir Charles Wood's Memorandum.

Considering the question of Reform under its two bearings—on the Franchise and on the Suffrage—the Queen thinks the proposal of merely adding neighbouring towns to the small boroughs an improvement on the original plan, which contemplated the taking away of members from some boroughs, and giving them to others. Thus the animosity may be hoped to be avoided which an attack upon vested interests could not have failed to have produced. Much will depend, however, upon the completeness, fairness, and impartiality with which the selection of the towns will be made which are to be admitted into the electoral district of others. Sir Charles Wood's Memorandum being only a sketch, the Queen hopes to see a more complete list, stating the principle also upon which the selection is made.

With regard to the Suffrage, the proposals of the Committee appear to the Queen to be framed with a due regard to the importance of not giving an undue proportion of weight to the Democracy. In the Queen's opinion, the chief question to consider will be whether the strengthening of the Democratic principle will upset the balance of Constitution, and further weaken the Executive, which is by no means too strong at present. The Queen is well aware of the difficulty of forming a correct estimate beforehand of the moral effect which such extensive changes may produce, but thinks that they cannot even be guessed at before the numerical results are accurately ascertained; she hopes therefore that the statistics will be soon in a state to be laid before her.

The Queen regrets that the idea of reviving the Guilds had to be abandoned, but can quite understand the difficulty which would have been added to the measure by its being clogged with such an additional innovation.

Queen Victoria to the King of the Belgians.

Osborne, *2nd December 1851.*

My dearest Uncle,—Accept my best thanks for your kind letter of the 28th. I am truly grieved to hear that you have got so bad a cold; nothing is more trying and annoying than those heavy colds, which render *all* occupation irksome and trying in the highest degree. I hope that it will soon be past.

It is a great pity that you do not venture to come to us, as I am sure you might do it easily. I do not think that there will be any outburst yet awhile in France....

I am rather unhappy about dear Uncle Mensdorff, who, I hear, has arrived at Vienna with gout in his head. I hope, however, soon to hear of his being much better....

349

Queen Victoria to the King of the Belgians.

Osborne, *4th December 1851.*

Dearest Uncle,—I must write a line to ask what you say to the *wonderful* proceedings at Paris, which really seem like a *story* in a book or a play! What is to be the result of it all?[28]

I feel ashamed to have written *so positively* a few hours before that nothing would happen.

We are anxiously waiting for to-day's news—though I should hope that the Troops were to be depended upon, and *order* for the present would prevail. I hope that none of the Orleans Family will move a limb or say a word, but remain perfectly passive.

I must now conclude. Ever your devoted Niece,

Victoria R.

Queen Victoria to Lord John Russell.

Osborne, *4th December 1851.*

The Queen has learnt with surprise and concern the events which have taken place at Paris.[29] She thinks it is of great importance that Lord Normanby should be instructed to remain entirely passive, and to take no part whatever in what is passing. Any word from him might be misconstrued at such a moment.

Lord John Russell to Queen Victoria.

Downing Street, *4th December 1851.*

(6 p.m.)

Lord John Russell presents his humble duty to your Majesty. Your Majesty's directions respecting the state of affairs in Paris shall be followed. Lord Normanby[30] has asked whether he should suspend his diplomatic functions; but the Cabinet were unanimously of opinion that he should not do so.

The result is very uncertain; at present the power is likely to rest in the Army, to whose memory of victories and defeats the President has so strongly appealed.

The King of the Belgians to Queen Victoria.

Laeken, *5th December 1851.*

My dearest Victoria,—Receive my best thanks for your dear gracious letter of the 2nd, the date of the battle of Austerlitz, and the *coup d'état* at Paris. What do you say to it?

As yet one cannot form an opinion, but I am inclined to think that Louis Bonaparte will succeed. The country is tired and wish quiet, and if they get it by this *coup d'état* they will have no objection, and let *le Gouvernement Parlementaire et Constitutionnel* go to sleep for a while.

I suspect that the great Continental powers will see a military Government at Paris with pleasure; they go rather far in their hatred of everything Parliamentary. The President takes a little of Napoleon already. I understand that he expressed himself displeased, as if I had too much supported the Orleans Family. I render perfect justice to the President, that hitherto he has not plagued us; but we have also abstained from all interference. I think that Hélène has been imprudent; besides, it is difficult for the poor Family to avoid to speak on these subjects or to express themselves with mildness.

If something like an Empire establishes itself, perhaps we shall for a time have much to suffer, as the *gloire française* invariably looks to the old frontiers. My hope is that they will necessarily have much to do at home, for a time, as parties will run high.... Your devoted Uncle,

Leopold R.

Queen Victoria to Lord John Russell.

Osborne, *6th December 1851.*

The Queen has to acknowledge Lord John Russell's letter of yesterday. She is glad to hear that the Cabinet occupy themselves assiduously with the Reform Question, but hopes that they will not come to a final decision without having first ascertained how the proposed plan will operate when practically applied to the present state of the Franchise and Suffrage. The Queen is very anxious to arrive at a definite opinion on this subject herself.

The Queen sees from the Manchester Speeches that the *Ballot* is to be made the stalking-horse of the Radicals.

The Marchioness of Normanby to Colonel Phipps.

Paris, *7th December 1851.*

My dear Charles,—I have an opportunity of writing to you *not* through the Foreign Office, which I shall take advantage of, as at present the Post is not to be trusted, and I am afraid I do not think the Office is either.

Palmerston has taken lately to writing in the most extraordinary manner to Normanby.[31] I think he wants to fix a quarrel with him, which you may be sure Normanby will avoid at present, as it would have the worst possible effect; but I do not understand it at all, and I wish you could in any way explain what it means. Palmerston seems very angry because Normanby does not unqualifyingly approve of this step here, and the results; the whole thing is so completely a *coup d'état,* and all the proceedings are so contrary to and devoid of law and justice and security, that even the most violent Tory would be staggered by them. (For instance, to-day *all* the English papers, even Normanby's, are stopped and prohibited; they will of course allow Normanby's to come, but it is to be under an envelope), and yet Palmerston, who quarrels with all Europe about a political adventurer like Kossuth, because he was defending the liberties and constitution of his country, now tries to quarrel with Normanby, and really writes in the most impertinent manner, because Normanby's despatches are not sufficiently in praise of Louis Napoleon and his *coup d'état.* There must be some *dessous des cartes* that we are not aware of. Normanby has always said, having been undertaken, the only thing now is to hope and pray it may be successful; but that is another thing to approving the way it was begun, or the way it has been carried out. The bloodshed has been dreadful and indiscriminate, no quarter was shown, and when an insurgent took refuge in a house, the soldiers killed every one in the house, whether engaged in the *émeute* or not.... It is very doubtful whether Normanby will be able to go on with [Palmerston] if this sort of thing continues, for he talks of "I hear this" and "I am told that," with reference to Normanby's conduct here, which no man in his position can stand, as, if Palmerston takes the *on-dits* of others, and not Normanby's own accounts, there is an end of confidence; but I must say his last letter appears to me a sort of exuberance of anger, which spends itself on many subjects rather than the one which first caused it, and therefore I suspect he has received some rap on the knuckles at home, which he resents here, or on the first person who is not of the same opinion as himself; but it is a curious anomaly that he should quarrel with Normanby in support of arbitrary and absolute Government. All is quiet here now, and will, I hope, continue so till the Elections, when I suppose we may have some more *émeutes*....

They have been told at the Clubs that they may meet, but they are not to talk politics. In short, I do not suppose that despotism ever reached such a pitch.... You may suppose what the French feel; it serves them all quite right, but that does not prevent one's feeling indignant at it. And this is what Palmerston is now supporting without restriction. We are entirely without any other news from England from any one. Would you not send me or Normanby a letter through Rothschild? I am rather anxious to know whether this is a general feeling in England; it could not be, if they know all that had happened here. Mind, I can quite understand the policy of keeping well with Louis Napoleon, and Normanby is so, and has never expressed to any one a hostile opinion except in his despatches and private letters to Palmerston.... I shall send this by a private hand, not to run the risk of its being read. Ever yours affectionately,

M. Normanby.

Queen Victoria to the King of the Belgians.

Osborne, *9th December 1851.*

Dearest Uncle,—Your kind letter of the 5th reached me on Sunday morning. Much blood has been shed since you wrote....

What you say about arbitrary and military Government in France is very true, and I daresay will do for a time; but I do not know *how* Louis Napoleon is to proceed, or how he will get over the anger and enmity of those he imprisoned. Still, I see that the Legitimists have all given in their adhesion. Every one in France and elsewhere *must wish* order, and many therefore rally round the President.

A most extraordinary report was mentioned to me yesterday, which, however, I never could believe, and which is besides *physically impossible*, from the illness of the one and the absence of the other, viz. that Joinville and Aumale had gone or were going to Lille to put themselves at the head of the troops,[32] which would be a terrible and a very unwise thing. It would be very awkward for *you* too.

I must now conclude, hoping soon to hear from you. You should urge the poor Orleans family to be very prudent in what they say about passing events, as I believe Louis Napoleon is very *sore* on the subject, and matters might get still worse. Ever your devoted Niece,

Victoria R.

The Marchioness of Normanby to Colonel Phipps.[33]

Paris, *9th December 1851.*

My dearest Charles,—I had written a long letter to the Queen, and upon second thoughts I have burnt it, because events have now become so serious between Normanby and Palmerston that I do not think that I should be the person to inform Her Majesty of it, in case anything was to be said upon the subject in Parliament. And yet as the affront has been given in Palmerston's private letters, I feel sure she does not know it. You have all probably seen Normanby's public despatches, in which, though as an Englishman he deprecates and deplores the means employed and the pledges broken—in short, the unconstitutional illegality of the whole *coup d'état*—yet he always says, seeing now no other refuge from Rouge ascendency, he hopes it may succeed. One would have supposed, from the whole tenor of his policy, from his Radical tendencies, and all that he has been doing lately, that Palmerston would have been the last person to approve of this *coup d'état*. Not a bit! He turns upon Normanby in the most flippant manner; almost accuses him of a concealed knowledge of an Orleanist plot—never whispered here, nor I believe, even imagined by the Government of Paris, who would have been too glad to seize upon it as an excuse; says he compromises the relations of the country by his evident disapproval of Louis Napoleon—in short, it is a letter that Morny might have written, and that it is quite impossible for Normanby to bear. The curious thing is that it is a letter or rather letters that would completely ruin Palmerston with *his* Party. He treats all the acts of the wholesale cruelties of the troops as a joke—in short, it is the letter of a man half mad, I think, for to quarrel with Normanby on this subject is cutting his own throat.... He has written also to Lord John. Louis Napoleon knows perfectly well that Normanby cannot approve the means he has taken; he talks to him confidentially, and treats him as an honest, upright man, and he never showed him more attention, or friendship even than last night when we were at the Elysée, though Normanby said not one word in approval....

There is another question upon which Normanby has a right to complain, which is, that two days before Palmerston sent his instructions here, he expressed to Walewski his complete approval of the step taken by Louis Napoleon, which was transmitted by Walewski in a despatch to Turgot, and read by him to many members of the Corps Diplomatique a day before Normanby heard a word from Palmerston. You will perhaps think that there is not enough in all this to authorise the grave step Normanby has taken, but the whole tone of his letters shows such a want of confidence, is so impertinent—talk of "we hear this," and "we are told that,"—bringing a sort of anonymous gossip against a man of Normanby's character and standing, that respect for himself obliges Normanby to take it up seriously.... In the meantime our Press in England is, as usual, *too* violent against Louis Napoleon. *We* have no friends or true allies left, thanks to the policy of Lord Palmerston; as soon as the peace of the country is restored the Army *must* be employed; it is the course of a Military Government; as much as an absolute Government is destroyed by the people, and the democracy again, when fallen into anarchy, is followed by Military Government. Louis Napoleon must maintain his position by acts: they will find out that Belgium should belong to France, or Alsace, or Antwerp, or something or other that England will not be able to allow, and then how are we prepared for the consequences?...

The more I think of Palmerston's letters, the less I can understand them; every sentence is in direct contradiction to his acts and words. He ridicules the idea of the Constitution; turns to scorn the idea of anything being due to the Members of the Assembly; laughs and jokes at the Club being fired into, though the English people in it were within an ace of being murdered by the soldiers; says that Normanby is pathetic over a broken looking-glass,[34] forgetting that the same bullet grazed the hand of an Englishman, "*a Roman citizen!*" who was between the window and the glass—in short, as I said before, he is quite incomprehensible, except, as I cannot help thinking, he read the private letter Normanby wrote to the Duke of Bedford upon the Kossuth business, wishing to take his advice a little upon a grave question, but which did not actually interfere with his position here. This would account for his extreme irritation....

All at present is quiet in Paris. There are Socialist risings in many parts of the country, but all these will do the President good, and strengthen his hands, for even the people who have been treated with indignity will pardon him if their châteaux are saved from an infuriated and brutal peasantry. The President told Normanby last night that the accounts of the cruelties and attacks in parts of the country were very serious, but he hoped they would soon be put down....

M. Normanby.[35]

Queen Victoria to Lord John Russell.

Osborne, *13th December 1851.*

The Queen sends the enclosed despatch from Lord Normanby to Lord John Russell, from which it appears that the French Government *pretend to have received* the entire approval of the late *coup d'état* by the British Government, as conveyed by Lord Palmerston to Count Walewski. The Queen cannot believe in the truth of the assertion, as such an approval given by Lord Palmerston would have been in complete *contradiction* to the line of strict neutrality and passiveness which the Queen had expressed her desire to see followed with regard to the late convulsion at Paris, and which was approved by the Cabinet, as stated in Lord John Russell's letter of the 6th inst. Does Lord John know anything about the alleged approval, which, if true, would *again* expose the honesty and dignity of the Queen's Government in the eyes of the world?[36]

Queen Victoria to the King of the Belgians.

Osborne, *13th December 1851.*

My beloved Uncle,—These lines are to express my *very warmest* wishes for *many, many happy* returns of your dear birthday, and for *every* earthly blessing you *can* desire. How I wish you could spend it *here*, or we with you! I venture to send you some trifles which will recall the Exhibition in which you took so much interest. The continuation of the work I send you, I shall forward as it comes out.

As I wrote so lately, and shall do so on Tuesday, I will not touch on politics—with one exception—that I think it of high importance that the Orleans should clear themselves of *all* suspicion of a *plot*, which *some people*, I am sure, wish to make it *appear* they *are* involved in; and that public contradiction should be given to the foolish report, *much* credited *here*, that Joinville has gone to Lille, or to some part of France, to head the Troops. Ever your devoted Niece and Child,

Victoria R.

How you will *again* miss your departed Angel!

Lord John Russell to Queen Victoria.

Woburn Abbey, *18th December 1851.*

Lord John Russell presents his humble duty to your Majesty. He received from Lord Palmerston yesterday an explanation of his declaration of opinion to Mr Walewski, which Lord John Russell regrets to state was quite unsatisfactory.

He thought himself compelled to write to Lord Palmerston in the most decisive terms.

Lord Palmerston requested that his letter might be returned to be copied.

The whole correspondence shall be submitted to your Majesty.

Your Majesty will find in the box a despatch of Lord Normanby of the 15th, and an answer of Lord Palmerston of the 16th,[37] which has been sent without your Majesty's sanction, or the knowledge of Lord John Russell.

The King of the Belgians to Queen Victoria.

Laeken, *19th December 1851.*

My dearest Victoria,—Receive my warmest and best thanks for your truly kind and gracious recollection of my old birthday, and your amiable presents.

Our angelic Louise had quite *un culte* for that day, and two have already passed since the best and noblest of hearts beats no longer amongst us. When one sees the haste and ardour of earthly pursuits, and how all this is often disposed of, and when one sees that even the greatest success always ends with the grave, one is tempted to wonder that the human race should follow so restlessly bubbles often disappearing just when reached, and always being a source of never-ending anxiety. France gives, these sixty years, the proof of the truth of what I say, always believing itself at the highest point of perfection and changing it a few weeks afterwards.

A military Government in France, if it really gets established, must become dangerous for Europe. I hope that at least at its beginning it will have enough to do in France, and that we may get time to prepare. England will do well not to fall asleep, but to keep up its old energy and courage....

Your truly devoted Uncle,

Leopold R.

Queen Victoria to Lord John Russell.

Osborne, *19th December 1851.*

The Queen has received several communications from Lord John Russell, but has not answered them, as she expected daily to hear of Lord Palmerston's answer. As Lord John Russell in his letter of yesterday's date promises to send her his correspondence with Lord Palmerston, she refrains from expressing a decided opinion until she has had an opportunity of perusing it; but Lord John will readily conceive what must be her feelings in seeing matters go from bad to worse with respect to Lord Palmerston's conduct!

Lord John Russell to Queen Victoria.

Woburn Abbey, *19th December 1851.*

Lord John Russell presents his humble duty to your Majesty, and has the honour to submit to your Majesty a correspondence with Viscount Palmerston, which terminates with a letter of this day's date.

Lord John Russell has now to advise your Majesty that Lord Palmerston should be informed that your Majesty is ready to accept the Seals of Office, and to place them in other hands.

Lord John Russell has summoned a Cabinet for Monday.

They may be of opinion that they cannot continue a Government.

But that is not Lord John Russell's opinion; and should they agree with him, he will proceed without delay to recommend a successor to your Majesty.

The Earl Granville appears to him the person best calculated for that post, but the Cabinet may be of opinion that more experience is required.

Queen Victoria to Lord John Russell.

Windsor Castle, *20th December 1851.*

The Queen found on her arrival here Lord John Russell's letter, enclosing his correspondence with Lord Palmerston, which she has perused with that care and attention which the importance and gravity of the subject of it demanded. The Queen has now to express to Lord John Russell her readiness to follow his advice, and her acceptance of the resignation of Lord Palmerston. She will be prepared to see Lord John after the Cabinet on Monday, as he proposes.

Queen Victoria to Lord John Russell.

Windsor Castle, *20th December 1851.*

With respect to a successor to Lord Palmerston, the Queen must state, that after the sad experience which she has just had of the difficulties, annoyances, and dangers to which the Sovereign may be exposed by the personal character and qualities of the Secretary for Foreign Affairs, she must reserve to herself the unfettered right to approve or disapprove the choice of a Minister for this Office.

Lord Granville, whom Lord John Russell designates as the person best calculated for that post, would meet with her entire approval. The possible opinion of the Cabinet that more experience was required does not weigh much with the Queen. From her knowledge of Lord Granville's character, she is inclined to see no such disadvantage in the circumstance that he has not yet had practice in managing Foreign Affairs, as he will be the more ready to lean upon the advice and judgment of the Prime Minister where he may have diffidence in his own, and thereby will add strength to the Cabinet by maintaining unity in thought and action. The Queen hopes Lord John Russell will not omit to let her have copies of his correspondence with Lord Palmerston, as he has promised her.[38]

Queen Victoria to Lord John Russell.

Windsor Castle, *21st December 1851.*

The Queen has received Lord John Russell's letter of to-day. She is not the least afraid of Lord Granville's not possessing sufficient public confidence for him to undertake the Foreign Affairs. He is very popular with the House of Lords, with the Free Traders, and the Peace party, and all that the Continent knows of him is in his favour; he had great success at Paris last summer, and his never having had an opportunity of damaging his character by having been mixed up in diplomatic intrigues is an immense advantage to him in obtaining the confidence of those with whom he is to negotiate.

Queen Victoria to the King of the Belgians.

Windsor Castle, *23rd December 1851.*

My dearest Uncle,—I have the greatest pleasure in announcing to you a piece of news which I know will give you as much satisfaction and relief as it does to us, and will do to the *whole* of the world. *Lord*

Palmerston is *no longer Foreign Secretary*—and Lord Granville is already named his successor!! He had become of late really quite reckless, and in spite of the serious admonition and caution he received only on the 29th of November, and again at the beginning of December, he *tells* Walewski that *he entirely* approves Louis Napoleon's *coup d'état*, when he had written to Lord Normanby by my and the Cabinet's desire that he (Lord Normanby) was to continue his diplomatic intercourse with the French Government, but to *remain* perfectly passive and give *no* opinion. Walewski wrote Palmerston's opinion (entirely contrary to what the Government had ordered) to M. Turgot, and when Normanby came with his instructions, Turgot told him what Palmerston had said. Upon this Lord John asked Palmerston to give an explanation—which, after the delay of a week, he answered in such an unsatisfactory way that Lord John wrote to him that *he could no longer remain Foreign Secretary*, for that perpetual misunderstanding and breaches of decorum were taking place which endangered the country. Lord Palmerston answered instantly that he would give up the Seals the moment his successor was named! Certain as we all felt that he could not have continued long in his place, we were quite taken by surprise when we learnt of the *dénouement*.... Lord Granville will, I think, do extremely well, and his extreme honesty and trustworthiness will make him *invaluable* to us, and to the Government and to Europe.

I send some prints, etc., for the children for Christmas. Ever your devoted Niece,

Victoria R.

Memorandum by the Prince Albert.

Windsor Castle, *23rd December 1851.*

Lord John Russell arrived here at six o'clock yesterday evening immediately from the Cabinet, and reported that the Cabinet had, without a dissenting voice, condemned Lord Palmerston's conduct, and approved of the steps taken by Lord John Russell, which was a great relief to him. Lord Lansdowne, to whom he had first written on the subject, had frightened him by answering that it was not possible to avoid the rupture with Lord Palmerston, but that he thought the Government would after this not be able to go on. When, however, this question was discussed in Cabinet, and Lord John had stated that he thought the Office could be well filled, they all agreed in the propriety of going on. The Members of the Cabinet were so unable to understand Lord Palmerston's motives for his conduct during these last months, that Mr. Fox Maule started an idea which once occurred to Lord John himself (as he said), viz. that he must have had the design to bring on a rupture! Lord Minto, who was absent from the Cabinet, expressed himself in a letter to Lord John very strongly about Lord Palmerston's *reckless conduct*, which would yet undo the country.

Lord John, after having received the concurrence of the Cabinet on the question of Lord Palmerston's dismissal, stated that Lord Granville was the person whom he would like best to see fill his office, and he knew this to be the feeling of the Queen also. The Cabinet quite agreed in Lord Granville's fitness, but Sir George Grey stated it as his opinion that it ought first to be offered to Lord Clarendon, who has always been pointed out by the public as the proper person to succeed Lord Palmerston, and that, if he were passed over, the whole matter would have the appearance of a Cabinet intrigue in favour of one colleague against another. The whole of the Cabinet sided with this opinion, and Lord John Russell now proposed to the Queen that an offer should in the first instance be made to Lord Clarendon.

The Queen protested against the Cabinet's taking upon itself the appointment of its own Members, which rested entirely with the Prime Minister and the Sovereign, under whose approval the former constructed his Government.... Lord John replied that he thought Lord Clarendon would not accept the offer, and therefore there would be little danger in satisfying the desires of the Cabinet. He had written to Lord Clarendon a cautioning letter from Woburn, apprising him of some serious crisis, of which he would soon hear, and speaking of his former wish to exchange the Lord-Lieutenancy for some other Office. Lord Clarendon at once perceived the drift of the hint, and wrote to the Duke of Bedford what he said he did not wish to write to his brother John, that, if it was that Palmerston was going, and *he* were thought of as a successor, nothing would be so disagreeable to him, as the whole change would be put down as an intrigue of his, whom Lord Palmerston had always accused of wishing to supplant him; that if, however, the service of the country required it, he had the courage to face all personal obloquy....

Lord John owned that Sir George Grey's chief desire was to see Lord Clarendon removed from Ireland, having been there so long; the Cabinet would wish to see the Duke of Newcastle join the Government as Lord-Lieutenant, which he might be induced to do. The Queen having mentioned Lord Clarendon as most fit to succeed Lord Lansdowne one day as President of the Council and leader in the House of Lords,

Lord John said that Lord Clarendon had particularly begged not to have the position offered him, for which he did not feel fit. Lord John would like him as Ambassador at Paris, and thought Lord Clarendon would like this himself; but it was difficult to know what to do with Lord Normanby.

In the course of the conversation, Lord John congratulated the Queen upon the change having been accomplished without her personal intervention, which might have exposed her to the animosity of Lord Palmerston's admirers, whilst she would have been precluded from making any public defence. I reminded Lord John that, as such was the disadvantage of the regal position, it behoved the Queen doubly to watch, lest she be put into the same dilemma with a new Minister, whose conduct she could not approve of. Lord Clarendon's appointment would be doubly galling to Lord Palmerston, whom Lord John might not wish to irritate further, a consideration which Lord John said he had also pressed upon the Cabinet. Upon a remark from Lord John as to Lord Granville's youth, the Queen replied: "Lord Canning, whom Lord Stanley had intended to make his Foreign Secretary, was not older...."

The conference ended by Lord John's promise to write to Lord Clarendon as the Queen had desired ... but that he did not wish to make the offer to Lord Granville till he had Lord Clarendon's answer. Lord Granville had been told not to attend the last Cabinet; Lord Palmerston had naturally stayed away.

I went up to Town at half-past seven to the Westminster Play, and took Lord John in my train to Richmond. We had some further conversation in the carriage, in which I asked Lord John whether it was true that Lord Palmerston had got us likewise into a quarrel with America by our ships firing at Panama upon an American merchantman; he said neither he nor Sir Francis Baring had received any news, but Sir Francis had been quite relieved by Lord Palmerston's quitting, as he could not be sure a moment that his Fleets were not brought into some scrape!

On my expressing my conviction that Lord Palmerston could not be very formidable to the Government, Lord John said: "I hope it will not come true what Lord Derby (then Lord Stanley) said after the last Ministerial crisis, when Lord John quizzed him at not having been able to get a Foreign Secretary—'Next time I shall have Lord Palmerston.'!"

Albert.

Lord John Russell to Queen Victoria.

Downing Street, *23rd December 1851.*

Lord John Russell presents his humble duty to your Majesty. He has just seen Count Walewski; he told him that he had an important piece of intelligence to give him; that your Majesty had been pleased to make a change in the Foreign Office, and to direct Lord Palmerston to give up the Seals.

He wished to give this intelligence that he might accompany it with an intimation that the policy towards France would continue to be of the most friendly character, and that there was nothing the Government more desired than to see a stable and settled Government in France; that they had every wish for the stability of the present French Government. Count Walewski said he had received various assurances of opinion from Lord Palmerston, which he supposed were adopted by Lord John Russell, and subsisted in force.

Lord John Russell said: "Not exactly; it is a principle of the English Government not to interfere in any way with the internal affairs of other countries; whether France chooses to be a Republic or a Monarchy, provided it be not a Social Republic, we wish to express no opinion; we are what we call in England a sheet of white paper in this respect; all we desire is the happiness and welfare of France." Count Walewski said it was of importance to the stability of the President that he should have a large majority; he would then give a Constitution.

Lord John Russell said each nation must suit itself in this respect; we have perhaps been in error in thinking our Constitution could be generally adopted; some nations it may suit, others may find it unfitted for them.

Queen Victoria to Lord John Russell.

Windsor Castle, *23rd December 1851.*

The Queen has just received Lord John Russell's letters, and is much rejoiced that this important affair has been finally so satisfactorily settled.

The Queen returns Lord Clarendon's letter, which she thinks a very good one.[39] The Queen hopes Count Walewski will have been satisfied, which she thinks he ought to be. The Queen will receive Lord Palmerston to deliver up the Seals, and Lord Granville to receive them, on Friday at half-past two.

Lord John Russell to Queen Victoria.

Downing Street, *24th December 1851.*

Lord John Russell submits a private note of Lord Palmerston,[40] which only shows how unconscious he was of all that the rest of the world perceived.

Queen Victoria to Lord John Russell.

Windsor Castle, *25th December 1861.*

The Queen has received Lord John Russell's letters, and she returns the enclosures.

The articles in the *Times* are very good; the other papers seem quite puzzled, and unable to comprehend what has caused Lord Palmerston's removal from office. Lord Palmerston's letter is very characteristic; he certainly has the best of the argument, and great care ought to be taken in bestowing any praise on him, as he always takes advantage of it to turn against those who meant it merely to soothe him. The Queen thought that there must be a Council for the swearing in of the new Secretary of State.

Memorandum by the Prince Albert.

Windsor Castle, *27th December 1851.*

Yesterday the Council was held, at which the change of Seals was to take place. We waited for one hour and a half, but Lord Palmerston did not appear; his Seals had been sent from the Foreign Office to Lord John Russell!

Lord John told us he had written to Lord Palmerston, announcing him the appointment of Lord Granville, and added that in his long political life he had not passed a week which had been so painful to him. Lord Palmerston's answer was couched in these terms: "Of course you will believe that I feel that just indignation at the whole proceeding which it must produce."

Lord Lansdowne seemed anxious particularly on account of the clear symptoms appearing from the papers that both Radicals and Protectionists are bidding for Lord Palmerston.

Lord Granville was very much overcome when he had his audience to thank for his appointment, but seemed full of courage and good-will. He said it would be as easy to him to avoid Lord Palmerston's faults as difficult to imitate his good qualities, promised to endeavour to establish a more decent usage between the Governments in their mutual communications, by setting the good example himself, and insisting upon the same on the part of the others; promised not to have anything to do with the newspapers; to give evening parties, just as Lord Palmerston had done, to which a good deal of his influence was to be attributed. He said a Member of Parliament just returned from the Continent had told him that an Englishman could hardly show himself without becoming aware of the hatred they were held in; the only chance one had to avoid being insulted was to say *Civis Romanus non sum.*

Lord Granville had been Under-Secretary for Foreign Affairs under Lord Palmerston for three years from 1837-40, but, as he expressed himself, rather the sandwich between his principal and the clerks. Lord Palmerston had in these three years hardly once spoken to him upon any of the subjects he had to treat.

Albert.

Queen Victoria to Lord John Russell.

Windsor Castle, *27th December 1851.*

The Queen forgot to remind Lord John Russell yesterday of his correspondence with Lord Palmerston, which he promised to let her have.

The Queen concludes from what Lord John said yesterday that he intended sounding the Duke of Newcastle relative to the Lord-Lieutenancy of Ireland.

Has Lord John ascertained the cause of Lord Palmerston's absence yesterday? If it was not accidental, she must say she thinks it most disrespectful conduct towards his Sovereign.

Lord John Russell to Queen Victoria.

Pembroke Lodge, *27th December 1851.*

Lord John Russell presents his humble duty to your Majesty, and submits a letter of Lord Palmerston, which explains his not going to Windsor. It appears to have arisen from a mistake in the message sent through Lord Stanley, and not from any want of respect to your Majesty.

Viscount Palmerston to Lord John Russell.

Carlton Gardens, *27th December 1851.*

My dear John Russell,—I am distressed beyond measure by the note from you which I have this moment received on my arrival here from Hampshire. I understood from Stanley that you had desired him to tell me that if it was inconvenient for me to come up yesterday, I might send the Seals to you at Windsor, and that my presence would be dispensed with.[41] Thereupon I sent the Seals up by an early train yesterday morning to Stanley, that he might send them down to you as suggested by you, and I desired that they might be taken by a messenger by the special train.

I shall be very much obliged to you if you will have the goodness to explain this matter to the Queen, and I beg you to assure Her Majesty how deeply grieved I am that what appears to have been a mistake on my part should have led me to be apparently wanting in due respect to Her Majesty, than which nothing could possibly be further from my intention or thoughts. Yours sincerely,

Palmerston.

Queen Victoria to Lord John Russell.

Windsor Castle, *28th December 1851.*

The Queen thinks the moment of the change in the person of Secretary of State for Foreign Affairs to afford a fit opportunity to have the principles upon which our Foreign Affairs have been conducted since the beginning of 1848 reconsidered by Lord John Russell and his Cabinet.

The Queen was fully aware that the storm raging at the time on the Continent rendered it impossible for any statesman to foresee with clearness and precision what development and direction its elements would take, and she consequently quite agreed that the line of policy to be followed, as the most conducive to the interests of England, could then only be generally conceived and vaguely expressed.

But although the Queen is still convinced that the general principles laid down by Lord John at that time for the conduct of our Foreign Policy were in themselves right, she has in the progress of the last three years become painfully convinced that the manner in which they have been *practically applied* has worked out very different results from those which the correctness of the principles themselves had led her to expect. For when the revolutionary movements on the Continent had laid prostrate almost all its Governments, and England alone displayed that order, vigour, and prosperity which it owes to a stable, free, and good Government, the Queen, instead of earning the natural good results of such a glorious position, viz. consideration, goodwill, confidence, and influence abroad, obtained the very reverse, and had the grief to see her Government and herself treated on many occasions with neglect, aversion, distrust, and even contumely.

Frequently, when our Foreign Policy was called in question, it has been said by Lord John and his colleagues that the principles on which it was conducted were the right ones, and having been approved of by them, received their support, and that it was only the *personal manner* of Lord Palmerston in conducting the affairs which could be blamed in tracing the causes which led to the disastrous results the Queen complains of.

The Queen is certainly not disposed to defend the personal manner in which Lord Palmerston has conducted Foreign Affairs, but she cannot admit that the errors he committed were merely *faults in form and method*, that they were no more than acts of "inconsideration, indiscretion, or bad taste." The Queen considers that she has also to complain of what appeared to her deviations from the principles laid down by the Cabinet for his conduct, nay, she sees distinctly in their practical application a *personal and arbitrary perversion* of the very nature and essence of those principles. She has only to refer here to Italy, Spain, Greece, Holstein, France, etc., etc., which afford ample illustrations of this charge.

It was one thing for Lord Palmerston to have attempted such substantial deviations; it will be another for the Cabinet to consider whether they had not the power to check him in these attempts.

The Queen, however, considering times to have now changed, thinks that there is no reason why we should any longer confine ourselves to the mere assertion of abstract principles, such as "non-intervention in the internal affairs of other countries," "moral support to liberal institutions," "protection to British subjects," etc., etc. The moving powers which were put in operation by the French Revolution of 1848, and the events consequent on it, are no longer so obscure; they have assumed distinct and tangible forms in almost all the countries affected by them (in France, in Italy, Germany, etc.), and upon the state of things now existing, and the experience gained, the Queen would hope that our Foreign Policy may be *more specifically defined*,

367

and that it may be considered how the general principles are to be practically adapted to our peculiar relations with each Continental State.

The Queen wishes therefore that a regular programme embracing these different relations should be submitted to her, and would suggest whether it would not be the best mode if Lord John were to ask Lord Granville to prepare such a paper and to lay it before her after having revised it.

This would then serve as a safe guide for Lord Granville, and enable the Queen as well as the Cabinet to see that the Policy, as in future to be conducted, will be in conformity with the principles laid down and approved.

Lord John Russell to Queen Victoria.

Pembroke Lodge, *29th December 1851.*

Lord John Russell presents his humble duty to your Majesty; he has received your Majesty's communication of yesterday, and will transmit it to Lord Granville.

It is to be observed, however, that the traditionary policy of this country is not to bind the Crown and country by engagements, unless upon special cause shown, arising out of the circumstances of the day.

For instance, the Treaty of Quadruple Alliance between England, France, Spain, and Portugal was contrary to the general principle of non-intervention; so was the interference in Portugal in 1847, but were both justified by circumstances.

Thus it is very difficult to lay down any principles from which deviations may not frequently be made.

The grand rule of doing to others as we wish that they should do unto us is more applicable than any system of political science. The honour of England does not consist in defending every English officer or English subject, right or wrong, but in taking care that she does not infringe the rules of justice, and that they are not infringed against her.[42]

Queen Victoria to the King of the Belgians.

Windsor Castle, *30th December 1851.*

My dearest Uncle,—Most warmly do I thank you for your kind and affectionate and interesting letter of the 26th, which I received on Sunday. All that you say about Lord Palmerston is but too true.... He *brouilléd* us and the country with every one; and his very first act precipitated the unfortunate Spanish marriages which was *le commence-ment de la fin*. It is too grievous to think how much misery and mischief might have been avoided. However, now he has done with the Foreign Office for ever, and "the veteran statesman," as the news-papers, to our great amusement and I am sure to *his* infinite annoyance, call him, must rest upon his laurels.... I fear much lest they should be imprudent at Claremont; the poor Queen hinted to Mamma that she hoped you would not become a friend to the President; no doubt you can have no sympathies for him, but *just because* you are related to the poor Orleanses, you feel that you must be doubly cau-tious to do nothing which could provoke the enmity of Louis Napoleon. I fear that poor Joinville *had* some *mad* idea of going to France, which, fortunately, his illness prevented. It would have been the height of folly. Their only safe policy is to remain entirely passive *et de se faire oublier*, which was Nemours' expression to me two years ago; nothing could be wiser or more prudent than he was then—but I don't think they were wise since. *La Candidature* of Joinville was in every way unwise, and led Louis Napoleon to take so desperate a course. Nemours told me also *last* year that they were not at all against a *fusion*, but that they could not *disposer de la France*, unless called upon to do so by the nation. I wish you would caution them to be very circumspect and silent—for all the mistakes made by others is in *their* favour; in fact, no good for them could come till Paris is old enough to be his own master—unless indeed they all returned under Henri V., but a Regency for Paris would be an impossibility....

We spent a very happy Christmas, and now wish you a very happy New Year—for many succeeding years. Also to the children, who I hope were pleased with the prints, etc.

We have got young Prince Nicholas of Nassau here, a pretty, clever boy of nineteen, with a good deal of knowledge, and a great wish to learn and hear, which is a rare thing for the young Princes, of our day in particular. I must stop now, as I fear I have already let my pen run on for too long, and must beg to be excused for this volumi-nous letter.

With Albert's love ever your devoted Niece,

Victoria R.

Queen Victoria to Lord John Russell.

Windsor Castle, *30th December 1851.*

The Queen has received Lord John Russell's letters of yesterday. She quite agrees with him and his colleagues in thinking it of importance to strengthen the Government, and she is pleased with his proposal to communicate with the Duke of Newcastle as to what assistance he and his friends can give to the Government.

The Queen expects better results from such a negotiation, with an ostensible head of a Party, than from attempts to detach single individuals from it, which from a sense of honour they always felt scruples in agreeing to.

Queen Victoria to Lord John Russell.

Windsor Castle, *31st December 1851.*

The Queen sees in the papers that there is to be a *Te Deum* at Paris on the 2nd for the success of the *coup d'état*, and that the Corps Diplomatique is to be present. She hopes that Lord Normanby will be told not to attend. Besides the impropriety of his taking part in such a ceremony, his doing so would entirely destroy the position of Lord John Russell opposite Lord Palmerston, who might with justice say that he merely expressed his personal approval of the *coup d'état* before, but since, the Queen's Ambassador had been ordered publicly to thank God for its success.

ENDNOTES:

[1]:Member of Parliament for Rye 1881-1832, and Ripon 1835-1843, afterwards a member of the Judicial Committee of the Privy Council: he became a Peer (Lord Kingsdown) in 1858, having declined a peerage on the present and other occasions.

[2]:Dr Lushington was judge of the Admiralty Court: he had been counsel for, and an executor of, Queen Caroline. He declined the offer now suggested, and the subsequent debates on the Wensleydale Peerage show that the proposed grant would have been ineffectual for its purpose.

[3]:Lord Palmerston had altered his mind as to certain proposed diplomatic changes, and suggested the appointment of Sir Hamilton Seymour to Berlin, Lord Bloomfield to Lisbon, Lord Cowley to Petersburg, Mr Jerningham, Sir Henry Ellis, or Sir Richard Pakenham to Frankfort.

[4]:On agricultural distress; the Motion was lost by fourteen only in a large House.

[5]:For equalising the County and the Borough franchise.

[6]:*Sic.*

[7]:With a view of uniting with the Peelites, Lord John drew up a Memorandum, printed in Walpole's *Lord John Russell*, vol. ii. chap, xxii., with the
following points:

A Cabinet of not more than eleven Members.

The present commercial policy to be maintained.

The financial measures of the year to be open to revision.

The Ecclesiastical Titles Bill to be persevered in so far as the Preamble and
the first clause, but the remaining clauses to be abandoned.

A Reform Bill for the extension of the Franchise.

A Commission of Enquiry into corrupt practices at elections in cities and
boroughs.

[8]:Published in Walpole's *Lord John Russell*, vol. ii. chap. xxii.

[9]:The Prince thereupon, at the Queen's request, communicated with Lord John
Russell, and after recounting to him the various successive failures to form
a Government, wrote that the Queen must "pause before she again entrusts
the commission of forming an Administration to anybody, till she has been
able to see the result of to-morrow evening's Debate." He added, "Do you
see any Constitutional objection to this course?"

[10]:See *ante*, p. 282 note 45.

[11]:*See* page 329.

[12]:The Queen's judgment was amply confirmed by the events of 1852. See
post, p. 404 note 50.

[13]:The Great Exhibition in Hyde Park was opened with brilliant ceremony on
the 1st of May.

[14]:Francis Joseph, who became Emperor in December 1848.

[15]:The Prince presided at the meeting commemorative of the one hundred and
fifty years' existence of the Society for the Propagation of the Gospel. His
speech was warmly praised by the Premier.

[16]:A ball in commemoration of the Exhibition took place at the Guildhall on
the 9th of July.

[17]:The Queen of Spain had expressed a desire through Lord Howden to receive the Order of the Garter.

[18]:Substance of the note to Lord John Russell, written down from recollection.

[19]:Lord Palmerston wished to receive Kossuth at the Foreign Office. In the
correspondence here referred to, which will be found in Russell's *Life*, the
Premier "positively requested" Lord Palmerston to decline to receive Kossuth. The rejoinder, written while the messenger waited, was: "There are
limits to all things. I do not choose to be dictated to as to who I may or may
not receive in my own house.... I shall use my own discretion.... You will,
of course, use yours as to the composition of your Government."

[20]:Draft sent to Lord John Russell.

[21]:The letter is printed in Lord Palmerston's *Life*. The Premier stated that the
question, being one of grave public importance, must be decided by argu-

ment, not passion, and would be considered by the Cabinet on the following Monday. *See* Walpole's *Russell*, chap. xxii.

[22]:The Cabinet met, and having listened to the statement of the Premier, which is printed in his *Life*, unanimously supported him. Lord Palmerston accordingly gave way for the time being. Lord John informed the Queen of the result.

[23]:Before ten days had elapsed, Lord Palmerston had resumed his high-handed methods.

[24]:After Kossuth's departure, addresses of thanks to Lord Palmerston, for his courteous attentions to Kossuth, were voted by ultra-Radical meetings in Finsbury and Islington, and he allowed a deputation to present the addresses to him at the Foreign Office, the Emperors of Austria and Russia being stigmatised therein as "odious and detestable assassins" and "merciless tyrants and despots." Palmerston, who expressed himself as "extremely flattered and highly gratified" by the references to himself, did not in terms reprehend the language used of the two Sovereigns, and added, in a phrase immortalised by Leech's cartoon, that "a good deal of judicious bottle-holding was obliged to be brought into play."

[25]:On the 4th of December the matter came before the Cabinet. No formal resolution was adopted, but regret was expressed at Palmerston's want of caution in not ascertaining in advance the tenor of the addresses, and in admitting unreliable reporters.

[26]:King Ernest died on the 18th of November, aged eighty, and was succeeded by his son, King George V., who reigned till 1866, and died in 1878.

[27]:Princess Mary of Saxe-Altenburg (1818-1907), wife of King George V. of Hanover.

[28]:On the 2nd of December, Louis Napoleon seized the Government of France, arrested his chief opponents, put an end to the National Assembly and Council of State, and declared Paris in a state of siege.

[29]:On the 3rd the tidings of the *coup d'état* reached London. Count Walewski announced it to Lord Palmerston, who expressed his approval of it, and wrote to Lord Normanby the letter printed in his *Life*, disavowing surprise that the President had struck the blow when he did, "for it is now well known here that the Duchess of Orleans was preparing to be called to Paris this week with her younger son to commence a new period of Orleans dynasty."

[30]:Lord Normanby, having applied for instructions as to his future conduct, was desired to make no change in his relations with the French Government, and to abstain from even the appearance of interference in her internal affairs. Having made a communication to this effect to M. Turgot, the latter replied that M. Walewski had notified to him that Lord Palmerston had already expressed to him his "entire approbation of the act of the President," and his "conviction that he could not have acted otherwise."

[31]:On the 6th, Lord Palmerston wrote to Lord Normanby the strange letter printed by Mr Evelyn Ashley in the *Life*, censuring Lord Normanby's sup-

posed hostility to the French President; Lord Normanby in reply defended his attitude, and asked for an explicit statement as to the Foreign Secretary's approval or otherwise of the conduct and policy of the President.

[32]:Mr Borthwick, of the *Morning Post*, had so stated to Lord Palmerston on the authority of General de Rumigny; seven years later Palmerston wrote the Memorandum on the subject printed in his *Life*.

[33]:Submitted to the Queen by Colonel Phipps.

[34]:The tone of Lord Palmerston's private letters to Lord Normanby at this time is best illustrated by the following extract:—

"Your despatches since the event of Tuesday have been all hostile to Louis Napoleon, with very little information as to events. One of them consisted of a dissertation about Kossuth, which would have made a good article in the *Times* a fortnight ago: and another dwells chiefly on a looking-glass broken in a Club-house; and you are pathetic about a piece of broken plaster brought down from a ceiling by musket-shots during the street fights. Now we know that the Diplomatic Agents of Austria and Russia called on the President immediately after his measure on Tuesday morning, and have been profuse in their expressions of approval of his conduct."

[35]:Lady Normanby wrote later:—

"I told you yesterday the President had no faith in him (Palmerston). The Treaty signed with Buenos Ayres, the Greek business, and the reception of Kossuth had long destroyed his confidence in Palmerston, and I believe he hates him and sees through his present adulations...."

[36]:On the 15th, Lord Normanby wrote to Lord Palmerston that he must now assume M. Walewski's report to be correct, and observed that if the Foreign Secretary held one language in Downing Street and prescribed another course to the British Ambassador, the latter must be awkwardly circumstanced. Lord Palmerston (in a letter not shown to the Queen or the Cabinet) replied that he had said nothing inconsistent with his instructions to Lord Normanby, that the President's action was for the French nation to judge of, but that in his view that action made for the maintenance of social order in France.

[37]:The letters are given in full in Ashley's *Life of Lord Palmerston*, vol. i. chap. vii., were Lord Palmerston's explanation of the 16th, in answer to the Premier's letter of the 14th, will also be found.

[38]:On the same day the Prince wrote to the Premier that the Queen was much relieved. She had contemplated dismissing Lord Palmerston herself, but naturally shrank from using the power of the Crown, as her action would have been criticised without the possibility of making a public defence; in his view the Cabinet was rather strengthened than otherwise by Palmerston's departure, and public sympathy would not be with him. The rest of the letter is published in *The Life of the Prince Consort*.

[39]:Lord Clarendon, in answer to Lord John Russell, expressed great reluctance to undertake the charge of the Foreign Office, on the ground that Palm-

erston, always suspicions of him, would insist that he had deliberately undermined his position: while Lord Granville would be popular with the Court and country.

[40]:In this letter, Lord Palmerston denied the "charge of violations of prudence and decorum," adding, "I have to observe that that charge is refuted by the offer which you made of the Lord-Lieutenancy of Ireland, because I apprehend that to be an office for the due performance of the duties of which prudence and decorum cannot well be dispensed with."

[41]:There is a fuller account given of Lord Palmerston's version of the whole affair in a letter to his brother, printed in Ashley's *Life of Lord Palmerston*, vol. i. p. 315.

[42]:A summary of Lord Granville's Memorandum in reply (which was couched in very general terms) will be found in Lord Fitzmaurice's *Life of Earl Granville*, vol. ii. p. 49.

INTRODUCTORY NOTE
TO CHAPTER XXI

Early in 1852, the Whig Government, impaired in public credit by the removal of Lord Palmerston, attempted once more a coalition with the Peelites, office being offered to Sir James Graham; the overtures failed, and soon, after the meeting of Parliament, the ex-Foreign Secretary, whose version of the cause of his dismissal failed to satisfy the House of Commons, succeeded in defeating the Government on their Militia Bill, affairs in France having caused anxiety as to the national defences. The Government Bill was for the creation of a local Militia, Lord Palmerston preferring the consolidation of the regular Militia. A Ministry was formed by Lord Derby (formerly Lord Stanley) from the Protectionist Party, but no definite statement could be elicited as to their intention, or the reverse, to re-impose a duty on foreign corn. Mr Disraeli, who became Chancellor of the Exchequer, and was the mainspring of the Government policy, showed great dexterity in his management of the House of Commons without a majority, and carried a Militia Bill in the teeth of Lord John Russell; but a plan of partial redistribution failed. The elections held in the summer did not materially improve the Ministerial position, and, on the meeting of Parliament in the autumn, the Fiscal Question had to be squarely faced. After much wrangling, Protection was finally abandoned, and the Government saved for the moment, but on their House-tax proposals they were defeated, after an impassioned debate, by a coalition of Whigs, Peelites, and Radicals, from whom Lord Lansdowne and Lord Aberdeen (and finally the latter alone) were called upon to construct a strong representative Government. The Duke of Wellington had died in September, and his funeral was the signal for an outburst of national feeling. During the year the Houses of Parliament designed by Sir Charles Barry, though not absolutely completed, were formally opened by the Queen; the new House of Lords had already been in use.

In France, the first result of the *coup d'état* was Louis Bonaparte's election as President for ten years by an immense majority; late in the year he assumed the Imperial title as Napoleon III., and the Empire was formally recognised by the majority of the Powers; the Emperor designed to add to his prestige by contracting a matrimonial alliance with Princess Adelaide of Hohenlohe. In the East of Europe a dispute had commenced between France and Russia about the Holy Places in Palestine. Simultaneously with the death of the Duke of Wellington, the era of European peace was destined to come to an end, and Nicholas, encouraged by the advent to power of Aberdeen (whom he had met in 1844, and with whom he had frankly discussed European politics), was hoping for the consummation of his scheme for the partition of Turkey.

To Great Britain the year was a memorable one, in consequence of the granting of a Constitution to New Zealand.

CHAPTER XXI

1852

Queen Victoria to the King of Denmark.

Windsor Castle, *4th January 1852*.

Sir, my Brother,—I received the letter which your Majesty addressed to me on the 24th of August last, and in which, after referring to the necessity for establishing some definite arrangement with regard to the eventual succession to the Crown of Denmark, your Majesty is pleased to acquaint me that, in your opinion, such an arrangement might advantageously be made in favour of your Majesty's cousin, His Highness the Prince Christian of Glücksburg,[1] and the issue of his marriage with the Princess Louisa of Hesse, in favour of whom the nearer claimants have renounced their rights and titles.

I trust I need not assure your Majesty of the sincere friendship which I entertain for you, and of the deep interest which I feel in the welfare of the Danish Monarchy. It was in accordance with those sentiments that I accepted the office of mediator between your Majesty and the States of the German Confederation, and it afforded me the sincerest pleasure to have been thus instrumental in re-establishing the relations of peace between your Majesty and those States.

With regard to the question of the eventual succession to both the Danish and Ducal Crowns, I have to state to your Majesty that although I declined to take any part in the settlement of that combination, it will be a source of great satisfaction to me to learn that an arrangement has been definitely determined upon equally satisfactory to your Majesty and to the Germanic Confederation; and whenever it shall have been notified to me that such an arrangement has been arrived at, I shall then be ready, in accordance with what was stated in the Protocol of the 2nd of August 1850, to consider, in concert with my Allies, the expediency of giving the sanction of an

European acknowledgment to the arrangement which may thus have been made.

I avail myself with great pleasure of this opportunity to renew to your Majesty the expression of the invariable attachment and high esteem with which I am, Sir, my Brother, your Majesty's good Sister,

Victoria R.

Queen Victoria to Lord John Russell.

Windsor Castle, *15th January 1852.*

The Queen has received Lord John Russell's letter last night, and wishes now shortly to repeat what she desired through the Prince, Sir Charles Wood to explain to Lord John.[2]

The Queen hopes that the Cabinet will fully consider what their object is before the proposed negotiation with Sir James Graham be opened.

Is it to strengthen their *case* in Parliament by proving that no means have been left untried to strengthen the Government? or really to effect a junction with the Peelites?

If the first is aimed at, the Cabinet will hardly reap any of the desired advantages from the negotiation, for, shrewd as Sir James Graham is, he will immediately see that the negotiation has been begun without a desire that it should succeed, and this will soon become generally known.

If the latter, the Queen must observe that there are two kinds of junctions—one, *a fusion* of Parties; the other, *the absorption* of one Party by the other. For a *fusion*, the Queen thinks the Peelites to be quite ready; then, however, they must be treated as a political Party, and no *exclusion* should be pronounced against particular members of it, nor should it be insisted upon that the new Government and Party is still emphatically the *Whig* party.

An *absorption* of the most liberal talents amongst the Peelites into the Whig Government, the Queen considers unlikely to succeed, and she can fully understand that reasons of honour and public and private engagement must make it difficult to members of a political Party to go over to another in order to receive office.

Having stated thus much, the Queen gives Lord John full permission to negotiate with Sir James Graham.

Queen Victoria to the King of the Belgians.

Windsor Castle, *20th January 1852.*

My dearest Uncle,—Your kind letter of the 16th I received on the 17th, with the newspaper, for which I return my best thanks. The papers which Stockmar communicated to us are most interesting, and do the writer the greatest credit. Watchful we certainly shall and must be. We shall try and keep on the best of terms with the President, who is extremely sensitive and susceptible, but for whom, I must say, I have never had any *personal* hostility; on the contrary, I thought that during 1849 and 1850 we owed him all a good deal, as he certainly raised the French Government *de la boue.* But I grieve over the tyranny and oppression practised since the *coup d'état,* and it makes everything very uncertain, for though I believe it in every way his wish and his policy not to go to war, still, *il peut y être entraîné.*

Your position is a peculiarly delicate one, but still, as I again repeat, I think there is no reason to be alarmed; particularly, I would *never* show it.

The poor Nemours were here from Saturday till yesterday evening with their dear nice boys, and I think it always does them good. They feel again as if they were in their own position, and they are diverted from the melancholy reality and the great sameness of their existence at Claremont. I found him very quiet and really *not* bitter, and disposed to be very prudent,—but seriously alarmed at the possibility of losing their property, which would be *too* dreadful and monstrous. I fear that the candidature and poor Hélène's imprudence in talking are the cause of this cruel persecution. The poor Orleans have really (and you should write them that) no *truer* and more faithful friends than we are—and it is for this reason that I urge and entreat them to be entirely passive; for *their day* will come, I feel convinced!

Now good-bye, my dearest, kindest Uncle. Ever your truly devoted Niece,

Victoria R.

Queen Victoria to Lord John Russell.

Windsor Castle, *27th January 1852.*

The Queen has received Lord John Russell's letter of yesterday with the draft of Bills, and likewise that of to-day enclosing a Memorandum on the probable effects of the proposed Measure.[3] She has perused these papers with great attention, but feels that any opinion upon the future results of the Measure must rest on surmises; she has that confidence, however, in Lord John's experience and judgment in these matters, and so strong a conviction that he will have spared no pains in forming as correct an opinion as may be formed on so problematical a matter, that she is prepared to come to the decision of approving the Measure on the strength of Lord John's opinion. She only hopes that the future may bear it out, and that the character of the House of Commons may not be impaired. Should this prove the case, the extension of the privilege of voting for Members will strengthen our Institutions. The Queen is glad that the clause abolishing the necessity for every Member of the Government to vacate his seat upon his appointment[4] should have been maintained. She hopes that the schedules showing which towns are to be added to existing boroughs will be drawn up with the greatest care and impartiality, and will soon be submitted to her. The Queen would be glad if the plan once proposed of giving to the Queen's University in Ireland the vacant seat for Sudbury were still carried out, as she feels sure that not only would it be a great thing for the University and the Colleges, but a most useful and influential Irish Member would be gained for the House.

The Queen takes it for granted that the Bill as approved by her will be stood by in Parliament, and that Lord John will not allow himself to be drawn on to further concessions to Democracy in the course of the debate, and that the introduction of the ballot will be vigorously opposed by the Government.

Queen Victoria to Lord John Russell.

Windsor Castle, *1st February 1852.*

The Queen has received the draft of the Speech. The passage referring to the proposed Reform Measure varies so materially from the one which was first submitted to her that she feels that she ought not to sanction it without having received some explanation of the grounds which have led the Cabinet to recommend it in its altered shape. The Queen will not object to the mode of filling the Offices still vacant which Lord John Russell proposes.

Queen Victoria to the King of the Belgians.

Buckingham Palace, *3rd February 1852.*

My dearest Uncle,—My warmest thanks for your kind little letter of the 30th. Matters are very critical and all Van de Weyer has told us *n'est pas rassurant.* With such an extraordinary man as Louis Napoleon, one can never be for one instant safe. It makes me very melancholy; I love peace and quiet—in fact, I *hate* politics and turmoil, and I grieve to think that a spark may plunge us into the midst of war. Still I think *that* may be avoided. Any attempt on Belgium would be *casus belli for us*; *that* you may rely upon. Invasion I am not afraid of, but the spirit of the people here is very great—they are full of defending themselves—and the spirit of the olden times is in no way quenched.

In two hours' time Parliament will be opened, and to-night the explanations between Lord John and Lord Palmerston will take place. I am *very* curious *how* they will go off. The curiosity and anxiety to hear it is very great.

I never saw Stockmar better, or more active and more sagacious, or more kind. To me he is really like a father—only too partial, I always think.

Albert grows daily fonder and fonder of politics and business, and is so wonderfully *fit* for both—such perspicacity and such *courage*— and I grow daily to dislike them both more and more. We women are not *made* for governing—and if we are good women, we must *dislike* these masculine occupations; but there are times which force one to take *interest* in them *mal gré bon gré*, and *I* do, of course, *intensely.*

I must now conclude, to dress for the opening of Parliament.... Ever your devoted Niece,

Victoria R.

Lord John Russell to Queen Victoria.

Chesham Place, *4th February 1852.*

Lord John Russell presents his humble duty to your Majesty, and has the honour to report that the Address was agreed to last night without a division.

The explanations between Lord Palmerston and himself were made. Lord Palmerston made no case, and was not supported by any

381

considerable party in the House. His approbation of the President's conduct seemed to confound the Liberal Party, and he did not attempt to excuse his delay in answering Lord John Russell's letter of the 14th.[5]

The rest of the debate was desultory and heavy. Mr Disraeli made a long speech for the sake of making a speech. Mr Roebuck was bitter without much effect.

Generally speaking, the appearance of the House was favourable. Sir James Graham says the next fortnight will clear up matters very much.

The tone of the House was decidedly pacific.

Queen Victoria to Lord John Russell.

Windsor Castle, *4th February 1852.*

We have learned with much satisfaction that everything went off so well in the House of Commons last night. Lord John Russell's speech is a most useful one, and he has given a most lucid definition of the constitutional position of the Prime Minister and Foreign Secretary opposite to the Crown. Lord Palmerston's speech is a very weak one, and he in no way makes out a case for himself. This seems to [be] the general impression.

The Houses of Lords and Commons being now almost completed, and the Queen having entered the House of Lords by the Grand Entrance (which is magnificent), the Queen thinks this will be the right moment for bestowing on Mr Barry the knighthood, as a mark of the Queen's approbation of his great work.

The Marquis of Normanby to Colonel Phipps.[6]

St George's Hotel, *5th February 1852.*

My dear Charles,—Yesterday morning I got a note from John Russell, saying that all had gone off so well the night before, and Palmerston had been so flat that he thought it better I should not revive the subject in the other House, as he had said nothing about me which in the least required that I should do so. I yielded, of course, to such an appeal, though there are several points in his speech on which I could have exposed inaccuracies. The fact is, John has never shown any consideration for me in the whole of these affairs; but I do not mean in any way to complain, and am very grateful to him for the very successful way in which he executed his task on Tuesday. Nothing can be more universal than the feeling of the utter discomfiture of Palmerston.[7] I am convinced that what floored him at starting was that letter of the Queen's,[8] because every one felt that such a letter would never have been written unless every point in it could have been proved like a bill of indictment; and then came the question, how could any man, even feeling he deserved it, go on under such a marked want of confidence?...[9]

Aberdeen, whom I saw at Granville's last night, told me that Cardwell had said to him, that often as he had felt indignant at the arrogance of "that man," he really pitied him, so complete was his overthrow. Disraeli said that he had watched him during Johnny's speech, and doubted whether the hanging of the head, etc., was merely acting; but before he had spoken two sentences he saw he was a beaten fox. Many said that the extreme flippancy and insolence of his manner was more remarkable than ever, from their being evidently assumed with difficulty. I have always thought Palmerston very much overrated as a speaker; his great power arose from his not only knowing his subject better than any one else, but being the only man who knew anything about it, and using that exclusive knowledge unscrupulously for the purposes of misrepresentation.

Thiers was at Lady Granville's last night, and was enchanted with the spectacle of the Opening. He said that he had been endeavouring for thirty years to support the cause of Constitutional Monarchy, as the best Government in the world, and there he saw it in perfection, not only in its intrinsic attributes, but in the universal respect and adhesion with which it was received. He said, though he did not understand a word of English, he could have cried at the Queen's voice in reading the Speech. He is very "impressionable," and I am convinced at the time he was quite sincere in his appreciation.

I am vexed at not having been able to say anything publicly about all this, as I believe I could have dispelled many misrepresentations; but it cannot be helped. I have endeavoured throughout not to be selfish, and I may as well keep up that feeling to the last. Ever, etc.

Normanby.

I told John Russell last night I regretted that he had vouched for the intentions of Louis Napoleon. He said he had not done that, but owned that he had said more than he ought. "The fact is, I did not know what to say next. I stopped as one sometimes does, so I said that; I had better have said something else!" Candid and characteristic!

Queen Victoria to Earl Granville.

Windsor Castle, *10th February 1852.*

The Queen returns the enclosed papers. She will not object to the proposed step[10] should Lord Granville and Lord John Russell have reason to expect that the Pope will receive Sir H. Bulwer; should he refuse, it will be doubly awkward. The Queen finds it difficult to give a decided opinion on the subject, as, first, she does not know how far the reception of Sir Henry at Rome will overcome the objections raised to his reception as Resident at Florence. Secondly, as she has never been able to understand what is to be obtained by a mission to Rome, a step liable to much misrepresentation here....

Lord John Russell to the Prince Albert.

Chesham Place, *16th February 1852.*

Sir,—I have seen the Duke of Wellington this morning, and have given him the Depôt plan.

It may be useful if your Royal Highness will see him from time to time in relation to the Army. On the one hand, your Royal Highness's authority may overcome the indisposition to change which he naturally entertains; and on the other, his vast experience may be of great use to your Royal Highness in regard to the future. I have the honour to be, Sir, your Royal Highness's most dutiful Servant,

John Russell.

Sir Francis Baring to Queen Victoria.

Admiralty, *15th February 1852.*

Sir Francis Baring presents his humble duty to your Majesty, and begs to state to your Majesty that despatches have this evening arrived from Commander Bruce in command of the African Squadron. Commander Bruce gives an account of an attack on Lagos[11] which was completely successful. The town of Lagos was captured and in great part burnt. The resistance appears to have been obstinate and directed with much skill. Your Majesty's naval Service behaved with their accustomed gallantry and coolness, but the loss amounted to fourteen killed and sixty-four wounded. Sir Francis Baring will forward to your Majesty copies of the despatches to-morrow, with his humble duty.

F. Baring.

Queen Victoria to Sir Francis Baring.

Buckingham Palace, *16th February 1852.*

The Queen has received both Sir Francis Baring's letters of the 15th. The news of the capture and destruction of the town of Lagos has given us the *greatest* satisfaction, as it will give a most serious blow to the iniquitous traffic in slaves. The Rev. Mr Crowther, whom the Queen saw about two months ago (and whom she believes Sir Francis Baring has also seen), told us that the slave trade on that part of the African coast would be at an end if Lagos, the stronghold of its greatest supporters, was destroyed. The Queen must express to Sir Francis Baring her sense of the services rendered by Commodore Bruce and the Officers under him.

Queen Victoria to the King of the Belgians.

Buckingham Palace, *17th February 1852.*

My dearest Uncle,—Your dear letter of the 13th reached me on Saturday here, where we are since Friday afternoon. I am glad that you are satisfied with Lord Granville's answer. The question shall certainly be borne in mind, and you may rely on our doing whatever can be effected to bring about the desired end. I think Louis Napoleon will find his decrees very difficult to carry out. I am very glad to hear that you quietly are preparing to strengthen yourself against the possibility of any attack from France. This will, I think, put Louis Napoleon on his good behaviour....

The extension of the Suffrage[12] was almost unavoidable, and it was better to do it quietly, and not to wait till there was a cry for it—to which one would have to yield. The deal there is to do, and the importance of everything going on at home and abroad, is unexampled in *my* recollection and *very* trying; Albert becomes really a *terrible* man of business; I think it takes a little off from the gentleness of his character, and makes him so preoccupied. I grieve over all this, as I *cannot* enjoy these things, *much* as I interest myself in *general* European politics; but I am every day more convinced that *we women, if* we *are* to be *good* women, *feminine* and *amiable* and *domestic*, are *not fitted to*

385

reign; at least it is *contre gré* that they drive themselves to the *work* which it entails.

However, this cannot now be helped, and it is the duty of every one to fulfil all that they are called upon to do, in whatever situation they may be!

Mme. van de Weyer thinks your children so grown and improved, and Charlotte as lovely as ever. With Albert's love, ever your devoted Niece,

Victoria R.

Lord John Russell to Queen Victoria.

Chesham Place, *20th February 1852.*

(9.15 p.m.)

Lord John Russell presents his humble duty to your Majesty, and has the honour to report that Lord Palmerston has just carried his Motion for leaving out the word "Local" in the title of the Bill for the Militia.[13]

Lord John Russell then declared that he could no longer take charge of the Bill. Lord Palmerston said he was astonished at the Government for giving up the Bill for so slight a cause.

Lord John Russell then said that he considered the vote as tantamount to a resolution of want of confidence, which remark was loudly cheered on the other side.

Sir Benjamin Hall said he wondered the Government did not resign, on which Lord John again explained that when confidence was withdrawn, the consequence was obvious.

Memorandum by the Prince Albert.

Buckingham Palace, *21st February 1852.*

Lord John Russell came this morning at twelve o'clock to explain that after the vote of yesterday[14] it was impossible for him to go on any longer with the Government. He considered it a vote of censure, and an entirely unprecedented case not to allow a Minister of the Crown even to lay his measure on the Table of the House; that he had expected to the last that the respectable part of the House would see all this, but there seemed to have been a pre-arranged determination between Lord Palmerston and the Protectionists to defeat the Government; that the Peelites also had agreed to vote against them. Sir James Graham and Mr Cardwell had stayed away, but Mr Gladstone and Mr S. Herbert had voted against them, the latter even misrepresenting what Lord John had said. No Government could stand against incessant motions of censure upon every imaginable department of the Executive Government. The Prime Minister would either have to take the management of all the departments into his own hands, and to be prepared to defend every item, for which he (Lord John) did not feel the moral and physical power, or he must succumb on those different points which the Opposition with divided labour could single out. Lord Palmerston's conduct was the more reprehensible as he had asked him the day before about his objections to the Bill, and had (he thought) satisfied him that the four points upon which he had insisted were provided for in the Bill.

He thought he could not (in answer to the Queen's enquiry) dissolve Parliament, and that Lord Palmerston had no Party. But he supposed Lord Derby was prepared to form a Protection Government. This Government would pass the estimates and the Mutiny Bill, and would then have to proceed to a Dissolution. Lord John had merely seen Lord Lansdowne, who had approved of the course he meant to pursue, though afraid of the imputation that the Government had run away from the Caffre debate. He had summoned the Cabinet, and would report their resolution. Speaking of Lord Palmerston, Lord John said he had heard that Lord Palmerston had said that there was one thing between them which he could not forgive, and that was his reading the Queen's Minute to the House of Commons.

At a quarter past four Lord John came back from the Cabinet, and formally tendered the resignations of himself and colleagues. The Cabinet had been unanimous that there was no other course to pursue, and that it would not be advisable to make use of the Queen's permission to advise a Dissolution. Lord Granville had ascertained through Dr Quin from Lord Lyndhurst that Lord Derby was prepared with an Administration, having obtained Mr Thomas Baring's consent to act as Leader of the House of Commons.

Sir Stratford Canning at Constantinople was supposed to be intended for the Foreign Office. Lord Lyndhurst said, though the materials were there, they were very bad ones, and it was a question whether they would stand long. He himself would keep out of place.

We advised Lord John to keep his Party well under discipline in Opposition, so that whilst there it did not commit errors which would become new difficulties for the future Government. He seemed disinclined for great exertions after the fatigues he had undergone these last years. He said he thought he would not go on with the Reform Bill out of office, as that was a measure which ought to be carried by a Government. If he had again to propose it, he would very likely alter it a little, reverting to his original plan of taking away one Member of the two returned by small boroughs, and giving their seats to some large towns, counties, and corporations like the Universities, etc.

Lord John defers taking his formal leave till a new Administration is formed.

Albert.

Queen Victoria to the Earl of Derby.

Buckingham Palace, *21st February 1852.*

The Queen would wish to see Lord Derby at half-past two tomorrow should he be in Town; if not, on Monday at twelve o'clock.

Memorandum by the Prince Albert.

Buckingham Palace, *22nd February 1852.*

... Lord Derby said that he could not command a majority in the House of Lords, that he was in a decided minority in the House of Commons, and thought that in the critical circumstances in which the country was placed both at home and abroad, he ought not to ask for a Dissolution. He must then try to strengthen himself particularly in the House of Commons by any means he could. There was one person whom he could not venture to propose for the Foreign Office on account of what had lately passed, and what he might be allowed to call the "well-known personal feelings of the Queen"; but Lord Palmerston was one of the ablest debaters, and might well be offered the post of Chancellor of the Exchequer.

The Queen ... would not, by refusing her consent, throw additional difficulties in Lord Derby's way; she warned him, however, of the dangerous qualities of [Lord Palmerston].

Lord Derby rejoined that he knew them, and thought them pernicious for the conduct of the Foreign Affairs, but at the Exchequer they would have less play; he himself would undertake to control him. His greatest indiscretion—that in the Kossuth affair—must have been with a view to form a Party; that if left excluded from office, he would become more dangerous, and might in fact force himself back at the head of a Party with a claim to the Foreign Office, whilst if he had ever accepted another Office, his pretensions might be considered as waived; he (Lord Derby) did not know in the least whether Lord Palmerston would accept, but in case he did not, the offer would propitiate him, and render the Government in the House of Commons more possible, as it would have anyhow all the talent of the late Government, Peelites and Radicals, to withstand.

To my question whether Lord Derby fancied he would remain Prime Minister any length of time, when once Lord Palmerston had got the lead of the House of Commons, he replied he was not afraid of him; he felt sure he could control him, although he would not have been able to admit him to the Foreign Office on account of the very strong strictures he had passed upon his Foreign Policy at different times—even if the Queen had allowed it.

The Earl of Derby to Queen Victoria.

St James's Square, *22nd February 1852.*

(*Half-past eight.*)

Lord Derby, with his humble duty, deems it incumbent upon him to submit to your Majesty without delay that having had an interview this evening with Lord Palmerston, the latter has, although in the most friendly terms, declined accepting the Office, upon the ground of difference of opinion, not on the principle, but on the expediency of the imposition of any duty, under any circumstances, upon foreign corn. This was a point which Lord Derby was willing to have left undecided until the result of a General Election should be known.

Although this refusal may add materially to Lord Derby's difficulties, he cannot regret that the offer has been made, as the proposal must have tended to diminish any feelings of hostility which might have been productive of future embarrassment to your Majesty's service, to whatever hands it may be entrusted....

The above is humbly submitted by your Majesty's most dutiful Servant and Subject,

Derby.

Memorandum by the Prince Albert.

Buckingham Palace, *23rd February 1852.*

Lord Derby reported progress at half-past two, and submitted a list of the principal Officers of the Government which follows, and which the Queen approved.

The Queen allowed Lord Lyndhurst (who has declined office—has been Lord Chancellor three times, and now entered upon his eightieth year) to be offered an Earldom—which he very much desired for the position of his daughters, having no son.

After he had kissed hands upon his entering upon his office, Lord Derby had a further conversation with me on Household appointments. I told him he must now, as Prime Minister, consider himself to a certain degree in the position of the Confessor; that formerly the Lord Chancellor was Keeper of the King's Conscience, the office might be considered to have descended on the Prime Minister. The Queen must then be able to confer with him on personal matters, or I, on her behalf, with the most entire confidence, and that she must be sure that nothing was divulged which passed between them on these matters, and he might repose the same confidence in us. As to the formation of the Household, the Queen made two conditions, viz. that the persons to compose her Court should not be on the verge of bankruptcy, and that their moral character should bear investigation. On the Queen's accession Lord Melbourne had been very careless in his appointments, and great harm had resulted to the Court therefrom. Since her marriage I had insisted upon a closer line being drawn, and though Lord Melbourne had declared "that that damned morality would undo us all," we had found great advantage in it and were determined to adhere to it....

Albert.

Queen Victoria to the Duchess of Sutherland.

Buckingham Palace, *23rd February 1852.*

My dearest Duchess,—I cannot say *how deeply* grieved I am to think that the event which has just occurred, and which Lord Derby's acceptance of office has to-day confirmed, will entail your leaving, for a time, my service. It has been *ever* a real pleasure to me to have you with me; my affection and esteem for you, my dearest Duchess, are great, and we *both* know what a kind and true friend we have in you.

I think that I may rely on your returning to me on a future occasion whenever that may be, and that I shall frequently have the pleasure of seeing you, even when you are no longer attached to my person.

I shall hope to see you soon. The Levée remains fixed for Thursday, and the transfer of the Officers of the new Government does not take place till Friday.

With the Prince's kindest remembrance, and ours to the Duke and Constance. Believe me always, yours affectionately,

Victoria R.

Queen Victoria to the King of the Belgians.

Buckingham Palace, *24th February 1852.*

Dearest Uncle,—Great and not *very* pleasant events have happened since I wrote last to you. I know that Van de Weyer has informed you of everything, of the really (till the last day) unexpected defeat, and of Lord Derby's assumption of office, with a very sorry Cabinet. I believe, however, that it is quite necessary they should have a trial, and then have done with it. Provided the country remains quiet, and they are prudent in their Foreign Policy, I shall take the trial as patiently as I can....

Alas! your confidence in our excellent Lord Granville is no longer of any avail, though I hope ere long he will be at the Foreign Office again,[15] and I cannot say that his successor,[16] who has never been in office (as indeed is the case with almost all the new Ministers), inspires me with confidence. I see that Louis Napoleon has again seized one of the adherents, or rathermore one of the men of business, of the poor Orleans....

There are some terrible stories from Madrid of people having told the poor Queen that the King had arranged this attack on her person, and that she was anxious to abdicate.[17] If you should hear anything of this kind, be kind enough to tell me of it. With Albert's love (he is well fagged with business), ever your devoted Niece,

Victoria R.

Queen Victoria to the Earl of Derby.

Buckingham Palace, *24th February 1852.*

The Queen thinks that it would be of the highest importance that not only Lord Malmesbury (as is always usual) should receive the necessary information from Lord Granville, but that Lord Derby should see him and hear from him the state of all the critical questions now pending on Foreign Affairs. Lord Granville has made himself master in a very short time of all the very intricate subjects with which his Office has to deal, and she must here bear testimony to the extreme discretion, good sense, and calmness with which he has conducted the very responsible and difficult post of Foreign Secretary.

The Earl of Derby to the Prince Albert.

St James's Square, *25th February 1852.* (*5* p.m.)

Sir,—I have delayed longer than I could have wished acknowledging the letter which I had the honour to receive from your Royal Highness last night, in hopes that by this time I should have been enabled to solve the difficulties connected with the Household Appointments; but I regret to say they are rather increased than otherwise. I will not trouble your Royal Highness now with any details; but if I might be honoured with an audience at any hour after the Levée tomorrow, I shall perhaps be able to make a more satisfactory report, and at all events to explain the state of affairs more fully.

In the meantime, it may save Her Majesty some trouble if I request that your Royal Highness will have the goodness to lay before Her Majesty the enclosed list of Appointments which, subject to Her Majesty's approval, I have arranged in the course of this day. The Admiralty List found its way most improperly into some of the morning papers before I was even aware that the Duke of Northumberland had finally obtained the assent of the Officers whom he had selected.

As it is possible that the Queen may not be acquainted with the name of Colonel Dunne, I have the honour of enclosing a letter respecting him which I have received from Lord Fitzroy Somerset, since I had intimated to him my intention of submitting his name to Her Majesty, and which is highly satisfactory.

I must beg your Royal Highness to offer to the Queen my most humble and grateful acknowledgment of the kindness which Her Majesty has evinced in endeavouring to facilitate the progress of the Household arrangements.

I have the honour to be, Sir, Your Royal Highness's most obedient Servant,

Derby.

Memorandum by Queen Victoria.[18]

Thursday, *26th February 1852.*

Lord Derby came to Albert at half-past three, and Albert called me in at a little after four....

Lord Derby told us he meant to proceed as speedily as possible with the defences of the country, and that his plan for the Militia entirely coincided with Albert's plan (viz. he (Albert) wrote on the subject to the Duke of Wellington, who *did not* like it),[19] and meant to try and avoid all the objections. On his observing that no one had entirely understood the Government Bill, I said that the Government had not even been allowed to bring it in, which was a most unfair proceeding; upon which Lord Derby reiterated his professions of this being no preconcerted plan of his Party's, but that it was "symptomatic"; he, however, was obliged to own that it was rather hard and not quite fair on the late Government.

I then explained to him the arrangement respecting the drafts from the Foreign Office going first to him before they came to me, and wished this should be continued, which he promised should be done, as well as that all important Colonial despatches should be sent to me. Touched upon the various critical questions on the Continent.... Lord Derby said that all Louis Napoleon's views were contained in his book *Idées Napoléoniennes* written in '39, for that he was more a man of "*Idées fixes*" than any one; and in this book he spoke of gaining territory by *diplomacy* and not by war. Lord Derby gave us a note from Louis Napoleon to Lord Malmesbury, congratulating him on his appointment, professing the most friendly and pacific intentions, and hoping the Cowleys would (as they do) remain at Paris.

Victoria R.

Memorandum by the Prince Albert.

Buckingham Palace, *27th February 1852.*

To-day the formal change of Government took place. The old Ministers who had Seals to give up assembled at half-past eleven, and had their Audiences in the following order:

Sir George Grey was very much overcome; promised at our request to do what he could to keep his friends moderate and united. Spoke well of his successor, Mr Walpole, and assured the Queen that he left the country in a most quiet and contented state.

Lord Grey was sorry that the resignation had taken place before the Caffre Debate, in which he had hoped to make a triumphant defence; he was sure it must have come to this from the way in which Lord John had managed matters. He had never had his measures thoroughly considered when he brought them forward. He (Lord Grey) had had to remonstrate very strongly about this Militia Bill, which had not even been laid, printed, before the Cabinet, and had not been discussed at all; he himself had objected to the greater part of it, and had always expected to have an opportunity of making his opinion heard; instead of spending Christmas at Woburn he ought to have digested his measures; this was not fair to his colleagues, and he could never have the same confidence in Lord John as before. We urged him to forget what had passed and to do the best for the future; that it was important the Party should be kept together and should unite if possible with the Peelites, so that the Queen might hope to get a strong Government. Lord Grey thought there was little chance of this. The next Government could never be as moderate again as this had been; this he had always dreaded, and was the reason why he lamented that Lord John had failed in his negotiation with the Peelites this winter, upon Lord Palmerston's dismissal; but the fact was Lord John had never wished it to succeed, and it had been unfair that he had not stated to them (the Peelites) that all his colleagues were ready to give up their places.

Lord Granville had seen Lord Malmesbury several times, who appeared to him to take pains about informing himself on the state of Foreign Affairs, but seemed inclined to be ambitious of acquiring the merit of being exclusively *English* in his policy; this was quite right, but might be carried too far; however, Lord Malmesbury was cautious and moderate.

The Chancellor of the Exchequer (*Sir Charles Wood*) was not surprised at the fate of the Government, although they had not expected to be defeated on the Militia Bill; in fact, a division had hardly been looked for, as Lord John had talked the day before with Lord Palmerston, and satisfied him that all his objections should be provided against in the Bill. He thought it was better, however, that the Caffre Debate had not been waited for, which must have been a personal and very acrimonious one. He thought Lord Grey had not been very discreet in his language to the Queen on Lord John. Sir J. Graham had been in a difficulty with his own Party, and therefore had not wished to encourage Lord John's negotiation with the Peelites. He promised that, for his part, he would do all he could to keep his Party from doing anything violent, but that he was afraid many others would be so, and that he and Lord Grey had in vain tried to persuade Mr Cobden to remain quiet.

Lord Derby had then an Audience to explain what should be done at the Council. He regretted the Duchess of Northumberland's declining to be Mistress of the Robes, on account of ill-health, which had been communicated to the Queen by her father, Lord Westminster. He proposed the Duchess of Argyll, whom the Queen allowed to be sounded (though feeling certain, that, considering the Liberal views of her husband, she will not accept it), and sanctioned his sounding also the Duchess of Athole, whom the Queen wished to make the offer to, in case the Duchess of Argyll declined. Lord Derby stated the difficulty he was in with Sir A. B., whose wife had never been received at Court or in society, although she had run away with him when he was still at school, and was nearly seventy years old. The Queen said it would not do to receive her now at Court, although society might do in that respect what it pleased; it was a principle at Court not to receive ladies whose characters are under a stigma.

We now proceeded to the Council, which was attended only by three Councillors, the other seventeen having all had to be sworn in as Privy Councillors first.[20]

[20]:See Disraeli's *Endymion* (chap. c.) for a graphic description of this remarkable scene.

After the Council Lord Hardinge was called to the Queen, and explained that he accepted the Ordnance only on the condition that he was not to be expected to give a vote which would reverse the policy of Sir R. Peel, to which he had hitherto adhered. He had thought it his duty, however, not to refuse his services to the Crown after the many marks of favour he had received from the Queen.

Lord Derby then had an Audience to explain what he intended to state in Parliament this evening as the programme of his Ministerial Policy. It was very fluent and very able, but so completely the same as the Speech which he has since delivered, that I must refer to its account in the reports. When he came to the passage regarding the Church, the Queen expressed to him her sense of the importance not to have *Puseyites* or *Romanisers* recommended for appointments in the Church as bishops or clergymen. Lord Derby declared himself as decidedly hostile to the Puseyite tendency, and ready to watch over the Protestant character of the Church. He said he did not pretend to give a decided opinion on so difficult and delicate a point, but it had struck him that although nobody could think in earnest of reviving the old Convocation, yet the disputes in the Church perhaps could be most readily settled by some Assembly representing the laity as well as the clergy. I expressed it as my opinion that some such plan would succeed, provided the Church Constitution was built up from the bottom, giving the Vestries a legislative character in the parishes leading up to Diocesan Assemblies, and finally to a general one.

On Education he spoke very liberally, but seemed inclined to support the views of the bishops against the so-called "management clauses" of the Privy Council, viz. not to allow grants to schools even if the parish should prefer the bishops' inspection to the Privy Council inspection.

Albert.

The Earl of Derby to Queen Victoria.

St James's Square, *27th February 1852.*

(*Half-past seven* p.m.)

Lord Derby, with his humble duty, hastens to acquaint your Majesty, having just returned from the House of Lords, that his statement, going over the topics the substance of which he had the honour of submitting to your Majesty was, as far as he could judge, favourably received. Earl Grey attempted to provoke a Corn Law discussion, but the feeling of the House was against the premature introduction of so complicated and exciting a topic. Lord Aberdeen, dissenting from any alteration of commercial policy, entirely concurred in Lord Derby's views of Foreign Affairs, and of the course to be adopted in dealing with Foreign Nations. Lord Derby did not omit to lay stress upon "the strict adherence, in letter and in spirit, to the obligations of Treaties," which was well received.

The King of the Belgians to Queen Victoria.

Laeken, *5th March 1852.*

My dearest Victoria,—I have to offer my affectionate thanks for a most gracious and long letter of the 2nd.

Within these days we have not had anything very important, but, generally speaking, there has been, at least in appearance, a quieter disposition in the ruling power at Paris. We are here in the awkward position of persons in hot climates, who find themselves in company, for instance in their beds, with a snake; they must *not move, because that irritates* the creature, but they can hardly remain as they are, without a fair chance of being bitten.... Your devoted Uncle,

Leopold R.

Queen Victoria to the King of the Belgians.

Osborne, *9th March 1852.*

My dearest Uncle,—Your dear letter of the 5th reached me just after we arrived here, at our sweet, peaceful little abode.

It seems that Louis Napoleon's mind is chiefly engrossed with measures for the interior of France, and that the serious question of Switzerland is becoming less menacing. On the other hand, Austria behaves with a hostility, and I must say folly, which prevents all attempts at reconciliation. All the admirers of Austria consider Prince Schwartzenberg[21] a madman, and the Emperor Nicholas said that he was "Lord Palmerston in a white uniform." What a calamity this is at the present moment!

We have a most talented, capable, and courageous Prime Minister, but all his people have no experience—have never been in *any sort* of office before!

On Friday the House of Commons meets again, and I doubt not great violence will be displayed.

With every kind love to my dear Cousins, ever your very devoted Niece,

Victoria R.

Colonel Phipps to Queen Victoria.

Buckingham Palace, *10th March 1852.*

Colonel Phipps' humble duty to your Majesty.

He has this day visited the Marionette Theatre, and feels quite certain not only that it would not be a suitable theatre for your Majesty to visit, but that your Majesty would derive no amusement from it.

The mechanism of the puppets is only passable, and the matter of the entertainment stupid and tiresome, consisting in a great part of worn-out old English songs, such as "The death of Nelson"! Colonel Phipps considers "Punch" a much more amusing performance. Lady Mount Edgecumbe, who was in a box there, would probably give your Majesty an account of it....

The report in London is, that Lord John Russell is to recommend moderation at the meeting at his house to-morrow. He has, very foolishly, subjected himself to another rebuff from Lord Palmerston by inviting him to attend that meeting, which Lord Palmerston has peremptorily refused. Since that, however, Lady Palmerston has called upon Lady John with a view to a *personal*—not political—reconciliation. Lady Palmerston, as Colonel Phipps hears, still persists in the unfounded accusation against Lord John of having quoted your Majesty's Minute in the House of Commons without giving Lord Palmerston notice of his intention.[22]

The King of the Belgians to Queen Victoria.

Laeken, *12th March 1852.*

My dearest Victoria,—I have to thank you for a most kind letter from peaceful Osborne, which must doubly appear so to you now, after all the troubles of the recent Ministerial arrangements. I am glad that you are struck with the good qualities of your new Premier. I am sure his great wish will be to make the best possible Minister of the Crown. His task will be very difficult. "Bread, cheap bread," "the poor oppressed by the *aristocratie*," etc.—a whole vocabulary of exciting words of that kind will be put forward to inflame the popular mind; and of all the Sovereigns, the Sovereign "People" is certainly one of the most fanciful and fickle. Our neighbour in France shows this more than any other on the whole globe; the Nation there is *still* the *Sovereign*, and this renders the President absolute, because he is the representative of the supreme will of the *supreme Nation*, sending us constantly some new exiles here, which is very unpleasant. We are going on very gently, merely putting those means of defence a little in order, which ought by rights always to be so, if it was not for the ultra-unwise economy of Parliaments and Chambers. Without, at least, comparative security by means of well-regulated measures of defence, no country, be it great or small, can be considered as possessing National Independence. I must say that in Austria, at least Schwartzenberg, they are very much intoxicated. I hope they will grow sober again soon. It was very kind of you to have visited the poor Orleans Family. Rarely one has seen a family so struck in their affections, fortunes, happiness; and it is a sad case. Those unfortunate Spanish marriages have much contributed to it; even angelic Louise had been caught by *l'honneur de la maison de Bourbon....* Your devoted Uncle,

Leopold R.

Queen Victoria to the Earl of Derby.

Osborne, *12th March 1852.*

The Queen must now answer Lord Derby on the questions which form the subjects of his three last communications.

With regard to the Militia Bill, she must admit that her suggestions are liable to the objections pointed out by Lord Derby, although they would offer advantages in other respects. The Queen will therefore sanction the measure as proposed, and now further explained by Lord Derby.

The despatches transmitted from the Foreign Office referring to the Swiss question[23] could not fail to give the Queen as much satisfaction as they did to Lord Derby, as they show indications of a more conciliatory intention, *for the present* at least. As Switzerland has yielded, France and Austria ought to be satisfied, and the Queen only hopes we may not see them pushing their demands further after a short interval!

The probability of a war with the Burmese is a sad prospect. The Queen thinks, however, that the view taken by Lord Dalhousie of the proceedings at Rangoon, and of the steps now to be taken to preserve peace, is very judicious, and fully concurs with the letter sent out by the Secret Committee. She now returns it, together with the despatch.

The despatches from Prince Schwartzenberg to Count Buol are satisfactory in one sense, as showing a readiness to return to the English Alliance, but unfortunately only under the supposition that we would make war upon liberty together; they exhibit a profound ignorance of this country.[24] The Queen is quite sure that Lord Derby will know how to accept all that is favourable in the Austrian overtures without letting it be supposed that we could for a moment think of joining in the policy pursued at this moment by the great Continental Powers. As Lord Derby's speech has been referred to by Prince Schwartzenberg, it would furnish the best text for the answer. The President seems really to have been seriously ill.

Queen Victoria to the Earl of Derby.

Osborne, *14th March 1852.*

The Queen has received this morning Lord Derby's letter respecting the St Albans' Disfranchisement Bill, and is glad to hear that Lord Derby means to take up this Bill as dropped by the late Government. Whether the mode of transferring these seats proposed by Lord Derby will meet with as little opposition in Parliament as he anticipates, the Queen is not able to form a correct judgment of. It may be liable to the imputation of being intended to add to the power of the landed interest. This might not be at all objectionable in itself, but it may be doubtful how far the House of Commons may be disposed to concur in it at the present moment. This will be for Lord Derby to consider, but the Queen will not withhold her sanction from the measure.

She knows that Lord John Russell meant to give the vacant seats to Birkenhead. Are not there two seats still vacant from the Disfranchisement of Sudbury? and would it not be better (if so) to dispose of all four at the same time? There is an impression also gaining ground that, with a view to prevent the Franchise being given exclusively to *Numbers*, to the detriment of *Interests*, it might be desirable to give new seats to certain corporate bodies, such as the Scotch Universities, the Temple and Lincoln's Inn, the East India Company, etc., etc.[25]

Mr Disraeli to Queen Victoria.

House of Commons, *15th March 1852.*

(*Monday night.*)

The Chancellor of the Exchequer, with his humble duty to your Majesty, informs your Majesty of what occurred in the House of Commons this evening.

Mr Villiers opened the proceedings, terse and elaborate, but not in his happiest style. He called upon the House to contrast the state of the country at the beginning of the year and at the present moment. But he could not induce the House to believe that "all now was distrust and alarm."

The Chancellor of the Exchequer, in reply, declined to bring forward in the present Parliament any proposition to change our commercial system, and would not pledge himself to propose in a future Parliament any duty on corn. He said a duty on corn was a measure, not a principle, and that if preferable measures for the redress of agricultural grievances than a five-shilling duty on corn (mentioned by Mr Villiers) could be devised, he should adopt them—a declaration received with universal favour on the Government side.

Lord John Russell replied to the Chancellor of the Exchequer in consequence of some notice by the former of the strange construction of a new Opposition to force a Dissolution of Parliament by a Minister who, three weeks ago, had declared such Dissolution inexpedient. It was not a successful speech.

The great speech on the Opposition side was that of Sir James Graham: elaborate, malignant, mischievous. His position was this: that Lord Derby, as a man of honour, was bound to propose taxes on food, and that if he did so, revolution was inevitable.

Mr Gladstone and Lord Palmerston both spoke in the same vein, the necessity of immediate Dissolution after the passing of the "necessary" measures; but the question soon arose, What is "necessary"?

Lord Palmerston thought the Militia Bill "necessary," upon which the League[26] immediately rose and denied that conclusion.

There seemed in the House a great reluctance to avoid a violent course, but a very general wish, on the Opposition side, for as speedy a Dissolution as public necessity would permit.

The evening, however, was not disadvantageous to the Government. All which is most humbly submitted to your Majesty, by your Majesty's most dutiful Subject and Servant,

B. Disraeli.

Queen Victoria to the King of the Belgians.

Osborne, *17th March 1852.*

My dearest Uncle,—I delayed writing till to-day as I wished to see the papers first, and be able to give you an account of the first Debate in the two Houses. They are not satisfactory, because both Lord Derby and Mr Disraeli refuse to give a straightforward answer as to their policy, the uncertainty as to which will do serious harm.[27] The Opposition are very determined, and *with* right, to insist on this being given, and on as early a Dissolution as possible. The Government will be forced to do this, but it is very unwise, after all *this* agitation for the last five years and a half, *not* [to] come forward manfully and to state what they intend to do. We tried to impress Lord Derby with the necessity of this course, and I hoped we had succeeded, but his speech has not been what it ought to have been in this respect.

The President seems more occupied at home than abroad, which I trust he may remain.

Stockmar is well.... *One* thing is pretty *certain*—that *out* of the *present state* of confusion and discordance, a *sound state* of *Parties* will be obtained, and *two Parties*, as of old, will again exist, without which it is *impossible* to have a *strong* Government. *How* these Parties will be formed it is impossible to say at present. Now, with Albert's love, ever your devoted Niece,

Victoria R.

Mr Disraeli to Queen Victoria.

House of Commons, *19th March 1852.*
(*Friday night, twelve o'clock.*)

The Chancellor of the Exchequer, with his humble duty to your Majesty, lays before your Majesty what has taken place in the House of Commons to-night.

At the commencement of public business, Lord John Russell, in a very full House, after some hostile comments, enquired of Her Majesty's Ministers whether they were prepared to declare that Her Majesty will be advised to dissolve the present Parliament, and call a new one, with the least possible delay consistent with a due regard to the public interest, in reference to measures of *urgent* and *immediate* necessity.

The question was recommended by Lord John Russell as one similar to that put to him in 1841 by Sir Robert Peel.

The Chancellor of the Exchequer in reply observed that there was a distinction between the position of the present Ministry and that of Lord John Russell in 1841, as in that and in the other precedents quoted in 1841 by Sir Robert Peel, the Ministry had been condemned by a vote of the House of Commons.

He said it was not constitutional and most impolitic for any Ministers to pledge themselves to recommend their Sovereign to dissolve Parliament at any stated and specific time, as circumstances might occur which would render the fulfilment of the pledge injurious or impracticable; that it was the intention of the Ministers to recommend your Majesty to dissolve the present Parliament the moment that such measures were carried which were necessary for your Majesty's service, and for the security *and good government* of your Majesty's realm; and that it was their wish and intention that the new Parliament should meet to decide upon the question of confidence in the Administration, and on the measures, which they could then bring forward in the course of the present year.

This announcement was very favourably received.

The discomfiture of the Opposition is complete, and no further mention of stopping or limiting supplies will be heard of.

All which is most humbly submitted to your Majesty by your Majesty's most dutiful Subject and Servant,

B. Disraeli.

Memorandum by the Prince Albert.

Buckingham Palace, *22nd March 1852.*

We came to Town from Osborne the day before yesterday, and saw Lord Derby yesterday afternoon, who is in very good spirits about the prospect of affairs. He told the Queen that he thought he might state that the Government had gained a good deal of ground during the last week, and that there was now a general disposition to let the necessary measures pass Parliament, and to have the dissolution the end of June or beginning of July. He hoped the Queen did not think he had gone too far in pledging the Crown to a Dissolution about that time; but it was impossible to avoid saying as much as that a new Parliament would meet in the autumn again, and have settled the commercial policy before Christmas.

To the Queen's questions, whether there would not be great excitement in the country produced by the General Election, and whether Parliament ought not to meet immediately after it, he replied that he was not the least afraid of much excitement, and that there was great advantage in not meeting Parliament immediately again, as the Government would require a few months to prepare its measures, and to take a sound view of the new position of affairs. He anticipated that there would be returned a large proportion of Conservatives, some Free Traders, some Protectionists; but not a majority for the re-imposition of a duty on corn, *certainly* not a majority large enough to justify him in proposing such a Measure. Now he was sure he could not with honour or credit abandon that Measure unless the country had given its decision against it; but then he would have most carefully to consider how to revise the general state of taxation, so as to give that relief to the agricultural interest which it had a right to demand.

He had received the most encouraging and flattering letters from the agriculturists of different parts of the country, all reposing the most explicit confidence in him, and asking him not to sacrifice the Government for the sake of an immediate return to Protection. They felt what Lord Derby must say he felt himself, that, after the fall of this Government, there would necessarily come one of a more democratic tendency than any the country had yet had to submit to. He thought most politicians saw this, and would rally round a Conservative standard; he knew that even many of the leading Whigs were very much dissatisfied with the company they find themselves thrown into and alarmed at the progress of Democracy.

Albert.

Queen Victoria to the King of the Belgians.

Buckingham Palace, *23rd March 1852.*

... Here matters have improved rather for the Government, and it seems now that they will be able to get through the Session, to dissolve Parliament at the end of June or beginning of July, and to meet again in November. And then Protection will be done away with. If only they had not done so much harm, and played with it for six long years! What you say of the advantage of having had Governments from all parties we have often felt and do feel; it renders changes much less disagreeable. In the present case our acquaintance is confined almost entirely to Lord Derby, but then *he is* the Government. They do *nothing* without him. He has all the Departments to look after, and on being asked by somebody if he was not much tired, he said: "I am quite well with my babies!..."

Victoria R.

Mr Disraeli to Queen Victoria.

House of Commons, *29th March 1852.*

(*Monday night.*)

The Chancellor of the Exchequer, with his humble duty to your Majesty, informs your Majesty of what has occurred in the House of Commons to-night.

Mr Secretary Walpole introduced the Militia Bill in a statement equally perspicuous and persuasive.

Opposed by Mr Hume and Mr Gibson, the Government Measure was cordially supported by Lord Palmerston.

Lord John Russell, while he expressed an opinion favourable to increased defence, intimated a preference for regular troops.

Mr Cobden made one of his cleverest speeches, of the cosmopolitan school, and was supported with vigour by Mr Bright. A division is threatened by the ultra-Movement party, but the Chancellor of the Exchequer hopes to ward it off, and is somewhat sanguine of ultimate success in carrying the Measure.

Queen Victoria to the King of the Belgians.

Buckingham Palace, *30th March 1852.*

My dearest Uncle,—Many thanks for your dear letter of the 26th, which I received on Saturday. Here we shall have some trouble with our Militia Bill, which all of a sudden seems to have caused dissatisfaction and alarm. Lord Derby is quite prepared to drop Protection, as he knows that the Elections will bring a Free Trade, though a Conservative majority. Mr Disraeli (*alias* Dizzy) writes very curious reports to me of the House of Commons proceedings—much in the style of his books....

Queen Victoria to the Earl of Derby.

Windsor Castle, *10th April 1852.*

The Queen hopes that both Lord Derby and Lord Malmesbury will give their earnest attention to the change in the politics of Italy, which is evidently on the point of taking place, according to the enclosed despatch from Mr Hudson.[28] What Count Azeglio[29] says in his Memorandum with respect to Austria is perfectly just. But France, as the champion of Italian liberty and independence, would become most formidable to the rest of Europe, and Louis Napoleon, in assuming for her this position, would be only following the example of his uncle, which we know to be his constant aim.[30]

Queen Victoria to the Earl of Derby.

Windsor Castle, *13th April 1852.*

The Queen has received Lord Derby's letter of the 11th inst., in which he states very clearly the difficulties which stand in the way of an active interference of this country in the affairs of Italy. The Queen did not mean to recommend in her letter of the 10th on this subject any active interference, as she is of opinion that our present want of due influence in Italy is chiefly owing to our former ill-judged over-activity. The Queen agrees therefore entirely with Lord Derby in thinking that "all that can be done now is carefully to watch the pro-ceedings of France and Austria in this matter, so as to profit by every good opportunity to protect the independence of Piedmont, and, if pos-sible, produce some improvement in the internal Government of Rome," and she would accordingly like to see her respective Foreign Ministers instructed in this sense.

The Queen continues, however, to look with apprehension to the possible turn which the affairs of Italy may take, proceeding from the political views of the President. It is not improbable that he may act now that he is omnipotent upon the views contained in his celebrated letter to Edgar Ney in 1849, which were at the time disapproved by the Assembly.[31] He will feel the necessity of doing something to compen-sate the French for what they have lost by him at home, to turn their attention from home affairs to those abroad, and to the acquisition of power and influence in Europe; and certainly, were he to head Italian liberty and independence, his power of doing mischief would be im-mense. After all, such an attempt would not be more inconsistent for him than it was for General Cavaignac, as President of the *République Démocratique*, to get rid of the Roman Republic, and to reinstate the Pope by force of arms.

The Queen wishes Lord Derby to communicate this letter to Lord Malmesbury, from whom she has also just heard upon this subject.

Mr Disraeli to Queen Victoria.

House of Commons, *19th April 1852.*
(*Monday night, half-past twelve.*)

The Chancellor of the Exchequer, with his humble duty to your Majesty, reports to your Majesty that, after a dull debate, significant only by two of the subordinate Members of the late Administration declaring their hostility to the Militia Bill, Lord John Russell rose at eleven o'clock and announced his determination to oppose the second reading of it.[32] His speech was one of his ablest—statesmanlike, argumentative, terse, and playful; and the effect he produced was considerable.

Your Majesty's Government, about to attempt to reply to it, gave way to Lord Palmerston, who changed the feeling of the House, and indeed entirely carried it away in a speech of extraordinary vigour and high-spirited tone.

The Ministers were willing to have taken the division on his Lordship sitting down, but as the late Government wished to reply, the Chancellor of the Exchequer would not oppose the adjournment of the debate.

The elements of calculation as to the division are very complicated, but the Chancellor of the Exchequer is still inclined to believe that the second reading of the Bill will be carried.

[32]:This tactical blunder, much condemned at the time, estranged many of the Whigs from Lord John.

Queen Victoria to the Earl of Derby.

Buckingham Palace, *25th April 1852.*

The Queen wishes to remind Lord Derby that the time for the presentation of the Budget to the House of Commons being very close at hand, none of the Measures referring to the finances of the country which the Government may have to propose have as yet been laid before her.

Queen Victoria to the Earl of Derby.

Buckingham Palace, *26th April 1852.*

The Queen has received Lord Derby's explanation of his views with regard to the Budget,[33] and will be glad to see him on Wednesday at three o'clock. She had been alarmed by vague rumours that it was the intention of the Government to propose great changes in the present financial system, which, with an adverse majority in the House of Commons and at the eve of a Dissolution, must have led to much confusion. She thinks the course suggested by Lord Derby to consider the Budget merely as a provisional one for the current year, by far the wisest, the more so as it will leave us a surplus of £2,000,000, which is of the utmost importance in case of unforeseen difficulties with Foreign Powers.[34]

Mr Disraeli to Queen Victoria.

House of Commons, *26th April.*
(*Monday night, twelve o'clock.*)

The Chancellor of the Exchequer, with his humble duty to your Majesty, reports to your Majesty that the Militia Bill has been carried (second reading) by an immense majority.

For 315

Against 165

The concluding portion of the debate was distinguished by the speeches of Mr Sidney Herbert and Mr Walpole, who made their greatest efforts; the first singularly happy in his treatment of a subject of which he was master, and the last addressing the House with a spirit unusual with him.

Queen Victoria to the King of the Belgians.

Buckingham Palace, *27th April 1852.*

My dearest Uncle,—I thank you much for your kind and affectionate letter of the 23rd. I have somehow or other contrived to lose my day, for which reason I can only write a very short letter. It seems to be generally believed that Louis Napoleon's assumption of the title of Emperor is very near at hand, but they still think war is not likely, as it would be such bad policy.

What you say about the ill-fated Spanish marriages, and the result of the poor King's wishing to have no one but a Bourbon as Queen Isabel's husband being that the *French won't* have *any* Bourbon, is indeed strange. It is a melancholy result.

I shall certainly try and read Thiers' *Révolution, Consulat, et Empire*, but I can hardly read *any* books, my whole *lecture* almost being taken up by the immense quantity of despatches we have to read, and then I have a good deal to write, and must then have a little leisure time to rest, and *de me délasser* and to get out. It is a great deprivation, as I delight in reading. Still, I will not forget your recommendation.

I am sorry to say *nothing* is definitely settled about our dear Crystal Palace. With Albert's love, ever your truly devoted Niece,

Victoria R.

Queen Victoria to Mr Disraeli.

Buckingham Palace, *1st May 1852.*

The Queen has read with great interest the clear and able financial statement which the Chancellor of the Exchequer made in the House of Commons last night, and was glad to hear from him that it was well received.

Queen Victoria to the Earl of Malmesbury.

Buckingham Palace, *13th May 1852.*

With respect to this despatch from Lord Howden,[35] the Queen wishes to observe that hitherto we have on all similar occasions declined accepting any Foreign Order for the Prince of Wales, on account of his being too young and not even having any of the English Orders. Might this not therefore be communicated to Lord Howden?

Queen Victoria to the Earl of Derby.

Osborne, *27th May 1852.*

The Queen returns the enclosed most interesting letters. It is evident that the President is meeting with the first symptoms of a reviving public feeling in France; whether this will drive him to hurry on the Empire remains to be seen. All the Foreign Powers have to be careful about is to receive an assurance that the *Empire* does *not* mean a *return to the policy of the Empire*, but that the existing Treaties will be acknowledged and adhered to.

The session seems to advance very rapidly. The Queen hails Lord Derby's declaration of his conviction that a majority for a duty on corn will not be returned to the new Parliament, as the first step towards the abandonment of hostility to the Free Trade on which our commercial policy is now established, and which has produced so flourishing a condition of the finances of the country.

Mr Disraeli's speech about Spain was very good, though he had certainly better not have alluded to Portugal.

We return to Town to-morrow.

Mr Disraeli to Queen Victoria.

House of Commons, *21st June 1852.*

(*Nine o'clock.*)

The Chancellor of the Exchequer, with his humble duty to your Majesty, reports to your Majesty that Lord John Russell introduced to the notice of the House of Commons to-night the recent Minute of the Committee of Council on Education.

Lord John Russell made a languid statement to a rather full House. His speech was not very effective as it proceeded, and there was silence when he sat down.

Then Mr Walpole rose and vindicated the Minute. He spoke with animation, and was cheered when he concluded.

Sir Harry Verney followed, and the House very much dispersed; indeed the discussion would probably have terminated when Sir Harry finished, had not Mr Gladstone then risen. Mr Gladstone gave only a very guarded approval to the Minute, which he treated as insignificant.

It was not a happy effort, and the debate, for a while revived by his interposition, continued to languish until this hour (nine o'clock), with successive relays of mediocrity, until it yielded its last gasp in the arms of Mr Slaney.

The feeling of the House of Commons, probably in this representing faithfully that of the country, is against both the violent parties in the Church, and in favour of a firm, though temperate, course on the part of the Crown, which may conciliate a vast majority, and tend to terminate dissension.

Queen Victoria to Mr Walpole.

Buckingham Palace, *1st July 1852.*

The Queen is much distressed at the account she has read in the papers of the dreadful riot at Stockport,[36] alas! caused by that most baneful of all Party feelings, *religious* hatred,[37] and she is very anxious to know what Mr Walpole has heard.

The King of the Belgians to Queen Victoria.

Laeken, *23rd July 1852.*

My dearest Victoria,—... We are very much plagued by our Treaty with France. Victor Hugo has written a book against Louis Napoleon, which will exasperate him much, and which he publishes *here*; we can hardly keep Victor Hugo here after that.[38] The great plague of all these affairs is their constant return without the least advantage to any one from the difficulties they created.... Your devoted Uncle,

Leopold R.

Queen Victoria to the Earl of Derby.

Osborne, *26th August 1852.*

The Queen has been considering the subject of the vacant Garter, and the names which Lord Derby proposed to her. She is of opinion that it would not be advisable on the whole to give the Garter to Lord Londonderry; that the Duke of Northumberland has by far the strongest claim to this distinction. At the same time, the Queen would have no objection to bestow it on Lord Lonsdale, if this is desirable, in order to facilitate any Ministerial arrangements which Lord Derby may have in contemplation.

The King of the Belgians to Queen Victoria.

Laeken, *10th September 1852.*

My dearest Victoria,—... That Mr Neild[39] should have left that great fortune to you delighted me; it gives the possibility of forming a private fortune for the Royal Family, the necessity of which nobody can deny. Such things only still happen in England, where there exists loyalty and strong affection for Royalty, a feeling unfortunately much diminished on the Continent of Europe, though it did exist there also....

F.M. The Duke of Wellington, K.G.

From a miniature at Apsley House

Memorandum by the Prince Albert.

Balmoral, *17th September 1852.*

The death of the Duke of Wellington[40] has deprived the Country of her greatest man, the Crown of its most valuable servant and adviser, the Army of its main strength and support. We received the sad news on an expedition from Allt-na-Giuthasach to the Dhu Loch (one of the wildest and loneliest spots of the Highlands) at four o'clock yesterday afternoon. We hurried home to Allt-na-Giuthasach, and to-day here, where it became important to settle with Lord Derby the mode of providing for the command of the Army, and the filling up of the many posts and places which the Duke had held.

I had privately prepared a list of the mode in which this should be done, and discussed it with Victoria, and found, to both Lord Derby's

and our astonishment, that it tallied in *every* point with the recommendations which he had thought of making.

I explained to Lord Derby the grounds upon which I thought it
better not to assume the Command myself, and told him of the old
Duke's proposal, two years ago, to prepare the way to my assuming the
Command by the appointment of a Chief of the Staff, on Sir Wil-
loughby Gordon's death, and the reasons on which I then declined the
offer. Lord Derby entirely concurred in my views, and seemed relieved by my explanation; we then agreed that for the loss of *authority*
which we had lost with the Duke, we could only make up by increase
in *efficiency* in the appointments to the different offices. That Lord
Hardinge was the only man fit to command the Army.

He should then receive the Command-in-Chief. The Ordnance
which he would vacate should be given to Lord Fitzroy Somerset,
hitherto Military Secretary (with the offer of a peerage).[41] The Con-
stableship of the Tower to Lord Combermere; the Garter to Lord
Londonderry; the Grenadier Guards and the Rifle Brigade to me; the
Fusiliers vacated by me to the Duke of Cambridge (or the Coldstream,
Lord Strafford exchanging to the Fusiliers); the 60th Rifles vacated by
me to Lord Beresford; the Rangership of the Parks in London to
George (Duke of Cambridge); the Wardenship of the Cinque Ports to
Lord Dalhousie; the Lieutenancy of Hampshire to Lord Winchester. I
reserved to me the right of considering whether I should not assume
the command of the Brigade of Guards which the Duke of York held
in George IV.'s time, to which William IV. appointed himself, and
which has been vacant ever since Victoria's accession, although inher-
ent to the Constitution of the Guards.

Lord Derby had thought of George for the Command-in-Chief, as
an alternative for Lord Hardinge, but perceived that his rank as a Major-General and youth would hardly entitle him to such an
advancement. He would have carried no weight with the public, and
we must not conceal from ourselves that many attacks on the Army
which have been sleeping on account of the Duke will now be forthcoming.

Victoria wishes the Army to mourn for the Duke as long as for a
member of the Royal Family.

Lord Derby proposes a public funeral, which cannot take place,
however, before the meeting of Parliament in November. He is to find
out how this is to be accomplished on account of the long interval.

The correspondence here following[42] shows what doubts exist as
to the person in whom the Command of the Army is vested in case of

413

a vacancy. I consider Lord Palmerston's letter as a mere attempt to arrogate supreme power for his Office,[43] which rests on no foundation. The Secretary at War has no authority whatever except over money, whilst the Commander-in-Chief has no authority to spend a penny without the Secretary at War.

Albert.

Queen Victoria to the King of the Belgians.

Balmoral, *17th September 1852.*

My dearest Uncle,—I am sure you will mourn *with us* over the loss we and this whole nation have experienced in the death of the *dear* and great old Duke of Wellington. The sad news will have reached you, I doubt not, on Wednesday or yesterday. We had gone on Wednesday, as I had mentioned, to our little Shiel of Allt-na-Giuthasach to spend two days there, and were enjoying ourselves very much on a beautiful expedition yesterday, and were sitting by the side of the Dhu Loch, one of the severest, wildest spots imaginable, when one of our Highlanders arrived bringing a letter from Lord Derby (who is here), confirming the report which we had already heard of—but entirely disbelieved—and sending me a letter from Lord Charles Wellesley, saying that his dear father had only been ill a few hours, and had hardly suffered at all. It was a stroke, which was succeeded rapidly by others, and carried him off without any return of consciousness. For *him* it is a blessing that he should have been taken away in the possession of his great and powerful mind and without a lingering illness. But for this country, and for us, his loss—though it could not have been long delayed—is irreparable! He was the pride and the *bon génie*, as it were, of this country! He was the GREATEST man this country ever produced, and the most *devoted* and *loyal* subject, and the staunchest supporter the Crown ever had. He was to us a true, kind friend and most valuable adviser. To think that all this is gone; that this great and immortal man belongs now to History and no longer to the present, is a truth which we cannot realise. We shall soon stand sadly alone; Aberdeen is almost the only personal friend of that kind we have left. Melbourne, Peel, Liverpool—and now the Duke—*all* gone!

You will kindly feel for and with us, dearest Uncle.

Lord Hardinge is to be Commander-in-Chief, and he is quite the *only* man *fit* for it.

Albert is much grieved. The dear Duke showed him great confidence and kindness. He was so fond of his little godson Arthur—who will now be a remaining link of the dear old Duke's, and a pleasant recollection of him. Ever your devoted Niece,

Victoria R.

The King of the Belgians to Queen Victoria.

Laeken, *17th September 1852.*

My dearest Victoria,—You will be much grieved at the loss of the Duke. It must give you satisfaction to think that you were always kind to him, and that he was very sincerely devoted to you and appreciated Albert. Since 1814 I had known much of the Duke; his *kindness* to me had been very *marked*, and I early discovered that he was very favourable to my marriage with Charlotte, then already in agitation. Since, he was *always kind* and *confidential*, even in those days of persecution against me, the result of the jealousy of George IV.; he never was influenced by it, or had the meanness of many who, in the days of misfortune, quickly leave one. The only case in which we were at variance was about the boundaries of Greece. He had some of the old absolute notions, which in that case were not in conformity with the real interests of England and of Europe. Even last year he spoke so very kindly to me on the subject of our Continental affairs. Rarely fickle Fortune permits a poor mortal to reach the conclusion of a long career, however glorious, with such complete success, so undisturbed by physical or moral causes. The Duke is the noblest example of what an Englishman may be, and to what greatness he may rise in following that honourable and straight line.

When one looks at the Manchester school, compared to the greatness to which men like the Duke raised their country, one cannot help to be alarmed for the future. You are enjoying the Highlands, but the weather seems also not very favourable; here it is uncertain, and at times very cold.... Your truly devoted Uncle,

Leopold R.

The Prince Albert to the Earl of Derby.

Balmoral, *22nd September 1852.*

My dear Lord Derby,—The Queen wishes me to answer your kind letter of yesterday.

Her letter to you and to Mr Walpole of this morning will have apprised you that she sanctions the Guard of Honour having been placed at Walmer, and the Duke's body having been taken possession of formally on the part of the Crown.

It would be a great pity if Lord Fitzroy were to be obliged to decline the Peerage on account of poverty; at the same time it may be difficult to relieve him from the payment of fees by a public grant. Under these circumstances, rather than leave Lord Fitzroy unrewarded, and a chance of his feeling mortified at a moment when his cheerful co-operation with Lord Hardinge is so important to the public service—the Queen would *herself* bear the expense of the fees. If this were to hurt Lord Fitzroy's feelings, you could easily manage it so that he need never know from what source the £500 came. The Queen leaves this matter in your hands. Ever yours truly,

Albert.

Queen Victoria to Mr Walpole.

Balmoral Castle, *22nd September 1852.*

The Queen has just received Mr Walpole's letter of the 20th, informing her of the difficulty of having the Funeral Service, *according* to the *Liturgy*, performed *twice*; she trusts, however, that means may be found to enable the Queen's intentions to be carried out, as communicated to Mr Walpole in Lord Derby's official letter. Whether this is to be done by leaving the body for two months without the Funeral Service being read over it, or by reading the Funeral Service now in the presence of the family, and treating the *Public Funeral* more as a translation of the remains to their final place of rest, the Queen must leave to be decided by those who have the means of personally sounding the feelings of the Duke's family, the dignitaries of the Church, and the public generally.

An impressive religious ceremony might certainly be made of it at St. Paul's, even if the actual Funeral Service should not be read on the occasion....

Queen Victoria to the Earl of Derby.

Windsor Castle, *23rd October 1852.*

Shortly after the formation of Lord Derby's Government, the Queen communicated to him a Memorandum respecting the necessity of attending to our national defences on a systematic plan. The Queen would now wish to hear how far we have advanced in this important object since that time. Lord Derby would perhaps call on the General Commanding-in-Chief, the Master-General of the Ordnance, and the First Lord of the Admiralty, as well as the Home Secretary, to make a report upon this. It will soon be necessary to consider what will have to be done for the future to complete the various plans. The Queen is no alarmist, but thinks that the necessity of our attending to our defences once having been proved and admitted by Parliament and two successive Governments, we should not relax in our efforts until the plans then devised are thoroughly carried out.

Queen Victoria to the King of the Belgians.

Windsor Castle, *26th October 1852.*

My dearest Uncle,—... I must tell you an anecdote relating to Louis Napoleon's entry into Paris, which Lord Cowley wrote over, as going the round of Paris. It is: that under one of the Triumphal Arches a Crown was suspended to a string (which is very often the case) over which was written, "*Il l'a bien mérité.*" Something damaged this crown, and they removed it—*leaving*, however, the *rope* and *superscription*, the effect of which must have been somewhat edifying!

It is not at all true that foreign Officers are not to attend at the funeral of the dear old Duke; on the contrary, we expect them from Prussia, Austria, and Russia, and the Duke of Terceira (whom we shall see to-night) is already come from Portugal to attend the ceremony.

I must now conclude. With Albert's love, ever your devoted Niece,

Victoria R.

Queen Victoria to the Earl of Malmesbury.

Windsor Castle, *8th November 1852.*

As we seem to be so near the declaration of the Empire in France, and as so many opinions are expressed on the subject of the title to be assumed by Louis Napoleon, the Queen is anxious to impress Lord

417

Malmesbury with the importance of our not committing ourselves on this point, and not giving our allies to understand that we shall join them in not acknowledging Napoleon III.[44] Objectionable as this appellation no doubt is, it may hardly be worth offending France and her Ruler by refusing to recognise it, when it is of *such* importance to prevent their considering themselves the aggrieved party; any attempt to dictate to France the style of her Ruler would strengthen Louis Napoleon's position; our object should be to leave France alone, as long as she is not aggressive.

All of this should be well weighed.

The Prince Albert to Viscount Hardinge.

Windsor Castle, *8th November 1852.*

My dear Lord Hardinge,—In reference to our conversation of yesterday, and the Queen's request to Lord Derby that he should call upon the different departments of the Admiralty, Army, Ordnance, and Home Office to furnish a report as to how far the measures begun last spring to put our defences in a state of efficiency have been carried out, and what remains to be done in that direction—I beg now to address you in writing. The object the Queen wishes to obtain is, to receive an account which will show what means we have *really* at our disposal for purposes of defence, *ready for action* at the shortest possible notice, and what remains to be done to put us into a state of security, what the supply of the wants may cost (approximately), and what time it would require.

As it will be not only convenient but necessary that the Horse Guards and Ordnance should consult together and combine their deliberations, I beg this letter to be understood to apply as well to Lord Raglan as to yourself, and that you would meet and give the answer to the Queen's questions conjointly.

(*A detailed list follows.*)

These questions would all present themselves at the moment when we received the intelligence of a threatened *coup de main* on the part of Louis Napoleon, when it would be too late to remedy any deficiency. The public would be quite ready to give the necessary money for our armament, but they feel with justice that it is unfair to ask them for large sums and then always to hear, *We are quite unprepared.* They don't understand and cannot understand details, but it is upon matters of detail that our security will have to depend, and we cannot

be sure of efficiency unless a comprehensive statement be made showing the whole.

I beg this to be as short as possible, and if possible in a tabular
shape. Ever yours truly,

Albert.

Queen Victoria to the Earl of Derby.

Windsor Castle, *13th November 1852.*

The Queen was very sorry to hear from Lord Derby and Mr Disraeli that Mr Villiers' Motion[45] will create Parliamentary difficulties.

With respect to the financial statement, she must most strongly
impress Lord Derby with the necessity of referring to our defenceless
state, and the necessity of a *large* outlay, to protect us from foreign
attack, which would almost ensure us against war. The country is fully
alive to its danger, and Parliament has perhaps never been in a more
likely state to grant what is necessary, provided a comprehensive and
efficient plan is laid before it. Such a plan ought, in the Queen's opinion, to be distinctly promised by the Government, although it may be
laid before Parliament at a later period

Mr Disraeli to Queen Victoria.

London, *14th November 1852.*

The Chancellor of the Exchequer, with his humble duty to your
Majesty, begs permission to enclose an answer to the Address for your
Majesty's approbation, and which should be delivered, if your Majesty
pleases, to the House of Commons to-morrow.

Referring to a letter from your Majesty, shown to him yesterday
by Lord Derby, the Chancellor of the Exchequer also begs permission
to state that, in making the financial arrangements, he has left a very
large margin for the impending year (April 1853-4), which will permit
the fulfilment of all your Majesty's wishes with respect to the increased defence of the country, as he gathered them from your
Majesty's gracious expressions, and also from the suggestion which
afterwards, in greater detail, His Royal Highness the Prince deigned to
make to him.

The Chancellor of the Exchequer will deeply consider the intimation graciously made in your Majesty's letter to Lord Derby as to the
tone on this subject to be adopted in the House of Commons, and he

will endeavour in this, and in all respects, to fulfil your Majesty's pleasure.

The Chancellor of the Exchequer fears that he sent to your Majesty a somewhat crude note from the House of Commons on Thursday night, but he humbly begs your Majesty will deign to remember that these bulletins are often written in tumult, and sometimes in perplexity; and that he is under the impression that your Majesty would prefer a genuine report of the feeling of the moment, however miniature, to a more artificial and prepared statement.

Queen Victoria to Mr Disraeli.

Windsor Castle, *14th November 1852.*

The Queen has received with much satisfaction Mr Disraeli's letter of this day's date, in which he informs her of his readiness to provide efficiently for the defence of the country, the call for which is *very* urgent. Lord Malmesbury, with whom the Prince has talked very fully over this subject, will communicate further with Mr Disraeli and Lord Derby on his return to Town to-morrow.

The Marquis of Dalhousie to Queen Victoria.

Government House, *23rd November 1852.*

The Governor-General still retains some hope of seeing general peace restored in India before he quits it finally, as your Majesty's Ministers and the Court of Directors have some time since requested him not to retire from its administration in January next, as he had intended to do.

Many private considerations combined to draw him homewards, even though the honour and the advantages of retaining this Office were willingly recognised. But the gracious approbation with which his services here have been viewed was a sufficient motive for continuing them for some time longer, if they were thought profitable to the State.

Your Majesty has very recently been pleased to bestow upon him a still further distinction, which calls not merely for the expression of his deep and humble gratitude to your Majesty, but for a further devotion to your Majesty's service of whatever power he may possess for promoting its interests.

That your Majesty should prefer him at all to an Office of such traditional distinction as the Wardenship was an honour to which the Governor-General would never at any time have dreamt of aspiring.

But by conferring it upon him thus—during his absence—and above all, by conferring it upon him in immediate succession to one whom he must all his life regard with reverence, affection, and gratitude—your Majesty has surrounded this honour with so much of honourable circumstance that the Governor-General is wholly unable to give full expression to the feelings with which he has received your Majesty's goodness.

The Governor-General is very sensible that in him, as Lord Warden, your Majesty will have but a sorry successor to the Duke of Wellington in every respect, save one. But in that one respect—namely in deep devotion to your Majesty's Crown, and to the true interests of your Empire—the Governor-General does not yield even to the Master he was long so proud to follow.

In every part of India the highest honours have been paid to the memory of the Duke of Wellington, which your Majesty's Empire in the East and its armies could bestow.

Even the Native Powers have joined in the homage to his fame. In the mountains of Nepaul the same sad tribute was rendered by the Maharajah as by ourselves, while in Mysore the Rajah not only fired minute guns in his honour, but even caused the Dusserah, the great Hindoo festival, to be stopped throughout the city, in token of his grief.

Excepting the usual disturbance from time to time among the still untamed mountain tribes upon our north-western border, there is entire tranquillity in India. The season has been good, and the revenue is improving.

Respectfully acknowledging the letter which he had lately the honour of receiving from your Majesty, and the gracious message it contained to Lady Dalhousie, who, though much improved in health, will be compelled to return to England in January, the Governor-General has the honour to subscribe himself with the utmost respect and gratitude, your Majesty's most obedient, most humble, and devoted Subject and Servant,

Dalhousie.

Queen Victoria to the King of the Belgians.

Windsor Castle, *23rd November 1852.*

My dearest Uncle,—What you say about Joinville has interested us very much, and we have confidentially communicated it to Lord

Derby, who is never alarmed enough. There is, however, a belief that the Orleans family have been very imprudent, and that Louis Napoleon has heard things and expressions used which did a great deal of harm, and Lord Derby begged me to warn them very strongly and earnestly on this point; *I* cannot do much, but I think *you* might, for in fact they might *unintentionally compromise us seriously*. The Government are rather shaky; Disraeli has been imprudent and blundering, and has done himself harm by a Speech he made about the Duke of Wellington, which was borrowed from an *éloge* by Thiers on a French Marshal!!![46]

You will have heard from your children and from Charles how very touching the ceremony both in and out of doors was on the 18th. The behaviour of the millions assembled has been the topic of general admiration, and the foreigners have all assured me that they never could have believed *such* a number of people could have shown such feeling, such respect, for *not* a sound was heard! I cannot say *what* a deep and *wehmtühige* impression it made on me! It was a beautiful sight. In the Cathedral it was much more touching still! The dear old Duke! he is an irreparable loss!

We had a great dinner yesterday to all the Officers. There is but one feeling of indignation and surprise at the conduct of Austria [47] in taking *this* opportunity to slight England in return for what happened to *Haynau*[48] for *his own* character. Ernest Hohenlohe was extremely anxious you should know the reason why he may *possibly* appear one evening at the Elysée (they are gone for three or four days to Paris).

Louis Napoleon being excessively susceptible, and believing us to be inimical towards him, we and the Government thought it would not be wise or prudent for *my* brother-in-law, just coming *from here*, purposely to avoid him and go out of his way, which Louis Napoleon would immediately say was *my doing*; and unnecessary offence we do not wish to give; the more so as Stockmar was presented to him at Strasburg, and received the *Légion d'honneur*. I promised to explain this to you, as Ernest was distressed lest he should appear to be *time-serving*, and I said I was sure you would understand it.

I must end in a hurry, hoping to write again on Thursday or Friday. Dear Stockmar is very well and most kind. He is much pleased at your children spending some time with him every day. Ever your devoted Niece,

Victoria R.

The Earl of Derby to Queen Victoria.

Downing Street, *25th November 1852.*

(*Thursday, four* p.m.)

Lord Derby, with his humble duty, in obedience to your Majesty's gracious commands of this morning, proceeds to report to your Majesty what he finds to have taken place and to be in contemplation; but the accounts of the latter are so conflicting and contradictory, that his report must be as unsatisfactory to your Majesty as the state of the case is unintelligible to himself.

On arriving in London, Lord Derby called on Mr Disraeli, and found that late last night he had had, by his own desire, a private interview with Lord Palmerston, who had come to his house with that object; that Lord Palmerston's language was perfectly friendly towards the Government; that he assured Mr Disraeli that his only object in offering his Amendment was to defeat Mr Villiers; that if that could be done, it was a matter of indifference to him which Amendment was adopted; and he concluded by declaring that though he sat by Mr Sidney Herbert in the House of Commons, and was an old personal friend, he did not act in concert with him or with Mr Gladstone; and that he did not see, on their part, any disposition to approach the Government! After this declaration Mr Disraeli felt that it would be useless and unwise to sound him farther as to his own ulterior views, and the conversation led to nothing.

As Lord Derby was walking home, he was overtaken by Lord Jocelyn, who stated, in direct opposition to what had been said by Lord Palmerston, that he, and the other two gentlemen named, were consulted upon, and had concocted the proposed Amendment; and that they were decidedly acting together. He was present at a dinner of the Peelite Party yesterday at Mr Wortley's, when Speeches were made, and language held about the reunion of the Conservative Party, resulting, however, in a declaration that if your Majesty's servants did not accept Lord Palmerston's Amendment, they, as a body, would vote in favour of Mr Villiers. Lord Derby has been farther informed that they are willing to join the Government, but that one of their conditions would be that Lord Palmerston should lead the House of Commons, Mr Gladstone refusing to serve under Mr Disraeli. This, if true, does not look like an absence of all concert.

To complete the general confusion of Parties, the Duke of Bedford, who called on Lady Derby this morning, assures her that Lord John Russell does not desire the fall of your Majesty's present Government, and that in no case will he enter into any combination with the Radical Party, a declaration quite at variance with the course he has pursued since Parliament met.

Of course Lord Derby, in these circumstances, has not taken any step whatever towards exercising the discretion with which your Majesty was graciously pleased to entrust him this morning.[49] He much regrets having to send your Majesty so unsatisfactory a statement, and has desired to have the latest intelligence sent up to him of what may pass in the House of Commons, and he will endeavour to keep your Majesty informed of any new occurrence which any hour may produce.

Half-past six.

Lord Derby has just heard from the House of Commons that Sir James Graham has given the history of the framing of the Amendment, and has expressed his intention, if Lord Palmerston's Amendment be accepted, to advise Mr Villiers to withdraw. Mr Gladstone has held the same language; there appears to be much difference of opinion, but Lord Derby would think that the probable result will be the adoption of Lord Palmerston's proposition. He fears this will lead to a good deal of discontent among the supporters of the Government; but a different course would run imminent risk of defeat.

Mr Disraeli to Queen Victoria.

House of Commons, *26th November 1852.*

(*Half-past one o'clock* a.m.)

The Chancellor of the Exchequer, with his humble duty to your Majesty, reports to your Majesty that the House of Commons has this moment divided on Mr Villiers' resolution, and in a House of nearly 600 members they have been rejected by a majority of 80.[50]

The debate was very animated and amusing, from the rival narratives of the principal projectors of the demonstration, who, having quarrelled among themselves, entered into secret and—in a Party sense—somewhat scandalous revelations, to the diversion and sometimes astonishment of the House.

The Chancellor of the Exchequer deeply regrets that, having been obliged to quit the House early yesterday, he was unable to forward a bulletin to your Majesty.

He has fixed next Friday for the Budget.

Memorandum by the Prince Albert.

Windsor Castle, *28th November 1852.*

Before the Council held yesterday we saw Lord Derby, who seemed much pleased with the result of the Division, though a good deal galled by the tone of the Debate.

Lord Derby had heard it said that Mr Sidney Herbert, although very bitter in his language, had not meant to be hostile to the Government, but felt that he owed the duty to speak out to the memory of Sir Robert Peel; that he was glad to have thrown the load off his mind. Lord Derby then read us a letter from Lord Claud Hamilton, who had seen Mr Corry (one of the Peelites), who had given him to understand that they would *not* serve under the leadership of Mr Disraeli; that they were ready, on the other hand, to serve under Lord Palmerston. This put all further negotiation out of the question, for, independently of the Queen objecting to such an arrangement, he himself could not admit of it. On my question why Mr Gladstone could not lead, he replied that Mr Gladstone was, in his opinion, quite unfit for it; he had none of that decision, boldness, readiness, and clearness which was necessary to lead a Party, to inspire it with confidence, and, still [more], to take at times a decision on the spur of the moment, which a leader had often to do. Then he said that he could not in honour sacrifice Mr Disraeli, who had acted very straightforwardly to him as long as they had had anything to do with each other, and who possessed the confidence of his followers. Mr Disraeli had no idea of giving up the lead.

We could quite understand, on the other hand, that the colleagues of Sir Robert Peel could not feel inclined to serve under Mr Disraeli.

Under these circumstances we agreed that nothing should be done at present, and that it must be left to time to operate changes, that much must depend upon the success which Mr Disraeli may have with his Budget, and that the knowledge that Lord Palmerston could not obtain the lead would oblige those who wished to join to think of a different combination.

Lord Derby owned (upon my blunt question) that he did not think Mr Disraeli had ever had a strong feeling, one way or the other, about

Protection or Free Trade, and that he would make a very good Free Trade Minister.

The Queen was anxious to know what Lord Derby thought Lord George Bentinck (if now alive) would do in this conjunction. Lord Derby's expression was "he would have made confusion worse confounded" from his excessive violence.

Albert.

Queen Victoria to the Earl of Malmesbury.

Osborne, *2nd December 1852.*

The Queen has received Lord Malmesbury's letter, and returns the enclosure from Lord Cowley. Under these circumstances the course recommended to be pursued by Lord Malmesbury[51] appears also to the Queen as the best. It is evident that we have no means of making Louis Napoleon say what he will not, nor would any diplomatic form of obtaining an assurance from him give us any guarantee of his not doing after all exactly what he pleases. Our honour appears therefore to be best in our own keeping. Whatever he may say, it is in our *note of recognition* that we must state *what* we recognise and what we do *not* recognise.

The Earl of Derby to Queen Victoria.

St James's Square, *3rd December 1852.*
(*Friday night, twelve o'clock* p.m.)

Lord Derby, with his humble duty, ventures to hope that your Majesty may feel some interest in hearing, so far as he is able to give it, his impression of the effect of Mr Disraeli's announcement of the Budget[52] this evening. Lord Derby was not able to hear quite the commencement of the Speech, having been obliged to attend the House of Lords, which, however, was up at a quarter past five, Mr Disraeli having then been speaking about half an hour. From that time till ten, when he sat down, Lord Derby was in the House of Commons, and anxiously watching the effect produced, which he ventures to assure your Majesty was most favourable, according to his own judgment after some considerable experience in Parliament, and also from what he heard from others. Mr Disraeli spoke for about five hours, with no apparent effort, with perfect self-possession, and with hardly an exception to the fixed attention with which the House listened to the exposition of the views of your Majesty's servants. It was altogether a most masterly performance, and he kept alive the attention of the House with the greatest ability, introducing the most important statements, and the broadest principles of legislature, just at the moments when he had excited the greatest anxiety to learn the precise measures which the Government intended to introduce. The Irish part of the question was dealt with with remarkable dexterity, though probably a great part of the point will be lost in the newspaper reports. It is difficult to foresee the ultimate result, but Lord Derby has no hesitation in saying that the general first impression was very favourable, and that, as a whole, the Budget seemed to meet with the approval of the House.

Queen Victoria to the Emperor of the French.

Osborne House, *4th December 1852.*

Sir, my Brother,—Being desirous to maintain uninterrupted the union and good understanding which happily subsist between Great Britain and France, I have made choice of Lord Cowley, a peer of my United Kingdom, a member of my Privy Council, and Knight Commander of the Most Honourable Order of the Bath, to reside at your Imperial Majesty's Court in the character of my Ambassador Extraordinary and Plenipotentiary. The long experience which I have had of his talents and zeal for my service assures me that the choice which I have made of Lord Cowley will be perfectly agreeable to your Imperial Majesty, and that he will prove himself worthy of this new mark of my confidence. I request that your Imperial Majesty will give entire credence to all that Lord Cowley shall communicate to you on my part, more especially when he shall assure your Imperial Majesty of my invariable attachment and esteem, and shall express to you those sentiments of sincere friendship and regard with which I am, Sir, my Brother, your Imperial Majesty's good Sister,

Victoria R.

To my good Brother,[53] the Emperor of the French.

Queen Victoria to the Earl of Malmesbury.

Osborne, *6th December 1852.*

The Queen has this morning received Lord Malmesbury's letter of yesterday, relative to Count Walewski's audience. The manner in which Lord Malmesbury proposes this should be done the Queen approves, and only wishes Lord Malmesbury to communicate with the proper authorities in order that the *Fairy* may be at Southampton at the right hour, and the Frigate, as suggested, in attendance off Osborne or Cowes, according to what the weather may be. The landing at Osborne Pier, in wet or stormy weather, is very bad, particularly for a lady.

The Queen wishes that the Count and Countess Walewski should come down here with Lord Malmesbury on *Thursday next*, and we should receive them at half-past one. We wish then that they should *all three dine and sleep here that day.*

Queen Victoria to the Earl of Malmesbury.

Osborne, *8th December 1852.*

The Queen was very much surprised to receive this morning in a box from Lord Malmesbury, without any further explanation, a secret Protocol[54] signed by the representatives of the four great Powers at the Foreign Office on the 3rd instant.

A step of such importance should not have been taken without even the intention of it having been previously mentioned to the Queen, and her leave having been obtained. She must therefore ask for an explanation from Lord Malmesbury. Though the purport of the Protocol appears to the Queen quite right, she ought not to allow the honour of England to be pledged by her Minister without her sanction.

The exact wording of a document of that nature is a matter of such serious importance that it requires the greatest consideration, and it is a question with the Queen whether it be always quite safe to adopt entirely what is proposed by Baron Brunnow, who is generally the *rédacteur* of such documents.

The Earl of Malmesbury to Queen Victoria.

Foreign Office, *13th December 1852.*

Lord Malmesbury presents his humble duty to the Queen. He thought it advisable to acquaint your Majesty as soon as possible with a conversation which Count Walewski had held of his own accord in reference to Her Serene Highness the Princess Adelaide of Hohenlohe,[55] and he requested Lord Derby to repeat it to your Majesty.

Lord Malmesbury was not mistaken in believing that the Count had not alluded idly to the subject, as he this day called on Lord Malmesbury, and stated to him that the Emperor of the French had not decided to negotiate a marriage with the Princess of Wasa;[56] but, on the contrary, was rather averse to such an alliance; that he was anxious, on the contrary, to make one which indirectly "*resserrerait les liens d'amitié entre l'Angleterre et la France,*" and that with this view he wished Lord Malmesbury to ascertain from your Majesty whether any objections would be raised on the part of your Majesty, or of the Princess Adelaide's family, to his contracting a marriage with Her Serene Highness. Your Majesty may suppose that he received this intimation by a simple assurance that he would submit the French Emperor's sentiments to your Majesty. and he added that he foresaw a serious difficulty to the project in the fact that the Princess was a Protestant. Count Walewski was evidently sincere in the earnestness with which he spoke of the subject, and the impatience with which he pressed Lord Malmesbury to inform your Majesty of his proposal.

Queen Victoria to the Earl of Derby.

Osborne, *14th December 1852.*

The Queen sends to Lord Derby a communication which she has received from Lord Malmesbury.

The Queen is sorry to have been put in a situation which requires on her part a direct answer, which to have been spared would have been in every respect more prudent and safe. As it is, however, the Queen is fully aware that the answer she is forced to give may really have, or may hereafter be made appear to have, political consequences disadvantageous to our political relations with France, and injurious to the Queen's personal character.

The Queen therefore encloses for Lord Derby a draft of the answer she intends to give to Lord Malmesbury,[57] asking that Lord Derby will not only give these matters his fullest consideration, but that he will return to the Queen the draft as soon as possible, with such of his suggestions or alterations as he may think advisable to propose to her.

The Queen must also express her decided wish that Lord Derby will not allow Lord Malmesbury to move a single step in this affair without it has been previously concerted with Lord Derby.[58]

He suggested that the following words should be substituted for the last paragraph: "And while she fully appreciates the desire expressed by Count Walewski on the part of his Government, '*de resserrer les liens de l'amitié entre l'Angleterre et la France,*' she feels bound to leave the consideration and decision of so serious a proposal to the unbiassed judgment of the parents of the Princess and the Princess her-self, the only persons to whom such a question can properly be referred. The Queen thinks it right to add that being fully persuaded of the strong religious persuasion of the Princess, of the extreme improb-ability of any change of opinion on her part, and of the evils inseparable from a difference of opinion on such a subject between the Emperor and his intended Consort, she wishes Lord Malmesbury to place this consideration prominently before Count Walewski, before he takes any other step in the matter, which he appears to have brought unofficially under the consideration of Lord Malmesbury."

Queen Victoria to the Earl of Derby.

Osborne, *16th December 1852.*

The Queen has received Lord Derby's letter of the 14th inst. She did not intend to complain personally of Lord Malmesbury, who, the Queen is sure, was most anxious to do the best he could under the cir-cumstances; but she still thinks that a question of such importance should not have been brought immediately before her for her decision; and although Lord Derby states his opinion that Lord Malmesbury had no alternative but to promise to Count Walewski that he would bring "*the Emperor's sentiments before the Queen,*" the very suggestion Lord Derby now makes, viz. "that Lord Malmesbury should be in-structed to treat the proposition as emanating, not from the Emperor, but *unofficially* from Count Walewski, and that he should also *unoffi-cially* dissuade him from pressing the matter further"—shows that there was an alternative.

Lord Derby and Lord Malmesbury alone can know, whether, after what may have passed in conversation between Lord Malmesbury and Count Walewski, this course still remains open.

There can be no doubt that the best thing would be to terminate this affair without the Queen being called upon to give any opinion at all.

Lord Derby seems to treat the matter as of much less importance than the Queen, but he will admit that, if the alliance is sought by the Emperor, "*pour resserrer les liens d'amitié entre la France et l'An-gleterre,*" the refusal of it on the part of the Queen must also have the opposite effect. The responsibility of having produced this effect would rest personally with the Queen, who might be accused of having brought it about, influenced by personal feelings of animosity against the Emperor, or by mistaken friendship for the Orleans family, or misplaced family pride, etc., etc., etc. The acceptance of the proposal, on the other hand, or even the consummation of the project without her *direct* intervention, cannot fail to expose the Queen to a share in the just opprobrium attaching in the eyes of all right-thinking men to the political acts perpetrated in France ever since 2nd December 1851. And, while it would appear as if her Family did not care for any such considerations, so long as by an alliance they could secure momentary advantages, it would give the other Powers of Europe, whom the Emperor seems to be disposed to treat very unceremoniously (as shown by Lord Cowley's last reports) the impression that England suddenly had separated herself from them, and bound herself to France for a family interest pursued by the Queen.

These are the dangers to "the Queen's personal character," which presented themselves to her mind when she wrote her last letter, and which Lord Derby says remained unintelligible to him.

The Queen wishes Lord Derby to show this letter to Lord Malmesbury, whom, under the circumstances, she thinks it best not to address separately. They will be now both in the fullest possession of the Queen's sentiments, and she hopes will be able to terminate this matter without the expression of an opinion on the part of the Queen becoming necessary.

The Earl of Derby to Queen Victoria.

St James's Square, *17th December 1852.*

(4 a.m.)

Lord Derby, with his humble duty, regrets to have to submit to your Majesty that the House of Commons, from which he has this moment returned, has rejected the resolution for the increase of the House Tax, by a majority of either nineteen or twenty-one.[59] This majority is so decisive, especially having been taken on a question which was understood to involve the fate of the Government, as to leave Lord Derby no alternative as to the course which it will be his duty to pursue; and although, as a matter of form, it is necessary that he should consult his Colleagues, for which purpose he has desired that a Cabinet should be summoned for twelve o'clock, he can entertain no doubt but that their opinion will unanimously concur with his own; that he must humbly ask leave to resign into your Majesty's hands the high trust which your Majesty has been pleased to repose in him. Lord

Derby, with your Majesty's permission, will endeavour to do himself the honour of attending your Majesty's pleasure this evening; but it is possible that he may not be able to find the means of crossing,[60] in which case he trusts that your Majesty will honour him with an audience to-morrow (Saturday) morning. Lord Derby trusts he need not assure your Majesty how deeply he feels the inconvenience and annoyance which this event will occasion to your Majesty, nor how anxious will be his desire that your Majesty should be enabled with the least possible delay to form an Administration possessing more of the public confidence. He will never cease to retain the deepest and most grateful sense of the gracious favour and support which he has on all occasions received at your Majesty's hands, and which he deeply regrets that he has been unable to repay by longer and more efficient service.

Memorandum by the Prince Albert.

Osborne, *18th December 1852.*

Yesterday evening Lord Derby arrived from Town formally to tender his resignation. We retired to the Queen's room after dinner with him to hear what he had to say on the crisis. He complained of the factiousness of the Opposition, which he and his Party hoped, however, not to imitate; was ready to support, as far as he could, any Administration which was sincerely anxious to check the growth of democracy. He said his calculations at the close of the Elections had been found almost to a man verified in the late vote: 286 members voting with the Government, and these were their regular supporters; the other half of the House was composed of 150 Radicals, 50 of the so-called Irish Brigade, 120 Whigs, and 30 Peelites. It was clear that, if all these combined, he would be outvoted, though none of these Parties alone numbered as much as half of his. However, he had heard lately from good authority that the Whigs and Peelites had come to an agreement, and were ready to form an Administration on Conservative principles, to the exclusion of the Radicals, under the lead of Lord Aberdeen. Although only 150 strong, they thought, that with all the talent they had at their command, they would be able to obtain the confidence of the country, and hold the balance between the two extreme Parties in the House. He felt that after having failed to obtain the confidence of Parliament himself, he could do nothing else than retire at once, and he advised the Queen to send for Lord Lansdowne, who knew better than anybody the state of Parties, and would give the best advice. He did not advise the Queen to send for Lord Aberdeen at once, because, if it were reported that he had given this advice, many of his Party—who had already been distressed at his declaration to them that if he was defeated he would withdraw from public life—would think it necessary to join Lord Aberdeen as their new appointed leader; and then the other half, which felt the deepest indignation at the treatment they had received from the Peelites, would throw themselves into a reckless alliance with the Radicals, to revenge themselves upon the new Government, so the great Conservative Party would be broken up, which it was so essential for the country to keep together and moderate.

I interrupted Lord Derby, saying that, constitutionally speaking, it did not rest with him to give advice and become responsible for it, and that nobody therefore could properly throw the responsibility of the Queen's choice of a new Minister upon him; the Queen had thought of sending for Lord Lansdowne and Lord Aberdeen together. This, Lord Derby said, would do very well; he knew that, strictly speaking, the Sovereign acted upon her own responsibility, but it was always said on such occasions, for instance, "Lord John advised the Queen to send for Lord Derby," etc., etc.

He then gave it rather jokingly as his opinion that he thought less than 32 could hardly be the number of the new Cabinet, so many former Ministers would expect to be taken in; the Whigs said 36. Lord John Russell was designated for the Home Office, Lord Canning for the Foreign, Mr Gladstone for the Colonial Department, Lord Clanricarde for the Post Office, Lord Granville for Ireland. These were the reports.

Albert.

Queen Victoria to the Marquis of Lansdowne.

Osborne, *18th December 1852.*

The Queen has received Lord Lansdowne's letter, from which she was very sorry to learn that he is suffering from the gout. Although the Queen was very anxious to have consulted with him before taking a definite step for the formation of a new Government consequent on the resignation of Lord Derby, she would have been very unhappy if Lord Lansdowne had exposed his health to any risk in order to gratify her wishes. Time pressing, she has now sent a telegraphic message to Lord Aberdeen to come down here alone, which, from the terms of the

Queen's first summons, he had thought himself precluded from doing. Should Lord Lansdowne not be able to move soon, Lord Aberdeen will confer with him by the Queen's desire immediately on his return to Town.

Memorandum by the Prince Albert.

Osborne, *19th December 1852.*

Lord Aberdeen arrived here at three o'clock and reported that he had seen Lord Lansdowne, and had come to a perfect understanding with him; he had also consulted with his friends, and with Lord John Russell. It would now depend upon the decision of the Queen whom she would charge with the formation of a Government. The Queen answered that she thought Lord Lansdowne was too old and infirm to undertake such arduous duties, and that she commissioned Lord Aberdeen. He replied he was fully aware of his own unworthiness for the task, and had expressed his disinclination to Lord Lansdowne, while Lord Lansdowne, on the other hand, had pressed him to take the responsibility himself; but since the Queen had commissioned him, he wished to say that it was of the greatest importance that only one person should be charged with the task and be responsible for it, and that the new Government should not be a revival of the old Whig Cabinet with an addition of some Peelites, but should be a liberal Conservative Government in the sense of that of Sir Robert Peel; he thought this would meet with the confidence of the country, even if excluding the Radicals. Lord Aberdeen said he meant to propose to the Queen Lord John Russell as Leader of the House of Commons and Secretary of State for Foreign Affairs, which *he* thinks he would accept. (The Queen sanctioned this.) He would then consult Lord John upon his appointments, but he (Lord Aberdeen) would be responsible, taking care that Lord John should be satisfied. There was no doubt that Lord John had full claims to be Prime Minister again, but that he could give him no greater proof of confidence, having been his opponent all his life, than to give him the lead of the House of Commons, which made him virtually as much Prime Minister as he pleased, and the Foreign Office combined with it would satisfy Lord John as following the precedent of Mr Fox. The Peelites would not have served under Lord Lansdowne, much less under Lord John; but a great many Whigs even objected to Lord John. This was a temporary and undeserved unpopularity, and still Lord John remained the first man in the country, and might be Prime Minister again. The Peelites would know and learn to respect him when meeting him in office. Lord Aberdeen hoped even many Conservatives now going with Lord Derby would support such a Government, but to preserve to it a Conservative character, two Secretaries of State at least must be *Peelites*.

We next talked of Lord Palmerston, whom we agreed it would be imprudent to leave to combine in opposition with Mr Disraeli. Lord Aberdeen had thought of Ireland for him; we felt sure he would not accept that. I gave Lord Aberdeen a list of the possible distribution of offices, which I had drawn up, and which he took with him as containing "valuable suggestions." He hoped the Queen would allow him to strengthen himself in the House of Lords, where there was nobody to cope with Lord Derby, by the translation of Sir James Graham or Mr S. Herbert, if he should find this necessary. Sir James might gain in moving from the House of Commons, as he lately fettered himself with inconvenient Radical pledges. He felt he would have great difficulty in the formation of his Government, for although everybody promised to forget his personal wishes and interests, yet when brought to the test such professions were often belied. The difficulty of measures lies chiefly in the Budget, as the Income Tax would have to be settled, and he was anxious to keep a good surplus. As to Reform, he felt that, considering the Queen to have recommended it by a Speech from the Throne, and Lord John to have actually introduced a Measure as Prime Minister, the door could not be closed against it; but it might be postponed for the present, and there was no real wish for it in the country.

He was very sorry that the Government had been upset, and if the Budget had been such that it could have been accepted he should much have preferred it. Lord Derby seemed very much offended with him personally for his speech in the House of Lords. Lord Aberdeen kissed hands, and started again at four o'clock.

The Earl of Aberdeen to Queen Victoria.

(*Undated.*)[61]

Lord Aberdeen, with his humble duty, begs to inform your Majesty, that on his return from Osborne last night, he saw Lord Lansdowne and Lord John Russell, and found them in the same disposition with respect to the formation of the new Administration. This morning, however, Lord John Russell, partly from an apprehension of the fatigue of the Foreign Office, and partly from the effect likely to be produced on his political friends by his acceptance of office, has expressed his unwillingness to form part of the Administration, although anxious to give it his best support. Lord Aberdeen has discussed this matter very fully with Lord John, and has requested him not to decide finally until to-morrow morning, which he had promised accordingly. In the meantime, Lord Aberdeen humbly submits to your Majesty that his position is materially affected by this irresolution on the part of Lord John. Had he not felt warranted in relying upon Lord John's co-operation, he would not have ventured to speak to your Majesty with the confidence he yesterday evinced. With the most earnest desire to devote himself to your Majesty's service, it becomes doubtful whether he could honestly venture to attempt the execution of your Majesty's commands should Lord John persevere in his present intention. At all events, nothing further can be done until this matter shall be decided; and Lord Aberdeen will have the honour of reporting the result to your Majesty.

Lord John Russell to Queen Victoria.

Chesham Place, *20th December 1852.*

Lord John Russell presents his humble duty to your Majesty, and is grateful for your Majesty's condescension in informing him that your Majesty has charged the Earl of Aberdeen with the duty of con-structing a Government.

Lord John Russell is desirous of seeing a durable Government, and he will consider with the utmost care how far he can, consistently with his own honour and his health and strength, contribute to this end.[62]

Mr Disraeli to the Prince Albert.

Downing Street, *20th December 1852.*

Sir,—I have the honour to return to your Royal Highness the State paper[63] which your Royal Highness entrusted to me. I have not presumed to keep a copy of it, but my memory is familiar with its contents, and in case hereafter there may be any opportunity formed to forward the views of your Royal Highness in this respect, I may per-haps be permitted, if necessary, again to refer to the document.

I hope I am not presumptuous if, on this occasion, I offer to your Royal Highness my grateful acknowledgments of the condescending kindness which I have received from your Royal Highness.

I may, perhaps, be permitted to say that the views which your Royal Highness had developed to me in confidential conversation have not fallen on an ungrateful soil. I shall ever remember with interest and admiration the princely mind in the princely person, and shall at all times be prepared to prove to your Royal Highness my devotion. I have the honour to remain, Sir, your Royal Highness's most obedient Servant,

B. Disraeli.

The Earl of Aberdeen to Queen Victoria.

London, *20th December 1852.*

Lord Aberdeen, with his humble duty, begs to inform your Majesty that Lord John Russell has finally decided not to undertake the Foreign Office, being influenced, Lord Aberdeen fully believes, by domestic considerations, and contrary to the advice of all the most important of his political friends. Lord Lansdowne has done his utmost to shake the resolution, but in vain. Lord John proposes to be in the Cabinet, without office, but to lead the Government business in the House of Commons. Lord Aberdeen thinks this arrangement objectionable, and a novelty, although the Duke of Wellington was Leader in the House of Lords for two years without office when Lord Hill was Commander-in-Chief. If the arrangement should be found untenable in a Parliamentary view, Lord John would consent to accept a nominal office, such as Chancellor of the Duchy. It is with great regret that Lord Aberdeen makes this announcement to your Majesty, as his own position is greatly weakened by this change; but he does not think it a sufficient reason for abandoning the attempt to serve your Majesty, which he feared might have been the case if Lord John had persevered in his intention of not forming part of the Administration.

Queen Victoria to the Earl of Derby.

Osborne, *21st December 1852.*

The Queen has to acknowledge the receipt of Lord Derby's letter. She has since read his Speech in the House of Lords announcing his resignation most attentively, and must express her doubts, whether that Speech was calculated to render easier the difficult task which has been thrown upon the Queen by the resignation of her late Government.[64]

Queen Victoria to the Earl of Aberdeen.

Osborne, *21st December 1852.*

The Queen received Lord Aberdeen's letter early this morning, the contents of which have filled her with no little anxiety.

Still, she relies on the spirit of patriotism which she knows animates all the parties concerned, and which she feels sure will ultimately prevail over all difficulties, and enable a strong Government to be formed, which the country so earnestly demands and requires. The Queen is not surprised at Lord John Russell's fearing the fatigue of the Foreign Office, together with the lead in the House of Commons, which Lord Aberdeen's wish to show him entire confidence had prompted him to offer to Lord John; but *this* difficulty, she trusts might easily be obviated. We intend leaving this place for Windsor to-morrow morning, and being there by two o'clock.

The Queen would wish to see Lord Aberdeen there in the course of the afternoon—either at three, four, or five—whichever time is most convenient to him, and requests him to let her find a line from him on her arrival, informing her of the hour at which he will come. Any letter, however, sent by the bag to-night or by a messenger will reach the Queen *here* to-morrow morning, as we do not go before a quarter to ten, and the Queen trusts therefore that Lord Aberdeen will let her hear as soon as possible how matters stand.

Queen Victoria to the King of the Belgians.

Osborne, *21st December 1852.*

My dearest Uncle,—Many thanks for your dear and kind letter of the 17th, which was as ever full of love and affection; but you know *very* well that your affectionate child will never allow any mention of *your* "leaving the premises." You know—too well—how sacred duties of any kind are, and above all, those of a King, and in these days; and how impossible it is for *us to shirk* or abandon any of those duties which God has imposed on us.

You will have heard of our crisis, and of the resignation of the Government; its overthrow was inevitable; but we must now get a strong and durable Government, one combined of the best Conservatives and Liberals, which is what the country expects, demands, and requires. Lord Aberdeen has undertaken the task, but I cannot yet announce, as I wish I could, the formation of the new Government. Ever your devoted Niece,

Victoria R.

You will receive a small parcel for my dear Charlotte for Christmas Eve, and I have directed some prize Christmas beef to be forwarded to Leo, which I hope he will approve of.

The Earl of Derby to Queen Victoria.

St James's Square, *22nd December 1852.*

Lord Derby, with his humble duty, learns with the deepest regret, by the note which he has just had the honour of receiving, that the statement which he felt it his duty to make in the House of Lords has appeared to your Majesty not calculated to render easier the difficult task which has been thrown upon your Majesty by the resignation of himself and his colleagues. Lord Derby begs humbly, but most sincerely, to assure your Majesty that nothing could have been farther from his intention than to let fall a single word which could increase the difficulties of the present position. He feels the full extent of those difficulties, and he may perhaps be forgiven if he entertains a strong opinion that a due appreciation of their magnitude might have been expected to have some weight with those Conservative statesmen, whose opposition thrown into the adverse scale turned the balance against your Majesty's servants, and rendered their retirement from office inevitable. Lord Derby does not affect to deny that he thinks he has some reason, personally and politically, to find fault with the course which they have pursued: but to suffer any such consideration to influence his public conduct, with regard to the Government now in process of formation, would be entirely at variance with his sense of public duty, and inconsistent with the deep gratitude which he must ever feel for the confidence with which your Majesty has honoured him. Lord Derby confesses himself at a loss to understand in what manner Lord Aberdeen can be enabled to reconcile the many and serious discrepancies, in matters both of Church and State, which would appear to exist among his presumed future colleagues; but it will give him unfeigned satisfaction to see these difficulties surmounted in such a sense as to enable him to give to the Government his independent support; and in the meantime it is his determination honestly to undertake the task, difficult as it must be, of keeping together a powerful

Party, without the excitement of opposition to a Government by which their own leaders have been superseded, and of some members of which they think they have reason to complain; and even to induce that Party to give it their support, whenever they can do so consistently, with their own conscientious convictions.

Memorandum by the Prince Albert.

Windsor Castle, *22nd December 1852.*

We arrived here from Osborne at half-past one, and saw Lord Aberdeen at half-past five, who reported the progress he had made in the formation of his Government.

The Chancellorship.—He had hoped to be able to offer to Lord St Leonards to remain, but Lord John Russell insisted, on the part of his Party (which he personally regretted to have to do), that the Chancellor should be a Liberal; Lord Aberdeen in consequence recommended Lord Cranworth.

The Presidency of the Council.—The Duke of Newcastle, who might have done for Ireland, but whose presence in the House of Lords would be a great support to Lord Aberdeen.

The Privy Seal.—The Duke of Argyll, to whom he had, however, not yet applied.

The Secretaries of State.—It appeared that Lord Palmerston had repented of his decision, for he had addressed Lord Lansdowne, and told him that he gave him his proxy—putting himself entirely into his hands, feeling sure that he would take care of his honour. Lord Lansdowne, who had been throughout very kind in his exertions to bring about the junction of Parties, was now engaged to prevail upon him to take the Home Office. We congratulated Lord Aberdeen upon this symptom, which augured confidence in his success. Lord Aberdeen said that when he saw Lord Palmerston, who then declined office, nothing could have exceeded the expressions of his cordiality; he had even reminded him that in fact they were great friends (!!!) of sixty years' standing, having been at school together. We could not help laughing heartily at the *Harrow Boys* and their friendship. The Foreign Office Lord John had again positively refused, contrary to the advice of all his friends, and to please Lady John. This arrangement failing, Lord Clarendon was to undertake it, but Lord Clarendon was now gone himself to try to persuade Lord, or rather Lady, John to accept— at least temporarily—declaring his readiness to take it off his hands at any time if he should find the work too heavy. Lord Aberdeen had no hope, however, of Lord Clarendon's success. Then there would come the grave Constitutional Question of establishing the novelty of a Leader in the House of Commons who held no office. Lord John had seen the danger of being exposed to the reproach that he had slipped into office without having gone through the popular ordeal of a re-election, and had proposed to obviate this by accepting the Steward-ship of the Chiltern Hundreds, and then having himself re-elected for the City of London. But this would not meet all the objections, for it would still be considered unconstitutional that he should lead the busi-ness of the Government in the House of Commons without the responsibility of office. The Leader of the House of Commons was an irresponsible person, and Lord John's saying: "I shall represent you (Lord Aberdeen) in the House of Commons," would be equally uncon-stitutional. Lord John must therefore be prevailed upon to take the Chancellorship of the Duchy of Lancaster, though he felt no inclina-tion to become the successor of Mr Christopher. Lord Aberdeen read a Memorandum of Lord John's, containing his political views on the crisis and the principles of the new Government, of which he is to send the Queen a copy.

For the Colonial Office.—Lord Aberdeen wavered between Sir J. Graham and Mr Gladstone; either could be this, or Chancellor of the Exchequer. Lord John wished Sir James as Chancellor of the Excheq-uer. We argued the greater capabilities of Sir James for the Administration of the Colonies, and Mr Gladstone for the Finances.

Chancellor of the Exchequer—therefore, Mr Gladstone.

Admiralty—Mr Sidney Herbert.

Board of Control—Sir C. Wood.

Board of Trade—Lord Granville.

Board of Works—Sir F. Baring.

(Baring and Wood being the two men whom Lord John had in-sisted on having on the Treasury Bench sitting by his side.)

Postmaster—Lord Canning.

Secretary-at-War—Mr Cardwell.

These would form the Cabinet. Upon Ireland no decision had been come to, though Lord Granville was generally pointed out as the best Lord-Lieutenant.

Lord Aberdeen was very much pleased with the entire confidence existing between him and Lord John. The Budget would be a formida-ble difficulty, as in fact the Government would be an Income Tax Government.

Lord Derby's intemperate and unconstitutional behaviour would do no good to the Government; many of his friends were disgusted. Lord Clanwilliam had called his speech in the House of Lords "a great outrage." The Radicals might be conciliated in some of the lower Offices by the appointment of Mr Charles Villiers, Sir William Molesworth, and others.

The Earl of Malmesbury to Queen Victoria.

Foreign Office, *23rd December 1852.*

Lord Malmesbury presents his humble duty to the Queen, and considers it right to inform your Majesty that Count Walewski again asked him yesterday where the Prince of Hohenlohe was now residing, adding that it was the intention of the Emperor to send a person to see him, and ascertain his feelings with respect to a marriage between him and the Princess Adelaide. Lord Malmesbury confined himself to replying that he did not know. Lord Malmesbury might perhaps in his private capacity endeavour to discourage these advances, but as long as he has the honour of being one of your Majesty's Ministers, it appears to him that your Majesty will be *personally* the least committed by his interfering as little as possible in the matter.

The Emperor is becoming extremely irritable at the delay of the three great Powers in recognising the Empire, and he has said to M. Hübner that, as they had plenty of time to agree among themselves what course they should pursue when it was proclaimed, he cannot understand how Austria and Prussia can in the face of Europe humiliate themselves by waiting for the orders of Russia—"*les ordres de la Russie.*"

Queen Victoria to the Earl of Malmesbury.

Windsor Castle, *23rd December 1852.*

The Queen has received Lord Malmesbury's letter. She thinks he is acting very judiciously in giving Count Walewski no advice whatever as long as he holds the Seals of Office.

Queen Victoria to the Earl of Aberdeen.

Windsor Castle, *23rd December 1852.*

The Queen has received Lord Aberdeen's communication of this morning, and was pleased to hear that Lord John has finally accepted the Foreign Office. She has also received the second communication, with the List of the distribution of Offices. The Queen thinks it of such importance that the Cabinet should be now announced to the world as complete, that she is unwilling to throw any difficulties in the way. At the same time, she must observe that in some instances the changes are, in her opinion, not for the better. Sir J. Graham will be very unpopular in the Navy; his achievements at the Admiralty in former times[65] were all *retrenchments*, and have since proved in many instances injurious to the Service. The Secretary-at-War ought properly to be left out of the Cabinet for the well working of the Army;[66] the President of the Board of Trade has always been in the Cabinet, and in Lord Granville's case, even the Vice-President. Lord Granville will have a difficulty as Chancellor of the Duchy of Lancaster, being one of the chief lessees of the Duchy, and, the Queen believes, even engaged in a law-suit against it. The Queen has no objection to Sir William Molesworth[67] at the Office of Works. She hopes that the Presidency of the Council will be filled at once, for which Lord Clarendon would be best.

Amongst the Under-Secretaries of State, the Queen wishes merely to express her objection at seeing Mr B. Osborne[68] at the *Foreign* Office. The Queen sees Lord Chandos's[69] name as Secretary to the Treasury; she would be very much pleased to see his services secured. All the other proposals she approves.

The Queen must repeat in conclusion that she considers the rapid completion of the Government of the first importance, even if none of the points the Queen has alluded to should be amended.

Queen Victoria to the Earl of Aberdeen.

Windsor Castle, *24th December 1852.*

The Queen has this moment received Lord Aberdeen's letter, reporting that new difficulties have arisen in the completion of the Government by new proposals made by Lord John Russell, since the Queen's sanction had been given to the arrangements submitted to her by Lord Aberdeen, which had then been agreed to by Lord John Russell. The Queen begins to fear serious mischief from the long duration of the crisis. It must weaken the prestige of the new Government, and, instead of smoothing difficulties, is, from the nature of things, rather calculated to invite new ones. The Queen has, in her letter of yesterday, stated some objections *she* felt, but added that she would waive them all for the satisfaction of the immediate want of the country (a strong Government), and she must express her hope that political par-

443

ties will not fall short in patriotic spirit of the example she has thus herself set.

Queen Victoria to the Earl of Aberdeen.
[Draft—from recollection.]

Windsor Castle, *24th December 1852.*

The Queen has received Lord Aberdeen's letter of this afternoon, and is very glad to hear that he has overcome the difficulties which he mentioned this morning, and that he has secured the services of Lord Lansdowne in the Cabinet. She hopes, however, that Lord Aberdeen will remain firm on the other points, as difficulties are never overcome by yielding to more than can be fairly demanded.

Memorandum by Queen Victoria.

Windsor Castle, *25th December 1852.*

Lord Aberdeen came this afternoon to announce the completion of his Cabinet.

From many of them answers have not yet been received.

The day before it looked very bad. Lord John Russell had sent in such a list of persons whom he required in the Cabinet (Sir Francis Baring, Sir George Grey, etc., etc.), that, having been very yielding hitherto, Lord Aberdeen was obliged to be peremptory in his refusal. Now that the Cabinet was formed on a due proportion, he was inclined to let Lord John have his own way pretty much with regard to the minor Offices, considering that he brought 250 followers, and he (Lord Aberdeen) only 50.

It was to Lord Clarendon that the persuasion of Lady John was finally due, but Lord Aberdeen had to add his own promise to that of Lord Clarendon, that the latter would take the Foreign Office whenever she thought Lord John ought to be relieved from it.

Lady Palmerston had been most anxious to bring her husband into office again; Lord Aberdeen had seen the first symptom of their joint wish in the earnestness with which Lord Palmerston's friends declared in all places that, had he been well enough, he would certainly have voted against the Government.

Lord Lansdowne's exertions and Lord Clarendon's disinterestedness were beyond all praise.

Of the Derbyites, he heard that most of them would be very quiet, and many would be very friendly.

Lord Breadalbane is to be Lord Chamberlain. We recommend a trial to get Lord Jersey to remain as Master of the Horse.

Victoria R.

The Prince Albert to the Earl of Aberdeen.
Windsor Castle, *26th December 1852.*

My dear Lord Aberdeen,—I have heard rumours of some appointments in the Household, for which the writs are to be moved tomorrow. As you have not yet placed before the Queen your recommendations, I merely write this to you, fearing that the "Whig Party" may deal out places before you have had an opportunity of taking the Queen's pleasure. Ever yours truly,

Albert.

Memorandum by the Prince Albert.
Windsor Castle, *27th December 1852.*

Lord Derby had his audience of leave yesterday afternoon. He repeated his thanks to the Queen for the support and countenance she had given him throughout the period he had been allowed to serve her, adding his regrets that his services could not have been more efficient or longer. One thing only distressed him in taking leave, and that was the idea that the Queen might think he had unnecessarily raised difficulties to the formation of a new Government by his Speech in the House of Lords. Now, it had been incumbent upon him to show to his Party that he had not quitted office on light grounds, after the sacrifices of opinion they had brought in order to support him; he had to prove that the vote in the House of Commons was not an accidental vote, but the preconcerted Union of all Parties (in opposition) against him, which gave them a real majority. We replied that it was not his opinion on the late division, to the expression of which the Queen had objected, but to that of an opinion on the character of the new Government which the Queen had not yet formed. It was of the greatest importance to keep that in suspense, and the declaration that Lord Derby knew Lord Aberdeen to profess Conservative opinions of his own (Lord Derby's) shade, had at once given the alarm to the Radicals, and made them insist upon a greater proportion of Liberals in the Cabinet. Lord Derby rejoined he had expressed his doubts as to how

445

these differences could be reconciled; and he did not see now how this was to be done. How could Lord Aberdeen and Lord John Russell agree upon the Foreign Policy, for instance? The Queen replied that Lord John's views were very sound and moderate, and that the line of Foreign Policy he had formerly had to pursue had been forced upon him by Lord Palmerston, who had never left a question for the decision of the Cabinet to which he had not already given a decided bias.

Did Lord Derby know that Lord Palmerston gave it out everywhere that, had he been well enough, he should certainly have voted *against* the Government? Lord Derby could only say that he had allowed his son-in-law, Lord Jocelyn, to go to Italy under the firm conviction that Lord Palmerston would refuse to join Lord Aberdeen or Lord John Russell!

Lord Derby took leave after five o'clock.

Albert.

The Countess of Derby to the Marchioness of Ely.[70]

St James's Square, *27th December 1852.*

My dearest Lady Ely,—Lord Derby told me that he saw you yesterday, but only for a moment. I think he was nervous about his audience of leave, but he returned deeply touched by the kindness of manner of the Queen and the Prince. I cannot resist saying to you that, during the last year, he has been more and more impressed with the admirable qualities of the Queen, and her noble straightforwardness on all occasions, and her unvarying kindness have inspired him with the strongest attachment (if I may venture so to express his feelings for Her Majesty). During that week of terrible suspense he continually said to me that his chief anxiety and regret were caused by the fear of leaving the Queen, particularly before he had had time and power to do more in her service. I am writing in haste, having much to do this last day in Town, but I have very often wished that the Queen knew how warmly and sincerely Lord Derby is devoted to her service. He is also very grateful to the Prince, for whose abilities he has the highest admiration, often speaking of his wonderful cleverness. I am delighted to hear that the Queen is so well; he said she was looking remarkably well yesterday. He told me that Her Majesty used some kind expression about myself. If you should have an opportunity of saying to Her Majesty how grateful I am for all her former kindness, I should be very much obliged to you. Ever yours very affectionately,

Emma Derby.

Memorandum by the Prince Albert.

Windsor Castle, *28th December 1852.*

The delivery of the Seals of Office of the outgoing Ministers into the Queen's hands, and her bestowal of them upon the new Ministers, took place to-day.

Of the former, Mr Disraeli seemed to feel most the loss of office.

We saw Lord Aberdeen for some time, who submitted the names of all the persons he recommended for the subordinate Offices, of whom he will send a list. We asked him what might have passed between the last Session and this to chill his feelings for Lord Derby, who maintained that up to the Dissolution he had sent him messages to say that he perfectly agreed with him, except on the Commercial Policy, and that he never would join the Whigs. Lord Aberdeen disclaimed all knowledge of such messages, though he acknowledged to have been very friendly to Lord Derby. At the General Election, however, it appeared to him that there was such a total want of principle in him and his Party, pledging themselves for Protection in one place and Free Trade in another, and appearing consistent only on one point, viz. their hatred to Sir Robert Peel's memory and his friends, that he became determined to have nothing to do with them.

The formation of the Government appeared to give satisfaction to the country, though of course the number of the disappointed must be even larger than usual on such occasions. Lord Canning seemed very much hurt at not being taken into the Cabinet, and felt inclined to refuse the Post Office. We agreed upon the impolicy of such a step, and encouraged Lord Aberdeen to press him. Lord Clanricarde, and particularly Lord Carlisle, were very much grieved at being left out altogether, but there was no help for it; for each man taken in from one side, two would be proposed from the other, and the Cabinet was just large enough to work.

We saw Lord Lansdowne after the Council, who seemed well satisfied with the Government, a combination he had so much and so long wished. Lord Carlisle's annoyance was the only thing which personally grieved him. He said that from the moment he had read Mr Disraeli's Budget he had felt sure that the Government would fall immediately; the country would never submit to a new tax with a surplus in the Exchequer.

Lord John Russell, whom we saw afterwards, seemed in very good health and spirits. He told us that the peaceful parting scene in the House of Commons had been his doing; he had told Mr Walpole that he thought Mr Disraeli ought to make an apology to the House for the language he had used, and which had given pain to a great many persons; and on Mr Walpole's saying that that was a very delicate thing to tell Mr Disraeli, he had allowed it to be told him as a message from him (Lord John). Mr Disraeli declared his readiness, provided others would do the same, and declared they had meant no offence.[71] We owned that we had been astonished to find them of a sudden all so *well bred*. We asked what Lord Palmerston had been about during the crisis? Lord John told us in reply that Lord Palmerston had certainly been disposed to join Lord Derby's Government, but always said he could not do so alone; that if eight of them were to join, then they would have the majority in the Cabinet. He also said that he believed Lord Palmerston would have voted *for* some parts of the Budget and against others. Lord John does not think that that large Party of Lord Derby's will long keep together, that some would vote for the Government, others might try to raise a Protestant cry.

Lord Palmerston looked excessively ill, and had to walk with two sticks from the gout.

Queen Victoria to the King of the Belgians.

Windsor Castle, *28th December 1852.*

My dearest Uncle,—Your dear letter of the 24th reached me on Monday, and I thank you warmly for it. The success of our excellent Aberdeen's arduous task and the formation of so brilliant and strong a Cabinet would, I was sure, please you. It is the realisation of the country's and our *most* ardent wishes, and it deserves success, and will, I think, command great support.... It has been an anxious week, and just on our happy Christmas Eve we were still very uneasy.

As I mean to write again before this year runs out, and I have a long Council with outgoing and incoming Ministers this afternoon, you will excuse my taking leave here. Ever your truly devoted Niece,

Victoria R.

The Princess Hohenlohe to Queen Victoria.

Langenburg, *30th December 1852.*

My dearest Victoria,—According to your wish and our promise, we send this servant with the most unwelcome news that yesterday morning M. de Jaux arrived here and told Ernest (as you will see by his letter to Albert) that the Count Walewski wishes to have an interview with him to confer on the subject we know of. A quarter of an hour before I received this letter from Uncle Leopold, which I sent in Ernest's letter to Ada, and in which he speaks his opinion that we ought not to say "*No*" *at once*, before telling Ada of it. This is very much against my wish and Ernest's, for we both would like to make an end of the affair as soon as possible, but cannot, as we see the truth of what Uncle Leopold says. I send a letter to Mamma to you, and one for Ada. Mamma knows of it, as she wrote to me the other day, and I leave it to you, dearest Victoria, if you or Mamma will tell the poor child of the transaction. She will be in great distress. I wish she may at once say "*No*," but am not sure of it; and in our letters we have not said anything for the thing, but nothing against also but what naturally is to be said against it. She will not know what to do, and I am sure you and Mamma will not put it to her in *too* favourable a light, as we are of the same opinion on the subject; but yet there may be some things in its favour too. I wish you would make Charles come to us—*if you think it wise to do so*—and he not only will try to engage us to it. But there may be so many reasons for or against which in a letter it is not possible to explain all, and which we could not answer in time; besides by him we might learn more accurately what Ada feels: but I leave it quite to your and Albert's judgment, if this would be a good plan. I am in great distress, you well may think, my dearest Victoria. Oh! if we could but say "*No*" at once!...

Many thanks, my dearest Victoria, for your kind letter of the 22nd. In the papers I have been following with the greatest interest what has been said on the formation of the new Ministry; there is one name though which frightens me—Lord Palmerston. Let me wish you joy of the New Year; may it *bring peace* not only to the nations, but also to us. Every blessing and happiness to you, dear Albert, and your children, and for me your love and affection, which is a blessing to your devoted Sister,

Feodora.

Ernest also wishes you all possible happiness. If Ada has the wish to see the Emperor before she decides, what is to be done?

Queen Victoria to the King of the Belgians.

Windsor Castle, *31st December 1852.*

My dearest Uncle,—On *this*, the last day of the old year, allow me to offer my most ardent wishes for *many* and happy returns of the New Year to you and yours. May it be one of peace and prosperity to us *all*, and may we have the happiness of seeing *you* again. May we still hope to see you this *winter* or not?

Our Government is very satisfactorily settled. To have my faithful friend Aberdeen as Prime Minister is a great happiness and comfort for me personally. Lord Palmerston is terribly altered, and all his friends think him breaking. He walks with two sticks, and seemed in great suffering at the Council, I thought. I must now conclude. Ever your devoted Niece,

Victoria R.

ENDNOTES:

[1]:Prince Christian of Schleswig-Holstein-Sonderburg-Glücksburg was named successor to Frederick VII., King of Denmark by a Treaty signed in London on the 8th of May 1852; and by the Danish law of succession (of the 31st of July 1853), he ascended the throne under the style of Christian IX., on the 15th of November, 1863. He was the father of His Majesty Frederick VIII., the present King of Denmark, and of Her Majesty Queen Alexandra of England; King Christian died in 1906, Queen Louise having predeceased him in 1898.

[2]:Lord John Russell having vainly attempted to secure the co-operation of the Duke of Newcastle, announced the wish of the Cabinet to make overtures to Sir J. Graham.

[3]:The Ministerial Reform Bill.

[4]:The Act of Settlement excluded (as from the accession of the House of Hanover) the Ministers of State from the House of Commons; but the 6 Anne, c. 7, modified this, and made them re-eligible on appointment.

[5]:See *ante*, p. 356.

[6]:Submitted to the Queen by Colonel Phipps.

[7]:It appears from a Memorandum made about this time by Prince Albert that when Lord Palmerston's retirement became known, the Radical constituency of Marylebone wished to present him with an Address of sympathy, and to invite him to stand at the next Election, promising him to bring him

in. Sir Benjamin Hall (one of the Members) told them that they had better wait till the explanation in Parliament had taken place, for at present they knew nothing about the merits of the case. This the Committee which had been organised consented to do. After the Debate on the 4th of February, Sir Benjamin called upon the Chairman of the Committee to ask him whether they would still carry out their intention. "No," said the Chairman; "we have considered the matter: a man who does not answer the Queen's letters can receive no Address from us."

[8]:See *ante*, p. 274.

[9]:*Cf.* Greville's account in his Journal, 5th February 1852. *See* also p. 368.

[10]:The Tuscan Government declined to receive Sir H. Bulwer, and it was then proposed to send him to Rome instead.

[11]:Notorious as a centre of the Slave Trade. The native king was deposed.

[12]:See *ante*, pp. 309, 340.

[13]:Events in France had revived anxiety as to the national defences, and the Government brought in a Bill for raising a local Militia. To this scheme the Duke of Wellington had been unfavourable, and Lord Palmerston, by a majority of eleven, carried an Amendment in favour of re-organising the "regular" instead of raising a "local" Militia.

[14]:On the Militia Bill.

[15]:Lord Granville held the Foreign Secretaryship in 1870-1874, and again in 1880-1885.

[16]:Lord Malmesbury.

[17]:The Queen was stabbed by a priest when returning from church.

[18]:Extract from Her Majesty's *Journal*.

[19]:This Memorandum is given in chap. xlv. of the *Life of the Prince Consort*.

[21]:Prime Minister of Austria. He died in the April following.

[22]:Palmerston, however, admitted the contrary (*Life of the Prince Consort*, vol. ii. chap. xliv.).

[23]:The French had been pressing the Swiss Government to expel refugees, and Austria supported the French President.

[24]:Lord Derby had urged that a more conciliatory message should accompany Lord Granville's last despatch, which, because of its unfriendly tone, Count Buol had delayed sending on to Vienna. The precise language (he said) must depend on what information Count Buol could supply.

[25]:The Government eventually proposed that the four seats taken from St Albans and Sudbury should be assigned to South Lancashire and the West Riding; but, on the ground that a Ministry on sufferance should confine itself to necessary legislation, Mr Gladstone induced the House by a great majority to shelve the proposal.

[26]:The members belonging to the Manchester School of Politics.

[27]:This uncertainty led to the Anti-Corn-Law League, which had been dissolved in 1846, being revived.

[28]:British Envoy at Turin.

[29]:Premier of Sardinia.

³⁰:Lord Derby in reply, after reviewing the whole matter, counselled non-interference, the keeping of a vigilant watch on French and Austrian actions, encouragement of Sardinia in her constitutional action, and the making use of any opportunity to secure both the independence of Piedmont and the reform of the Papal Administration.

³¹:In this letter the President of the Republic had expressed his admiration at the conduct of the French troops in the Roman expedition under General Oudinot, and his warm approval of the policy that led to the campaign.

³³:Its chief feature was a renewal of the expiring Income Tax.

³⁴:Accordingly, no financial changes were proposed until after the General Election. See *post*, p. 406.

³⁵:British Minister at Madrid.

³⁶:The Church question was brought into the political arena in the General Election, which was now in progress; much violence was manifested during the contest.

³⁷:"It is additional proof, if more were wanting," wrote Mr Walpole in reply, "that all Parties should forbear as much as possible from the ostentatious parade of anything that can provoke either the one or the other."

³⁸:Victor Hugo (1802-1885) had founded the journal, *L'Evénement*, in 1848: he was exiled in 1851, and published *Napoléon le Petit* in Belgium. After the fall of the Empire he returned to France, and in 1877 published his *Histoire d'un Crime*.

³⁹:John Camden Neild, an eccentric and miserly bachelor, nominally a barrister, died on the 30th of August, bequeathing substantially the whole of his fortune (amounting to half a million) to the Queen. As there were no known relatives, the Queen felt able to accept this legacy; but she first increased the legacies to the executors from £100 to £1000 each, made provision for Mr Neild's servants and others who had claims on him, restored the chancel of North Marston Church, Bucks, where he was buried, and inserted a window there to his memory.

⁴⁰:The Duke passed away at Walmer on the 14th of September, in his eighty-fourth year.

⁴¹:He became Lord Raglan.

⁴²:These letters, which are of no special importance, contained a statement from Lord Palmerston to the effect that the appointment to the Commandership-in-Chief was vested in the Secretary at War.

⁴³:Lord Palmerston had held the office of Secretary at War from 1809 to 1828.

⁴⁴:Louis Napoleon himself claimed no hereditary right to the Imperial dignity, but only that conferred by election: he acknowledged as national all the acts which had taken place since 1815, such as the reigns of the later Bourbons and of Louis Philippe. (See *Memoirs of an ex-Minister*.)

⁴⁵:This Motion, intended to extort a declaration from the House in favour of Free Trade, and describing the Corn Law Repeal as "a just, wise, and beneficial measure," was naturally distasteful to the Ministers. Their *amour-*

propre was saved by Lord Palmerston's Amendment omitting the "*odious* epithets*" and affirming the principle of unrestricted competition.

[46]:Marshal Gouvion de St Cyr.

[47]:In sending no representative to the funeral of the Duke of Wellington.

[48]:See *ante*, p. 276.

[49]:The Queen had allowed him to enter into negotiations with the Peelites and Lord Palmerston on the distinct understanding that the latter could not receive the lead of the House of Commons.

[50]:Lord Palmerston's Amendment (See *ante*, p. 419.) was carried instead, and Protection was thenceforward abandoned by Mr Disraeli and his followers.

[51]:Lord Malmesbury advised that a formal repetition of the interpretation and assurances as to the use of the numeral "III" in the Imperial title, already verbally made by the President and the French Ambassador, should be demanded. This was duly obtained. On the 2nd of December, the anniversary of the *coup d'état*, the Imperial title was assumed; on the 4th, the Empire was officially recognised.

[52]:Increase of the House Tax, reduction of the Malt and Tea duties, and relaxation of Income Tax in the case of farmers, were the salient features of the Budget.

[53]:The Czar persisted in addressing him as *Mon cher Ami*.

[54]:By this Protocol Louis Napoleon was to be recognised as Emperor by Great Britain, Austria, Prussia, and Russia.

[55]:The Queen's niece, daughter of Princess Hohenlohe.

[56]:The Princess Caroline Stéphanie, daughter of Prince Gustavus de Wasa, who was son of the last King of Sweden of the earlier dynasty.

[57]:Queen Victoria to the Earl of Malmesbury.

[*Draft.*]

Osborne, *14th December 1852.*

The Queen has received Lord Malmesbury's letter of yesterday, reporting his conversation with Count Walewski, who had asked him to ascertain from the Queen "whether any objections would be raised on her part or on that of the Princess Adelaide's family to his (the Emperor's) contracting a marriage with Her Serene Highness."

In a question which affects the entire prospects and happiness of a third person, and that person being a near and dear relation of hers, the Queen feels herself conscientiously precluded from forming an opinion of her own, and consequently from taking the slightest part in it either directly or indirectly. The only proper persons to refer to for the consideration of and decision on so serious a proposal are the parents of the Princess and the Princess herself.

[58]:In his reply Lord Derby observed that it did not appear to him that the matter was at present in so critical a position. Lord Malmesbury would have little difficulty in showing Count Walewski, without any interruption of a friendly *entente*, that the intended overtures were not likely to be favourably received. He suggested that Lord Malmesbury should be instructed to

treat the proposition as emanating, not from the Emperor, but unofficially, from Count Walewski; and that he should, also unofficially, dissuade him from pressing the subject further; such course could have no injurious effect upon the political aspect of Europe. Lord Derby could not understand how the affair, however it might turn out, could affect the Queen's "personal character."

[59]:This memorable debate and its sensational ending, with the notable speeches from Disraeli and Gladstone, has been repeatedly described. See, e.g., Morley's *Gladstone* and McCarthy's *History of our own Times*. The *Times* leader (quoted by Mr Morley) was cut out and preserved by the Queen.

[60]:To Osborne.

[61]:Apparently written on the 20th of December 1852.

[62]:He consulted Lord Lansdowne, and Macaulay, happening to call, threw his influence into the scale in favour of his serving under Aberdeen (Walpole's *Russell*, chap, xxiii.).

[63]:It is impossible to ascertain what this was; it was probably one of the Prince's political Memoranda.

[64]:Lord Derby severely attacked Lord Aberdeen, in his absence, and declared himself the victim of a factious combination.

[65]:From 1830 to 1834.

[66]:The Secretary-at-War was not a Secretary of State.

[67]:M.P. for Southwark; well known as a philosophical writer, the first member of the Radical Party included in any Ministry.

[68]:Mr Bernal Osborne, a well-known speaker at the time, became Secretary of the Admiralty.

[69]:Afterwards, as Duke of Buckingham, Secretary for the Colonies and Governor of Madras.

[70]:Submitted to the Queen by Lady Ely.

[71]:"Mr Disraeli ... with infinite polish and grace asked pardon for the flying words of debate, and drew easy forgiveness from the member (Mr Goulburn), whom a few hours before he had mocked as 'a weird sibyl'; the other member (Sir James Graham), whom he could not say he greatly respected, but whom he greatly regarded; and the third member (Sir C. Wood), whom he bade learn that petulance is not sarcasm, and insolence is not invective. Lord John Russell congratulated him on the ability and the gallantry with which he had conducted the struggle, and so the curtain fell." Morley's *Gladstone*, Book III. chap. viii.

INTRODUCTORY NOTE
TO CHAPTER XXII

The opening of the year 1853 saw a strong Coalition Ministry in power; the necessity of a cordial understanding with France was obvious, but bitter and indiscreet attacks on the Emperor of the French were made by certain members of the Government, for which Mr Disraeli took them severely to task. Lord John Russell, who had been appointed Foreign Secretary, resigned that office in February, in favour of Lord Clarendon, being unable to bear the twofold burden of the Leadership of the House and the Foreign Office. Though the arrangement was questioned, he continued during the year to lead the House without office. A Canadian Clergy Reserves Bill, an India Bill, introducing competitive examination into the Civil Service, and various measures of Metropolitan improvement were passed. A more important feature of the Session was Mr Gladstone's first Budget, dealing comprehensively with the Income Tax, and imposing a duty on successions to real property.

The Eastern Question, however, overshadowed all other interests. For some time a dispute had existed between the Latin and Greek Churches as to the guardianship of the Holy Places (including the Church of the Holy Sepulchre) in Palestine. After long negotiations between the French and Russian Governments, as representing these Churches, an indecisive judgment was pronounced by the Porte, which, however, so incensed Russia that she began to make warlike demonstrations, and sent Prince Menschikoff to Constantinople to make peremptory requisitions as to the Holy Places.

In the meanwhile, the Czar had made confidential overtures to Sir Hamilton Seymour, the British Ambassador at St Petersburg, representing the Sultan as a very "sick man," and suggesting that, on the dissolution of his Empire, a concerted disposal of the Turkish dominions should be made by England and Russia; these conversations were

reported at once to the British Government. Lord Stratford de Redcliffe, who had been sent to represent British interests at
Constantinople, arrived there after Prince Menschikoff, and a settlement of the disputes as to the Holy Places was then easily effected,
Lord Stratford insisting on this question being kept independent of any
other issue. But Prince Menschikoff had come to the conference with
instructions to keep an ulterior object in view, namely, to advance a
claim, by means of a strained interpretation of the Treaty of Kainardji
of 1774, of a Russian protectorate over the Christian subjects of the
Sultan. Influenced by Lord Stratford, the Porte rejected the claim, and,
in retaliation, the Czar occupied the Danubian Principalities of Wallachia and Moldavia, characterising the step not as an act of war, but a
material guarantee of Russia's just rights. The French Emperor, anxious to divert the attention of his subjects from domestic politics, was
making preparations for war; and similar preparations were also being
made in England.

Negotiations took place between the Powers with a view of averting war, and a document known as the Vienna Note, to which Great
Britain and France were parties, and which Russia accepted, was prof-
fered to the Sultan: again Lord Stratford interposed to prevent its
acceptance, and, when the Russian Government subsequently announced its own interpretation of the Note, it was apparent that the
Western Powers had been mistaken as to its purport.

An Ultimatum, requiring the evacuation of the Principalities, was
sent by the Porte to Russia and rejected: war broke out, and the first
encounter at Oltenitza, on the 4th of November, resulted in favour of
Turkey. Meanwhile both the British and French fleets had been sent to
the East, and, on the declaration of war, the British Admiral was instructed to take any action he thought fit to prevent Russian aggression
on Turkish territory. On the 30th of November the Turkish Fleet in
Sinope Harbour was destroyed by the Russian squadron, this occurrence provoking profound indignation in England, though it had been
urged both within the Cabinet and outside that the despatch of the
combined Western Fleets through the Dardanelles was more likely to
appear as a defiance to Russia than a support to Turkey.

Earlier in the year Lord Aberdeen had desired to retire, but en-
quiry soon disclosed that Lord John Russell no longer had the
influence necessary to form a Ministry, and in the face of danger Lord
Aberdeen remained at his post. But there were sharp dissensions in the
Cabinet, especially between Lord Palmerston, representing the anti-
Russian party, on the one hand, and on the other Lord Aberdeen, who

distrusted the Turks, and Mr Gladstone, who disavowed any obligation to uphold the integrity of the Ottoman Empire. In December, Lord Palmerston resigned office, the ostensible reason being his opposition to the contemplated Reform Bill of the Government. The real cause was his opinion that apathy was being shown by his colleagues in reference to the Eastern Question; however, after arrangements had been made for replacing him, he was, at his own desire, re-admitted to the Cabinet.

CHAPTER XXII

1853

Queen Victoria to the King of the Belgians.

Windsor Castle, *4th January 1853.*

My dearest Uncle,—... Our new Government will really, I think, command a large support, and, I trust, be of duration, which is a great object. Their only difficulty will be the Budget.

The coldness and tardiness of the Northern Powers in recognising *our* new *bon Frère* annoys him very much, and produces a bad effect in France. I don't think it is wise. Unnecessary irritation may produce *real* mischief. To squabble about *how* to call him, after having praised and supported him after the *Coup d'État*, seems to me very *kleinlich* and inconsistent, and I think our conduct throughout has been much more dignified....

I have read with pleasure the loyal addresses of the Chambers, and with peculiar satisfaction the allusion to Leopold's visit to England. Let him and Philippe come here often and regularly, and let them study this country and her laws *à fond*—it will do them more good than all the studying and reading in the world. They all three express most warmly to us their hopes of returning to us soon. Do let us have the hope of seeing you in February. It would be delightful!... I must now wish you good-bye. Ever your devoted Niece,

Victoria R.

The Earl of Aberdeen to Queen Victoria.

London, *9th January 1853.*

... Lord Aberdeen also begs to mention to your Majesty that he saw Dr Hawtrey yesterday and in signifying your Majesty's gracious intentions[1] towards him, took an opportunity of expressing in very strong terms the great importance cf the choice of his successor as Headmaster of Eton, and described the requisite qualifications for such a situation, as well as the objections to which some appointments might be liable. Lord Aberdeen was perfectly understood by Dr Hawtrey, although no name was mentioned; and the subject was regarded as being of the utmost importance, not only to the school itself, but to the nation at large.

Lady Augusta Bruce to the Duchess of Kent.

Rue de Varennes 65, *31st January 1853.*

Dearest Madame,—I fear that I shall not be able to add much to the newspaper account of yesterday's ceremony,[2] for it was one the impression of which is best conveyed by a simple and accurate description of the scene, and of those arrangements and details which combined to render its effect gorgeous and dazzling. Apart, however, from the historical interest attached to it as one of the very curious acts of the extraordinary Drama now enacting in France, the impression produced was one that would be called forth by a magnificent theatrical representation, and little more. This seemed to be the public feeling, for though multitudes thronged the streets, the day being dry, they appeared to be animated by curiosity chiefly, and that *sober* curiosity which now characterises the people of Paris, wearied as they are of *novelty* and excitement. As far as one can judge, it does not seem that the lower orders take much interest in this marriage; the ambition and vanity of *his* partisans have been wounded by it, and, of course, his enemies do not scruple to calumniate and slander the unfortunate object of his choice disgracefully.

It is very difficult to ascertain anything like truth as regards her, but her beauty and engaging manners will, it is thought by many, gain for her, for a time at least, a greater amount of popularity than his friends who now blame the marriage expect. That he is passionately in love with her no one doubts, and his countenance on late occasions, as well as yesterday, wore a radiant and joyous expression very unusual. She, on the contrary, showed a considerable amount of nervousness at the Civil Marriage, and was as pale as death yesterday—however, even with the high and determined spirit she is supposed to have, this might be expected. Lady Cowley had been kind enough to send us an invitation, of which we were tempted to avail ourselves.[3] Nothing could be more splendid than the decorations of the Cathedral—velvet and ermine—gold and silver—flags and hangings of all colours were

459

combined and harmonised with the splendid costumes of the Clergy, the uniforms, civil and military, and the magnificent dresses of the ladies. The greatest mistake was the *conflict* of lights—the windows not having been darkened, though countless thousands of wax candles were lighted. The music was very fine.... The object of our neighbours seemed to be to scan and criticise the dress of the Bride, and the wonderful penetration and accuracy of their eagle glances was to us something incredible! Certainly, though unable ourselves at such a distance to appreciate the details of her dress or the expression of her countenance, we saw her distinctly enough to be able to say that a more lovely *coup d'œil* could not be conceived. Her beautifully chiselled features and marble complexion, her nobly *set-on head*, her exquisitely proportioned figure and graceful carriage were most striking, and the whole was like a Poet's Vision! I believe she is equally beautiful when seen close, but at a distance at which we saw her the effect was something more than that of a lovely picture, it was aerial, ideal. On the classically shaped head she wore a diamond crown or diadem, round her waist a row of magnificent diamonds to correspond, and the same as trimming round the "basques" of her gown. Then a sort of cloud or mist of transparent lace enveloped her, which had the effect of that for which, when speaking of the hills in Scotland, Princess Hohenlohe could find no English word, "*Duft*." I hope your Royal Highness will not think me very much carried by what pleases the eye. I felt all the while that one could view the matter but as an outside show; as such, in as far as she was concerned, it was exquisitely beautiful—and I suppose that a sort of national prejudice made me attribute the grace and dignity of the scene, for what there was of either came from her, to the blood of *Kirkpatrick!!!*

The carriages were ugly and the Procession by no means fine, and those in which the Bridal party afterwards travelled to St Cloud, were driven by individuals in the famous theatrical costume of the well-known "Postillon de Longjumeau!"[4]

The King of the Belgians to Queen Victoria.

Laeken, *4th February 1853.*

My dearest Victoria,—Receive my best thanks for your gracious letter of the 1st. Since I wrote to you *le grand événement a eu lieu!* We truly live in times where at least variety is not wanting; the only mischief is that like drunkards people want more and more excitement, and it therefore will probably end by what remains the most exciting of all—War. Amusing and interesting war is, it must be confessed, more than anything in the world, and that makes me think that it must be the bouquet when people will be *blasé* of everything else. I enclose a letter from our Secretary of Legation at Madrid, Baron Beyens, who married a great friend of the Queen, Mademoiselle de Santa Cruz, and is much *au fait* of all things that interest the public just now. It seems by what I learned from Paris that the Empress communicated to a friend a communication of *son cher époux* when she expressed her sense of her elevation to such eminence; as it may interest you and Albert, I will make an extract of it here: "Vous ne me parlez, ma chère enfant, que des avantages de la position que je vous offre, mais mon devoir est de vous signaler aussi ses dangers; ils sont grands, je serai sans doute à vos côtés l'objet de plus d'une tentative d'assassinat; indépendamment de cela, je dois vous confier que des complots sérieux se fomentent dans l'armée. J'ai l'œil ouvert de ce côté et je compte bien d'une manière ou d'autre prévenir toute explosion; le moyen sera *peut-être la guerre*. Là encore il y a de grandes chances de ruine pour moi. Vous voyez donc bien que vous ne devez pas avoir de scrupules pour partager mon sort, les mauvaises chances étant peut-être égales aux bonnes!"

I was sorry to hear of Lord Melbourne's, *i.e.*, Beauvale's, death. I knew him since 1814, and found him always very kind. For poor Lady Melbourne, who devoted herself so much, it is a sad blow. We are longing for a little cold, but it does not come though we have some east wind. I am held back in some of the *most essential* measures for the defence of the country by the tricks of the Chamber. I see that the Manchester party shines in unusual Bright-ness and Cobden-ness by a degress of absurdity never as yet heard of. In the American War the Quakers refused to fight; they did not besides like the extremities the States had gone to against the mother country; but not to defend its own country against probable invasion is truly too much.

Pray have the goodness to give my best love to Albert, and believe me, ever my dearest Victoria, your devoted Uncle,

Leopold R.

Queen Victoria to the King of the Belgians.

Windsor Castle, *8th February 1853.*

My dearest Uncle,—I have to thank you for two most kind letters of the 4th and 7th (which I have just received) with very interesting enclosures, which shall be duly returned. The little report of what the Emperor said to the Empress is very curious, and tallies with what I have also heard of his thinking much more of the insecurity of his position than he used to do. The description of the young Empress's character is an interesting one, and also agrees with what I had heard from those who know her well. It may be in her power to do much good—and I hope she may. Her character is made to captivate a man, I should say—particularly one like the Emperor.

I am sorry that you have had trouble with your Parliament. Ours begins its work on Thursday. The accounts of the support which our Government will receive are most satisfactory, and the Cabinet is most harmonious.... Ever your devoted Niece,

Victoria R.

The Earl of Aberdeen to Queen Victoria.

London, *8th February 1853.*

... Lord John Russell read at the Cabinet a despatch received from your Majesty's Minister at St Petersburg, giving an account of an interview with the Emperor, at which His Majesty appeared to expect an early dissolution of the Turkish Empire, and proposed in such a case to act in perfect concert with the British Government. Lord John also read the rough draft of a proposed answer to this despatch, which, with slight alterations, was fully approved.[5]

Lord Aberdeen does not think there is anything very new in this demonstration by the Emperor. It is essentially the same language he has held for some years, although, perhaps, the present difficulties of Turkey may have rendered him more anxious on the subject....

Lord John Russell to Queen Victoria.

Chesham Place, *12th February 1853.*

Lord John Russell presents his humble duty to your Majesty; he has waited till to-day in order to be able to give some account of the appearance of the House of Commons.

Lord John Russell's statement of measures to be proposed was well received, but as it did not contain reform was a disappointment to a part of the House. Mr Walpole spoke privately to Lord John Russell as to his future position in leading the Government in the House of

Commons without office. Mr Walpole said it was neither illegal nor unconstitutional, but might prove inconvenient as a precedent.

The Speaker said in conversation there was clearly no *constitutional* objection, but that the leadership of the House was so laborious that an office without other duties ought to be assigned to it....

Queen Victoria to Lord John Russell.

Windsor Castle, *13th February 1853.*

The Queen has received Lord John Russell's letter of yesterday, and was very glad to hear that he considers the aspect of the House of Commons as favourable to the Government.

Lord John alludes for the first time in his letter to a question on which the Queen has not hitherto expressed her opinion to him personally, viz., how far the proposed new arrangement of Lord John's holding the leadership of the House of Commons without office was constitutional or not?[6] Her opinion perfectly agrees with that expressed by Mr Walpole to Lord John. If the intended arrangement were *undoubtedly illegal* it would clearly never have been contemplated at all; but it may prove a *dangerous precedent.*

The Queen would have been quite prepared to give the proposition of the Speaker "that the leadership of the House of Commons was so laborious, that an Office without other duties ought to be assigned to it," her fullest and fairest consideration, upon its merits and its constitutional bearings, which ought to have been distinctly set forth before her by her constitutional advisers for her final and unfettered decision.

What the Queen complains of, and, as she believes with justice, is, that so important an innovation in the construction of the executive Government should have been practically decided upon by an arrangement intended to meet personal wants under peculiar and accidental circumstances, leaving the Queen the embarrassing alternative only, either to forego the exercise of her own prerogative, or to damage by her own act the *formation* or *stability* of the new Government, both of paramount importance to the welfare of the Country.

Lord John Russell to Queen Victoria.

Chesham Place, *13th February 1853.*

Lord John Russell presents his humble duty to your Majesty. He cannot forbear from vindicating himself from the charge of forming or being party to an arrangement "intended to meet personal wants under peculiar and accidental circumstances, leaving the Queen the embarrassing alternative only, either to forego the exercise of her own prerogative, or to damage by her own act the *formation* or *stability* of the new Government—both of paramount importance to the welfare of the Country."

Lord John Russell has done all in his power to contribute to the formation of a Ministry in which he himself holds a subordinate situation, from which nearly all his dearest political friends are excluded, and which is held by some to extinguish the party which for eighteen years he has led.

He has done all this in order that your Majesty and the Country might not be exposed to the evil of a weak Ministry liable to be overthrown at any moment, formed whether by Lord Derby, or by himself at the head of one party only.

But in consenting to this arrangement he was desirous to maintain his honour intact, and for this purpose he asked before the Ministry was formed for the honour of an Audience of your Majesty, that he might explain all the circumstances of his position.

This Audience was not granted, and Lord John Russell has never been in a situation to explain to your Majesty why he believes that his leading the House of Commons without office is not liable to any constitutional objection.

The Speaker and Mr Walpole both concur that no constitutional objection to this arrangement exists, but should your Majesty wish to see the arguments briefly stated by which Lord John Russell has been convinced, he should be happy to be allowed to lay them before your Majesty.

The Earl of Clarendon to Queen Victoria.

25th February 1853.

Lord Clarendon presents his humble duty to your Majesty, and humbly begs to state that Count Colloredo[7] called upon him this afternoon.... Count Colloredo then said that he had another and more disagreeable subject to discuss with Lord Clarendon. He commenced by reading a note from Count Buol[8] complaining bitterly of the refugees, and the manner in which they abused the hospitality afforded them in this country, and attributing in great measure to the proclamations of Kossuth and Mazzini the late insurrection at Milan, and the attempt on the Emperor's life.[9] This note expressed a hope and belief that some measure would at once be adopted by your Majesty's Government to remove the just complaints of Allied Governments, and intimated that should this hope not be *spontaneously* realised some measures on the part of those Governments would become necessary for their own protection as well as to mark their sense of the wrong done to them by England.

Lord Clarendon said that your Majesty's Government were as indignant as that of Austria could be at the disgraceful abuse of the protection afforded to these refugees; but he could hold out no hope of any legislation for the purpose of sending them out of the country.

Count Colloredo did not disguise his annoyance and disappointment at this, and seemed to attribute it to want of goodwill on the part of your Majesty's Government, which he felt sure would have the support of public opinion in proposing such a measure as his Government desired.

The discussion became rather warm, and Lord Clarendon thought it right to remark that too much importance might be given to these proclamations and too little to the causes which at home might lead the subjects of Austria to manifest their discontent by revolutionary outbreaks, nor could we conceal from ourselves that the complaints about the refugees were occasionally directed against the free institutions which gave them protection, and that we were not always viewed with favour as presenting the single but prosperous exception to that system of government which otherwise would now almost be uniform in Europe.[10]

Queen Victoria to Viscount Palmerston.

Buckingham Palace, *9th March 1853.*

The Queen has received Lord Palmerston's letter, and the reports on the Militia which she returns, having marked several parts in them which show an absence of the most important requisites. Already in October the Queen observed upon the want of arms for the Militia, and was invariably answered that they would be immediately provided. But by these reports this seems still not to be the case.

The King of the Belgians to Queen Victoria.

Laeken, *18th March 1853.*

My Dearest Victoria,—Receive my best thanks for your gracious letter of the 15th. I trust that the bitter cold weather we have now again will not displease you. I fear Albert's heavy cold will not be the better by the east wind which makes one shiver. I am thunderstruck by a telegraph despatch from Marseilles of the 17th, which declares that Prince Menschikoff has not succeeded, and has therefore given orders for the Russian fleet to come to Constantinople.[11] Heaven grant that these news may not be true, though bad news generally turn out correct. I am so sorry to see the Emperor Nicholas, who had been so wise and dignified since 1848, become so very unreasonable. In Austria they are still a good deal excited. One can hardly feel astonished considering circumstances; I trust that reflection may induce them to modify their measures. The Italian Nobles have shown themselves great fools by acting as they have done, and thereby giving an opening to social revolution. By some accident we have been within these few days well informed of some of the movements of the good people that enjoy an asylum in England. Kossuth is now the great director and favourite, and Republics are everywhere to spring up, till he (Kossuth) is to be again Dictator or Emperor somewhere.... Europe will never recover that shock of 1848.

My dearest Victoria, your truly devoted Uncle,

Leopold R.

The Earl of Aberdeen to Queen Victoria.

London, *22nd March 1853.*

Lord Aberdeen presents his humble duty to your Majesty. He encloses a letter from Lord Cowley, which shows a considerable degree of irritation on the part of the French Government, and of embarrassment in consequence of the rash step they have taken in ordering the departure of their fleet from Toulon to the Greek Waters.[12] If no catastrophe should take place at Constantinople, as Lord Aberdeen hopes and believes, this irritation will probably subside, and they may find us useful in assisting them to escape from their difficulty with respect to the "Holy Places."

Lord Aberdeen has seen the Instructions of Prince Menschikoff, which relate exclusively to the claims of the Greek Church at Jerusalem; and although these conditions may humiliate Turkey, and wound the vanity of France, there is nothing whatever to justify the reproach of territorial aggression, or hostile ambition. If the Turkish Government, relying upon the assistance of England and France, should remain obstinate, the affair might become serious; but even then, Lord Aberdeen is convinced that no final step will be taken by the Emperor, without previous communication to England.

Much depends upon the personal character of Prince Menschi-koff. If he can command himself sufficiently to wait for the arrival of Lord Stratford, Lord Aberdeen does not doubt that the matter will be settled, without coming to extremities....

Queen Victoria to the Earl of Aberdeen.

Windsor Castle, *23rd March 1853.*

The Queen has received Lord Aberdeen's letter of yesterday, and returns Lord Cowley's. Everything appears to her to depend upon the real nature of the demands made by Russia, and the Queen was therefore glad to hear from Lord Aberdeen that he found nothing in Prince Menschikoff's instructions to justify the reproach of territorial aggression or hostile ambition. Still the mode of proceeding at Constantinople is not such as would be resorted to towards a "sick friend for whose life there exists much solicitude." This ought clearly to be stated to Baron Brunnow, in the Queen's opinion.

The two Drafts to Sir H. Seymour and Lord Cowley struck the Queen as very temperate, conciliatory, and dignified.

The Earl of Clarendon to Queen Victoria.

29th March 1853.

Lord Clarendon presents his humble duty to your Majesty, and humbly begs to state that he had this afternoon a satisfactory interview with the French Ambassador, who told him that the Emperor had to a certain extent been deceived upon the Eastern Question, and that he had given his decision without fully considering the matter in all its bearings. But that he had since viewed it in a different light, and had so far recognised the propriety of the course adopted by your Majesty's Government, that if the sailing order had not been improperly published in the *Moniteur* the French Fleet should not have quitted Toulon.

Count Walewski further stated that *the Persons* who had thus advised the Emperor, finding that their views were not supported by facts as they hoped, had endeavoured to throw the blame upon England and to show that France had been abandoned and Russia preferred by your Majesty's Government, and that hence had arisen the want of cordiality and good feeling with respect to which Lord Clarendon some days ago spoke to Count Walewski. He, however, assured Lord Clarendon that all this had now passed away, and that the Emperor was as anxious as ever for a good understanding with England, and particularly upon all matters connected with the East. Lord Clarendon expressed great satisfaction that this momentary difference between the two Governments should be at an end.

Count Walewski in confidence requested Lord Clarendon to impress upon Lord Cowley the necessity of often seeing the Emperor, and not trusting to the Minister, when any question of difficulty arose.

Count Walewski said the Emperor was particularly anxious that your Majesty should know that the liberation of the Madiai[13] was owing to the interference which the French Legation had been instructed by the Emperor to use in their behalf.

Queen Victoria to the King of the Belgians.

Windsor Castle, *29th March 1853.*

My dearest Uncle,—I have to thank you very much for your kind letter of the 25th....

I hope that the Oriental Question will be satisfactorily settled. From all the confidential reports we have received from the Emperor of Russia, I think I may safely say that though he has treated the Sultan rather overbearingly and roughly, there is *no* alteration in his views— and *no wish whatever* on his part to appropriate Constantinople or any of those parts to himself—though he does not wish us, or France or Austria *or Greece*, to have it either. But he thinks the dissolution of the Ottoman Empire very imminent, which I really think is not the case. The Russians accuse us (as we have preached moderation) of being too French—and the French of being too Russian!....

Now with Albert's love, ever your devoted Niece,

Victoria R.

Queen Victoria to Lord Clarendon.

Windsor Castle, *30th March 1853.*

The Queen has received Lord Clarendon's letter with great satisfaction. We are now reaping the fruits of an honest and straightforward conduct, and the Queen hopes Lord Clarendon will likewise in all future cases of difficulty arrest the mischief, sure to arise from a continuance of mutual suspicion between this Country and any Power, by at once entering upon full and unreserved explanations, on the first symptoms of distrust.

As the Emperor deserves great credit, if he really caused the liberation of the Madiai, the Queen wishes Lord Clarendon to express to Count Walewski her feelings on this subject.

The Emperor of Russia to the Prince Albert.

St. Petersburg, le 8 Avril – 20 Avril, 1853

Monseigneur,—J'allais Vous adresser mes félicitations sincères pour l'heureuse délivrance de Sa Majesté la Reine, quand Votre aimable lettre est venue me prévenir.[14] Veuillez donc, Monseigneur, être persuadé, que c'est avec grande joie, que ma femme et moi, nous avons appris cet heureux événement, et j'ose aussi vous prier de déposer aux pieds de Sa Majesté mes humbles hommages et félicitations. Je me flatte n'avoir pas besoin de Vous assurer tous deux, Monseigneur, de toute la sincérité des sentiments d'affection que je Vous porte. Cette fois j'ose y joindre mes remercîments bien sentis à Sa Majesté la Reine, pour l'indulgence et l'attention qu'Elle a daigné prêter aux communications dont j'avais chargé directement Sir Hamilton Seymour, qui a le mérite seul d'avoir su transmettre mes intentions avec une fidélité et une exactitude parfaites.

Je crois que dans peu Sa Majesté la Reine sera dans le cas de se persuader, que *Son sincère et fidèle ami* l'a prévenue à temps de ce qu'il prévoyait devoir infailliblement arriver; non certes dans l'intention d'être un *prophète de mauvais augure*, mais dans la conviction intime, que ce n'est que la confiance la plus intime, la plus complette et la plus parfaitte identité de vues entre Sa Majesté et Son très humble serviteur, c. à. d. entre l'Angleterre et la Russie, que peuvent commander aux événements et conjurer de terribles catastrophes!

Maintenant nous nous entendons, et je m'en remets à Dieu pour tout ce qui doit arriver.

C'est avec la plus haute considération et la plus sincère amitié que je serais, toujours, Monseigneur, de Votre Altesse Royale le tout dévoué Cousin,

Nicolas.

Queen Victoria to the King of the Belgians.

Buckingham Palace, *18th April 1853.*

My dearest Uncle,—My first letter is *this* time, as last time, ad-dressed to you; last time it was because dearest Louise, to whom the first had heretofore always been addressed, was with me—alas! *now*, she is no longer amongst us! I can report very favourably of myself, for I have never been better or stronger or altogether more comfort-able.

Stockmar will have told you that *Leopold* is to be the name of our fourth young gentleman. It is a mark of love and affection which I hope you will not disapprove. It is a name which is the dearest to me after Albert, and one which recalls the almost *only* happy days of my sad childhood; to hear "Prince Leopold" again, will make me think of all those days! His other names will be George Duncan Albert, and the Sponsors, the King of Hanover, Ernest Hohenlohe, the Princess of Prussia and Mary Cambridge.

George is after the King of Hanover, and Duncan as a compli-ment to dear Scotland.... Ever your devoted Niece and Child,

Victoria R.

Lord John Russell to Queen Victoria.

Chesham Place, *19th April 1853.*

Lord John Russell presents his humble duty to your Majesty, and is happy to say that Mr Gladstone's statement last night was one of the most powerful financial speeches ever made in the House of Com-mons.[15]

Mr Pitt in the days of his glory might have been more imposing, but he could not have been more persuasive.

Lord John Russell is very sanguine as to the success of the plan, both in the House of Commons and in the country.

The Prince Albert to Mr Gladstone.

Buckingham Palace, *19th April 1853.*

My dear Mr Gladstone,—I must write to you a line in order to congratulate you on your success of last night. I have just completed a close and careful perusal of your speech, which I admire extremely, and I have heard from all sides that the effect it has produced is very good. Trusting that your Christian humility will not allow you to become dangerously elated, I cannot resist sending you the report which Lord John Russell made to the Queen for your perusal; knowing that it will give you pleasure, and that these are the best rewards which a public man can look for. Ever yours truly,

Albert.

Mr Gladstone to the Prince Albert.

Downing Street, *19th April 1853.*

Sir,—I have to offer my most humble and grateful thanks to Her Majesty for graciously allowing me to know the terms in which Lord John Russell's kindness allowed him to describe the statement made by me last night in the House of Commons; and to your Royal Highness for the letter which your Royal Highness had been pleased to address to me.

The reception which you, Sir, gave to my explanation on the 9th instant of the propositions I had to submit to the Cabinet, was one of the first and best omens of their favourable fortune.

As a Servant of the Crown, deeply sharing in that attachment which all servants of Her Majesty must feel both to her Throne and Person, I venture to hope that the propositions of the Government declared through me, are in accordance with our faith and loyalty to Her Majesty.

For myself, Sir, I am most thankful, if it can be said that I have not by my own defects injured a good and an honest cause; my only title to reward lies in sincerity of purpose, and by such testimony as that of your Royal Highness I am already much more than duly rewarded....

I return the letter of Lord John Russell, and I pray your Royal Highness to believe me, Sir, your most dutiful and most obedient Servant,

W. E. Gladstone.

Queen Victoria to the Earl of Aberdeen.

Osborne, *27th May 1853.*

The Queen has read Lord Aberdeen's letter of yesterday with great concern. She had been much surprised to hear from Lord John Russell on the 24th that "in concert with Sir Charles Wood and Sir

James Graham, he had settled last night to propose to the Cabinet on Wednesday to delay the measure (on the Indian Government) till next Session, and that Sir James Graham had stated that Lord Aberdeen would be ready to assent to this course."[16] She did not answer Lord John until she should have heard from Lord Aberdeen himself. From the explanation he has now given to the Queen, she must say that it would have a *very bad* effect if the measure were withdrawn at the eleventh hour, and after all that has been publicly and privately stated.[17] Nothing damages a Government more than the appearance of vacillation and uncertainty of purpose, and no Government ought to shun this more than the *present*. The fact of a dissension in the Cabinet on a vital point, which it cannot be hoped will remain concealed, must besides much impair its vigour and power....

The Queen earnestly hopes that it will not become necessary to change the course announced by the Government.

The King of the Belgians to Queen Victoria.

Laeken, *3 June 1853*.

My dearest, best Victoria,—... The young Emperor[18] I confess I like much, there is much sense and courage in his warm blue eye, and it is not without a very amiable merriment when there is occasion for it. He is slight and very graceful, but even in the *mêlée* of dancers and Archdukes, and all in uniform, he may always be distinguished as the *Chef*. This struck me more than anything, as now at Vienna the dancing is also that general *mêlée* which renders waltzing most difficult.... The manners are excellent and free from pompousness or awkwardness of any kind, simple, and when he is graciously disposed, as he was to me, *sehr herzlich und natürlich*. He keeps every one in great order without requiring for this an *outré* appearance of authority, merely because he is the master, and there is that about him which gives authority, and which sometimes those *who have the authority cannot succeed in getting accepted or in practising*. I think he may be severe *si l'occasion se présente*; he has something very *muthig*. We were several times surrounded by people of all classes, and he certainly quite at their mercy, but I never saw his little *muthig* expression changed either by being pleased or alarmed. I trust that this family connection may mitigate the only impression which in Austria has created a hostile feeling, viz. the suspicions in Palmerston's time that it had become a plan of England *to destroy* the Austrian Empire. After the *attentat* on the Emperor the impression on those who are attached to their country was, and still is, that in England a sort of menagerie of Kossuths, Mazzinis, Lagranges, Ledru Rollins, etc., is kept to be let occasionally loose on the Continent to render its quiet and prosperity impossible. That impression, which Lord Aberdeen stated in the House of Lords at the end of April, is strong everywhere on the Continent, in Prussia as it is in Austria, and even here our *industriels* are convinced of it. About what is to be done by way of graciousness on your part we will consider.... Ever, my dearest Victoria, your devoted Uncle,

Leopold R.

The Duke of Newcastle to Queen Victoria.

7th June 1853.

The Duke of Newcastle presents his humble duty to your Majesty, and has the honour of bringing under your Majesty's notice a desire for some time past felt by the Archbishop of Canterbury, and by others interested in the welfare of the Church of England in the Colonies, that the extensive See of Capetown should be divided, and that a new Bishopric of Grahamstown should be erected.

An endowment of £10,000 for the proposed See has lately been provided by the Society for the Propagation of the Gospel in Foreign Parts.

The Duke of Newcastle under these circumstances hopes that your Majesty will approve of the erection of this new See, and has the honour to recommend to your Majesty that, in that case the Rev. J. W. Colenso should be appointed to it.

Mr Colenso at present holds a living in the Diocese of Norwich, he was second wrangler at Cambridge, and was at one time tutor to two of the sons of the late Sir Robert Peel at Harrow.

The Duke of Newcastle has received a very high character of Mr Colenso from his Diocesan, and the Archbishop of Canterbury considers him a fit person to be recommended to your Majesty.

Queen Victoria to the King of the Belgians.

Buckingham Palace, *22nd June 1853.*

My dearest Uncle,—Many thanks for your kind letter of the 17th, which I could not answer on my usual day (yesterday), as we were the whole day at the Camp, where there was a Review, at which I rode. It was a very fine sight, but my enjoyment was a good deal spoilt by the nervousness which I was in at having my poor blind cousin[19] *on* horseback next to me—*led*. It is a sad sight, and one which keeps me in a constant state of anxiety, as one is afraid of saying or doing anything which may pain or distress him, or of his meeting with any accident; but he manages it wonderfully well, hardly ever makes a mistake, and manages so well at dinner. He is very cheerful, kind, and civil, and would be very good looking if it were not for his poor eyes. He likes to go everywhere and do everything like anybody else, and speaks of things *as if he saw* them....

The Oriental Question is at a standstill. It is the Emperor of Russia who must enable *us* to help him out of the difficulty. I feel convinced that *War will* be *avoided*, but I don't see *how* exactly. Our Troops looked beautiful yesterday. I wish your young people could see our Camp.[20]

With Albert's love, believe me, ever, your devoted Niece,

Victoria R.

The Earl of Dalhousie to Queen Victoria.

12th July 1853.

Lord Dalhousie presents his humble duty to your Majesty, most gratefully acknowledging the gracious words which your Majesty has addressed to him in the time of his great affliction.[21]

Your Majesty has been pleased for many years to honour him with frequent marks of personal distinction. He is indeed most keenly sensible of the favour which bestowed them all. But his deep gratitude must ever be given to the goodness which dictated the touching assurance he has now received of your Majesty's interest in the piteous fate of one who for eighteen years has been all the world to him, whose patient, gentle spirit, and whose brave heart had turned aside so many perils, and who yet has sunk at last under the very means on which all had securely reckoned as her certain safety.

Lord Dalhousie ought not perhaps to have uttered even this much of his sorrow, but your Majesty's truly gracious words have melted it from his heart; and still encourage him to believe that your Majesty will not regard it as obtrusive.

Lord Dalhousie will not mingle the other topics, on which it is his duty to address your Majesty, with this respectful expression of the enduring gratitude, with which he has the honour to subscribe himself, your Majesty's most obedient, most humble, and most faithful Subject and Servant,

Dalhousie.

The Earl of Aberdeen to Queen Victoria.

London, *11th September 1853.*

Lord Aberdeen presents his most humble duty to your Majesty....

Lord Aberdeen has by no means forgotten the conversation to which your Majesty has referred; but after full consideration he believes that the safest and best course has been adopted.[22] Trusting to your Majesty's gracious condescension, and the confidence with which Lord Aberdeen has been honoured, he will humbly venture to lay before your Majesty, without any reserve, the motives which have induced him to offer this advice to your Majesty.

The situation of Lord Palmerston is peculiar.[23] Unless he should continue to be a cordial member of your Majesty's Government, he may very easily become the leader of Opposition. Lord Aberdeen is at this moment ignorant of his real views and intentions. He has been recently more than once thwarted in his endeavours to press a hostile policy upon the Cabinet; and it has been reported to Lord Aberdeen that he has expressed himself in terms of great hostility. This cannot perhaps be avoided, and is only the result of taking different views of the public interest; but it is very essential that Lord Palmerston should have no personal or private cause of complaint against Lord Aberdeen. From his office of Home Secretary he might naturally expect to have the honour of attending your Majesty; and should this not be the case he might probably resent it and attribute it to the jealousy and ill-will of Lord Aberdeen. But whether he did this, or not, himself, the Public and the Press would not fail to do so, and would convert this neglect into the ground of the most hostile and bitter attacks.

Your Majesty may perhaps be aware that there is no amount of flattery which is not offered to Lord Palmerston by the Tory party, with the hope of separating him altogether from the Government.

Lord Aberdeen fully admits that this step which he has humbly proposed to your Majesty may fail to produce any good effect, and that it may even be turned hereafter to the injury of the Government; but, at all events, Lord Aberdeen's conscience will be clear; and if Lord Palmerston has any generous feelings, it is not impossible that he may appreciate favourably a proceeding which cannot but afford him personal satisfaction.

Queen Victoria to the Earl of Clarendon.

Balmoral, *24th September 1853.*

The Queen has this morning received Lord Clarendon's letter of the 22nd inst. She has not been surprised at the line taken by Austria, who, Lord Clarendon will remember, the Queen never thought could be depended upon, as she is not in that independent position which renders a National Policy possible. The accounts from Constantinople are very alarming, and make the Queen most anxious for the future. She quite approves of the steps taken by the Government. The presence of the Fleets at Constantinople in case of general disturbance will take from the Emperor of Russia what Lord Cowley calls his *coup de Théâtre à la Sadlers Wells*, viz.: the part of the generous protector of the Sultan and restorer of Order.[24]

Queen Victoria to the Earl of Aberdeen.

Balmoral, *25th September 1853.*

The Queen has received Lord Aberdeen's letter of the 23rd, and is very thankful to him for this full and lucid statement of the present very critical situation.

She transmits to him a memorandum containing our views, drawn up by the Prince with the desire he might also communicate it to Lord Clarendon.[25]

The Queen must say she now rejoices the Fleets should be on their way to Constantinople.

God grant that any outbreak at Constantinople may yet be averted.

"It is evident" (it was added) "that Russia has hitherto attempted to deceive us in pretending that she did not aim at the acquisition of any *new* Right, but required only a satisfaction of honour and a re-acknowledgment of the Rights she already possessed by Treaty; that she *does intend* and for the first time lays bare that intention, to acquire *new* Rights of interference which the Porte does *not* wish to concede and cannot concede, and which the European Powers have repeatedly declared she *ought not* to concede....

"If the views of Russia, for instance, with regard to 'Modification III. of the Note,' were to prevail, the extension of the advantages and privileges enjoyed by Christian communities, in their capacity as *for-*

eigners, to the Greeks generally, with the Right granted to Russia to intercede for them to this effect, would simply make foreigners of 10,000,000 of the subjects of the Porte, or depose the Sultan as their sovereign, putting the Emperor of Russia in his place."

The Earl of Aberdeen to Queen Victoria.

London, *6th October 1853.*

... The Cabinet will meet to-morrow; and Lord Aberdeen will have the honour of humbly reporting to your Majesty the result of their discussions. It will be Lord Aberdeen's endeavour to prevent any rash decision; and, above all, to keep open the possibility of peaceful communications. No doubt, it may be very agreeable to humiliate the Emperor of Russia; but Lord Aberdeen thinks that it is paying a little too dear for this pleasure, to check the progress and prosperity of this happy country, and to cover Europe with confusion, misery, and blood.

The Earl of Aberdeen to Queen Victoria.

London, *7th October 1853.*

Lord Aberdeen presents his humble duty to your Majesty. As your Majesty will expect to hear from him to-day, he has the honour of addressing your Majesty, although he could wish that it had been in his power to give your Majesty a more full and satisfactory account of the decisions of the Cabinet. The meeting was very long, and considerable difference of opinion prevailed in the course of the discussion. At length, however, Lord Aberdeen is happy to say there was such an agreement as ensured a certain degree of unanimity. With this view, it was determined to adhere to a defensive principle of action in the East. The Fleets may perhaps be already at Constantinople; but, at all events, they are to be brought there forthwith, and to be stationed either there or in the Bosphorus, unless the Russians should cross the Danube, or make any attack upon the Turkish possessions on the coast of the Black Sea. In this case, the combined Fleets would enter the Black Sea, for the defence of the Turkish territory.

Considering the position we have already assumed in this unfortunate affair, perhaps it was impossible to do less than this; and as there is very little chance of Russia undertaking any active hostilities of the nature apprehended, it may reasonably be hoped that no actual collision will take place. At the same time it must be recollected that

477

Russia will regard the entrance of line of battle-ships into the Black Sea as a virtual declaration of war against herself.

There is yet no confirmation of the actual declaration of war by the Porte, and although there is no reason to suspect any serious impediment to the decision of the Divan being fulfilled, it is rather strange that intelligence to this effect has not been received. If Lord Stratford should see great cause for apprehension at the prospect of the Turks in the prosecution of hostilities, it is just possible that by his influence he may have arrested the progress of their warlike measures; but probably this is too much to hope. At all events, Lord Aberdeen trusts that the path of negotiation is not finally closed, and that, notwithstanding the equivocal position of Great Britain in this contest, it may still be possible to employ words of conciliation and peace....

Memorandum by the Prince Albert.

Balmoral, *10th October 1853.*

I had a long interview with Sir James Graham this morning, and told him that Lord Aberdeen's last letter to the Queen and him[26] made us very uneasy. It was evident that Lord Aberdeen was, against his better judgment, consenting to a course of policy which he inwardly condemned, that his desire to maintain unanimity at the Cabinet led to concessions which by degrees altered the whole character of the policy, while he held out no hope of being able permanently to secure agreement. I described the Queen's position as a very painful one. Here were decisions taken by the Cabinet, perhaps even acted upon, involving the most momentous consequences, without her previous concurrence or even the means for her to judge of the propriety or impropriety of course to be adopted, with evidence that the Minister, in whose judgment the Queen placed her chief reliance, disapproved of it. The position was morally and constitutionally a wrong one. The Queen ought to have the whole policy in spirit and ultimate tendency developed before her to give her deliberate sanction to it, knowing what it involved her in abroad and at home. She might now be involved in war, of which the consequences could not be calculated, chiefly by the desire of Lord Aberdeen to keep his Cabinet together; this might then break down, and the Queen would be left without an efficient Government, and a war on her hands. Lord Aberdeen renounced one of his chief sources of strength in the Cabinet, by not making it apparent that he requires the sanction of the Crown to the course proposed by the Cabinet, and has to justify his advice by argument before it can be adopted, and that it does not suffice to come to a decision at the table of the Cabinet. Sir James Graham perfectly coincided with this view and offered to go up to Town immediately. The Queen wrote the letter to Lord Aberdeen ... which Sir James takes up with him. He shall arrive at Windsor on Friday (14th), and Lord Aberdeen is to have an Audience on Saturday. Sir James will tell him that the Queen wants his deliberate opinion on what course is best to be followed, and that the course once adopted should be steadily and uninterruptedly pursued.

Albert.

Queen Victoria to the Earl of Clarendon.

Balmoral, *11th October 1853.*

The Queen has received Lord Clarendon's letter. She had written to Lord Aberdeen that she felt it her duty to pause before giving her consent to the measures decided on in the Cabinet, until she should have received an explanation on the views which dictated that decision, and of the ulterior steps involved in it; and Sir James Graham is gone up to Town, verbally to explain more fully the Queen's feelings. She has now received and read the Despatches, which have in the meantime been sent off to their points of destination without having received her sanction!

The draft to Vienna the Queen thinks very ably argued, and justly to define the present position of the question at issue.[27]

The instructions to Lord Stratford,[28] on the other hand, appear to her very vague, and entrusting him with enormous powers and a latitude of discretion which is hardly to be called safe. As matters have now been arranged, it appears to the Queen, moreover, that we have taken on ourselves in conjunction with France all the risks of a European war, without having bound Turkey to any conditions with respect to provoking it. The hundred and twenty fanatical Turks constituting the Divan at Constantinople are left sole judges of the line of policy to be pursued, and made cognisant at the same time of the fact that England and France have bound themselves to defend the Turkish Territory! This is entrusting them with a power which Parliament has been jealous to confide even to the hands of the British Crown. It may be a question whether England ought to go to war for the defence of so-called Turkish Independence; but there can be none that if she does so, she ought to be the sole judge of what constitutes a breach of that

479

independence, and have the fullest power to prevent by negotiation the breaking out of the war.

The Queen would wish copies of the enclosed papers to be sent for her use as soon as convenient.

Memorandum by the Prince Albert.

Windsor Castle, *16th October 1853.*

We saw Lord Aberdeen yesterday. He went with us through the whole of the proceedings of the last six weeks with respect to the Eastern Question. Regretted Count Nesselrode's Note,[29] which Baron Brunnow owned nobody would regret more than the Count himself, acknowledged the weakness of Austria, felt sure of Lord Stratford's insincerity towards him and the Government,... as he had to Lord Aberdeen's certain knowledge called "the conduct of the Government infamous" and declared "he would let the world know that his name was Canning." He acknowledged the disadvantage of the course adopted by the Cabinet, which left the Turks at liberty to do as they pleased; he had to concede this to the Cabinet, which would otherwise have been broken up by Lord John and Lord Palmerston. Had he known what the Queen's opinion was, he might have been more firm, feeling himself supported by the Crown, but he had imagined from her letters that there was more animosity against Russia and leaning to war in her mind.

Yet, under all the adverse circumstances Lord Aberdeen saw still reason for hope that a peaceable settlement could be obtained. The French were ready to do anything we pleased, go to war, remain at peace, etc., etc.; in fact, Louis Napoleon had experienced the great advantage for his position of the Alliance with England.... Lord Stratford was thoroughly frightened, and had made a proposal himself, which accordingly he would support *con amore*. The Emperor of Russia had failed in his attempt to form a Northern League against the Western Powers.... The Emperor complained bitterly of the conduct of the Powers, who had disgraced him before the world by making him accept a Note, and sanctioning its alteration by Turkey; "now they should do what they pleased and settle matters with Turkey first, and bring him only what was settled and fixed, he was wearied of the whole business, and anxious to get rid of it for ever."

What Lord Aberdeen now proposed was to follow the Emperor's advice and agree with Turkey upon a Note, leaving out all that she had objected to in the Vienna Note as Lord Stratford recommended, and taking as much as possible Redschid Pasha's own words to found the proposal of it upon the declaration made by the Emperor at Olmütz to the Powers, that he sought for *no new* right, privilege, or advantage, but solely for the confirmation of the legal *status quo*, but accompanying this with a declaration, that if Turkey created needless difficulties and tried to evade a peaceful settlement the Powers would withdraw their support and leave her to fight her own battle. We went over the Documents which are not yet settled, even between Lord Aberdeen and Lord Clarendon, and will require the greatest caution in their wording. It is evident that the Turks have every inducement not to let this opportunity slip in going to war with Russia, as they will probably never find so advantageous a one again, as the whole of Christendom has declared them in the right, and they would fight with England and France actively on their side!

At home, Lord Aberdeen said matters do not stand much better. Lord John has convinced himself that, under present circumstances it would not do for him to ask Lord Aberdeen to retire from the Prime Ministership and let him step in in his place; perhaps he has found out also that the Peelites will not serve under him; his own Whig colleagues would very much regret if not object to such a change, and that Lord Palmerston could not well submit to the arrangement. So he told Lord Aberdeen that he had given up that idea; it was clear, however, that he was now looking for an opportunity to break up the Government on some popular ground, which it was impossible to hope that he should not find. He now had asked for the immediate summoning of Parliament, called for by the state of the Oriental Question. This would create the greatest alarm in the country, and embarrassment to the Government, and was therefore resisted. Lord Aberdeen told Lord John quite plainly he knew what the proposal meant—he meant to break up the Government. "I hope not," was Lord John's laughing reply.

The Queen taxed Lord Aberdeen with imprudence in talking to Lord John of his own readiness to leave office, which he acknowledged, but called *very natural* in a man of seventy. Lord John was dissatisfied with his position;... upon Lord Aberdeen telling him that he had the most powerful and honourable position of any man in England as leader of the House of Commons, he answered, "Oh, *there* I am quite happy!"

I asked how under such circumstances that all-important measure of Parliamentary Reform, upon which the future stability and well-being of the Country so much depended, was to be matured and brought forward? Lord Aberdeen replied that Lord John had it all ready and prepared in his pocket, and told Lord Aberdeen so, adding, however, that under present circumstances there was no use in bringing it forward, to which Lord Aberdeen added: "You mean unless you sit in the chair which I now occupy?" Lord John laughed.

We discussed the probable consequences of Lord John's retirement. Lord Aberdeen thought that Lord Palmerston, Lord Lansdowne, and even Lord Clarendon would secede with him, but this by no means implied that the whole party would; Lord Palmerston would not coalesce with Lord John, but try for the lead himself; Lord Clarendon quite agreed with Lord Aberdeen, and had been very angry with Lord John, but was personally under great obligations to him, and Sir James Graham had (as he said) been very much struck with the change of tone in Lord Clarendon at the last meeting of the Cabinet. Most of the Liberals seemed very much pleased with their situation. Sir James Graham had, of his own accord, told Lord Aberdeen that, in the event of Lord John's secession, he himself could not well sit in the House of Commons under so much younger a man as Mr Gladstone as Leader. He knew that there would be objections to his assuming the lead himself, but he would be quite ready to go to the House of Lords to support Lord Aberdeen.

Albert.

The Emperor of Russia to Queen Victoria.[30]
Tsarko, ce 18 Octobre – 30 Octobre, 1853.

Madame,—Votre Majesté connaît, je l'espère, les sentiments d'affection sincère qui m'attachent à Sa personne, depuis que j'ai eu l'honneur de L'approcher. Il m'a semblé qu'Elle daignait aussi m'accorder quelque bienveillance. A la veille d'événements, peut-être fort graves, qu'Elle daigne donc excuser si je m'adresse droit à Elle, pour essayer de prévenir des calamités, que nos deux pays ont un égal intérêt à éviter. J'ose le faire avec d'autant plus de confiance, que longtemps encore avant que les affaires d'Orient eussent pris la fâcheuse tournure qu'elles ont acquise depuis, je m'étais adressé directement à votre Majesté, par l'entremise de Sir Hamilton Seymour, pour appeler votre attention, Madame, sur des éventualités, alors encore incertaines, mais déjà fort probables à mes yeux, et que je désirais éclaircir, *avant tout*, avec le Cabinet Anglais, pour écarter autant qu'il m'était possible, toute divergence d'opinion entre nous. La correspondance d'alors, qu'Elle daigne de la faire relire atteignit son but, car elle mettait le Gouvernement Anglais au fait de mes plus intimes pensées sur ces graves éventualités, tandis que, je devais au moins le penser ainsi, j'obtiens en réponse un égal exposé des vues du Gouvernement de votre Majesté.

Sûrs ainsi de ce que nous désirions de part et d'autre, par quelle fatalité devons-nous donc, Madame, en venir à une mésintelligence aussi prononcée, sur des objets qui paraissaient convenus d'avance, *où ma parole est engagée vis-à-vis de votre Majesté*, comme je crois *celle du Gouvernement Anglais engagée de même vis-à-vis de moi*.

C'est à la justice, au cœur de votre Majesté que j'en appelle, c'est à Sa bonne foi et à Sa sagesse que je m'en mets qu'Elle daigne de décider entre nous.

Devons nous rester, comme je le souhaite ardemment, dans une bonne intelligence également profitable à nos deux États, ou juge-t-Elle, que le pavillon Anglais doive flotter près du croissant, pour combattre la croix de Saint André!!!

Telle que soit la détermination de votre Majesté, qu'Elle veuille être persuadée de l'inaltérable et sincère attachement avec lesquels je ne cesserais d'être, de votre Majesté, le tout dévoué frère et ami,

Nicolas.

Je prie votre Majesté de vouloir bien faire mes amitiés à Monseigneur le Prince Albert.

Queen Victoria to the Earl of Aberdeen.

Windsor Castle, *5th November 1853.*

Although the Queen will have the pleasure of seeing Lord Aberdeen this evening, she wishes to make some observations on the subject of Lord Stratford's last private letters communicated to her yesterday by Lord Clarendon.[31] They exhibit clearly on his part a *desire* for war, and to drag us into it. When he speaks of the sword which will not only have to be drawn, but the scabbard thrown away, and says, the war to be successful must be a "*very comprehensive one*" on the part of England and France, the intention is unmistakable, and it becomes a serious question whether we are justified in allowing Lord Stratford any longer to remain in a situation which gives him the means of frustrating all our efforts for peace. The question becomes still graver when it is considered that General Baraguay d'Hilliers seems from Lord Cowley's account of his conversation with him equally anxious for extreme measures.

The Queen must express her surprise that Lord Stratford should have coolly sent on so preposterous a proposal as Redschid Pasha's note asking for a Treaty of Alliance, the amalgamation of our Fleets with the Turkish one, and the sending of our surplus ships to the "*White*" Sea (!) without any hesitation or remark on his part. As the note ends, however, by saying that the Porte desires *que les points ci-dessus émenés (sic) soient appréciés par les Cours d'Angleterre et de France, et que ces Cours veuillent bien déclarer leur intention d'agir en conséquence*, this appears to the Queen to afford an admirable opportunity for stating plainly and strongly to the Turkish Government that we have *no intention* of being used by them for their own purposes. This time such a declaration might be *handed in* to the Turkish Government, so that there can be no mistake about the matter for the future.

The Queen encloses the letter and note, and wishes Lord Aberdeen to show her letter to Lord Clarendon.

Queen Victoria to the Emperor of Russia.

Windsor Castle, *ce 14 Novembre 1853.*

Sire et très cher Frère,—C'est avec une profonde et sincère satisfaction que je viens de recevoir la lettre que V.M.I. a bien voulu m'écrire le 18/30 Octobre. Je suis vivement touchée des sentiments affectueux que vous m'y témoignez. V.M. me connaît assez pour savoir combien ils sont réciproques.

Je vous remercierai également, Sire, de la franchise avec laquelle vous me parlez des complications actuelles; je ne saurais mieux répondre aux loyales intentions de V.M. qu'en lui exprimant à mon tour, et avec toute droiture, mes opinions à ce sujet, car c'est là, j'en suis sûre, le meilleur moyen de conserver utilement une amitié bien véritable.

J'ai, mon cher Frère, conformément à votre désir, relu les communications confidentielles que vous avez bien voulu me faire, ce printemps, par l'intermédiaire du bon Sir Hamilton Seymour, et les réponses que mon Gouvernement a reçu l'ordre d'adresser à V.M.

Bien qu'une différence d'opinion très notable devînt alors évidente entre V.M. et moi relativement à la manière d'envisager l'état de la Turquie et l'appréciation de sa vitalité, le Mémorandum de V.M. en date du 3/15 Avril vint néanmoins dissiper de la manière la plus heureuse ces fâcheuses appréhensions; car il m'annonçait que, si nous n'étions pas d'accord sur *l'état de santé* de l'Empire Ottoman, nous l'étions cependant sur la nécessité, pour le laisser vivre, de ne point lui faire des demandes humiliantes, pourvu que tout le monde en agît de même, et que personne n'abusât de sa faiblesse pour obtenir des avantages exclusifs. V.M. dans ce but, daigna même se déclarer prête "à travailler de concert avec l'Angleterre à l'œuvre commune de prolonger l'existence de l'Empire Turque, en évitant toute cause d'alarme au sujet de sa dissolution."

J'avais de plus la conviction qu'il n'existait et ne pouvait exister au fond aucune divergence d'opinion entre nous au sujet des réclamations relatives aux Lieux-Saints, réclamations qui, j'avais droit de le croire, constituaient le seul grief de la Russie contre la Porte.

Je mets, Sire, la confiance la plus entière dans la parole que V.M. a bien voulu me donner alors, et, que les assurances subséquentes, dues à votre amitié, sont venues confirmer, en me donnant la connaissance de Vos intentions. Personne n'apprécie plus que moi la haute loyauté de V.M., et je voudrais que les convictions que j'ai à cet égard pussent seules résoudre toutes les difficultés. Mais quelle que soit la pureté des motifs qui dirigent les actions du Souverain même le plus élevé par le caractère, V.M. sait que ses qualités personnelles ne sont point suffisantes dans des transactions internationales par lesquelles un État se lie envers un autre en de solennels engagements; et les véritables intentions de V.M. ont été à coup sûr méconnues et mal interprétées, à cause de la forme donnée au réclamations adressées à la Porte.

Ayant à cœur, Sire, d'examiner ce qui avait pu produire ce fâcheux malentendu, mon attention a été naturellement attirée par l'article 7 du Traité de Kainardji; et je dois dire à V.M. qu'après avoir consulté, sur le sens qui pouvait avoir été attaché à cet article, les personnes les plus compétentes de ce pays-ci; après l'avoir relu ensuite moi-même, avec le plus sincère désir d'impartialité, je suis arrivée à la conviction que cet article n'était point susceptible de l'extension qu'on y a voulu donner. Tous les amis de V.M. ont, comme moi, la certitude que vous n'auriez point abusé du pouvoir, que vous eût ainsi été accordé; mais une demande de ce genre, pouvait à peine être acceptée par un Souverain qui tient à son indépendance.

Je ne cacherai pas davantage à V.M. l'impression douloureuse qu'a produit sur moi l'occupation des Principautés. Cette occupation a causé, depuis les quatres derniers mois, une perturbation générale en Europe, et pourrait amener des événements ultérieurs que je déplorerais d'un commun accord avec V.M. Mais, comme les intentions de V.M. envers la Porte sont, je le sais, amicales et désintéressées, j'ai toute confiance que vous trouverez le moyen de les exprimer et mettre à exécution de manière à détourner de plus graves dangers, que tous mes efforts, je vous assure, tendront sans cesse à empêcher. L'attention impartiale avec laquelle j'ai suivi les causes qui ont fait échouer jusqu'à présent toutes les tentatives de conciliation, me donne la ferme conviction qu'il n'existe pas d'obstacle réel qui ne puisse être écarté ou promptement surmonté avec l'assistance de V.M.

Je n'abandonne point l'espoir de cet heureux résultat, même après les tristes conflits qui ont fait couler le sang dans les Principautés; car j'ai la foi en Dieu que lorsque de toute part les intentions sont droites et lorsque les intérêts bien entendus sont communs, le Tout-Puissant ne permettra pas que l'Europe entière qui contient déjà tant d'éléments inflammables, soit exposée à une conflagration générale.

Que Dieu veille sur les jours de V.M.; et croyez, Sire, à l'attachement sincère avec lequel je suis, Sire et cher Frère, de votre Majesté Impériale, la bien bonne Sœur et Amie,

Victoria R.

Albert est très sensible au souvenir de V.M. et me prie de le mettre à vos pieds.

The Earl of Aberdeen to Queen Victoria.

London, *26th November 1853.*

Lord Aberdeen presents his humble duty to your Majesty. The Cabinet met to-day for the consideration of the overtures made by the French Government for the settlement of the Eastern Question.[32] These proposals were in substance adopted; although a considerable change was made in their form, and in some of their details. The step now taken is evidently wise; but Lord Aberdeen can scarcely venture to hope that it will be attended with success. Pacific language is accompanied with insulting and hostile acts; and it remains to be seen what effect will be produced on the Emperor of Russia by the entrance of English and French ships of war into the Black Sea, under the pretext of bringing off Consuls from Varna, and of looking after the grainships at the Sulina mouth of the Danube. This information has hitherto been only communicated by telegraph; but it is calculated to lead to serious consequences, of which Lord Stratford must be perfectly well aware.

Queen Victoria to the Earl of Aberdeen.

Osborne, *27th November 1853.*

The Queen has received Lord Aberdeen's letter of yesterday. She is sorry to find that after all a considerable change was made in the form of the French proposal. She is not aware at present of what that change consists in and is therefore unable to form an opinion as to the effects of its introduction, but she quite concurs in Lord Aberdeen's apprehensions with regard to the effect of Lord Stratford's orders to the Fleet. The perusal of Lord Stratford's Despatches of the 5th inst. has given the Queen the strongest impression that, whilst guarding himself against the possibility of being called to account for acting in opposition to his instructions, he is pushing us deeper and deeper into the War policy which we wish to escape. Wherefore should three poor Turkish steamers go to the Crimea, but to beard the Russian Fleet and tempt it to come out of Sebastopol, which would thus constitute the much desired contingency for our combined Fleets to attack it, and so engage us irretrievably!

The Queen must seriously call upon Lord Aberdeen and the Cabinet to consider whether they are justified in allowing such a state of things to continue!

The Emperor of Russia to Queen Victoria.

S. Pétersbourg, le 2 *Décembre – 14 Décembre, 1853.*

Madame,—Je remercie votre Majesté d'avoir eu la bonté de répondre aussi amicalement que franchement à la lettre que j'ai eu l'honneur de lui écrire. Je la remercie également de la foi qu'elle accorde à ma parole,—je crois le mériter, je l'avoue,—28 années d'une vie politique, souvent fort pénible, ne peuvent donner le droit à personne d'en douter.

Je me permets aussi, contrairement à l'avis de votre Majesté, de penser, qu'en affaires publiques et en relations de pays à pays, rien ne peut être *plus sacré* et ne l'est en effet à mes yeux que la parole souveraine, car elle décide en dernière instance de la paix ou de la guerre. Je ne fatiguerais certes pas l'attention de votre Majesté par un examen détaillé du sens qu'elle donne à l'article 7 du Traité de Kainardji; j'assurerais seulement, Madame, que depuis 80 ans la Russie et la Porte l'ont compris ainsi que nous le faisons encore. Ce sens-là n'a été interrompu qu'en derniers temps, à la suite d'instigations que votre Majesté connaît aussi bien que moi. Le rétablir dans son réception primitive et la justifier par un engagement plus solennel, tel est le but de mes efforts, tel il sera, Madame, quand même le sang devrait couler encore contre mon vœu le plus ardent; parce que c'est une question vitale pour la Russie, et mes efforts ne lui sont impossibles pour y satisfaire.

Si j'ai dû occuper les Principautés, ce que je regrette autant que votre Majesté, c'est encore Madame, parce que les libertés dont ces provinces jouissent, leurs ont été acquises *au prix du sang Russe, et par moi-même Madame les années* 1828 *et* 29. Il ne s'agit donc pas de *conquêtes*, mais à la veille d'un conflit que l'on rendait de plus en plus probable, il eût été indigne de moi de les livrer sûrement à la main des ennemis du Christianisme, dont les persécutions ne sont un secret que pour ceux qui veulent l'ignorer. J'espérais avoir répondu ainsi aux doutes et aux regrets de votre Majesté *avec la plus entière franchise.* Elle veut bien me dire qu'Elle ne doute pas qu'avec mon aide le rétablissement de la paix ne soit encore possible, malgré le sang répandu; j'y réponds de grand cœur, *Oui*, Madame, si les organes des volontés de votre Majesté *exécutent fidèlement ses ordres et ses intentions bienveillantes. Les miennes n'out pas varié dès le début de cette triste épisode. Reculer devant le danger, comme vouloir maintenant autre chose que je n'ai voulu en violant ma parole, serait au-dessous de moi*, et le noble cœur de votre Majesté doit le comprendre.

J'ajouterais encore que son cœur saignera en apprenant les horreurs qui se commettent déjà par les hordes sauvages, près desquels flotte le pavillon Anglais!!!

Je la remercie cordialement des vœux qu'Elle veut bien faire pour moi; tant que ma vie se prolongera ils seront réciproqués de ma part. Je suis heureux de le Lui dire, en l'assurant du sincère attachement avec lequel je suis, Madame, de votre Majesté, le tout dévoué Frère and Ami,

Nicolas.

Je me rappelle encore une fois au bon souvenir de Son Altesse Royale le Prince Albert et le remercie également de ses paroles obligeantes.

The Earl of Aberdeen to Queen Victoria.

London, *6th December 1853.*

... As Lord John Russell will have the honour of seeing your Majesty to-morrow, he will be able to explain to your Majesty the present state of the discussions on Reform, and the progress of the Measure.[33] Lord Aberdeen feels it to be his duty to inform your Majesty that on Saturday evening he received a visit from Lord Palmerston, who announced his decided objection to the greater part of the proposed plan.[34] He did this in such positive terms that Lord Aberdeen should imagine he had made up his mind not to give the Measure his support; but Lord John entertains considerable doubt that such is the case.

Lord Aberdeen thinks it by no means improbable that Lord Palmerston may also desire to separate himself from the Government, in consequence of their pacific policy, and in order to take the lead of the War Party and the Anti-Reformers in the House of Commons, who are essentially the same. Such a combination would undoubtedly be formidable; but Lord Aberdeen trusts that it would not prove dangerous. At all events, it would tend greatly to the improvement of Lord John's Foreign Policy.

"My dear Lansdowne,—I have had two conversations with Aberdeen on the subject of John Russell's proposed Reform Bill, and I have said that there are three points in it to which I cannot agree.

"These points are—the extent of disfranchisement, the extent of enfranchisement, and the addition of the Municipal Franchise in Boroughs to the pound; 10 Householder Franchise....

"We should by such an arrangement increase the number of bribeable Electors, and overpower intelligence and property by ignorance and poverty.

"I have told Aberdeen that I am persuaded that the Measure as proposed by John Russell and Graham will not pass through the two Houses of Parliament without material modifications, and that I do not choose to be a party to a contest between the two Houses or to an Appeal to the Country for a Measure of which I decidedly disapprove; and that I cannot enter into a career which would lead me to such a position, that, in short, I do not choose to be dragged through the dirt by John Russell. I reminded Aberdeen that on accepting his offer of Office, I had expressed apprehension both to him and to you, that I might find myself differing from my Colleagues on the question of Parliamentary Reform.

"I have thought a good deal on this matter. I should be very sorry to give up my present Office at this moment: I have taken a great interest in it, and I have matters in hand which I should much wish to bring to a conclusion. Moreover, I think that the presence in the Cabinet of a person holding the opinions which I entertain as to the principles on which our Foreign Affairs ought to be conducted, is useful in modifying the contrary system of Policy, which, as I think, injuriously to the interests and dignity of the Country, there is a disposition in other quarters to pursue; but notwithstanding all this. I cannot consent to stand forward as one of the Authors and Supporters of John Russell's sweeping alterations. Yours sincerely,

Palmerston".

The Prince Albert to the Earl of Aberdeen.

Osborne, *9th December 1853.*

My dear Lord Aberdeen,—The Queen has consulted with Lord John Russell upon the Reform plan, and on the question of Lord Palmerston's position with regard to it; and he will doubtless give you an account of what passed. She wishes me, however, to tell you likewise what strikes her with respect to Lord Palmerston. It appears to the Queen clear that the Reform Bill will have no chance of success unless prepared and introduced in Parliament by a *united* Cabinet; that, if Lord Palmerston has made up his mind to oppose it and to leave the Government, there will be no use in trying to keep him in it, and that there will be danger in allowing him to attend the discussions of the Cabinet, preparing all the time his line of attack; that if a successor to him would after all have to be found at the Home Office, it will be unfair not to give that important member of the Government full opportunity to take his share in the preparation and deliberation on the measure to which his consent would be asked. Under these circumstances it becomes of the highest importance to ascertain—

1. What the amount of objection is that Lord Palmerston entertains to the Measure;

2. What the object of the declaration was, which he seems to have made to you.

This should be obtained *in writing*, so as to make all future misrepresentation impossible, and on this alone a decision can well be taken, and, in the Queen's opinion, even the Cabinet could alone deliberate.

Should Lord Palmerston have stated his objections with the view of having the Measure modified it will be right to consider how far that can safely be done, and for the Queen, also, to balance the probable value of the modification with the risk of allowing Lord Palmerston to put himself at the head of the Opposition Party, entailing as it does the possibility of his forcing himself back upon her as leader of that Party.

Should he on the other hand consider his declaration as a "notice to quit," the ground upon which he does so should be clearly put on record, and no attempt should be made to damage the character of the Measure in the vain hope of propitiating him. Ever yours truly,

Albert.

Memorandum by the Prince Albert.

Osborne, *16th December 1853.*

Lord Aberdeen arrived yesterday and returned to-day to meet the Cabinet to-morrow. Lord Palmerston has sent in his resignation in a short note to Lord Aberdeen, a further correspondence with Lord John and Lord Lansdowne, Lord Aberdeen put into my hands, and I have copied the two most important letters which follow here.

Lord John is reported as very angry, calling Lord Palmerston's conduct "treacherous," a term Lord Aberdeen hardly understands, as against him he has been perfectly consistent with regard to the Reform Measure, from the beginning, and had frequently denied the necessity of Reform.... Lord Aberdeen had advised Lord John to show boldness and energy, and to undertake the Home Office at once himself; this would have a great effect under the difficulties of the circumstances, would show that he was in earnest and determined to carry his Reform Measure. Lord John seemed hit by the idea, but asked for time to consider; after seeing *Lady* John, however, he declined.

Lord Aberdeen's fears are still mainly as to the Eastern Question, Lord John pressing for war measures. Lord Aberdeen had followed my advice, and had a long explanation on the subject, in which they both agreed that their policy should be one of Peace, and he thought matters settled when Lord John now asks for contingent engagements to make war on Russia if her forces cross the Danube (which Lord Aberdeen thinks quite uncalled for), and to convoy the Turkish expeditions in the Black Sea, even if directed against Russian territory, etc., etc. The Cabinet is certain not to agree to either of these propositions.

When Lord Aberdeen announced the intended rupture with Lord Palmerston to Lord John, he drily said: "Well, it would be very awkward for you if Palmerston quarrels one day with you about Reform, and I the next about Turkey!"

There can be no doubt that Lord Palmerston will at once try to put himself at the head of the late Protectionist party, and, with the present indifference of the Country upon Reform, the fate of the Bill is by no

491

means certain. On the question of Peace or War, Lord Aberdeen is quite certain that the House of Commons will adopt no war resolutions.

Much will depend, however, on the line taken by Lord Lansdowne, who has great influence in the House of Lords, and whose secession would spread great alarm over the Country as to the real tendency of the Measure (which the Duke of Newcastle describes as in fact a great increase of power to the land[35]). We agree that the Queen should write to him to prevent any hasty step.

The Queen sanctioned the offer of the Home Office to Sir George Grey, and of a seat in the Cabinet to Mr Cardwell (the President of the Board of Trade).

Albert.

Queen Victoria to the Marquis of Lansdowne.

Osborne, *16th December 1853.*

The Queen has been made very anxious by the Resignation of Lord Palmerston, but still more so by hearing that Lord Lansdowne has not been able to reconcile himself to the Measure of Reform as now proposed in the Cabinet, which has caused Lord Palmerston's withdrawal. Lord Lansdowne is aware of the paramount importance which the Queen attaches to a safe settlement of that question, and to the maintenance of her present Government; and she would press upon Lord Lansdowne not to commit himself to a final determination before she shall have an opportunity of seeing him. The Queen will go to Windsor on Thursday, and hold a Council on Friday, at which it may perhaps be convenient to Lord Lansdowne to attend, and it will give the Queen the greatest pleasure to find that Lord John Russell has succeeded in removing Lord Lansdowne's objections.

Queen Victoria to the Earl of Clarendon.

Osborne, *17th December 1853.*

The Queen returns the enclosed Draft and Despatch to Lord Clarendon.

She has never been so much perplexed respecting any decision she has had to make, as in the present instance. She has read Lord Stratford's Despatch (358) over several times, and she is struck, every time more, with the consummate ability with which it is written and argued; but also with the difficulty in which it places the person reading it to extract distinctly what the Porte will be prepared to concede.

The concluding passage of the Draft involves the most important consequences. As the Queen understands it, it promises war with Russia in a given contingency, but the contingency is: Russia rejecting terms which are "in their spirit and character such as Your Excellency sets forth in your Despatch." The Queen finds it impossible to make such tremendous consequences dependent upon such vague expressions. The more so, as "the spirit and character" alluded to, appears to her to be, as if purposely, obscure.

When Lord Stratford says, that the Turks would be satisfied "with a renewal in clear and comprehensive terms of the formal Declarations and Treaties already existing in favour of the Porte"—the Queen cannot understand what is meant—as all the former Treaties between Russia and Turkey have certainly not been in favour of the Porte. Nor is it clear to the Queen whether "the clear and unquestionable deliverance from Russian interference applied to spiritual matters" is compatible with the former treaties.

Whilst the Queen, therefore, perfectly agrees in the principle that, should Russia "for its own unjustifiable objects, show herself regardless of the best interests of Europe" by rejecting every fair term, the time will have arrived "for adopting measures of more active coercion against her"—she cannot sanction such a Declaration except on terms which are so clear in themselves as to exclude all misinterpretation.

Queen Victoria to the Earl of Clarendon.

(Undated.)

The Queen has received Lord Clarendon's letter of the 19th, and enclosures. She approves the Draft to Vienna, and asks to have a copy of it, together with the Despatch from Lord Westmorland to which it refers.

She also approves of the Draft to Lord Cowley, with certain exceptions, viz., on the second page our accordance with the views of the French Government "upon the utterly unjustifiable course that Russia has pursued," etc., is stated. If, as the Queen must read it, this refers to the affair at Sinope,[36] it is a dangerous assertion, as we have yet no authentic account of the circumstances of the case, which would make it possible to judge what degree of justification there might have been. The sentence should, at any rate, be qualified by some expression such as "as far as we know," or "should present accounts prove correct," etc.

The word "utterly" might under any circumstances be left out, as a state of War is in itself a justification of a battle.

On page four the words "by sea" will have to be added to make the statement precise and correct.

The concluding sentence, the Queen must consider as tantamount to a declaration of war, which, under the guarded conditions however attached to it, she feels she cannot refuse to sanction. It would, in the Queen's opinion, be necessary, however, distinctly and fully to acquaint the Russian Government with the step now agreed upon.

Lord Palmerston's mode of proceeding always had that advantage, that it threatened steps which it was hoped would not become necessary, whilst those hitherto taken, started on the principle of not needlessly offending Russia by threats, obliging us at the same time to take the very steps which we refused to threaten.

The Queen has to make one more and a most *serious* observation. The Fleet has orders now to prevent a recurrence of such disasters as that of Sinope. This cannot mean that it should protect the Turkish Fleet in acts of aggression upon the Russian territory, such as an attack on Sebastopol, of which the papers speak. This point will have to be made quite clear, both to Lord Stratford and the Turks.

The Queen would also wish to have copies of the Draft, when corrected, of Lord Cowley's Despatch.

Memorandum by the Prince Albert.

Windsor Castle, *25th December 1853.*

Lord Aberdeen had an Audience of the Queen yesterday afternoon. He reported that some of his colleagues, Sir C. Wood, the Duke of Newcastle, and Mr Gladstone, had been very anxious that Lord Palmerston should be readmitted into the Cabinet; they had had interviews with him in which he had expressed his hope to be allowed to reconsider his step. Lady Palmerston had been most urgent upon this point with her husband. All the people best conversant with the House of Commons stated that the Government had no chance of going on with Lord Palmerston in opposition, and with the present temper of the public, which was quite mad about the Oriental Question and the disaster at Sinope. Even Sir W. Molesworth shared this opinion.

Lord Palmerston had written a letter to Lord Aberdeen, in which he begs to have his resignation considered as not having taken place, as it arose entirely from a misapprehension on his part, his having believed that none of the details of the Reform Measure were yet open for consideration, he had quite agreed in the principle of the Measure! Lord Aberdeen saw Lord John and Sir J. Graham, who convinced themselves that under the circumstances nothing else remained to be done. Lord Aberdeen having asked Lord John whether he should tell the Queen that it was a political *necessity*, he answered: "Yes, owing to the shabbiness of your colleagues," to which Lord Aberdeen rejoined: "Not shabbiness; *cowardice* is the word."

Lord Aberdeen owns that the step must damage the Government, although it ought to damage Lord Palmerston still more. Lord John's expression was: "Yes, it would ruin anybody but Palmerston."

Lord Aberdeen thinks, however, that he can make no further difficulties about Reform, and he, Lord John, and Graham were determined to make no material alterations in the Bill. Graham is suspicious lest the wish to get Palmerston in again, on the part of a section of the Cabinet, was an intrigue to get the Measure emasculated. Lord Aberdeen does not believe this....

Lord Aberdeen describes Lord John's feeling as very good and cordial towards him. He, Lord John, had even made him a long speech to show his gratitude for Lord Aberdeen's kindness to him.

Albert.

The Earl of Aberdeen to Queen Victoria.

London, *26th December 1853.*

Lord Aberdeen, with his most humble duty to your Majesty, has the honour of enclosing copies of Lord Palmerston's letter to him,[37] and of his answer. Lord Aberdeen was not without some apprehension of receiving a rejoinder; but instead of which, a note arrived this morning, merely asking if a Cabinet was likely to be summoned in the course of the week, as he was going into the country; in fact, a note just as if nothing whatever has taken place!

ENDNOTES:

[1]:Dr E. C. Hawtrey was advanced to the Provostship of Eton upon the death of the Rev. Francis Hodgson. Dr C. O. Goodford succeeded to the Headmastership.

[2]:The Emperor of the French was married to Mademoiselle Eugénie de Montijo on the 29th of January. William Kirkpatrick, her maternal grandfather, had been a merchant and American Consul at Malaga, and had there married Françoise de Grivegnéc. Their third daughter, Maria Manuela, married, in 1817, the Count de Téba, a member of an illustrious Spanish family, who in 1834 succeeded his brother as Count de Montijo, and died in 1839. His widow held an influential social position at Madrid, and her elder daughter married the Duke of Alba in 1844, while she herself, with Eugénie, her younger daughter, settled in Paris in 1851.

[3]:Lord Cowley had been specifically instructed by the Government to attend the marriage and be presented to the Empress.

[4]:A comic opera, written by Adolphe Adam, and performed at Paris in 1836.

[5]:*See* Introductory Note, p. 455. The Emperor had, no doubt, misunderstood the attitude of the British Ministry in 1844 on this subject, and regarded Lord Aberdeen as in full sympathy with himself.

[6]:See *ante*, pp. 436, 441.

[7]:Austrian Ambassador.

[8]:Austrian Prime Minister.

[9]:Kossuth and Mazzini were in England, prosecuting their schemes against Austria; the Austrian Government attributed to them the Milanese rising, and the recent attempt to assassinate the Emperor Francis Joseph at Vienna.

[10]:The Refugee Question was debated in the House of Lords on the 4th of March.

[11]:*See* Introductory Note, *ante*, pp. 455-6.

[12]:Even before the Conference met, Menschikoff's overbearing conduct and demeanour had induced Napoleon to despatch the French Fleet from Toulon to Salamis, to watch events.

[13]:Two persons, husband and wife, domiciled in Florence, who had embraced the English reformed religion. In 1852 they were seized, imprisoned in separate dungeons, and subjected to great hardships. Lords Shaftesbury and Roden went to Florence and appealed to the Grand Duke on their behalf, but were unsuccessful. In March 1853, however, after the British Government had interposed, the two were released, a pension being provided for them by public subscription.

[14]:The fourth son of the Queen and Prince, afterwards Duke of Albany, was born on the 7th of April at Buckingham Palace.

[15]:Mr Gladstone's Budget imposed a duty for the first time on the succession to real property; he retained the Income Tax for two years longer, at its then rate of sevenpence in the pound on incomes above £150, and extended it, at the rate of fivepence in the pound, to incomes between £100 and £150. Ireland was made subject to the tax, but received relief in other directions. Remissions of indirect taxes were also made, and one of these, the repeal of the Advertisement Duty, was carried against the Government.

[16]:The India Bill, which passed during the Session, threw open the lucrative patronage of the Company (whose existence was continued but with less

absolute control) to competition. The Mutiny, and the resulting legislation of 1858, tended subsequently to overshadow Sir Charles Wood's measure.

[17]:The matter had been referred to a Cabinet Committee, reported upon, agreed to in full Cabinet, proposed to and sanctioned by the Queen and announced to Parliament.

[18]:Francis Joseph, Emperor of Austria.

[19]:King George V. of Hanover.

[20]:Lord Stratford de Redcliffe had insisted that the disputed points as to the guardianship of the Holy Places, and the Russian demand for a Protectorate over the Christian subjects of the Sultan, should be kept distinct. After the former had been arranged and the latter had been rejected by the Porte acting under Lord Stratford's advice, Menschikoff abruptly quitted Constantinople, and the Russian troops, crossing the Pruth, invaded the Danubian principalities of Moldavia and Wallachia (now united as Roumania). In England, meanwhile, a military encampment had been established at Chobham.

[21]:Lady Dalhousie died on the 6th of May, on her passage home from India.

[22]:Lord Aberdeen had suggested that it would be advisable for several reasons that Lord Palmerston should be invited to Balmoral as Minister in attendance, and he accordingly went there on the 15th of September.

[23]:Lord Palmerston and Lord John Russell led the war party in the Cabinet; but the latter was pledged to the introduction of a Reform Bill, while the former was opposed to the scheme. Lord Aberdeen's pacific views were making him increasingly unpopular in the country.

[24]:Even after the Russian occupation of the Principalities, which the Russian Minister, Count Nesselrode, had described as not an act of war, but a material guarantee for the concession by Turkey of the Russian demands, the resources of diplomacy were not exhausted. The Four Powers—England, France, Austria, and Prussia—agreed, in conference at Vienna, to present a note for acceptance by Russia and the Porte, to the effect (*inter alia*) that the Government of the Sultan would remain faithful "to the letter and to the spirit of the Treaties of Kainardji and Adrianople relative to the protection of the Christian religion." This was most unfortunately worded, but, however, the clause had obtained the sanction of the English Government, and the Czar expressed his willingness to accept it. Lord Stratford, however, saw the danger underlying the ambiguity of the language, and, under his advice, the Porte proposed as an amendment the substitution of the words "to the stipulations of the Treaty of Kainardji, confirmed by that of Adrianople, relative to the protection by the Sublime Porte of the Christian religion." The Russian Government refused to accept this amendment, and from that moment war was inevitable. The British Fleet under Admiral Dundas had been sent from Malta to the East at the beginning of June.

[25]:The Memorandum stated that it would be fruitless further to attempt to settle the dispute by the "Rédaction" of Notes to be exchanged between Turkey and Russia, or the choice of particular words and expressions in

public documents designed in order to avoid naming the real objects in dispute.

26 *The Earl of Aberdeen to Sir James Graham.*
Submitted to the Queen.

Argyll House, *8th October 1853.*

My dear Graham,—... When we met, Clarendon made a sort of *résumé* of what had taken place before we all separated, but ended with no specific proposal. After a few interlocutory remarks from different quarters, Palmerston proposed his plan. Lord John faintly supported it in general terms, but did not seem much in earnest about it. I said that it appeared to involve the necessity of a declaration of war against Russia, and the calling together Parliament forthwith. Gladstone strongly argued against the proposal. Clarendon then read an outline of his proposed instructions, which were a great abatement from Palmerston's plan. We came at last to a sort of compromise; our great difficulty being now to deal with the question of entering the Black Sea. I consented to this being done, provided it was strictly in defence of some point of attack on Turkish territory. I have no fear that this will take place; and as long as we abstain from entering the Black Sea, Peace may be possible between us and Russia. We have thus assumed a strictly defensive position, which for the moment may be sufficient, and will enable us to carry on negotiations; but this cannot last long. Under the character of defensive war, we should inevitably become extensively engaged. Should the Turks be at all worsted, which is probable, of course we must increase our assistance. We should have a French army, and perhaps English money—all for defence.

The aspect of the Cabinet was, on the whole, very good. Gladstone, active and energetic for Peace; Argyll, Herbert, C. Wood, and Granville, all in the same sense. Newcastle, not quite so much so, but good; Lansdowne, not so warlike as formerly; Lord John warlike enough, but subdued in tone; Palmerston urged his views perseveringly, but not disagreeably. The Chancellor said little, but was cordially peaceful. Molesworth was not present, there having been some mistake in sending the notice.

On the whole, therefore, yesterday passed off well enough; but we shall see what to-day will bring us. Not a syllable was said in the Cabinet on any other subject. Lord John seemed in good humour; he came to see me a few minutes before the Cabinet. I told you that I had spoken to Gladstone very fully; but I did not press any decision respecting *domestic* matters, as it would at this moment be quite unseasonable. Nevertheless, it must not be forgotten altogether. Yours, etc., etc.,

Aberdeen.

27:In this despatch Lord Clarendon, after referring to the interpretation which Count Nesselrode had put upon the Vienna Note, and the Russian rejection of it as amended by the Porte, told Lord Westmorland that it would be useless and dishonourable to recommend it in its unaltered form, that the Czar was contending for privileges for Christian subjects of the Porte not hitherto enjoyed by them, and that a war embarked upon in such a cause would be without parallel in history.

[28]:Authority had been given to Lord Stratford to employ the British Fleet in the manner he might deem most fit for defending Turkish territory from aggression, and he was instructed that if the Russian Fleet left Sebastopol, the British Fleet was to pass through the Bosphorus.

[29]:In this despatch to Baron Meyendorff, the Austrian Foreign Minister, the Count had disclosed the fact that the Russian interpretation of the Vienna Note differed from that of the other Powers.

[30]:Greville calls the writing of this letter an unusual step; but in sending it to Lord Aberdeen and Lord Clarendon, the Queen observed that its despatch was an important and advantageous fact, as it both committed the Czar personally, and enabled her to state certain truths to him, as well as to explain privately the views which guided her own and her Ministers' conduct.

[31]:Lord Stratford had written that Redschid Pasha was unable to make head against his warlike colleagues, and that unless some proposal of a decidedly satisfactory kind should come from Vienna very soon, there would be no chance of avoiding hostilities. Lord Stratford added that he had obtained a promise that no act of hostility should take place on the Turkish side before the expiration of fifteen days, and concluded with the words: "I fear that war is the decree of Fate, and our wisest part will be to do what we can to bring it to a thoroughly good conclusion."

[32]:The Emperor had made certain suggestions to Lord Cowley, which the British Government were willing to adopt; but the anti-Russian feeling was increasing daily in the nation, and, as will be seen from the Queen's letter of the 27th of November, Lord Stratford seemed resolved on war.

[33]:On the 19th of November Lord John had written to the Queen outlining the Reform proposals of the Committee of the Cabinet. The Queen subsequently wrote to make additional suggestions, *e.g.*, for finding a means of bringing into the House official persons or men without local connections, and for dealing with Ministerial re-elections.

[34]:Lord Palmerston wrote to Lord Lansdowne, giving an account of the affair:—

"Carlton Gardens, *8th December 1853.*

[35]:*I.e.*, the landed interest.

[36]:On the 30th of November the Russian Fleet from Sevastopol attacked the Turkish squadron in the harbour of Sinope, a naval station in the Black Sea, and destroyed it. The feeling in the country against Russia was greatly inflamed by the incident, which was referred to as the "massacre of Sinope."

[37]:Lord Palmerston wrote: "I find ... that I was mistaken in inferring from your letter that the details of the intended Reform Bill had been finally settled by the Government, and that no objection to any part of those details would be listened to." He went on to say that, under the circumstances, he could not decline to comply with the wish of many members of the Government that he should withdraw his resignation.

Also from Benediction Books ...
Wandering Between Two Worlds: Essays on Faith and Art
Anita Mathias
Benediction Books, 2007
152 pages
ISBN: 0955373700

Available from www.amazon.com, www.amazon.co.uk

In these wide-ranging lyrical essays, Anita Mathias writes, in lush, lovely prose, of her naughty Catholic childhood in Jamshedpur, India; her large, eccentric family in Mangalore, a sea-coast town converted by the Portuguese in the sixteenth century; her rebellion and atheism as a teenager in her Himalayan boarding school, run by German missionary nuns, St. Mary's Convent, Nainital; and her abrupt religious conversion after which she entered Mother Teresa's convent in Calcutta as a novice. Later rich, elegant essays explore the dualities of her life as a writer, mother, and Christian in the United States-- Domesticity and Art, Writing and Prayer, and the experience of being "an alien and stranger" as an immigrant in America, sensing the need for roots.

About the Author

Anita Mathias is the author of *Wandering Between Two Worlds: Essays on Faith and Art.* She has a B.A. and M.A. in English from Somerville College, Oxford University, and an M.A. in Creative Writing from the Ohio State University, USA. Anita won a National Endowment of the Arts fellowship in Creative Nonfiction in 1997. She lives in Oxford, England with her husband, Roy, and her daughters, Zoe and Irene.

Visit Anita's website
    http://www.anitamathias.com,
and Anita's blog
    http://dreamingbeneaththespires.blogspot.com, (Dreaming Beneath the Spires).